Social science in an age of change

Donald W. Calhoun
University of Miami

Social science in an age of change

Harper & Row, Publishers, New York, Evanston, San Francisco, London

PHOTOGRAPHIC CREDITS

The numbers refer to the pages on which the photographs appear.

J. Clark, 147. Colos, 14, 183. Contemporary Films/McGraw-Hill, 105. Michel Cosson, 31, 42, 58, 158, 180, 203, 238. Culver Pictures, 170, top right 218, 227, 233, 338, 340, 344. Carol Cutler, top left 249. Hilton Hotels Corp., 193. IBM, 61. Thomas McAvoy (courtesy LIFE Magazine. © Time-Life, Inc.), 148. Monkmeyer Press Photo Service: 10 (Fujihira), 18 (Louise Jefferson), 27 (Ron Batzdorff), 47, left and right 69 (Fujihira), center 69 (Wolfram Knoll), 86 (UNICEF), 98, 185, right 185 (Hugh Rogers), 210 (Pro Pix), bottom 218 (Sybil Shackman), 225 (Fritz Henle), bottom right 248, center left 248 (Bernard Silberstein), center left 249 (Fujihira), 257 (Hans Mann), bottom left 259 (Tiers), bottom right 259, 267 (Gregor), 299 (Eric L. Brown), 389 (Minoru Aoki), 404 (Pitkin), 413 (Hilda Bijur), 416 (Fritz Henle), 439 (Eric L. Brown), 466 (Delmar Lipp), 478, 485 (Eric L. Brown), 490 (Julian E. Caraballo), 494 (Delmar Lipp). John Myrick, 1A, 426. NASA, 78. New York Daily News, 104, Sovfoto, top 330, 393, 396. Wide World, 35, 127, 310, 311, 318, 321, bottom 331, 343, 350, 355, 401, 411, 420, 431, 436, 452, both 458.

SOCIAL SCIENCE IN AN AGE OF CHANGE

Standard Book Number: 06-041117-1

Library of Congress Catalog Card Number: 71-151336

Excerpt on page 264 from The People, Yes by Carl Sandburg, copyright, 1936, by Harcourt Brace Jovanovich, Inc.; renewed, 1964, by Carl Sandburg, reprinted by permission of the publishers.

For Constance-Leigh
Colleague, student, and dear friend

Contents

Preface

This book is, first of all, a text in general education. In the year of the American Declaration of Independence, Adam Smith wrote of the double danger of extreme specialization: the narrow specialist is not only improverished in his inner life, but is inadequately equipped to be a citizen of his community. This text is written for those courses, in both senior and junior colleges, whose aim is to present social science so as to contribute both to the student's personal enrichment and to his ability to participate in democratic decision making.

This is, further, an integrated text in social science, not a survey in which the student is exposed briefly, in series, to the different social-science disciplines. In our specialized world, we are likely to take the separation of disciplines for granted, as though it had existed from the beginning of time. When we try to present an overall view of social science (or any other area of knowledge), we are likely to assume that the way to do it is to add together the findings of the separate specialties. But reality existed before the separate sciences, and it continues to exist. For purposes of advanced research and study, the division of labor into disciplines is, of course, necessary. Even here, however, we have learned that some of the most important and exciting scientific problems appear on those border lines that are the property of no single discipline: social psychology, biochemistry, political economy. The integrated approach simply begins by assuming this immediate wholeness of life.

I have tried to stress integration with other areas as well as within the sphere of social science. For example, on the border line of the so-called "natural" sciences, I have given more attention than is usual in social-science texts to the interplay of human society with its biophysical environment. This emphasis on human ecology stresses the impact of population density, climate, terrain, and nutrition—the last an area with a wealth of new relevant material not generally considered by social scientists. In another dimension I have introduced the possible implications for man and society of recent research in mystical experience and extra-sensory perception. I believe that these approaches should give both a new breadth and a new excitement to the exploration of social science.

The emphasis in this book is upon principles of social behavior rather than historical sequence. This choice does not in any sense imply a bias against history. I believe it is impossible to generalize about the present without knowing the past and have used both contemporary and historical data accordingly. What I have not tried to do is to present a chronological course in world history.

The teacher and student will find this book marked by as much emphasis on questions as on answers. It is obviously impossible to master all the significant data in the social sciences, or any other field, in one year's study. What the general student needs in a course outside his special field is first of all to understand and be moved by the most pressing questions in the area. Then he needs to begin to understand some of the methods and principles that have been developed in the attempt to answer the questions. Such a task is not too comprehensive for a relatively short course. Once he is moved by the significant questions, the student may have the impetus to spend the rest of his life trying to answer them. Thus this book stresses basic concepts as tools for approaching relevant problems, with the emphasis on the combination of both. It begins with the kind of world that the student is going to have to face—a world of manifold revolutionary change —and plunges him immediately into its crises and dilemmas. Then, and only then, does it begin to ask how social science approaches such a world. At the end it considers how the social-science principles that make up the bulk of the book may be applied in some crucial areas of life.

The structure is rather like that of a sandwich, in which practical problems constitute the "bread" and basic principles the "filling." Part one introduces the student to seven of the significant revolutions of our time and to the methods by which social science endeavors to comprehend the kind of world they reflect. Part two is an examination of the physical, social, psychological, and cultural bases that underlie all social life. In terms of disciplinary areas, the emphasis is primarily sociological, psychological, and anthropological. The subject matter of Part three is political economy in the original sense. Against the background developed in Part two, the structure of Part three is a counterpoint in which are interwoven the economic and the political dimensions of social life. Part four focuses upon the problem of social values in a very concrete way. It asks whether we may establish standards for health and pathology, in the individual and society, and it explores the question by examining the possibility of such standards in a number of different areas of social experience.

A final word. This book has a point of view. I have never been able to accept the argument that one can be objective only about those things in which he is not emotionally involved. I think the opposite is closer to reality: only the person who cares about the world in which he lives is going to want to take the trouble to see things as they really are. Teachers and students will discover what my point of view is. I should rather not label it now. I hope that among other things the book will teach that premature labeling can be a barrier to thought. Because my point of view is a point of view, one of several possible approaches, I hope that teachers *and students will explore and use all possible ways of challenging it—supplementary readings, speakers who are in disagreement, fact-finding projects to test the validity of my statements. If it can catalyze controversy and exploration, the book may contribute to a learning situation that is as real and challenging as the world it studies.*

Donald W. Calhoun

Social science in an age of change

Part one
Social change and social science

In our first two chapters we shall deal with the role of social science as a human activity in the world in which we live. We might be interested in learning about society just for the sake of knowing. A more pressing reason, however, is that life in society, and in our own society, poses problems which urgently need to be solved. In Chapter 1 we shall examine some of these problems. This examination will be an analysis of the age in which we live. In Chapter 2 we shall examine the nature of social science as a part of scientific effort. We shall ask how it is related to the other sciences, to nonscientific branches of knowledge, and to the social world which it investigates.

Chapter one
The revolutions of our time

You who study this book will live in the last third of the twentieth century, and the first half of the twenty-first. The purpose of this text is to help you prepare for the kind of world that you may expect. You will note that the title is *Social Science in an Age of Change.* This title was not picked by accident or because the words sounded good. We are now living in what is probably the most rapid period of change in the history of the world. The turn of the next century, at which you will have reached the prime of your life, will probably see even more spectacular changes. In the world in which you will live, those who are not prepared for change will simply not be prepared for life.

A few of you will find, after this course, that you wish to be specialists in social science. For you, this book will be a beginning to your life career. Most of you will not become professional students of society. You will discover, nevertheless, that it is impossible to be really effective in any career that you may undertake, including that of housewife and mother, without an understanding of the society in which you live. You will also find that this kind of understanding is essential if you are to participate intelligently as a citizen of your world.

Let us look briefly at what we shall do in this book. This chapter will be devoted to examining seven concrete revolutionary changes that have been taking place in our lifetimes. There have, of course, been other important changes with which we shall be concerned throughout the book, but none more significant. In Chapter two we shall ask how social science fits into the whole social picture—what it is about, what it does, how it can contribute to solving the problems of a changing society. Most of the book will be concerned with the actual substance of what social science has found about our social world. In the final chapter we shall return to some of the most pressing problems facing people and society and see what light social science can throw upon them.

Before analyzing them one by one, we can summarize briefly the seven major social revolutions of our time. (1) New *technology* has affected every aspect of society. (2) Among the great problems related to changing technology is the explosive growth of *population.* (3) Our modern society has crowded increasing numbers of people into *urban* areas. (4) Technological and other changes have led to *rising expectations* and revolutionary aspirations on the part of depressed peoples throughout the world. (5) In every area of life, we see the growth of vast *organizations.* (6) We also see changes in values and morality, none of which are more spectacular than the changes in *sexual* patterns. (7) One aspect of technological change, *weapons* technology, has revolutionized warfare and diplomacy, and threatens the future existence of mankind.

THE TECHNOLOGICAL REVOLUTION

Technology consists of all those devices and methods through which man manages his environment. For about 200 years, since that great development that we call the Industrial Revolution, human technology has been growing at an ever-increasing rate. Clearly we live today in a world dominated by technology, one that would be utterly amazing, for example, even to George Washington or Benjamin Franklin, who lived at the beginning of the Industrial Revolution.

The horse and buggy of Washington's day has been succeeded by the interplanetary space capsule. On earth we shall soon be flying passenger schedules at 2000 miles per hour, so fast that in terms of the clock, a plane leaving New York will land in Los Angeles "before" it takes off. Before long we shall no doubt have instant worldwide television. We have already televised the far side of the moon. One of the most dramatic applications of technology is in production. Computers have been programmed to roll steel, machine engine blocks, make textiles, run oil refineries, and sort bank checks. Junior executives have been displaced because computers could do a better job of giving credit ratings and picking television advertising spots.

No aspect of society escapes the impact of technology. An example is government functions. Warehouses of social security files have been replaced by electronic tapes. A national information bank is proposed which would contain exhaustive computerized data on all citizens. The Russians are actually experimenting with using computers to plan their economic system. Other activities are equally affected. In Houston sports now take place in an enclosed, weather controlled environment. Closed circuit television replaces the "live" teacher; computerized objective exams take the place of written tests; and teaching machines and language laboratories teach mathematics, languages, and other skills.

No one can yet estimate the effect of the "pill" upon sexual patterns, but we know what a change was wrought by the automobile in "putting sex on wheels." The role of the housewife has been drastically changed by processed food, mechanized kitchens, and ever-available restaurants. Church members are urged to "worship Christ in air-conditioned comfort," while biochemical technology explores the mysteries of the cell and (sometimes) brings back a verdict of "no soul." Most dramatic of all the impacts of technology is perhaps the release of atomic energy. As one writer put it, before 1945 *men* were exterminable, but since 1945, *man* is exterminable.

The development of modern technology has been a blessing to mankind, but from the beginning there have been those who feared that it was not a complete blessing. The English poet, Lord Byron, made his first speech in the House of Lords in defense of laborers who had wrecked machines because they feared they would take away their jobs. Mary Shelley, wife of another English poet, wrote the famous story of Frankenstein, the scientist who created an intelligent machine who got out of hand and destroyed its maker. Today many fear what may happen if automated computer systems continue to take the place of men. Many also fear that our destructive military technology may lead us to the fate of Frankenstein.

Let us begin our examination of the technological revolution with a little historical perspective. Human civilization rests on a fairly limited number of basic discoveries and inventions, which have increased man's ability to manipulate his environment. For more than a million and a half years of human existence, according to our latest reckoning, men got along with only two of these discoveries: fire and simple tools of wood, bone, or stone. Fire enabled man to cook his food, to frighten away predators, to clear land, to work wood and hardened wooden spear points, to make use of chemical reactions in preparing metals for use. Without tools man would hardly be human. The caveman's simple tools are the basis for all later technology.

There have been two great technological bursts in human history: one about 5000 B.C., the other about A.D. 1750. Between 5000 and 3000 B.C., in the general area of Egypt, Mesopotamia, and India, man added to his repertoire the plow, the harnessing of animals, the use of wheeled vehicles, the solar calendar, the use of writing, the use of numbers, and the use of bronze. He also added irrigation, the sailboat, orchards, the loom, fermentation, the production of bricks, glazing, and the arch. The next 2500 years (3000 to 500 B.C.) gave us the use of decimals, the alphabet, the construction of aqueducts, and the use of iron. The early part of this technological revolution gave us agriculture, which enormously increased man's productive powers. The latter part gave us the city, which has always been associated with advanced civilization.

For over 2000 years there was relatively little more technical advance. Then, in the eighteenth century (some would say earlier), began another massive surge of technological growth. The Industrial Revolution has centered around (1) a few basic machines, (2) new materials, and (3) new sources of power. Among the fundamental machines have been the clock, the spinning wheel, the power loom, the blast furnace, the steam engine, and the internal combustion engine. In succession the new basic materials have been high-grade steel, aluminum, and plastics. The basic new sources of power have been steam, gasoline, electricity, and atomic energy.

Industrial technology began in England around 1770, spread to the United States in the early nineteenth century, and developed in western Europe in the middle of that century. Japan began to adopt it around 1870. Except for Japan, at the time of World War I, industrialism was still largely confined to the rim of the Atlantic Ocean. After 1917 it spread to Russia; after 1925, to China, India, and South America; and since then to Africa.

The years since 1930 have brought another development in technology— automation. What ordinary mechanization primarily does is to substitute machine power and skill for human muscle. Automation substitutes machine control for the human brain. Its most important characteristic is feedback. If a system of operations deviates from a desired pattern, forces are set in motion that correct the deviation. For example, if a thermostat is set for a given room temperature, a rise or fall in air temperature will "feed back" into the thermostat, which will then regulate the heating supply accordingly. Some people see automation as simply another form of mechanization and feel that it will create no essentially new problems. Others regard it as a revolutionary new step in technology, which will be as far-reaching as the technology of the agricultural and industrial revolutions. The second view is probably nearer the truth.

The most direct result of technology has been a rise in the standard of living. The purpose of technology is to produce more satisfaction with less effort. The advantages have not always come immediately to the industrial worker, but there has clearly been a gain in the long run for the average person. No one can doubt that there are more material conveniences and luxuries in any industrial nation today than there were 200 years ago or than there are in today's industrially underdeveloped nations. Technology has also brought aspirations to those who do not yet enjoy its fruits: this is the "revolution of rising expectations."

The results of technology have, however, gone far beyond increased production. So far have they gone, indeed, that some people—balancing the gains against the costs—wonder whether it is all worth it. The new techniques introduced in the eighteenth century changed the organization of work, and with it the whole structure of society. For technical reasons the workshop was replaced by the factory. Large numbers of machines, run by steam rather than water power, were massed at the sites of large sources of power, and masses of workers came to the machines. Thus was born the modern industrial city, which has altered people's whole pattern of living. It broke down people's close ties to small rural communities and often left them part of an urban mass without a real sense of belonging. As never before industrial technology separated man from nature. We shall explore these and other effects in the section on the urban revolution.

One of the unintended effects of technology has been a great wave of population growth. The reason is simple. When it is first introduced to an area, technology generally raises the living standard, improves housing, brings better sanitation, improves nutrition, and brings better public health measures. There is thus a drop in the death rate. If the birth rate does not change or drops more slowly than the death rate, then population will increase. In the section on the population revolution, we shall see that this is one of the greatest problems of the modern world.

New technology tends to throw men out of work. It is "labor saving"—that is why it exists—and its first effect is therefore to reduce the number of workers. This is why early in the Industrial Revolution, groups of enraged workers called the Luddites began smashing machines. In the long run, it is argued, displaced workers are rehired in new jobs. At best, however, this may mean a long period of unemployment and learning an entirely new occupation. At worst it may mean that one's son may find a new job, but that one is himself too old by the time that the "long run" catches up. In the early nineteenth century, the famous English economist, David Ricardo, said:

I am convinced that the substitution of machinery for human labour is often very injurious to the interests of the class of labourers. . . . The opinion entertained by the labouring class, that the employment of machinery is frequently detrimental to their interests, is not founded on prejudice and error.[1]

There is a serious question as to whether "technological unemployment" always cures itself, even in the long run. Britain went from 1920 to 1940 with only a brief period in which fewer than ten percent of her workers were unemployed. Whether the unemployment created by automation will correct itself is not certain. According to one expert estimate, automation is eliminating two million jobs a year. Optimists think that new jobs created by an automated society will keep pace with the displacement of workers. Pessimists feel that automation may well stabilize itself with all production being carried on by only a part of the available workers. Some way will have to be found, it is held, to support millions of people for whom there will no longer be gainful employment.

Technology has changed the nature of work itself. Before the Industrial Revolution, the worker tended to make a whole product. To a considerable extent, at least, he set his own pace of work. When he used tools, he controlled the tools. His work carried the mark of his personal skill. This was more the case, it is true, with skilled independent artisans—shoemakers, tailors, watchmakers, silversmiths, and the like—than with agricultural peasants. Nevertheless, modern technology changed the life of all. The factory or office worker comes to the job on schedule and works on schedule. His pace is likely to be set by the needs of the whole operation. He does not control the machine; he is, rather, a part of the machine. He usually performs only part of the process of making a prod-

1. David Ricardo, *Principles of Political Economy and Taxation,* London, G. Bell & Sons, Ltd., 1929, pp. 379, 383.

uct. When it is finished, the work typically bears no personal touch.

It is true that the most advanced technology is likely to feature the semi-skilled worker, with some control over his activity, rather than the completely unskilled person. However, the slogan of Frederick Winslow Taylor, one of the exponents of "scientific management" in industry, still largely holds true: "In the past the man has been first; in the future the system must be first."

Technology has also changed the relationship of the worker to the employer. The life of a serf on a medieval manor left much to be desired, but he did usually have a sense of personal relationship to his lord. The typical workmen's shop before the Industrial Revolution employed only a few men, who were thus personally related to the shop master. With the massing of large numbers of workers into factories, the personal relationship was almost inevitably lost. The worker had no sense of working for a person, only for a vast impersonal organization. The employer or manager did not know his workers as people. Thus, for both, labor became simply a *commodity,* to be bought and sold and used for a price. Only these impersonal conditions, in all likelihood, could have permitted the situation in England in the early Industrial Revolution, where women worked naked in the mines, or in the United States, where 40 to 60 percent of all factory work before 1860 was done by children.

It was of this kind of impersonal degradation that the poet William Blake wrote when, in the early days of industrialism, he described the streets and the people of London themselves as "chartered," that is, bought and sold. Almost two centuries later, actress Kim Novak voiced the same problem in the movie industry: "The trouble with this business is that they buy and sell you like a hunk of meat." Moreover, technology has generally turned the individual employer himself into a dependent worker selling his labor as a commodity. In 1800 four out of five Americans were self-employed. In 1950 the figure was one out of seven.

One of the obvious results of technology is the changed attitude toward time. The clock was actually the first of all automatic machines and may be considered the basic machine of technological civilization, for the organization of technology requires that time be subdivided and measured. Before modern technology time was more like "farmer's time"—flowing with the sun, the moon, and the seasons, not divided into any clearly marked intervals. The world of technology is a very different time world. The carefulness and punctuality with which time is observed is a rather good measure of technical advance. There is a much more casual attitude toward time in Latin America or in Africa than in the United States or most of western Europe. The close division of time into hours, minutes, and seconds probably did not take place until the late fourteenth century. Since then, people have come more and more to run their lives by the clock. This is true not only of work but also of leisure. Time has become a commodity to be bought and sold by the "piece"—so much work, so much advertising exposure. Also, one "kills time," or "wastes time."

Submission to time illustrates the fact that in a technological world, technology and its results tend to become the most important values. The machine is the most evidently successful aspect of our life. To many people all that is real or important seems to be machine-like. Thus religion and its values tend to vanish. The technical world becomes a "secular" world, in which nothing is sacred. Or, rather, the machine and its products come to be worshipped. In education all other subjects tend to take second place to technology and the physical sciences.

Technology brings a new attitude toward nature, one of exploitation. Machine technology tends to take the natural world and use it for its immediate purposes without thought for other results. Thus natural beauty is likely to be replaced by man-made ugliness in the name of technical progress. The soil itself is depleted by exploitation until it washes away, blows away, or loses its fertility. What we have just described is actual history in many parts of the world, especially the United States.

Such exploitative results of technology have led in very recent years to an increased concern with the problems of *ecology:* the total impact of man's actions upon his biophysical environment. A significant event in this ecological rethinking was the publication in 1962 of Rachel Carson's *Silent Spring,* in which she described our destruction of the biological environment by chemical poisons.

One of the chief results of technology is increased interdependence. Freedom, in the sense of individual independence from broad social forces, is decreased. A few years ago, for example, a large part of the northeastern United States was blacked out by a technical failure in the power-grid system serving the area. The size of the area of failure, which was the area of technical interdependence, is a measure of the development of technology. Dependence of the worker is another example. In George Washington's time, the average person owned land with orchards, a garden, and various livestock. He could fall back on his farm and be fairly self-sufficient in hard times. With the advances of technology, his grandchildren became factory or office workers with little or nothing to fall back on in depression. Thus they were completely dependent upon business prosperity. A third example is weapons technology, to which a section of this chapter is devoted. There is on earth "no place to hide" from modern instruments of destruction, and therefore no independence from the power struggles of armed nations.

Armaments illustrate how technology has made the earth "one world."

In this trend both transportation and communication technology have broken down barriers. It is hard to believe that as late as World War II, the English Channel served as an effective barrier against Nazi invasion of England. Today the largest oceans are no barriers against jet bombers or intercontinental missiles. Today military "isolationism" is dead. Other kinds of isolation are too. Behind much of the "revolution of rising expectations" is the fact that modern communications —for example, movies and transistor radios—have invaded the most remote areas of the earth, bringing the story of the affluence of the technically developed nations. An outstanding student of technology, Norbert Wiener, has said that such technical problems as broadcasting and air transport are bound to require some kind of world state. As it has spread, technology has also tended to create "one world" by destroying local customs and substituting the ways of technology. In all those parts of the world that have been reached by the technological revolution, there is a growing sameness in architecture, form of cities, eating habits, dress, music, and all other patterns of life.

Technology tends to bring centralization of power, and with it a shrinking of the power of the individual. The activities of government must increase. Radio and television channeling, electrical networks, water pollution, the atmosphere of cities all demand government intervention. A careful 1949 report by the United States government held that atomic energy could be properly developed only by public agencies. The largest new jet planes are too expensive to be built except by government aid.

Whether they work for government or not, the number and powers of "experts" also increase. As everything becomes more technical, the number of people capable of understanding and making specific decisions becomes smaller. It becomes increasingly difficult for the "many" to exercise control over the expert "few." In military affairs, in economic life, in science and medicine, in the educational system, in the operations of government, experts increasingly insist that only they can provide right answers. If they are correct, there arises a serious question as to whether democracy is any longer possible in an advanced technological age. In his book *The Making of a Counter Culture,* Theodore Roszak has taken a very dim view of the rise of a "technocracy" of experts.

THE POPULATION REVOLUTION

In the early days of the Industrial Revolution in England, Thomas Malthus wrote his famous *Essay on Population.* To those who saw the new world of scientific and technological progress as bringing increased happiness and enlightenment to men, Malthus replied that biological facts about man made this impossible. If unchecked, the human ability to reproduce tends to follow a geometric ratio (1, 2, 4, 8, 16, 32, etc.). Man's ability to increase his food supply is limited to approximately an arithmetic ratio (1, 2, 3, 4, 5, 6, etc.). Apart from the preventive check of sexual abstinence, population must always be held in check by famine, disease, or war. The level, moreover, at which it normally balances is just that which enables the poorest survivors to stay alive.

Since Malthus' time, two new factors have entered the picture. Technology has greatly increased our ability to grow food. The opening up of North and South America and Australia have given new "elbow room." Artificial methods of contraception have added a new, effective check to population. The problem posed by Malthus has not, however, been solved.

Any attempt to measure the population of the whole world today can be only a rough estimate, and figures for the past must be even rougher. We can be sure, however, about what has in general been happening. At the time of Christ, the United Nations calculates, there were about 200 to 300 million people in the world. Sixteen centuries later, when the Pilgrims settled in America, the figure was only perhaps twice that much—500 to 550 million. In the next two centuries, the world population doubled again, reaching one billion between 1820 and 1830. These were centuries of commercial and industrial expansion. In the next century, the population doubled once more, to 2 billion in 1930. To add the third billion took only about 30 years—population reached the 3 billion mark in the early 1960s.

If present trends continue, the figure will be about 7 billion in the year 2000. The *increase* in the population of Asia between 1960 and 2000 will probably about equal the whole population of the world in 1958. The increase in Latin American population between 1950 and 2000 may be as great as the increase for the whole world from the dawn of man to the settlement of America. Should present rates of increase continue beyond the year 2000, world population would be more than 100 billion in 2100, and around 500 billion in the year 2200. If such a figure were reached—about 165 times the present world population—it would mean that if people were spread evenly over the whole land surface of the globe, including deserts, jungles, mountains, and the frozen polar regions, the density would be a little less than that of Washington, D.C., in 1960.

As we shall see, the situation in the United States is less severe than in the world as a whole. Nevertheless, the population is now growing at the fastest rate in American history (although a slowdown may have begun in 1961 and 1962). The increase between 1953 and 1963 was equal to the whole growth of the country from 1620 to 1860. To keep abreast of present population growth in the United States will require new housing roughly equal to the building of a new Chicago every year. If the rate of population increase since World War II were to be sustained, the United States would within a century contain a billion people, or about five times as many as at present.

These figures for what world and United States population *might* become do not mean that population *will* in any likelihood get that large. Before that happens, wider use of contraception will have prevented births, or the "Malthusian checks" of hunger, disease, and war will have killed many people. Actually, in the world as a whole, both things will have happened. Contraception is slowly spreading, to peoples who have not previously used it. There is famine in the world, and there will almost certainly be much more in the next few decades. The point is that the basic biological problem stated by Malthus is still with us.

Figures for the earth as a whole actually underestimate the seriousness of the population problem. Increase is not spread equally over the globe. Rather, it tends to be highest in just those areas that can least afford it— the poor, economically underdeveloped areas of the world.

We have seen that the advance of modern technology increases population by lowering the death rate. In general we can distinguish three stages in the population pattern that accompanies technology. (1) In the traditional, pretechnological society, both birth and death rates are typically high. Thus population is fairly stable. (2) As technology is introduced, the death rate falls, but not the birth rate. There is therefore a "population explosion." (3) As technology develops still further, the birth rate tends to fall. Contraception is used. More people remain single or childless. Others prefer to bring up a few children well. There are many other reasons. Thus both the birth and death rates are low. This has been true of all nations that have become urbanized. Thus the underdeveloped nations typically have a birth rate of about 40 per thousand population per year, with five children for each

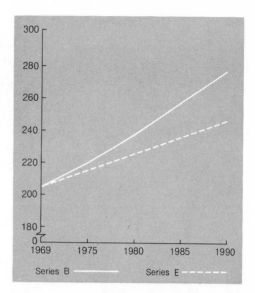

Figure 1.1. *United States population—projections to 1990.*
Source: U.S. Department of Commerce, Bureau of the Census, *Statistical Abstract of the United States, 1970.*

bearing mother. Europe, on the other hand, has a birth rate of about 20 per thousand, with two or three children to a family.

The areas of the world that now have a low or moderate rate of growth are North America, temperate South America, Australia, New Zealand, the Soviet Union, Europe, and Japan. These are the industrialized areas. Together, they have only about a third of the world's population, and this percentage will drop by the year 2000. The areas of rapid growth are Africa, Central America, tropical South America, Southwest Asia, the Pacific Islands, the Caribbean, Central South Asia, Southeast Asia, and East Asia except for Japan. These are almost entirely the economically underdeveloped nations. They have about two-thirds of the world's population, and by the year 2000 will have more than three-fourths.

Even today most of the existing population of the world is badly fed. An oft-quoted estimate, which is probably not exaggerated, is that two-thirds of all humanity go to bed hungry every night.

In the 1950s the Food and Agricultural Organization estimated that to feed the world's population adequately in the year 2000, it would be necessary to quadruple food production. There are a number of ways in which this might possibly be done. Existing land might be cultivated more intensively through use of machinery, seeds, and fertilizers. New agricultural areas might be brought into use, as through desert reclamation. It might be possible to catch many more fish. Marine plankton or algae might be used for food, or special yeasts used to process new foods.

One of the biggest problems, however, is that the countries that need help most are those least likely to be able to develop these new food sources. Raymond Ewell thinks that improved agricultural techniques could keep up with population growth for only 20 to 30 years. Even if we could feed 7 billion people well in 2000, there is no way in sight to feed 100 billion in 2100, or 500 billion in 2200, or to keep up with the biologically possible increase along the way.

Population increase hangs like a millstone around the poor nations of the world, not only because it brings the threat of famine, but because it holds back all economic growth. Before it can industrialize, a country must first feed its people and have something left over to spend on technology. In countries like India and Egypt, economic development has been barely able to keep up with the population explosion. This is a matter of concern not only to the poor nations but to the affluent ones. The best market for the products of economically "developed" nations like the United States lies in other developed nations. If they keep most of the world economically backward, overpopulation and hunger deprive the wealthy nations of a chance to sell their products.

The political threats posed by the population explosion are equally serious. They are totalitarianism and war. We can be quite safe in saying that democratic institutions will not develop in any nation that has not solved its population problem. Mass participation in government requires literacy and education, and these require a fairly high degree of economic development. People on the edge of starvation will always be illiterate, ignorant, and unequipped for political participation. Population pressure is also likely to lead to war. Overpopulated nations may try to colonize some of their surplus population through conquest, as did Italy in Ethiopia, or as Communist China might do in Russian Mongolia or, conceivably, in Australia. Rulers threatened by mass misery and discontent at home may use the age-old formula of diverting people into military ventures.

It should be clear that no increase in food production can keep up for, at most, more than perhaps fifty years with the increase in population of which man is biologically capable. Population must be curbed by one or another method of birth limitation if immediate or ultimate disaster is to be avoided. The question of techniques is the first problem. As late as 1960 an authoritative book on population could say that "There is no single, cheap, simple, effective, acceptable, and available contraceptive that provides a 'solution.' "[2]

Today this is probably not true. The intrauterine device (IUD), a simple piece of plastic in a variety of shapes that is inserted into the uterus, would seem to meet these requirements. The much publicized and much used birth control pill, which suppresses the formation of ova, is reliable, but its safety has been questioned by a number of researchers. Since it involves counting, it is also actually too complicated for many poor and illiterate women who most need help. The problem may be simplified by the so-called "morning-after pill."

Aside from technique, population control faces powerful obstacles. The traditional position of the Catholic Church has been that no contraceptive method is legitimate except abstinence or avoidance of fertile days in the menstrual cycle (the "rhythm" method). This view is still a strong factor in Latin America and in the United Nations and related international organizations. It was reinforced by a 1968 papal encyclical. The traditional position does not represent the view of many Catholics. Several hundred Catholic theologians openly criticized the papal statement. The words of Msgr. George W. Casey of St. Brigid's, Lexington, Massachusetts, doubtless represent the kind of thinking that has influenced many Catholic clergymen: "I first began to modify my adjectives against birth control when, without bitterness or self pity, a man told me that his wife had borne him nine tiny monstrosities in a row, who lived but a few weeks each."[3] Dr. John Rock, a Catholic physician, was one of the developers of the pill. Although not in as large numbers as non-Catholics, Catholic couples in the United States use artificial contraceptives. A number of Catholic countries—Belgium, France, Italy, Spain, and Portugal—have lower birth rates than the United States.

In addition to religious resistances, strong obstacles remain that go to the heart of the problem of underdeveloped nations. Preindustrial societies are likely to regard many children as a blessing rather than a curse. When death rates were higher, many children needed to be born if a few were to survive to reproduce. In an agricultural community, each new child tends to be looked upon as another strong back for

2. Richard M. Fagley, *The Population Explosion and Christian Responsibility,* New York, Oxford University Press, 1960, p. 93.

3. George W. Casey, "The Pastoral Crisis," *Commonweal, 80,* no. 11 (June 5, 1964), 317.

the work of the farm. Where there is no government social security, one is likely to feel that many children will make his old age more secure.

As with the traditional Chinese and the Old Testament Hebrews, agricultural people are likely to feel it important to have many heirs to honor their memory. Men feel that an abundance of children testifies to their manhood; women are likely to regard continuous childbearing as their main function. People who have known nothing but abject poverty and deprivation may be unwilling to take the trouble to use contraceptives because they feel that nothing they can do will really make their condition either much better or much worse. Some leaders of the underdeveloped nations actually feel that population control is a Western plot to reduce their numbers and power.

History seems to indicate that as a society adopts modern technology and becomes economically developed, these anticontraceptive attitudes may be expected to change. But if the attitudes do not change first, economic development may never take place.

With fairly adequate contraceptives now available, there is reason for some hope that resistances can be overcome by organized effort in time to prevent considerable suffering. Japan, the first non-Western country to take steps to control population, cut her birth rate nearly in half after World War II. This example does not mean very much for underdeveloped nations, since Japan was already fairly highly industrialized. However, in Singur, outside Calcutta, fairly untrained personnel, using simple contraceptive methods, reduced the birth rate about 15 percent in four years. The birth rate of a comparable group without a program remained the same. In Ceylon a Swedish mission reduced the birth rate of a group of women by about one-third. Peasant women were the subjects of both programs. Other programs have been established or announced in Formosa,

Singapore, Korea, Turkey, Egypt, Hong Kong, Chile, Puerto Rico, and Costa Rica. The last three, we may note, are predominantly Catholic.

In the early 1960s, United States government funds were used for the first time to establish public birth control clinics. Although the United States as such is not an underdeveloped country, the poverty groups who most need birth control are almost an island of underdevelopment in an affluent society. Also, this program represents a change in attitude on the part of the wealthiest and most powerful government in the world, which will help create an atmosphere more favorable to population control everywhere.

THE URBAN REVOLUTION

Urbanization is like the twin brother of industrial technology. In 1790 only one person in 20 in the United States was urban, that is, lived in a settlement of 2500 or more. In 1965, 7 out of 10 Americans were urban or suburban. It is expected that in 1980, over 90 percent of the population will be urban. In 1790 there was no city over 50,000. In 1960 there were 106 cities over 100,000, and five over a million. On a lesser scale, the same thing has happened in the world as a whole. In the year 1800, it is estimated, 1.7 percent of the world's population lived in cities. In 1950 the figure had risen to 13.1 percent.

Clustering in cities has been characteristic of industrial society. We must, however, also notice two other trends. Since about 1910 there has been a tendency for business, industry, and residence to move out of the "central city" and into industrial or residential suburbs. The departure of the middle and upper classes, who are mainly white, has left low-income Negroes as the largest element in many central cities. Our most critical urban problems center around this fact.

This movement from the central city has also produced a new phenomenon called "conurbation." Instead of being clustered in sharply defined cities, urban population and urban functions are spread out over wide areas, some of which may not be included in any incorporated city. A strip from Boston to Washington is fast becoming one solid area of conurbation, and indeed now contains 60 percent of the entire population of the United States. There is a similar tendency in the Los Angeles-to-San Francisco strip, in a strip from Seattle south to Eugene, Oregon, and in the "Gold Coast" of the southern Florida peninsula. A less dignified term for conurbation is "slurb": "sloppy, sleazy, slovenly, slipshod semi-cities."

Why exactly have cities arisen? Although industrialism has clearly spurred city growth, there were cities before the Industrial Revolution. What advantages draw people to cities? On the other hand, for about sixty years people have been trying to escape the central city. Why do they want to get away?

Let us begin our examination by looking briefly at the history of urbanization. There have really been two urban revolutions. City life began in about 3000 B.C., primarily in Egypt, Mesopotamia, and India. This first urban revolution followed the earlier revolution in agriculture for a simple reason. City people do not feed themselves. In order that there may be cities, there must be an agricultural surplus large enough to support the city population. As soon as the technological revolution had increased agricultural production, people began to cluster in cities. This sequence of agricultural and urban revolutions has been followed throughout the world wherever technology has spread and is occurring today.

The nineteenth- and twentieth-century city growth that has accompanied the Industrial Revolution is not simply a continuation of earlier urbanization. It is a second urban revolution, which has changed the whole pattern of human living. Before this revolution, although some people lived in cities,

they were an exception. Everywhere the population was predominantly rural. Today the situation is reversed. The sociologist Kingsley Davis sees the human species as moving rapidly in the direction of an almost totally urban existence. The city itself has changed in size and complexity, giving birth to something new that is called "megalopolis." At its height Athens was about as large as Yonkers, New York. Florence at the peak of the Renaissance was not as large as New Haven. Imperial Rome was considerably bigger, but never in a class with modern New York, Chicago, Los Angeles, London, Paris, Tokyo, or other megalopolises.

A clear reason for cities is that they are centers for the massing of labor, power, and equipment. The diking of the Nile in ancient Egypt or the draining of Mesopotamian swamps would have been difficult or impossible without a clustering of population. The Industrial Revolution required masses of people to man the factories. Once it had begun, clustering attracted other groups: retail merchants, wholesalers and distributors, bankers, office personnel to coordinate these operations, and a range of service people from priests to prostitutes.

Clustering was enhanced because it promoted specialization. Many specialized services cannot take place unless there is a mass of people large enough to support them. Large libraries, art galleries, symphony orchestras, or professional athletic teams are much more easily supported in large cities. This is also true of specialized medical services, for example. A small town or even a small city cannot ordinarily support a doctor specializing in a small part of the eye or in an infrequent operation on the ear. Cities tend to draw both individuals who have specialized skills to offer and people who desire their services.

People are also drawn by the impersonality of city life. In small towns and villages, one is likely to lead his life under the close and watchful eyes of

his neighbors. In the city a person is usually free of this restraint. Unmarried schoolteachers who want to have some freedom in their sex life, for example, will generally be drawn to large cities. One of the reasons the city can offer such freedom is simply anonymity —in the city, one need not know his next door neighbor. If he does know him, his neighbor will probably not be connected with his job or other interests, and will therefore probably not be in a position to hurt him. In addition, since the city dweller is typically less bound by traditional religion and morality than are people in town or country, his neighbor is less likely to care what he does.

Another appeal of cities lies in the variety of experience. In rural and small-town life, there tends to be a single pattern which has perhaps remained relatively unchanged for generations. The city is generally marked by a variety of patterns. A great cosmopolitan city like ancient Rome, medieval Florence or Venice, or modern New York or Paris is a crossroads for the whole world. There a person

can sample a wide range of ways of living and perhaps shape his own way so as to include a great many of them. The coming together and clashing of different ways of life tend to create an atmosphere both exciting and stimulating to creative effort.

Cities are attractive because they are, in the words of Lewis Mumford, "museums of culture." Libraries, art galleries, and museums physically preserve the specialized products of art and civilization. The great historic traditions of art, music, and literature are also preserved by the stage, concert hall, lecture hall, and other specialized cultural institutions, and in the everyday way of life of city people who have grown up to appreciate them.

The advantages of the city are, however, only one side of the picture. Perhaps all the disadvantages are related to the fact that the city creates an artificial environment for man.

The impersonality of urban life, for example, is found only in the city. Everywhere else people live, and have lived, in fairly close communities. Impersonality may of itself be a serious shortcoming. One can get desperately lonely in the city. There are two sides to the situation where "nobody cares." Especially when one is sick or troubled, he may long for more personal relationships. Single people may find it hard to meet possible mates.

Impersonality threatens society as well. When one ceases to feel responsible to others, he may be limited only by what he can get away with. This loosening of inner controls is an important factor behind crime and juvenile delinquency in the city. It helps explain how a woman can be sexually attacked and murdered in full view of a number of people and how all the observers can be too afraid of getting "involved" to do anything about it.

At this point it is worth noting that, according to the FBI, serious crimes increased 98 percent from 1950 to 1960, while the population increased 12 percent. Juvenile delinquency more than doubled from 1951 to 1960. There was a murder every 58 minutes in the United States in 1960, a rape every 38 minutes, a robbery every 6 minutes, a car stolen every minute, and an "aggravated assault" every 15 seconds. Not all of these offenses are, of course, urban, but the rise is certainly connected with urbanization.

The city birth rate reflects the fact that there is something unfavorable about the urban environment. Arthur Morgan, a life-long student of human communities, says that there is only one case in history (and that a doubtful one) where a long-standing urban community has maintained its population through birth alone. In all other cases, the city would have slowly lost numbers had it not been fed by more fertile rural areas. "City populations," said the distinguished anthropologist Ralph Linton, "do not and never have reproduced themselves."[4] Why is this so? The individualism that causes people to remain single and to place individual pleasures above those of

having children is one reason. Another may perhaps be biological. Studies of overcrowding in animal populations show a loss of fertility. The same thing may be true for man.

In recent years increasing attention has been given to the kinds of biological stress caused by city life. Many animal studies have shown that overcrowding leads to abnormal results. An Oxford biologist cites the case of monkeys and apes, who seldom fight in the wild, but establish brutal dictatorships with periodic violence when overcrowded in zoos. Studies of overcrowding in laboratory rats have shown increased infant and maternal mortality, homosexuality, cannibalism, predatory aggression, and sexual "wolfism." In some areas of Harlem, the density is so great that if it were continued over three New York boroughs, it would equal the whole population of the United States. We may wonder about the psychological and physiological results of such crowding.

The head of the psychology department at Manhattan College thinks that exposure to noise may create violent outbursts, and a professor of environmental medicine at the University of Texas thinks that noise is related to anxieties and duodenal ulcers. Other studies have shown that the noise in a subway will cause constriction of the cardiovascular system even if one is asleep. Such urban stress may be one of the reasons why a Chicago medical study in the early 1950s showed death rates from cardiovascular diseases to be 100 percent higher in Chicago than in adjoining rural areas for men 35 to 54, and almost 300 percent higher for those 55 and over.

No problem of the artificial urban environment is greater, or shorter of any solution, than the problem of traffic. The city creates a constant stream of movement between the central city and the suburbs and outlying areas. The automobile is by far the most widely used vehicle. Since World War II it has put out of business about 150 rapid transit systems. What has

---

4. Ralph Linton, *The Tree of Culture,* New York, Vintage, 1959, p. 39.

happened is suggested by the case of New York City. In the early years of this century, one could cross lower Manhattan faster by horse and buggy than he can now cross it by car. Such congestion has led some city planners to advocate banning all automobiles from downtown areas. San Francisco has built a very expensive rapid transit system, and other cities are considering similar plans. The success of any move to replace the automobile is likely to be thrown in doubt, however, by a study of Chicago commuters which showed that only 18 percent of them would be willing to give up their automobiles even for free transportation. Half would not travel by public transportation even if they were paid $.35 a ride.

"Every time you take a glass of water from a faucet in St. Louis . . . you are drinking from every flush toilet from here to Minnesota."[5] Thus did one newspaper story, perhaps overdramatically, describe the St. Louis water supply. Only one-fifth of all factories and less than one-half of all municipalities treat their waste before dumping it into streams. The Detroit, Miami, Hudson, and Potomac rivers in this country, the Seine and the Rhine abroad, are badly contaminated. In 1964 Stewart Udall, then secretary of the interior, gave impressive testimony to a congressional committee about destruction of fish and birds by pesticides washing from farms into rivers and lakes in widely scattered parts of the United States. The amount of pesticides in New Orleans water in 1964 was so high that if it had been milk, it could not have been sold in interstate commerce. Because there is not enough fresh water, many city dwellers drink water that has been cleaned once or more. It has been estimated that if pollution continues, present chemical methods of treatment will not be able to provide clean water in many cities by 1980. Suburbs with wells and septic tanks are a menace. In Peoria, Illinois,

and Dania, Florida, septic tank seepage has been found in well water. The Minnesota Health Department found the water in 24 percent of the wells in a subdivision near Minneapolis–St. Paul unfit for use in babies' formulas.

Urban air is perhaps the most serious of all the problems of cities. Ever since the term "smog" was coined in 1905, the situation has been getting worse. In 1965 Clair Patterson, a geochemist at California Institute of Technology, told the *New York Times* that, because of lead contamination of the air, the lead content in the blood of the average American was then 100 times the content in the normal human level. In 1953 New York City suffered an attack of smog so severe that had it not been for a fortunate wind to sea, an incredibly large segment of the population might have died. A year earlier 4000 deaths had been attributed in London to a week of smoke and soot. Solutions made from particles filtered from Los Angeles air have produced skin cancer in 75 percent of mice. Some estimates have held that in a day in Birmingham, Alabama, one breathes as many cancer producing irritants as are contained in two packs of cigarettes. Moscow planned to allow only natural gas as fuel after 1965; Soviet scientists had found that air pollutants can change human brain waves. Durban, South Africa, Kobe, Japan, the Po valley of Italy, and even Paris and Budapest suffer from air pollution.

In 1958 Dr. James P. Dixon, Commissioner of Health for Philadelphia, said that gas masks may be as common in a hundred years as shoes are today. In Osaka, Japan, for a little under three cents, one can now get twenty seconds' worth of clean oxygen from a vending machine. In 1965, however, Dr. Morris Neiberger of the University of California at Los Angeles, a world expert on air pollution, saw little hope in any kind of defense. He felt that smog, and not a nuclear war, would destroy mankind. He envisions human civilization gradually suffocating in its own wastes.

5. Quoted in Mitchell Gordon, *Sick Cities,* New York, Macmillan, 1963, p. 84.

We should note, in closing this section, that the megalopolis which followed the Industrial Revolution may conceivably have had some reason for existence before about 1900, but not since then. At that time the coming of electric power and electric communication had made it unnecessary to bring together such vast collections of people. Decentralization was technologically practical. It is also noteworthy that cities began decentralizing themselves to a degree at about that time. In the Metropolitan Region Study of New York, Raymond Vernon pointed out that since about 1910, housing, retail trade, wholesale trade, and manufacturing have all been moving from the central city to the suburbs. It is also important to note that between 1950 and 1961, more people between the ages of 20 and 30 left the city than entered it. New York lost 21 percent of her people in this age group; Chicago, 24 percent; Oklahoma City, 15 percent; Portland, 30 percent.

Rather than solving the problems of cities, however, these movements have for the most part increased the area of "slurb." They have taken wealth out of the central cities and often left them too poor to pay for needed services. The central cities, now heavily populated by racial minorities, suffer from increasing noise, dirt, and pollution; from summer heat and winter cold; from unemployment; from discrimination; from inadequate and crowded housing; and from insufficient schooling, recreation, and other public facilities. Meanwhile television and other media bring back news of the affluence that surrounds the central city. Thus urban blight coupled with "rising expectations" have made the central city America's most explosive social problem.

THE NEGRO REVOLUTION

In April 1968, following the assassination of Martin Luther King, the nation's Capitol was ringed by fires set by looters and rioters who, often unchecked, roamed the streets. Nothing could have dramatized more clearly the gravity of the racial crisis.

Weeks before, the National Advisory Commission on Civil Disorders, chaired by Governor Otto Kerner of Illinois, had published its analysis of the racial situation in the United States. The Kerner Commission was composed of "moderates," two Negro and nine white. Extremists were conspicuously absent. It saw three possible directions in which race relations might move.

The first was a continuation of present policies. "If this road was taken," said the commission, "large-scale and continuing violence could result, followed by white retaliation, and, ultimately, the separation of the two communities in a garrison state."[6]

A second possibility was a program for enrichment of life in segregated Negro ghettos, but without efforts to integrate Negroes into the whole society. "This," said the commission, "is another way of choosing a permanently divided society."

A third line of action was ghetto enrichment combined with positive programs to integrate "substantial numbers" of Negroes into society outside the ghetto. This the commission saw as the only workable solution. "The primary goal must be a single society, in which every citizen will be free to live and work according to his capabilities and desires, not his color."

To see why a committee of essentially middle-of-the-road Americans (including, among others, the chief of police of Atlanta) could see integration of races as the only solution, we need to look at the past and present position of Negroes in the United States.

A question often asked is why Negroes are different from other American minorities, who have in time succeeded in winning acceptance without

6. *Report of the National Advisory Commission on Civil Disorders,* GPO, March 1, 1968, p. 10, *et passim* (referred to hereafter as the Kerner Commission Report).

A street in Washington, D.C., after the 1968 riots.

special programs. The answer is simple. No American minority has been treated as have Negroes, and indeed few groups in the history of the world have been.

Other ethnic groups, such as Jews, Italians, Germans, Irish, and Poles, have brought with them rich social traditions and a meaningful group life. American Negroes, too, came from a rich background in Africa. Life in Africa in 1600 was not primitive savagery. It was quite highly developed in family organization, in political organization, and in arts and crafts. When they were seized as slaves, however, Negroes were severed from this background as suddenly and completely as an infant is severed from its mother by the cutting of the umbilical cord. Villages and families were broken up, and Negroes were relocated on American plantations which were usually rather widely separated. They were forbidden to form legal marriages, and it was thus impossible to reestablish a stable family life. Man and woman could be separated by the master at will. Thus the American Negro came about as close to having no social heritage as any group has ever come. In this respect he has been altogether different from other minorities.

Although most American minorities have at some time suffered exploitation and discrimination, none have suffered as systematically and continuously as have Negroes. Negro history in the United States may be roughly divided into five periods. (1) From the first landing of Negroes at Jamestown in 1619 to the introduction of the cotton gin around 1800, slavery was practiced but did not assume overwhelming importance. Many leading people in the North and South hoped for its abolition. (2) The cotton gin brought a rapid expansion of the cotton economy in the South, which raised the number of slaves from 1 million in 1800 to 4 million in 1860. (3) Legal freedom after the Civil War was followed by the increasing legalization of discrimination in the last years of the nineteenth century. (4) The organization of the National Association for the Advancement of Colored People in 1909–1910, and of the Urban League in 1911, brought several decades of organized efforts and slow gains. (5) The *Brown* v. *Topeka* decision of the United States Supreme Court in 1954, invalidating school segregation, was rapidly followed by the rise of a militant protest movement.

Throughout, Negroes have been second-class citizens, in law or in fact. The slave could not own property, make any legal contract, defend himself legally against abuse, or assemble publicly without a white person present. The dehumanized view of Negroes held even by the founding fathers is indicated by the fact that a slave was to be counted as three-fifths of a person in apportioning congressional representation. Even legally free Negroes, of whom there were a good many before the Civil War, had no freedom to move in the South, could associate with neither whites nor slaves, and were in constant danger of being enslaved themselves.

In the first years of the Civil War, Negroes in the Union army received less pay than whites. After the war organized groups such as the Ku Klux Klan conspired to deprive Negroes of their new legal rights. In New Orleans, Negroes meeting to discuss their right to vote were massacred by the mayor and police. In the late years of the nineteenth century, segregation and discrimination were written into the laws of the southern states, and treatment was little different in the North.

> *On trains all Negroes, including those holding first-class tickets, were allotted a few seats in baggage car. Negroes in public buildings had to use freight elevators and toilet facilities reserved for janitors. Schools for Negro children were at best a weak imitation of those for whites, as states spent 10 times more to educate white youngsters than Negroes. Discrimination in wages became the rule, whether between Negro and white teachers of similar training and experience or between common laborers on the same job.*[7]

With some changes, this summary by the Kerner Commission was true of large areas of the South into the 1960s.

The 1896 decision of the United States Supreme Court in *Plessy* v. *Ferguson* legalized "separate but equal" facilities. In 1913 Congress enacted segregation in federal offices, shops, restaurants, and lunch rooms. During World War I, Negroes were placed in separate units in the Army, barred from the Marines, and given menial jobs in the Navy. In World War II, Negroes were also in separate units, and their blood was segregated in blood banks. War industry often practiced the kind of discrimination openly advertised by one West Coast firm: "The Negro will be considered only as janitors and in other similar capacities. . . . Regardless of their training as aircraft workers, we will not employ them."[8]

The American Negro has been largely cut off from a social heritage, and faced everywhere with the opinion that he is a second-class human being —or no human being at all. No other minority has had this double experience. The result is usually severe damage to the Negro's sense of himself as a person. As we proceed in this book, we shall see that a large part of anyone's "self-image" comes from (1) his sense of his social roots and (2) what others think of him. With this background it may be easier for us to understand why Negroes today are so concerned with Negro history and "black power."

Negro discontent and protest began very early. In 1712 and 1741 Negro rebellions in New York resulted in the death of both blacks and whites. Slave uprisings were led by Gabriel Prosser in 1800, Denmark Vesey in 1822, and Nat Turner in 1831. In 1816 a group of Negroes were transported to Sierra Leone, in Africa, by a Negro shipowner. Frederick Douglass was a powerful Negro figure in the movement for abolition of slavery. Free Negroes as well as whites participated in an underground railroad, through which escaped slaves made their way to freedom. Since the Civil War there have been periodic race riots—New York in 1900, East St. Louis in 1917, Chicago in 1919, and many others. These could, however, be better described as white than as Ne-

---

7. *Ibid.*, p. 100.

8. *Ibid.*, p. 104.

gro riots, since it was Negroes who were primarily attacked.

There were organized Negro betterment movements in the nineteenth century. The National Negro Convention Movement, founded in 1830, called for an end of slavery and indignities against Negroes. Effective Negro movements became better established, however, around the beginning of this century. Booker T. Washington promoted a program for enabling Negroes to win white acceptance by attaining education, business success, and white moral standards. The Urban League, founded in 1911, has tried especially to expand employment for Negroes in cities. In 1914 Marcus Garvey founded the Universal Negro Improvement Association, whose main aim was emigration of Negroes to Africa. Garvey also worked to promote Negro businesses. His "separatism" reminds us of the present movement for black power.

Probably the most important step in the early part of the century was the formation of the National Association for the Advancement of Colored People by Negroes and white liberals in 1909–1910. The NAACP's most effective work has been done in the courts. Over the years it has, for example, won cases outlawing the famous "grandfather clause" which restricted Negro voting in southern states; outlawing racial discrimination by municipalities; abolishing the primary limited to whites; and, in 1954, invalidating school segregation. The CIO, although not a Negro organization, played an important part in black equality after 1935 because its policy was nondiscriminatory and its program called for mass organization of workers in large industries. An important step was the threat by A. Philip Randolph in 1941 to call a march on Washington to protest discrimination in employment. President Roosevelt responded by establishing a Fair Employment Practices Commission to promote nondiscrimination in hiring and firing.

The recent militant wave of Negro protest might well be dated back to 1942–1943, when CORE (Committee of Racial Equality) was established under the sponsorship of pacifists, mostly white. It began using nonviolent techniques in sit-ins and other demonstrations. In 1947 CORE sponsored a "Journey of Reconciliation" by an interracial group on a bus into the South. The great turning point of Negro protest was, however, the mass boycott against bus segregation in Montgomery, Alabama, in 1955–1956, which brought Martin Luther King to the fore. The Montgomery protest was followed by similar activities in Tallahassee, Florida, and Talladega and Birmingham, Alabama. In 1957, under the leadership of Dr. King, the Southern Christian Leadership Conference (SCLC) was founded to apply the Gandhian methods of active nonviolence to Negro protest.

A new dimension was added in 1960 with the beginning of student sit-ins at Greensboro, North Carolina. In the same year the Student Non-Violent Coordinating Committee (SNCC) was formed. The entrance of students shifted leadership from the "old guard" of Negro leaders and made the movement more militant and more urgent in its demands. In 1961 the freedom rides on buses by racially mixed groups through the South resulted in an order by the Interstate Commerce Commission banning segregation on public vehicles. In 1963 a march on Washington brought 250,000 people to the nation's capital, 20 percent of them white. Such pressures clearly influenced the passage of the Civil Rights Act of 1964, which outlawed discrimination in public accommodations. The mass demonstrations against voting discrimination at Selma, Alabama, in 1965 were followed by federal legislation protecting Negroes' right to vote.

At this point large gains had been made, but they served to make many Negroes more discontented. Increasing numbers of Negroes were voting, and public accommodations were opening. But only the surface of segregation had been scratched. The 1954 decision against school segregation had been enforced only to a limited degree. Negro income was actually rising more slowly than that of whites. "What's the use of being able to sit at a lunch counter," Negroes asked, "if you can't afford a cup of coffee?" There began a marked shift in the emphasis of the Negro movement

> . . . *from legal to direct action, from middle and upper class to mass action, from attempts to guarantee the Negro's constitutional rights to efforts to secure economic policies giving him equality of opportunity in a changing society, from appeals to the sense of fair play of white Americans to demands based upon power in the black ghetto.*[9]

There was also a movement away from nonviolence. Protest arose against the role of white liberals in the movement. CORE, founded primarily by whites, in 1965 voted to limit white leadership. The Black Muslims, organized around 1930, brought to the fore the dramatic figure of Malcolm X, who rejected collaboration with whites and the philosophy of nonviolence. In 1966 a march from Memphis to Jackson, Mississippi, led by James Meredith, brought to a focus the concept of black power, which was made famous by Stokely Carmichael. Black power has meant many things to many people: establishment of a separate Negro state, a separate Negro economy, an emphasis upon Negro tradition and history, a glorification of things black. "Black is beautiful." The term "Negro" has itself been rejected in favor of "black." The heart of black power is a belief that even the best intentioned white people cannot be trusted to protect or promote Negro interests. It calls therefore for an effort to mobilize every possible strength of the black community to struggle as a group for black objectives. Militant groups like SNCC and

the Black Panthers call for independent political action by blacks outside the major parties, and regard riots as legitimate forms of rebellion.

Not even a brief sketch of the Negro revolution can be complete unless it is related to (1) American poverty and unemployment and (2) other oppressed peoples throughout the world. The greatest problem of Negroes is that they are, as a group, desperately poor. There are approximately 50 million people in the United States living in poverty, that is, with family incomes of under $3000 a year. Of this "other America," as Michael Harrington called it in his influential book of that name, a majority are white, but this is only because whites make up about nine-tenths of the whole population. In terms of percentages, 37.3 percent of all nonwhite families had poverty incomes in 1964. Only 15.4 percent of whites were in poverty, considerably less than half that percentage.

The average Negro family income in the United States is a little more than half that of whites. Even Negro college graduates receive considerably lower pay than white graduates. Negroes have always been the last hired and the first fired. The Negro rate of unemployment is higher than that of whites. Negroes are concentrated in the lowest paying jobs.

Especially as discrimination in some areas has been somewhat relieved, Negroes have increasingly focused on economic discrimination. First of their objectives has been equal access to jobs with equal pay for equal work. But this is only the beginning of a solution, for an extremely high percentage of Negroes are unqualified at present for any but the lowest paying jobs. This is not their fault. It is simply the result of centuries of prejudice and discrimination, which have barred Negroes from better jobs and from the opportunity to train for them. It is, however, a hard fact. A second objective is, therefore, training opportunities, such as those afforded by the Job Corps, which will upgrade the skills of Negroes.

9. *Ibid.,* p. 107.

More still is required than this, however, for the incapacity of Negroes is more than lack of technical skill. It is lack of the total educational and social background, including language skills, necessary for higher paying jobs. Thus a third objective is the upgrading of all educational and social opportunities for Negroes, beginning before the school years, as in the Headstart program.

Some of the most informed Negroes, however, think that the remedy is more difficult than any of those just mentioned. Equal opportunity, upgrading of technical qualifications, enrichment of educational and social background will get jobs for Negroes only if jobs are available. Technological advance, especially automation, has raised a question as to whether there will be employment available for all in the future. These leaders, such as A. Philip Randolph, Martin Luther King, and Bayard Rustin, have stressed therefore that the Negro's economic problem can be solved only by long-range government policies that will ensure jobs and eliminate poverty for all, black and white. They have also stressed that these policies cannot be promoted successfully by Negro separation, but only by a united effort of all interested Negroes and whites. In this they have been joined by white liberal and labor leaders.

It is also important to recognize that the Negro revolution in the United States is not an isolated event. It is one aspect of a worldwide revolution of historically subjected peoples, especially in Asia, Africa, and Latin America. This revolution may be the most important event of our time.

The revolution has been brought about by a number of factors, one of the most important of which is the "revolution of rising expectations." An old folk proverb tells us that "eating breeds hunger." As long as they remained isolated in the rural South or in urban ghettos, knowing little of the outside world, Negroes were more able to accept their lot. But as they became able to contrast their poverty and deprivation with the affluence and opportunity of much of the rest of society, their own condition became intolerable. As long as Negroes were barred from voting, from public accommodations, and from any kind of real participation in the majority society, the reaction of a large number was resigned hopelessness. As soon as they were able to participate in American society to some degree, however, they began to demand much more. Similarly, as subjected peoples throughout the world have been brought face to face, by communications technology, with how the "haves" live, and as they have begun to share some freedom and opportunity, their discontent has risen. The "haves" customarily say of the "have-nots," "Give them an inch and they'll take a mile." This is exactly what we mean by the "revolution of rising expectations." The statement is generally true, for it is usually at least a mile to equal opportunity.

The unity of the Negro revolution with the larger world revolution is recognized by a large number of Negroes, especially since most of the rising peoples of Asia, Africa, and Latin America are nonwhite (or non–Anglo-Saxon). It is also recognized by the rising peoples elsewhere, who see subjection of American Negroes as part of a long-time and worldwide subjection of nonwhites by whites. It is important that we as students of social science be no less aware of the connection.

THE ORGANIZATIONAL REVOLUTION

Our age is one of large organizations. When groups of machines were substituted for human hands and tools, the size of productive operations increased enormously. The large factory replaced the craftsman's shop. Masses of laborers and supervisors took the place of a handful of skilled workers. Large amounts of money were necessary to finance this new scale of operation. Thus arose "big business." Today the biggest private business in the United States, the American Telephone and Telegraph Company, employs three-quarters of a million people.

The large business, operating a factory or system of factories, has become the model for all areas of modern life. Marketing has been taken over to a large extent by large chain organizations. Labor unions have grown to a size resembling big business, with a form of organization that also resembles it. The large modern university has been compared to a factory, with students as its "product." Communications has become a vast industry, dominated by national newspaper chains and radio and television networks. Advertising and public relations are likewise big business.

The Catholic Church has long been a vast organization. Today all the major Protestant and Jewish religious groups also have large overall organizations employing extensive personnel and having large budgets. Professional and amateur sport, from the Superbowl to the Olympic Games to the Little League, is operated by large organizations. Welfare and charity are managed by large bodies, such as the Community Chest, the United Fund, and organizations concerned with individual diseases or particular community problems. "Informal" social life has to a considerable extent become organized, as for example by national or international fraternal organizations like Rotary, the Shrine, and the Knights of Columbus.

The biggest of all organizations is government. The government of the United States spends annually over one hundred billion dollars, about one-fifth of the total national income.

Why is our world so dominated by large organizations? The development of the factory suggests a central reason. Large organizations are more efficient than small ones for doing certain things. Labor unions suggest a second reason. In a world of big organizations, one may need to be as big as those with whom he competes or deals (in this particular case, corporations). At the same time, unlimited size is not necessarily more efficient. Many of the things done by big organizations in our society could probably be done better by smaller and more informal groups. We shall return to this question later in the book.

Large organization in our society is marked not only by bigness, but by *bureaucracy.* To some people "bureaucracy" is very often an uncomplimentary word, as when we speak of "those bureaucrats." The term refers, however, simply to a particular way of organizing to do things. Bureaucracy is the type of organization designed to accomplish large-scale administrative tasks by systematically coordinating the work of many individuals.

The organization of bureaucracy is based on *specialization:* each of its members is an expert at performing one specific task. It also involves *hierarchy of authority.* This is shown by the typical "organizational chart," which is a pyramid wide at the bottom and narrow at the top, with authority passing from the top to the bottom. The military is the best example. Bureaucracy also involves a system of rules to which every person is subject. No one, even the foreman or "top boss," is supposed to make decisions arbitrarily. He can exercise only the authrotiy that is given him by the rules of the organization. Bureaucratic organization is also *impersonal.* The rules are supposed to be applied, not on the basis of personal preference, friendship, or feeling, but impartially according to the merits of the situation. It will be good for us to try to understand these characteristics by thinking of large organizations with which we have had personal experience—schools, government, business, the military, and so on.

The goal of bureaucracy is *rational efficiency,* that is, it seeks to find the shortest and best way to a given goal. Bureaucracy has become so widespread in our world, says its great student, Max Weber, because of its superior, machine-like ability to do the job. However, this is not necessarily true for all the things we want to do, and Weber overlooked some weaknesses of bureaucracy.

Bureaucratic organization is at its best when goals have been established and we want to waste the least motion in achieving them. It is not a very good instrument for making decisions when we do not know what we want. Thus it may work better in a factory turning out a given model of airplane than in a laboratory investigating possible new types of planes, or in a political party trying to establish a policy on cutting back air power. Some "nonrational" human activities are poorly suited for bureaucracy. It is not very well fitted to promote love, artistic creativity, or new religious experience. Since it is governed by a set of rules, bureaucracy is better suited to an unchanging situation than to meeting new problems. Needed change is likely to get fouled up in bureaucratic red tape. This problem is particularly important in an age of change. Impersonality may damage efficiency. If people feel that they are robots, their morale may suffer.

In actual fact bureaucracies are usually somewhat less rigid than their formal structure would make them appear. In a famous study of the Western Electric Company,[10] it was found, for example, that informal cliques of workers were more important in setting rates of work than were formal rules. Members of one clique almost always worked harder than those of the other. Supervisors who overlooked some of the rules, such as "No Smoking" signs on occasion, were generally more effective than those who enforced them strictly. Students of bureaucracy have thus found that alongside the formal organization there is always an informal organization which may be just as important in determining what really happens. This makes bureaucracy somewhat more flexible and human

than might appear at first view. It does not, however, change its main effect.

Large bureaucratic organization has given rise to *mass society*. By this we do not mean simply a lot of people or a high density of population. In fact, mass society is usually found in the industrialized parts of the world, which are generally among the less densely populated. Mass society refers to a situation where the individual is confronted by vast bureaucratic organizations and does not have effective small, informal, and personal groups in between.

In a preindustrial society, a person usually has strong ties to a large family spanning several generations. He belongs to a relatively small neighborhood or community. He participates in voluntary social, recreational, political, religious, and other groups which are usually small and local. In the industrial, urban, organizational society, these groups tend to weaken. The clan family breaks up into small households of individual parents and children. As we have seen, the personal neighborhood tends to be replaced by the impersonal city. Local churches, town meetings, labor unions, social and fraternal groups tend to become part of, or to be replaced by, large bureaucracies. Thus the individual tends to be related only to large, impersonal organizations: the corporation, the political party, the large school or university, the bureaucratically organized religious denomination, the organized recreational program, the public charity, and so on.

Part of mass society is *mass production*. Again, this does not mean simply quantity of production, but rather the standardization of products with the average person as the target. As Henry Ford first showed with the Tin Lizzie, the use of standardized machinery and standardized procedures to produce large numbers of identical products enables a large organization to produce them cheaply, because costs are spread over a large volume. This is what bureaucratic organization tends

10. Fritz J. Roethlisberger and William J. Dickson, *Management and the Worker*, Cambridge, Mass., Harvard University Press, 1947, chap. 23.

to do. Production for the taste of a few requires different machines or procedures and is more expensive. Thus people who are much taller or much stouter than the average find it difficult to buy clothes, if they do not live in a metropolitan area with "tall and big" shops. School and college courses intended for the "mass student" are not likely to have much imagination or depth; to include these to benefit a few serious students might make the courses too difficult for the many who must get by. Religious programs for a mass audience are not likely to contain many profound insights. Political candidates are likely to pitch their appeals to the less informed voters. The need for special educational TV stations speaks for the usual level of the commercial networks. The best buy for the tourist is often a standard "packaged" tour.

All this does not mean that people in a mass production society are always worse off because of it. People in less organized and affluent societies are, for example, rarely able to buy even standardized clothing, or any kind of tour abroad, packaged or otherwise.

The organizational society tends to standardize the person as well as the product. In the first place, we have become an "employee society." As we have seen, six out of seven people in the United States depend for their livelihood on selling their talents to an employer. Increasingly, the employer is likely to be a large corporation. On the job the person who works for such an organization must fit into the particular specialized slot for which he is hired. This is not all, however. His dependence on his employer does not end at the close of the working day. His whole life is likely to be under the scrutiny of the organization for which he works. The schoolteacher is not generally free in his off hours to choose his own personal habits, his sexual morals, or his politics. The federal government employee is likely to have had the most intimate details of his personal life scrutinized before he is employed. Private corporations are likely to screen not only the job candidate himself, but also his wife, his children, and his friends. The tendency is to leave no personal life that is one's own.

Several writers have stressed the pressures toward individual conformity. One example is *The Organization Man,* by William H. Whyte, Jr. American society, says Whyte, has traditionally honored the individual, the self-made man, the person who is his own master, whose ideas are his own. Today, he feels, we are more likely to honor the person who has really given himself up to the organization; who has no important ideas in conflict with the organization; who, in fact, thinks he has no *right* to have any such ideas. "When a young man says that to make a living these days you must do what somebody else wants you to do he states it not only as a fact of life that must be accepted but as an inherently good proposition."

General Electric, at the time of Whyte's book, trained its employees in techniques that would help them become good managers. One was "Never say anything controversial." One company president is quoted by Whyte as advising young executives: "The ideal is to be an individualist privately and a conformist publicly." (He did not advise, it appears, where and how it was safe for the young man to lead his "private" life.) A professor in a theological seminary said that, in contrast to students twenty years earlier, "The present generation of students are less inquiring of mind, more ready to accept an authority, and indeed most anxious to have it 'laid on the line.' "[11] We must bear in mind that *The Organization Man* was written in the 1950s, which was more a decade of conformity than the one that followed. Nevertheless, Whyte's ideas are well worth examining.

David Riesman, in a book entitled

11. William H. Whyte, Jr., *The Organization Man,* Garden City, N.Y., Doubleday, 1956, pp. 6, 135, *et passim.*

The Lonely Crowd, developed the idea that the typical individual in our society today is the "other-directed personality." Historically, the individual associated with the great social changes of the last few hundred years has been the "inner-directed" person. He has an inner sense of selfhood, conscience, and worth. He is guided, so to speak, by an internal gyroscope which determines his course. Today, Riesman thinks, he has been replaced to a large extent by the "other-directed" person. His guiding mechanism is a sort of inner radar that searches out what other people think and what they would like him to do and to be.

One of the great problems of bureaucratic organization is that of individual *responsibility.* The person in a bureaucracy tends to feel responsible to the rules and decisions of the organization rather than to his own judgment or conscience. Adolf Eichmann, who ordered massive extermination in the Nazi concentration camps, defended himself on the ground that he himself was only carrying out orders from his superiors. The trials at Nuremburg after World War II established the principle that people in a situation like that in Nazi Germany are obligated to disobey orders. However, there have been elected and appointed officials in the American government who have felt certain aspects of American foreign policy to be morally indefensible, and yet they have felt obliged to go along with their government. It is probably safe to say that a majority of Americans believe that draftees should unquestioningly accept the policies of their superiors, right or wrong.

It is not only in the largest affairs of national policy, however, that the problem arises. There is no bureaucratic organization in which the conscientious individual does not at some time face the choice between organization policy and his sense of morality. The pressures of bureaucracy are likely to urge, "Forget your conscience. Who are you to question?"

The problems raised by modern bureaucratic organization have given rise to what we may call the *antiorganizational revolution.* This is dramatized most strongly by the hippies, but it includes far more people, both young and older. The hippie movement is essentially a rebellion against the Establishment—the whole structure of the organizational society. This counterrevolution sees bureaucratic organization as destroying spontaneity, individuality, responsibility, and natural relationships among people.

The hippie's dislike for regular work is a protest against an economic organization that turns people into "organization men." His rejection of conventional dress, short hair, and conventional standards of order and cleanliness are a rejection of values that to him symbolize surrender to the Establishment. His campaign against established educational practices is for him a protest against a system that turns out standardized parts for an organizational society. His rejection of military life and of military conscription is a protest against the most thoroughly developed and destructive of bureaucratic organizations.

Rejection is accompanied by affirmation. The hippie affirms spontaneity (although his appearance and behavior may sometimes be as standardized in their own ways as are those of the organization man). He asserts the value of sex and of natural relationships of love among people. In the midst of the depersonalization of an organizational society, he is likely to be found in sensitivity and encounter groups which seek openness and honesty and stress the importance of immediate communication between "real selves." Here he may touch and handle the bodies of others physically as an antidote to the "distancing" which he feels to be imposed by the Establishment. Flowers express a relatedness to nature as opposed to bureaucratic regimentation. "Pot" and other drugs are a way out of the world of the Establishment into a wider consciousness.

Although older people may share in

it, the anti-Establishment revolution is essentially a revolution of the young against the old, in which older generations are seen as representing an oppressive social system aimed at mechanizing and depersonalizing all relationships and at suppressing the rising expectations of all dispossessed people. Of these the young feel themselves to be special spokesmen. Youth serves as the driving wedge of a strong and often bitter cleavage which seems to pit the young, the poor, the non-white, and the female against the old, the affluent, the white, and the male. One side charges its opponents with destroying all natural human relationships and aspirations. The other believes itself to be the defender of organized society against an inner tribe of "barbarians" who would annihilate it.

THE SEXUAL REVOLUTION

A famous anthropologist, after reviewing the practices of all peoples known to his science, concluded that almost nowhere has sexuality been more strongly controlled than in Western civilization. The strongest antisexual influence has been the Christian Church. In the beginning it was strongly opposed to sex and the "flesh," and it has not entirely lost that point of view. After the Protestant Reformation in the sixteenth century, Puritanism "turned with all its force against one thing: the spontaneous enjoyment of life and all it had to offer."[12] It shaped much of the life of western Europe. It did not shape all of it; the Restoration period after Cromwell in England and the period of the Enlightenment in France before the revolution were hardly periods of strict sexual morality. The Puritan influence has been particularly strong in the United States. In spite of many influences to the contrary, on balance the United States has been one of the most antisexual of countries.

It is equally clear that the United States has recently been undergoing a revolution in sexual attitudes and behavior. We cannot be altogether sure as to just when it began. In *Sexual Behavior in the Human Female,* published in 1954, Kinsey found that premarital intercourse by women born after 1900 was substantially greater than among women born before that time. There were no great differences, however,

12. Max Weber, *The Protestant Ethic and the Spirit of Capitalism,* trans. Talcott Parsons, New York, Scribner, 1958, p. 166.

among women born at different dates after 1900. If we are inclined to see the last decade as having brought something entirely new in sexual patterns, we should remember that the Roaring Twenties were also a rather "swinging" decade. We have no real proof that there is more sexual intercourse among college students today than there was in the 1920s, or later, for that matter. Yet we do suspect that there is more.

In some respects sexual change has clearly been moving very rapidly in recent years. In the late 1960s, movies were being seen by the general public that could not possibly have been released twenty-five years earlier, or in some cases probably even five years earlier. Nudity and actual sexual intercourse were shown on the screen. In 1939 the word "syphilis" was spoken in moving pictures for the first time. Thirty years later most of the obscene and profane terms in general use were appearing on the screen. Twenty years ago it was still illegal and dangerous to describe any contraceptive device in public print. Today "family" magazines offer detailed information.

In the 1960s some college health services were providing contraceptives for students, and many more college administrators were discussing whether they should. In the late 1950s, "intervisitation" of men and women in each other's dormitory rooms began in some more radical colleges. A decade later intervisitation was more widespread, and the doors were very often no longer kept open. In some college dormitories, unmarried couples were living together, although probably nowhere with official approval. College officials were discussing, however, the possibility of frankly coeducational dormitories for unmarried students. Another fairly recent change in sexual patterns has been the more open sexual talk and activity among young adolescents and preadolescents.

There are a number of reasons for the sexual revolution. Not the least of them is *technology*. Contraception has eliminated a large part of the fear of pregnancy which previously deterred people from sexual relations. The development of the condom and the diaphragm in the late nineteenth century and the introduction of the birth control pill and the intrauterine device (IUD) in recent years have been the main advances in the technology of contraception. We are not clear as to the exact effect of these contraceptives on sexual expression, but it is likely that all have promoted freer sexual behavior. Perhaps no less important has been the automobile. Since Henry Ford's Tin Lizzie, lovers have been able to get away from parents and neighbors to a degree impossible before. The car has provided two of the most common places for premarital and extramarital sex: the back seat and the motel.

A second important reason for the sexual revolution has been urbanization. As we have seen, one's neighbors in the city are less likely than one's neighbors in the town or country to (1) know about one's sex life or (2) to care if they do know or (3) to be able to harm one if they do care. One of the reasons that city dwellers are less likely to censure one's behavior is that their own standards have become secularized. In the city, not only sexual morality, but all values are less likely to be governed by traditional religious codes and more likely to be determined by practical or pragmatic results. Thus the small-town girl, confronted with sexual intercourse, may ask, "Is it sinful to do this?" The more secular approach of the city girl may be, "Will I get pregnant?" Or, on a more complex level, she may ask, "How will this affect my relationship with this man, or with my future husband and family, or my stability and growth as a person?"

One of the strong influences toward the sexual revolution has been science. The scientific approach tends to secularize all thinking and acting. It stresses experiment, observation, and prediction of probable results rather than reliance on established authority.

For many science has "disproved" religion, and thus undermined the strongest source of traditional sexual morality. Others disagree that science has invalidated religion and believe that both can contribute to sexual and other values. In either case, however, rigid and dogmatic codes are likely to be replaced by more flexible standards. Today even the orthodox religious person who believes in virginity before marriage is less likely to think that a person who "slips" has committed a virtually irreparable sin. Many deeply religious people will, indeed, find positive values in certain kinds of serious sexual relationships between unmarried people.

In addition, the scientific study of sexuality has greatly influenced sexual codes. Perhaps the greatest factor has been the work of Sigmund Freud (1856–1939). We shall examine this in some detail in later chapters. Freud made sex a subject to be discussed factually and objectively by physicians, scientists, and laymen. This was a very important breakthrough at the end of the Victorian period, when even a leg might be referred to only as a "limb." What Freud had to say about sex was just as revolutionary as the fact that he talked about it at all. In his therapy and research he claimed to have discovered that sexual disturbances lie behind all mental disorders. Freud himself was rather conservative about prescribing changes in sexual behavior. To some people, however, his work meant that all suppression of sexuality is harmful and that freedom from virtually all restraint is justified in the name of science. To others it meant at least that existing sexual morality is injurious and that psychological health requires greater sexual freedom.

Also extremely influential was the research of Alfred C. Kinsey (1894–1957) and his associates at Indiana University. The main works were *Sexual Behavior in the Human Male* (1948) and *Sexual Behavior in the Human Female* (1954). These are the most extensive studies of sexual behavior ever made. They were actually misnamed. They should have been called *Sexual Behavior in Some American Males and Females.* The basis for the Kinsey research was in-depth interviews in which volunteers provided extensive sexual histories. The research revealed interesting differences in sexual behavior between different educational levels, between different religious groups, between rural and urban dwellers, and between other social groups.

Like most important scientific researches on controversial topics, the Kinsey reports were strongly criticized from many quarters. An important question was whether respondents selected by the volunteer method were representative of the whole population. Nevertheless, it seems likely that most of what Kinsey reported was not very far from the actual behavior of Americans. Revelations of widespread premarital, extramarital, and homosexual relations may not have been new to many people, but to see them in print in a scientific report was rather a social shock.

Many people were inclined to conclude that "whatever is, is right," and to believe that what had been shown by Kinsey to be widespread was therefore justified. This conclusion does not, of course, necessarily follow, although Kinsey himself was inclined to encourage it. Some of Kinsey's findings about causal relationships were, in any case, quite important. The reports showed, for example, that frigidity was substantially higher among orthodox religious married women than among nonorthodox women. This suggested that the sexual standards of orthodox religion seem to promote sexual maladjustment in marriage. Women who had experienced orgasm in premarital intercourse were found much less likely to be frigid after marriage than those who had not experienced it (whether because they remained virgins until marriage or because their premarital sex experience was unsatisfactory). These findings raised serious questions about general taboos on premarital sex.

Human Sexual Response, published in 1966 by William H. Masters and Virginia E. Johnson, marked another high point in the sexual revolution. This was a study of physiological responses in volunteers who actually performed sexual intercourse under laboratory conditions. It is not likely that the whole spontaneous response of lovers in privacy can be duplicated in the laboratory; nevertheless, Masters and Johnson accumulated a large mass of new data on the physiology of sexual response. This has been used by them as a background for treating sexual disturbances. It is too early to judge how great an effect the Masters-Johnson study will have upon sexual behavior. It is hardly likely that it can fail to have a liberalizing effect. The very fact that the study could be made and published without great shock or protest in itself indicated a great change in sexual attitudes.

Another significant, although probably less influential, event was the release to the general public in 1965 of *Love and Orgasm,* by the psychoanalyst Alexander Lowen. This was based on the work of Wilhelm Reich, who had first used the term "sexual revolution" as the title of a book in 1930, and whose sexual theories were much more radical than those of Freud. Indeed, less than a decade before Lowen's book, a number of Reich's publications had actually been burned by the United States government. The impact of Lowen's work may perhaps not be wide, but neither its title nor its content would have been acceptable to a major publisher ten years before.

A final major factor behind the sexual revolution has been the *declining influence of parents over children.* Urbanization is partly responsible for this. On the farm families are likely to be close, and sons and daughters tend to learn from their parents the same activities of farming and homemaking that have been carried on for generations. In the city most children do not participate in their parents' work activities, and most are interested in preparing for vocations other than those of their parents. Thus family ties are weakened, and the school rather than the home tends to be the center of children's lives. The opinion of peers (their own age group) tends to become more important than that of parents. Thus when sex patterns are shifting, parents may have little power to influence children to hold to the old patterns. Some sociologists believe that we have developed in our high schools and colleges an almost distinct "adolescent culture," which has little respect for the values of the adult world.

Partly as a result of the sexual revolution itself, large numbers of parents have been more permissive with children from their earliest years and may be reluctant to try to influence their sexual behavior. The very rapidity of change, in sex patterns and elsewhere, is likely to make children regard their parents as "old fogies" and lead them to be contemptuous of their opinions and standards. Sheer numbers are also on the side of the sexual revolution: the population is growing increasingly younger, and today over half the population of the United States is under 25.

Although we have talked about the sexual revolution, it is in fact only a partial revolution. On the one hand, many people have rejected the old morality which restrained sexual behavior. On the other, however, there is little opportunity for real sexual freedom. Adolescents are claiming the right to free sexual expression, but society is still unclear as to whether to grant situations (such as completely coed dormitories) where it can take place in a normal atmosphere. This is true for older adolescents and even more true of younger adolescents. Youth in their early teens are now aware of their sexual drives, and many have access to contraceptives. But American and other Western societies are not yet prepared to do as many primitive societies (where sexual intercourse is expected to begin at puberty) do, that is, provide "bachelor huts" or other recognized facilities. It is not

clear, on the other hand, what will happen to the newly awakened drives of young adolescents if they are not provided with opportunity.

Another area of incompleteness in the sexual revolution is uncertainty as to the whole meaning of sexual expression. A good many young people, casting aside old sexual morals, have taken the position that sex is purely a matter of physical release in which a personal relationship is unnecessary. All social science shows this view to be false, for gratifying sex always involves a relationship between two whole personalities. However, the very efforts to prevent premarital sexuality have tended to make sex a mechanical act rather than a deep personal relationship. In automobile seats in fear of policemen, in homes in fear of parents, in dormitories in fear of house mothers, or in motels in fear of possible discovery, there is little chance for sex to be a relaxed and meaningful experience. Instead, it is likely to awaken the anxieties and guilt feelings associated with the old sexual morality.

While the less serious sometimes copulate more or less promiscuously and mechanically, serious young people are trying to answer the question as to when sexual relations are justified, and when they are not, and what their meaning in a total life can be. In doing so they are trying to reject both promiscuity and the old morality, but the halfway nature of the sexual revolution—rejection of old standards with little real opportunity for wholesome new experiences—make their task very hard.

The status of women also illustrates the halfway nature of the sexual revolution. Over the past 200 years, women have gained access to jobs previously confined to men, have become able to vote and hold office, and have been recognized as capable of the same sexual desire and satisfaction as men. Brides no longer promise to "obey" their husbands. But women typically find themselves paid less than men for the same work, are still barred from important economic, political, and social positions, are confined to the home by tasks of childbearing and child care, and are often exploited as sexual objects for male gratification. (In this sense *Playboy* is an illustration of the incompleteness of sexual change.) As a result there has arisen a movement for "women's liberation" which regards the female sex as one of the world's dispossessed groups and uses the same militant tactics and language employed by blacks and student protesters.

THE WEAPONS REVOLUTION

If we think of sexual change as explosive, another revolution has been literally so. Technological development has given rise in the last twenty-five years to an incredible increase in man's capacity to destroy. The central theme has been the development of explosive devices. Through World War II, the explosive generally used for bombing was TNT. In 1945 at Hiroshima, there was used in war for the first time a bomb whose power depended upon the fission of atoms. Seven years later, in 1952, the atomic bomb was followed by the hydrogen, or thermonuclear, bomb, whose explosive power lay in atomic fusion.

It is hard—perhaps really impossible —for us to grasp the figures that describe the weapons revolution. World War II blockbusters carried a little more than 20 tons of TNT. The atomic fission bomb dropped at Hiroshima was 1000 times as powerful. It was the equivalent of 20,000 tons (20 kilotons) of TNT. A 20-megaton thermonuclear fusion bomb is a thousand times as powerful as the atomic bomb, or one million times as powerful as a blockbuster. It is the equivalent of 20 million tons of TNT. This is not even the largest bomb already exploded. One 20-megaton thermonuclear bomb exceeds the power of all the bombs dropped on Germany and Japan during World War II.

Figure 1.2 describes the increase in destructive power graphically. If one foot of height represents the blockbuster, the Hiroshima bomb would equal the height of the Empire State Building, and the thermonuclear bomb the height of the orbit of the first Sputnik.

If a 10-megaton bomb were dropped on a city, the immediate *blast* effect would probably destroy virtually all buildings within a radius of about fourteen miles. With a 100-megaton bomb, the radius would be about thirty miles. This is, however, only the beginning. Even heavy, prenuclear bombing, as in Hamburg and Tokyo in World War II, created great fire storms, which sucked air into the bombed area and turned it into a virtual blast furnace. In an atomic attack, most people who survived the initial blast would either be quickly incinerated or suffocated by withdrawal of oxygen. A third effect is that of radiation. This would be relatively intense and could cause quick death to those exposed within and around the blast area. More damaging in the long run, however, would be radioactive fallout from contaminated material sucked up into the atmosphere and slowly deposited. The 15-megaton hydrogen bomb, Bravo, exploded in the Pacific in 1954, spread deadly radiation over an area of 7000 square miles.

In war bombs would not, of course, be used singly, but in massive attacks. In 1956 General James M. Gavin testified before a Senate committee that a large nuclear attack by the United States on the Soviet Union would probably kill hundreds of millions of people. If the wind were blowing east, people might die as far away as the Philippines. If it blew west, much of the population of western Europe might be killed. It was with such an attack that President Kennedy threatened Russia during the 1962 missile crisis. It has been estimated that an all-out attack of less than 20,000 megatons (fewer than 1000 20-megaton bombs) could destroy the United States as a nation, with possible virtual annihilation of our people, cities, villages, forests, and farmland. If she does not have this many bombs now, Russia can have them shortly. The United States and Russia together have nuclear weapons at least equal to ten tons of TNT for every person in the world. As long ago as 1958, the Federation of American Scientists calculated that existing nuclear weapons could cover the earth with enough radiation to make any life on land impossible for a period of ten years.

The development of carriers for bombs has been equally revolutionary. World War II bombers traveled about 300 miles per hour. One of these would have required about sixteen hours to fly with an atomic load from Washington to Moscow. An attack by such planes could be detected fairly easily and met with conventional defensive planes. With 650-mph jet bombers, the job of defense would be harder, but perhaps manageable. With rocket-powered missiles, however, the situation has been entirely changed.

After World War II, the United States decided to try to develop a ballistic missile capable of carrying an atomic warhead. At first the task seemed almost impossible, but in 1957 the first Atlas missile was launched. By 1962 it was reported that the Air Force had 126 Atlas missiles. Today both the United States and the U.S.S.R. have enough intercontinental ballistic missiles (ICBM) to carry massive nuclear attacks. These could make the trip from Washington to Moscow, or Moscow to Washington, in thirty minutes. In this short time, detection becomes much more difficult. Detection devices have not always been successful even in distinguishing missiles from meteors and other phenomena. Even if an attack should be detected, effective defense is probably impossible. Today both nations are prepared to launch attacks from both land bases and submarines. China has also developed nuclear bombs and carrying missiles.

This weapons revolution has changed the whole nature and meaning of warfare. Before 1945 it was possible at least to conceive of a defense against any possible kind of offensive. It was possible to talk of being so strong that

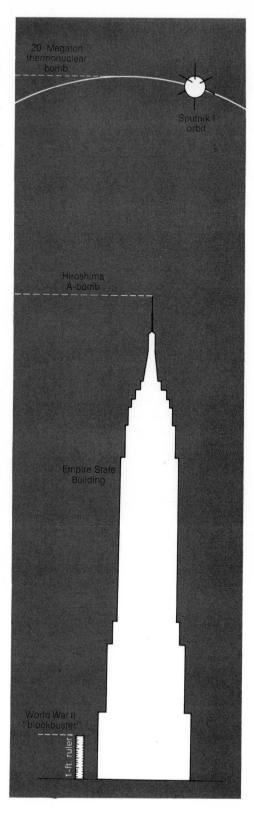

Figure 1.2. Relative explosive power of weapons developed in the twentieth century.

no other nation would dare attack. If war came, it was possible to conceive of winning it. In addition, one could feel that under the worst circumstances, his nation would in all likelihood survive.

None of these things is true any more. If a large proportion of the world's existing nuclear weapons were used in a nuclear war, it is quite conceivable that civilization would be destroyed or human life rendered impossible. Even short of such a total catastrophe, all participants would almost certainly be so damaged that the restoration of their way of life would be unlikely.

It is very doubtful that there is, or can be, any effective defense against massive nuclear attack. Previous methods of defense against nonnuclear weapons have been content with stopping a relatively small part of the attack. In World War II, for example, the British eventually defeated the German Luftwaffe by shooting down only about 10 percent of their planes. Such a percentage would be totally inadequate for nuclear defense. Trying to stop ICBMs with countermissiles has been compared to trying to stop bullets with bullets, and it is noteworthy that no one has yet developed an effective defense against the bullet. Passive defense through massive programs of underground shelters might save some lives, but such a program would be enormously costly. The task of moving and keeping a population underground for an indefinite period would be enormous. The problems of coming out and trying to reestablish a society in the face of almost total physical destruction and massive radioactivity would probably be overwhelming.

Some people hope that the sheer power of nuclear weapons will prevent their use by deterring all nations from attack. This might happen, it is reasoned, if one nation should have a large superiority in nuclear armament. This was the case in the first few years after Hiroshima, when the United States was the only atomic power. It is not likely to happen again, for other nations have joined the "atomic club," and more may join. It is important to note here a very important difference between conventional and nuclear weapons. A nation with a large advantage in conventional weaponry may be relatively safe from attack. A nation with a large superiority in nuclear weapons might, however, very conceivably be attacked by a nation much less powerful, provided the attacker felt itself strong enough to knock out the larger power with a first strike so that it could not retaliate. In 1962 the United States, with 60,000 missiles, did not feel safe at the prospect of even 40 in Cuba.

The hope for peace through deterrence must thus rest on mutual rather than one-sided deterrence. All nations with atomic weapons will be so strong, it is hoped, that no one will dare to attack. To a considerable extent this has been the case for some years with the United States and Russia. The Cuban missile crisis was a dramatic example. Again, however, there is always the possibility that one nation will try to get in a devastating first strike to which the other will be unable to retaliate effectively. The nation that did so might not even intend to be an aggressor.

Let us imagine nations A and B, each armed (like the United States and the U.S.S.R.) with enough power to destroy the other (and more besides). Neither intends to strike first, but both want to be sure of being able to retaliate with an effective second strike if attacked. In order to increase its sense of security, nation A increases its nuclear forces. Nation B interprets this as preparation to launch a first strike. To prevent this, nation B attacks, hoping to beat nation A to the punch. Thus the very effort to deter the enemy has actually produced an attack instead. Any nuclear "balance of terror" is very shaky and runs the risk that the very show of strength intended to prevent war may instead start it.

The balance of terror is precarious in other ways. Accident or the act of a mentally disturbed person might start an unintended war. A few years ago a thermonuclear bomb dropped from an American plane in North Carolina with all but one of its "fail-safe" devices released. Had it exploded, it is conceivable that this might have been interpreted as an attack by a foreign power and have led to retaliation. Former Secretary of Defense James Forrestal was mentally ill and eventually killed himself. What might such a person do if he had access to a nuclear "button"? The longer the nuclear arms race continues, the higher the probability that at some time an unintended war will be started.

At present nuclear powers appear to have decided that all-out use of nuclear weapons would be mutually disastrous. They continue, however, to carry on conventional wars under the nuclear "umbrella." There is always the danger that a conventional war will escalate into a nuclear war. This has been a constant danger in the war in Vietnam. At some point the situation may become like the game "chicken," in which two drivers approach each other at high speed, each straddling the same center line, and the first to turn is the loser and coward. Two nuclear powers in a conventional war might both become so "committed" that one, or both, might feel it better to use nuclear weapons than to lose "face." The situation is complicated by the fact that both American and Russian conventional forces are now armed with "tactical" nuclear weapons for use in the field. They have not been used yet, but should they be employed, escalation into a large-scale nuclear war would be much harder to prevent.

Smaller nations in the nuclear "club" might trigger a war between major powers. Should Israel or Egypt, for example, obtain and use nuclear weapons, it might drag the United States or Russia into a major nuclear exchange. Cuba illustrates how possession of nuclear weapons by a smaller power might set off a major nuclear conflict.

In concentrating our attention on the threat of nuclear weapons, we have so far ignored the development of chemical and bacteriological warfare. This has also reached the point where it would be at least theoretically possible to exterminate mankind. Nerve gas has now been developed to the point where "a few good breaths or a few drops on the skin kill in a matter of minutes." It has been estimated that there is enough nerve gas in the Rocky Mountain arsenal to kill everybody on earth. The U.S.S.R. is also stockpiling nerve gas. Biological toxins and bacteria that would start massive epidemics have also been stockpiled. One glass of botulism toxin contains enough poison to kill the whole human race. So far methods for distributing chemical and biological poisons are imperfect. One problem is that these poisons may back up and kill people in the nation using them. One of the great threats, however, lies in the ease with which small nations as well as large can produce them.

For all these and other reasons, the statement made early in the nuclear age by a group of scientists still holds true, or is more true than ever:

In the end, only the absolute pre-vention of war will preserve human life and civilization in the face of chemical and bacteriological as well as nuclear weapons. No ban of a single weapon, no agreement that leaves the general threat of war in existence, can protect mankind suffi-ciently.[13]

The problem is how to move in this direction, in the face of fears of dis-armament. So far, four major steps have been taken away from an uncon-trolled nuclear race. (1) In 1963 a treaty was signed banning nuclear tests above ground. (2) In 1966 the United States and Russia banned the use of nuclear (or any other high ex-plosive) weapons in outer space. Early in 1967 this agreeent was ratified by sixty nations. The United States and the U.S.S.R. also agreed at this time to discuss mutual reduction of nuclear stockpiles. (3) Later in 1967 the Treaty of Tlatelolco forbade the production of nuclear devices in Latin America. The ban extended to production for indus-trial as well as military uses. (4) In 1968 a nonproliferation treaty pledged the United States, the Soviet Union, and Great Britain not to make nuclear weapons available to nations not now possessing them. A number of nonnu-clear countries agreed not to accept nuclear arms. None of these agree-ments has included Communist China.

Aside from the threat of extermina-tion itself, the weapons revolution has produced two other great problems. One is the increasing role of the mili-tary in national life. Today the United States spends about 15 percent of its total national product for military pur-poses. The U.S.S.R., with a less pro-ductive economy, spends about 25 percent. The United States Department of Defense is the largest organization of any kind in the world. In 1960 it owned an area approximately equal to

that of Rhode Island, Delaware, Con-necticut, New Jersey, Massachusetts, Maryland, Vermont, and New Hamp-shire combined. It had assets and per-sonnel three times as great as the combined total for United States Steel, American Telephone and Telegraph, Metropolitan Life, Standard Oil of New Jersey, and General Motors.

The military tends to oppose all efforts at disarmament; in the United States it bitterly fought, for example, the 1963 nuclear test ban. This is partly because military men, like other people, like to keep their jobs and see their profession strong. It is partly be-cause most military men, like many others, are unable to see that the ways of doing things which prevailed before 1945 simply do not apply to the world of the weapons revolution.

Extension of military power is a threat to democratic institutions. In the first days of the United States, Alex-ander Hamilton warned that excessive dependence upon soldiers might ele-vate the military state above the civil state. In 1835 in *Democracy in America,* the great French observer of American life, Alexis de Tocqueville, pointed out, "All those who seek to destroy the liberties of a democratic nation ought to know that war is the surest and the shortest means to ac-complish it. This is the first axiom of the science."[14] In his farewell ad-dress, President Dwight D. Eisenhower warned against increase in power on the part of the "military-industrial com-plex."

One example of how military power destroys freedom is the role of scien-tific research. Today the best scientific minds in the nuclear powers are preoc-cupied with preparations for destruc-tion. The central feature of science is the free exchange of results, but in the nuclear age a considerable part of scientific research is classified and un-available to other scientists. Univer-sities, which are supposedly dedicated

13. *Proceedings of Pugwash Conference of Inter-national Scientists on Biological and Chemical Warfare,* Pugwash, Nova Scotia, August 24–30, 1959, pp. 5–6.

14. Alexis de Tocqueville, *Democracy in America,* New York, Knopf, 1945, vol. 2, p. 269.

to the free search for truth, collaborate in these restrictions upon freedom of thought and inquiry. In many cases they have become so heavily subsidized by the military that they have become dependent upon it.

A final problem of the weapons revolution is the kind of responsibility that it places upon those who make political and military decisions. Before 1945, when a nation declared war or used military threats to back up its policies, only its own citizens and those of the enemy were generally involved. Today, when they threaten to use nuclear weapons, political and military leaders threaten the extermination of neutral peoples and perhaps of the human race. They say, in effect, that the political interest of their nation justifies the possibility of depriving of life untold numbers of people both innocent and unborn. In doing this they are assuming powers of judgment and decision which before 1945 were given only to God. In a democratic society, at least, all people share to some extent this responsibility of playing God. The historian Arnold Toynbee has said that future generations must look back upon us—who would take such risks with the human fate for the sake of uncertain political ends—as criminals on a monstrous scale. It is hard to escape his judgment.

The drastic nature of the weapons revolution has led to antimilitary movements that are equally revolutionary. One is direct personal war resistance. The War Resisters League of which

Albert Einstein was once a sponsor, has as its slogan, "Wars will cease when men refuse to fight." An increasing number of young people seem to find this thought a meaningful answer to the weapons revolution. Until fairly recently personal war refusal was usually limited to religious conscientious objectors. In recent years in the United States, it has spread to the point where many young men, rather than just accepting the draft, weigh emigration, jail, and the military as equally real alternatives. Related to war resistance is the spread of the philosophy of nonviolence as a method of social action. While some of the dispossessed call strongly for revolutionary violence as a way of changing things, an increasing number feel that leaders like Gandhi, King, and Chavez have been right in rejecting the whole method of violence.

In this first chapter we have discussed seven major revolutions of our time. These are, of course, not separate, but interrelated. No one can understand any one without understanding at least some of the others. It will be a good exercise to take each revolution in turn and illustrate specifically for ourselves how it is related to other revolutions.

These first pages should have impressed upon us why it is important to understand and, if possible, influence our changing society. We shall now examine what social science is, and what it may be able to contribute to our revolutionary times.

Suggestions for further reading

At the end of each chapter we shall discuss briefly a number of readings that may enable students (and teachers) to enrich their understanding of the material of that chapter. These are books which have been useful to the author in his thinking on the subject of the chapter, as well as other books of the kind which should be part of the experience of any educated person. They may be used throughout the book as a basis for special class reports and discussion.

There are, of course, many good books on

the revolutions of our time. A fine and thorough treatment of the long-run development of technology is Technics and Civilization, *by the cultural historian LEWIS MUMFORD (available in paper, Harcourt Brace Jovanovich, 1963). The impact of twentieth-century technology upon the American scene is treated in GILBERT M. OSTRANDER's* American Civilization in the First Machine Age: 1890–1940 *(Harper & Row, 1970). A widely read book on the revolution in mass communications is MARSHALL McLUHAN's* Understanding Media *(McGraw-Hill, 1966). An* important and provocative view of the technological revolution appears in The Technological Society (*Knopf, 1964*), by the contemporary French writer *JACQUES ELLUL*. Those who wish to project technological development into the future may do so with *HERMAN KAHN* and *ANTHONY J. WEINER* in their forecast, The Year 2000 (*Macmillan, 1967*).

Every educated person who lives in the era of the population explosion should be acquainted firsthand with *THOMAS MALTHUS'* "Essay on the Principles of Population" (1798). A useful current collection of readings is Population, Evolution, and Birth Control, *assembled by GARRETT HARDIN* (2nd ed., W. H. Freeman, 1969).

A balanced presentation of the social role of the urban life is found in *LEWIS MUMFORD's* The City in History (*Harcourt Brace Jovanovich, 1961*). *MITCHELL GORDON's* Sick Cities (*Pelican, 1966*) is a dramatic but highly factual and readable treatment of the modern urban scene. Those who are more optimistic about city life may find support for their hopes in The Secular City by *HARVEY COX* (*Macmillan, 1966*). Cox stresses the positive role of urbanization in liberating people from arbitrary tribal controls.

With respect to the revolution of rising expectations, no one can claim to be really informed unless he is acquainted with *GUNNAR MYRDAL's* classic study of the American Negro in An American Dilemma (*rev. ed., Harper & Row, 1962*). Of great importance among recent materials is the Report of the National Advisory Commission on Civil Disorders—*the KERNER COMMISSION report* (*Dutton, 1968*). It is hard to get inside the thinking of many dispossessed groups unless one is familiar with the highly influential book by the French Negro psychiatrist, *FRANTZ FANON*, who wrote The Wretched of the Earth (*Grove, 1968, paper*). Similar in view and also very influential is Soul on Ice (*McGraw-Hill, 1968*), the prison writings of Black Panther *ELDRIDGE CLEAVER*, one of the best cultural critics now writing. *WILLIAM H. WHYTE, JR.'s* The Organization Man (*Doubleday, 1956, paper*) and *DAVID RIESMAN's* The Lonely Crowd (*rev. ed., Yale University Press, 1950*) are such influential treatments of the organizational revolution that it can hardly be discussed without reference to them. Another thorough treatment by a university social scientist is *PETER BLAU's* Bureaucracy in Modern Society (*Random House, 1956*). Another approach by a very able political scientist is The Organizational Society, by *ROBERT V. PRESTHUS* (*Vintage, 1962, paper*).

The title volume for current sexual change is The Sexual Revolution, by the radical psychoanalyst *WILHELM REICH* (*Noonday, 1963, paper*). (Incidentally, Reich is the only social scientist to have his writings officially burned by the United States government. His ideas have also been very influential in recent sensitivity and encounter groups.) The *KINSEY* volumes, Sexual Behavior in the Human Male (*Saunders, 1948*) and Sexual Behavior in the Human Male (*Saunders, 1954*) are important not only for the information they contain, but as documents that shaped the thinking of a generation. The more recent *WILLIAM MASTERS–VIRGINIA JOHNSON* study, Human Sexual Response (*Little, Brown, 1966*), is worth reading as a much debated study in sexual physiology, and also as an example of the changing temper of our times.

An authoritative account of the revolution in weapons technology is The Weapons Culture (*Norton, 1968*), by nuclear scientist *RALPH LAPP. FRED J. COOK's* The Warfare State (*Macmillan, 1960*) is a thorough description of the growth of military power in American society. In Sanity and Survival (*Vintage, 1968*) psychiatrist *JEROME D. FRANK* analyzes how the weapons revolution has shaped our thinking in a way which he believes is pathological.

Chapter two
What is social science?

Social science is part of man's effort to understand his universe through the methods called science. All through history some people have thought about their society and tried to understand it. To a large extent, however, it has only been in the last 200 years that their thinking was combined with systematic observation.

Social science has been in large measure a result of the technological revolution and the social changes that have accompanied it. Society before the Industrial Revolution was not unchanging, but the rise of technology made change much more rapid and shattered the traditional patterns of life without providing new ones to take their place. Social science arose in part out of the effort to find new patterns. The misery of the working classes in the new industrial cities of the nineteenth century led, for example, to a number of systematic studies of the urban poor. The destruction of authoritarian political regimes in the English, French, and American revolutions led to a more open attitude toward society. No longer were the answers given by the authority of kings. Participation by more of the people in the processes of government led to a more experimental attitude toward the way society operates. The secularization of life led people to look to science more than to religion for answers, in the social as well as the physical world.

To understand social science, we must first ask how scientific investigation is distinguished from other kinds of human activity and knowledge. We must ask how social science differs from physical or natural science. We must ask, also, how it is related to the other sciences. We need to look also at how social science is related to those studies that we call the humanities and how it is different from them. We must look at the particular methods that social scientists use. We need to examine the different fields or disciplines into which social science is divided and to know how these fields are separated and also how they are interrelated.

In this chapter we shall also be concerned with how science, and social science in particular, is related to society as a whole. In particular, how free are scientists to investigate? What barriers to science exist? What kinds of social interests favor science, and what kinds oppose it? How do these interests influence scientific investigators? Are the barriers to free investigation greater or fewer in the social sciences than in the other sciences?

THE NATURE OF SCIENCE

Science, of which social science is a part, rests first of all upon *systematic observation,* which is different from several other methods of getting knowledge. One of these other methods is casual observation in which broad conclusions are drawn from a small number of facts not very carefully gathered. Another is common sense,

For there are two modes of acquiring knowledge, namely, by reasoning and experience. Reasoning draws a conclusion and makes us grant the conclusion, but does not make the conclusion certain nor does it remove doubt so that the mind may rest on the institution of truth, unless the mind discovers it by the path of experience; since many have the arguments relating to what can be known, but because they lack experience they neglect the arguments, and neither avoid what is harmful, nor follow what is good. For if a man who has never seen a fire should prove by adequate reasoning that fire burns and injures things and destroys them, his mind would not be satisfied thereby, nor would he avoid fire, until he placed his hand or some combustible substance in the fire, so that he might prove by experience that which reasoning taught. But when he has actual experience of combustion his mind is made certain and rests in the full light of truth. Therefore, reasoning does not suffice, but experience does.

—Roger Bacon (1214?–1294), Magnum Opus, *from W. S. Fowler*, The Development of Scientific Method, *New York, Pergamon Press, 1962, p. 36.*

which science has often shown to be completely wrong. A third is pure reason, which attempts to arrive at knowledge of the world through mental processes alone.

Aristotle was a great biologist because, unlike his contemporaries, he observed animals with scrupulous care and was thus able to present descriptions, many of which are still valid today. His physics was, however, mainly "armchair" science, most of which had to be revised later by the careful observations of Galileo, Newton, and many others. Aristotle's contributions to biology, great as they had been, were improved upon in the Renaissance when taboos against dissection of bodies were broken down. During the Middle Ages, scholars tended to look to reason alone, or reason based upon a few unsystematic observations, for their knowledge of the world. Roger Bacon, who himself lived in the thirteenth century, effectively pointed out the limitations of this method (see the quotation above).

In social science generalizations about poverty became more reliable in the nineteenth century when factory inspectors in England and social scientists like Le Play in France studied systematically the life conditions and spending habits of working class people. Discussions about sex or prejudice have become less armchair when based upon systematic studies like the Kinsey reports, the Carnegie study of the American Negro in *An American Dilemma,* or the American Jewish Committee's investigation of the social and psychological characteristics of the authoritarian personality. Generalizations about military life were made more solid by Samuel Stouffer's study of the American soldier, which showed that a number of common sense beliefs about the attitudes of soldiers were simply contrary to fact.

It would be completely wrong, however, to suppose that science is simply a collection of observations. It is, rather, a system of organized statements concerning *relationships* among observations. These statements are called hypotheses, theories, and laws.

If, as legend reports, Newton observed an apple falling, what was important was not the fall of the apple, but his conclusion that the forces at work upon the apple were universal forces which could also be found operating in the orbits of planets. The observation of the apple was significant because it led to the hypothesis of a universal gravitational force, which underlies the whole Newtonian view of the universe. This abstraction from observation had tremendous power to change the modern world. To use an example suggested by the modern physicist Max Planck, the scientist is like the student of human population growth who plots on a chart the actual observed population of the world at different times and then connects the points with a curve that enables him to predict future population. Darwin's own careful and extensive observations, including those made as a naturalist on H.M.S. *Beagle,* began to fit together into the theory of universal organic evolution after he had read the writings of Thomas Malthus on the struggle for existence which keeps populations in check.

It is very important to emphasize that the hypotheses, theories, and laws that make up the body of science are abstractions about observed relationships. As Einstein has said, science can tell us something about the chemical composition of soup, but it can never give us the taste of the soup. We must look elsewhere for this. We must also look elsewhere if we want not abstractions about social relationships, but the whole actual experience of social events. Social science can generalize about the causes or results of race riots, but as such it cannot give us the concrete experience of being in a riot.

It is not enough merely to generalize from observations; hypotheses must be capable of being tested. They must be formulated in such a way that one can say, "If this hypothesis is valid, then this can be observed under these conditions." The process of constructing hypotheses from observations is called "induction"; the process of inferring observations from hypotheses is called "deduction." Both are inseparable parts of science.

Let us take the hypothesis that tobacco smoke, or smog, is a cause of cancer. A deduction would be that if tobacco tar, or smog particles, are ap-plied to the skin of laboratory mice, in time the mice will develop cancer. If this result actually occurs, we can say that the hypothesis has been in some measure verified. (It can never be completely proved, as any scientific hypothesis cannot, because the result may actually be due to some other factors that we have overlooked.) One may hypothesize that taboos on premarital sex are likely to impair sexual adjustment in marriage. From this hypothesis it might be deduced that people with satisfactory premarital sex experience will have better experience after marriage. Kinsey's studies would support this inference, although not conclusively.

We will note here that a scientific hypothesis should specify procedures that would test it; these procedures should be such that other competent investigators can repeat them and agree upon the observed results. The ideal form of testing is perhaps through the controlled experiment, in which all factors except one variable are held constant. For example, if one takes two plants from the same stock, waters and fertilizes them in the same manner, but places one in the sunlight and the other in the shade, he may reasonably conclude that any observed differences in their growth are related to the variable factor of sunlight. If two groups of women are similar in all known respects except that one has had access to contraceptives and the other has not, then differences in the rate of pregnancy may reasonably be attributed to the variable factor of contraception.

Hypothesis, theory, and law represent stages in verification. A statement of relationships that has not received considerable verification is a hypothesis. If it is supported by a substantial number of observations, preferably by independent observers, it may be accepted as an established theory. Further verification may give it the status of a law. For example, Einstein's speculation that space is curved was a hypothesis until it was supported by observa-

Social science is the study of the group behavior of human beings.

tions of the path of light around the planet Mercury. Darwin's conclusions about the origins of species have received enough verification to be referred to as the "theory of organic evolution." Newton's generalizations about the behavior of bodies at rest have conformed to so many observations as to be considered laws within the body of physics. These distinctions among hypothesis, theory, and law are not extremely important, for they shade into one another. What is significant is that theory, in the general sense, is not wild, unconfirmed speculation, but the most important thing in science.

Science is a *body* of observation and theory. It is a *method* of verification. It is also an *attitude*. The scientist is committed to learning more about how things are, regardless of how his findings affect his personal interests or prejudices. That is, he tries to be objective. Science, said one famous physicist, is "doing your damndest with your mind, no holds barred." The true scientist, said the philosopher

Bertrand Russell, is able to "look into the face of hell and not be afraid." Few scientists, perhaps none, are so objective, but objectivity is at least a scientific ideal.

THE NATURE OF SOCIAL SCIENCE

What now is social science? We can begin with a rough working definition which will become sharper as we proceed through the book. *Social science is the study of the group behavior of human beings.* It is concerned with the behavior of families, factories, churches, communities, nations, and other groups. It is also concerned with the behavior of individual people insofar as this is influenced by their belonging to groups. Social science is not concerned with inanimate objects, as such, or with other species of plants or animals, as such. These are the subject matter of astronomy, geology, physics, chemistry, and biology. Neither is it concerned with that behavior of human beings that is not influenced by their participation in groups. Such behavior is, in fact, very hard to find. Insofar as it exists, it is studied by psychology. Many people would include at least some of psychology within the social sciences. Sometimes the term "behavioral science" is used instead of "social science" to include all sciences concerned with human behavior.

What do social scientists do? Broadly, they do the same things that all scientists do: they observe, they generalize, they verify. We shall see shortly that the nature of the subject matter they study limits the methods that social scientists can easily use. This is, however, true of all sciences.

Some of the basic methods by which social scientists gather data are illustrated by two of the early social investigations already referred to. In connection with legislation to protect industrial workers, the British government employed staffs of investigators to study the condition of the poor. Staff members interviewed employers, clergymen, other local authorities, and workers themselves. In an investigation conducted from 1840 to 1842, investigators filled out prepared tables with data on the employment of children and conditions of work. Twenty staff members held personal interviews with workers. Investigators went into the mines to study conditions firsthand, and some even became ill while there.

In the 1890s a Liverpool ship owner, Charles Booth, gave much of his time and money to studying poverty in England. He conducted extensive interviews with London school inspectors, who were responsible for working-class children. He employed people to study the major trades in England. He summed up data dealing with millions of individuals. He personally lived in poor areas. He divided the people he studied into classes according to income. In each class he selected individual families for personal interviews. On the basis of these studies, Booth was able to make specific recommendations for dealing with poverty.

Methods of social science research have been refined since these early studies. They illustrate, nevertheless, some of the most important techniques of investigation now in use:

Field observation *dealing with a specific problem. The use of tables,* or schedules, *on which data are plotted as the problem is studied.*

The use of personal interviews.

Use of statistical data *to give an overall, generalized picture.*

Case studies *of individual workers and their families, to furnish more concrete detail.*

The technique of the participant observer, *who becomes personally engaged in the data he studies.*

Social scientists today also have at their disposal methods of observation not available to nineteenth-century investigators, or significant improvements upon their techniques. We can name some important areas of advance.

Statistics

Government agencies, such as the Bureau of the Census, the President's Council of Economic Advisors, and agencies of the United Nations, make available extensive and complex statistical data. Private agencies, including foundations, also collect such statistics. New methods make the data more easily available and more easily used. Today Booth would not need to get vast numbers of cases, but could use sampling techniques such as those employed by public opinion polls. With these it is possible to let a small number of cases represent a large population. Methods of statistical correlation make it possible to summarize a degree of relationship between two (or more) sets of data in a single figure. For example, school performance scores will generally show a positive "coefficient of correlation" with family income. The techniques of probability statistics enable a researcher to measure through a single figure the likelihood that an observed result could have occurred by chance. Thus it may be found that a difference as large as that found between the percentages of Democrats and Republicans in an upper-class district could have occurred by chance only one in a hundred times. It is not likely that such a difference is accidental.

Depth analysis

Here the investigator is able to probe farther into the privacy of the individual than earlier techniques of observation and interviewing allowed. Investigators who worked with Kinsey secured long personal histories involving intimate details of sexual behavior. The American Jewish Committee's study of authoritarianism made use of an "F scale" which measured hidden fascist tendencies in individuals. Investigators secured data detailing the loves, hates, and anxieties of people with authoritarian leanings. Modern advertising research often employs methods such as hypnosis, or "projective techniques" like the Rorschach test, which diagnoses personality through responses to standardized ink blots. Through such depth analysis, it is felt that new information is secured about the factors underlying the choices of consumers.

Designed observations

In the broad sense, these are experiments in which the investigator has interfered with natural conditions. (They may not be experiments in the stricter sense that all variables except one have been controlled.) The psychologist Lewin, for example, studied the influence of democratic and authoritarian environments upon the performance of children by deliberately constructing groups organized in a democratic and authoritarian manner. In the famous Robbers' Cave Experiment, two groups of boys were manipulated so as to create strong antagonisms between the groups. Then situations were constructed in which the need to cooperate was so strong as to overcome these antagonisms. In obedience experiments at Yale University, a laboratory situation was set up in which participants were ordered to move handles that would supposedly give electric shocks to other participants. No shocks were actually given, but those moving the levers did not know this. Nevertheless, under command most of the subjects could not resist "giving shocks" that they believed were strong enough to injure seriously or kill their "victims." (For further discussion see Chapter fourteen.)

Simulation and models

All these experiments were intended to set up situations that would tell something about wider social behavior. Sometimes models are established that are even more definitely intended to imitate, or simulate, the behavior of real-life social groups. At Carnegie Tech, for example, a "management game" has been devised which enables students of business administration to play intricate roles in a business operating in a competitive market. This game is used for research as well as training. War games have for some time been played by the military and other investigators in an effort to predict behavior in a real wartime confrontation. Conflict simulation in psychological laboratories puts individuals in interpersonal conflict situations that may throw light on the conflicts and solutions found in international relations. An internation game has likewise been used as a model for the world of international diplomacy.

A related way of simulating social reality is through theoretical models. For many years economists have used a mental blueprint of a self-regulating system which is kept in balance by the forces of supply and demand. This has been supposed to be close enough to real economic behavior so that it can be used to understand the actual economic world. (Whether it does is a matter of debate.) One sociologist has used data fed into a computer to simulate the intricate network of leadership, followership, and clique membership found among high school students.

Ideal types are one kind of theoretical model. These describe some aspect of social behavior or organization in an exaggerated or pure form. In discussing large organizations in Chapter one we used Weber's ideal type of a bureaucracy that is completely impersonal and efficient. In Chapter four we shall study the difference between primitive and modern societies by using an ideal type that exaggerates the characteristics found in primitive life—face-to-face contacts, simplicity of organization, and so on.

We have outlined some of the methods, both simple and sophisticated, used by social scientists in gathering and working with their data. Not all the work of social science is so organized and systematic. Generalizations may also be suggested by material in newspapers or magazines or by the reading of fiction. As in all science, one of the chief sources of data is simply the investigator's intelligent and imaginative use of his everyday experience.

In general social science has not advanced as far as have the other sciences in the systematic construction and verification of theories. A good deal of social science is still simply descriptive material, attempted experimental or theoretical models of reality, or hypotheses that have not been very precisely tested. We shall compare shortly some of the characteristics of social and natural science.

THE FIELD OF SOCIAL SCIENCE

In the course of its development, social science has been specialized into separate social sciences. This trend is part of the specialization typical of modern life. In this book we shall be more concerned with social science as a whole than with its separate specialties. Nevertheless, to understand social science as it is organized today, we must understand the disciplines into which it is divided.

The oldest discipline dealing with social data is *history.* This begins, at the latest, with the early Greeks. The American historian, Henry Steele Commager, has said that history has three aspects. It is a record of the past, a pattern of the past, and an interpretation of the past. As a record, it is concerned with the details of what happened—at the battle of Thermopylae, the inquisition of Galileo, the Constitutional Convention, the assassination of Lincoln, the Yalta Conference. Historians seek, however, to weave records of individual events into larger patterns. Examples are Thucydides' history of the Peloponnesian war, Pirenne's study of the medieval city, Burckhardt's account of the Renaissance in Italy, Toynbee's work on the Industrial Revolution. In addition, historians try to develop broader generalizations and interpretations to explain the course of history. Examples are Bury's account of the development of the idea of progress, Mumford's work on the role of the city in history, Turner's theory of the part played by the frontier in developing American democracy, Marx's interpretation of history in terms of class conflict, Spengler's prophecy of the decline of Western civilization.

Strictly speaking, history is not a science because it is concerned not with generalizing about phenomena that repeat themselves, but with depicting a stream of unrepeatable events. The preceding paragraph suggests, however, that historians have tried to make generalizations about historical patterns and sometimes to discover "laws" that will explain historical trends. In any case, history does furnish material with which other social scientists can work in forming their hypotheses. It is only with this latter aspect that we shall be concerned in this text. History as such—the chronological record of the unrepeatable human past—is the subject of other courses.

Among the social sciences with which we shall be chiefly concerned, the first to develop was *economics,* and the first important economist was Adam Smith (1723–1790). It was not accidental that his great work, *The Wealth of Nations,* was published in England in the early days of the Industrial Revolution.

Economics studies how men organize to deal with natural scarcity. Human beings will always have more needs and desires than it is possible to satisfy. They have always sought to manage the resources available to them so as to satisfy the largest possible number of desires. That is, they economize. This involves seeking the most efficient methods of production and organizing systems for distributing what is produced. In all advanced societies, people specialize and exchange at least some of their products. All these activities require some method of coordinating production, distribution, and exchange.

Most primitive and many civilized peoples have solved these problems through traditional patterns passed down through the generations. Tradition is not enough, however, for rapidly changing modern societies. They have chosen variations of two methods. One is the market, in which economic decisions are made chiefly through the free play of supply and demand. The other method is planning, in which basic decisions are made by authoritative bodies. Most economics is concerned with the principles and problems involved in organizing economic life through the market or planning.

Economics developed first in the form of political economy, which dealt with the relationship of economic life to government. Later the study of political institutions split off into the separate discipline of *political science.* Some social scientists would call Aristotle (384–322 B.C.) the first political scientist. Others would find the beginning of the discipline in *The Prince,* by Niccolò Machiavelli (1469–1527). Although the first official teaching of political science in the United States began at Columbia University in 1858, many political scientists would place the beginning of their discipline in this country at the publication of Arthur F. Bentley's *The Process of Government* in 1908.

The political scientist studies political behavior. Every society has a political system, which is marked by three important characteristics. It extends to all the members of the society, as other organizations, such as churches or labor unions, do not. It has the ultimate power to use force to require obedience. Other organizations have only a limited power to do this. Finally, the political system is generally recognized as having not only the power, but the *right,* to exercise final authority, by force if necessary. In technologically advanced societies, political behavior centers in specialized organs of government. This is not necessarily true in primitive societies.

Historically, political scientists have had two major interests. They have tried to reason about what forms of political organization would promote the greatest justice and welfare. Thus they have tried to judge, for example, among democracy, aristocracy, monarchy, and dictatorship. This branch of political science has sometimes, although by no means always, been closer to armchair philosophy than to systematic observational, or empirical, science. Political scientists have been relatively late in developing an interest in observing and generalizing from everyday political processes, that is, political party behavior, pressure groups, evolutionary and revolutionary political change, and the like. There is a good deal of controversy between the old-style "political theorists" and the more recent "empiricists."

Psychology as a science is frequently dated from the psychological laboratory established at Leipzig in the nineteenth century by Wilhelm Wundt (1832–1920). As we have said, psychology is concerned with the principles governing individual behavior. It is particularly interested in such questions as how we perceive the world, how we learn, how we respond emotionally to our experience, how our responses develop from infancy to adulthood, and how we become emotionally disturbed or "mentally ill."

If these processes were isolated within the individual's skin or did not involve any other people, but only the nonhuman environment, then we should not include psychology at all in our discussion of the social sciences. Experience and research have taught us, however, that all the processes named actually involve and influence social experience. Our perceptions of beauty, for example, differ from one society to another: some primitive belles would be hopelessly fat by our standards. In addition, there is a special field called "social psychology" which deals with the psychological phenomena found in social groups, and the behavior of individuals as it is affected by their group participation. In actuality, almost all psychology is social psychology. This field really occupies the borderline between psychology and sociology, and courses in social psychology are commonly taught in both disciplines.

The name of the discipline of *sociology* was first coined by the Frenchman Auguste Comte (1798–1847). It was only toward the end of the nineteenth century, however, that sociology developed as a systematic science. Although there have been very important German, French, and Italian sociologists, the greatest development of sociology has been in the United States.

Sociology studies group life. It is concerned with social institutions, such as the family, religion, government, and the like, which are found in all or almost all societies. It is also concerned with voluntary groups, such as lodges, athletic clubs, and political parties. Social stratification—the division of society into classes, castes, and status groups—is another important field for research. So is social control, through which people are led to play their parts in groups. Demography, the science of population growth and movement, lies on the borderline of sociology. In the field of social psychology, sociologists study groups such as crowds, masses, and publics. Social psychologists also study the way in which an individual takes on the patterns of his society, the process that sociologists customarily call "socialization."

Not all, but a considerable part of *anthropology* is social science. Anthropology is literally the "science of man." Its branches are physical anthropology, which investigates the physical characteristics of man; linguistics, which studies his language patterns; archaeology, which unearths the remains left by past men; and cultural anthropology, which studies man's social organization. Only cultural anthropology, and perhaps to some degree linguistics, can be called social science.

The difference between sociology and cultural anthropology is not very clear. One distinction often made is

This scene would have different significance to an historian, an economist, a political scientist, a sociologist, and a geographer.

that the sociologist studies society, while the anthropologist studies culture. We shall see that the term "society" refers to the way in which the ongoing life of a group is organized at a particular time, whereas culture consists of the group habits passed down by learning from one generation to another. In actual life, however, it is impossible to separate the two. A more practical distinction is that sociology usually studies technologically advanced societies, while anthropology usually studies primitive societies. Although each discipline has intruded somewhat on the other's ground, this distinction describes what has happened historically.

Two other disciplines straddle the borderline between social and physical science. Human *geography* studies how climate, terrain, and other geographic factors influence the distribution, organization, and way of life of human settlements. Human *ecology* is part of the broader field of ecology, which is concerned with the relationship of biological organisms to their physical and biological environment. The human branch of ecology deals, of course, with the environmental relationships of man as a biological species. How an urban population secures food, water, and air; disposes of its waste products; and responds psychologically to man-made inanimate surroundings is, for example, a problem in human ecology.

In this book we shall be more concerned with the overlapping and teamwork of the disciplines than with their separateness. We have seen that economics and political science, psychology and sociology, and sociology and anthropology are very close together. Life itself does not generally appear as the subject matter of a particular discipline, but as *social* life, requiring many or all disciplines to understand it. The problem of how any one of us has, for example, become what he is, is a psychological, sociological, political, *and* economic problem. A grave social problem, such as the racial crisis in the United States, requires the combined efforts of all the social sciences. The aim of this book is to investigate how whole social problems may be approached by the whole body of social science.

SOCIAL AND NONSOCIAL SCIENCES

We need now to consider the relationship between the social and the physical and biological sciences. (These are sometimes called the "natural" sciences, but this implies that the social sciences are outside nature, which is not true.) There are several points of view on this subject. Some people hold that the study of social phenomena is not a science, and never can be. Others believe that social phenomena can be studied scientifically, but require different methods from those used in the other sciences. Others hold just the opposite, that the social sciences will never be scientific until they adopt the same methods as the physi-

cal and biological sciences, especially those of physics.

First of all, the basic methods of science—observation, generalization, and verification—apply in the study of social events just as in the study of biological and physical events. The methods emphasized in securing and testing data may, however, need to be different. This fact does not make the social sciences unique. Geology and astronomy, for example, do not often make use of the controlled experiment preferred in physics. There is no single right method of securing data either in science as a whole or in one particular science.

As a general proposition, the physical and biological sciences are better able to predict and control phenomena than are the social sciences. Manned space flight, for example, probably has no counterpart in social science or social engineering. The laws of social science are generally less precise than those of physics. The point can, however, be exaggerated.

A Princeton astronomer once told a sociologist that "your data are more accurate than ours." Even physicists, like social scientists, encounter "bugs" when they try to bring their work out of the laboratory into the more complex real world. The physical and biological sciences are not very successful in predicting such phenomena as epidemics or hurricanes, or even the next day's weather. "30 percent probability of showers" is often about the best they can do. It would probably be much easier to predict the number of absences in a class with a strict attendance policy during a given month (a social phenomenon) than to predict the month's weather (a physical phenomenon). Human population censuses, and data on birth, death, and migration, are generally more accurate than data on deer, dogs, or fish. We make many reliable social predictions in ordinary life. There is a high probability that the next scheduled meeting of your class will take place. When we mail a letter, we assume that it will be delivered. Every time we go on the highway we bet our lives on our predictions of the behavior of other drivers.[1]

Why, nevertheless, are prediction and control generally better in the non-social sciences? The most obvious answer is that the objects they study are simpler. Varying complexity of phenomena is not peculiar to social science, however. Chemistry is more complex than physics. Biology is more complex than chemistry, for life is more complex than inanimate objects. (This fact led the great biologist Cuvier to assert wrongly that biology could never become a science.) People are probably the most complex forms of life known; thus individual psychology is more complex than biology. The fact that man is a social animal adds yet more complexity. Although this does not mean that human social life cannot be studied scientifically, it does mean that the results of social science will probably always be somewhat less exact.

Part of the complexity of social life lies in the fact that human beings, unlike stones and hurricanes, have an inner mental life as well as external behavior. We not only act, but are aware of our actions and give them a meaning. (This is also true, to a lesser degree, for other forms of life.) Some social scientists believe that this fact is irrelevant, that human behavior can be studied entirely from the outside without taking any account of inner mental processes. Others feel that we cannot understand social life without understanding how people inwardly experience it. Some would hold that access to this inner life gives social scientists an advantage that physical and biological scientists do not have.

Because human events are so complex, experimentation in the strict sense must probably play a smaller part in social science than in the physical sciences. We have already seen,

however, that in some of the physical sciences experimentation is relatively unimportant. Social scientists have sometimes found experimental situations when they could not construct them. The anthropologist Walter Goldschmidt, for example, wanted to study the effects of small- versus large-scale farming on community life. He was able to find and compare two California farm communities which he felt were essentially the same in all respects except the size of farms. Such an experiment is not necessarily inferior to one artificially produced in a laboratory.

Some people believe that human beings have free will and that social science can therefore never make predictions, as can the other sciences. We cannot examine at length the question of whether or not human wills are, in fact, "free," that is, in part undetermined by events outside themselves. Whether or not they are free, however, we do make social predictions. Free will or not, we do not expect many drivers to go through a red light where a police car is visibly stationed. People may feel that they exercise a free choice at the election booth, yet recent public opinion polls have generally been quite accurate in predicting election results. Even if free will should make impossible any *certain* predictions in social science, the situation would not be essentially different from that in the other sciences. Even physicists now speak in terms of probability rather than certainty.

It is sometimes claimed that social data are unique, while biological and physical data repeat themselves. This is, however, not true. It is a commonplace that "one can never step twice in the same stream." *All* events are unique. We can, however, generalize about their common characteristics, whether the problem be the dynamics of water flow or the dynamics of crowd behavior.

It is also sometimes said that physical (and perhaps biological) laws are universally true, for all space and time, whereas generalizations about social

1. Most examples in this section are from Ralph Thomlinson, *Sociological Concepts and Research*, New York, Random House, 1965.

life are perhaps true only for particular societies. The atomic weight of manganese is presumably the same on the most remote star as it is on earth. Generalizations about competitive behavior which may be true for the average American may, however, not be true for the less competitive Hopi Indian. As we shall see in this book, however, all human beings are enough alike so that there are many generalizations which we can make about social behavior anywhere on this globe. Whether they would hold true for life on other planets remains, of course, to be seen.

Finally, it may be that social science is more difficult because social scientists are more influenced by their prejudices and therefore find it harder to be objective. Investigation of the sex life of wasps is less disturbing to the average researcher than study of human sexual customs, and the meteorology of Mars is less likely to cause mental blocks than is the investigation of human religion. We shall discuss this problem of bias and objectivity at greater length shortly.

Social science is, then, part of the whole venture of science. Its data are in general the most complex known to science, and this fact causes special problems. But there are also differences in complexity among the physical and biological sciences. Social science is less able than the other sciences to use certain methods, but also has available methods to which they do not have access. Similar differences hold between the other sciences. The distinctions between the social and nonsocial sciences are therefore only of the same kind as exist among the biological and physical sciences.

SOCIAL SCIENCE AND THE HUMANITIES

Social science is also related to that body of knowledge that we call the "humanities." These are made up primarily of philosophy, literature, and the arts.

It is probably best to describe philosophy in terms of its major fields, rather than trying to give an abstract definition. *Epistemology* deals with the nature of knowledge and how it can be obtained. *Logic* is concerned with the rules of valid reasoning. *Ethics* tries to generalize about what is good. *Aesthetics* endeavors to define the nature of beauty. *Metaphysics* is concerned with the ultimate nature of things, literally with questions of reality "beyond physics."

Philosophy is related to science and to social science primarily in two ways.

First, philosophy is concerned with the procedures and assumptions that underlie scientific investigation. Although some scientists will deny it, all science rests on certain metaphysical assumptions about the nature of reality. For example, the scientist cannot begin his work without assuming at least that the world is real, that it is not a chaos but follows some orderly pattern, and that the pattern is at least somewhat knowable. The question of whether or not the human will is free is a metaphysical problem which, as we have seen, may affect the work of social scientists. Empirical science rests on the epistemological assumption that observation is a better way to know reality than reasoning without observing, or than depending on pure intuition or direct divine revelation. Logic tells us what procedures of reasoning are valid in scientific investigation, for example, what conclusions we can reasonably draw from the results of our experiments.

Second, philosophy uses the findings of social science, as well as other sources, as material for generalizations which go beyond the possibility of scientific verification. Ethics may use the results of social science as a basis for asserting that there are no absolute moral standards, but that which is ethical depends entirely upon time and place. Similarly, aesthetics may point to the varying standards of beauty held in different societies and claim that there are no absolute criteria for the beautiful. On the other hand, either ethics or aesthetics may claim that there are absolute standards beyond the differences discovered by social science. Metaphysics may also use the material of science in generalizing about ultimate reality. When he said that his scientific experience led him to feel that the universe resembles a vast intelligence more than a vast machine, Einstein was using his observations as a physicist to make a metaphysical statement that is neither provable nor disprovable by ordinary scientific procedures.

How, then, is social science related to literature, painting, sculpture, music, architecture, and the other arts?

Both social science and the arts seek to *communicate about the world in which we live* in such a way as to increase our experience and understanding of that world, and perhaps our ability to control it. As we have said, the language that science seeks to communicate is that of *abstract generalization.* The arts, on the other hand, seek primarily to evoke *concrete experience.*

The physicist will analyze the spectrum. An impressionist painter like Turner or Monet will try to capture the experience of light at dawn or around a cathedral at dusk. The sociologist will devise a scale for predicting success and failure in marriage. A poet like Shelley or the author of the Song of Solomon will try to capture the immediate experience of love. A marine biologist will analyze the possibility of expanding food sources from the sea. A novelist like Melville or Conrad will depict the emotional experience of the men who ''go down to the sea in ships.'' A social statistician will analyze the physical and human costs of war. A novel like Crane's *The Red Badge of Courage* or Remarque's *All Quiet on the Western Front* will convey what it means actually to be a soldier at war.

The philosopher and psychologist William James once distinguished between knowledge about the world and knowledge of the world. Knowledge about is general and abstract and can be secondhand, though it need not necessarily be. Knowledge of is concrete and ultimately must always arise from personal experience. Typically, science gives us knowledge about; literature and the other arts seek to give us knowledge of.

No social scientist can be very effective unless, in addition to his knowledge of social science generalizations, he also has knowledge *of* the subject he studies. One can hardly be competent to generalize about race relations unless he is a Negro or has in some way worked intimately with or in a Negro community. An expert on a foreign country is suspect if he has never been there. To generalize about mental illness, one should preferably have been either a psychiatrist, an attendant in a mental hospital, or a psychiatric patient. Something is missing in the work of an expert on the family who has never been married. Without immediate experience social scientists are likely to lack the observations necessary to formulate the most meaningful hypotheses. They will also lack the concrete, in-depth detail that must ''fill in'' their generalizations if their knowledge is to give the most useful understanding.

Some of this is true also of the nonsocial sciences. We should suspect the qualifications of an archaeologist who has never been on a dig, an astronomer who has never looked through a telescope, a biologist who has never performed a dissection, or a chemist who has never done a qualitative or quantitive analysis. We feel that in order to generalize successfully, one must somehow ''get his hands dirty.''

It is not enough, however, to have been on the scene of scientific investigation. Our ability to experience even those things to which we are closest is very limited. The humanities represent a selection of the greatest human experiences of reality. A social scientist may be well trained in social science methods and theory and have lived with his problem firsthand, yet he will be scientifically impoverished if he knows nothing of what the most insightful writers and artists have communicated about human experience. It is impossible to imagine a complete social scientist who had never experienced the works of Dante, Shakespeare, Beethoven, Rembrandt, or Ibsen. This is equally true of the physical scientist. Moreover, it is probably true that every great scientist has something of the artist in him. We speak of the "elegance" of a finely constructed scientific theory. The expression tells us that creative scientific work is itself a thing of beauty. It is no accident that two of the greatest of modern physicists, Einstein and Planck, were also accomplished musicians.

It is equally true that the most sensitive writer or artist is impoverished if he knows nothing of the world of science, either social or nonsocial. We cannot imagine a complete writer or artist to whom the theories of Copernicus, Newton, Adam Smith, Sigmund Freud, and Albert Einstein were completely foreign. The most creative writers and artists have intimate access to the insights and material afforded by the social and nonsocial sciences. Yet in his much discussed essay, *The Two Cultures,* the British scientist and novelist C. P. Snow has made a strong case that just as physical scientists (perhaps not social scientists) are generally very ignorant of literature and the arts, so most writers are equally ignorant of the most elementary scientific concepts.

The right relationship between social science and the humanities is suggested by Lewis Coser's book, *Sociology Through Literature.* In this book Coser illustrates social science concepts through selections in which they are treated by the great writers of fiction. Ideally, social science and the humanities do not conflict, but support each other. The knowledge of reality that is conveyed by the artist cannot be objectively verified by the methods of science. On the other hand, science can never give experience of the concrete details of life. To "know" the world we must in some degree be both scientists and artists.

SOCIAL SCIENCE AND VALUES

Social science can without doubt tell us something about how the world *is.* It can help us, in some measure, to change it. What, however, can it tell us about what *ought* to be? How is social science (and science in general) related to the problem of human values?

Clearly, social science can describe values, that is, tell us what forms of behavior different societies have considered right and wrong. It can tell us that somewhere, at some time, monogamy, polygamy, capitalism, communism, fascism, cannibalism, slavery, head hunting, human sacrifice, the killing of infants, exposure of the aged, and even incest have been approved forms of behavior. William Graham Sumner's book, *Folkways,* and the much more recent cross-cultural survey at Yale University are valuable sources for such information. But what can the description of how people have behaved and felt, or do behave and feel, tell us about how they should behave and feel?

Let us look at four answers to the problem.

One view of values is that they are revealed and absolute. To the orthodox Jew or Christian, the Ten Commandments are such a source of revealed ethics. Since they do not cover all possible acts, they may be supplemented by the reasoning of rabbis, priests, and other ethical thinkers. This reasoning generally deduces other ethical principles from the revealed laws, rather than appealing to observed consequences. Another source of revelation may be the inner conscience, which to many is the "still, small voice of God" giving intuitive moral guidance.

Revealed ethical standards are likely to be absolute; that is, their validity does not depend on observed consequences. The person to whom stealing is wrong may not steal even to feed his family. The person for whom premarital sex is a sin may not be interested in arguments about whether sex experience may be a better preparation for marriage. The absolute conscientious objector cannot participate in war, no matter what the probable consequences of defeat. If truth is an absolute value, one might not be able to lie even to save his loved ones from the secret police. To ethics of this kind, science, with its prediction of consequences, is largely irrelevant.

A second view holds that science can contribute to ethics by predicting consequences of action, but that values are in the last analysis beyond science. The scientist is limited to "if-then" statements. "If we want to avoid worldwide famine, we will spread contraception." "If we want better sex adjustment in marriage, we must have widespread public sex education." "If we want to eliminate poverty, we must have a positive national economic policy." "If we want racial equality, we must provide equal job and educational opportunities." "If we want to preserve civil liberties, we must control the military branch of government." "If we want peace, we must control arms." (These statements may not all necessarily be true, but they are the kind of if-then statements that can be empirically tested.) *If* people want to have good sexual adjustment, to avoid famine, to eliminate poverty, to secure racial equality, to preserve civil liberty, to achieve peace, *then* such statements can help them decide what they ought to do. According to this second view, science cannot, however, tell them whether or not they should want these things.

Scientific presentation can also influence people's ethical choices by dramatically calling facts to their attention. Friedrich Engels influenced reform and revolutionary movements by summarizing factual data on the condition of the British working classes in 1845. Émile Zola stimulated moral

The Ten Commandments are an example of revealed or absolute ethical standards. (Courtesy of the Museum of Modern Art Film Stills Archives.)

indignation and political action by his depiction of the famous Dreyfus case. The picture of the American racial crisis put forward in *An American Dilemma* led to new concern and action. Kinsey's depiction of American sex patterns undoubtedly had some effect in changing sexual morality. Michael Harrington's picture of poverty in *The Other America* stimulated indignation and action. All that such factual presentations can do, however, according to this point of view, is to reinforce or activate moral choices that people have already made. If they have not made them, science cannot tell them that they should.

According to this view, a person's ultimate moral choices may be purely personal and arbitrary—"there is no disputing taste." They may reflect the traditional standards of right and wrong accepted in society. They may, perhaps, come through some form of revelation. From one source they cannot come, however. One cannot derive an *ought* from an *is,* an ethical standard from a factual statement.

A third position on the relationship of social science to values holds that basic ethical standards can be derived from factual knowledge. There can be no ethical standards, it is held, beyond what is done in one's society. "When in Rome, do as the Romans do." If most Americans practice extramarital sex relations, this is simply how things are, and one will probably do best to adjust. If Moslems typically have four wives, that is their accepted pattern, and non-Moslems have no basis for judging them. If the Russians want to practice a version of communism, and the Americans a version of capitalism, that is their choice, and no outsider can criticize. From this standpoint the best ethical guide is a thorough scientific description of what is practiced and accepted in a society.

A fourth view also contends that ethics can be derived from science, but for a different reason. One can describe wide varieties of social patterns, this view holds, but there are common human standards above the patterns of any single society. "Always and everywhere," said the sociologist Charles Horton Cooley, "men seek honor and dread ridicule, defer to public opinion, cherish their goods and their children, and admire courage, generosity, and success."[2] A quite different writer, the Russian Communist Lenin, spoke of "the elementary rules of social life that have been known for centuries and repeated for thousands of years in all school books. . . ." People everywhere have common needs and desires, and live under common human conditions. By accurately presenting their needs and conditions, science can guide men to ultimate values.

Social science can say, for example, that a society that practiced widespread incest would so disrupt family life that it would perish. Incest cannot therefore be a general value in any society that hopes to continue. Science can perhaps say, as did John F. Ken-

nedy, that if mankind does not eliminate war, war will eliminate mankind. If this is true, it would hardly seem that warfare can continue to be ethical behavior. Science can perhaps demonstrate that monogamy serves deeper and broader human needs than do other forms of marriage. It can show that rape, sadism, sexual promiscuity, homosexuality, and also rigid Puritan morality are expressions of frustrated human needs and will tend to disappear as deeper needs are gratified. If this is true, then they cannot represent basic human values. Perhaps social science can also show that the great religious values of compassion and forgiveness represent the most profound needs and desires of all normal human beings.

From this last point of view, sharp distinctions between facts and values are arbitrary: the deeper our understanding of man and his society, the more we shall approach agreement on ethical standards. Although the author believes that there is some truth in each of the positions described, this is the view to which he himself comes closest. Our final chapter will be devoted to the question of what social values may be derived from our study of social science.

SOCIAL SCIENCE AND SOCIETY

Albert Einstein once said that science carries forward the call of the Hebrew prophets for a better and more just world. Social science, we have seen, developed in the last two centuries as part of man's attempt to improve his society. It has become a very large enterprise, substantially supported by society.

Industry has used social science for such varied purposes as increasing production and influencing consumer choices. Government has employed social scientists to collect and use census data, plan community programs, improve the morale of the army, strengthen wartime propaganda programs, plan economic measures to

2. Charles Horton Cooley, *Social Organization*, New York, Schocken, 1962, p. 28.

stabilize the economy, and in many other capacities. Foundations subsidize large numbers of social science research programs. With or without their aid, universities are also centers of social science research. Nationwide polls of public opinion have become perhaps the best known social science research and an important part of our political system.

It would be a mistake, however, to suppose that social science has always been received with open arms. Indeed, science in general has often been far from welcome.

Galileo was forced to deny his scientific findings, and Bruno burned at the stake, both at the hands of the Catholic Church. The chemist Lavoisier was executed in the French Revolution, probably for his scientific as well as his political views. The Hungarian physician Semmelweiss was driven to suicide by colleagues who refused to recognize his statistical evidence on the benefits of antiseptic practice in childbirth. The author knows personally of a social scientist who was once warned that his promotion might be denied if he did not stop investigating extrasensory perception, of a young physiologist who declined to make objective tests of a controversial cancer cure because he was afraid his funds would be withdrawn, of a physician in excellent standing who would not investigate the same cure because of fear of his medical association.

In the social sciences the difficulties are on the whole greater than in the other sciences. The history of social science in the United States includes, for example:

a distinguished sociologist who was dropped from a West Coast university because his social views conflicted with economic interests that strongly supported the university;

an economist and sociologist, author of several books, but a socialist, who lost his last university job over half a century ago and has never held another since;

a historian who lost his college teaching position because of his opposition to war and military conscription;

a sociologist and historian whose appointment was terminated after he taught a course about the Russian Revolution at a YMCA;

a sociologist who lost his job after he circulated a sex informaton questionnaire among his students at a leading eastern women's college;

a political scientist whose appointment to a western university was canceled because of his antiwar views;

a politically active social philosopher who lost his job under pressure upon his university from the state legislature;

a biologist who investigated human sexual behavior and was subjected to pressure—eventually unsuccessful— to relieve him of his job or withdraw his research funds;

a sociologist offered a job under the condition that he not speak about the views that made him a conscientious objector.

We can recognize two important aspects of resistance to social science, one more general and one more specific.

Social science tends to *disturb social patterns.* The job of social science is to investigate the prevailing economic practices, governmental organization, family structure, sex patterns, religious beliefs and practices, arrangement of social classes, relations between races, and the general beliefs and values of a society. The social scientist tries to examine his own society as objectively as he would study a group of primitive people, or as a biologist would study a shellfish, or a chemist an unidentified compound. This is not the way, however, in which people usually view their own customs. Rather, the members of any society are likely to grow up believing in the rightness and wisdom of their traditional ways. They feel confused and threatened if these are questioned.

They are likely to react to the social scientist, therefore, with fear and hostility, especially when he questions sensitive areas such as religion, sex, or form of government. The more deeply the findings of social science conflict with cherished social patterns, the greater is likely to be the fear and hostility. The most effective ways in which to challenge the social scientist are to threaten his job or his funds for research. Other things being equal, the more deeply the work of a social scientist questions the established order, the more his livelihood, his status, or his promotions are likely to be jeopardized. Thus there is always the temptation, in research and teaching, to "play it safe."

A second obstacle to objective social science lies in *vested interests.* Particular individuals or groups have a special stake in keeping things as they are. Powerful corporations may not welcome investigation of the extent of their power or the methods by which they have gained it. Labor union leaders may similarly resist investigation of the internal structure of their unions. Organized religious bodies may resist objective discussion of the merits of contraception or of the techniques by which they hold their members. Universities may resist disclosure of the influences exerted by businessmen on their boards of trustees or by government agencies that grant funds. Politicians may not welcome study of their sources of financial support. In general, any large and long-standing organization is likely to develop vested interests and to resist change. This is true even in science itself. Scientists achieve position, prestige, and income by working within an established body of observations and theories. They may not be very objective about new approaches that question and perhaps threaten the work they have been doing.

The social scientist is always tempted, therefore, to avoid offending powerful interests, even in his own profession. More than this, vested interests may welcome and support his work if he is on their side. Some of the largest support for social science comes from business, government agencies, and the military. One student of the work of social scientists stated to the American Association for the Advancement of Science that in both Russia and the United States, the main function of social science is "to support the policies of those in political and economic power."[3]

Resistance to social science has been greatest in the totalitarian countries. Nazi Germany and fascist Italy had little place for objective study of society. The situation is more complicated in the Soviet Union. The observer just quoted has said that social science in Russia has the lowest position on the ladder of science, that it is concerned mainly with methods of propaganda, and that it is very little concerned with experimentation or other methods of objective verification. There is no room for objective study of the social relations among classes or of the way in which political leadership maintains its power. These are also, incidentally, touchy subjects in the United States.

In general, in a totalitarian society we find both kinds of resistance to social science sharpened. More clearly than elsewhere, there is an official ideology which holds the existing social arrangements to be the ideal form of society. In Russia the ideology is Marxism. What is already the best form of human social organization cannot, obviously, be improved by social investigation! Vested interests in a totalitarian country are more centralized and in a better position to supress investigations that threaten them and to pay the bills for research that they can use to their advantage.

Although social science is most threatened in the dictatorships, there is no resistance there for which we do not

3. Russell L. Ackoff, "Scientific Method and Social Science: East and West," *Soviet Science,* ed. Conway Zirkle, Washington, D.C., American Association for the Advancement of Science, 1952, p. 52.

find parallels in the nondictatorial countries. Nowhere is the person welcome, or likely to receive great financial support, who would simply seek truth and report it as he finds it. The social scientist, and the serious student of social science, must everywhere contend not only with the scientific difficulties of investigation, but also with the resistance of established social patterns and of the "powers that be."

Suggestions for further reading

Scientific method of the middle and late twentieth century originated in the physical sciences. A good background book was written when the "new" physics was still new: PERCY W. BRIDGMAN's The Logic of Modern Physics *(Macmillan, 1927). This work by an outstanding Harvard physicist is thorough, readable, humane, and at times humorous. For a more recent treatment of general scientific method, see A. CORNELIUS BENJAMIN,* Science, Technology, and Human Values *(University of Missouri Press, 1965).*

Discussion of the methods peculiar to social investigation and their relation to the other sciences appears in Sociological Concepts and Research, *by RALPH THOMLINSON (Random House, 1965).* Social Thought from Lore to Science *by HARRY ELMER BARNES and HOWARD W. BECKER (Dover, 1966, paper) is a very comprehensive study of the historical development of social science.*

A recent controversial discussion of the relationship between the sciences and the humanities appears in The Two Cultures and a Second Look *(Cambridge, 1969), by the British physicist and novelist C. P. SNOW. How social science and the humanities may work together is demonstrated concretely in LEWIS COSER's* Sociology Through Literature *(Prentice-Hall, 1963, paper). Coser's material can also be used profitably at later times in the study of this book.*

RUSSELL ACKOFF's article "Scientific Method and Social Science: East and West" is an interesting and provocative comparison of the methods and problems of social scientists in the United States and the Soviet Union. Ackoff's article appears in Soviet Science *(arranged by Conway Zirkle and published in Washington, D.C., in 1952 by the American Association for the Advancement of Science).*

Part two
The bases of human life

In the next five chapters, which make up a major part of this book, we shall explore four bases of human life. As human beings, we are *physical* animals living in a physical and biological environment. We always live in organized *social* relationships with other people. In addition to having an external physical and social environment, we also have a world of *psychological* experience. Finally, the way we act is shaped by a *cultural* environment of common habits and life patterns passed down from generation to generation.

Chapter three
The physical basis

This chapter is concerned with exploring how our physical nature and environment affect our social life. There is no doubt that man is a remarkable creature. It has been said that if we think of the whole age of the earth as a single year, man as we know him would not have appeared until about 11:45 on the evening of December 31, and the period for which we have recorded history would be little longer than the last minute of the year! To put it otherwise, the earth is estimated to be about four billion years old. *Homo sapiens,* or modern man, goes back from 50,000 to 100,000 years, and written history begins not much more than 5,000 years ago. Yet in his final minute of the year, man has changed the face of the earth far more than all previous living beings. How has he been able to do so much in so little time?

In attempting an answer, we must first look at man as an animal. We will need to introduce ourselves to some findings of archaeology and physical anthropology.

MAN AS AN ANIMAL

What makes man such a unique animal? His success in changing his environment rests upon his special ability to manipulate it. More than any other animal, man is able to take hold of his surroundings and physically reshape them. Even more remarkable is his ability to manage his environment symbolically, through translating it into symbols which he then manipulates. Verbal language, mathematics, and the use of computers are examples of such symbolic manipulation.

The computer is an advanced illustration of the human capacity for *tool making,* which began with the earliest chipping of stone implements hundreds of thousands of years or more ago. The famous anthropologist L. S. B. Leakey has defined man as a creature who makes tools. The ability to extend hands and sense organs with tools and machines is possessed by man alone, and explains much of his unique achievement.

Another characteristic of man is the flexibility of his behavior. He is relatively unspecialized. He uses his brains and his toolmaking ability to defend himself, rather than being limited by a shell like a turtle. He can adapt to more different climates than can any other animal. He can eat a wide variety of foods. In his history he has almost certainly been both an almost complete vegetarian and an almost complete meat eater. By comparison with other species, man has few fixed, inborn behavior patterns. Most of his behavior is acquired through experience, his own or that of other people. Not being limited by inborn patterns, he has a wide ability to adapt, which is increased by his ability for abstraction and symbols.

Not being very strong or even especially agile as an individual, man has become a *cooperative* animal. "In union there is strength," through the pooling of physical powers and experience. Collectively man has been able

The computer is an advanced illustration of man's capacity for toolmaking.

to find and grow food he could not secure alone, to shelter himself, to defend himself against enemies. Through collective labor he carries on vast projects which only skilled cooperation can make possible.

Human cooperation rests upon man's skills in *communication.* His ability to create symbols and language gives him a capacity far beyond that of any other animal for creating what social scientists call "culture"—a system of habits, skills, and values that is transmitted by learning from one generation to another. Thus each human individual shares in a collective knowledge and wisdom cooperatively acquired. Each human generation is able to start, not from scratch, but from the point which the previous generation reached. Man's development is cumulative.

These differences in behavior rest upon differences in man's makeup as an animal. The fact that he is *upright in stature* gives man an advantage in seeing and maneuvering in his environment. Standing upright has specialized his hind paws as feet and left his forepaws free for something else—grasp-

ing and handling objects. Of special importance is man's *opposable thumb,* which enables him to seize objects between his thumb and other fingers. Without this grasping ability of the hands, he could neither make nor use tools. Man also has *binocular vision,* that is, his eyes, located on the front of his head and functioning as a unit, give him depth vision of a three-dimensional world, and thus help him enormously in reacting to and managing his surroundings. Man possesses in his brain highly developed centers of *speech.* (No other animal, even apes, can imitate sounds.) Upon the ability to vocalize depends most of man's capacity for abstraction, symbolization, language, and culture. The development of speech centers is only part of the development of man's *large and highly convoluted brain.* Man has a larger brain, in proportion to his body weight, than any other animal. Even more important, he has a highly organized and developed brain, as indicated by the greater number of ridges or convolutions, especially in the fore part, or cerebrum.

How did man get this way? When we

go back millions of years before history, as we must, our answers have to involve a good deal of guesswork. Fortunately, there is evidence enough for some fairly good guesses. We can find clues in the experiences of the animal family to which we are most closely related, the primates. These include man; the apes, such as the chimpanzee, the gorilla, and the orangutan; the monkeys; and two small animals, the tarsius and the lemur, which are now found only in very limited areas of the world.

Contrary to some impressions, we are not descended from either apes or monkeys. We are certainly, however, very close relatives and are descended from common ancestors. The skeleton of a man and an ape are amazingly similar, and a visit to a zoo is likely to leave small doubt that the apes are our cousins. We even possess the remnants of a tail (the coccyx), and babies are occasionally born with a more fully developed tail which must be removed surgically.

An interesting test, involving what is called antiserum, demonstrates quite definitely our membership in the primate family. If one takes blood from one animal family (for example, from a dog) and injects it into a member of another family (a rabbit, for example), the blood of the receiving animal will form defensive substances. If the rabbit's blood is then injected into a dog, or any other member of the canine family, a clouding and precipitation will occur in the canine's blood. This will not happen if the antidog serum is injected into a cat, or a horse, or a man, or any other animal outside the dog's family group. Now, let human blood be injected into the rabbit. The antiman serum that forms will create varying degrees of precipitation if injected into a man, a gorilla, a howler monkey, a lemur, or a tarsius—but not in a cat, a dog, or a goat. Man and the other primates are all "of the same blood."

Man is by far the most intelligent and successful manipulator among the primates. Yet all the primates, especially the apes, possess some of the traits that make man outstanding. Probably these traits arose from the fact that the primates have been tree dwellers. This kind of life made demands, and had advantages, which probably led toward the kind of physical and intellectual development we see in human beings.

Swinging from branch to branch requires strong, grasping hands. It demands a high degree of coordination of the nervous and muscular systems, and is helped enormously by depth

---

It is worth nothing, however, that man is by no means a perfect specimen. His development, particularly his upright posture, has left him with some physical qualities which are far from ideal. He has even been described as "a walking museum of antiquities."

The presence and distribution of body hair on man is an obvious vestige; it has long since become so slight and atrophied as to be without value; indeed, its superfluity is such as to give rise to a flourishing depilatory business in our culture. . . . The third molar, or wisdom tooth, in the reduced jaw of man is another organic superfluity. It is healthy and useful in the other primates, but there is hardly a place for it in our dentition. Overcrowding causes frequent impaction; it is more subject to decay than the other teeth. . . .

Indeed, if one takes the pessimistic point of view enunciated by the physical anthropologist Hooten, it seems as if most of the human body is formed of anatomical lags, many of which, although

*they function . . . do so with lamentable insufficiency. For alas,
in standing on his hind legs man throws undue stresses and
strains upon his bodily structure for which it was not originally
constructed in the days when our mammalian quadruped ancestors
ran on all fours. The convex arch of the spine of the quadruped
is a fine supporting structure, but the S-curved columnar spine of
man is apt to be too weak for its job; more than this, it throws too
much weight on the wedge-shaped sacrum. The frequently
lamentable result is sacroilian displacement. To add to our woes,
our visceral organs no longer rest in a neat underslung casket
of ribs; instead, they drape down into a poorly supported
abdomen. Result: rupture of the abdominal wall or the
displacement of internal organs.*

*We also carry a crowded tangle of unnecessarily long (for our
type of diet) intestines, a heritage from our herbivorous ancestors.
Our overstrained hearts must work excessively hard to pump
an adequate stream of blood to our enlarged brains, now in a
position above the heart instead of on the same level with it, as
among quadrupeds.*

—*E. Adamson Hoebel,* Man in the Primitive World, *2nd ed., New York,*
McGraw-Hill, *1958, pp. 24–25.*

---

vision. (In the long run, which means millions of years, those primates who were poorly coordinated or could not see "in depth," were probably eliminated in favor of those better adapted.) When the body hangs between the arms, there is need for a strong pelvis to support the intestines, which were previously supported by the ribs and abdominal wall. This development no doubt prepared the way for fully upright posture when man's near ancestors finally came down out of the trees. Tree swinging is much more efficient with shoulders that can rotate freely, and such shoulders in turn prepare the way for the throwing of rocks and spears and the swinging of clubs. All these developments are related to a better developed and coordinated nervous organization.

Even though it brought the primate family a long way, development in the trees did not produce man. This required that the primates come down to earth. Possibly several millions of years ago, perhaps in Africa, a long period of drought—itself perhaps a million years long—destroyed the forests in which our primate ancestors lived. They then may have had either to use their physical and mental abilities to develop radically new ways of eating and defending themselves or else perish before predatory animals and starvation. Perhaps these were the conditions that led preman to pick up stones, bones, and branches and use them as tools and weapons. Perhaps this led to the great step by which some preman first shaped a tool instead of simply finding it. At that point man the toolmaker, as Leakey defines him and as we know him, had arrived.

We need now to establish a few signposts in man's development. This is not the place for a detailed account of human prehistory and archaeology. For one thing, these are highly technical subjects. Most of our knowledge is put together from fragments of skeletons millions of years old—a tooth here, a piece of a jawbone here, a fragment of a hip there. To reconstruct a picture of a skeleton from a few pieces requires a detailed and imaginative knowledge of anatomy. To date a fragment this old may require the use of methods based upon radioactive traces of carbon or potassium. Obviously, these procedures are too specialized for a general course, and here all we can know is what kinds of data archaeologists employ and how they use them. Moreover, since our knowledge of prehistory is very limited, very possibly the most important evidence is yet to be uncovered. The picture we have of man's ascent may thus change radically at any time with an important new archaeological find.

We do, however, have a fairly good collection of men and man-like creatures to begin working with. Until fairly recently it was generally thought that the birthplace of man was probably in Asia. In 1890 and 1891 a skull was unearthed in Java which was given the name *Pithecanthropus erectus* ("erect man-ape"). Java man's small brain indicated that he was probably not outstanding in intelligence, but development of the areas of speech indicates that he may have used language. His age is estimated to be somewhere around 500,000 years.

For a long time Java man was considered to be the oldest true man. In the 1920s a number of fossils were found southwest of Peking and named *Pithecanthropus pekinensis* ("apeman of Peking"). *Pekinensis* appears to have been a close relative of Java man and to have lived about the same time, but he had a considerably larger brain and thus was probably more intelligent. In his caves are remnants of fashioned tools and charred animal bones, indicating that he had probably learned to use fire. In fact, cracked fossil skulls indicate that he probably ate the roasted brains of other *Pekinenses*.

In 1907 there had been unearthed in Europe a specimen named *Homo heidelbergensis* (Heidelberg man), whose name denoted where he was found. He probably lived at roughly the same time as Java and Peking man, about half a million years ago. He seems to have been rather similar to them, and probably was a relative.

Today, however, we think that the place of man's origin was most likely in Africa. In 1925 Professor Raymond

Dart uncovered a skull that he named *Australopithecus* ("southern ape"). Living perhaps as early as a million years ago, this primate probably walked erect, inhabited caves, used objects for tools and weapons, but did not make tools. We guess this from the residues that he left in his caves. A considerable number of *Australopithecus* fossils have since been discovered. In 1959 Leakey uncovered a specimen that he named *boisei Zinjanthropus* ("East Africa man"). Evidence indicated that he stood erect and used bones, stones, and pieces of trees as crude tools. His age was estimated at from 1¾ to 2 million years. The most recent important African find, made in 1964, is *Homo habilis* ("capable man"), discovered by the native Negro archaeologist Kimeu while working with Leakey. *Habilis* was found more deeply buried than *Zinjanthropus,* and this is dated at the earlier time of about 1,850,000 B.C. He was, however, apparently a more advanced user of tools.

In Europe we find important later links in the chain that binds modern man to his earliest ancestors. One of the best known and very earliest of all fossil men to be discovered there is *Homo neanderthalensis,* or *Neanderthal* man, who was found in Germany in 1856. He is the figure we are likely to visualize when we think of the cave man—short (about five feet four inches), bullnecked, with slanted forehead and no chin, loping along with a club in one hand and a female in the other. Neanderthal man dominated Europe from perhaps 150,000 to 50,000 B.C. and was also found in North Africa and southwest Asia. He had a brain a little larger than ours, but less convoluted with less frontal development. He made hand axes, sharp-edged scrapers for dressing skins, and flint-pointed spears or darts. He lived in separate families rather than in tribes, sometimes buried his dead in ways which suggest a belief in the hereafter, and at times got arthritis in his later years.

Around 50,000 B.C. Neanderthal man began to be displaced in Europe by *Homo sapiens,* who seems to have come from the area of Palestine. The Latin name means "wise man." This is our not very modest evaluation of modern man, ourselves, for it is to *Homo sapiens* that we belong. *Homo sapiens* is distinguished from earlier men and other primates by a combination of several anatomical characteristics: smaller canine teeth, a definitely formed chin, a depression in the bone beneath the eye (the canine fossa), a brow ridge over the eyes formed by two overlapping bones, and a particular form of the tympanic plate, the bone surrounding the ear hole.

We know most about early *Homo sapiens* from the fossils of Cro-Magnon man (the French is pronounced *crow mahn-yon*), first found at Les Eyzies in south central France. Cro-Magnon man was completely erect, over six feet in height, light boned, with high brows, had a less ape-like face than Neanderthal or any earlier type, and had a better brain development than any except perhaps Neanderthal man. He had a tribal form of life. By 30,000 B.C. he was apparently firmly established in Europe, and *neanderthalensis* had disappeared. Cro-Magnon was not only the finest primate specimen yet to appear up to his time, his accomplishments were in some ways outstanding even by present standards. Around 18,000 to 15,000 B.C. he painted on the walls of caves in the French valley of the Dordogne remarkable pictures of animals whose detail and vitality rival the skill of any later artist. In terms of man's physical and mental capacity, from that point in time there is little more to say. There have probably been no substantial changes in man as an animal since then.

Archaeologists generally agree that the New World is indeed new to human habitation, as well as to European discovery. It is believed that there was no human life in North or South America before the time when *Homo sapiens* was well established in Europe. It is

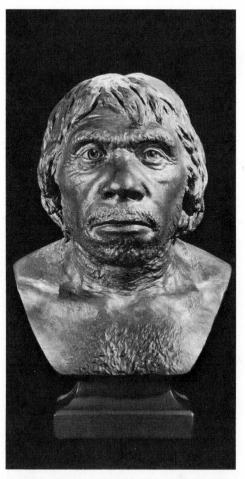

A reconstruction of Homo neanderthalensis. (*Courtesy of the American Museum of Natural History.*)

thought that the first men to reach the Western hemisphere came via the Bering Sea from Siberia to Alaska, at a time when a great drop in ocean level had left a land bridge. Their arrival is dated not later than 10,000 and not earlier than 30,000 B.C. Fossil remains have been found, especially in the Southwest of the United States, which date back to this period. It is generally thought, also, that the great American Indian civilizations—Inca, Mayan, Aztec—were developed by the descendants of these immigrants, independent of the development of civilization in the Old World.

We may close this section with a little note that may encourage a healthy skepticism about archaeological dates. Certainly one of our most fascinating scientific questions is: When did man begin? The discovery of *Zinjanthropus* and *Homo habilis* in southern Africa has set back our date for the beginnings of true man about a million years. Yet both *Zinjanthropus* and *habilis* may be only about 600,000 years old, or not much older than Java, Peking, and Heidelberg men. On the basis of geological evidence at the site where they were unearthed, Leakey himself thought this to be the case. But analysis of potassium traces, in an American laboratory, gave the much earlier figures of 1,750,000 and 1,850,-000 years. On such precarious evidence our guesses about the origins of man rest.

PHYSICAL STOCKS AND RACES

Certainly one of the most important facts about the human animal is that people are physically different from one another. The color of a person's skin, the texture of his hair, and the shape of his nose may be of enormous significance in determining the kind of life he will lead. Many people are convinced that individuals with certain physical traits and background are physically, morally, or intellectually superior to others. They may believe that too close contact between physically different groups is undesirable or dangerous. These beliefs are embodied in customs, laws, and institutions that discriminate among separate groups. Sometimes these patterns are accepted with little or no open protest. Sometimes they are enforced with brutal violence. Today many of these patterns are breaking down, often with violence on both sides. Race riots and race wars are part of the revolution of rising expectations.

In this section we shall examine, not primarily people's beliefs about human physical difference or their behavior based upon these beliefs, but the facts about difference. What are the important physical differences that we find in the world's population? Is the species *Homo sapiens* divided into clear-cut races that are easily distinguished? How did physical differences arise? What function do they serve? Do physical differences denote superiority and inferiority, and if so, in what sense? How important are physical differences among people as compared with differences in social experience and opportunity? What are likely to be the biological results of intermixture of physically different individuals?

Some of the characteristics in which human beings differ physically are obvious to anyone. Others are familiar only to specialists. *Skin color,* determined by the amount of melanin pigment, is probably the most ordinarily obvious difference, and the one most likely to excite emotion. People differ widely in hair *color* and *texture* (straight, wavy, or kinky), and in distribution of hair on the body. Individual groups have different *eye formation,* particularly with respect to eye color, and the epicanthic eye fold, which distinguishes the Chinese and other people. *Nose shape* is an important distinction. One measure of this is the nasal index, the ratio of nose width to length. Human beings differ widely in *stature;* in Africa, height ranges from the Pygmies, who are under five feet, to the Nilotic peoples, who may approach seven feet. Groups as well as individuals differ in their typical *body build.*

Facial shape, especially the size and prominence of teeth and jaw, is an important difference. *Head shape* is one of the measures longest used by anthropologists. Some people are round-headed, others very long-headed. The numerical measure used is the cephalic index—the ratio of head width to length. Fairly recent is the discovery that *blood composition* differs among human groups. Some groups are more likely to have A, B, O, or other blood type, and to have positive or negative Rh factors. Sickle-shaped red cells, which are associated with a particular kind of anemia, are present only in certain groups. An interesting recent discovery is that human individuals have apparently inherited differences in their ability to *taste* certain substances, and that this ability is also greater in some groups than in others. The testing agent most frequently used is phenylthiocarbamide (PTC).

How did these differences arise, which distinguish the black Congolese Negro and the blond Swede, the long-headed Spaniard and the round-headed Ukrainian, the slant-eyed Chinese, the diminutive Pygmy or Bushman? To some extent physical differences may be the result of the immediate environment. The anthropologist Boas found that even the head shapes of immigrants to the United States changed over several generations, perhaps because of nutritional changes. Japanese in Hawaii were at one time found to be much heavier and taller than their less generously fed relatives back in Japan. But certainly a large part of physical difference is hereditary. Since hereditary patterns are carried primarily in the genes, we speak of these as *genetic* differences.

Physical differences have undoubtedly arisen, to a large extent, out of genetic *mutations.* These are sudden changes in the genes which are then passed down to succeeding generations. Mutation has achieved public prominence since we have learned that atomic radiation may change genetic structure, but it is a process that has been going on at all times. Once mutations have occurred, *natural selection* tends to take place. Those mutations that are favorable to survival and the production of offspring tend to continue, while others that are not adapted to the environment are eliminated. We can see that in asking how physical differences in the genus *Homo sapiens* have arisen, we are simply asking the whole question of how biological evolution has occurred. (Most scientists rule out another possibility, that traits acquired during a lifetime—for example, darkening of the skin—can be transmitted to offspring. The "inheritance of acquired characteristics" is, however, somewhat more open to debate than it used to be.)

A third factor in producing physical types is *genetic drift,* through which a trait may disappear or be accentuated "by chance." Suppose that there is a population with the average number of genes for red color blindness, and that this population splits into smaller groups who separate and migrate. One of the groups, by chance, may carry an unusually high number of color blindness genes, while another may carry none at all. Finally, human physical types as we know them are all the product of a long history of *intermixture.* Almost all people in the world today are the product of miscegenation ("mixture of genes"), which has blended groups with distinct physical traits and produced hybrid physical types.

It is likely that a large number of the physical differences among human beings represent survivals of types adapted to different environments. Dark pigmentation serves to protect, among other things, against skin cancer in a tropical climate. It loses its function in more northerly climates and when clothes are worn. Heavy, bulky bodies conserve heat in cold climates, while more rangy frames evaporate moisture and thus cool themselves more efficiently under hotter conditions. Long noses may help to moisten or warm air on its way to the lungs in dry or cold climate, while broad flat noses suffice in humid tropical areas. Thick, kinky, dark hair protects the head and brain against the tropical sun; only in cooler areas can blondness, grayness, or baldness be afforded.

Large teeth and jaws are an advantage among primitive people who chew food in its natural state. Smaller jaws and teeth are likely to be found among people who have for a long time had technically advanced methods of growing and preparing food. Small people with low nutritional needs may have an

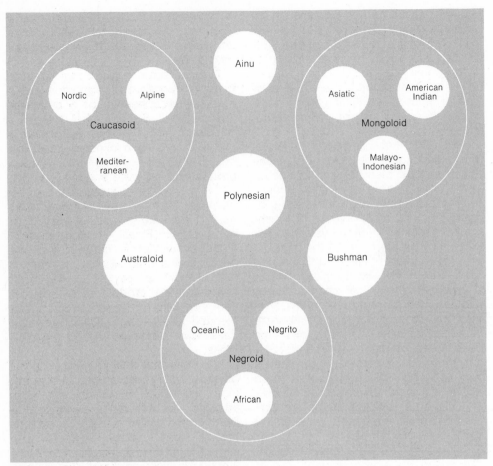

Figure 3.1. Major races and subraces of mankind.
Source: E Adamson Hoebel, *Man in the Primitive World*, 2nd ed., New York, McGraw-Hill, 1958, p. 132; modified from Kroeber.

advantage in surviving in areas where food is very hard to get. Visual defects like color blindness are likely to be able to survive only when people become technically advanced and cease to depend on acute vision for spotting food and enemies. Sickle cells in the blood appear to help protect against tropical malaria, but lose their function in areas where malaria is not present. Blood types may represent adaptations to different kinds of diet—to predominantly vegetarian and predominantly meat diets, for one thing.

It should be emphasized that almost all physical traits have been influenced by migration and intermixture. Also, the kinds of connections drawn in the last

two paragraphs are hypotheses rather than proved conclusions. Too, one factor alone seldom determines anything. Nevertheless, it is likely that the better we learn to understand physical differences, the more we shall discover that most of them are not just "accidents" but serve some function in survival, or have done so in the past.

Can we refer to different physical types as "races"? In the first place, let us look at some things with which race is often confused, but which it clearly is not. A race is not a national population. It is incorrect to speak of the "British race," for the inhabitants of England are a mixture of many physical stocks. Neither is a race a group of people

Representatives of the three major races: Negroid, Caucasoid, and Mongoloid.

who share a common cultural background. *Most* Jews share a long and rich cultural heritage, but social scientists do not generally classify Jews as a racial group.

So far as it does have meaning, the term "race" is a group of people that has been relatively isolated and interbred and has thus developed an inherited (genetic) physical similarity. Among biologists in general, a race is defined as a "subspecies," a distinct group within an animal species. Unlike different species, subspecies or races can interbreed successfully with one another. For reasons that we shall examine shortly when we come to naming human races, it is impossible to find agreement even among experts. Figure 3.1, adapted from the anthropologist A. L. Kroeber, is probably as good a classification as any.

We will note three major races: Mongoloid (yellow), Negroid (dark), and Caucasoid (white). Each is divided into three subgroups. There are then four groups that are difficult to classify in any single race: the Polynesians, the Bushman hunters of South Africa, the native aborigines of Australia, and the "white" and hairy Ainus, early residents of Japan, some of whom survive today.

Mongoloids are slant-eyed (possessing the epicanthic fold), brown-eyed, brown or yellowish tan with straight black hair. They are usually round-headed, squat-nosed, and short in the legs. Infants have a purplish, triangular area at the base of the spine, called the "Mongoloid patch." It is relatively easy for us to visualize the three Mongoloid types: the Chinese or Japanese, the Indonesian, and the American Indian.

Negroids are dark, generally long-headed, broad-nosed, sparse of beard and body hair, medium in height, with thick musculature in the legs. We have perhaps a general image of a typical African Negro, as distinct from a Pygmy, who belongs to the Negrito group. The Oceanic Negroes first came to attention when American GIs entered the South Sea islands in World War II. Unlike the African Negro, the Oceanic is likely to have a prominent hooked nose and thinner lips.

Caucasoids have eyes from blue to dark brown. Hair may be any color, straight or wavy, but rarely kinky. There is often much body hair in the male. The nose tends to be narrow and high, and the lips thin. Stature is medium to tall. We think of the Scandanavian as the typical Nordic Causasoid. He is likely to be tall and slender, blond, with light eye color, long-headed, with sparse hair on the body and head. A good many of the Alpine stock are now in the Communist satellite countries of east central Europe. They are typically round-headed, solid and heavy, with a medium or short body, brown to black eyes and hair, and olive skin. The Mediterranean is found mainly in Spain, Italy, North Africa, and India. He has dark or black hair, a long head with a narrow, high forehead, light brown or olive skin, a narrow high-bridged nose, and is likely to be slight in youth with a tendency to fatness in maturity.

Some of the material in the preceding paragraphs is new and technical. Much, however, deals with things with which we already have some familiarity. As we think seriously about this classification of races, we may feel some dissatisfaction.

For one thing, in these descriptions of racial groups, is there not a lot of overlapping? There do not seem to be many traits that sharply and clearly belong to one and only one racial group. In large measure this objection is justified. A few traits are "all or none" qualities. For example, only Mongoloids have the Mongoloid patch at the base of the infant spine. Only Negroes have sickle cells in their blood. There are no Rh negative genes in Chinese, Australian aborigines, or American Indians. But for most traits, it is not a question of presence or absence, but of how much.

Consider the head shape of Alpine Caucasoids and Negroes, for example. We say that Alpines are round-headed and Negroes are long-headed. But if we measured all Alpine heads, we would actually get a *frequency distribution,* a curve with most heads fairly round, a few extremely round, and some rather long. A measurement of all Negro heads would show most to be quite long, a few extremely long and narrow, and a few relatively round. If we would combine these two frequency distributions, we would find that they

do overlap—*some* Alpines are longer-headed than *some* Negroes. We could plot other traits similarly. If we compared Caucasoid and Mongoloid skin color, we would find that most Caucasoids are lighter than most Mongoloids, but that *some* Caucasoids are darker than *some* Mongoloids.

Another question may occur. How many traits must a group share to be a race? Are one or two—say, skin color and head shape—enough? If a race is a group that, some time in the past, has developed in adaptation to an isolated environment, ought not its members to be similar in a large number of the important traits by which races are distinguished? Is this true of the major groups we have defined?

Do all Africans, including the seven-foot Masai and the five-foot Pygmy, deserve to be included in the same race because they have dark skins? Do the Oceanic Negroes, with their hooked noses and thin lips, belong? Do the Australian aborigines, or "blackfellows," who are dark but have heavy body hair? Do the very dark peoples have enough other physical qualities in common for us to believe that they all came originally from one isolated interbreeding group?

What about the Mongoloids? Can we include the American Indian, who possesses many Mongoloid characteristics but who, for example, has no B-type blood while other Mongoloids have it? If all came from the same original stock, how do we explain this difference?

And what about the Caucasians? Do Swedes, Italians, and Hungarians show enough other similarities, apart from the fact that they are all relatively light skinned, to justify our believing that they came from a single original stock?

On such questions social scientists take various positions. Perhaps the most extreme scientific defender of the idea of human physical groups as distinct biological races is the anthropologist Carleton Coon. He believes not only that the human races are real biological subspecies, but that they were distinct even before *Homo sapiens* developed from our earlier ancestors. He holds, for example, that Peking man was already Mongoloid 500,000 or more years ago, and that the early African men were probably already Negroid. This view of human origins is called "polygenetic" ("several origins"). It holds that *Homo sapiens* did not evolve once and then split into races, but that each race evolved separately into *Homo sapiens.* Coon also believes that the races probably evolved into modern man at different times, so that some races have been *Homo sapiens* longer than others.

Coon has supported his views with a detailed study of the physical traits of the known fossil men and premen. Most archaeologists, however, reject the polygenetic view, and hold that human races have evolved from a single *Homo sapiens* stock, perhaps in the last 100,000 years. This we call the "monogenetic" view of the origin of modern man.

Some of the holders of this view agree with the anthropologist Ashley Montagu that it is remarkable enough that a creature like *Homo sapiens* evolved at all, and that it stretches the imagination to suppose that he evolved independently, several times, in different parts of the world. Many of the followers of the monogenetic view believe that we do have human stocks that are genuine biological races or subspecies. Support for this view comes from some of the most recent work in genetic differences among races. Chinese, Australian aborigines, and American Indians, for example, not only share important traits in physical structure, but are also like one another and distinguished from Caucasoid people in that none of them has Rh negative genes and all are able to taste PTC.

Other social scientists (and biologists) believe that the term "race" or "subspecies" cannot properly be applied to the major human physical groups we know. Not only is Coon wrong in believing that races are older

than *Homo sapiens,* they hold, but evidence from fossils does not suggest that at any time physical types were any "purer" than they are now. Ashley Montagu has expounded this view in his book, *Man's Most Dangerous Myth: The Fallacy of Race,* and in more recent publications. Holders of this position believe that the concept of race has been so long associated with wrong ideas that continued use of it actually hinders objective study of physical differences. They believe that the word "race" should be dropped from use in any discussion of human differences. Some biologists believe that the concept of race is of doubtful value in the study of any biological species.

Whatever we may think about the word "race," there remains the question of whether some human physical types are superior to others. Let us now look at the evidence.

Some people believe that some physical groups (or races) are biologically more primitive than others. Coon's theory that Negroes probably developed into *Homo sapiens* later than Caucasians is an example of such a view. Often certain physical characteristics are taken to mark one group as closer to the other primates than is another. For example, the typically greater length of Negro arms in proportion to the body is sometimes considered evidence that Negroes are more "ape-like" (simian). Mongoloids (especially Japanese at the time when they were enemies of America) have sometimes been compared to monkeys.

If one will review a number of important physical traits, however, he will see that each major group is more "ape-like" in some characteristics and less so in others. Negroids are more simian in the shape of nose, the capacity of the skull, and the shape of the jaw. They are, however, the least "ape-like" group in shape of head, form and length of head and body hair, and form of lips. Mongoloids are most simian-like in head shape, hair form, and lip form, but least simian in jaw shape and eye form. Caucasoids are closest to the ape in hairiness of the body; more simian than Negroids in head shape, hair form, and form of lips. One anthropologist has said that in a number of important physical characteristics, Negroes are least ape-like in six and Caucasoids in only three. But there is no real evidence that one group significantly is more "animal" than any other.[1]

Another question relates to brain size. The best studies available indicate that the average Negro brain is slightly smaller than that of Mongoloids and Caucasoids. In general, if one compares animal species, higher intelligence is associated with a larger brain in proportion to body size. However, the size of the frontal lobe and the number and complexity of convolutions are more important than sheer size. In terms of brain size alone, for example, Neanderthal man would have to be judged more intelligent than modern *Homo sapiens*. His smaller frontal lobe and the simpler convolutions of his brain suggest, however, that this was not the case. There is no evidence that any existing human type is superior to any other in frontal lobe development or brain convolutions. Among Caucasoids who have been studied, there appears to be some relationship between intelligence and size of head. Probably, however, this is because people who are brought up well, nutritionally and otherwise, tend to be brighter and also larger in body and head. If brain size alone were evidence of intelligence, we should have to rate as more intelligent than Caucasoids the Eskimos and the Negro Zulie and Amaxsosa, all of whose brains are larger in proportion to body. The evidence on this problem is thus inconclusive, and in any case difference between human groups in brain size is so small as to be unimportant in comparison with other factors.

1. See E. Adamson Hoebel, *Man in the Primitive World*, 2nd ed., New York, McGraw-Hill, 1958, chap. 9.

There are other possible evidences advanced for difference in intelligence among physical groups. During World War I, the American Army undertook the first widespread testing of the intelligence of members of all racial groups. In the Army alpha and beta tests, given routinely to recruits, Negroid and Mongoloid recruits (the latter mostly American Indians) rated definitely below Caucasoid recruits. These tests seemed to some people to give clear proof of white superiority.

It was soon clear, however, that more had to be taken into account in interpreting the Army tests. The question that must always be asked in comparing the performance of test groups arose: *Did the tests measure inborn ability or amount of social opportunity (or both)?* Evaluation of the tests with this question in mind brought interesting results. If black and white draftees were broken into four groups—northern Negro, northern white, southern Negro, and southern white—they rated on the tests in this order:

1. *Northern white*
2. *Northern Negro*
3. *Southern white*
4. *Southern Negro*

What did this mean? Do northern Negroes have more inborn intellectual ability than southern whites? No such conclusion was necessary. In all likelihood the northern Negroes scored higher because they had gone to better schools and had better cultural backgrounds and opportunities. The same explanation probably held for all the other differences. It was not proved, of course, that the results do not reflect some inborn differences, but since the scores of all four groups corresponded to their amount of cultural opportunity, it is more likely that the explanation lies largely or entirely there.

The difficulty in attributing differences on tests to differences in inherited ability is that it is probably impossible to construct a "culture-free" intelligence test, that is, one that measures innate ability alone without measuring social experience. There are in the United States children of school age who have never seen a mirror or a book. Regardless of inborn ability, such children are going to score lower on any kind of test than most children who have had rich family and cultural opportunities.

The efforts of the psychologist Porteus to test the mental ability of the native Australian "blackfellows" show why we cannot draw from intelligence tests conclusions about native aptitude. Most intelligence tests measure the ability to solve problems on one's own, but this is not the way the blackfellows solve problems, for they always work them out together. They felt, indeed, that Porteus should have helped them with the test, especially since one tribe had made him a member. Most intelligence tests have a time factor; the score depends upon speed. But the Australian natives gave no importance to ability to perform rapidly. The intelligence tests available to Porteus were constructed in a society that emphasizes individualism and speed. The aborigines naturally showed up very poorly. If a test based upon their type of experience and approach could have been constructed, Westerners might have scored equally poorly.

It has not been proved that no racial differences in native intelligence exist. In fact, it is perhaps unlikely that groups differing in inborn physical traits will be exactly the same in inherited mental qualities. Adaptations to different environments may well have emphasized certain qualities of adjustment in one group and other qualities in another. However, differences may be simply differences, rather than denoting general inferiority and superiority. In any case, we have little or no direct evidence on this problem. We do know that most of the group differences yet found on tests can be explained in terms of difference in social experience. It is also likely that if they do exist among groups, native differences are relatively unim-

portant when compared with the effects of cultural environment.

Some people believe that different levels of technology and social organization demonstrate differences in ability among physical groups. Neither the Mongoloid nor the Negroid peoples, they contend, have produced on their own the kind of civilization achieved by Western Caucasoid man.

This point of view raises, however, several problems. We are likely to assume our modern technological civilization to be superior and to rank all others as inferior. The Chinese have, however, had a continuous rich culture and an advanced social and political organization since before the time of Christ. Though until recently they have not emphasized technology, they would never have admitted their way of life to be inferior. Quite the contrary, as we shall see in the next chapter. The Negroid peoples of central Africa have not produced a civilization of the complexity of either the Chinese or that of Western white man. However, their tribal political development has been much less simple than we may imagine, and African art has recently come to be held of considerable value in the West. It may be, also, that the climate of the tropics has been unfavorable to the development of a complex technological civilization in the predominantly Negroid areas. We shall examine this problem later in this chapter.

Also, we need to take a long view. Recorded history is only about 5,000 years out of the 50,000 to 100,000 years of modern man. Modern Western technology, which distinguishes Caucasoid achievement, is only 400 or 500 years old. There have been constant changes in the social development of different peoples, although genetically they have probably changed little. The descendants of the Greeks who built the Parthenon let Athens deteriorate by the nineteenth century into a squalid village. The Roman Cicero said of the Britons: "Do not obtain your slaves from the Britons, for the Britons are so stupid and dull that they are not fit to be slaves." The Romans held a similar view of the Germanic tribes. How do the descendants of Romans, Germans, and Britons compare on the scale of development today?

In the Middle Ages, European technology and science fell to a low level, while in North America the Mongoloid Mayan Indians had developed a thriving civilization. At the same time, the Mohammedan Moors, with considerable Negroid ancestry, were definitely superior in science and technology to Caucasoid Christian Europe, and so regarded themselves. Today Chinese, Japanese, and Africans have all shown themselves able to master complex technology and social organization in a relatively short time. All this does not finally prove that all physical stocks are exactly equal in capacity for civilization. It does indicate, however, that opportunities and challenges in the physical and social environment are more important than any possible genetic differences.

What, finally, about "race mixture"? Will failure to keep the races sexually separate result in "mongrelization"? The idea that it will may rest on the notion that some groups are superior and that their level will be brought down by mixture. The preceding paragraphs should suggest that there is little reason for anxiety. Perhaps it is feared that traits which have become specialized in some groups might be lost by mixture. What would happen to the peculiar resonance of many Negro singing voices (undoubtedly related to physical differences in nasal and sinus formation) if all people mixed indiscriminately? There are undoubtedly other group traits with a physical basis which might also disappear.

Biologically, there is no clear evidence for or against hybridization as such. When one wishes to accentuate special qualities, as in breeding fast horses or dogs, he avoids a mixture of strains. There is a question, however, as to whether a thoroughbred horse or dog may not be too "fine" for survival

except under protected circumstances. We know that inbreeding tends to bring out recessive genetic traits—gene qualities that are carried by an individual, that are not expressed in the physical body of the carrier, but that may appear in the offspring if two carriers mate. The recessive qualities thus brought out may be either positive or negative—color blindness or tendencies toward nervous instability, perhaps, on the one hand, and possibly predispositions to musical or mathematical genius on the other. Either favorable or unfavorable, joining of recessive genes is less likely to occur where intermixture is common. Hybridization, by joining two lines of genes, also gives a larger "pool" of possible adaptations. From this standpoint, hybrids have an advantage in the struggle for existence.

If physical types represent adaptations to specific environments, then mixture might weaken adaptation. For example, if Negroid skin is an adaptation to intense sunlight, and sickle cells help resist malaria, then miscegenation with Mongoloid or Caucasoid stock might weaken the capacity to adapt. The opposite might be true in northern, malaria-free climates. It should be clear by now that there is no open and shut case, biologically, for or against mixture of physical stocks. But civilized man has learned to adapt so well to different environments that it is doubtful whether any biological advantages of "race purity" that may exist are of much importance. It should also be clear that if miscegenation were as disastrous as some people think it to be, the human race could not have survived as long and as well as it has. If any of us traces his family tree far enough and widely enough, he will discover that he is already a mongrel.

BODY TYPE AND TEMPERAMENT

We must now give some attention to another kind of connection which has been drawn between physique and psychological and social phenomena. This is the idea that personal temperament and social events are influenced by the body build of individuals.

The belief that body type is associated with personality, or character, is very old. In Shakespeare's *Julius Caesar* we find this interchange between Caesar and Antony:

Caesar

*Let me have men about me that
    are fat;
Sleek-headed men, and such as
    sleep o'nights:
Yon Cassius has a lean and
    hungry look;
He thinks too much: such men
    are dangerous.*

Antony

*Fear him not, Caesar; he is
    not dangerous;
He is a noble Roman, and well
    given.*

Caesar

Would he were fatter! . . .

In the twentieth century, the study of body, or "somatic," type is especially connected with a German psychiatrist, Ernst Kretschmer, and an American psychologist, William Sheldon.

Kretschmer's findings were presented in the book *Physique and Character,* published in 1925. He distinguished three human body types, not associated with any particular race.[2]

The *asthenic* type ("without strength") is "a lean narrowly built man (or woman), who looks taller than he is, with a skin poor in secretion and blood, with narrow shoulders, from which hang lean arms with thin muscles, and delicately boned hands; a long, narrow, flat chest, on which we can count the ribs . . . a thin stomach, devoid of fat, and lower limbs which are just like the upper ones in character."

2. Ernst Kretschmer, *Physique and Character,* New York, Harcourt Brace Jovanovich, 1925, pp. 21, 24, 29.

The *athletic* individual is "a middle-sized to tall man, with particularly wide projecting shoulders, a superb chest, a firm stomach, and a trunk which tapers in its lower region, so that the pelvis, and the magnificent legs, sometimes seem almost graceful compared with the size of the upper limbs."

The *pyknic* type is characterized by "middle height, rounded figure, a soft broad face on a short massive neck, sitting between the shoulders; the magnificent fat paunch protrudes from the deep *vaulted* chest which broadens out toward the lower part of the body. The shoulders are not broad and projecting as with the athletics, but (especially among older people) are rounded, rather high, and pushed forward together."

Kretschmer's interest in body types grew out of his desire as a psychiatrist to find an explanation for types of mental disease. He believed that he had found an association between his three somatic types and two major forms of severe mental illness (psychosis). *Schizophrenia,* which is characterized by a psychological withdrawal from reality, he believed to be associated with the asthenic and athletic body forms. *Manic depression,* in which there is an alternation of extremely elated periods with periods of deep depression, he believed is found chiefly among people of pyknic build.

Kretschmer believed that the association of body traits and temperament is true not only for mentally ill people but for all people. Everyone, he thought, is either a schizothyme, living a large part of his life in a world of ideas and fantasy, or a cyclothyme, much more enmeshed in "real" everyday life, but prone to swings of elation and depression. In Kretschmer's view, these bodily and temperamental types have important social consequences. He discussed connections which he felt exist in science and philosophy, in art, and in social leadership.

In science and philosophy, the cyclothyme is likely to be skilled in observation and description, but weak in organizing or theorizing about his findings. There are very few pyknic philosophers. The schizothyme is likely to be a formal, abstract thinker, a pure mathematician or a metaphysician. Pyknic artists are likely to have a strong and realistic visual and descriptive sense. Schizothymic artists are likely to produce works that are abstract, romantic, or dreamy.

The two temperamental types produce two kinds of social leaders. Pyknic leaders are likely to be tough, simple fighters, confident and practical organizers, successful diplomats. Kretschmer considered Martin Luther and the French revolutionary leader Mirabeau examples of this kind of leader. The schizothymic leader is more likely to be an idealist, a moralist, a "cold calculator," a fanatic, a despot. Kretschmer gives Savanarola, the fanatical Florentine monk, and Robespierre, the leader of the terror in the French Revolution, as cases of schizothymic leaders. John Calvin, one of the great founders of Protestantism, he saw as a typical and historically very influential schizothyme. Calvin, he said, was a typical asthenic, with a "haggard, very long face, abnormal length of the middle face, long sharp nose. . . ."

Sheldon's work is summarized in his book *The Varieties of Temperament.* Sheldon's three somatic types are the *endomorph,* the *mesomorph,* and the *ectomorph.* "When endomorphy predominates, the digestive viscera are massive and highly developed, while the somatic structures are relatively weak and undeveloped. Endomorphs are of low specific gravity. They float high in the water. . . . The mesomorphic physique is high in specific gravity and is hard, firm, upright, and relatively strong and tough. . . . The hallmark of mesomorphy is uprightness and sturdiness of structure, as the hallmark of endomorphy is softness and sphericity. . . . The ectomorph has long, slender, poorly muscled extremities with delicate, pipestem bones, and

he has, relative to his mass, the greatest surface area and hence the greatest sensory exposure to the outside world. He is thus in one sense overly exposed and naked to his world."[3]

We can see the resemblance to Kretschmer's types:

KRETSCHMER	*SHELDON*
pyknic	*endomorph*
athletic	*mesomorph*
asthenic	*ectomorph*

Corresponding to the three body types are three characteristic temperaments. The endomorph tends to be *viscerotonic:* "the personality seems to center around the viscera. . . . The digestive system is king." The viscerotonic person loves physical comfort and takes great pleasure in eating, especially with other people. He likes people with what Sheldon calls an "indiscriminate amiability." When in trouble, he seeks the comfort of other people. The mesomorph tends to be *somatotonic*— the most important thing to him is his muscles. For him, "action and power define life's primary purpose." He loves physical activity and adventure. He has little sensitivity for the feelings of others and may be ruthless. The ectomorph tends to be *cerebrotonic*—to live mainly in his brain and nervous system. The cerebrotonic person is tight and restrained. He loves privacy. He is afraid of people and is extremely sensitive to pain. When in trouble, he strives to be alone.

According to Sheldon, somatotypes are related to the structure of society as well as to individual temperament. Ectomorphs are at their best, for example, in universities, and play a prominent role there. Different religions represent emphasis on one or another somatic and temperamental type. Buddhism is predominantly viscerotonic (we may visualize the picture or statue of Buddha). Christ is typically depicted

3. William H. Sheldon, *The Varieties of Temperament,* New York, Harper, 1942, pp. 7, 8, *et passim.*

as an ectomorph. Sheldon described Christianity as an "antisomatic revolution," that is, as a reaction against the vigorous, muscular, aggressive life. Nationalism, which has to a considerable extent become a religion in modern times, is typically somatotonic. Nazi Germany was an example of the uncontrolled dominance of the somatotonic temperament.

Sheldon saw war as an explosion of muscular, aggressive, ruthless somatotonia. In social and economic life, he saw somatotonia as associated with the ruthless pursuit of power and status. Sheldon believed that we have had a "somatotonic revolution since World War I." He felt that in its stress on war and ruthless competition, our twentieth-century society has become a "predatory culture" which has given too much prominence to somatotonic individuals and qualities. He hoped for a more balanced society which would stress equally the qualities of more relaxed enjoyment (viscerotonia) and reflective intelligence (cerebrotonia).

We do not have enough evidence to give anything like a final evaluation of the views of Kretschmer and Sheldon. It is important, however, that we know what these men have said, and are able to weigh it in our own thinking as we attempt to understand the variety of influences which shape society.

MAN AND HIS HABITAT

So far in this chapter, we have been concerned with the influence of man's physical and biological structure upon his social life. Now we turn to his relationship to the physical and biological world outside him—the *habitat* in which he dwells. We shall ask how this affects his social relationships.

Our relationship to our habitat is fourfold. Man lives in relation to an *atmosphere.* It is arresting to think that of all the space in our solar system, only a thin area surrounding the earth is capable of providing the oxygen necessary to support life. A few thousand feet above the ground life becomes difficult, and a few thousand more it becomes impossible without artificial sources of oxygen. It is also arresting to think that the waste products of man's civilization have already made some areas of the atmosphere incapable at times of supporting life for some people, and that there are scientists who predict that man may within a very short time conceivably make the whole atmosphere unlivable. Life's balance with the atmosphere is precarious.

Man also lives in relation to a *hydrosphere.* Most of the earth's surface is water, surrounded by which we are all really island animals. Life originally came from the sea, and the composition of our blood and other bodily fluids, very close to that of ocean water, bears evidence of our origins. We can live only a short time without replenishing these fluids from the hydrosphere. The sea has furnished both a barrier and a challenge to human activities. Oceans and rivers have provided channels for migration and commerce. In times no older than Cro-Magnon man, the frozen hydrosphere in the form of glaciers pushed down from the North and profoundly affected human life. Melting ice has changed the level of oceans and submerged some human habitations. In the course of time, both glaciation and melting may very well happen again.

Man is related to a *geosphere,* the solid part of the earth. In order to keep a proper perspective, it is good to remind ourselves again that the "solid" ground on which we live is a very thin shell over a mass molten at the center. Our deepest mines carry us not so far proportionally as the thickness of the shell of an egg. The surface of the geosphere, broken into mountains, plains, and river valleys, shapes man's movements and his forms of life. From the geosphere (in cooperation with hydrosphere and biosphere), man gets the food that maintains his body. From it, largely, he also derives the raw materials for the technology on which his civilization rests.

Finally, man is part of a *biosphere*. We are one species among a multitude of species of flora (predominantly grasses, plants, and trees) and fauna (insects, birds, wild and domestic animals). Intermediate between animal and plant life are bacteria, viruses, enzymes, and other borderline forms of life. With the biosphere we live in complex relationships. In the universal biological struggle for existence we are in competition with many species; without control, they would drive us from the earth. But we also live in cooperation. Without plant or animal food, without the cooperation of other life in food production, without the "friendly" bacteria and fauna which help control our "enemies," we also could not continue to live.

Those aspects of our social life which involve our relationship to our physical and biological environment we call "ecological" relationships. The word "ecology" comes from the Greek word for house or home, *oikos*. Ecological relationships are thus concerned with making our home in our habitat. Ecology is as wide as life, for all living forms are part of the same fourfold environment. We must all adapt together to it and to one another. We are all part of an ecological community. In a famous illustration, Darwin pointed out the relationship between the number of cats and the crop of red clover in the ecological community. Only bumble bees can fertilize red clover. Field mice kill bumble bees. Cats kill field mice. Therefore, the more cats, the larger the clover crop. Someone has added that since old maids keep cats, the clover crop depends on the supply of old maids!

Let us look at three important groups of relationships in which our participation in our fourfold habitat involves us.

Climate and geography

The first of these is man's relationship to climate and geography. These factors vary enormously over the earth's surface. How are these differences reflected in man's social life? We have already seen that adaptation to climate seems to have been one of the most important factors in the development of racial groups. What similar connections can we find?

The most important elements in climate are temperature, humidity, and wind velocity. Clearly some parts of the globe are climatically unsuitable at present for any organized social life. In others it is possible, but only under difficulty. Some areas are well or very well suited.

The geographer C. E. P. Brooks has classified nine types of climatic areas, in terms of their suitability for human life.[4] Extreme polar areas, high mountains, deserts, and areas of combined high humidity and heat are at, or over, the borderline of human habitation. In areas like Alaska, northern Canada, Labrador, and farther north, life is

4. C. E. P. Brooks, *Climate in Everyday Life*, London, Ernest Beun, 1950.

possible most of the time only with extremely heavy clothing. In high mountains, like those at Cerro de Pasco, Peru (altitude 14,200 feet), no children are born, hens do not lay eggs, and no purebred dog can live. Desert climate, marked by rainfall under ten inches a year, is very injurious to machinery, there is always danger of cramps and sunstroke, and the dry, hot air makes tempers likely to be habitually short. In highly tropical "deterioration" areas, metals corrode, clothing molds, the natives are likely to be lethargic, and nonnatives are able to maintain themselves only with regular periods of absence.

Other types of areas present rather severe problems, but can support social life well. Climates like that of Egypt, with intense solar radiation and maximum temperatures of 110 to 120° F., have many of the drawbacks of deserts, but may be fertile under irrigation, although one rarely tries to work in midday. In areas like the West Indies and part of the southeastern United States, conditions are on the whole favorable, but buildings have to be constructed against the risk of hurricane damage. Climates with long, icy winters, like those of the north central United States and the center of the Eurasian continent, require insulation, heating devices, and extra strong or pitched roofs, and sometimes pose serious transportation problems.

Brooks thinks that probably the most favorable climates for human life and productivity are Mediterranean and temperate. On the coast of the Mediterranean Sea and in southern California, winters are very pleasant, although summers are too hot for sustained outdoor activity. Temperate areas like the northeastern United States, parts of Canada, northwest Europe, Japan, southeast Australia, and New Zealand usually have enough but not too much rain, seldom experience great extremes of heat or cold, and are changeable enough to be highly stimulating to human effort.

Judgment about climatic areas assumes that some conditions are best for the human organism. What is best depends on what one is doing. The optimum temperature for sleeping or sitting in the shade is quite different from that for digging ditches. The best temperature for mental activity is probably somewhere in between. It has been suggested that the best temperature is one where a person at rest neither perspires nor shivers. Thus a temperature range of about 60 to 75° would be most favorable. When it is hotter, bodily activity slows down in order to keep the body from being overheated. When it is cooler, one is compelled to be physically active or to seek artificial sources of heat. It is likely that, other things being equal, a climate between 70 and 75° has the lowest death rate.

There is a question to be raised, however. Can a climate be *too* favorable, so that people lack stimulation? Writers as early as the great Greek physician Hippocrates and as recent as the contemporary British historian Arnold Toynbee have stressed the importance of challenge from the environment in promoting social development. Perhaps the best temperature, at least for social progress, is one a little too cold for comfort, one which will spur people into activity.

Temperature cannot be separated from humidity. Higher or lower extremes of temperature can be borne if the air is relatively dry. The best humidity is probably not lower than 30 percent or higher than 70 percent, and indeed a climate with a steady humidity near 70 will be too oppressive. In line with the idea that variation is favorable, the geographer Ellsworth Huntington has also done a good deal of research which he feels demonstrates that a climate with fairly frequent storms is very stimulating to human activity.

Can we find connections between climate and the course of history? From the days of the Greeks and Romans, writers have drawn such conclusions. Aristotle held that people of the middle latitudes are superior to those of either the extreme North or the extreme South—and the ideal climate was that of Greece! The Roman philosopher Pliny followed the same line of thought—but found the ideal a little farther north, in Rome! Since these ancient days, the center of civilization in the Western world has moved much farther to the North. This fact has given rise to the theory of the "coldward course of civilization"—the idea that civilization began in rather warm regions (Egypt, Mesopotamia, India) and has moved gradually toward colder areas. This idea has been developed by many people, one of the most famous of whom was the nineteenth-century British historian, Henry Thomas Buckle.

It does appear that the early great civilizations of Egypt, Mesopotamia, and India fall roughly along the 70° isotherm—a line which marks points with an annual average temperature of 70° F. In the European and American world, the center of civilization has moved gradually to areas where the average temperature is under 60°. We will note that 70° falls well within the optimum range suggested for human comfort. Why, then, did the center move northward—first to Greece and Rome, eventually to London and Paris, New York and Moscow?

Perhaps because what matters is not the natural outdoor temperature alone, but the temperature which nature plus man's *technology* is able to maintain. When man learned to heat his houses fairly efficiently (as in Greece and Rome), he was able to create a year-round climate that was tolerable in winter and more stimulating in summer than that of Egypt, Mesopotamia, and India. It was not until the nineteenth century, it is true, and then mainly in the United States, that winter was effectively mastered through efficient central heating of houses. Nevertheless, heating methods had been good enough to make central and northern Europe livable and had been accompanied by the northward shift of civilization.

But why did it shift just because it became possible to live in the North? As suggested earlier, perhaps the southern climates, which were the first to make civilization possible, were too comfortable to promote the most vigorous kind of development. Buckle thought that northerly climates, where survival depends upon human ingenuity rather than the "bounty of nature," are more likely to promote social progress. It has also been proposed that the rotation of seasons, by making the storage of food over winter necessary, led to habits of foresight and planning which were unnecessary farther south.

If all this is true, what will happen in the future? In the mid-twentieth century, air conditioning has done for the southern climates what central heating did for the North. Will the subtropics and perhaps even the tropics be able to manufacture the kind of comfortable and also stimulating climate that will support vigorous civilization? Is it conceivable that the center of civilization might even shift to an area like central Africa?

The course of history is determined by many variables. So far as climate is a variable, it makes a good deal of sense to think of it in terms of (1) natural climate, (2) human technology, and (3) environmental challenge. We are left, however, with unresolved problems. Perhaps the "coldward course of civilization" applies most to the technological aspects which we in the Western world have come to regard as most progressive. It has been suggested that the world's greatest religious leaders have come from near the 70° isotherm and that religious leadership has not followed technology northward. We may think of the Hebrew prophets (Palestine), Zoroaster (Persia), Buddha (India), Jesus (Israel), and Mohammed (Arabia). In fact, a good case could be made that the desert climates, which we have called borderline for human habitation, have been by far the most productive of great religious spirits. It is better at this point to leave a question than to attempt an answer.

Location with respect to space and geographical factors has equally important social influences. People who are geographically isolated are likely to be provincial, to have little acquaintance with other people's ways and to assume that their own ways are right. The Basques of the Spanish-French frontier and the Appalachian mountaineers in this country are examples. Such people are likely to be suspicious of strangers, but very hospitable once they accept a person. They are also likely to be independent and individualistic. The islanders of Tristan da Cunha, well out in mid-Atlantic and off any main trade route, are an interesting study in isolation. Of mixed English and African ancestry since the early nineteenth century, they have developed a society almost completely apart from the rest of the world. When a volcano threatened to cover their island, they emigrated temporarily to England. Most of the islanders, however, found "civilized" life incompatible with their simple and individualistic ways and returned to Tristan when the danger was past.

Insulation from external threat has important social effects. In the years before 1400 B.C., Crete developed a peculiarly free and expressive society, probably in part because water freed the Cretans from the necessity of military activities. The development of England is without doubt related to the fact that the English Channel has insulated her from invasion since 1066. Location on the seacoast, especially at or near a major port, is likely to produce qualities the opposite of those created by isolation. People here are likely to be cosmopolitan, "citizens of the world" at home with a variety of social patterns. From the standpoint of more isolated peoples, the moral standards of seaport areas are likely to seem "loose." Location at a geo-

graphical crossroads tends to produce similar cosmopolitan qualities. This has been the case with Persia (now Iran), a crossing point of trade routes since almost the dawn of history. Rome, to which "all roads once led," is another historic example.

Breaks in transportation are likely to lead to the formation of important settlements. A study of maps will show how many cities are located at points where goods must be transferred from ocean vessels to river or land transportation (New York or any large ocean port). Other types of breaks of transportation occur at the end or junction points of railways or highways (Chicago); at the "head of navigation" of rivers where water transportation gives rise to other forms (Minneapolis–St. Paul); and at junction points of rivers (St. Louis). Location with respect to natural resources is extremely important: Pittsburgh and coal, Duluth and iron, Johannesburg and diamonds, Miami and sunshine.

One of the subjects most studied by human ecologists has been the spatial pattern of human settlement. The earth's population is obviously not settled evenly over the land surface. Rather, a very large proportion lives in fairly dense clusters while most of the land area has very little or no settlement. The obvious reason for this clustering is that there are things which people want to do (defend themselves, carry on production, find companionship, promote cultural activities, and so on) which require that they live near one another. Human communities tend to form concentric zones in space (see Figure 3.2). Primitive settlements typically show (1) at the center a village, often surrounded by a stockade; (2) outside this a zone of gardens; and (3) on the very outside, lands for hunting and gathering of food. A study of the modern American settlement pattern in areas of grain and dairy farming showed these concentric zones: (1) a commercial area; (2) a zone of intense residential use; (3) a zone occupied

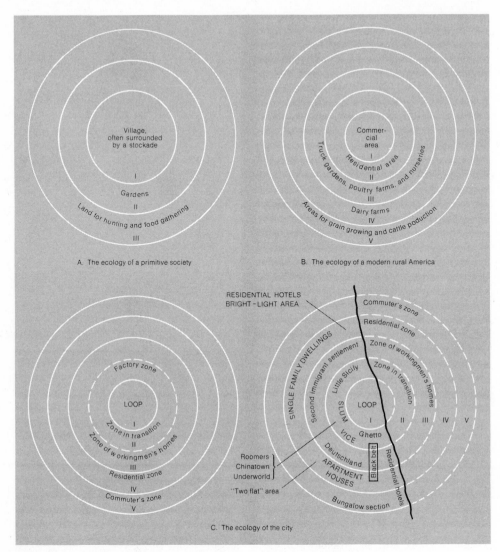

Figure 3.2. Zonal patterns of human settlement.
Source: Robert E. Park and Ernest W. Burgess, *The City,* Chicago, University of Chicago
Press, 1961, pp. 50, 55.

primarily by truck gardens, poultry farms, and nurseries; (4) a zone of dairy farms; and (5) a zone of grain crops and cattle production.

One of the most famous descriptions of spatial distribution was put forth by the sociologist Ernest W. Burgess in describing the ecology of cities.[5] Burgess saw (1) a central business district, (2) a zone in which property is

deteriorating and becoming obsolete, (3) a zone of workingmen's homes, (4) a zone of middle-class residences, and (5) a zone of commuters' homes. Studies using Burgess' scheme have appeared to show that certain social characteristics are spatially distributed. For example, each urban zone has a particular form of family life: zone 1, general absence of family dwelling; zone 2, unconventional or "bohemian" sex and family patterns; zone 3, strong father-dominated fami-

5. Robert C. Park and Ernest W. Burgess, *The City,* Chicago, University of Chicago Press, 1967.

lies typical of European immigrants; zone 4, stable "democratic" families with authority divided between husband and wife; zone 5, female-centered families with the father absent a large part of the time. Another instance was distribution of mental illness. Schizophrenia has appeared to be concentrated in the central zones of the city, with manic depression in the more outlying areas.

Why the zonal pattern of distribution? The answer lies largely in what has been called the "friction of space." The closer one gets to the center of an area of settlement, the more accessible he is to the largest number of people in the area. The total distance to all points in a circular area is smallest from the center. Once they have settled at the core, important functions draw large numbers of people and thus also draw other interests seeking customers or patrons. Lines of transportation develop as radii leading to the center of the circle. Many interests want to be located where the largest number of customers or patrons is available or the most interesting activities are going on. Land values are highest where the greatest number of people want space. Thus those functions that can afford to pay the highest price for space locate near the core. Each successive zone outside the core contains interests that are able to pay increasingly less for space.

Although social scientists disagree about particular descriptions of zonal patterns, such as that of Burgess, the basic principles underlying the relationship of human concentration to space can hardly be questioned.

We can observe some other ways in which geography and climate influence major areas of social life. Economics is one instance. An interesting case is the relationship between geographic terrain and slavery in the American colonies. Why did the slave system develop in the South but not to any extent in the North? Since New England Puritan sea captains did not hesitate to trade in slaves, it was not a matter of morals.

Rather, it had to do with the fact that the low, flat lands of the southern tidewater (coastal area) were well suited to production of cash crops, such as indigo, cane, and cotton, on large plantations with mass labor. The hilly, rocky, infertile land of New England was suited mainly to small family holdings, on which people simply grew their own livelihood. Where geographical conditions were reversed, economic and social facts also changed. Small individual farms with no slaves were the rule in the southern Piedmont, or hilly uplands, while in the rich river valley land of Rhode Island, slavery did take hold.

To take another illustration, in the modern industrial world, economic and political leadership generally goes to those nations that possess rich natural resources, especially iron for structural materials and coal, oil, or water for power. The struggle over natural resources is central to all international relations. Or we may consider how the entire social life of an area is colored by its natural resources. The tourist culture of south Florida, whose main natural resource is physical climate, is quite different from the culture of West Virginia or western Pennsylvania, which are based upon the mining of coal, or Iowa, whose main resource is deep, fertile farm land.

We can find many influences of climate and geography on government. Perhaps the most famous writer on the relationship between habitat and government was the Frenchman Baron de Montesquieu (1689–1759). In his discussion of government in the book *The Spirit of the Laws,* Montesquieu said that laws "should be in relation to the climate of each country, to the quality of its soil, to its situation and extent, to the principal occupation of the natives, whether husbandmen, herdsmen or shepherds."[6] He described some of the factors that he believed lawmakers

6. Baron de Montesquieu, *The Spirit of the Laws,* trans. Thomas Nugent, New York, Hafner, 1949, pp. 6, 222.

should take into account. One was the effect of climate on peoples of different countries. "The inhabitants of warm countries are, like old men, timorous, the people in cold countries, like young men, brave." Thus warm countries are poorly suited for freedom, and are easily conquered and ruled by more northerly peoples. It is also easier, said Montesquieu, to maintain a despotic central government in wide open spaces than in areas that are broken up by geographical barriers.

Montesquieu's conclusions have been debated. They are food for thought: What hot climate democracies do we know? What cold climate dictatorships? Of what bearing is recent experience which seems to show that it is difficult to conquer or hold by force mountainous areas like the European Balkans or jungle areas like Southeast Asia, where mass armies are of little use against guerrilla resistance?

The relationship between geography and diplomatic and military affairs is the basis for that branch of study known as geopolitics. We cannot understand the history of isolationism in the United States—the idea, going back to George Washington, that America should "avoid entangling alliances"—without taking into account the separation of the United States from other continents by two oceans. In understanding Russian foreign policy under both czars and soviets, we must reckon with the desire to have assured access to warm water ports which will not be closed by winter ice, like those on the Arctic and north Pacific. To understand the historic foreign policies of England and Japan, we must realize the position of each as a power desiring to be industrial but lacking some of the basic resources for industrialism. The lack in Britain has been food, most of which has had to be imported. Thus Britain has sought to control areas that can feed her industrial population and markets in which she can exchange manufactured goods for foodstuffs. Japan lacks fuel and structural materials, the basic

foundation of industrialism. She has sought to control areas and markets in which she can secure these.

Religion is another area in which we can see the influence of the habitat. In the Norse, Hindu, Greek, and Roman religions, as among many primitive peoples, an important part is played by gods representing climatic or geographical forces—deities of sun, wind, rain, sky, earth, and sea. The winter solstice (return of the sun) and vernal equinox (first day of spring) have been the occasions for religious celebration among both primitive and civilized peoples. In Christianity the winter solstice is celebrated at Christmas, the vernal equinox at Easter. Religious symbolism is geographically colored. Consider, for example, the prominence of the figure of shepherd and sheep in the Judaeo-Christian tradition.

An interesting example of climatic influence on religion is the conception of hell. The Judaeo-Christian tradition originated in a desert environment where the worst thing that could be imagined is unending intense heat; so the Judaeo-Christian hell is hot. But not all hells are hot. In the ancient religious traditions of Norway, hell is cold. The case of Indian and Tibetan Buddhism is very instructive here. In the area of India where Buddha lived, temperatures are well over 100° much of the time. The concept of eternal torment is that of unending heat. But in the high, wintry steppes of Tibet, Buddhism developed a conception of hell as cold.

There may be significance in the fact that all three of the great monotheistic religions in the modern world (Judaism, Christianity, and Islam) have arisen in the desert. It has been suggested that the contrast between the vast unbroken unity of the desert vista and the smallness and powerlessness of individual man might well give rise to a sense of dependence on a single, omnipotent Creator. The jungle, by contrast, might be likely to develop a religion based upon a multitude of gods representing the various aspects and threats of that many-sided environment. The unbounded sea, like the desert, also tends to give rise to overwhelming religious feelings. Sailors, although often profane, tend to have an underlying religious feeling about their life and environment. Herman Melville's *Moby Dick* communicates this sense very well.

How shall we sum up the influence of climate and geography on society? Some connections, like the optimum temperature for physical and mental functioning, are fairly objectively established. Others, such as the location of cities at breaks in transportation or the tendency of mountaineers to individualism, are based upon fairly solid common sense observations. Still others, such as the relationship of climate to democracy or of deserts to monotheism are suggestive hypotheses which need to be explored further. Views on the importance of geography and climate to society run all the way from those of geographical determinists, who would see habitat almost completely determining society, to those of critics who believe habitat to be of little significance in shaping social patterns.

Clearly, geography and climate are not sole factors absolutely determining the form of society. The nineteenth-century philosopher Hegel pointed out that in (presumably) the same geographical setting, "The Turks have come to dwell where formerly the Greeks dwelt." He was emphasizing the contrast between "the glory that was Greece" and the decadence of Turkish occupation. The Hopi and Navaho Indians, with the same habitat, have quite different social forms. One prominent French geographer, Jean Brunhes, has said that the environment is never purely physical and apart from man, but that the habitat in which man lives is itself always partly man-made. Buckle said that the influence of habitat has decreased as civilization has advanced. The "coldward course of civilization" is one example of man's ability to use technology to lessen his dependence on habitat. However, the advance of machine technology may also make man more dependent on nature's supply of raw material resources.

This discussion suggests a concluding question. In the past few centuries we have developed vast cities, an environment of steel, glass, and concrete containing few signs of organic life. Man has evolved for millions of years as a living animal in a living environment. Can he also thrive in an artificial, nonliving habitat? There is no strictly scientific answer available, but the evidence we have suggests that it is very doubtful. Many people are now moving from the center of cities to the hope of grass, trees, and flowers in the suburbs. If they can afford it, those who remain may have summer homes in the country! If they cannot, they are likely to take summer vacations, perhaps camping out in the woods. Those who cannot do either perhaps cherish "a tree grown in Brooklyn," and dream of retiring to the country when they become older. Even (or perhaps, especially) slum and delinquent children have been deeply moved or almost completely transformed by camping experiences in natural surroundings.

Before this chapter is over, we shall confront several other aspects of this same ecological question: To what degree can man declare himself independent of his natural habitat?

Food and society

A second vital ecological relationship involves the securing of food.

Food getting involves us in ecological interdependence with all four aspects of our environment. From the atmosphere we secure indirectly the carbon and the nitrogen which are essential to all living cells. The hydrosphere provides the water which forms most of the substance of all tissue and is the solvent in which solid matter becomes usable by our bodies. The geosphere furnishes mineral substances for our nourishment and is the structure in which plant food grows. The contributions of the biosphere are

hunger explains the loss of all ambition, the lack of initiative, on the part of the marginal populations of the world; in diet and not elsewhere are the origins of Chinese submissiveness, of the fatalism of the lower classes in India, of the alarming improvidence of certain populations in Latin America. . . . The sadness of the Mexican Indian, for example, is the result of his scant and deficient diet based on corn. . . . The conception of the Latin American native sitting indolently on his doorstep, contemplating with weary eye a magnificient landscape of luxurious tropical vegetation which he lacks the spirit and energy to dominate, is essentially a picture of hunger.[7]

It is a well-established fact in social science that revolutions do not occur when people are completely depressed economically and socially, but when they are on the way up. We might not go so far as Josué de Castro in suggesting that hunger is the only important factor involved, but we really need no further explanation of why very depressed peoples just accept their lot than the simple fact that they are too hungry to do anything else.

In the United States we are likely to believe that we are the best-fed people on earth and that there are no serious nutritional problems. Objective studies, however, show otherwise. A 1953 survey of 2536 teenage boys and girls showed that three-fourths were not eating enough calories to supply adequate energy; nearly half were receiving inadequate protein; none had enough calcium or phosphorous; 48 percent suffered from fidgeting, blinking, twitching, nail-biting, and other nervous disturbances attributable to nutritional deficiency; and three-fourths suffered from eye trouble traceable to poor diet. An even more extensive study in 1958, by the New Jersey Nutritional Council, covered 9000 students and found that

especially impressive and absolutely necessary. With the aid of sunlight, plants synthesize carbohydrates out of water and carbon dioxide in the air. Bacteria attached to the roots of leguminous plants fix nitrogen from the air and make it available for the formation of protein. Other soil bacteria help make soil minerals available to plant and animal life. The roots of trees draw from deep underground minerals that may not be available at the surface. Animals furnish manure and labor power for the growing of plant food, or eat the plants and are themselves eaten by man. There is no better example of the working of the ecological community.

Food is of dramatic importance in the social scheme. It is impossible to understand how the world is organized without knowing that probably most people on earth are hungry most or all of the time. The Brazilian geographer Josué de Castro, in his book *The Geography of Hunger,* says that

7. Josué de Castro, *The Geography of Hunger,* Boston, Little, Brown, 1952, pp. 68, 69, 77.

four out of five New Jersey teenagers had inadequate diets.

Exploration of the social impact of food takes us into some of the most interesting and dramatic material in the social sciences. For example, ever since the voyages of discovery revealed the South Seas to white men, the natives of Polynesia have been famous for their fine bodies and teeth. But when young Tahitian women appeared in the film *Mutiny on the Bounty,* nearly all were wearing false dentures supplied by Metro-Goldwyn-Mayer as part of their wages. Today, says an official of the World Health Organization, nearly 50 percent of Tahitian women need false teeth by the time they are in their teens. Why are these beauties becoming toothless? Because, said this official, they have changed from native diets to the foods of civilization.

This is not an isolated case. In 1964 a government health officer from the Canadian province of Alberta reported that when the Eskimos lived on their native foods, their teeth seldom decayed. But those who eat the same refined sugar and starch foods as other Canadians have the same cavities. A New Guinea health officer reported in 1963 that certain natives on the Sepik River have perfect teeth until they die. They live on snakes, crocodiles, opossums, lizards, fish, taro roots, sago, and yams. Perhaps not a very appealing diet to some of us, but it seems to do the job! In 1950 the resident physician at a Swedish Lutheran mission in southern Rhodesia said that the civilized diet brought to the natives by the British has also brought them cancer, gallstones, dental caries, and appendicitis, from all of which they had previously been free.

One of the most striking reports of the effects of nutrition is that of Dr. Robert McCarrison. In the early part of this century, McCarrison was sent as a physician for the British government to the remote people called Hunzas, in the mountains of Pakistan. After seven years with the Hunzas, McCarrison re-

ported that he had had virtually nothing to do, since the Hunzas were almost never sick, either with infectious diseases or with the diseases of age common in our society. About all the doctoring he did was to set a few broken bones, which typically healed quickly. McCarrison attributed the amazing health of the Hunzas to the rugged natural outdoor life they led, but especially to their food, which was not in itself unusual, consisting of fruits, vegetables, and some milk and meat. Apricots were a particularly important item. What seemed significant was that the Hunzas grew their own food, ate it fresh and unprocessed, and took great care with their gardens, which were carefully terraced on the mountain slopes. These they fertilized liberally with natural manures, and it appeared that the water supply from the mountains was rich with minerals.

So impressed was McCarrison with the contrast between the health of the Hunzas and that of the civilized peoples he knew, that he undertook extensive laboratory experiments. To one group of about 1000 rats he fed over a five-year period a diet very similar to that of the Hunzas. The result was that there was no case of illness, no death from natural causes, no maternal mortality, no infant mortality. To another group of rats McCarrison fed a diet similar to that typical of the British working classes—white bread, margarine, tea with a little milk, boiled cabbage, canned meat, and canned jam. The result was severe damage to the endocrine glands—adrenals, thymus, thyroid, pituitary, gonads—which either shrank or swelled, and finally ceased to function. McCarrison's studies were reported in 1921 in his book *Studies in Deficiency Disease.*

In 1939 there appeared another remarkable study of food habits and their outcome in *Nutrition and Physical Degeneration,* by Weston A. Price. A dentist, Price had observed the contrast between the usually excellent teeth of native peoples and the cavity-filled mouths of the civilized patients he treated. He believed that the difference was related to diet and personally undertook a worldwide investigation which took him to every continent except Asia. In each area he visited groups of native people who continued to eat their native diet and groups who had begun to eat civilized foods. His study included Swiss, Eskimos, Canadian Indians, Seminole Indians, Polynesians, Africans, Australian aborigines, Malay Indians, the Maori of New Zealand, and the Indians of Peru. In every case he found that tooth decay in modernized groups far exceeded that of primitives of the same racial and social heritage. He also found in the modernized groups malformations of jaw and facial structure, narrowing of the pelvis, brain defects, diminution of vision, difficulty in giving birth, and reduced capacity to reproduce.

We may understand more fully the data presented in this section so far if we will ask just how food is related to individual life and to society, and then look at some of the historic changes in human diet.

There is an old German play on words, "Man ist was er isst"—"one is what he eats." There is much more, of course, to man and society than eating, but food is one inescapable variable in the human equation. The level of energy, the vigor and skill of physical effort, and the quality of mental activity of an individual or a group can be no better than the level of nutrition. Recognition of this fact led the great medieval philosopher Thomas Aquinas to advise that, in choosing a place to settle, people should examine the animal life in the area for goodness of food.

The most obvious form of malnutrition throughout the world is simple lack of calories (energy units). These are most commonly provided by carbohydrates (sugars and starches) and fats. During World War II a number of young conscientious objectors volunteered for starvation experiments at the University of Minnesota as an alternative to military service. Dr. Ancel Keys kept 36 of them on a low calorie diet for 24 weeks. The result was "depression, narrowing of interest, social introversion [turning into self], preoccupation with thoughts of food, decrease in spontaneous activity (physical as well as mental), and marked diminution of libido [sexual drive]."[8]

One writer tells of the effect of hunger on some Russian radicals after the Revolution of 1917:

Here I saw men and women who had lived all their lives for ideas, who had renounced material advantages, liberty, happiness and family affection for the realization of their ideals —completely absorbed by the problem of hunger and cold.[9]

Experiences in prisoner-of-war and concentration camps showed similar results. Although these are only extreme cases, most of the people of the world do not eat enough calories to maintain normal animal life. Even in the 1953 study of American teenagers, 75 percent did not have enough calories.

Performance may also be impaired by lack of protein. This provides the nitrogen essential to all tissue, including the blood, and for the secretions of the internal glands which regulate metabolism. Severe protein starvation ("kwashiokor") is fairly common in the underfed areas of the world and is marked by swollen bellies, peevishness, dullness, and apathy. Some pre-Communist Chinese authorities believed that protein deficiency in China had traditionally been responsible for "lethargy, inefficiency, indecision and lack of stamina." There is no conclusive answer to the question of how much protein is best for a human being. There is such a thing as too much protein, for nitrogenous waste products may be hard on the organs of

8. Elizabeth C. Bell, "Nutritional Deficiencies and Emotional Disturbances," *Journal of Psychology*, 45 (1958), 61.
9. Angelica Balabanoff, *My Life as a Rebel*, New York, Harper & Row, 1938, p. 204.

elimination. Some students of the subject believe that the industrial nations, with their high consumption of meat and milk, may suffer from too high a protein intake.

We are constantly learning more about the results of vitamin deficiency and about how common it is in our country as well as elsewhere. The B vitamins have been the subject of much research. As early as 1938 it was found at the Mayo Clinic that people with deficiencies of vitamin B_1 (thiamine) suffered changes in attitudes and behavior and found it hard to perform tasks that had previously been easy. The subjects became irritable, depressed, uncooperative, quarrelsome, and fearful that some misfortune awaited them without knowing why. Two felt that life was no longer worth living and threatened suicide. In extreme cases B_1 deficiency may lead to the disease beriberi (which, significantly, means "I can't"). Deficiency of B_2 (riboflavin) may result in nervous depression and nerve degeneration, a general weakness and lowering of tone, diminished vitality, shortening of life expectancy, and an undue early onset of the aging process. Severe lack of vitamin B_3 (niacin, or nicotinic acid) may result in pellagra, which was for many years widespread in the American South. Pellagra begins with a loss of appetite, weakness, nervousness, failure of mental activity, fatigue, and irritability. In extreme cases it leads to psychosis. In 1943, 73 percent of the population of the South lived on a deficient diet. Undoubtedly, pellagra and other B vitamin deficiencies have been responsible for much of the lack of energy and ambition traditionally associated with poor southern whites and Negroes.

One of the most spectacular examples of the effects of vitamins has been the use of B_3 in treating schizophrenia patients. Similar results have been achieved by the use of other B vitamins with various types of mental patients. One patient who had been unable to walk more than two steps walked two miles within 24 hours of receiving a 50-milligram injection of vitamin B_6 (pyrodoxine). A patient suffering from extreme depression and mental confusion became mentally organized and oriented after injections of vitamin B_{12} (cobalamine). It is worth noting that B vitamin deficiencies do not usually occur singly, so that the most effective treatment usually uses the whole "B complex."

It will, in fact, include all other vitamins as well. Vitamin A is necessary for the thyroid gland, which is very important in emotional balance and body function. It is also important for vision; deficiency may lead to "night blindness." Vitamin C is essential to the adrenal glands, and thus to the body's whole system of defense and aggression. Deficiency is likely to result in lack of energy and emotional stability and lowered resistance to disease. Deficiency of vitamin D impairs the body's ability to use calcium (see the next paragraph) and to form teeth and bones. Because the synthesis of vitamin D in the body requires sunlight, which is in short supply in Britain, the extreme form of D deficiency known as rickets used to be referred to as the "English disease." Cattle fed a diet deficient in vitamin E appeared healthy, but suddenly dropped dead. Vitamin E deficiency causes nervousness and irritability in children.

To function adequately human beings also need a number of key minerals. Calcium is essential for the brain and nervous system. People suffering from deficiency may be irritable, nervously unstable, mentally unclear. (We will remember that in the 1953 study of American teenagers, *none* of the 2536 had enough calcium.) Potassium deficiency may be marked by dullness, apathy, or restlessness. Lack of sodium is likely to result in depression, anxiety, and loss of strength. Inadequate supply of iron may lead to anemia and lassitude, emotional instability, irritability, and fear. Iodine deficiency is likely to be marked by apathy and mental sluggishness. Lack of magnesium has changed "friendly, out-going, cooperative individuals" into "surly, belligerent, apathetic ones." On the other hand, the effect of magnesium on the nervous system is such that it has been successfully used even to treat epilepsy. Phosphorous is also essential to metabolism, but deficiencies are rare except in real starvation. Other trace minerals, such as zinc, chromium, and cobalt, also are necessary for physical and mental health.

Normal functioning is also impossible without adequate enzymes. These are biological substances which aid digestion and other metabolic processes. Most raw foods contain enzymes which help in their digestion. The phosphatase in wheat, for example, serves this purpose. Raw papaya and pineapple contain particularly effective digestive enzymes. The effect of enzymes is destroyed or lessened when foods cease to be fresh, or are cooked or otherwise processed. This is also true of some vitamins, some proteins, and other food elements.

This may explain the remarkable and significant results of an experiment by Dr. Francis X. Pottenger, in which he divided 900 cats into one group which ate all uncooked food (raw milk and raw meat), and other groups which ate partly or entirely cooked food. The "all cooked food" cats showed symptoms which remind us of McCarrison's rats fed on the British working class diet: arthritis, pyorrhea, constipation, bone degeneration, stomach and intestinal ulcers, heart enlargement, and liver congestion. In the third generation all the "cooked food" cats died before they were six months old. They became so infertile that "raw food" cats— which were free from disease—had to be brought in for breeding purposes. Apparently the absence of elements present only in raw food causes deadly deficiencies.

How well a society is nourished will depend on how well it is supplied with the food elements we have just discussed—and others. Price analyzed the content of six important food elements in the diets of the various groups he studied (see the table on p. 91). These elements were calcium, phosphorous, magnesium, iron, and vitamins A and D. In almost every case he found that the amount of these elements was very much higher in the native diets. A historical change had brought about a nutritional change which could be analyzed in the laboratory. Let us look at some of the historical events which have changed human nutrition.

Three major ones are (1) man's adoption of meat eating, (2) his move to northern climates, and (3) the evolution of his ways of securing food.

Earliest man, or his immediate forerunners, in all likelihood ate a "monkey diet" like his primate relatives—fruits, roots, leaves, nuts, honey, and perhaps insects, worms, and small animals. Somewhere, from a near or complete vegetarian, he became a meat eater. Perhaps a million-year African drought brought one of our primate ancestors down out of the trees to hunt for game which would replace the disappearing vegetation. Perhaps it was a later move into northern winters that made man a carnivore. Some students of the subject see in this a great advance; once a near-vegetarian primate became an omnivore (eater of everything), he had acquired the flexibility to adapt himself almost everywhere and had really become man. So well has man adapted to eating meat, they may say, that now he cannot really be healthy without it. Others feel that adoption of meat eating was a change for which man's primate body was never intended. Meat eaters like the cat, they contend, have large livers (to neutralize the poisons in meat) and short intestines (so as to get rid of meat before it rots in body heat). Man, like other primates, has a small liver and long colon. Thus the adoption of meat eating was a damaging mistake, and man would be much healthier if he would return to his original primate diet. Wherever the truth may lie, the change was a significant one.

**RELATIVE QUANTITIES OF FOOD ELEMENTS IN
"PRIMITIVE" DIETS COMPARED WITH "CIVILIZED" DIETS***

	CALCIUM	PHOS-PHOROUS	MAGNESIUM	IRON	VITAMINS A AND D
Eskimos	5.4	5.0	7.9	1.5	10.0
North Canadian Indians	5.8	5.8	4.3	2.7	10.0
Swiss	3.7	2.2	2.5	3.1	10.0
Gaelics	2.1	2.3	1.3	1.0	10.0
Australian aborigines	4.6	6.2	17.0	50.6	10.0
Maori	6.2	6.9	23.4	58.3	10.0
Melanesians	5.7	6.4	26.4	22.4	10.0
Polynesians	5.6	7.2	28.5	18.6	10.0
Coastal Peruvians	6.6	5.5	13.6	5.1	10.0
Andean Peruvians	5.0	5.5	13.3	29.3	10.0
African cattle people	7.5	8.2	19.1	16.6	10.0
African agriculturalists	3.5	4.1	5.4	16.6	10.0

* In all cases the "civilized" constant is 1. In other words, Eskimos eating a modernized diet consumed 1 unit of calcium as opposed to the 5.4 units of calcium in the diet of Eskimos eating their "primitive" native foods.

Source: Weston A. Price, Nutrition and Physical Degeneration, Los Angeles, American Academy of Applied Nutrition, 1948, pp. 275–276. Reprinted by permission of the Price-Pottenger Foundation.

When men moved north, winter significantly changed their food supply in more ways than meat eating. They became dependent for long periods of the year on storing food rather than eating it fresh. In all likelihood the move north increased the amount of cooking. This had the advantage of extending man's diet to include starches which are not easily eaten raw. But in the winter months the diet lost most of the factors present in fresh, raw food. People were likely to be very short of vitamin C, which is found mainly in fresh fruits and vegetables and is highest in the fruits of the tropics and subtropics. The covering of the body against cold also made vitamin D a problem, unless one could eat the livers of fish in place of exposing himself to sunlight. Only recently, after perhaps hundreds of thousands of years of habitation of the North, has modern transportation of food begun to provide an adequate winter diet (fresh orange juice and cod liver oil, for example, for English babies). This history has never been written, but through all the centuries before that, serious winter deficiencies

must have almost certainly been the rule among northern peoples. Primitive peoples like the Eskimo are an exception, because they have traditionally lived on freshly killed meat or fish. For the same reason, perhaps Neanderthal and other cave men, if they killed and ate fresh game through the winter, may have fared better than did later civilized man.

The third important factor that has affected nutrition is changes in methods of food getting. Basically, men have found three ways to get food: (1) collect it, (2) grow it, (3) buy it. Let us look at these three methods and see some of the effects of each.

For most of human life, man has been a hunter and gatherer. His method has been essentially that followed by his primate relatives, or that followed today among the Bushmen of South Africa, among whom the women spend most of their time digging for edible roots and the men spend most of theirs hunting game with simple weapons. If we think of man's whole time on earth as a 24-hour day, until about ten minutes before midnight he hunted and gathered. Only since 23:50 on the clock has he used other methods. Today some peoples are still in the hunting and gathering stage, for example, the Bushmen, the Tierra del Fuegians on the extreme tip of South America, the Sakai and Semang of Malaya, some Australian aborigines, some Eskimos. The Indians of the Great Plains lived this way into the nineteenth century.

It is easy to think of the disadvantages of this method. This was a hand-to-mouth existence, with little or no storage of food. Most of us are too accustomed to knowing where the next meal is coming from to be well suited for such a life. As long as they were hunters and gatherers, men spent just about all their time and energy staying alive. There was little time for any of the "higher" things that characterize human civilization.

On the other hand, there were certain characteristics of food in the hunting and gathering stage which we should look at carefully and compare with later stages.

Freshness. *The other side of lack of storage was that food was usually eaten immediately, before vitamins, enzymes, and other perishable food elements had been lost.*

Rawness. *Until man discovered how to use fire, presumably all food (except that accidentally roasted by forest fire, perhaps) was eaten raw. Even after that time much food, even meat, was eaten without cooking.*

Wholeness. *Hunters, for example, did not generally eat the muscle meat and throw away the skin, liver, brains, and eyeballs. As a rule they ate them all, and as a result got a more complete fare than later muscle eaters.*

Natural State. *Seeds and grass were eaten as they came from nature, not processed into refined flour. Fruits and honey were not reduced to refined white sugar. There were no preservatives, additives, or "conditioners" in food in the hunting and gathering stage, as there are today.*

There was no canning and no packaging.

Variety. *Like their primate relatives, hunters and gatherers tended to nibble as they roamed. Thus they were likely to eat a large number of different foods. A study of certain Australian aborigines, for example, showed that they had 75 different plants which they used for food. It is not easy to get a diet containing all the food elements described earlier, and other necessary ones of which we are probably not yet aware. The more different things a person eats, the greater his chance of getting everything he needs. (Also, the more he eats his food whole, the greater the likelihood.) The more his diet is restricted to a few foods, the greater his chance of deficiencies.*

About 7000 B.C. (23:50 on the human clock) there took place what may have been the most important revolution in human history. Man became an agriculturalist cultivating his own food. This revolution involved, in different places or the same place, both the cultivation of plants and trees and the domestication of animals. It used to be thought that man had evolved from hunting and gathering into the pasturing of herds, and thence to farming. We no longer believe that things always, or generally, happened in this order. The agricultural revolution developed first in the area from Egypt to India, around wheat, barley, oxen, sheep, the goat, and the pig. (It later developed independently in North America around maize and the potato.) In China agriculture arose, perhaps independently, around millet and the pig. By 5000 B.C. the agricultural revolution had reached eastern Europe, and by 3000 B.C. it had reached Britain.

The development of agriculture brought epoch-making changes. It meant that man had settled down in permanent communities, which meant the beginning of civilization. The increased productivity made possible a great increase in population; it has been estimated that hunting and gathering generally cannot support more than two or three people per square mile. Agricultural methods created for the first time an economic surplus. It became possible to support groups of people who did not have to engage in food getting—poets, dancers, sculptors, musicians, philosophers, scientists, priests. Thus the "higher" things of life, which especially distinguish man, began to flourish. Cities began to develop. They, again, require enough food so that some people can live apart from the land. Since there was now for the first time more than enough to go around, a struggle began to take place for possession of the surplus. Thus both class divisions and war arose for the first time. Historian Arnold Toynbee has said that before a surplus there was no spare time or resources for war. Certainly these changes were not all totally desirable, but they were all part of the agricultural revolution.

Of particular importance in the development of an economic surplus was the introduction of the plow, for with only hand labor production is limited. With the plow was associated the manuring of fields. The plow seems to have been in use in Egypt and Mesopotamia before 3000 B.C. The civilization of the Old World seems to have developed and spread with the plow. Even as late as A.D. 1500 the use of the plow was almost entirely confined to Europe, Asia, and north and northeast Africa, those places that constituted the "civilized" area of the globe.

Aside from providing more food, what changes did agriculture bring in the quality of nutrition? To a large extent agriculture has given grains a greater prominence in the human diet. There are those who think that this has not been a good thing. The explorer Steffanson, who spent a great deal of time experimenting with diet, concluded that man became physically adapted over many thousands of years to eating either a monkey diet like other primates or a meat diet. He felt that the human body is not really suited to starchy grains. Possibly in another couple of hundred thousand years of evolution it may be! Meanwhile, Steffanson felt that the agricultural revolution, by emphasizing grains, has led to an increase of tooth decay and other kinds of physical degeneration. Many people, of course, disagree and regard grain as the very staff of life, an excellent food. Steffanson's ideas are set forth in his book *Not by Bread Alone.*

Less controversial is the decrease in variety of food which has followed the introduction of agriculture. Where one engages in the work needed to domesticate plants and animals, he is likely to specialize and concentrate his labor on a few items. His diet may become quite narrow. Thus his chances of incurring nutritional deficiencies may be greatly increased. The same is true of the nonfarmer who may be fed by the agriculturalist.

Another very important factor has been the change in land ownership following the agricultural revolution. Typically, a few people have acquired most of the land and wealth, leaving only a relatively small portion for the vast majority of people. This is the social scheme, for example, in most of the Middle East and Latin America today. The masses of agricultural people may then be left plots of land too small to provide an adequate food supply. Although we shall shortly have some good things to say about traditional Chinese farming, this has been true in China for several centuries. It is true in India today.

Some people, completely without land, have become wage laborers on large plantations, such as the rubber plantations of Malaya, the tea plantations of Ceylon, the coffee plantations of Brazil, the sugar plantations of the Caribbean, the cotton plantations of the old American South. Here they have either bought food with wages or had it furnished by the plantation owners. In either case it has usually been the cheapest kind of food, high in starches and sugars, which produce quick energy, and low in everything else. This is the kind of diet that Mc-Carrison used to produce deficiency diseases in his rats and that Price found among the modernized natives. The traditional diet of the poor Southerner—cornbread, hominy grits, fat pork, white sugar, saved only by turnip greens—is typical.

Thus the system of landholding developed by the agricultural revolution has probably greatly worsened the nutrition of most of the human race.

Around 200 years ago (about 23:59: 30 on the human clock) there occurred another great historical change. The Industrial Revolution began to remove most people completely from the land and place them in cities where their only way of getting food was to buy it. The beginnings of this change, of course, reach back as far as the agricultural revolution, but since the late 1700s it has swept forward at a rapid rate. In the United States since the Civil War, new agricultural machinery has brought about such a vast increase in produce that already only a very small part of the population produce anything that they eat. The trend is spreading throughout the world.

It is easy to see some of the advantages which this newest revolution in food getting has brought. The quantity of food has been greatly increased. New methods of preservation have made it possible to keep food for long periods of time and transport it widely. This can widen the variety of food in all seasons for those who realize their needs and can pay the price. Another advantage is that we have given more study to the subject of food and gained scientific nutritional knowledge of the kind introduced earlier in this section. The ability of a small minority of food growers to support a large majority of industrial workers has raised the material standard of living, and given people of all social levels more money with which to buy food.

We need to look carefully, however, at the negative side of the picture.

Some of the data presented at the beginning of this section would suggest that there is one. We may be able to see this best by going back to the characteristics of food in the hunting and gathering stage, and seeing what changes have taken place between the hunt and the supermarket.

Freshness. In the industrial urban world, food is a commodity, an item produced by one person to be sold to another. This means that there is almost always a time gap between the growing and the eating, in which perishable nutritional factors are lost. Modern techniques of preservation may bring some food to the consumer nearly fresh. But it is only nearly so, by comparison with the food which has come right from the wild berry bush or fruit or nut tree, or the farmer's garden, orchard, or slaughterhouse.

Rawness. Man is the only creature who cooks his food. Cooking widens his range of nutrition, by making some poisonous foods (like manioc) edible, and some relatively indigestible foods (like raw grains) digestible. It has opened up all of the pleasures that accompany "good cooking." On the other hand, with the exceptions named, cooking usually lowers the nutritive value of food. In a society where food is a commodity, raw food is perishable and thus a handicap. Cooking is one of the most convenient ways of preserving it. Thus the world of the supermarket is one where most foods are packaged or canned. Poor or unimaginative people can easily fall into the kind of diet that destroyed the bodies of Pottenger's "cooked food" cats —hamburgers and cokes, for example.

Wholeness and natural state. As we have seen, instead of whole grains, fruit sugars and honey, and the whole bodies of animals, we are likely to eat white bread, white sugar, and the muscle meat alone. In general, food is most nutritious when it is in its whole natural state, but it will generally keep better if it is *not* in that condition, but refined down to a fraction of the whole food. Whole sugar and whole wheat spoil easily, for example, but white sugar and white flour keep very well. For the very reason that they are not so nutritious as the whole food, insects and rats will generally leave them alone. The human beings who finally eat them are likely to suffer. Refined flour and sugar lack the vitamins and minerals that are needed by the body. Instead, they draw out of the body's own supply. Thus white sugar is linked with calcium loss and tooth decay. White flour created the vitamin E deficiencies that cause cattle to drop dead. White sugar is clearly linked to diabetes, a disease of sugar metabolism, and to hypoglycemia, an ailment marked by rapid swings from high to low blood sugar. Some research also links white sugar with heart disease.

The desire to preserve food leads to the addition of various kinds of preservatives—sodium nitrite in meat, sodium propionate in bread, for example. When food is a commodity sold for profit, it may also be advantageous to add a cheaper material as filler, or other substances which may improve its appeal to most consumers. Part of the process of preserving food involves the use of poisonous insecticides, both on the farm and on the way to the consumer. A customer who reads the labels in his supermarket will know that it is almost impossible to get any food in its natural state, free from additions or subtractions. If he is aware of research data from agencies such as the Federal Food and Drug Administration, he knows that almost all commercial foods carry insecticide residues.

Variety. Even those people in the food buying society who have the money to take advantage of the many foods offered on the market generally eat a far smaller variety than the hunter and gatherer. Those without means of nutritional knowledge usually have an even smaller range.

We should be aware of one more im-

portant aspect of the transition from food growing to food buying. At the beginning of this section we saw that food getting is an excellent example of man's ecological interdependence with this habitat. Through almost all of human history and prehistory, man has followed the ecological law of return: *from* his environment he takes organic life as food, and *to* his environment he returns organic material to replace that taken away.

In the primitive forest, the material taken for food is constantly being replaced by the refuse of meals, by animal and human excrement, and eventually by the bodies which come from the earth and return to it.

When he settled down and began agriculture, man continued to return as he took, fertilizing his fields with the manure of animals, enriching them with plants and grasses turned under after letting land lie fallow. The book *Farmers of Forty Centuries* furnishes an excellent case study of the law of return as practiced by Chinese farmers for 4000 years.[10] Returning every scrap of organic material possible to the earth (including human manure, a practice with questionable sanitary aspects), they maintained its fertility undiminished despite millennia of annual crop after crop.

Within the last 200 years, this has tended to change. Stimulated by the desire for quick profit through the sale of farm products, man gave less attention to the law of return. He exploited the soil instead, "mining" virgin land without replacement and then moving on to new land when the fertility was gone. By 1937, according to the United States Department of Agriculture, 61 percent of all farmland in the United States had become infertile. The red gullied hills of the South and the dustbowl lands of the West were examples. In parts of Africa, China, and Ceylon the same thing had happened. Realizing what was happening, farmers tried

10. Franklin H. King, *Farmers of Forty Centuries,* New York, Harcourt Brace Jovanovich, 1927.

to replace the annual loss with inorganic plant food synthesized in factories. But this could not take the place of the deep-rooted trees bringing minerals from underground and depositing them as rotting leaves, or of the manure of animals, or of the residue of fallow crops.

Although the quantity of farm production increased immensely, evidence indicated that quality decreased. Experiment station figures in the 1940s and 1950s, for example, showed a decline in the protein content of Missouri corn and Kansas wheat, and in the food value of California pears.

Today soil bank programs pay farmers to grow cover crops to enrich soil. Commercial fertilizers often contain substantial amounts of organic matter. Some cities are helping "return" by processing their sewage into organic fertilizers. There is a lively movement of people interested in using only natural fertilizers on their gardens and fields. Perhaps man has begun to ask whether it is really possible to repeal the ecological law of return which governed food getting until 23:59:30 on the human clock.

People and resources

The problem of food leads us logically back to a third important ecological relationship which we have already introduced in Chapter one, the balance of population with resources.

It is rather generally recognized that organisms tend to multiply to the number which the food supply of their habitat can support, but not beyond. Careful studies of certain birds in the North Atlantic, which live on the one-celled plankton, have shown that the bird population in any area varies with the density of the plankton population in the water. Laboratory studies of guppies, fruit flies, flour beetles, and mice reveal that they also will reproduce up to the point where population is just enough for the food supply, and then the increase will stop.

The same appears orginally to have been true of human beings. In his book of 1922, *The Population Problem,* the famous student of population trends, Alexander Carr-Saunders, did a careful study of available anthropological data on primitive people. He was impressed by the fact that they usually seemed to be well nourished and not on the brink of starvation. He came to the conclusion that primitive men, like other animals, automatically tended to balance their population at the "optimum number" which their habitat will support.

There is, that is to say taking into account the abundance of game, the fertility of the land, the skilled methods in use, and all other factors, a density of population which, if attained, will enable the greatest possible income per head to be earned; if the density is greater or less than this desirable density, the average income will be less than it might have been. Obviously it must be a very great advantage for any group to approximate to this desirable density.[11]

If there were fewer than the optimum number, there would not be enough people to use the resources to best advantage. If there were more, there would not be enough food to go around. Like other animals, primitive men did not wait for overpopulation to reduce their number through starvation, for this would have been disastrous. They anticipated the problem and stabilized their numbers before there were too many for the food supply. In the long course of evolution, presumably, those groups that had developed effective population control mechanisms survived, while those that had not done so were gradually eliminated. When we say "developed," we do not mean that men in large part were conscious of what they were doing, but simply that a pattern of group adjustment did arise.

11. Alexander Carr-Saunders, *The Population Problem,* Oxford, Clarendon Press, 1922, p. 213.

How does limitation of population to the optimum number take place? We can distinguish checks that come from outside a group and those that come from inside. Death from predators of one kind or another—whether they be lions or bacteria—is one kind of limitation. Death through accident or natural disaster is another. There is little reason, however, to suppose that accidents, earthquakes, or death by lions will decrease when food is plentiful and increase when it is necessary for population to slow down. The important checks are therefore internal.

Carr-Saunders named three checks that he felt to be especially important among primitive peoples: abstention from intercourse, abortion, and infanticide (killing of babies). In animals which have been studied, and perhaps in man, other mechanisms have been found: reduction in the number of female eggs produced, resorption of embryos by the mother, eating of the eggs or of the young, desertion of the young, exclusion of the mature young from opportunity to breed. Modern man, of course, uses artificial techniques of contraception. Emigration of members of the group in the face of the threat of hunger is frequent. Some students of the subject believe that good nutrition tends to reduce fertility and poor nutrition to increase it. There are studies in rats which seem to confirm this theory. This idea is, however, far from generally accepted.

A contemporary ecologist, V. C. Wynne-Edwards, has written a book entitled *Animal Dispersion in Relation to Social Behavior,* in which he emphasized the roles of territoriality and group status in controlling population in a wide variety of animal species. Division of the habitat into a limited number of territories each held by an individual (or family) or a tribal group, he believes, ensures that population will not exceed resources. Wynne-Edwards says that territorial organization is typical not only of man at all periods of history, but of a wide variety of forms of animal life. The naturalist Konrad Lorenz, in his well-known book *On Aggression,* has emphasized this same territoriality, as has Robert Ardrey. Ranking members of the group in terms of status is a way of designating those "low on the totem pole" who will not be allowed to breed or to eat if resources become too scarce. "Lek" behavior in many birds, in which territories are staked out with extravagant competitive displays of plumage and acrobatic agility may serve this purpose. Wynne-Edwards believes that the main reason why status ranking arose in the first place was that it provided an organized system of population balance. We shall discuss territoriality and status more in the next chapter.

So far we have dealt with the problem of population balance as though there were only one species (plus its food supply) in a habitat. This is, of course, never the case. Any balance is thus a joint balance worked out by many species. Modern Western man must still compete for food and space with domestic and sometimes wild animals, cockroaches, weeds which threaten his gardens, boll weevils, Japanese beetles, and other insects that would like to eat his crops. His cities compete with trees and grass. In India man coexists with vast numbers of cows who, because of religious taboos, sometimes eat while men die of starvation.

There is not only the relationship of competition for food, but also that of predators and prey. In the modern world, man is one of the chief predators. The relationship between predators and their victims is very informative, for it illustrates the whole principle of ecological balance. We might suppose that predators, having greater strength or skill, would eat their prey at will. But if they did so, they would "kill the goose that lays the golden egg." Therefore there always tends to be, between predator and prey, a balance which always keeps enough prey alive to continue producing future victims. Man, for example, acting as a predator

Man has changed from a cooperator in nature to an exploiter.

of animals and of primitive peoples than of modern man. Primitive men follow group ways almost without thinking. Modern man is a more choosing individual. Thus he seems to have weakened or lost the automatic balancing mechanisms of primitive group life. Especially in the last few centuries, man has developed such an extensive technology that he has constantly expanded his supply of food and resources rather than curbed population. Sometimes he has believed that the population problem no longer exists, because his power to produce food is unlimited. This belief is, however, false. Already, for lack of ecological checks, population has gone beyond the food supply to the point where hunger is typical of most human beings, and large numbers are actually starving. Moreover, it takes only a little simple arithmetic to show that at man's potential capacity to reproduce (about a doubling each generation) no technology could provide food enough very long. The problem of ecological balance of population and food has not been eliminated; it has only been postponed or evaded.

Even if food production could be unlimited, the need for an ecological balance would remain, for food is not the only factor involved in an optimum population. Studies have shown that rats become less fertile, tend to avoid sex, and show many of the population-limiting mechanisms we have discussed, when they are overcrowded in terms of sheer space, even though food is plentiful. Overcrowding appears to set in motion physiological stress mechanisms which in the long run increase the death rate. (Stress is discussed in Chapter five.) City populations generally have higher death rates and lower fertility rates than town and country populations. While there are no doubt a number of reasons, the same biological mechanisms operating in rats may be operating in humans. Some of the disorganized behavior found in cities, which resembles that in overcrowded rat cages, may also be a

in killing whales throughout the oceans of the world, has been forced to enter into international agreements on limitation of whale fishing in order to keep his prey from being exterminated. He has not always been so wise in his self-limitation on use of land, forests, or animal resources.

On the surface the automatic ecological balancing of numbers and resources would seem to be much truer direct response to lack of physical space. The whole problem of ecological population balance is thus one that is still very much with us.

We are led, finally, to an ecological problem that is largely that of modern man: his relationship to his environment as a consumer of raw materials. Other species, primitive man, and even civilized man up to recent centuries have been very limited in their demands upon their environment. As we have seen, food production naturally tends to take place in such a way that the materials used are eventually returned to the earth. The raw materials needed for the simple tools and machines used until the Industrial Revolution scarcely touched the surface of the vast resources of the geosphere.

In the past four or five centuries, however, man has changed from a co-operator in nature, who largely returned what he took, to an exploiter of nature, who takes on a vast scale without replacing. As our section on food suggested, this has been true of his attitude toward forests and plant and animal life in general. Planned conservation of these resources has only re-

cently endeavored to restore an ecological balance. But in particular, the progress of industrialism has meant a constant drain upon the earth's fuel resources, especially coal and oil. It has meant the extension of mining for structural metals into veins constantly harder and more expensive to reach. The problem is not changed by the advent of atomic power as long as it is dependent upon limited mineral resources, whether uranium or something else. Man's technology exists largely by exploiting and destroying resources in the geosphere which, in terms of world history, must be exhausted in a very short time. His long-run future is thus very precarious unless he can find—perhaps in the atmosphere and hydrosphere, and to some extent in the manufacture of plastics—sources of power and structural materials that are not exhaustible.

We thus close this chapter with another reminder of the fact that since 23:59:30 on the human clock man has to a large extent tried to deny his ecological interdependence with his habitat, and that where this course is leading him is very uncertain.

Suggestions for further reading

A good, readable source on prehistoric man is E. A. HOEBEL's book now entitled Anthropology, The Study of Man *(3rd ed., McGraw-Hill, 1966). A solid study of the physical basis of racial differences is BOYD's* Genetics and the Races of Man *(p. 244A). Another authoritative book on physical stock is* Man's Most Dangerous Myth: The Fallacy of Race, *by ASHLEY MONTAGU (World, paper, 1965). The most famous scientific statement of the idea that racial superiority and inferiority are rooted in a separate (polygenetic) origin of races is found in CARLETON S. COON and W. E. HUNT, JR.,* Living Races of Man *(Knopf, 1965). For another scientific work which defends the idea of race inequality, see the report of biologist WESLEY CRITZ GEORGE to the governor of Alabama, entitled* The Biology of the Negro *(National Putnam Letters Committee, 1962).*

The basic works on the relationship of body type to personality are Physique and Character *by ERNST KRETSCHMER (Harcourt Brace Jovanovich, 1925) and WILLIAM H. SHELDON's* Varieties of Temperament *(Harper & Row,*

1942). One of the most thoroughgoing (and controversial) students of the influence of geography was ELLSWORTH HUNTINGTON. His findings are presented in Mainsprings of Civilization *(Wiley, 1954).*

An excellent study of the history of food getting is Plough and Pasture, *by E. C. CURWEN and GUDMUND HATT (Macmillan, 1961, paper). JOSUÉ DE CASTRO's* The Geography of Hunger *(Little, Brown, 1952) is a thorough and dynamically written account of malnutrition in the modern world. SIR ROBERT McCARRISON's experimental work on the diets of British and Indian social groups will be found in* Studies in Deficiency Disease *(p. 244A, 1921). WESTON A. PRICE's worldwide studies on the relationship of dental structure to nutrition are reported (with dramatic photographs) in* Nutrition and Physical Degeneration *(Hieber, 1939).*

An analysis of the psychological effects of nutritional deficiency by an American scientist is "Nutritional Deficiency and Emotional Disturbances," by ELIZABETH C. BELL (Journal of Psychology, 1958). A very interesting and practical account of the relationship of nutrition to physical and psychological health is Let's Get Well, by nutritionist and biochemist ADELLE DAVIS (Harcourt Brace Jovanovich, 1965).

No treatment of the ecology of food getting can be complete without the book which opened the whole public controversy over the effect of insecticides, RACHEL CARSON's Silent Spring (Crest Fawcett-World, 1964, paper). Also interesting is FRANKLIN H. KING's Farmers of Forty Centuries (Harcourt Brace Jovanovich, 1927), an account of how Chinese farmers returned nutrients to the soil in such ways as to maintain its fertility for over 4000 years. V. C. WYNNE-EDWARDS's Animal Dispersion in Relation to Social Behaviour (Hafner, 1962) is a basic and exhaustive study of the controls which establish the balance of human and other populations with their food supply and other resources. It is fundamental for anyone interested in nutrition, population, or ecology.

Chapter four
The social basis

Every one of us, in addition to living in a physical and biological environment, is born into a system of social relationships that existed before we were born and will probably continue to exist long after we are gone. We live in society.

THE WEB OF SOCIETY

Society is not a special social science term. We use it in our ordinary conversation. "The criminal paid his debt to society." "He is a useful member of society." "The child must learn to adjust to society." "Under a dictatorship the individual is swallowed up by society." President Lyndon Johnson introduced the term "the great society." We know what is meant by the hope that some day we will realize a "world society."

We can distinguish these uses of the term from another meaning of the word, which refers to "high society." Only a few people belong to the Four Hundred, or the Social Register, or appear on the "society" pages, but everybody is a member of society in the wider, social science sense of the word.

What do we mean when we say that each of us is a member of society? We mean that none of us acts simply as he pleases, as though he were the only person in the world, but each fits his action into an organized and ongoing system of activity which involves other people. Nor do we invent our own ideas and actions in a vacuum, but rather derive them to a large extent from this organized system, or rather, from organized systems, for each of us fits into many different overlapping societies of which "society" in the broad sense is the most general.

To a considerable extent we may look at these societies as concentric circles. Suppose that you live in Concord, New Hampshire. What are the circles that constitute your social environment, as contrasted with your biological and physical environment? The smallest society to which you belong, the smallest and most immediate system of social activity, is your family. A larger circle may be your neighborhood, or possibly your clique, "gang," crowd. Social scientists refer to this group of people your own age as your "peer group." A still larger circle may be the community of Concord. Wider still is the society of New Hampshire (you may have a certain common feeling of interest and loyalty with all other citizens of the state). Wider still is New England society (as distinguished from the society of the South, or the Middle West). Beyond this, you are an American, with a membership in American society. Then you are a member of the society of the Western world as distinguished from the Orient. Finally, you are a member of human society, the network of relationships that embraces the whole human race. You may perhaps, with Albert Schweitzer, even feel yourself a part of a still wider society that includes all living things.

Let us now look at some of the

things involved in your relationship to your society, or your societies.

The first thing we observe is *interdependence.* Probably the first society in which you were involved was that of yourself and your mother. At birth as, of course, before birth you were utterly dependent. Without this society you would have died in a short time. What you needed most of all was food. But you also needed the warmth, the closeness, the loving embrace of your mother (or mother substitute). Studies show that without these, a person's whole physical and psychological development is likely to be stunted. Your mother also needed you. A woman who nurses her child is less likely to hemorrhage in the days immediately after birth, and her uterus returns to normal size more rapidly. She also derives a deep emotional satisfaction which is vitally important to her.

The "symbiosis" (living together) of child and mother is the model for all later social relationships. If you will look at yourself today, you should see that you are no less dependent on a web of social ties than you were in the womb or at birth. If you had to start from scratch today and provide all your own food supply, you would probably have a very hard task keeping alive. Certainly your whole standard of living would be sharply reduced if you had to provide everything for yourself. Without society where would be the orange juice you drink for breakfast, your wheat cereal, the clothes you wear, the motorcycle you ride or the car you drive? If you will stop just to think of everything you use in one day that was made by someone else and think of where it came from, you will begin to become conscious of the worldwide social network of which you are a part.

In the atomic age, we are particularly aware of how much our physical survival depends on world society, or what we sometimes call the "world community." As was said of the American colonists at the time of the Declaration of Independence, on a world scale today we must "hang together or hang separately." If the world society fails to keep the peace, there will in all likelihood be no hiding place from atomic war, no place to escape from the web of common fate. International agreements like the nuclear test ban and international agencies like the United Nations are part of the machinery by which we strive to create a society as wide as our mutual interdependence and need for common survival.

A second characteristic of societies is a set of *common values.* Members of a society tend to think and feel the same way. Sometimes these common values are referred to by the Greek term *ethos* (the common feelings of a people). Among the simple, "primitive" Hopi Indians, for example, the ethos is so noncompetitive that it is difficult to organize a contest because no one wants to win. Sharply different are the Kwakiutl Indians of British Columbia, who engage in an intense striving for prestige by competitively throwing away or destroying their possessions in contests called *potlatches.* The passive attitude toward life characteristic of the Arapesh of New Guinea is strikingly different from the warlike ethos of the American Plains Indians.

The traditional society of New England has emphasized those values that we call Puritanism. The society of the Old South had a set of values that included belief in Negro inferiority, a strong respect for tradition, a deep feeling for propriety and formal courtesy, and a strong feeling for the land and distrust of city ways. The ethos of the American West has stressed a rough-and-tumble individualism. The Communist society of modern Russia is marked by the subordination of the individual to state goals, an emphasis upon technology, and a distrust of any activity that does not seem to advance the Communist revolution—all this grafted to a much older, Russian, nationalistic pride. The ethos of modern society in the United States has often been described in such terms as belief in bigness, in progress, in formal education, in competition, in individual initiative, in material values, in success. One of the problems in forming an effective world society lies in the seeming lack of strong common values held by all human beings.

The sharing of common values is likely to be associated with what one social scientist called a "consciousness of kind." One feels that he "belongs" with other members of his society, that he and they are in a sense set apart with respect to all other people. He has a sense of loyalty and obligation to them which he does not feel toward those not of his social group. This kind of feeling is particularly strong in families, although in our present world it is generally weaker than it used to be. New Englanders and Southerners have traditionally had a strong sense of common belongingness. When this consciousness of kind is felt toward members of a common national group, we call it patriotism. Again, one of the difficulties in forming a world society lies in the fact that most people's sense of common humanhood is less strong than their sense of national, sectional, or local loyalty.

Behavior in society is marked by *roles.* In a large sense, Shakespeare was right when he asserted that "all the world's a stage." In the family role is distinguished by age and sex. The role of the father is obviously not that of the mother, nor is the role of any of the children. The father cannot have babies, and neither the pregnant mother nor the children are very well equipped to earn the family living. Sons and daughters generally follow sex roles. In Western society these have traditionally called for the male child to be more aggressive and the girl more passive and "ladylike." Among the Tchambuli tribe of New Guinea, however, according to anthropologist Margaret Mead, these roles seem to be reversed. We know, too, that the first-born child's role is different from that of the "baby" of the family. If there are middle children,

their roles are different from those of either the first or last. The role of the only child is different from that of any child who has siblings (brothers and/or sisters).

In the traditional South, the sex roles were sharply stressed. The role of the gallant, protective gentleman contrasted strongly with that of the fragile lady. The role of the master was entirely different from that of the Negro slave or, later, hired hand. Even slaves had different roles according to whether they worked in the fields or were attached as domestics to the master's house. Both the master and slave had different roles from those of the tobacco- and cotton-farming poor whites. In an industrial society, the specialization or division of labor which we already find in the family or in the largely rural society of the Old South is increased to a marked degree. A large part of formal education is geared toward fitting one for a specialized role in society—doctor, farmer, merchant, lawyer, politician, or one of thousands of other specialties. These roles are geared together in a very complex way, so that every one of us becomes capable of doing fewer and fewer of the things necessary for his life, and more and more dependent on others to do them for him. In all the cases we have cited, becoming a functioning member of society is to a large extent a matter of finding a satisfactory role in the total network.

Division into roles is closely related to common *expectations.* However cynical we may be about our fellow men, to live in society at all we must trust them in all kinds of ways. Without essential faith in other drivers, for example, we could never venture onto the highway. Nor could we carry on most of our activities—going to class, theater, or beauty parlor—did we not trust the promises that people have made to be at certain places at certain times doing certain things. To belong to a society is to know, to a large extent, what to expect of other people, and to conform to what they expect of us.

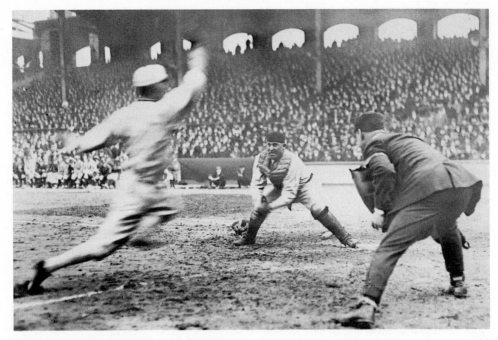

Out at home: disappointment of a team's common expectations.

A noted social scientist, George Herbert Mead, took a baseball game as an illustration of common expectations. In a ball game, you must know what to expect of every other player on your team in every ordinary (and, hopefully, extraordinary) situation. If you are a second baseman, it is particularly imperative that you and the shortstop share common expectations, but it is also necessary that you and the right fielder and the catcher do so. In football success to a large extent depends on the degree to which practice has welded an effective society where each person's assignment on every play is known to every other. Mead suggested that the game of life in the larger society is only an extension of the ball game.

We sometimes become aware of this matter of expectations very dramatically, when we move into a new social situation. Going to college may be an example. We become involved in a whole new set of expectations that must be learned: with roommates and dormitory mates, with faculty members, with the administration, with the opposite sex. It takes a passage of time and often considerable psychological pain before we learn to gear our expectations with those of all these different people so that we can function without undue strain as members of the college society. It requires perhaps as much practice as becoming a member of the football team.

We may have much the same problem in moving into a new country. A visitor to the German settlers of Southwest Africa relates, for example, that he was almost assaulted physically by his host because he had lifted a glass to this man's wife in a dinner table toast. The host considered this to be virtually an improper advance. Clearly the two men had different systems of expectations. The formation of a marriage is a particularly good example of the problem of developing common expectations. Most people who marry are relative strangers. Only after long experience together—and often never at all—do a man and a woman reach the point where they have learned to know what to expect of each other in all the complex relationships that constitute the society we call marriage.

It should be clear by now that behavior in society is organized and patterned. Social scientists have distinguished several kinds of patterns.

The most general is that of the *folkways,* designated by the great early social scientist, William Graham Sumner. The word is closely related to the general term "custom." The folkways are habitual ways of behaving typical of a group of people. There are folkways for every aspect of life. In the United States today, our folkways of dress prescribe suits for men, skirts for women. Our folkways of eating call for three meals a day of typically "American" foods—orange juice, packaged cereal, baked potatoes, fried chicken or country ham, apple pie or ice cream, and so on. Our economic folkways stress the value of hard work. Our political folkways include ritual handshaking and babykissing. Our folkways of recreation give a large role to competitive spectator sports. Our folkways of courtship feature a pattern of dating unknown to many peoples. Our folkways of birth include the distribution of cigars by the father; our folkways of death, the use of black to symbolize mourning.

Folkways arise spontaneously; no one invents a folkway deliberately. Why do most Americans eat the evening meal between 6 and 8, while the Spanish are more likely to eat it between 9 and 11? The reasons are lost in history; certainly no one at any time sat down and invented either pattern. The folkways are not written down or codified. They are so taken for granted that we are not usually even conscious of following them. They are passed from generation to generation by word of mouth and by example. In this respect they are "folk" in the same sense as are "folk music" and "folk art" (as contrasted with recorded and more formalized music and art). Another characteristic of folkways is that, as such, they are considered as the right

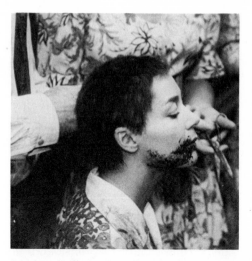

A scene from the film Hiroshima Mon Amour *in which a girl in Nazi-occupied France has her head shaved by neighbors as censure for her love affair with a German soldier.*

or customary way to do things, but violation is not considered immoral. The violator may be regarded as queer, but hardly as wicked.

Some social scientists have felt that the concept of folkways applies rather well to a primitive or nonindustrial society, but that the idea has to be amended if it is to fit our industrial world. A large number of our patterns, they suggest, have not arisen slowly out of a long period of growth, but have come into being more quickly, as adaptations to technical inventions and change. These patterns have sometimes been called *technicways.* Thus we have technicways of dress, such as the use of wash-and-wear fabrics; technicways of eating, such as the frozen, precooked dinner; technicways of work, such as the forty-hour week; political technicways, such as the spot TV ad paid for by one's supporters; technicways of birth, such as the hospitalization of the mother, and of death, such as the embalming of the body for presumed public-health reasons. Probably it is best to think of the technicway as a special kind of folkway.

When folkways are felt by a society to be vitally important to its welfare, we call them "mores" (pronounced "more-rays." This is a Latin term, and the singular is *mos,* not *more*). Violation of the mores is considered immoral. It is punished by informal action of the group: by shunning of the offender, by public censure, by banishment, sometimes by death. When occupied France was freed from the Nazis, women who had consorted with the enemy were sometimes forced to parade with their heads shaved to the taunts and jeers of their fellow townsmen. Usually a member of a society learns also to punish himself for violation of the mores; he feels shame or guilt. Generally the mores are connected with religion, so that violation is considered an offense to God or the gods, and the violator often fears divine punishment.

Eating at a customary hour is a matter, of the folkways, but for a Jew or Moslem to eat pork is a violation of the mores. To wear a foreign garment may be contrary to the folkways, but to wear a dress much more revealing than the present fashion will probably violate the mores. One tends to dance the dances prescribed by the folkways of his society. On the other hand, for some groups all dancing is contrary to the mores, and for most Americans dancing with a member of another race has traditionally been a violation. Drinking is in many circles a social folkway, but public drunkenness generally violates the mores. Remaining seated while the national anthem is played or refusing military service is usually a breach of the mores. For a professional man to give an outsider an objective appraisal of a competitor may contradict those mores that we call "professional ethics." When it says that a book may be held obscene if it violates "contemporary community standards," the Supreme Court is referring to an infringement of the mores of the majority.

In most primitive societies, social control is imposed almost entirely through folkways and mores. There is little formal government and no enacted legislation. In technically advanced and literate societies, however, we find that a considerable part of the pattern of social organization consists of formal and written *law.* This is the part of the pattern of which we are perhaps most aware.

We still do not have any final answer to the question of the whole relationship between law and the folkways and mores. Sometimes we are inclined to overemphasize the importance of law and to think that if we want to change things, all we need to do is pass a law. We forget that laws that go counter to the mores are very hard to enforce. Whatever the written law may say, for example, it is often very hard to convict a man who has caught a rival in a sexual situation with his wife and has killed him on the scene. The jury is likely to follow the "unwritten law," which says that his action is a justified defense of his rights. On the other hand, many people (including some social scientists) have been inclined to say that no law that is in conflict with the mores can ever be effective. "You can't legislate morals." This, too, is a doubtful generalization. Recent history seems to show that civil rights legislation, by making long-standing patterns of segregation illegal, has changed some of the mores of race relations in a relatively short time. An example is travel in public buses. It is equally true, of course, that what civil rights legislation has been able to do in the face of widespread "public opinion" is sharply limited. This fact is illustrated by the slowness of school integration.

In any case, folkways, mores, and law shade into one another. Perhaps most of the time law puts into writing existing customs and morals. Audiences which were shocked by Clark Gable's famous "I don't give a damn" in *Gone With the Wind* in 1939 now take in stride movies like *Midnight Cowboy* or *The Boys in the Band.* The rulings of the courts and of extralegal censors have changed to keep pace. Changing attitudes toward contraception have resulted in elimination of most laws against birth control information and devices. But, at least some of the time, law leads the way in changing mores. It is worth noting, too, that sometimes the folkways and mores, even when unwritten, have all the force of law. When courts can find no precedents in written law for their decision, they may reach one based upon the unwritten common law. The author, once seeking to eat in a Southern restaurant with Negro friends, was told by the proprietor that if they insisted he could not refuse to serve them, since under the English common law the proprietor of an eating place was required to serve anyone.

Folkways, technicways, mores, and laws tend to group themselves into clusters around certain social interests and to form what we call *institutions.* Marriage is an example of such a cluster. In every society the social pattern determines how many men shall be married to how many women—one man to one woman, one man to several women, one woman to several men. It determines how courtship shall take place. It determines the form of the marriage ceremony itself. It shapes the family roles, determining what are the rights and obligations of the husband toward the wife, and of the wife toward the husband; of parents toward children and children toward parents; of children toward one another. It determines to a large extent who shall wield what authority in the home. It is likely to prescribe whether the wife shall go to live with her husband's family, the husband with the wife's family, or whether they shall set up a separate household. It determines how property shall be inherited. It sets up rules to deal with extramarital sex relations, yet in some societies it may obligate the husband to lend his wife or daughter to his overnight guest. The whole cluster of folkways, technicways, mores, and laws that governs these human relationships we refer to as the institution of marriage.

Social scientists have distinguished two kinds of institutions. Those that we call "crescive" are like Topsy; they just grow without deliberate plan or intent.

To a large extent our pattern of marriage is this kind of institution. There are a small number of areas, common to all societies, where institutions seem spontaneously to grow.

Economic institutions develop around the interest in making a living. From the need for formal social control there originate government or political institutions. Around sex and reproduction there emerge marriage and family institutions. Around man's relationship to his widest values arise religious institutions. Around the training of the young there emerge educational institutions. Around the systematic pursuit of knowledge emerge scientific institutions. Around the prevention and cure of disease develop therapeutic institutions. From interests in play and sport develop recreational institutions. Around aesthetic interests develop artistic institutions.

Eventually, as a society becomes more complex and more technically advanced, people begin deliberately to create institutions. These we refer to as "enacted" institutions. Examples are banks, national governments, colleges, museums, baseball leagues, scientific foundations, medical and chiropractic associations, birth control foundations, churches, synagogues, and mosques. Through these enacted institutions, the interests of the original crescive institutions are served in a more conscious and purposeful way. In a later chapter, we shall deal more at length with social institutions and their interrelationships.

We may well ask at this point just how the vast pattern of society is related to individuals. Clearly, all societies we know existed before the people who now participate in them. In all likelihood they will survive long after they are dead. Especially in the United States, with our strong tradition of rugged individualism, it often seems hard for us to realize that this is the case. We tend to think of society as simply a collection of isolated, self-made individuals. But in reality, there are no such isolated persons.

There is, in the history of social sci-

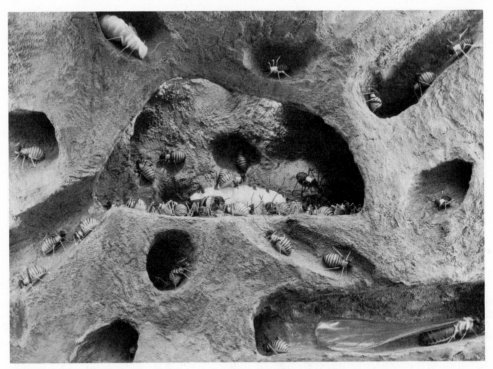

Termites, often called "white ants," live in a highly developed society. (*Courtesy of the Buffalo Museum of Science.*)

ence, a "once upon a time" story. According to this account, man once lived without a society, in a "state of nature." Eventually he found this so unworkable that he agreed to form a "social contract," and thus society came into being. This story is, however, just a fairy tale. Human individuals could never survive without social relationships. Social scientists today agree that just as long as there have been people, there must have been societies. We shall see shortly that there were, in fact, animal societies before there were people.

It is equally true that as long as there have been human societies, there have been people. Society could not exist apart from the activities of individuals. For this reason we might seem to be justified in concluding that a society is just the sum of individuals in it at any one time. But this is not true. Each generation of us inherits at birth a whole pattern of folkways, technicways,

mores, laws, and institutions that are not of our making. In a sense this pattern is apart from us all and shapes our acts and feelings just as does our physical environment. It leads or forces us as individuals to do things we would rather not do. Indeed, even as groups, society can lead us to do things that no member of the group alone would do.

In the novel and movie *The Ox-Bow Incident,* by Walter Van Tilburg Clark, there is a scene at the end in which the participants in a lynching, the deed done, sit at a bar with the realization growing over them that what they have done no one wanted to do, but each felt compelled to do because he felt carried along by all the others. There are, no doubt, many communities in both North and South where almost everyone has resisted a change in racial customs, not necessarily because of strong conviction, but because each felt that his neighbors would otherwise condemn him. Many industrialists pollute our air and water, not in most cases because they are unusually wicked men, but because each feels that the pressure of a competitive system makes it impossible for him to do otherwise. It is conceivable that the Cold War and the atomic arms race may force us into a nuclear war which, literally, nobody wants. Men on all sides, who individually would make peace, may be so caught in a deteriorating situation that they will feel forced in spite of themselves to push the button. If this happens, their position may not be very much different from that in which many Germans claimed, at Nuremberg, to have found themselves under Hitler. The whole pressure of society, they asserted, was so great that they had no real choice, for example, other than to help send Jews to the gas chambers.

The fact that most people in such circumstances find themselves unable to resist does not mean that no one can. We are not just social robots. In each such case some people do refuse to conform. But most of us, when the whole pressure of society seems to be against us, are not heroes.

A society is a vast system of both liberation and compulsion. Some social rebels, viewing oppressive social pressures like those we have just examined, feel that society is nothing but a burden. But without it, none of us could enjoy the richness of life we do enjoy. In fact, we would not even be alive at all. Society does, however, restrict us. In every society we know, there are restrictions of two kinds. There are those limitations upon our freedom that are rationally necessary for the survival of all members of the group. To take the most widespread of these restrictions, all societies forbid incest, because in a group that permitted unlimited incest, family life would be hopelessly disrupted and the society would be too chaotic and strife-torn to survive. Some conservatives feel that almost all traditional social restrictions are of this kind, so that it is our duty to conform almost completely to existing society. But there are always limitations upon individual freedom which are not rationally necessary. Today, for example, more and more people are coming to feel that discriminations based on race, sex, or religion are this kind of restriction. There are also those who—whether rightly or wrongly—view the draft, our sex mores, compulsory social security, the fluoridation of water, or our marriage and divorce laws as unjustified compulsion. One of our most important tasks as students of society and as human beings is to distinguish between rational and irrational social restrictions.

HUMAN AND PREHUMAN SOCIETIES

At first thought we might believe that society is peculiar to human beings. This is not, however, at all the case. We have many well-studied examples of societies among the lower animals. Human society is only one part of a vast scheme of social life which is much broader in scope.

One of the most carefully studied forms of animal social organization is the pecking order of chickens. Every chicken roost is organized into a system of rank ("hierarchy") in which each chicken has a status. This is determined by a series of encounters of pairs of chickens, in which one emerges the victor and thereafter has the right to "peck" the other, while the other submits. Each chicken pecks all below it and submits to all above. Generally males peck females, older chickens peck younger, the stronger or more intelligent peck the less strong or intelligent. Chickens high on the pecking order are more likely to obtain food and generally have greater freedom. At the same time, the organization of the roost around the pecking order is a form of peace which prevents constant struggles for dominance. The pecking order of chickens is a very stable and "authoritarian" form of organization in which "top" chickens almost always dominate lower chickens. In pigeons, on the other hand, the organization of pecking seems to be looser, more flexible and "democratic."

Many insects are noted for their social life. The anthill is a complex social system with a high degree of specialized interdependence. The queens are limited to the function of reproduction, as are the males. The other females are specialized into workers and soldiers. The workers may be subdivided into as many as a dozen different types, including one so tiny that it can ride on the queen's antennae. The hills of some ants may cover as much ground as a small cottage. Inside are nests, roads, and vaulted galleries for storage of food. Ants may keep slaves or "cows" (aphids) whom they "milk" for food. They fight wars. A similarly complex social organization is found in bee and termite societies.

In the ocean we may find floating an even more tightly organized social system—the *Halistemma,* related to the Portuguese man-of-war. This is a group consisting of different specialized members attached to a long string, which culminates at the top in a float. Below the float are swimmers, who have no mouths and can only propel the colony. Farther down are the hunters, who secure and digest food, and distribute it to the rest of the colony through connecting stems. There are also members who serve as soldiers, stinging, paralyzing, or capturing victims. Finally there are forms without mouths or tentacles, whose sole function is to reproduce, and thus create new colonies. Whether or not we call this colony a society, in the strict sense, it is an intricate interdependent grouping of members who can live only as part of a group.

It would seem that social relationships are found, indeed, where any kind of animal life is found. No known form of animal lives its entire life span alone. Biologists who have studied the matter feel that a primitive, perhaps largely unconscious tendency toward sociality is probably characteristic of all animals. Kinsey, the zoologist who studied human sexual behavior, remarks that the first impulse of any living organism, upon touching another object, is to press against it. Another biologist, W. C. Allee, who studied the social life of animals extensively, found, for example, that an isopod (a small crayfish-like creature) will swim upstream when placed alone in moving water, but when placed in the same water with other isopods will move instead toward them. When sponges— actually colonies of cells—are macerated and passed through sieves, they will under appropriate conditions reform themselves into new sponges. Human sociality seems to be but one expression of a very primitive biological "consciousness of kind." And it is a relatively recent one. Human life on earth has lasted only about one and a half million years. By contrast, preserved fossils of ants have been found that are estimated to be 50 million years old. They were already highly specialized, thus members of long-standing and complex social groups. Yet ants are themselves relative newcomers in biological history, when compared, for example, with the much older termites, and all land-dwelling species are relatively young when compared with marine life.

In the long history of life on earth, sociality has developed, in part at least, because it gives members of a species greater power to survive. A dramatic demonstration of such survival was performed by Allee, with goldfish. When placed in a solution poisoned with colloidal silver, groups of goldfish survived significantly longer than did isolated fish. The reason lies in the fact that the fish are able to secrete a slime which partly neutralizes the poison. In a group the power of this neutralizing slime becomes concentrated, while with a single individual it becomes diluted too fast to be effective. Flatworms exposed to ultraviolet rays survived longer in groups than singly. Many kinds of birds and mammals are able, by grouping, to defend

No living being is solitary. Animals, especially, sustain multiple relations with the organisms of their environment, and without mentioning those that live in permanent intercourse with their kind, nearly all are impelled by biological necessity to contract, even if only for a brief moment, an intimate union with some other individual of their species. Even among organisms devoid of distinct and separate sexes, some traces of social life are manifested, both among the animals that remain, like plants, attached to a common stock and among the lowly beings which, before separating from the parental organism, remain for some time attached to it and incorporated with its substance. Communal life, therefore, is not an accidental fact in the animal kingdom; it does not arise here and there fortuitously and as it were capriciously; it is not, as is so often supposed, the privilege of certain isolated species in the zoological scale, such as the beavers, bees, and ants, but on the contrary . . . a normal, constant, universal fact. From the lowest to the highest forms in the series, all animals are at some time in their lives immersed in some society; the social medium is the condition necessary to the conservation and renewal of life.

—*Alfred V. Espinas, quoted in William M. Wheeler,* The Social Insects, *New York, Harcourt Brace Jovanovich, pp. 5–6.*

---

themselves against more powerful predators which could destroy them singly. Man is, of course, such a mammal.

One of the advantages of social life is that it protects the young, enabling a larger number to survive to the age where they will in turn produce offspring. Thus social groups are likely to have an advantage over their less social fellows in the struggle for existence. Group life also makes a species more adaptable to changes in its environment. Sexual reproduction is perhaps the most elementary social relationship. Through it, each offspring bears two sets of genes, and thus a species that reproduces sexually has more potentialities for adaptation than a species that simply duplicates a single parent. A large population has a wider variety of genes than a small, isolated one, and thus again a better chance of producing offspring who will be able to adapt to environmental changes. There are other survival advantages in group life. Fish have been shown to eat better in a group than alone. Ants and men work more effi-ciently in groups. For all these and other reasons, Allee says, a minimum amount of massing of animals is necessary for the best chance of development and survival. Either overcrowding or undercrowding decreases vitality and the chance of survival.

What similarities and differences are there between human societies and the social organizations of lower species? Clearly, many of the traits of human society are not unique but are found in prehuman groups. The family is a widespread social grouping, probably the grouping out of which most societies of all kinds develop. Animal societies are characterized, as are ours, by interdependence and specialization. Animals, like ourselves, have statuses in their groups, perform roles, and live up to expectations. Underlying all human and prehuman societies there seems to be a deep "consciousness of kind." Slavery and other forms of domination of one group by another are found among animals as among men. So are both tightly knit totalitarian organizations and more loosely bound democratic structures.

On the other hand, human societies seem to have qualities that are essentially not found in animal groups. Man has a smaller number of inherited behavior patterns. He depends more upon learning and is much more capable of learning. This is to say that he is far more intelligent. The differences between animal and human societies are closely related to these differences. We can hardly speak of animal folkways, animal mores, animal values, or animal institutions. The words themselves seem to signify something uniquely human.

We are not yet sure how much of a social pattern, such as an anthill, is innate and how much may be learned behavior, but we can say that there is little cumulative learning in subhuman groups. An ant society is essentially the same from one generation to the next, perhaps even over millions of years. This is not true of any human society, especially of any technically advanced one. Each human generation builds upon the accumulated experience of its predecessors; that is, human societies possess *culture,* which is simply a cumulative pattern of folkways and institutions, developed in experience and transmitted by learning from one generation to the next. While the higher animal societies may possibly be said to possess some rudiments of culture, for practical purposes we can say that only human societies are culture making. We shall have much more to say about culture a little later.

PRIMITIVE AND CIVILIZED SOCIETIES

As great as is the difference between human and prehuman societies, it is perhaps no greater than the difference between primitive and civilized human groups. If human societies are very recent by contrast with prehuman ones, so civilized society has occupied only a small fraction of man's life on earth. The last 5000 years belong to historic man, the previous one and a half million years to our prehistoric ancestors. We know relatively little about their social life, but we are sure that they were much less advanced than any primitive society now existent. Yet, even the primitive peoples now alive have a life so different from ours that if we really try to imagine ourselves in their societies, it is hard to believe that we live on the same planet.

We cannot fully understand precivilized people, or understand ourselves, or understand what happens when noncivilized people encounter civilization without analyzing the differences beween the two kinds of societies.

Let us dramatize the extremes by comparing the life of New York City with the life of one of the most primitive peoples now known. The Bushmen of the Kalahari Desert of South Africa are a Stone Age people who know no metal tools other than those borrowed recently from the white man. They still live, in a sparse and arid desert region, by hunting game with simple weapons and by digging roots. They have no developed agriculture. As far as we know, they have changed their way of life but little over thousands of years. New York City is, of course, the symbol of our dynamic technological civilization, in its most advanced form. The New Yorker uses the most sophisticated scientific technology. He, too, practices no agriculture, but only because he has passed beyond it to dependence on a commercial food supply. In New York City we find a vast, complex formal machinery of government, a world center for the publication of the written word, and constant change as the way of life.

In comparing the Bushman with the New Yorker, we need first to notice that in spite of their differences, they are both human beings and do live on the same planet. They have much the same biological structure and drives. They both breathe air, eat and drink, experience fear and sexual desire, deal with heat and cold, with calm and storm, confront the same physical,

Bushmen of the Kalihari Desert, Africa. (Courtesy of the American Museum of Natural History.)

chemical, and biological laws, and eventually die. Both make a living, speak a language, recognize some organized social control over their lives, practice a religion, grow up in a family, educate their young, play as well as work, make or experience works of art, have some scientific knowledge of the world, and have some measures to protect physical and psychological health. As one anthropologist, Clark Wissler, has put it, they share (with each other and with all other human groups) the same *universal culture pattern*. That is, each performs, in an organized manner, a number of basic human functions.

But if the Bushman and the New Yorker carry on the same fundamental human activities, how differently they perform them!

The primitive society is *preliterate*. The Bushman has no written language. Civilized man can set his knowledge apart from himself, can store and transmit it in the form of symbols. Primitive man must carry all his knowledge, so to speak, in his head. The difference enormously affects the possibilities of each type of society. The amount of knowledge the minds of any one generation can carry is narrowly limited; while the capacity of books and libraries, magnetic tapes, microfilms, and computers is almost infinite.

Modern anthropologists, indeed, generally prefer to use the term "preliterate" to describe the simpler societies. They feel that primitive suggests inferiority, while preliterate simply describes the factual absence of writing. Can we say, they would ask, that because of the greater complexity which written language makes possible, the New Yorker is necessarily more advanced in terms of ultimate values than the Bushman? One can, of course, make a strong argument that he is, but the South African writer Laurens Van der Post tells us that in his experience the Bushman has shown a natural religious and artistic relationship to his environment and a spontaneous moral sense toward his fellow men which the less primitive white man has usually lost. The use of the term "preliterate" enables us to describe differences objectively without implying judgment as to which way may be better.

The society of the Bushman is *technologically simple.* Digging sticks, a bow and arrow, and a hunting spear are his most important tools. Unless it has been introduced by the white man, the wheel is unknown to him. As we have seen, so is the use of metal. He is typical of a simple, preliterate society in that he has few secondary tools, that is, tools to make other tools. The variety and complexity of the New Yorker's technology—his skyscrapers, subways, jet planes, television, computers —are so different that to a Bushman he might well seem to be another species. The Bushman has few technicways, the New Yorker, many.

Again, is it better or worse to be technologically primitive? We in the technically advanced West are likely to assume without much question that our technology is entirely desirable. We are likely to believe that it not only gives us more material security, but that it also enables us to develop the higher things of life. Preliterate peoples, coming in contact with the white man's world for the first time, are likely to agree and to be fascinated by the products of advanced machinery. But sometimes they also react like the isolated inhabitants of the remote South Atlantic island of Tristan da Cunha. Transplanted to England because of the threat of a volcanic eruption and later given the choice of remaining, almost all of these people chose *not* to stay in the modern world of noise, mass production, and omnipresent TV. The philosophy of the Orient has typically looked upon technology as of doubtful value and regarded simplicity as preferable to material affluence. "One is the road that leads to wealth," say the Buddhist scriptures, "another the road that leads to Nirvana [union with the infinite]." A philosopher from the edge of the East admonished his followers to take their example from the lilies, who "toil not, neither do they spin." Even in the Western world we are troubled by the story of Frankenstein, who was destroyed by the machine he created.

The Bushman is also relatively *unspecialized.* Another way to express this is to say that he has a low degree of division of labor. Everyone tends to do very much the same thing as everyone else. Men and women do generally have different roles which, as everywhere, grow out of men's inability to bear children and the relative helplessness of the pregnant woman. But aside from this, there is little specialization. In this respect the Bushmen are like the transplanted Tristan islanders. One of these said: "At home I am a sailor, a farmer, a carpenter, a shepherd, a lumberjack—all these things. In England I am simply: Unskilled." It is an interesting exercise in comparison to take the classified telephone directory of New York, and see the intricate specialization of life in that city. One can take a particular category, such as physician, and compare the degree of specialization not only with that of the Bush medicine man, but with that shown in the yellow pages of smaller cities. He can then see how the degree of specialization increases with size of community. While in a town of 1,000 there may be only general practitioners, in a city of 10,000 there may be a specialist in diseases of the eye, ear, nose, and throat; in a city of 100,000, doctors specializing in the eye alone; and in New York, specialists in various branches of eye surgery.

Specialization is related to the fact that preliterate people tend to be economically self-sufficient, while highly civilized people depend on exchange. Few of us, as we pointed out earlier, produce much of what we consume. We typically exchange our services, through the medium of money, for those of others. Even such exchanges as take place among preliterate people are more likely to be on the basis of gifts or barter rather than through a medium of exchange. The preliterate person is likely to starve or know want chiefly because of natural scarcity, disaster, or his low technology and lack of specialization. The Bushman is often hungry and seems generally undernourished simply because there is not much food in a desert, and what there is is hard to get with his Stone Age tools. On the other hand, the highly civilized person may live in hunger and poverty seemingly because of his high technology and division of labor. His specialization has made him so dependent on others that if automation or a business recession deprives him of a job, he may have nothing to fall back on and may suffer extreme want in the midst of affluence.

The preliterate society is to a large extent *nonhistoric*. The use of written words to store knowledge gives the New Yorker a sense of standing at the end of a long series of generations which reaches back through almost 10,000 years of recorded history. He also projects his sense of history back further into the past and can think of a prehistory reaching back millions and even billions of years. Even though these reaches of time are too vast for an individual "six feet and seventy years long" really to comprehend, he can at least construct a timetable of the biological and geological past. New York man also projects his sense of history into the future; one social scientist has even written a book called *The Future as History*. New York man imagines supersonic jets carrying a thousand passengers, space trips to Venus, the possibility of a world where the population explosion will have left "standing room only," or where automation may have abolished a large part of work, and so on.

All this is impossible for the Bushman. Without writing, he can remember only as much of the past as can be transmitted by word of mouth. Some observers believe that primitive peoples have more accurate memories than we do. Even at best, however, they cannot have more than three or four generations of history. The times of Lincoln or Washington, much less of Shakespeare or Jesus or Moses—all potentially real to us through recorded history—are beyond the records of the Bushman. He lives, so to speak, only in a "now" world which quickly fades off into forgetfulness. The anthropologist Dorothy Lee, writing of the Trobriand Islanders of Melanesia, says that they so lack a sense of past-present-future that they have no sharp grammatical tenses to reflect a difference in time. An incident in the life of one's grandfather may be described in the same tense as one happening today: "When Grandfather is a little boy he goes . . . ."

The Bushman society is also mostly a *static* one. Here we find a most important contrast. The New Yorker, like most Americans, takes change for granted. He has hardly bought his car, his TV set, his hi-fi, his electric razor, and dishwasher (and probably not paid for them) before he is pressed to buy a newer—and of course better—model. While he may accept new ideas less easily than new gadgets, he usually finds himself compelled to adjust to the fact that the ways of his children in music, in grammar, or in sex are not his ways. He usually learns to adjust to new ideas even in economics, politics, and religion.

For the Bushman, on the other hand, there may have been no new model in digging sticks or hunting spears in a thousand years. Neither has there probably been one in habits of family life, group organization, or religious beliefs. Tradition is the dominant force in Bushman society. The Bushman follows the "conservatism of the tested": the ways of his father and his great grandfather have been tried and found successful in enabling them to survive in difficult circumstances. To propose to abandon them for new and untried patterns is not only unnecessary but dangerous, for it may threaten the tribe's very capacity to survive.

New York man not only takes change for granted, but generally feels that it means progress. He can hardly imagine how anyone could want to, or could even endure, living in a society that was not progressing. He might perhaps be willing to accept the fact that progress could have little meaning at all to a native Stone Age Bushman, but he will probably be very much surprised to learn that the idea of progress is itself fairly new even among civilized people. Most people living before perhaps the sixteenth century, even the classical Greeks, had very little idea of progress. They took it for granted that a repetition of the past rather than constant change is the desirable way of life. The idea of progress has also traditionally been alien to much of the Orient.

The Bushman avoids the risk which is always involved in trying the new. He avoids the confusion and disorganization which are always involved in change. His is a stable and, in this sense, a more emotionally secure so-

ciety. But he also loses the opportunity for improvement of his material standard of life, the excitement of breaking new paths, and the opening up of new possibilities for development of his human potentialities, all of which may be the life of the New Yorker. There is no final answer as to whether conservatism or change is better. Each has its assets and liabilities, and we should learn to evaluate both.

The preliterate society is *isolated and immobile*. Unless he enters the white man's world, the Bushman rarely or never sees anyone outside his own tribe. Bushmen, being hunters and gatherers, are actually somewhat more mobile than some less primitive but settled agricultural peoples, but their wanderings do not take them beyond a relatively small area. The Bushman is rooted in this area, with one group of people, usually from birth to death. The sharply different mobility of the New Yorker may be symbolized by the constant flights to and from Kennedy Airport or by the traffic on Fifth Avenue. The range of his contacts may be symbolized by the United Nations building. The New Yorker may be poor, living in an area like one studied in Chicago, where it was found that the average person moved every nine months. He may be a teacher always on the lookout for a move up the academic ladder. Or he may be an organization man, always ready to pull up stakes as his corporation moves him to another job.

Because his society is isolated, and also fairly unspecialized, the Bushman's social contacts are *homogeneous*, that is, the people he encounters are all much the same. They contrast sharply with the heterogeneity and variety of the New Yorker's experiences with people. Comparing the range of human possibilities with the spectrum of colors, the anthropologist Ruth Benedict has suggested that each society develops only a small arc of the whole spectrum. Because of his isolation, the experience of the Bushman is limited to his one narrow arc. The New Yorker, on the other hand, coming in contact with many varied people, may experience a far larger part of the whole range of human possibilities. The Bushman's awareness is largely limited to his tribe, whereas the New Yorker's may encompass the world.

The previous paragraph suggests something that may have already occurred to us. Because of the homogeneity of Bushman society, it is fairly easy to make statements that apply to all Bushmen. There are, however, so many different kinds of New Yorkers that it is hard to generalize about *the* New Yorker. In some areas of Harlem there are undoubtedly people who have never seen Times Square. Many immigrants may still not venture forth very often or very far from their ghettos. One million people in New York City still live in poverty, large numbers of them in the most primitive physical conditions, with few of the advantages of civilized technology. When we speak of the New Yorker, as contrasted with the Bushman, we are describing that kind of person who possesses the qualities that we most associate with civilization—literacy, mobility, specialization, affluence, sophistication. We probably will find more of his kind in New York than in any other one place.

The social relationships of the Bushman are, for the most part, what social scientists call *primary relationships,* while those of the New Yorker are mainly secondary ones. The term "primary group" was first used by the social scientist Charles Horton Cooley to describe those relationships that are normally found in such groups as the family, the child's playgroup, and the neighborhood. These groups are crescive, that is, they just grow. The typical form of secondary relationship is found in enacted groups—clubs, organizations, associations—whose members draw together deliberately for specific purposes. Relationships in primary groups are typically close and personal, as contrasted with the impersonal and relatively superficial relationships which characterize life in large-scale organizations and in the city.

Because most Bushmen are isolated, their relationships with one another tend to be relationships of long acquaintance. In such a preliterate society, except for additions by birth and subtractions by death, one lives his whole life with the same people. For the same reason, his contacts with them are frequent. New York man, on the other hand, encounters many more people in a lifetime, but with few of them does he typically have long-term relationships—he moves too often for that. Likewise, moving about and seeing more people as he does, he is likely to see each of them less often.

The New Yorker tends to meet other individuals as simply performers of specialized roles and to know them in only one aspect of their total personalities—as salesman, bus driver, waitress, policeman, movie usher, minister, checkout girl, physician, and so on. Because he is relatively unspecialized and because his contacts are frequent and lifelong, the Bushman is much more likely to know others as whole people, in all their life activities. Along with this greater breadth of knowledge is likely to go greater depth. The New Yorker usually knows many of the people who are involved in his life only on a superficial and impersonal level. He is likely to have little emotional involvement with most of them. The Bushman, on the other hand, is likely to know the members of his society on a much deeper level, to identify with and share their most profound joys and sorrows, their pains, frustrations, and fears. Among other things, this is possible because his society is smaller. As one sociologist has pointed out, if the dweller in a large city were to react to all the people he meets with the same intensity he gives to his immediate family relationships, he would simply tear himself apart.

Primary group relationships have both their assets and their liabilities. Without them, it is doubtful whether anyone can survive in emotional health, or indeed, even in physical health. Even monkeys, for example, when deprived of close emotional contact in infancy, fail to develop normal social or sexual interests. Children brought up in institutions may waste away physically from simple emotional deprivation, and in any case are unlikely to develop healthy personalities. It seems certain that adults also need some close emotional relationships in order to be healthy human beings.

On the other hand, continued close emotional contact in tightly knit primary groups can be not only monotonous, but very limiting and confining. Primary groups may grant their members little freedom or privacy, so youths from preliterate tribes may be drawn to the apparently greater variety and freedom of the city. Yet, having experienced it, they may in turn feel profoundly rootless and alone and long to return to the close emotional relationships of the tribe. One of the most important tasks of social science is to suggest ways in which we can have deeply satisfying primary relationships without the limitation of freedom and individual development which they so often require.

The preliterate society is *close to nature*. The advanced civilized society is separated from nature by its technology. The Bushman lives intimately with sky, sun, wind, and rain. He is in constant contact with the earth. His life is guided by the seasons; he suffers the heat of summer and the cold of winter. New York man lives in a world of steel, glass, and concrete. Towering buildings block his view of sky and sun. He is separated from the earth by concrete pavements. Central heating in winter and air-conditioning in summer may create for him an almost constant indoor environment with no seasons. The Bushman constantly engages his muscles; the New Yorker is moved and served by technology. The primitive is almost always closely involved with the growth and death of plant and animal life. The New Yorker seldom sees plants and animals in their natural habitat except on a visit to the country. The Bushman breathes fresh air, sometimes mixed with sand; drinks, if he is fortunate, from a perhaps muddy water hole; eats his food as he catches or

digs it. New York man breathes conditioned or polluted air; drinks filtered and chemically treated water; eats food bought from the supermarket or from a slot machine.

In spite of the cosmopolitan New Yorker's "emancipation," there is little doubt that the Bushman has a more natural sense of, less fear of, his own body. He is more direct and spontaneous in his sexual and emotional life. He typically has a greater sense of primary emotional closeness to his fellows. He is much more likely to have a spontaneous religious sense of oneness with all his universe. Thus, for example, at the end of an exhausting hunt, when he has finally killed a giraffe, he may pause in recognition of the great gap which has been left in Creation by the death of his prey. Such an experience of belonging to one's whole environment is probably rare among New Yorkers. As in all the differences we have examined, there are here advantages in being close to nature in the raw, and advantages in the civilized mastery of nature. We need to ask, again, to what extent it may be possible to have the best of both worlds.

All through this comparison, we have dealt only with two extremes. If what we have said told us only about Bushmen and New Yorkers, it would be interesting, but of limited value. It can, however, do far more than this. It is a tool for understanding all kinds of societies, for there are, of course, many gradations between Bushman and New York man. In fact, almost all human societies could be arranged somewhere between these two poles. According to their nearness to one or the other pole, they would share its characteristics, but in less extreme form. We would then have a continuous series of societies, or a continuum, graded by small variations from the most simple to the most complex.

Suppose we imagine a continuum on which, for the sake of simplicity, we add between Bushman and New York society only six other societies. The first, and nearest to the Bushman, might be

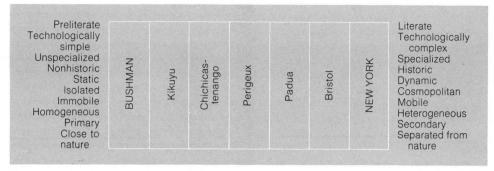

Figure 4.1. Bushman–New Yorker continuum.

the more advanced Kikuyu tribe of African Kenya, who practice settled agriculture. Farther along the scale is Chichicastenango, a peasant village in the hills of Guatemala. The next society is that of Perigeux, a small town of 10,000 in southern France. The next is Padua, an Italian city of 75,000. The last, and nearest to New York, is Bristol, an English city of 500,000.

The continuum would then look like Figure 4.1.

Many of our greatest social problems are related to the Bushman–New York continuum. A large part of the earth's population in the so-called underdeveloped areas is beginning to move from preliterate tribal society into civilization, or from a simple agricultural society into a complex industrial society. The whole civilized world, particularly the highly industrialized portion, appears to be moving toward the end of the continuum represented by New York City. What conflicts are these trends creating? What will be their results in terms of human values? What will be gained and what lost?

SIZE AND GROUP STRUCTURE

The preceding comparison of a small society with a mass society suggests that size makes a great difference in the structure of groups. This is true regardless of the nature and purpose of the groups. We must explore this difference more explicitly.

We can start with the smallest groups, the dyad (group of two) and triad (group of three). "Two's company, three's a crowd." What does the folk saying reflect? What is the difference between company and a crowd? In a love affair, we can see the difference, and we can see it in families. When the couple becomes a threesome, a profound change takes place in the group life. A smaller change occurs when the threesome becomes four. A family of twelve, on the other hand, is quite different in its group life from a family of three.

We have other experiences of the significance of group size. How big is a party? How many people do we have to invite lest it be too small? And at what point will it become too big to serve the purpose for which we are having it? We are all aware of the difference that size makes in a college class. A class of 3, 15, 50, or 250 presents a quite different teaching and learning experience. Similarly, we are aware that a small college and a large university are two different things. Recent plans for breaking up large universities into "cluster colleges" and large dormitories into small residence halls reflect awareness of the difference. It is no different with other group life, although perhaps not so close to our everyday experience. The medieval manor or the workmen's guild was quite different from today's corporation farm or General Motors. A New England town meeting had a different structure from the General Assembly of the United Nations. The twelve disciples of Jesus formed a group quite different from the Roman Catholic Church.

That group size makes a difference is common sense. Let us try to analyze systematically what some of the differences are.

Increasing numbers bring many kinds of increased *efficiency.* People in large numbers can do things simply because there are so many of them. Thus in ancient times were the Egyptian pyramids built, the Nile diked, the swamps of Mesopotamia drained. More primitive societies could not have done these things. Large numbers make possible specialization that would be impossible in smaller groups. A major political party, for example, can employ professional researchers and public relations agencies, while a minor party must do these things on an amateur basis. A large university can support research programs impossible for a smaller college. Numbers have other competitive advantages. A large business has the capital to buy expensive machinery to do things that a smaller competitor must do by hand. A large business can purchase in bulk lots at low prices, while the smaller business pays high prices for small quantities. These are some of the kinds of efficiencies of size that favor large groups.

Numbers also bring *depersonalization.* In terms of the concepts introduced in the previous section, primary relationships tend to give way to secondary ones. Intensity of personal relations is generally possible only where numbers are small. We can see this in a large party or classroom situation. With size, contacts become more superficial. It is easier to be detached about people in large groups. This is an advantage in many inevitable situations, such as those where people must be disciplined or fired, where medical judgments must be made as to which patient to save when there are not time or resources to save all, or where there is only so much welfare

money available and some children must go without milk. On the other side, size may reduce people to figures on ID cards or translate human flesh and blood into abstract news service statistics of military "casualties." Depersonalization may deaden the sense of personal responsibility for one's actions toward others.

A related aspect of growth in size is *formalization.* The amateur jack of all trades is replaced by the specialist with an assigned niche in a hierarchy with its levels of authority. Face-to-face decisions give way to indirect communication through memoranda passed up and down chains of command. Verbal communication is replaced by the instruction to "put it in writing." The larger the organization, the greater the danger of that kind of breakdown in communication where "the left hand knoweth not what the right hand doeth." We can illustrate this in any large organization. Indirect and formal communication is likely to lead to red tape, the situation where the machinery of communication becomes more important than the thing being communicated. It may also lead to buck passing, the easy shifting of responsibility to someone else in the hierarchy.

The greater the size of the group, the greater is likely to be the *centralization* of decision making. People lose their ability to participate in decision making directly. If they take part at all, it is likely to be through delegates to representative bodies. This is true in corporations, labor unions, churches, political parties, professional organizations, and organizations of many other types. Again, there is likely to be a weakening of the individual's sense that he is responsible for the group life and decisions.

The specialization that accompanies growth in size is apt to give rise to *bureaucratization.* Specialized divisions or bureaus of the organization are set up; these are supposed ultimately to be responsible to central authority, but often have a considerable degree of independence. They are very likely to develop their own interests, sometimes at the expense of the organization as a whole. If action is taken against them, they are likely to protest that only they really understand the specialized job they are doing and that their critics are just ignorant bureaucrats. Government bureaus, divisions of business, and university departments, among other groups, often behave in this way.

An important feature of size is the increasing *weight of administration.* Beyond a certain point, as groups become larger, an increasingly greater percentage of their personnel and resources has to go into simply keeping the organization functioning. The characteristics already discussed should make clear why this is so. The larger the army, the larger is likely to be the ratio of officers to enlisted men. The larger the university, the larger the ratio of vice presidents and deans to faculty and students. The larger the business or government bureau or charitable organization, the greater the percentage of its budget that is likely to go to overhead, as distinguished from the actual services it performs. Once it has been established, the branch of administration tends to grow and to resist any reduction. Thus organization becomes subject to Parkinson's Law, put forth somewhat tongue in cheek by the political scientist G. Northcote Parkinson: in organized life, whatever time exists will always be filled.

All these processes tend to result in *institutionalization,* the tendency of an institution to become an end in itself and seek its own survival rather than the aims for which it originated. This is true both of the organization as a whole and of its separate individual branches. It is true of student organizations, churches, and revolutionary political organizations, as it is also true in business, government, and other areas.

Group life of all sizes is clearly a balance of advantages and disadvan-tages of number. The fact that we have listed more disadvantages of size should not lead us to forget the very great significance of the advantages of numbers. Is there somewhere, however, an optimum size for an organization beyond which losses outweigh gains?

An amoeba divides into two rather than increase beyond a certain critical size. The dinosaur was not so fortunate and became extinct. We have seen that animal populations tend to maintain an optimum size in relation to their environment. Plato said that a city should not exceed the number of people who can listen to a single orator. When they threatened to exceed a certain size, the Greek city states tended to divide (like the amoeba) by colonizing the surplus population overseas. A modern city planner, Ebenezer Howard, proposed that cities be prevented from exceeding a maximum size by surrounding them with "greenbelts" of forest, and that when this limit was reached, new cities be started.

Is there a critical size for human groups, or rather, are there critical sizes for different types of groups? We think we know the optimum size for a love affair, though the polygamous populations of the world might disagree. What is the optimum size for a college class? for a university? for a legislative body? for a steel mill? for a government? for a church? for a city? How many of our modern organizations have passed the point of optimum advantage? How should we go about correcting this situation, if it exists? Here may well lie some of our most important social problems.

IN-GROUPS AND OUT-GROUPS

One of the most important facts in social behavior is the sharp distinction that most people make between the groups to which they belong and those to which they do not belong—between "in-groups" and "out-groups." An in-group may be any group to which one belongs by virtue of the geographical area in which he lives, his race, religion, sex, age, cultural, or professional interest, or any other criterion. An out-group is a corresponding group to which one does not belong. To a man, for example, males are a sexual in-group, females a sexual out-group. To a cadet at the Military Academy, the Naval Academy is an out-group. To the religious Jew, Gentiles constitute an out-group. To a Chinese, the United States is an out-group.

Although each kind of in-group is different, certain attitudes are typical of all in-group behavior. These can be described by the word "ethnocentrism." (The Greek root *ethnos* refers to people or ethnic group.) This term, first used by the sociologist Sumner in his book *Folkways,* "is the technical name for this view of things in which one's own group is the center of everything, and all others are scaled and rated with reference to it." The insert from *Folkways* which appears on this page describes the ethnocentric attitudes of different societies, or cultural groups. We can notice several elements in the ethnocentric attitude.

1. The members of the in-group assume their superiority to all out-groups. This superiority is not demonstrated or argued; it is simply taken for granted. To the Carib Indians cited by Sumner, the world was divided into two kinds of individuals: Caribs and non-people. It did not even occur to them to question this division. Some Americans feel the same way about their own "tribe" in relation to foreigners.

2. The in-group assumes that its ways are the right ways. The Chinese of the Middle Kingdom, about whom Sumner also speaks, did not objectively compare the traditions he had inherited from Confucius with the ways of other people. Of course, the traditional ways were the right ways, the only ways in which any civilized person would act! Some American tourists feel insulted if they are expected to speak the native language in a foreign country. Don't all people who really are people speak English?

3. Strong loyalty to the in-group is combined with hostility toward the out-group. A nation may maintain internal order as long as there is an enemy to fight but break into disorder when the war is over. Indeed, it is known that a foreign war is one of the most effective ways to reduce conflict and increase the spirit of cooperation in the name of "national unity." Mussolini, faced with internal dissension, found it convenient to direct the aggressions of Italians against the Ethiopians. An out-group at home may serve the same purpose; this was almost certainly the case of the Jews in Nazi Germany.

4. The in-group has a double standard for judging actions, according to whether they are performed toward in-group members or toward an out-group. An intense "honor among thieves" may lead a juvenile delinquent or criminal to die rather than betray a gang member at the same time that he shows no scruples toward the police or toward society at large. The Old Testament commandment "Thou shalt not kill" was considered to apply to the members of the Hebrew tribes, but did not keep them from invading other lands and massacring the inhabitants. Nations, even today, practice this double standard.

5. Members of the in-group tend to identify themselves psychologically with the group. This means that whatever happens to the group happens, so to speak, to them personally. The attitudes that others feel toward the in-group are felt to apply to them personally. We all know the athletic fan for whom victory or defeat for his team is a personal triumph or disaster. In the case of socially powerful in-groups, this identification is very important. An individual who might otherwise feel personally insignificant and worthless may feel very significant and powerful as a member of such a group. An underprivileged white person may find it very important to maintain white supremacy because it enables him as a member of the white in-group, to feel superior to any member of the Negro

out-group. Or the in-group may be reversed, and a personally powerless Negro may be carried away by the chant of "Black Power."

As suggested earlier, almost any characteristic that differentiates people may give rise to in-group feelings and behavior. Sumner originally applied the concept of ethnocentrism primarily to in-groups that have a common geographical location and a common way of life, or culture. The members of a modern nation state, such as Yugoslavia or the United States, differ in having more than one cultural background. Be this as it may, nationalism is the most powerful form of in-grouping in the modern world. It is a very useful exercise to see how the ethnocentric mechanisms of superiority, rightness, hostility, double standard, and identification apply to modern nations, our own included. Sections within a nation state—such as Protestant Northern Ireland, or New England, or the South—may likewise show many strong ethnocentric characteristics.

A group does not have to have a common geographical location, however, to behave and feel as an in-group, with corresponding attitudes toward out-groups. Jews, even when dispersed throughout the world for centuries, maintained a sense of identity as God's chosen people. We may think of them as having been an ethnic group, or a nation, without geographical boundaries. Settlement of a large number of Jews in the common homeland may intensify this traditional in-group feeling by giving it the form of modern Zionism, but it has not created the feeling.

Although many Jews are nonreligious, to a large extent we may also think of the historic Jewish people as a religious in-group. As such they share many of the same ethnocentric characteristics as do Christians and Mohammedans. All three faiths, in their orthodox forms, believe in their own superiority, consider their doctrine the only true doctrine, and think of themselves as God's elect. Not all religions are so

---

Each group thinks its own folkways the only right ones, and if it observes that other groups have other folkways, these excite its scorn. Opprobrious epithets are derived from these differences. "Pig-eater," "cow-eater," "uncircumcised," "jabberers," are epithets of contempt and abomination. The Tupis called the Portuguese by a derisive epithet descriptive of birds which have feathers around their feet, on account of trousers. For our purpose the most important fact is that ethnocentrism leads a people to exaggerate and intensify everything in their own folkways which is peculiar and which differentiates them from others. It therefore strengthens the folkways. . . .

When Caribs were asked whence they came, they answered, "We alone are people." The meaning of the name Kiowa is "real or principal people." The Lapps call themselves "men," or "human beings." The Greenland Eskimo think that Europeans have been sent to Greenland to learn virtue and good manners from the Greenlanders. Their highest form of praise for a European is that he is, or soon will be, as good as a Greenlander. The Tunguses call themselves "men." As a rule it is found that nature peoples call themselves "men." Others are something else— perhaps not defined—but not real men. In myths the origin of their own tribe is that of the real human race. They do not account for the others. The Ainus derive their name from that of the first man, whom they worship as a god. Evidently the name of the god is derived from the tribe name. When the tribal name has another sense, it is always boastful or proud. The Ovambo name is a corruption of the name of the tribe for themselves, which means "the wealthy." Amongst the most remarkable people in the world for ethnocentrism are the Seri of Lower California. They observe an attitude of suspicion and hostility to all outsiders, and strictly forbid marriage with outsiders.

The Jews divided all mankind into themselves and Gentiles. They were the "chosen people." The Greeks and Romans called all outsiders "barbarians." In Euripides' tragedy of Iphegenia in Aulis, *Iphegenia* says that it is fitting that Greeks should rule over barbarians, but not contrariwise, because Greeks are free and barbarians are slaves. The Arabs regarded themselves as the noblest nation and all others as more or less barbarous. In 1896 the Chinese minister of education and his counselors edited a manual in which this statement occurs: "How grand and glorious is the Empire of China, the middle kingdom! She is the largest and richest in the world. The grandest men in the world have all come from the middle empire." In all the literature of all the states equivalent statements occur, although they are not so naively expressed. In Russian books and newspapers the civilizing mission of Russia is talked about, just as, in the books and journals of France, Germany, and the United States, the civilizing mission of these countries is assumed and referred to as well understood. Each state now regards itself as the leader of civilization, the best, the freest, and the wisest, and all others as inferior.

—*William Graham Sumner,* Folkways, *Boston, Ginn, 1940, pp. 13–14.*

---

ethnocentric. A Hindu, for example, may see no reason why he cannot be a good Christian or Jew also. The opposite belief would be impossible for a devout follower of the Christian or Jewish faith. Atheists also may show very ethnocentric attitudes toward believers.

Racial distinction is one of the most significant forms of in-grouping. Ethnocentric feeling toward Negroes is found almost everywhere in the United States—by no means only in the South —and, of course, in many other countries. Most Americans have similar feelings toward Orientals, and as Sumner suggests, these may be returned. In World War II Americans and Japanese fought each other with a ferocity and ruthlessness seldom matched on the German front, for each regarded the other as somewhat less than human. Similar racial feelings on both sides make the problem of relations between the United States and China today quite different from those with France, or even with Russia, which is still also a "white" nation.

In the United States we find an interesting and important example of how the in-groupings of ethnic origin, religion, and race may work together. This is the dominance in American society of the WASP—White Anglo-Saxon Protestant. Negroes have achieved few positions of prominence in American society, but they are not the only group that has been outside in terms of equal opportunity. The American melting pot has never produced a president of southern or eastern European origin (although it has produced a vice president)—Italian, Polish, Czech, or Greek. It is only in local areas where these ethnic groups are concentrated that their members have often been elected to political office. Only recently have eastern and southern European names begun to appear in substantial numbers on university faculties. There has never been a Jewish president, and there have been few Jews in high political office; anti-Semitism, though not generally as intense as anti-Negro feeling, is perhaps as widespread in the United States. The election of our one Catholic president was accompanied by widespread self-congratulation that we had for once overcome our traditional prejudices.

Social classes are extremely significant in-groups. Middle-class people often have strong feelings about the rightness of their ways, especially with regard to cleanliness, thrift, sexual restraint, and control of violent emotions. They are likely to look upon those "below" them as violent, dirty, and immoral. The behavior of the upper classes is likely to be regarded by them as extravagant and morally loose. Working-class in-group feelings are appealed to by Marxism, against the bourgeois out-group, as in the opening words of the "Internationale":

> *Arise, ye prisoners of starvation,*
> *Arise, ye wretched of the earth.*
> *For justice theatens condemnation,*
> *A better world's in birth.*

Upper-class groups may justify their position in society by doctrines of the inferiority of other classes. Alexander Hamilton said: "All communities divide themselves into the few and the many. The first are the rich and well-born, the other the mass of the people [who] seldom judge or determine right."

There are also ethnocentrisms of age. There may never, in history, have been a generation of parents that has been able to understand its children or that has not complained with "superior" moral righteousness that its offspring are going to the dogs. The children, in turn, have cockily cast their parents into outer darkness as hopelessly outdated. There is always likely to be hostility between the generations

because parents see children taking their place and resist the takeover. This is even more likely to happen in an age of rapid change like our own. Urban technology and mass education have led more and more young people away from the family farm and have thus tended to separate the generations. Some sociologists think that we have developed in our high schools and colleges an almost distinct adolescent culture, which looks upon parents and teachers as "preatomic" and has little respect for the values of either. Parents and educational administrators, on the other hand, are likely to underestimate the maturity of the young and insist unbendingly upon their own superior wisdom and right to make important decisions that concern them. At the other end of the life cycle, the increase in the number of older people has created a group of "senior citizens" with a sharp sense of its own identity and special interests.

Sex divides the human race into two halves which show many of the characteristics of in-groups. It is hard to remember that little more than a century ago women were widely considered intellectually incapable of higher education. Until 1920 the federal government had not guaranteed women the right to vote. Until relatively recently, feminists and suffragettes were often considered the wildest of radicals. Advocates of women's liberation still are. In our society preadolescents typically separate into one-sex gangs hostile to the opposite sex. Sexual relationships before marriage have traditionally taken the form of a kind of combat in which the male tries to seduce the female and she is supposed to resist his advances. Sexual disturbances, such as frigidity, impotence, and homosexuality, suggest that many people have a strong fear of the opposite sex. The battle of the sexes is reflected in widespread sexual humor: "Who was that lady I saw you with last night?" "That was no lady, that was my wife." There is an area of social life largely closed to women—men's clubs, men's business

This wall marked the boundary of the ghetto in Warsaw. The ghettos of Europe, established by tradition and law, were an expression of ethnocentrism.

contacts, men's athletic events, men's magazines. Men tend to resent any invasion. There is a similar closed area of women's clubs, bridge clubs, sewing circles, and women's social causes.

All the institutions of society tend to create in-groupings. We know the intense rivalry between educational institutions, especially when it is connected with athletics. There is often great political ethnocentrism in the members of the Democratic or Republican parties, in the Liberal, the Conservative, the Socialist, the Communist, or the John

Bircher. Art may divide its followers into sharply contending devotees of classical, jazz, or rock music, of traditional or contemporary painting. Professional interests are apt to develop ethnocentric in-groups, with strong feelings of superiority and rightness. In a society that grants them much prestige, this is likely to be true of the scientist, the engineer, the medical doctor, and the military. Other professions —public school teachers, osteopaths, insurance agents, social scientists— are likely to show exaggerated in-group characteristics in their efforts to convince themselves and others that they are equally deserving of prestige. There is often great antagonism between intellectuals and practical men, the latter often deriding the former as "eggheads" and being derided in turn as mindless muddlers.

Each of us should become aware of the in-groupings in his own life and ask whether the characteristics we have described apply to his attitudes. Then we might well ask: Why is ethnocentrism so widespread?

Some answers suggest themselves. No person can be attached to everyone else in the world with the same intensity. We all tend to feel closer to "our own," whatever the particular interests that draw us together. Also, we want and need to feel that those groups and activities with which our lives are most closely engaged are significant. There is also the attraction of the familiar. It is easier to follow habit, individual or collective, than to examine possible new ways. There is the threat that new patterns may, if we open our minds to them, destroy the balance of our group. Certainly this has happened, for example, in many cases where primitive peoples have been introduced to some of civilized man's ways.

But why the intense antagonism, the sharp downgrading of the outsider? One possible answer is that this behavior is rooted in human nature. Perhaps all people simply have a natural drive for status, an innate desire to be better than others. Perhaps there is so much inborn human aggressiveness in each of us that we can maintain peace within our in-groups only by directing our hostility toward outsiders. The founder of psychoanalysis, Sigmund Freud, held that religions can successfully preach love only if they also preach hatred of other religions. Perhaps we need enemies in order to be able to live with our friends.

A related answer is that ethnocentrism may not be inborn, but is still inevitable because it grows out of frustrations which all human beings must experience. None of us, so this view goes, can live and avoid being severely frustrated. We compensate for this frustration by inflating ourselves, by downgrading out-groups, and by taking our hostility out on these groups. We need some out-group and will create one if we do not find it. There is a sense of this in a conversation which a psychologist recounts with an SS guard at one of Hitler's concentration camps. The psychologist was being prepared for release, and told the guard that he was planning to go to the United States. As they spoke of America, the SS man said, "If we'd had the Negroes in Germany, we wouldn't have had to do this to you Jews."

Simple and convincing as they may seem, answers in terms of innate human nature are likely to be superficial. In this case they must clearly be modified in the light of the recent findings of studies on the authoritarian personality. These suggest that at least the extreme forms of in-group behavior cannot be attributed to human nature, but rather to a form of psychological sickness.

In the late 1940s, the American Jewish Committee undertook research whose aim was to understand the extreme kind of ethnocentrism that had led the "Aryan" Nazis to throw the Jewish out-group into gas chambers. In their study they used tests that distinguished people on the basis of their amount of ethnocentrism. They then related the strength of their in-group feelings to their life histories. There were three important findings.

1. People differ greatly in their degree of ethnocentrism. Some are relatively free from strong in-group attitudes, while such attitudes are central to the lives of others.

2. Ethnocentrism (or lack of it) is a general attitude in an individual's personality. One is seldom ethnocentric toward only a single group. An American, for example, who has ethnocentric feelings toward Negroes is also likely to have them toward Jews, other American ethnic groups, labor unions, foreigners, and Communists.

3. How ethnocentric a person will be depends primarily on how deeply gratified or frustrated he is in his life in general. The most important factor is whether he has grown up in an atmosphere of love and security or in an atmosphere of rejection, anxiety, and hostility. The person who can love others generally accepts difference without necessarily thinking of it in terms of inferiority and superiority. The person who is inwardly dominated by insecurity, fear, and hostility is likely to see all life as a battle in which the all-important question is, who is on top. He downgrades others to compensate for his sense of insecurity and uses them as targets for his great hostility.

We shall discuss these authoritarian personality studies again in later chapters. At this point they should show us that at least some ethnocentrism is less than inevitable, provided we can remove some of the sources of human frustration.

SOCIAL STRATIFICATION

We have already referred to the pecking order that exists among human beings, as in other species. We know that people are designated not only as different, but also as superior and inferior in terms of the power and privi-

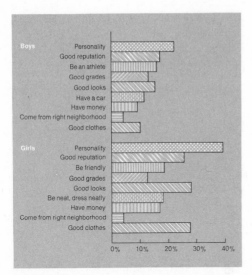

Figure 4.2. School status rating: attributes seen by high school students as important for inclusion in a leading crowd, by sex.
Source: James S. Coleman, *The Adolescent Society*, New York, Free Press, 1961, p. 40.

leges each enjoys. To use another figure, we can think of human society as like the layers of rock which we see in the wall of a highway cut. It is stratified into different social levels.

Three terms are important in discussing social stratification. These are *status, class,* and *caste.*

Every advanced society, at least, has a collective social "map" which its members carry around in their heads. Status refers to the position a person holds on the collective map. First of all, in every large organization there is a formal hierarchy or ranking of its members. This can be represented on an organization chart, which generally takes the form of a pyramid, with a few people at the top and increasing numbers on each level as one approaches the bottom. Military organization and the hierarchical structure of the Catholic Church are perhaps the best examples of highly organized formal status.

In the ordinary life of factory, office, school, hospital, and other organizations, we can see how important a part status plays. A nurse must be aware of the way doctors with whom she works

are ranked in the hospital hierarchy, on the basis of experience, income, skill, and other considerations. Top and junior executives are distinguished by the size of their offices and desks, the thickness of the carpet on the floor, the name plates on the desk or office door, the possession of a private secretary. A college professor, especially a young one in a small school, may be offended if he is not addressed as doctor, although in the higher status schools he might prefer to be called professor or just mister.

There are also statuses that are not ranked on any formal organization chart. In a factory office workers will almost always consider themselves above production line workers and may refuse to eat at the same lunch counter. In the adolescent society of the high school or college campus, each person has a position determined by looks, dress, family, personality, athletic ability, and even, to some extent, by grades! Figure 4.2 shows the qualities necessary to win membership in the "leading crowd" in a sample group of ten high schools studied by James S. Coleman. The adolescent's striving for status is a preparation for status seeking in adult business and social life.

In society as a whole, we recognize the existence of social classes. We know that there are a so-called right and a wrong side of the tracks. Most of us are likely to distinguish at least three classes—lower, middle, and upper.

There are two important elements in social class, an objective and a subjective one. The objective aspect concerns people's outward position in society, regardless of what they themselves or others may think or feel about it. Objectively, the way people make a living tends to divide them into groups with common interests. Particularly important is the occupation they pursue and whether or not they own their own means of livelihood. The subjective aspect of class involves the way in which people place themselves and are placed by others on the collective social map. Subjectively a class is a group of people who feel themselves and are felt by others to be a class. It is a group that shares a common social status.

In this argument for the American Constitution in the *Federalist Papers,* James Madison spoke of objective factors which divide society into conflicting groups:

> *The most common and durable source of factions has been the various and unequal distribution of property. Those who hold and those who are without property have ever formed distinct interests in society. Those who are creditors, and those who are debtors, fall under a like discrimination. A landed interest, a manufacturing interest, a mercantile interest, a moneyed interest, with many lesser interests, grow up of necessity in civilized nations, and divide them into different classes, actuated by different sentiments and values. The regulation of these various and interfering interests forms the principal task of modern legislation.*[1]

The most famous and influential treatment of class in terms of objective position appeared in 1848, in the *Communist Manifesto* by Karl Marx and Friedrich Engels.

> *The History of all hitherto existing society is the history of class struggles. . . . In the earlier epochs of history we find almost everywhere a complicated arrangement of society into various orders, a manifold gradation of social rank. In ancient Rome we have patricians, knights, plebians, slaves; in the Middle Ages, feudal lords, vassals, guild masters, journeymen, apprentices, serfs; in almost all of these classes, again, subordinate gradations.*
> *The modern bourgeois society*

> *that has sprouted from the ruins of feudal society has not done away with class antagonisms. It has but established new classes, new conditions of oppression, new forms of struggle in place of the old ones.*[2]

In the society of 1848, Marx and Engels distinguished the lower-middle class, the small manufacturer, the shopkeeper, the artisan, and the peasant, as well as the two classes which they thought most significant; the *bourgeoisie,* or large capitalists, and the *proletariat,* or industrial workers.

If we were to study occupational groups in the United States today, and ask how they have changed in the last 75 years, we would reach a classification somewhat like this:

> *Independent farm owners and tenant farmers, who have declined in proportion to the population.*
> *Farm laborers, who have likewise declined in percentage.*
> *Unskilled industrial workers, who have declined percentage-wise.*
> *Independent business and professional people, who have declined proportionately.*
> *Semi-skilled and skilled (blue collar) workers, who have increased proportionately.*
> *White collar workers, salaried professional people, people in service trades, government employees, all of whom have increased enormously.*
> *Large corporation ownership and management, who remain about the same percentage-wise.*

Many modern social scientists have felt that economic or other objective factors are not enough to make a class, unless people are conscious of having common interests and a common position. They have, therefore, brought the subjective approach into the study of class. The best-known

1. Henry Steele Commager, *Living Ideas in America,* New York, Harper & Row, 1951, p. 166.

2. Harold J. Laski, Karl Marx, and Friedrich Engels, *Harold J. Laski on The Communist Manifesto,* New York, Random House, 1967, pp. 131, 132.

study of social class in America, the famous Yankee City survey of Newburyport, Massachusetts, in the 1940s, was one of this type. W. Lloyd Warner set about to classify the people of Newburyport by asking each person (1) where he placed himself and (2) where he placed other types of people. The result was a system of six classes, which picturesquely divided each of the lower, middle, and upper classes into two. The accompanying table shows the size of classes in Newburyport and also how they were related to objective economic position.

When the sociologists Davis and Gardner took Warner's scheme to the deep South, they had to add another important dimension, for they found color castes—groupings of people who held a status from which they could not escape. There were much the same six classes as in Warner's study, but there were also two groups, whose status was determined by birth, from which there was no exit to any other group.

Negroes, like whites, had their class distinctions, although there were *few* or *none* in either of the two upper classes. But every white person, no matter how low in status, outranked even the highest Negroes in, for example, ability to eat at a white restaurant, attend a white school, or play golf at a white country club. White and Negro, as Davis and Gardner found them, were not separated quite so completely as the hereditary castes of India, but they were arranged in a semi-caste system which looked like the accompanying diagram. (The situation has changed markedly in many parts of the South, but we should not underestimate the amount of color caste today in either the South or the North.)

Clearly one's position in the social pecking order shapes his behavior, his ideas, and his privileges. In 1955 the average income of the top one-tenth of the American population, after taxes, was 27 times that of the bottom one-tenth. Social classes are likely to have different economic attitudes. Middle-

class people in our society have traditionally placed a strong emphasis on hard work and thrift. "A penny saved is a penny earned" is a typical middle-class motto. It is much less likely to appeal to a lower-class person who sees little hope of getting ahead or to an upper-class individual who "has it made." Political preference is so much influenced by class that one can usually tell, in driving through any part of a city, whether it is predominantly Democrat or Republican. The wrong side of the tracks is likely to be Democrat, the right side, Republican. The Democratic "solid South" has been an exception, but even that is developing Republican areas, mainly upper-middle and upper class. Religious membership and behavior tend to follow class lines. Among Protestant groups an Episcopalian is likely to be higher on the social scale than a Methodist, a Congregationalist higher than a member of the Holiness sects.

Different classes bring up their children differently. Until recently middle-class mothers were likely to wean their children and toilet train them earlier than working-class mothers and were more likely to discourage sexual exploration and physical violence. In recent years, on the contrary, college-trained mothers have often become more permissive. In his famous researches on sexual behavior in 1948 and 1954, Kinsey found strong class differences in sexual activity and attitudes. Working-class boys, for example, were likely to begin having sexual relationships with girls much earlier than middle-class boys. (In fact, Kinsey found that by knowing a young adolescent boy's sexual activity, one could predict fairly accurately his social status as an adult. If he was having intercourse with girls, a boy of fourteen would very likely wind up as a mechanic or a store clerk. If masturbation was his typical sexual outlet, the chances were good that he would eventually be a businessman, a lawyer, a doctor, or a college professor.) On the other hand, he found that lower-

Upper-upper	1.4%	Birth and inherited wealth
Lower-upper	1.6	Finance, industry, professions
Upper-middle	10.0	Professions and large businessmen
Lower-middle	28.0	Small business, white collar, skilled workmen
Upper-lower	33.0	Semiskilled, service, a few small tradesmen
Lower-lower	25.0	Semiskilled, unskilled

class people accepted nudity much less easily than those higher on the social ladder. We can observe that one rarely sees a working-class man, for example, in shorts. Kinsey found that working-class people generally insisted on remaining partially clothed even when having sexual intercourse.

Some class differences are more dramatic. When the steamship *Titanic* went down in mid-Atlantic in 1912, first-class passengers were loaded into lifeboats while many third-class passengers were held in the steerage at the points of guns. This is only one illustration of the fact that one's life chances differ according to his social class. Because they come from the middle class or have developed middle-class values, most teachers are likely (even though often unaware of what they are doing) to be prejudiced against lower-class children and to give them poorer grades. The poor have a greater chance of contracting almost any disease, of being drafted into the Army, of dying at birth or in infancy. A famous New Haven study by Hollingshead, a sociologist, and Redlich, a psychiatrist, showed that the amount of treated mental illness in the lowest social class was about three times as great as the rate in any higher class. The treatment was also inferior! Upper-class people were likely to get extensive and expensive psychiatry, while lower-class people were more likely to receive shock treatment or lobotomy (brain surgery).

The disadvantages of lower-class position have commonly motivated people to move upward. Movement up or down the social scale is called *vertical mobility,* by contrast with horizontal, or geographical, movement from place to place.

Caste is an example of very high

vertical immobility. Under feudalism, the social system typical of the Middle Ages in Europe and of much of South America and Asia today, vertical mobility has been greatly restricted, though not so severely as in a caste system. The birth of modern technological society in the Commercial and Industrial Revolution produced two factors that increased vertical mobility. New, uninhabited geographical frontiers all over the world enabled people caught in rigid class situations to migrate and begin afresh. New economic frontiers—expansion of commerce and industry, the development of new occupations and skills—also enabled many people to rise. The United States, with its vast frontier lands and vast natural resources developed privately, and with its slogans of "from rags to riches" and "from log cabin to White House," became the extreme example of this mobility.

When the geographical frontiers had been settled, however—as in the United States about 1890—the individual became increasingly at the mercy of ever-larger organizations. At least as far as movement to the top is concerned, American society has become less mobile in the last century. A study by the sociologist C. Wright Mills concerning the origins of very rich men showed that in 1890, 39 percent had come from the lower class of small farmers, storekeepers, and white-collar and wage workers. In 1950 only 9 percent had come from this class. The percentage of rich men who had been born rich was 39 percent in 1890 and 68 percent in 1950. In the last 25 years, mass education has opened new opportunities for lower-class young people to rise to the status of upper-middle class. In fact, formal education has become the chief ladder of vertical mobility in the United States. Negroes have become less caste-bound and more vertically mobile than 10 or 15 years ago. There are no longer, however, many physical frontiers in the world. If we are to continue to have much vertical mobility in the future, we will need many new frontiers of economic invention and opportunity.

Throughout human history there have always been dreams of the maximum vertical mobility, a classless society with no stratification at all. Every society has had the myth of a lost Golden Age of greater freedom and equality. Since the days of ancient Israel, prophets have always exhorted us to "seek justice, correct oppression; defend the fatherless, plead for the widow." Since the early days of Christianity, people have periodically set up voluntary communities based upon a primitive "communism" involving equality and common ownership of property. (The kubbutzim [communal farms] in Israel are a modern-day example.) When modern capitalism first arose, many people saw it as the avenue to a society of many small independent farmers and craftsmen in which old inequalities would be eliminated. The scientific socialism of Marx looked forward to a final revolution in which class rule would be brought to an end, and social inequality would wither away.

Are such dreams at all realistic? To answer this question we must ask why social stratification exists.

The human pecking order, many would argue, is rooted in the individual desire for security and the collective desire for social peace. These desires go back to our animal ancestors, as observed both in nature and the laboratory. There are never enough resources to assure plenty for everyone. Status is one way for an animal to assure itself food, sexual mates, and other advantages. For the animal or human society, establishment of a pecking order serves to bring an armistice in the struggle for existence. Thereafter everyone knows where he,

and others, stand and accepts the situation.

It is also argued that stratification grows out of a natural inequality in the members of any group. "Society," said the twentieth-century Spanish philosopher, Ortega y Gasset, "is always a dynamic unity of two factors: minorities and masses. . . . The minorities are individuals or groups of individuals who are specially qualified. The mass is the assemblage of persons not specially qualified."[3] One often hears the argument that if all wealth were divided equally, in a very short time the strong, intelligent, and ambitious would again have the largest share of money and privilege.

It is also held that stratification is a necessary result of the specialization, or division of labor, which exists in any technologically advanced society. At the Bushman end of the continuum, society is fairly homogeneous, and the problems of group life are simple. There may therefore be relatively little difference in status, although in some cases there is great difference. (A famous study of Cooperation and Competition Among Primitive Peoples, edited by the anthropologist Margaret Mead in 1936, found strong status systems among the South Sea Manus, the Kwakiutl Indians of British Columbia, and the Ifugao of the Philippines. On the other hand, there was hardly any sense of status among the Zuni and Ojibwa Indians, the Eskimo of Greenland, and the Arapesh of New Guinea.) When, however, a society becomes complex so that the activities of many kinds of people have to be coordinated on a large scale, it is necessary to establish levels of command. Those who make more of the necessary decisions acquire wealth, power, and privilege. This, it is argued, is inevitable in any complex social organization.

Finally, it is contended that historic facts argue against the possibility of a

3. José Ortega y Gasset, The Revolt of the Masses, London, Allen & Unwin, 1951, p. 9.

classless society. The German political scientist, Robert Michels, who grew up in the Socialist dream of equality, saw liberal and Socialist regimes, once in power, establishing the same kind of hierarchy that they once condemned. From this observation he formulated the "iron law of oligarchy" (rule by the few): we can never have an end to rule by a minority, but only an exchange of minority groups. Capitalist dreams of an equalitarian society of small producers have given way to a society dominated by large, centralized organizations. The Bolshevik Revolution in Russia has resulted in rule by a new class of bureaucrats who have taken the place of the czar and the bourgeoisie. Colonial peoples have freed themselves from the white man only to fall under native dictators.

Strong as these arguments are, there are those who do not accept them as final. Status is most necessary for security, they rejoin, in poor societies. When there is a relative abundance of food, it becomes less important. This is demonstrated in some animal groups. As we learn to use our technology to produce enough for everybody, social rank may become less important. Status is also less necessary when people are psychologically secure. This we say in observing that the anxiety-ridden individual needs to have others beneath him, while the more emotionally secure person has less need for such compensations. As we are able to increase people's inner sense of security, we may reduce their need for status. Then differences in the division of labor need not necessarily lead to general ratings of superiority and inferiority. People may simply recognize that everyone has his own peculiar combination of capabilities and also of shortcomings. We might then become like the Wintu Indians of California and the Trobriand islanders of Melanesia, among neither of whom could the anthropologist Dorothy Lee find any comparisons made between individuals.

The systems of power and privilege which we have known through most of recorded history, it may be argued, have arisen more out of force and deception than out of inequality in socially useful talents. There are clearly innate differences among people, but we do not know that social stratification represents these differences. There may be a higher percentage of people with intelligence and other inborn capabilities among the upper classes than among the lower, but this has not been proved. We do know that, as has happened in the case of the American Indian and Negro, people have very often been deprived of opportunity, and then they and their descendants have been charged with being inferior. Historic social stratification, the argument continues, has not advanced the interests of society as a whole as much as it has advanced the interests of a few. We may be able to learn how to incorporate much of the equality and mutual respect of the simpler, nonprehistoric peoples into a technologically advanced society and be both more productive and happy as a result of the change.

We shall not attempt now to reach a final resolution of this debate. Let us rather see what light the rest of the book throws on it.

CONFLICT AND COOPERATION

From the question of class differences, we move logically to the role of antagonistic and cooperative forces in society. Are competition and conflict the main factors in human relations? Is cooperation normal and antagonism a form of pathology, or are both natural, so that all life is what one social scientist called "antagonistic cooperation"? Is struggle between classes and other groups a natural condition or a disturbance of healthy social relationships? Does economic competition express natural human tendencies, or would a cooperative economy be more desirable and "human"? Is war natural and inevitable, or is it a form of social sickness that we can hope to overcome?

We can see that some of our most important human questions fall in this area. They have been answered in sharply different ways. Let us look first at some answers which have emphasized the social role of conflict.

Somewhat more than a century ago, there came to prominence a view of social life known as Social Darwinism. This took Darwin's theories of evolution and applied them to society, specifically to the world of nineteenth-century free enterprise capitalism. According to Darwin the central fact in biological life is the universal struggle for existence. In this struggle the weak or unfit are eliminated and the fit remain. It is through this constant biological competition and conflict that evolutionary progress has taken place; that is, we have seen the development and survival of individuals and species constantly better adapted to their environment.

Social Darwinism holds that human social life operates, and should operate, in the same way. In society every individual struggles to secure money, power, and other social values. How well he succeeds depends on his capacities, energy, and initiative. Social stratification is, on the whole, a measure of fitness in this social struggle— the fit move to the top, the unfit remain or fall to the bottom. Free enterprise capitalism is the ideal economic expression of this social struggle for existence. Under capitalism every person is free to compete with his talents against everyone else. Those who fail are eventually eliminated. Thus economic competition serves the evolutionary purpose of improving human society through survival of the fittest.

Socialism, which would replace economic competition by cooperation, would, in this view, defeat the evolutionary process. Progressive social legislation to protect workers—child labor laws, workmen's compensation laws, minimum wage laws, laws protecting union organization—also impedes the natural working of competition. Even welfare legislation to help the poor is likely to be socially undesirable, for it will probably encourage dependency on others rather than on their own initiative, or keep them reproducing when they should be eliminated by the natural process of selection.

A related view of conflict stresses the naturalness of war. There will always be wars and rumors of wars, it is contended. Contemporary writer Robert Ardrey holds that war is rooted in two basic aspects of human nature. First, man, like all other animals, naturally stakes out a territory and defends it. The territorial drive is very likely even stronger than the sex drive. Second, man is by nature a hunter and killer. Archaeological research, says Ardrey, shows that his most distinguishing feature is the use of weapons. Modern war is an acting out of the natural territorial and predatory impulses.

War, it has also been argued, is a positive force in many ways. The needs of war have often stimulated invention and technological development; radar was developed in Britain under the impetus of World War II. As was the case with the thirteen American colonies, war may help form larger and more inclusive political units (in that case, the United States). War, it has been contended, is a way of ensuring the survival of the fittest. It strengthens people's fiber and promotes values of self-assertion and courage which are likely to lag in peacetime. The Fascist leader Benito Mussolini felt that war brought out people's greatest energy and nobility.

We have already touched on the view that there are conflicts between classes or other groups that cannot be reconciled. There are two ways of viewing the class struggle. The conservative version sees an elite of competent people and a mass of incompetent people who would overthrow it. "I hold," said John C. Calhoun in his defense of slavery in the Senate in 1837, "that there never has yet existed a wealthy and civilized society in which one portion of the community did not, in point of fact, live on the labor of the other." Nine years earlier he had written, "There is and always has been in an advanced stage of wealth and civilization a conflict between labor and capital." He predicted that capitalist society would divide into two classes, capitalists and operatives, and that the former would make the latter propertyless and poverty stricken and create a revolutionary crisis. He hoped that the capitalists of the North and South would join in self-defense against this threat.

Marx and his followers held a similar view of the class struggle in general and of the situation under capitalism, but their sympathies were with the other side. They hoped to bring about a revolution, for they felt that only through such conflict are mass injustices overcome. Marx was willing to believe that conflict between classes might sometimes be resolved peacefully, although he was not very hopeful. Some (not all) anarchists, like the nineteenth-century Russian, Michael Bakunin, have, on the other hand, glorified the role of violent conflict itself as a necessary means of social improvement. "Let us put our trust," said Bakunin, "in the eternal spirit which destroys and annihilates only because it is the unsearchable and creative source of all life. The urge to destroy is also a creative urge."[4]

Those who stress the role of conflict are likely to feel that their position is based on a realistic view of human nature. "To his fellow man," said Sigmund Freud, "man is a wolf; who has the courage to dispute it in the face of all the evidence in his own life and in history?" People who emphasize conflict tend to consider themselves realistic and toughminded and to regard ideas of a more cooperative, humanitarian, and peaceful society as romantic, sentimental, and tender-minded.

Freud spoke rather contemptuously of well-meaning optimists who try to deny the reality of conflict "with their lullaby-song of Heaven."[5]

How shall we evaluate these views which stress human antagonism?

Clearly all life involves struggle for existence in an environment which is far from being entirely friendly to our desires. The fact that every species has excess fecundity is evidence of this; that is, each species is capable of producing many more offspring than would be necessary to maintain it were not the surplus killed off by accident, disease, or combat. Nature, so to speak, expects a large percentage of life to perish in the struggle for survival.

As Darwin said, there is not only struggle against nature, but struggle among species. Different forms of life compete for the available food supply, as every farmer who has tried to keep insects from eating his crops knows. The very act of eating involves the destruction of one or another form of life, so that the only way for an individual to avoid destroying other plant or animal organisms is to commit suicide. There is also competition within species. As long as land, food, wealth, or other desired values are less than sufficient to satisfy the desires of all people, there must be some kind of competition for them. One social scientist put it:

As the saying is, we all want the earth. We all have a multiplicity of desires and demands which we seek to satisfy. There are very many of us but there is only one earth. The desires of each continually conflict with or overlap those of his neighbors.[6]

It is possible, however, to overestimate the role of conflict. In the nine-

4. George Woodcock, *Anarchism,* Cleveland, World, 1962, p. 151.

5. Sigmund Freud, *Civilization and Its Discontents,* trans. Joan Riviere, New York, Cape & Smith, 1930, p. 85.

6. Roscoe Pound, *Social Control Through Law,* New Haven, Yale University Press, 1942, p. 64.

teenth-century world of rugged individualism, people tended to see only one side of the struggle for existence. They forgot that cooperation is at least as basic as antagonism.

This overemphasis was criticized by the Russian geographer, Peter Kropotkin. As a young man, Kropotkin spent many years studying the animal life of Siberia. He came to the conclusion that conflict and battle play a smaller part in the life of wild animals than most followers of Darwin had supposed. On the other hand, he was impressed by the extent of cooperation in animal life. In 1902 he set forth his conclusions in the famous book, *Mutual Aid: A Factor in Evolution.*

> *Two aspects of animal life impressed me most during the journeys which I made in my youth in Eastern Siberia and Northern Manchuria. One of them was the extreme severity of the struggle for existence which most species of animals have to carry on against an inclement Nature; the enormous destruction of life which periodically results from natural agencies; and the consequent paucity of life over the vast territory which fell under my observation. And the other was, that even in those few spots where animal life teemed in abundance, I failed to find—although I was eagerly looking for it— that bitter struggle for the means of existence, among animals belonging to the same species, which was considered by most Darwinists (though not always by Darwin himself) as the dominant characteristic of struggle for life, and the main factor of evolution.[7]*

The Social Darwinists, said Kropotkin, had confused struggle against the environment and struggle within species. Darwin was generally very careful to support his theories with evidence, but of the struggle *within* species he had not offered "even one single instance." Here, contrary to the ideas of Social Darwinism, cooperation and mutual aid were far more prevalent than competition and conflict. We have already seen the depth to which social impulses and behavior are rooted, not only in man, but in all life. Kropotkin agreed with Espinas' observations on the universal nature of cooperative behavior, without which no species could survive—sexual cooperation, cooperation in rearing the young, cooperation in the economic division of labor, cooperation in mutual defense.

The higher we get on the evolutionary scale, he said, the more important and conscious is mutual aid. Man is the greatest example of the animal which has survived because he is cooperative. It is our high capacity for mutual aid that has made us supreme in the evolutionary competition. Darwin, indeed, far from regarding the natural condition as an endless war within species, had spoken of the central role of cooperation.

> *Those communities which included the greatest number of the most sympathetic members would flourish best, and rear the greatest number of offspring. . . . The small strength and speed of man, his want of natural weapons, etc., are more than counterbalanced, firstly, by his intellectual faculties; and secondly, by his social qualities, which led him to give and receive aid from his fellow men.[8]*

The dog-eat-dog struggle of every man for himself thus works against the evolutionary survival of man. Had early man behaved like a nineteenth-century rugged individualist, the species could never have continued. The aborigines of Australia, among the most primitive peoples known to anthropology, had a clan organization so complex that it is

7. Peter A. Kropotkin, *Mutual Aid: A Factor in Evolution,* Boston, Extending Horizons Books, 1955, p. vii.

8. Charles Darwin, *The Descent of Man,* London, John Murray, 1881, pp. 107, 164.

difficult for us even to learn all the different relationships among people which their language distinguishes. Among other survivals of Stone Age peoples—the Papuans of New Guinea, the Eskimos, the Fuegians of Patagonia—we find not individual struggle, but communal ownership. Kropotkin believed that there was good reason to think that this was how our early ancestors typically lived. Slavery introduced intergroup struggle. Yet, for the most part, civilized man has typically lived in small agricultural villages, with a long tradition of mutual aid in construction, planting, cultivation, and harvest. In western Europe, business and industry were first organized in guilds which strictly limited competition. It is only with the rise of the modern state and modern capitalism in the last 400 or 500 years, said Kropotkin, that competitive individualism has become widespread.

Anthropologists have not found universal competition. In Margaret Mead's study of *Cooperation and Competition Among Primitive Peoples,*[9] two primitive groups, the Ifugao of the Philippine Islands and the Kwakiutl of British Columbia, showed an intense competition for wealth and prestige resembling that of Western individualism. More common was the emphasis on cooperation shown by the Zuni and Hopi Indians of the American Southwest, the Dakota Indians of the American Plains, the Iroquois of the American East, the Bathonga natives of South Africa, and the native Maori of New Zealand. Among these peoples individual competition for wealth and status was generally unimportant or positively discouraged.

Instead, widespread cooperation was typical in such activities as the holding of land; the storing and distribution of food; the planting, cultivation, and harvest of crops; the building of villages; and the conduct of arts and crafts. Among the Bathonga it was reported that there was a striking absence of competitive activities. Prestige among the Dakota depended most of all upon good personal relations. Among the Iroquois there was great pleasure in working together. The highest status, aside from that given of birth, was awarded to those who were outstanding in cooperation. With the Zuni anyone who accumulated extra property distributed it to the tribe at the winter festival. Among them, said the report, "It is . . . the cooperative person, ready to share his food with his relations and needy friends, ready to assist his neighbor or religious or clan colleague in agricultural labor, who is most respected in the community."[10]

Contrary to the claims of the Social Darwinists, where competition does prevail, there is no guarantee that those who survive are fittest from the standpoint of societal welfare. Competitive success may, it is true, reflect superior ability to contribute to society. Very often, however, it is the result of little more than, for lack of a better term, luck. It may also reflect ability to "feather one's own nest" at the expense of society. In this case those who survive may be about the least fit from the social standpoint. "In a sewer," said the French novelist Victor Hugo, "the sewer rats survive."

The findings of anthropology on the subject of war likewise question the inevitability or desirability of conflict. In the Mead study, the competitive societies were warlike, both toward outsiders and within the group itself. But the cooperative peoples, under favorable conditions, were mostly peaceful. The people of the remote Atlantic Island of Tristan da Cunha, described by the anthropologist Peter Munch, not only do not have war, but have no memory even of a fight. If we define war as an "organized clash of armed forces aiming at the enforcement of a tribal policy," it is, according to the anthropologist Bronislaw Malinowski, ab-

9. Margaret Mead, *Cooperation and Competition Among Primitive Peoples,* revised ed., Boston, Beacon, 1961.

10. *Ibid.,* p. 314.

sent in a large number of primitive peoples. Examples of peoples without war are the aborigines of Australia, the Eskimos of Greenland and the Bering Straits, and the Veddahs of Ceylon.

There are anger, cruelty, head hunting, and fighting for sport among many primitive peoples, but in few is there any organized warfare, says Malinowski. This begins only with the development of slavery. Then war serves as a means of getting slaves. Organized warfare is also connected with the rise of agriculture. After men formed permanent agricultural settlements, about 8000 years ago, there was a surplus of wealth to be gained by organized raiding. This organized warfare is an institution developed in a relatively recent history—the last several thousands of years out of man's million and a half on earth.

In 1936, before the Atomic Age, Malinowski said that, whatever positive contributions it had made in the past, war is now obsolete. The historian Arnold Toynbee has held that no past war had enough benefits to be justified. Many students of the subject would claim more benefits in the past, but agree with Malinowski about war in our age. Undoubtedly war has stimulated invention in the past and continues to do so. There are, however, certainly equally effective and less dangerous ways of stimulating technology. In World War II, whatever technical gains that would not have been made without the war have to be weighed against the tremendous human and physical destruction. Should World War III occur, it is even less likely that there could be a balance of technological gain. War undoubtedly demands much courage, but so do other "moral equivalents of war," as the philosopher William James described them. One can become a Peace Corps worker in a backward and hostile country, or a civil rights worker in a violent segregationist area. It is hard to find much support for the argument that war improves the human stock for the evolutionary struggle. Traditionally, war has killed the physically most fit and allowed the physically weakest to survive. In modern war whole populations are destroyed indiscriminately.

There is certainly a common tendency in men, as in other animals, to stake out and defend a territory. Certainly the sense that "a man's home is his castle" is very strong. This leads to the impulse to defend one's country, which is one of the most powerful appeals of war. Every war, even the most aggressive, is justified as a defense against invasion, now or later. Except where there is actual invasion, however, men do not seem to flock spontaneously to war. On the contrary, every major nation must draft its young men in order to get them to exercise their "territorial imperative" (as Ardrey calls it). The territorial impulse does not seem very closely related to the motives that lead modern nations or soldiers to fight.

The claim that war and conflict grow out of a predatory impulse is equally doubtful. Ardrey may very well be right in claiming that our most immediate ancestor, the ape man *Australopithecus Africanus* of central Africa, was unique in that he had learned to use weapons to hunt and kill. But hunting is not war. Neither does it mean that the hunter is necessarily cruel, hostile, or generally violent. Hunting peoples can, like the Bushmen, be quite peaceful and friendly. The use of weapons may have been merely a better way to eat. The habits of a remote man-ape ancestor can tell us very little about man today, and certainly very little about the complex institution of modern war. War undoubtedly satisfies cruel and destructive impulses, however they may arise, for some people. For most soldiers, however, it provides mostly boredom, fear, and the compulsion to perform cruel acts in spite of their kinder impulses. Again, if man had a primitive, predatory impulse that somehow led him to war like lemmings to the sea, it would hardly be necessary to draft him to fight.

The problem of war illustrates the

fallacy of trying to explain complex social institutions in terms of simple biological instincts. In the section on The Psychological Basis we shall discuss further the problem of human nature in relation to social institutions. It is enough to say here that the relationship is very much more complex than it is often thought to be.

While questioning the arguments in favor of the inevitability or usefulness of conflict, we must however recognize that absence of open conflict is not always what it may seem. Well-intentioned people concerned with promoting good human relations are sometimes quick to see the problems associated with conflict, while they overlook the problems that it may resolve.

There are undoubtedly married couples who never quarrel because they have no serious disagreements, but the couple who claim never to have exchanged a harsh word may be preserving the peace of their marriage by blinding themselves to their real differences. Americans who look back at the "good" race relations which supposedly existed before "agitators" stirred up the Negro population, are likely to be closing their eyes to the inequality and misery which lay beneath racial peace. The same is true of many who blame Communists for creating class struggle. Good industrial relations between capital and labor may simply mean that workers lack the strength or insight to protest. International peace may mean simply submission to tyranny.

Those who deplore the visible damage done in open conflict often forget the less visible "violence of the status quo" (things as they are). They ignore the undramatic suffering of people who lead "lives of quiet desperation" under unjust conditions. The Indian leader Gandhi believed that creative conflict should be nonviolent. He led a successful nonviolent revolution against imperial Britain, yet Gandhi said that it is better to use violence than to submit to injustice because one fears conflict.

Such considerations are behind the contentions of those who argue the beneficial effect of intergroup or class struggle. It is not that they themselves desire conflict, they usually say. They would much rather settle matters through rational discussion, but groups in power often are unwilling to allow change to take place. Thus civil rights leaders have felt forced to take to the streets in racial demonstrations as the only alternative to submission. Revolutionary leaders in the underdeveloped nations have felt that only pressure could move the colonial powers.

It is encouraging that we have succeeded in setting up national legislation (such as civil rights laws) and international machinery (such as United Nations agencies) for settling many differences that would previously have led to physical violence. It is encouraging to find some groups, such as colonial Britain, willing at times to give up power peaceably. It is also encouraging that, where conflict has seemed unavoidable, underprivileged groups have begun to develop nonviolent methods—as in India, in the civil rights movement, and in the organization of migrant farm workers. It is encouraging that even the most ardent advocates of class and race struggle do not generally value conflict for its own sake, but look forward to a time when it will no longer be necessary because the causes will have been removed.

Among the most important causes of conflict is certainly scarcity of resources. It would be too simple to expect that economic plenty would bring complete social peace. If this were so, the United States should already be Utopia, for while many people are still poor, we have enough resources that they need not be. In the Mead study, the Ifugao Filipinos were competitive and hostile despite a rich food supply, while the Hopi were highly cooperative with very poor economic resources. Nevertheless, on the whole, we cannot expect miserable and poverty-stricken people to be peaceful and cooperative unless they have been so degraded that they lack the energy and will to

resist. If we can use our technical resources to relieve the scarcity that is
still the lot of most of the human race,
we shall without doubt have taken a
very long step toward a more peaceful
world.

Suggestions for further reading

*Although there are many more recent books on
the subject, WILLIAM GRAHAM SUMNER's*
Folkways (*Ginn, 1940*) *is still a basic and
fascinating work on the structure of society.*

*Two fundamental books on subhuman social
life are* Social Life Among the Insects, *by
WILLIAM MORTON WHEELER (Brace, 1923) and*
The Social Life of Animals *by W. C. ALLEE
(Beacon, 1958).*

*Background for the Bushman-New Yorker
continuum will be found in* Peasant Society and
Culture (*University of Chicago Press, 1956*), *by
the anthropologist ROBERT REDFIELD, whose
major area of professional experience was the
Mexican folk society of Yucatan. Background of
another kind appears in the beautiful and
moving accounts of the Bushmen by South
African writer LAURENS VAN DER POST. An
excellent example is* The Heart of the Hunter
(*Apollo, 1966, paper*).

*Two important analyses of in-grouping (in this
case, racial) are JOHN DOLLARD's* Caste and
Class in a Southern Town (*Doubleday, 1957,
paper) and* Killers of the Dream (*Doubleday,
1963, paper), by the Georgia novelist LILLIAN
SMITH. The second is perhaps the most revealing single book on the fundamentals of race
relations in the historic South. A timely study of
age in-grouping is* The Adolescent Society, *by
JAMES S. COLEMAN (Free Press, 1961). The*
Authoritarian Personality, *edited by T. W.
ADORNO et al. (Norton, 1969, paper) reports
the American Jewish Committee's attempts to*

*understand scientifically the kind of in-group
feeling which leads to ethnocentric expressions
like Nazi anti-Semitism.*

*The most famous study of the class system
of the United States is the "Yankee City" survey
by W. LLOYD WARNER, PAUL L. LUNT, and
others,* The Status System of a Modern Community (*Yale University Press, 1942; rev. by
P. Smith, 1960). A useful broad collection on
social stratification is* Class, Status, and Power,
*edited by SEYMOUR MARTIN LIPSET and
REINHARD BENDIX (Free Press, 1953). The
dramatic findings of AUGUST B. HOLLINGS-
HEAD and FREDERICK C. REDLICH on class
differences in frequency and treatment of mental
disorder are reported in* Social Class and Mental
Illness (*Wiley, 1958*).

PETER KROPOTKIN'S famous study, Mutual
Aid: A Factor in Evolution, *first published in
1902, was most recently made available by
Extending Horizons Books (Sargent, 1955).
More recent anthropolitical work on the subject
is edited by MARGARET MEAD in* Cooperation
and Competition Among Primitive Peoples (*rev.
ed., Beacon, 1961, paper). Those interested in
the idea that combat is an innate and inevitable
part of social relations may wish to read
KONRAD LORENZ,* On Aggression (*Harcourt
Brace Jovanovich, 1966) and ROBERT ARDREY,*
The Territorial Imperative (*Atheneum, 1966).
See also WYNNE-EDWARDS,* Animal Dispersion
in Relation to Social Behaviour, *in suggested
readings for Chapter three.*

Chapter five
The psychological basis

To understand society and its possibilities, we must look at it not only from the outside, but from the inside. Social life involves not only an organization of human relationships, but also the experience of human beings. All of us have needs and impulses which we strive to gratify. We find ways that are successful and tend to repeat them. We try ways that prove unsuccessful and tend to reject them. In the whole process we are shaped by our environment, and we also shape it.

We need to examine how our experience is related to our society. This examination is important because, in the first place, we as people are the goal of social institutions. The welfare of human beings is the ultimate reason for the existence of social science. Such examination is also important because social behavior cannot be understood without a knowledge of what goes on inside people.

HUMAN NATURE

A good place to begin is with the problem of human nature. People are the building blocks of society. The kind of society we can construct is limited by the kind of human material with which we must work. What kind of material are we? How is human nature different from the nature of animals? To what extent are we shaped by rather inflexible inborn patterns (instincts, drives, urges) which we inherit? To what extent are we plastic material which can

be molded to fit almost any variety of social patterns?

There is a strong tendency to explain social institutions in terms of inborn and unchangeable qualities in human beings. In the previous chapter we saw how war and economic competition have been identified with human nature. Firm discipline is justified as a necessary way to bring a child's willful nature in line with social demands. Sex discrimination was long defended on the ground of the natural inferiority of women. Television violence is regarded by some as a healthy outlet for natural destructive impulses. Slavery was once upheld on the ground that some people are born to rule and others to be ruled. Real democracy is sometimes held to be impossible because people naturally shirk responsibility and want to be led. Such explanations of social behavior are usually accompanied by the statement that "you can't change human nature."

Views of this kind are closely related to the belief that man has rather fixed instincts. In the early part of this century, this kind of explanation received a good deal of acceptance among social scientists. The great philosopher and psychologist, William James, defined instinct as "the faculty of acting in such a way as to produce certain ends without foresight of the ends, and without previous education in the performance." Instincts were thus (1) inborn, (2) without conscious purpose, and (3) unlearned. James listed 28 important instincts. A famous explanation of human behavior in terms of instinct was that of William McDougall, who listed thirteen instincts along with their accompanying emotions.

These classifications by James and McDougall appear in the table above. We should neither accept nor reject them at this point, but it will be helpful to study them carefully and ask ourselves the question: To what extent do these instincts, as we see them expressed in our own experience, meet William James's definition? To what degree, for example, are hunting, cleanliness, shyness, hoarding, and parental love hereditary, unpurposeful, and unlearned?

Such formulations as those of James and McDougall came under criticism by psychologists and other social scientists. One problem was that not all the listed instincts, though supposed to be inborn, are present at birth. Sucking is, but the carrying of objects to the mouth, crawling and walking, speech, sexual reproduction, and hunting all arise considerably later. If these are innate and unlearned behavior, where are the instincts in the interval before they actually make their appearance? Advocates of the instinct theory were likely to reply with the concept of *maturation:* not all instincts appear at birth, but some make their appearance only after a period of preparation. The question arose, if many kinds of social learning have taken place before the instinct appears, how can we know that it is really inborn and not (at least in part) learned?

Another difficulty was found in the fact that the instincts listed had different degrees of complexity. Crying, clasping, and biting are simple, fairly uncomplicated actions. But modesty, jealousy, parental love, shyness, cleanliness, and constructiveness are entirely different and far more complex forms of behavior. Only in the simplest reflex action, such as the knee jerk, the eye blink, the gag reflex, the curling of a baby's toes around a finger (Babinski reflex), is an act performed in essentially the same way on every occasion. In other kinds of actions claimed to be instinctive—hunting, fighting, loving, exploring, self-asserting, constructing, laughing, submitting —there are certainly similarities from time to time, place to place, society to society, but there are also great differences. In such complex behavior, there must at least be, in addition to an innate, instinctive core, a good deal of learning, of intelligent adjustment, and of patterning by one's particular society.

Studies by sociologists and anthropologists raised further questions about human instincts. They showed how behavior that is considered human nature in one society is changed markedly, or even seems to disappear completely, in another. Jealousy, for example, may seem to be instinctive in an individualistic, monogamous society. In a polygamous society, however, several wives (or husbands) can seemingly share a mate without resentment or conflict. Where is the instinct of pugnacity among the inhabitants of Tristan da Cunha, who cannot remember a fight? Where is the acquisitive instinct among the Zuni when they redistribute their surplus property? What has happened to the cooperative instinct, on the other hand, among a people like the Dobuans, who live in mutual hostility and will go out of their way to insult and harm one another? How does the parental instinct fit into those societies that practice the exposure of children?

Margaret Mead's study of three South Sea people—the Arapesh, the Mundugumor, and the Tchambuli— seemed to show that even the differences between sexes which we assume to be innate are not so. We are likely to consider males to be more aggressive than females. We expect them to be more interested in sex and thus to make the sexual advances. We consider artistic interests and backyard gossip to be primarily feminine. Among the Arapesh, however, Mead found both sexes typically showing the "soft," passive personality traits which we consider feminine in our society. In

TWO CLASSIFICATIONS
OF INSTINCTS AND EMOTIONS

*WILLIAM JAMES**

1. *Sucking*
2. *Biting, chewing, licking, grimacing, spitting out (in infants)*
3. *Clasping*
4. *Carrying to the mouth*
5. *Crying*
6. *Turning the head (aside as a gesture of rejection)*
7. *Holding head erect*
8. *Sitting up*
9. *Standing*
10. *Vocalization*
11. *Locomotion*
12. *Limitation*
13. *Emulation*
14. *Pugnacity*
15. *Sympathy*
16. *Hunting*
17. *Fear*
18. *Acquisitiveness*
19. *Constructiveness*
20. *Play*
21. *Curiosity*
22. *Sociability and shyness*
23. *Secretiveness*
24. *Cleanliness*
25. *Modesty*
26. *Love*
27. *Jealousy*
28. *Parental love*

WILLIAM McDOUGALL†

Instincts

1. *Flight*
2. *Curiosity*
3. *Repulsion*
4. *Pugnacity*
5. *Self-abasement*
6. *Self-assertion*
7. *Paternal*
8. *Reproduction*
9. *Gregariousness*
10. *Construction*
11. *Acquisition*

Emotions

1. *Fear*
2. *Wonder*
3. *Disgust*
4. *Anger*
5. *Subjection*
6. *Elation*
7. *Tender emotion*

* *William James,* The Principles of Psychology, *New York, Dover, 1950.*

† *William McDougall,* Outline of Psychology, *New York, Scribner's, 1923.*

---

the Mundugumor society, both sexes showed the self-assertive, aggressive qualities which we consider masculine. Among the Tchambuli the females were more assertive. The males were more artistic, while the women supervised the economic life. The women dressed plainly, while the men decorated themselves with feathers. The men were the gossipers. They complained about the women's stronger sexual demands. In other words, the sexual roles which we consider to be natural and innate seemed to be reversed.

The instinctivist view had maintained that a very large part of our behavior is the outgrowth of fixed inherited traits. Some critics tended to swing, like a pendulum, to the opposite extreme. They argued that inheritance plays virtually no role at all. The English philosopher John Locke had spoken of the mind at birth as a *tabula rasa* (blank slate). What appears upon it, he said, is the result of subsequent experience. The behaviorist psychologist, John B. Watson, who believed in the almost un-

limited possibilities of learning, said, "Give me the baby and my world to bring it up in and . . . I'll make it a thief, a gunman, or a dope fiend. The possibility of shaping in any direction is almost endless."

Some sociologists and anthropologists developed extreme views of cultural relativism. They held that human nature is entirely relative to a particular society, that whatever drives, urges, or impulses we have are infinitely plastic. To the extreme cultural relativist, human nature is whatever a particular society makes it. The cultural relativist view actually said two things—one factual, the other ethical. Factually it held that society can shape people to accept any kind of social pattern—infanticide, cannibalism, head hunting, human sacrifice, totalitarianism, genocide. Ethically it held that there is no standard by which we can make moral judgments about what any whole society accepts. For a whole society, "whatever is, is right." Sumner had said, "The mores can make anything right and prevent condemnation of anything." He meant this in both the factual and the ethical sense.

Neither extreme, exaggerated instinctivism nor complete cultural relativism is adequate. There are no instincts in the old sense of complex, inflexible, unlearned behavior. Of inflexible innate responses, we have only the simple reflexes. On the other hand, the human organism is not born a blank slate on which experience can write whatever the society wishes. A famous anthropologist is reported to have said to the equally famous Margaret Mead, when she was relating how society shapes sex roles, "But really, Margaret, do you know of any society where the men have the babies?" Dr. Mead, of course, did not, nor had she claimed that she did.

How shall we answer—can we answer?—the question: What is human nature? All people do, in fact, share many things in common. We all do have essentially similar biological organisms. We live under physical life conditions which, with all their differences, are essentially similar. We all live in society. We do, therefore, share common physical, biological, and social *imperatives.* These are not inflexible instincts, but common factors in human experience which inevitably lead all human life in certain directions, toward the solution of common problems. We shall not try to make a complete and final tabulation of these, but rather suggest a basis for further thinking.

As we have seen, we share, with all organisms, nutritional imperatives. In the broad sense, these have to do with maintaining the structure and temperature and energy level of our bodies. In this sense they include food, shelter, and clothing. They underlie all struggles for material security. They are still the uppermost concern of most human beings.

Food is, under most conditions, the most imperative of the three. It illustrates the relationship of human imperatives to society. There is no society where people do not eat any more than there is one where the females impregnate the males. Maintenance of life demands food. We have seen that physical, psychological, and social health requires quality as well as quantity of food. There is, however, a fairly wide range of things that people can eat and an equally wide range of ways in which they can schedule meals, prepare food, and observe the actual meal. Here we can see how a given kind of behavior can be absolutely essential and yet leave room for wide social flexibility.

We may find it hard to believe that *social* needs can be almost as imperative as hunger. As late as the second decade of this century, says the physician and anthropologist, Ashley Montagu, almost all infants in foundling institutions died before they were one year old. A large cause of death was a wasting disease, *marasmus,* in which the baby ate but did not gain weight and eventually wasted away. The main factor associated with marasmus was absence of human contact and response. Caught in time, marasmus could be cured by applying intense "mothering."

Where the results are not so extreme, failure to satisfy the imperative of social response may still lead to severe psychological damage. Even monkeys, deprived of social contact in infancy, fail to develop normal personalities and may become so withdrawn that they have no interest in the opposite sex, even when biologically mature. It has been similarly shown that the personalities of human infants deprived of social relationships may be almost irreversibly damaged. On the other hand, social contact is the deepest source of psychological security. Okinawan children, brought up as infants in unusually warm personal relationships, withstood bombing and the terrors of invasion in World War II with a remarkable freedom from panic. A religious writer once said, with great truth, "Perfect love casteth out fear."

It is not so clear to what extent other imperatives in our relationship to others are an inevitable part of the human condition. We have seen it suggested that man is naturally a territorial animal. It may well be that we must all feel dissatisfied and rootless until we have staked out a part of the earth's surface that is our own. (If so, our society will need considerable changing.) We have seen that there is room for question as to whether the need for status is a universal human imperative. Likewise, many people have felt that a need for power over others is ingrained in human nature, while others have regarded it as a compensation for lacks in one's life.

No one is likely to deny that *sexual* imperatives are very strong, and exert great influence over social behavior. Next to love of life, the philosopher Schopenhauer contended, the sexual impulse

> shows itself the strongest and most powerful of motives, constantly lays claim to half the powers and thoughts of the younger portion of mankind, is the ultimate goal of almost all human effort, exerts an adverse influence on the most important events, interrupts the most serious occupations every hour, sometimes embarrasses for a while even the greatest minds . . . breaks the firmest bonds, demands the sacrifice sometimes of life or health, rank and happiness, nay, robs those who are otherwise honest of all conscience, makes those who have been hitherto faithful, traitors.[1]

We do not die, directly, from sexual frustration. Psychiatric case records and other sources do, however, indicate that people can be severely damaged. Many people have, of course, lived lives of celibacy. Their number includes many of the great individuals of history. Even many Catholic priests and nuns are today, however, beginning to question whether this is a natu-

ral or healthy way to live. Much evidence supports the view that there is no completely satisfactory way of releasing sexual tensions except through genital activity.

So far we have been dealing with imperatives which we share, in varying degrees, with all animals. We are unique, however, in being human animals. We must beware of drawing completely sharp lines between the human and the nonhuman. Traces of the distinctively human traits we shall describe—the sense of shame, for example—may perhaps be found in an ape or a puppy. Nevertheless, the human situation is different from the situation of any other animal. It gives us a nature different from that of any other species. The ways in which we express our nutritional, social, and sexual imperatives are all shaped by our uniquely human experience.

What is our special nature as human beings?

We are *self-aware*. Each of us is conscious of himself, is an object to himself. We can step, so to speak, into the shoes of others and look at ourselves as they look at us. Our selves, our egos, become objects of value to us. Higher animals—dogs, monkeys, apes—may have some self-awareness, but if they do, it is extremely limited. Our self-consciousness makes individual human experience and human society unique. We shall see shortly how this self-awareness develops.

Human *imagination* extends enormously the world of time and space of which we are conscious. In comparing modern and primitive man, we observed how all our collective record of the past is part of our today. The difference is even more striking when we compare human beings with lower animals. Moreover, the human animal has *foresight*. Think at this moment of how much of your present life is governed by images of a career, of the draft, of marriage, of yourself 15 years from now. Human acts are unique in that remote events, distant future goals, are "causes" of our present behavior. The

1. Arthur Schopenhauer, *The World as Will and Idea*, trans. R. B. Haldane, London, Routledge & Kegan Paul, 1948, vol. 3, p. 339.

more we develop humanly, the wider also is the spatial universe of which we are conscious. The dog's world is bounded by a few blocks, the primitive's by perhaps the next village or water hole. The space to which we modern men relate ourselves includes the other side of the globe and stars millions of light years away.

Because we are self-conscious and imaginative, *self-expression* is a human imperative in a sense that is not true for other species. We not only adapt ourselves to our environment, but adapt the environment to ourselves. Moreover, we seem to be impelled to shape it in a way that puts our own individual stamp upon it, even if it means doing such things as carving our names in public places. Our consciousness of self gives us an imperative to create, which is uniquely human.

Being conscious of self in ourselves, we are also aware of self in others. When we relate ourselves to other human beings, we have an imperative to *identify* ourselves with them, to put ourselves in their place. Our consciousness of selves and our capacity for imagination thus strengthen the social imperatives which seem to characterize all animal life. Only a human being can say, with John Donne:

> *No man is an island, entire of itself; every man is a piece of the continent, a part of the main. If a clod be washed away by the sea, Europe is the less, as well as if a promontory were, as well as if a manor of thy friend's or of thine were: any man's death diminishes me, because I am involved in mankind.*[2]

It seems that, somewhere in our nature, all of us have the imperative to feel this way, although it often clashes with other individualistic imperatives.

2. John Donne, "Devotions Upon Emergent Occasions," *Complete Poetry and Selected Prose*, ed. John Hayward, London, Nonesuch Press, 1929, p. 538.

Thus part of our human nature is *altruism* (a feeling for others) and a *sense* of *responsibility* for other people and for the effect of our actions upon them. Our individual imperatives for creative self-expression are shaped into the social desire to *serve others.* When we focus our identification upon a single person, upon whom are also focused our sexual imperatives, then we experience sexual love. The wider our range of imagination in time and space, the wider is likely to be the number of people with whom we identify. The ultimate human limit is love of mankind.

Human identification is related to the fact that man has a *conscience,* a sense of right and wrong. We may feel that animals such as the dog have a sense of shame and wrongdoing. This may in some sense be so, but it is little developed as compared with human conscience. There are some human beings who seemingly have no conscience—the technical term for such people is "psychopathic (or sociopathic) personality"—but we recognize this condition as a form of pathology. Our conscience develops in experience as part of the normal human condition, but it is not inborn. A little later we shall see how it develops. Closely related to conscience is the sense of guilt. Some people think that feelings of guilt are a normal part of being human. Others regard guilt as a sickness of conscience which should be treated. In either case guilt is characteristically a human experience.

One of the most important aspects of the human situation is that man is the only creature who *foresees his own death.* This is one of the results of our general capacity for foresight. Not only do we know that we "are all condemned to death with indefinite reprieves," but we also know that we may die at any time. We may ask ourselves how different individual experience and social life would be if we did not have this knowledge of death, though it may be hard to envision the answer. "Existentialism" is a philosophy that stresses the human relation-

ship to death. "Eat, drink and be merry, for tomorrow you may die," is an old existentialist philosophy. Realization of our existential state leads other people, however, to quite different conclusions, such as the determination to give their lives as long as they last to human service. The point is that only a human being has the knowledge to make either choice in an existential way.

The qualities of the human condition that we have named make a man the only animal who has an imperative to find *meaning* in his life. Only human beings become aware of themselves, of their relationship to other people, to time and space, infinity and eternity, right and wrong, life and death. Only human beings ask, "What is the significance of it all? What is the significance of my life?" Only man tries to live so as to relate himself meaningfully to the whole universe he knows. The

search for meaning colors every other imperative. Eating and drinking, social intercourse, accumulation of property, the search for status, the lust for power, drugs, creative self-expression, human service, sexual love—each may be someone's vehicle for finding meaning. To say that man's life is such that he naturally seeks meaning is to say that we are inescapably religious animals, unorthodox as some of our "religious" answers may be.

We have not exhausted human nature. We have introduced some significant elements that are part of the human situation. These are not fixed instincts. They may express themselves more clearly in some individuals and in some societies than in others, but they are part of man, as such, everywhere. Some of them we share with other animals. Others, we do not. It is impossible to understand what happens in individuals or in society

without taking into account these common human imperatives.

INDIVIDUAL AND ENVIRONMENT

In this section we shall focus on the interaction between an individual human being and his environment. We must begin by getting a perspective on the whole problem. To modern science there is no such thing as an isolated object separate from all other objects. Every object is part of a "field" of forces, within which it is constantly interacting and from which it cannot be separated. To point out this interrelationship of everything, the great natural scientist and theologian, Teilhard de Chardin, has reminded us that any motion that occurs anywhere is eventually felt, though in very minute form, in every other part of the universe. Let us splash a foot in the ocean on the Atlantic coast of the United States, and eventually the wave, though extremely small, will be felt on the shores of Spain and India. Every word that has ever been spoken is still reverberating in space, and if we only had sensitive enough receivers we could hear all past conversations.

That we cannot be separated from the field in which we live was dramatically shown in experiments by the psychologist, Donald Hebb. He suspended people in a tepid bath of water, so as to cut them off as far as possible from all stimuli. Within a few hours their minds began to wander, they ceased to be able to think coherently, and their sense of personality seemed to be disintegrating. Our very sense of our selves apparently depends on constantly receiving stimuli from our environment. Cut off these stimuli for a relatively short time, and the characteristics that make us human begin to disappear. They will return when the experimental isolation is ended.

These goslings follow Dr. Konrad Lorenz because he was presented to them at a critical stage just after hatching and thus became their substitute "mother."

What is true of our physical environment is equally true of our social environment. We will recall the studies of primitive cooperation in animal life cited in the previous chapter. The German naturalist, Konrad Lorenz, tells us that the first normal act of a newborn animal is to turn toward and try to follow its mother or mother substitute. The psychoanalyst Ian Suttie points out that among human beings dependence on the mother takes the place of instincts in lower animals. The helpless human baby must depend on another person for things that innate patterns enable a kitten or puppy to do for itself. Repeated studies have shown that a normal personality depends on social stimulation and interaction and cannot develop without it. Harry Harlow showed this in the studies of monkeys which we have already cited. Rene Spitz demonstrated it in studies of human infants deprived of maternal care. It is supported by Kingsley Davis' famous studies of a human child brought up for six years in an attic with only the minimum amount of contact necessary to maintain life. The child showed hardly any human traits.

In our interaction with the field of our environment, a good deal is harmonious; this is pleasant. But long before a child is born, he has already experienced conflict with his surroundings. The problem may be sudden sounds, which we now know can be heard in the womb, or the shock of a mother's fall. It may be the nicotine or alcohol from his mother's cigarette or cocktail, or the surge of adrenaline which accompanies his mother's fear or anger. This conflict calls for the constant adaptation to his environment which will go on as long as he lives—which is, in fact, life.

Let us look at this process of adaptation, for it is at the heart of all personal and social life. In a book entitled *The Wisdom of the Body,* the physiologist, Walter B. Cannon, gave us the concept of homeostasis (Greek *homoios,* "similar," and *stasis,* "position"). This was based upon the conception of the French physiologist, Claude Bernard, that the body endeavors to keep its internal state constant or the same. Whenever the body deviates from its normal state, a tension is set up, and the body takes steps to relieve the tension and return to the normal condition.

In the chemistry of the body, there are a host of homeostatic mechanisms, which tend to restore any deviations, for example, from the normal level of sugar, protein, calcium, insulin, or adrenaline in the blood. Antibodies tend to restore the equilibrium disturbed by invasion of bacteria or foreign proteins (such as pollen). Our thermostatic mechanism, by which sweating (to cool) or shivering (to heat)—and other reactions—adjust any deviation from the normal 98.6° F. is an excellent example of this process. Thermostasis, that is, is a form of homeostasis. Eating, elimination, sexual release of tension, are all examples of homeostatic processes which normalize a state of tension. We might carry the concept farther and find homeostatic adjustment in our search for social response, in curiosity, in play, in creativity, even in the religious search for meaning. Each reduces a particular kind of tension. Finally, we might see in a religious revival, a lynching, a race riot, a revolution, or a war, mechanisms for restoring a social homeostasis by bringing a *state of tension back to normal.*

Homeostasis can explain much, but it is limited as an explanation of the most significant human behavior. Consider, for example, a football game or other athletic event. Why do you go? Not only in order to reduce accumulated tension to a normal level. Rather, you go in part at least because you enjoy the tension itself. Of course, you also anticipate the release of tension which will come with the end of the game, perhaps with victory for your side. You would not want to live the rest of your life at the height of a goal line stand! What you seek, then, is neither the reduction of tension alone, nor heightened tension alone, but the *cycle* of heightened tension followed by release. The experience you seek at the football game does not look nearly so much like this homeostatic picture

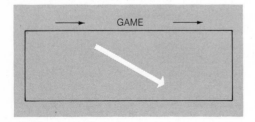

as like this tension relaxation curve.

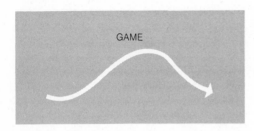

The most important aspects of human life involve not mechanical homeostasis, but the desire for tension followed by release. We are far from mere tension-reducing machines. To maintain the easiest homeostatic level is to be a vegetable. To be a human being is to be a purposeful tension-builder as well as a tension-releaser.

In creative work, for example, even though the work is hard and full of tension, we seek it, not only for the rest that follows, but for the satisfaction of the tension itself. Some of us, at least, have had this experience in study or in the laboratory. The artist, in painting a picture, writing a score, or sculpting a statue, has the same experience. Often, as in Irving Stone's account of Michelangelo, the artist goes through an agony which is also an ecstasy. John Dewey, in the book *Art as Experience,* has described all artistic experience as involving this gratifying succession of tension and resolution.

Adventure and discovery—the climbing of a mountain, for example—involve intense stress followed by completion. Children enjoy struggling with the most difficult tasks if they have hope of being able to resolve them. We know that a great deal of hunger can be enjoyed if it is in anticipation of a good meal, that the tension release in the meal is, in fact, not so gratifying without the hunger. Sexual tension is enjoyable, and in love making people continually seek to heighten it, in anticipation of final release.

We may note here again one important qualification. Anyone who has ever engaged in petting knows that sexual tension is not in itself painful, but the contrary. On the other hand, he may have discovered an important principle; tension becomes painful when there is no prospect of release. Ungratified hunger, unresolved sexual excitement, frustration in work are painful, not pleasurable. We do not seek *this* curve (although, if we will examine it carefully, we will recognize it as an extremely familiar one).

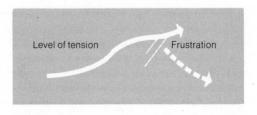

Let us now look a little further at some of the built-in responses through which we adapt ourselves to our environment. The psychiatrist Karen Horney has said that our life activities are of three kinds: movement *toward* our environment, movement *away from* it, and movement *against* it. We relate ourselves through approach, withdrawal, and aggression. Each response is accompanied by inner states or emotions.

We have seen that our first spontaneous response, that of all animals, is to move toward other objects. Approach is a *nonemergency* response, the way we act when things are going well. Observation of any normal child or animal will show him engaging in the approaching activities that we describe as curiosity, play, and love. We do not need any explanation of why we are curious, why we play, why we love. These are ultimately the way life expresses itself when there are no reasons (such as fatigue or threat) for doing otherwise. The emotions that typically accompany these activities are *pleasure* and *joy.*

Let a frustration or threat arise and deep emergency responses come to the fore. One may take flight physically. A primitive runs from a dangerous animal, a child from a bully. An army goes into retreat, refugees take flight from totalitarianism, a draftee crosses the border. One may also take flight psychologically, into himself. If poison is put into a solution containing an amoeba, the one-celled creature, which has been "approaching" his environment by pushing out little pseudopodia ("false feet"), contracts into a tight sphere. A child who has been frustrated or rejected may sulk. If the frustration or rejection is persistent, he may become passive, shy, or withdrawn. A disappointed, hurt, frustrated, or bereaved adult may go into depression. A mentally ill patient may go into a catatonic withdrawal in which he becomes so unresponding that it may be possible to use him as a human pincushion. The emotion that typically accompanies physical or psychological flight is *fear.*

One need not, however, always respond to frustration or threat by withdrawing. One may, instead, move against the offending object or situation. Broadly, we call such activity *aggression.* It is important to note that aggression may mean several things which are not the same.

It may mean *manipulation* of the environment for the purpose of removing obstacles. A child moves a chair that stands in his way. He develops wiles for managing his parents, "wrapping them around his little finger," in order to get what he wants. Pioneers clear a forest for settling and planting. Space scientists work to remove obstacles to landing on the moon or Mars. The emotions that accompany such activities may be fairly low key: a sense of frustration or challenge and satisfaction at removal of the source of difficulty.

Aggression may mean *combat.* This occurs in animals, in children, and in adults and needs no complicated description. It may happen when highly important values are challenged: food supply, sexual opportunities, territory, possessions, status, life or safety of oneself or those close to one. The emotions that are likely to accompany combative fighting are anger and rage and usually also fear.

Aggression may mean *sadistic destruction.* Here the dominant emotions are *hatred* and *pleasure in giving pain.* Neither of these is necessarily present in simple, spontaneous combat. There is usually a good deal of sadistic destructiveness in a prison or a concentration camp. We find it in the cruelty of a lynch mob, and it is very often in the behavior of both races in race riots. It draws people to bullfights and prize fights. It expresses itself in battered babies and battered wives.

Aggression may mean, finally, *impersonal destruction.* This is organized violence marked by no strong emotion. In fact, the absence of emotion—cold, feelingless calculation—may be more typical. A good deal of concentration camp cruelty is of this kind rather than sadistic. The guard is just "doing his job." So is the soldier in much of the mass destruction of war. He is not so much angry, or sadistic, as he is simply a machine operating under orders.

We need to distinguish these four kinds of aggression, all of them very familiar to our ordinary experience, for a reason. They are very often confused, and the term "aggression" is used to lump together in a single package things that are quite different. From this loose use of the word, very questionable conclusions arise.

For example, we see a race riot (aggression) as expressing the same thing as we see in a child's slapping his parent in momentary anger (aggression). We see in the mass torture and destruction of a concentration camp simply the same "natural human aggressiveness" involved in a primitive hunt or in a civilized worker's killing of hogs for food in a slaughterhouse. We equate the mass activity of an army invading and laying waste the crops, land, and people of a distant country with an individual's defending his home against invasion or his sister against rape. That is, we use the simpler forms of aggression, which we take to be "just human nature"—and use them to explain the others.

Let us look more closely at the differences. Simple manipulation of the environment to remove obstacles involves no necessary hostile emotion. It may be simple necessity, as in the case of hunting. Sometimes it shades over into approach and even love. One may have to overcome many obstacles in order to attain the object of his love or even of his simple or scientific curiosity. Such aggression is a normal human activity. As Lorenz has demonstrated in his studies of aggression in animals, and as we may observe in children, a certain amount of combat is probably natural. However, spontaneous combat among animals as well as children usually stops well short of death.

Sometimes the anger of simple combat shades over into hatred, especially when something or someone of deep value to an individual is being defended. Yet sadistic destruction, which plays so important a part in human society, is probably a distinctly human activity. Mark Twain said that man is the only creature with malice. Under ordinary circumstances probably only man hurts or kills for pleasure. Some social scientists, as already suggested, are inclined to see mass sadism, such as we find in class or race conflicts, concentration camps, and war, as simply expressing man's natural aggression. It is more likely that hostility and cruelty express deep frustration. If we examine a hostile child, we will probably find a child who has been deeply misused and frustrated. Examine a hostile adult, and we will probably find a person whose basic life imperatives have been persistently thwarted. Finally, as Malinowski suggested, cool, impersonal mass destruction is also uniquely human, has little to do with simple manipulation or spontaneous personal combat, and may be characteristic only of fairly recent societies.

Aggression is one way of solving conflicts between one's impulses and his environment. One can also try to deal with the problem by blocking his impulses. *Inhibition* is one of the most important methods of adaptation. One resists an impulse to hit a superior officer or a smaller or weaker person. He "keeps his mouth shut" to avoid trouble. He stops at a particular point in a petting session. He turns down a drink before driving. Each of us is constantly inhibiting all kinds of specific acts.

We may also inhibit certain general kinds of behavior more or less permanently. A child learns to inhibit his impulses to touch stoves and run across busy streets. A person who is overweight learns to push himself away from the table. A child who has been punished repeatedly for fighting may inhibit most of his aggressive impulses. Told that masturbation is wicked, he may develop inhibitions against all sexual activity. When his efforts at social contact are repeatedly blocked, he may inhibit his social impulses and become chronically withdrawn or hostile. If he is punished for asking questions (perhaps sexual ones), he may inhibit most of his impulses of curiosity.

Inhibition is very likely to lead to *ambivalence,* the state of simultaneously wanting and not wanting to do something. A certain amount of ambivalence is part of most life decisions. We usually are not 100 percent convinced of whether we should study or go on a date, take a particular job, move to a new home, go to a particular college, or marry a particular person. Hamlet felt ambivalent about life itself—"To be or not to be. . . . " When we have developed more or less permanent inhibitions of strong impulses, we are almost always ambivalent about their expression: whether to ask questions or squelch our curiosity, to assert ourselves or to accept injustice, to approach others or to avoid the risk of rejection, to express or suppress our sexual desires.

All these problems become more complex because inhibition is likely to pass into *repression.* Sometimes we are quite aware of the impulses we are inhibiting and of our conflict over them. On the other hand, we may also block our awareness of the conflict and of the impulse itself. This is particularly likely to happen when we are required to inhibit strong impulses in childhood. The reason is in a way clear. If a child hates his parent or sibling, it may be easier simply to deny the hatred than to be forever in conflict. Thus, the person who has repressed his hostile impulses may feel that he is really a very peaceful person who has no desire to fight. A person who has repressed his social impulses toward people may feel that he really hates everybody and has no desire for close relationships. A person who has been brought up to conform to rigidly atheistic parents may be unable to admit to himself any religious needs. A person who has repressed his childhood desires to masturbate may become unable to feel sexual desire at all. It should be clear that repression as a method of adaptation may create severe problems.

Clearly, inhibition and repression involve *learning.* The ability to learn from our experience is obviously one of our most important devices for adaptation. On the other hand, mislearning can create serious problems in our relationships to our environment. Let us examine how and what we learn.

To a large extent we may view learning as *generalizing,* that is, applying our experience to situations that are (or seem to be) related. Learning always involves generalization from past to present: we apply now the responses we made to a similar situation in the past. "The burnt child dreads the fire"—when we have suffered pain once, we expect similar situations in the future to repeat it. A person who has almost drowned as a child may intensely fear water all his life. Learning may also involve generalization from an individual case to a group in which the case is believed to belong. The burnt child dreads not only the particular stove, but perhaps all forms of fire. An unfortunate experience with one individual of a given national or racial group may be generalized: "All members of group X are bad (or good)." Psychiatry shows that we tend to generalize our experience with one type of authority figure (parents) and react the same way to all authority figures, such as bosses, officers, judges, policemen, or deans. The reaction may be submission, rebellion, or perhaps an ambivalent mixture.

We also generalize from one part of a total situation to another. The most famous case is Pavlov's conditioned response. A dog was presented with meat, and secretion of saliva followed. Then a bell was rung as the meat was presented. Finally, the bell was rung without the meat, and the dog still salivated. The meat was the unconditioned stimulus, the bell, the conditioned one. Watson introduced a child to a white rat, and the boy was attracted to it. Then a metal bar was clanged as the rat was presented. After a number of repetitions, the boy feared the rat as well as the sound. Much of language involves this kind of learning. A child hears the word "dog" as a dog is presented. The next time the word "dog" is pronounced, he may look for the dog, because the word arouses in his memory the whole situation in which it was first pronounced. A large number of psychiatric problems are related to this kind of generalization. A child's brother or sister dies on a dark and stormy day. In adult life he may find himself unaccountably depressed and fearful in stormy weather.

Generalization is obviously a convenient and economical procedure. It makes one experience serve for many. There is also, however, the possibility of misgeneralizing. Apparent similarities may not be very useful, or be positively harmful. If one cannot conquer an overwhelming childhood fear of water, later swimming situations, when water is only a relative danger which can be mastered, may be difficult. One or two people from a group may not really be representative of the group. Rats do not need to be feared and totally avoided because they were once associated with a frightening sound. A good deal of psychiatric trouble derives from just this kind of misgeneralizing or mislearning.

We may also view learning as *repetition of gratifying responses*. In the beginning we select responses that are satisfying. As long as they continue to be satisfying, we tend to repeat them. Psychologists say that satisfying behavior is reinforced. If the reinforced responses fail, we are likely to abandon them, either suddenly or gradually. As already suggested, however, in many cases we cling to responses that do not seem to work very well.

One method of selection is through *trial and error*. A hungry cat is placed in a slatted box with food outside. The box contains a button which will open a door to the food. When placed in the box, the cat slashes around, trying all possible ways of getting the food, until finally by accident he hits the button. Eventually, when placed in the box, he will push the button at once. A child tries a number of ways of getting his mother to let him stay up ten minutes longer at night. Then he hits upon one —perhaps asking for a last glass of water—which is successful, and this becomes part of his going-to-bed pattern.

Another situation in which selection takes place is *planned reinforcement.* Training through reward or punishment

is an example. It is hoped, at least, that people will repeat behavior that is rewarded and not repeat that that is punished. This method is widely used by parents and teachers. An interesting case is that of an Englishman who could not shake himself free from a sexual affair with a neighbor. Finally, with the consent of both the neighbor and his wife, he entered upon an experiment. A psychologist agreed to present him repeatedly with photographs of his wife and his mistress. Each time the neighbor's picture was shown, he received an electric shock. After a number of repetitions he was ''cured'' of his attraction to the neighbor.

The psychologist, B. F. Skinner, has been remarkably successful in using reinforcement techniques in training. By feeding two hungry pigeons when they pushed a ball, and then feeding them again when one pushed the ball past the other, he taught them to play a modified game of Ping-Pong. With the same methods he has ''taught rats to use a marble to obtain food from a vending machine . . . and dogs to operate the pedal of a refuse can so as to retrieve a bone,'' and ''has trained pigeons to coordinate their behavior in dancing in a cooperative manner which rivals the skills of most able human dancers.'' Upon the same principles he pioneered the teaching machines which are widely used today in educational institutions.[3]

Another important method of selection is *identification with models* who are deemed successful. The child learns to eat at the table or go to the toilet ''like Mommy and Daddy.'' The girl puts on her mother's high-heel shoes and makeup. The boy may become a ''chip off the old block.'' Or he may identify with Spaceman, Batman, cowboys, Indians, war heroes, or gangsters, or swagger like a coach or a famous athlete.

A fourth example of selection of sat-

3. Examples taken from Morris L. Bigge, *Learning Theories for Teachers*, New York, Harper & Row, 1964, chap. 5.

isfactory responses is that of *creative insight.* The forms of learning described so far seem rather passive and mechanical. They largely happen *to* one. But a large part of learning involves an active sizing up, a grasping of a total situation, and an intelligent selection of the best solution.

Let us look at a very significant experiment by the psychologists Tolman and Honzik.[4] Rats were put in the maze depicted in Figure 5.1. After ten trials they soon learned to select the shortest route, Path 1. Then a barrier (Block A) was placed in Path 1. The rats had to return to the junction with Paths 2 and 3, and choose. About 93 percent of them selected the shorter Path 2. Presumably their trial and error had taught them that this was shorter. Then Block B was placed so as to cut both Paths 1 and 2 off from the food. Again the rats started up Path 1, were blocked, and had to return to the intersection of Paths 2 and 3. Would they take the shorter Path 2? Or would they size up the pattern of the whole maze and see that Path 3 was the only route open? To do this, said Tolman, would require intelligence of a kind not found in ordinary trial and error. If their learning was merely trial and error, we would expect them to have picked Path 2. In actuality, of 15 rats, 14 took Path 3, the longest route, but the only one open.

A psychologist gives from everyday life an example of insightful learning:

> Army rifles have a powerful recoil or kick. A soldier is supposed to "squeeze" the trigger gradually and smoothly until the rifle fires. Recruits usually anticipate the recoil and jump before the shell explodes; thus, their aim is completely spoiled. The problem for a noncom was to teach his "pupil" not to make the anticipatory jump. Recruits were convinced that they really did not jump until after the explosion, and thus

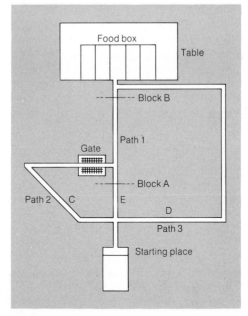

Figure 5.1. A maze used to test insight in rats. The paths become established as a hierarchy according to length, Path 1 preferred to Path 2, Path 2 to Path 3. If Path 1 is closed by Block A, the rats run by Path 2. If Path 1 is closed by Block B, the rats run by Path 3 if they have "insight" that the barrier closes Path 2 as well as Path 1.
Source: Ernest R. Hilgard, *Theories of Learning,* New York, Appleton-Century-Crofts, 1956, p. 194.

> hours of blankety-blankety-blanks had little, if any, effect. Corporal Jones helped his "pupil" gain an insight. He "scolded" him several times for jumping, with no avail. Then while his pupil's attention was diverted to a fellow sufferer, the corporal slipped a fired cartridge into the firing chamber. The recruit aimed, started to squeeze, and again jumped out of his skin. He thereby gained an insight. He was jumping before his rifle fired and thus ruining his aim. His jumping before the rifle had fired then ceased.[5]

Our highly developed capacity for intelligent, insightful learning distinguishes us from other animals, even

4. Ernest R. Hilgard, *Theories of Learning,* New York, Appleton-Century-Crofts, 1956, p. 194.

5. Morris L. Bigge, *Learning Theories for Teachers,* New York, Harper & Row, 1964, p. 178.

intelligent rats. We are also distinguished by the role of foresight in our learning. The rifleman was not merely reacting to past conditioning. He was preparing for the future. To go back to a proposition made at the beginning of this section, we always make choices and learn in relation to the total field in which we act. The total situation for a human being always includes future goals as well as past and present experience. Our learning is pulled by our tomorrows as well as pushed by our todays and yesterdays.

We may close this section by discussing briefly one of the most important and dramatic findings on man's effort to cope with his environment. This grows out of the work of the Austrian-Canadian physician, Hans Selye, on *stress*. Selye's research extends Cannon's work on homeostasis. We all have a common sense idea of what we mean by "stress." Selye describes stress as the "wear and tear of life." It involves especially the activities of flight, aggression, and inhibition which we have described, but it may also include approaching activities. Love making, for example, involves considerable physiological stress. In summary, stress is the whole relationship of tension between an organism and its environment.

The object or situation that gives rise to a specific stress is a stressor. It may be physical, psychological, or social. Cold, heat, high humidity, deprivation of oxygen, thirst, hunger, overeating, overexposure to sunlight, wounds, poisons, and bacteria are examples of physical stressors. Among the psychological stressors are frustration, repression, fear, anger, excitement, boredom, disappointment, depression, and grief. Social stressors include such factors as famine, economic insecurity, economic competition, population crowding, war and threat of war, status anxiety, overstimulation, suppression of personality, intoxication of food, air, and water.

Selye's great contribution consists in pointing out that all types of stressors produce essentially the same general bodily reactions. The physiological response to such diverse stressors as intense cold, grief, or acute fear of losing status may be almost identical. The stress reaction goes through three typical stages. Taken together, these constitute the general adaptation syndrome (GAS).

In the alarm reaction, which is fairly brief, bodily forces are mobilized for emergency action. A triad of symptoms is typically seen: shrinking of the thymus gland, increase in size of the adrenal glands, and inflammation and bleeding of the lining of the stomach and duodenum. In the stage of resistance, the body, so to speak, settles down to live with and adapt itself to a continued stress situation. Particularly involved are the pituitary gland and the adrenal cortex, whose hormones mobilize overall bodily reactions of defense or counterattack. This stage may last for years. In the third phase, the *stage of exhaustion*, the body's adaptive powers are spent, and it ceases to be capable of resistance. A body exposed to cold, for example, will after an initial alarm reaction settle down into a period in which it is more capable of resisting cold, but eventually its resistance will fail, and it will be less resistant than it initially was. Life itself represents a general adaptaton syndrome. Constantly beseiged by stressors, we work out adaptations, but our capacity to adapt finally wears out, and the environment overcomes us.

We had suspected, before Selye, that stress could lead to disease. He points out specifically how "diseases of adaptation"—diseases caused by the body's own defenses against stress —may occur. By administering pituitary and adrenal-cortical hormones and thus creating artificially the conditions of stress, Selye and others have produced kidney disease, high blood pressure, other diseases of the heart and arteries, allergies, ulcers, arthritis and other rheumatoid diseases, diseases of the liver, diabetes, and a general lowering of resistance to all stress. We will recognize here, significantly, the "degenerative diseases" which are especially marked in modern societies.

To what extent must prolonged stress lead to diseases of adaptation? In our complex and competitive situation, we are relieved from some of the stresses of a simpler society, such as, ordinarily, the fear of being eaten by lions. But it is likely that we live to an unusual degree in a state of psychological seige. We appear, therefore, to be peculiarly liable to the diseases of stress.

Is it possible to avoid or reduce the damage of stress under these conditions?

The answer is clearly, in part, yes, by certain methods, some of which are suggested by Selye. An earlier chapter indicated that stress increases greatly the need for vitamins and minerals. Those who supply these extra needs are in the best position to survive stress without disease. Those who are most successful in dealing with stress are likely to follow the old adage, "Know thyself." They learn what are their typical forms of stress and the way in which they respond to it. They are able to watch consciously, for example, for tendencies to become overly "wound up" (probably a sign of excessive hormone production). They can then deliberately break the routine, rest, relax, and "wind down." They learn when and when not to resist the stressors in their life situations—how, so to speak, to "roll with the punches." They are likely to follow the adage, "Change those things which can be changed, accept those things which cannot be changed, and know the difference between them." When confronted with piled up stress, they turn their energies into less blocked channels. They know how to let off steam in physical activity. Most important of all, perhaps, they have in their lives channels for gratifying self-expression.

Each individual seems to have only a very limited ability to reduce the stress of life in the modern world. Perhaps every person's central problem, therefore, in his relationship to his environment, is how to minimize the damage done in adapting to that stress.

THE SELF

There are few if any objects that are of as much interest and concern to us as our selves. Certainly there are few, if any, that seem as close. But what is the self? To one point of view, the self is an eternal unchanging entity which became attached to us at the moment of conception or some time later. To another, it is simply the role (or roles) that we play in social life. (It is interesting that the word "person" is derived from the Latin word *persona,* the mask that the Greek and Roman actors wore in the drama.) "All the world's a stage, and all the men and women merely players." From another point of view, the self is "illusion," and salvation and happiness lie in being rid of self. There are still other interpretations.

Each of us has a self, so let us begin our investigation with self-observation. When we think of our selves, we do think of something that changes, and yet has a core which seems to remain the same. As you remember the person you were ten years ago, and anticipate the person you expect to be ten years from now, each is a different individual from the self you are today. Yet you also have a sense of continuity. Some Hindu philosophy tells us that just as one cannot step twice in the same stream (because the water always flows and is never the same), so we are never twice the same person (because the stream of our life is always changing). There is certainly some truth in this view. Nevertheless, common sense seems to tell us that the stream really exists and so does our self.

What is it that exists? As we look at ourselves, each of us will find a unique pattern which is duplicated by no other person. Out of all the possibilities in the world, you typically engage in certain *activities,* and not in others. You

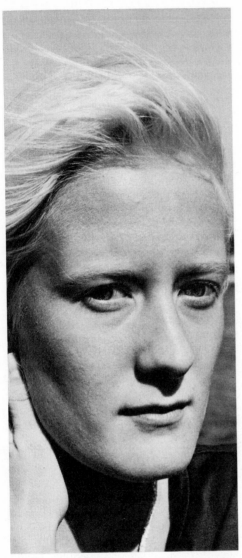

The self: role, illusion, or unchanging entity?

meet frustration with withdrawal or aggression, are highly repressed or relatively uninhibited. Moreover, you are to a considerable degree aware of all these things. You are an *object* to yourself. Your attitude toward yourself is marked by awareness, value, concern, by consciousness of your social roles, and probably by some pride, some shame, and some guilt.

The self, then, is a pattern—sometimes we use the German word *Gestalt* —of activities, interests, attachments, attitudes, and emotional responses of which you are aware. Let us look at the self in the field in which it lives.

First of all, when and how does it originate? Whatever else we can say about the self, we have some idea about when and how self-consciousness arises. At birth there is no distinction of any object as such. Since "myself" is an object, there can be no awareness of self. The young infant— as also the foetus—is conscious, but not *self*-aware. Slowly it learns to differentiate objects. Its mother is typically the first. Developing a sense of self requires, as we have said, the ability to take the role of others. Language is a great help in doing this. A child may learn, from hearing other people, to speak his name and simultaneously to point to himself. Later he may not only say "bye-bye" to objects he recognizes—children, mother, horses, dogs. He may also, in the role of another, call "bye-bye" to himself, using his name. At this point it is clear that he has begun to become an object to himself.

Charles Horton Cooley, who developed the concept of primary groups, also gave us a suggestive figure to describe the nature of our self-awareness. He spoke of the "looking-glass self." It is as though other people were mirrors. We look into these mirrors, and what they reflect is our conception of ourselves. We see ourselves as others see us—or, more accurately, as we *think* they see us. The most important "mirrors" are likely to be those of our close primary groups. In early

have certain abilities. You play a certain role in your society. People expect certain things of you. You have certain *interests,* which include both the things you yourself do and the things you observe others doing. You have attachments of varying intensities to certain people, things, and places. You have a particular set of *attitudes* toward people, things, places, the activities of individuals and groups. You have certain typical *emotional responses;* you are predominantly reserved or outgoing, childhood the chief mirror is likely to be our family. In later childhood, our play group or peer group (group of equals) becomes more important. In adulthood, our neighborhood or community may be most influential. As we grow up, in Cooley's view, what we feel ourselves to be is a composite of what we feel our family, our peers, and our neighbors see us to be.

In the previous chapter, we discussed George Mead's description of how a child learns, through the baseball game, to fit into the expectations of his group. Mead saw two important stages in the development of the sense of self. The first is represented by a young child's very typical private conversations with imaginary playmates. In carrying on such conversations, in taking the role of the other and talking to himself, he gains a sense of the self to whom he is talking. This, said Mead, is a first step in self-formation. Mature self-development requires, however, a relationship to a social group—as Mead put it, a "generalized other"—as contrasted with a single other.

To conform to the expectations of all the other players in the game, the child must have a composite sense of himself in his whole role in the game, as it appears to *all* the other players more or less simultaneously. What is true of one's relationship to the specific game situation, Mead believed, holds also for the child's general self-awareness in relation to all the continuing activity of his group. Later his sense of self will be further developed in relation to adult groups and society as a whole. Always, the sense of self, said Mead, is the sense of how the "generalized other" sees us. Self-awareness always involves a social relationship to a group.

We need, however, to be on guard against a narrow interpretation of the self. We cannot wrap up a whole person in any single formula. One such formula which has proved inadequate, for example, is the view that the self is entirely the product of one's society. Thus, if we can only get people early and long enough, we can mold their selves to any kind of social arrangement. We will recognize this as the extreme cultural relativist view of human nature discussed earlier in this chapter. By this standard 50 years and two new generations of totalitarian indoctrination should have molded Russian selves into complete conformity with Soviet society. Yet the passage of time sees more selves demanding freedom and individuality, not fewer. There is never a self without a social environment, but the self is more than the social environment.

We need to get a broad view of several dimensions or components of the self. By "components" we do not mean separate, isolated parts which are added together mechanically to make a person. We mean, rather, interrelated *aspects* of the self.

We will recognize, first of all, a *biological* component. This is composed particularly of those imperatives that we share with other animals: self-preservation and maintenance, sex, aggression, physical and emotional contact. Sometimes these biological imperatives lead us into cooperative or loving relations with others and into a spontaneous and pleasant empathy with our environment. At other times they lead us into aggressive manipulation of our environment, and into manipulation of, or combat with, people. This deep part of our selves is often in conflict with the inhibitions, repressions, habits which represent the folkways, mores, technicways, laws, and institutions of society. Freud used the German word *Es* ("it") to designate this component of the self. English translations have employed the Latin word *Id*. Freud employed the neuter pronoun to distinguish this deep, involuntary biological component from the *Ego* (German *Ich,* English *I*), which is the more conscious and rational self. He also distinguished both from the *superego,* roughly, the conscience.

We can recognize, next, a *social* component. This is made up of those qualities that arise from the experience of living as a human being in a social life with other human beings. Cooley held that this component is the product mainly of primary group experience (in family, peer group, and community) as contrasted with experience in secondary organizations and institutions. He believed that although technology and secondary organizations vary quite widely, the basic relationships in primary groups are essentially the same everywhere. He spoke of

> *those sentiments and impulses that are human in being superior to those of lower animals, and also in the sense that they belong to mankind at large, and not to any particular race or time . . . particularly, sympathy and the innumerable sentiments into which sympathy enters, such as love, resentment, ambition, vanity, hero-worship, and the feeling of social right and wrong. . . . Where do we get our notions of love, freedom, justice and the like which we are ever applying to social institutions? Not from abstract philosophy, surely, but from the actual life of simple and widespread forms of society, like the family or the playground. In these relations mankind realizes itself, gratifies its primary needs, in a fairly satisfactory manner, and from the experience forms standards of what it is to expect from more elaborate associations. Since groups of this kind are never obliterated from human experience, but flourish more or less under all kinds of institutions, they remain an enduring criterion by which the latter are ultimately judged.*[6]

The process of attaining those qualities essential for successful participation in social life we call *socialization*.

The Swiss psychologist Jean Piaget went somewhat further than Cooley in studying the development of the social self. Socialization is, as Mead said, learning how to play the game of social life. Piaget studied how children learn, using as the object of his study the way in which they learn to play the game of marbles.

In his study he found two different attitudes toward the game. In very young children he found that the rules of the game of marbles were taken, by the child, on authority, without question. He was likely to feel that the rules had always been this way and always must be the same. At this time children's lives were generally under the sway of arbitrary rules laid down by their parents. Piaget called this stage "heteronomy" (Greek *heteros*, other, and *nomos*, law)—"rule by another." The child's relationship to the parent he called "unilateral constraint," meaning that all the rules of life were imposed upon him one-sidedly without his participation.

By the time the child had reached the age of seven or eight, however, Piaget found that he no longer accepted the rules of marbles just because they were given to him that way. He felt that they were man-made (or child-made!), and could be changed if they were unsatisfactory. Piaget called this stage "autonomy" (Greek *autos*, self, and *nomos*, law)—"self-rule." At this time the main influence on the child was no longer his parents, but his peer group. Rules were no longer imposed by authority, but worked out by a process of cooperative give and take. This relationship of the child to the source of the rules Piaget called *reciprocity*. There are, Piaget concluded, a heteronomous sense of the rules, which develops under one-sided authority, and an autonomous sense, which develops in a more democratic group situation. What applies to marbles is true for all the game of life.

> *We have recognized the existence of two moralities in the child, that of constraint and that of cooperation. The morality of constraint is that of duty pure and simple and of heteronomy. The child accepts from the adult a certain number of commands*

6. Charles Horton Cooley, *Social Organization*, New York, Schocken, 1962, pp. 28, 32.

to which it must submit whatever the circumstances may be. Right is what conforms to these commands; wrong is what fails to do so. . . . But, first parallel with this morality, and then in contrast to it, there is gradually developing a morality of cooperation, whose guiding principle is solidarity and which puts the primary emphasis on autonomy of conscience.[7]

One of the important things Piaget found was that the young child, although he *says* he has great respect for the rules, may not actually follow them very carefully. The older child, on the other hand, says they can be changed, but is more likely to accept them as long as his group has agreed upon them. We may have observed children brought up under rigid discipline, who break the rules as soon as they feel they can get away with it. We may also know children who have been brought up to feel a part of family rule making and who accept reasonable social restraints much better. Authoritarian discipline may seem in the short run the best way to socialize a child, but in the long run it defeats itself. Piaget clearly felt that real socialization requires a cooperative, democratic atmosphere of the kind that develops autonomy. His conclusion implied that homes and schools with a good deal of freedom and give and take will provide better socialized individuals than those governed by arbitrary discipline and authority. In general, Piaget's view is supported by the studies of the authoritarian personality which were cited earlier.

A third aspect of the self is the *cultural* component. What we are and feel ourselves to be depends upon the particular cultural tradition in which we have grown up, as well as upon our common human experience.

Every cultural group has a distinctive core of common qualities of personality—as the sociologist Don Martindale says,

a set of traits (attitudes and evaluations, conceptions of the nature of the natural and social world, notions of appropriate and inappropriate ways of solving life's problems) that the members of a community come to share with one another over and beyond their individual differences and the personality traits that they share as members of some subcommunity formation (as members of a social class or ethnic group, or of familial, religious, economic, educational, or other institutions).[8]

Not everyone shares the typical cultural personality or shares it to the same degree. We are speaking of what is typical.

The Mead studies of sexual "selves" among the Arapesh, Mundugumor, and Tchambuli, cited in the previous chapter, were among the earliest demonstrations of how cultural background can influence personality. A famous study contrasting cultural personalities was *The Psychological Frontiers of Society*, by Abram Kardiner and Ralph Linton. They compared the South Sea people of the island of Alor with the Comanche Indians of the American Plains. The Alorese were typically given almost no affection by their mothers in infancy. They typically lacked self-confidence, were habitually anxious and hostile, and were incapable of close personal relationships. The Comanche usually began with warm and confident family relationships in infancy. In adulthood they were characteristically self-reliant and cooperative and relatively free from anxiety even though as warriors they led a constantly dangerous life.

It is more difficult to find common personality traits in a technically advanced society than among a simple

7. Jean Piaget, *The Moral Judgment of the Child*, trans. Marjorie Gabain, New York, Free Press, 1948, pp. 334, 335.

8. Don Martindale, *Annals of the American Academy of Political and Social Science*, March 1967, p. ix.

primitive group. Nevertheless, there is reason to believe, for example, that respect for authority, efficiency, and power have been prominent in the German personality for at least several generations. This quality is found in the patriarchal (father-centered) family, in the stern patriarchal conception of God, in the authoritarian role of "Herr Professor" in education, and in the constant prominence of the military. Many observers feel that there is in the Swedish people a tendency to meet the description of "emotional coldness and distance together with stress on achievement and work rather than the warmth of interpersonal relationships."

The Chinese self is described by the sociologist Francis L. K. Hsu as:

centered on the family and clan
marked by a strong sense of security, continuity and permanency
practicing reverence toward parents and ancestors
having close feelings of mutual dependence
having a strong sense of "place" in society
concerned with conventionality, face, and ritual
without a strong desire for social change.

The national personality of Hindu India is described by the same author as:

marked by strong attachments to the mother
strongly oriented to mystical relationships with the supernatural
strongly related to the caste of one's birth
dependent on the gods rather than personal effort
unable to feel strongly
unable to carry through sustained efforts
lacking the Western sense of the importance of time.

Hsu characterizes the typical American self as:

individualistic and self-reliant
distrustful of being dependent or depended upon
not given to strong permanent ties
oriented toward secondary associations
preoccupied with the problem of finding "meaning"
believing in Good and Evil with few shades between
dynamically oriented to change.[9]

Even the best studies of the national character of modern societies are, however, subjective and impressionistic rather than scientifically controlled. We need to be very careful of loose and hasty stereotypes which may justify prejudice rather than increase understanding. Nevertheless, there is little doubt that there are wide national differences in the sense of self and that as a starting point for our own thinking and observation, studies like those of Hsu are very useful.

Each of the peoples named, like all people we know, have been through what may be called a "cultural brainwashing," that is, all have been indoctrinated with cultural values under tremendous psychological pressure. Every culture we know submits its members, from infancy on, to an intensive program for fitting their "selves" into the cultural mold. It is always easier to see this process in a person from another culture than in ourselves. This blindness to our own brainwashing is itself evidence of how effective it usually is.

Each child is born into a world where he is small and helpless, utterly dependent at first upon powerful adults. These adults, chiefly his parents, have themselves been brought up in the existing folkways, mores, and institutions. They largely accept them and expect that he will learn to accept them. They reward compliance and punish deviation. Thus the family is the first, and usually the most powerful, agent of cul-

9. Francis L. K. Hsu, *Clan, Caste, and Club,* New York, Van Nostrand Reinhold, 1963.

tural indoctrination. Religion usually gives powerful support. God, or the gods, are usually held to have great power to reward or punish, through Heaven, hell fire, or in other ways. Though religious institutions may try to be universalistic, that is, to treat all peoples and cultures alike, in most cases they largely support existing cultural values. In wartime, for example, both sides are almost always supported by their respective religious bodies.

In advanced societies schools and colleges generally continue the process of indoctrination begun in the home. Educational institutions often try to be objective and to examine their own cultural ways as objectively as any others. As we saw in an earlier chapter, however, even in a democratic society they are always subject to strong pressures from vested interests that wish them to "toe the cultural line." Teachers and administrators have themselves been through the cultural brainwashing. Government in modern society exercises an increasingly strong influence on personality. Rituals like the flag salute strengthen cultural values. The management of news by government is an example of pressure on the individual. The mass media often employ the most advanced psychological techniques for selling both advertisers' products and dominant cultural (and political) values. Children begin to be exposed to these even before they can walk or talk, and their early words often show the influence of television and other media. It is not surprising, then, that even among college students in a democratic society the overwhelming majority conform largely without serious question.

The process of incorporating the cultural component of the self is *enculturation.* Though the words are often used interchangeably, this is not necessarily the same thing as socialization, which is development of the basic qualities necessary for cooperative social living. If the authoritarian upbringing of a Ger-

Man with a Hoe *by Jean Francois Millet. (Private Collection, San Francisco.)*

man child made him better able to adapt to a job as guard in an extermination camp, his enculturation was in sharp conflict with real social learning. The enculturation of the Hindu, which makes him resist contraceptive techniques which could reduce death by famine, is opposed to rational social values. If the American reduces his tension over competitive success by drinking which ends in an automobile accident, he may be very well enculturated, but he is not socialized. The social and the cultural components of the self are not necessarily in harmony.

A fourth component of the self is the *economic.* This is that aspect of the personality that is shaped by the way one makes his living and, secondarily, by the way he spends his income. It is actually a subdivision of the cultural component. It is, however, so important that it requires special attention. The reason for its importance is simple. Throughout history, making a living has been the dominant fact of life for most people.

Consider some illustrations of how the way one makes a living shapes the self. Inspired by a painting by the French artist Millet, the American poet Edwin Markham penned the famous "Man with the Hoe." This poem describes untold millions of farm laborers from ancient Babylonia and Egypt to the present day.

Bowed by the weight of centuries he
leans
Upon his hoe and gazes at the
ground,
The emptiness of ages in his face,
And on his back the burden of the
world.
What made him dead to rapture
and despair,
A thing that grieves not and that
never hopes,
Stolid and stunned, a brother to
the ox?

Slave of the wheel of labor, what to
him
Are Plato and the swing of Pleiades?
What the long reaches of the peaks
of song, ·
The rift of dawn, the reddening of the
rose?[10]

In the days of the Industrial Revolution in England, William Blake wrote of the London he saw. Everything and everybody seemed to be "chartered," that is, made into a commodity to be bought and sold. (The situation might not be much different today.)

I wander through each chartered
street,
Near where the chartered Thames
does flow,
And mark in every face I meet
Marks of weakness, marks of woe.

In every cry of every man,
In every infant's cry of fear,
In every voice, in every ban,
The mind-forged manacles I hear.[11]

These two poems describe the "self" as it still exists in a large part of the agricultural and industrial world. Nor does affluence necessarily remove the economic pressures on the self. The psychoanalyst Erich Fromm describes the marketing personality, who would like to be creative and productive, but feels he has to "sell himself" in a competitive society.

Only in exceptional cases is success predominantly the result of skill and of certain other human qualities like honesty, decency and integrity. . . . Success depends largely on how well a person sells himself on the market, how well he gets his personality across, how nice a "package" he is. . . . A person is not concerned with his life and unhappiness, but with becoming salable . . . his feeling of identity . . . is constituted by the sum total of roles one can play: "I am as you desire me."[12]

In *The Organization Man,* Whyte depicts the way in which the demands of the job may shape the "executive ego."

More and more the executive must act according to the role that he is cast for—the calm eye that never strays from the other's gaze, the easy, controlled laughter, the whole demeanor that tells onlookers that here certainly is a man without neurosis and inner rumblings. . . . "The ideal," one company president recently advised a group of young men, "is to be an individualist privately and a conformist publicly."[13]

The executive is an example of how one's personality may be shaped by his occupational role. People who share a common occupation tend to have common qualities of self, just as do people with a common culture. This is because their occupation subjects them to similar demands and conditions of life. Consider some of the qualities that we often associate with different trades. (These, again, are im-

10. Edwin Markham, *Poems of Edwin Markham,* New York, Harper & Row, 1950, pp. 30, 31.
11. William Blake, "London," *Poems of William Blake,* ed. William Butler Yeats, New York, Book League of America, 1938, p. 77.

12. Eric Fromm, *Man for Himself,* New York, Holt, Rinehart and Winston, 1947, pp. 69, 70, 73.
13. William H. Whyte, Jr., *The Organization Man,* Garden City, N.Y., Doubleday, 1956, p. 172.

pressionistic rather than carefully scientific.)

The sailor: tough, profane, cosmopolitan, superstitious, sex-starved, fatalistic
The banker: sedentary, conventional, reserved, efficient, professional
The bureaucrat: detached, impersonal, bored, formalistic, unimaginative
The salesman: gregarious, persistent, plausible, genial, confidential, "sincere"
The mass media personality (advertising, public relations, radio, television): compulsive, chain-smoking, fast-talking, facile, superficial, cynical

Social class does not correspond perfectly with economic position, but we have seen that it is very closely related. There tends to be a class personality as well as an occupational and a cultural personality. We have seen how class position makes it more or less likely that the self will break down in mental illness or be unable to continue its family relationships. We have seen how basic attitudes toward the emotions and self-expression differ among social classes. There are other significant differences.

Those who "have it made," especially those who have inherited wealth rather than earned it, are oriented to life in a way quite different from that of people who have to work for a living. The upwardly mobile classes, with hopes of advancement in income and status, have self-feelings quite different from people in hereditary poverty who have lost hope of escape. Whether one works primarily with objects, with people, or with symbols is very important. Work that is dirty has a quite different effect on the self from work that is clean.

How one consumes also affects his self-image. One of the most famous books in social science is *The Theory of the Leisure Class,* written in 1899 by the economist and sociologist Thorstein Veblen. In it Veblen pointed out that in a simple society people may work just in order to live or to satisfy creative impulses. As society becomes more complex, however, people come to work more and more in order to be able to impress their neighbors, and thus, themselves. For this behavior he coined the term "conspicuous consumption."

In order to stand well in the eyes of the community, it is necessary to come up to a certain, somewhat indefinite, conventional standard of wealth. . . . Those members of the community who fall short of this . . . normal degree of . . . property suffer in the esteem of their fellow men; and consequently they suffer also in their own esteem, since the usual basis of self-respect is the respect accorded by one's neighbors. Only individuals with an aberrant temperament can in the long run maintain their self-esteem in the face of the disesteem of their fellows.[14]

One's self-esteem thus tends to depend on his ability to consume. He is pressed to conform in his occupational role for, by and large, society requires conformity as the price of high income and status. More than this, he must largely conform in his cultural personality, not only on the job, but in his whole life.

Economics is thus one of the most powerful levers of cultural brainwashing. In some primitive societies, the nonconformist may be an established part of society; the homosexual or the psychotic may, for example, be a medicine man. In modern society this is not usually the case. In *The Organization Man* Whyte included a section on "How to Cheat on Personality Tests," in

14. Thorstein Veblen, *The Theory of the Leisure Class,* New York, Macmillan, 1899, p. 30.

which he said that the way to take job-qualifying tests is to score "as near average as possible without submerging one's whole real personality." Students often ask the writer how becoming involved in protest activities will affect their job chances later. One cannot give a very encouraging answer. Today one may usually eat while not conforming, but the promotions and raises necessary for the conspicuous consumer generally go to those whose "selves" conform fairly closely to the cultural average.

The last component we shall discuss is the *spiritual.* This does not necessarily imply an immaterial or supernatural spirit or soul apart from the body. In ordinary language we use the term "spiritual" to refer to an element in ourselves that transcends both our common animal heritage and our everyday cultural life. We usually think of it as a "higher" or "wider" part of ourselves. When the philosopher George Santayana said that "life is all animal in its origin and all spiritual in its possible fruits," he was not necessarily speaking of God or an immortal soul, but he was speaking of a higher or wider element in human experience.

An excellent guide to this dimension is found in the ideas of the French philosopher Henri Bergson. He pointed out that our everyday experience, and our selves which are attuned to it, are only a part of human potentialities. In order to deal with the practical realities of life, we have to put on blinders, so to speak, which shut out many possibilities. A primitive hunter in hot pursuit of food cannot stop for relaxed admiration of a sunset. A person engaged in scientific research or political activity may feel bound to put all his time and energy into his work. A conspicuous consumer in hot pursuit of status and money may have no time for nature, art, religion, or love. Moreover, science and technology in themselves are not concerned with the immediate wholeness of experience. They take a rose, a human body, a sunset, a love affair, a mystical religious experience and dissect it, analyze it, select and abstract certain parts for study. This is the nature of their approach.

Our minds or intellects, said Bergson, focus on the practical tasks of *manipulating* our environment. They filter out and exclude those things that would interfere with this manipulation. The intellect, and the technology that it has developed for manipulating and mastering the world, are of great practical importance. They have provided the material means for civilization. But the manipulation of our environment is only part of our life. "The intellect," said Bergson, "can never comprehend reality," that is, the immediate wholeness of experience.

What is the spiritual component that transcends the everyday life of farm, factory, shop, office, laboratory? All of us have had some experiences of it. In love we feel transported into a dimension of life and of ourselves wider than everyday experience. An old folk saying tells us that "every man has two selves—one to meet the world with, and one to show a woman when he loves her." Art is another avenue to the spiritual. Great experiences of music, the theater, painting, poetry, and sculpture may give this sense of an immediate widening of ourselves. Experiences with nature, especially in its grander aspects, such as mountains, forests, deserts, ocean, and sky, may have the same effect. Creative people in any field are likely to have had this experience. People have found in the civil rights movement, in underground activity or open warfare against tyrants, in the peace movement, in the labor movement, and in other social causes an experience of transcending their ordinary selves. Religious experience which is not merely formal, but really moves us, gives the same sense of self-expansion. Many young people who are experimenting with drugs are seeking to open up areas of experience and selfhood which seem to them unattainable in the ordinary world.

Certain things tend to be common to all experiences of the spiritual dimension of the self. It is experienced as different from ordinary life. It is often felt to be much more significant and real. Very often—in love, art, nature, commitment, creativity, religious experience—there is a sense of discovery and revelation. One feels that he has found the meaning of his life. Sometimes he feels that he has discovered his real self, beside which his ordinary cultural self seems narrow and shallow.

In the modern Western world, where we have developed to a high degree the practical management of things and people, large numbers of individuals are largely cut off from this component of their personalities. Our environment tends to be something to be manipulated and mastered with machines, technology, and intellect rather than something to be immediately experienced and lived with. This may be more true of our civilization than of any previous human society. Many anthropologists who have lived with primitive peoples have found in them a spontaneous relationship to the whole of life which many of us seem to lack. The Orient has, on the whole, been less concerned with technical manipulation of the environment and more with other ways of experiencing it, and ourselves. Of course, no one has made the tremendous material gains we have made with our science and technology. Often, however, we get preoccupied with them and forget there is anything more to life than technology and anything more to self than a cultural machine.

How is the spiritual component re-

In 1876 my only sister, a young lady of eighteen years, died suddenly of cholera in St. Louis, Mo. My attachment for her was very strong, and the blow a severe one to me. A year or so after her death the writer became a commercial traveler, and it was in 1876, while on one of my Western trips, that the event occurred. I had "drummed" the city of St. Joseph, Mo., and had gone to my room at the Pacific House to send in my orders, which were unusually large ones, so that I was in a very happy frame of mind indeed. My thoughts, of course, were about these orders, knowing how pleased my house would be at my success. I had not been thinking of my late sister, or in any manner reflecting on the past. The hour was high noon, and the sun was shining cheerfully into my room. While busily smoking a cigar and writing out my orders, I suddenly became conscious that some one was sitting on my left, with one arm resting on the table. Quick as a flash I turned and distinctly saw the form of my dead sister, and for a brief second or so looked her squarely in the face; and so sure was I that it was she, that I sprang forward in delight, calling her by name, and, as I did so, the apparition instantly vanished. Naturally I was startled and dumbfounded, almost doubting my senses; but the cigar in my mouth, and pen in hand, with the ink still moist on my letter, I satisfied myself I had not been dreaming and was wide awake. I was near enough to touch her, had it been a physical possibility, and noted her features, expression, and details of dress, etc. She appeared as if alive. Her eyes looked kindly and perfectly natural into mine. Her skin was so lifelike that I could see the glow or moisture on its surface, and, on the whole, there was no change in her appearance, otherwise than when alive.

Now comes the most remarkable confirmation of my statement,
which cannot be doubted by those who know what I state actually
occurred. This visitation, or whatever you may call it, so
impressed me that I took the next train home, and in the presence
of my parents and others I related what had occurred. My father, a
man of rare good sense and very practical, was inclined to
ridicule me, as he saw how earnestly I believed what I stated;
but he, too, was amazed when later on I told them of a bright red
line or scratch on the right-hand side of my sister's face, which
I distinctly had seen. When I mentioned this my mother rose
trembling to her feet and nearly fainted away, and as soon as she
sufficiently recovered her self-possession, with tears streaming
down her face, she exclaimed that I had indeed seen my sister, as
no living mortal but herself was aware of that scratch, which
she had accidentally made while doing some little act of
kindness after my sister's death. She said she well remembered
how pained she was to think she should have, unintentionally,
marred the features of her dead daughter, and that unknown to
all, how she had carefully obliterated all traces of the slight scratch
with the aid of powder, etc., and that she had never mentioned
it to a human being from that day to this. In proof, neither my father
nor any of our family had detected it, and positively were
unaware of the incident, yet I saw the scratch as bright as if just
made. So strangely impressed was my mother, that even after she
had retired to rest she got up and dressed, came to me and
told me she knew at least that I had seen my sister. A few weeks
later my mother died, happy in her belief she would rejoin her
favorite daughter in a better world.

—F. W. H. Myers, Human Personality and Its Survival of Bodily Death,
New Hyde Park, N.Y., University Books, 1961, pp. 222–224.

lated to other aspects of the self? The biological component represents the heritage common to all animals. The spiritual component is the most distinctively human aspect of ourselves. Yet, sexual love, for example, which is one of our highest spiritual experiences, is impossible without adequate biological functioning. The social component can be very close to the spiritual. The goals of love, justice, and human brotherhood, which Cooley saw originating in primary groups, are certainly spiritual values. The relationship of the spiritual to the cultural component is complex. The creative artist uses the media provided by his culture; the creative scientist, its heritage of knowledge; the religious prophet, its traditional symbols. Yet each goes be-yond his culture. Culture is almost always conservative. The spiritual dimension is usually considered too "far out," and is viewed as a threat. It is thus almost always in conflict with cultural conformity.

We cannot close this section without referring back to a question left open earlier. We said that the spiritual component need not necessarily be immaterial or supernatural. What is it? Materialists or naturalists will say that there is nothing in it that cannot be explained by known laws of nature. There are also other views. Studies in extrasensory perception (ESP) appear to have demonstrated that there is some kind of direct communication between human minds—or influence of minds over matter—which is not explainable by presently known natural laws. It might be explained by natural laws not yet known. This research suggests, at any rate, that the spiritual in man may not be altogether separate or insulated, but may have some direct relationship to the spiritual in other people. Some psychologists have held that our selves are part of a "collective unconscious." Research in ESP suggests that the spiritual component in each of us may in some way be part of a common spiritual pool.

It is a widespread belief that the spiritual represents an element of a supernatural God which is present in every person. Millions of people have believed that the spiritual is, or is related to, an immortal and immaterial soul in man. One outstanding student of personality, F. W. H. Myers, in a book entitled *Human Personality and Its Survival of Bodily Death* (1903), held that there are many aspects of the self, but that one opens up, so to speak, upon a realm of supernatural reality. He was one of a number of scholars and scientists who, under the auspices of the British Society for Psychical Research, studied by the most rigorous scientific procedures the evidence for the survival of the self after death. Some of the researchers, like Myers, were firmly convinced of its survival. Others were equally persuaded of the opposite.

PSYCHODYNAMICS

We now have a background with which to examine some ideas that have grown out of the contributions of Sigmund Freud (1856–1939). Whatever we may think of his theories, Freud has without doubt been one of the most important and influential figures of the past century. His views have challenged and changed much of our framework of thinking in social science and in most spheres of life.

Freud was a physician and a psychiatrist, trained first of all in neurology. He was primarily concerned with psychological health and illness. His theories were the outcome of his long clinical practice of the technique of psychoanalysis, in which the patient was (and still is) treated by encouraging him to talk freely, without inhibition, about whatever came into his mind. It is important to remember that Freud's theories and concepts were not spun out of thin air, but were his way of summarizing a lifetime of practice as a physician. We can really understand them only by becoming familiar with his work, and then by trying to apply his concepts concretely in understanding our own lives. Many people too easily get a glib name-dropping acquaintance with Freudian terminology without really understanding much of it at all.

Freud was concerned with the quest of the self for happiness. He saw the problem as one of *psychodynamics* (Greek *psyche,* mind or spirit; *dynamis,* power or energy). The self, or the personality, he regarded as an organization or expression of the life force—*libido,* or psychic energy. This continually presses toward expression. Sometimes the energy of our impulses is expressed directly. At other times it is inhibited, suppressed, repressed. Much of the time it is deflected into channels other than its original one. For example, the sexual drive may be expressed directly in a love affair, suppressed by a vow of celibacy, or deflected into a love poem. Since the libido never ceases to demand some outlet, the happiness and health of the personality depend on how successful one is in finding satisfactory and acceptable outlets for his psychic energy.

Freud's concept of psychodynamics applied not only to the individual but to social groups, for he saw society as to a large extent an organization of psychic energies. Thus a family, a community, a military combat unit, even a nation may be bound together by affectional ties of the members to each other or to a common leader. On the

Sigmund Freud

other hand, each may also be united by hatred of a common out-group.

Freud saw the libido, or life energy, as essentially sexual in nature. By this he meant, first of all, that the aim of life is to secure pleasure and avoid pain. "It is simply the pleasure principle which lays down the program of life's purpose." Pleasure is the reduction of tension. Sexual orgasm is the most intense pleasure. All other pleasures—in work, play, art, companionship, communion with nature—are simply lesser expressions of the same drive. All are influenced by an individual's sexual experience.

To understand the libidinal problems of an individual, said Freud, we must pay special attention to his early infancy and childhood, for sexuality does not begin at adolescence, but is present from the beginning of life. In making this point, Freud referred to a study of strong heterosexual "love affairs" of children as young as three or four, made by the American psychologist Sanford Bell before 1900. Even the youngest infant has, he claimed, ex-

periences of a sexual nature and significance. Certain zones of his body, certain people, certain kinds of activities become sources of strong tensions and impulses toward pleasure. Since, as we have seen, early patterns of learning tend to persist strongly, these experiences of infantile sexuality have great significance for later life. While most would agree with Freud that sexuality begins well before adolescence, many would not give to infantile sexuality the great importance he gave it.

What are these experiences, specifically? First we must understand Freud's view of psychosexual development with respect to erogenous zones. At no age are all areas of the body equally great sources of pleasure. Always some are more erogenous (productive of pleasure) than others. The first erogenous zone is the mouth. The young infant's relationship to the world is primarily "oral," his main pleasure, the reduction of tension through sucking. Somewhat later—perhaps from the end of the first year to the third year— urination and, particularly, defecation become important sources of tension and pleasure. The significance of this "anal" phase of development may be increased by the fact that adults place a great importance on toilet training and often instill severe conflicts and anxieties in children (and often in themselves). As he becomes more independent, a child begins to take an increasing interest in his genital organs. This "genital" phase may begin quite early; Kinsey's *Sexual Behavior in the Human Female* records genital masturbation by a 6-month-old girl in her crib. Normally there is a shift in erogenous zones from oral to anal to genital, and the genitalia remain the chief erogenous zone throughout the rest of life.

We must also understand the significance to Freud of the infant's and child's choice of sexual objects. As we have seen, the first figure who emerges, as the child in the early oral phase of infancy begins to distinguish objects, is his mother. She is the center of his universe, of his strivings, the ultimate source of security and protection. This is true for both the boy and the girl, and the experience is never fully forgotten.

As the child enters the genital phase of development, however, a new factor is added. A cross-sexual choice develops. The boy's libidinal interests remain attached to his mother, but in a genital rather than an oral form. (He may have erections, for example, when held by her.) The girl's chief love object ceases to be her mother and becomes instead her father. The stimulus for these choices comes partly from within, through the child's own awareness of sex differences and their significance. It comes partly from the parents' choice; the father tends to favor the little girl, the mother the little boy.

Freud described these childhood sexual attachments, in terms of Greek mythology, as Oedipal, after the myth of Oedipus, who slept with his mother and killed his father. These attachments lead to the *Oedipus conflict*. The young child has a rival. For the boy his father stands in the way of his obtaining sole possession of his mother, which is what he wants. The mother stands in the way of the girl. Each would like to eliminate his rival. But this would remove a person upon whom the child is deeply dependent and whom he loves. Also, he is afraid that if he tried, he himself would be removed instead! The Oedipal wish thus becomes so fraught with anxiety that it is banished from consciousness —repressed. This fear and repression are the reason why most of us would so strongly deny ever having wanted to possess our father or mother sexually, and sometimes might even be willing to fight a person who suggested it.

The Oedipal repression leads, in about the sixth year of life, to the *latency period*. From this time until adolescence, the child's sexuality seems to have disappeared. Actually it has only been driven underground. The reason is that it is associated with his forbidden Oedipal desires. (In addition, a child is likely to have been actively punished or threatened for masturbation, sexual curiosity, or sexual play.)

At puberty biological changes strengthen the sex drive and tend to bring it out into the open again, but the unmarried person has two problems to deal with. One lies in the taboos and punishments which society places upon premarital sex. The other, and in the long run perhaps more serious problem, lies within. A girl's first experience with sexual love for a male (her father) and a boy's first experience with sexual love for a female (his mother) were both impossible of fulfillment. They were associated with deep anxiety. The emotional attitudes of fear and denial developed toward the first sexual object tend to be generalized to any future love object. Thus a girl may respond to a sexual relationship with a man as though she were a child realizing her wish to remove her mother and go to bed with her father. She may become frigid or flee the whole relationship, and the man may thus become impotent, ungratified, or be unable to treat the girl lovingly. One psychiatric expert, Dr. Marie Robinson, estimates that 40 percent of married women are to some degree frigid. The large amount of frigidity and sexual maladjustment among legally married people indicates that marriage is no sure solution at all to sexual problems. (In terms of our discussion of learning, this is a dramatic and tragic case of mislearning or wrong conditioning.)

This problem, said Freud, is so central and universal that it can be said that a person's main task in achieving psychological health and happiness is to overcome his Oedipal fears and establish a mutual love relationship free from infantile anxieties. This is not only a sexual problem, but a problem of one's whole life. One's work, his play, his creative capacity, and his ability for social relationships are all affected by his sexual experience. Neurosis, or mental illness, affects the whole personality, but to Freud, it was fundamentally a failure to achieve a satisfactory release of libido in genital love.

To many people much of this sounds bizarre, absurd, or impossible. It might, indeed, be all these things if people were rational and fully conscious of their acts. This is, however, Freud pointed out, quite clearly not the case. By far the larger part of our experience is *not* conscious. A human being is like an iceberg: looking from above the water, we see only the mass above the surface and think that it is the whole iceberg, whereas in fact by far the larger part is hidden from view. We can never understand either individual or social behavior if we assume that it is largely conscious or rational or what it appears to be on the surface.

A young child, said Freud, is not ordinarily conscious of desiring his cross-sexual parent sexually or of wanting to remove his rival parent. When a young (or older) man or woman responds to a sexual relationship as though he were going to bed with a forbidden parent, he is not ordinarily conscious of his responses. This is just the point of the whole matter. If he were conscious of the connection, he could probably deal with the problem fairly easily. The difficulty is that he has learned without knowing either how or what he has learned. Thus, said Freud, the basic task in psychotherapy is to bring hidden infantile fears and conflicts to the surface where they can be handled—to make the unconscious conscious.

It was here that Freud was led to his threefold division of the self into id, ego, and superego. These he conceived as *functions* of the personality. No one should suppose that anatomical dissection will reveal the place where any of them is located!

The *id,* as we saw earlier, is essentially the biological component of the self. A large part of it, although by no means all, is below the level of con-

sciousness. Freud saw the id as dominated by two primary impulses: love and aggression. Love includes sexuality and all the affectional and social impulses that bind people together. It includes work, play, art, and creativity. In his earlier years, Freud thought that aggression was simply a reaction to frustration of libidinal impulses. Later he was inclined to believe that in addition to frustration of libido, there is an inborn urge for manipulation, power, and destruction. The life of an individual (and of society) he felt to be a constant tension between the two components of the id—Eros (libido, love) and Thanatos (destruction, death).

The *superego* we may describe, with some reservations, as the conscience. To Freud, this was largely the product of the child's experience in the family. The family acts as the representative of society and transmits social mores. The superego is the internalized representative of society and the parents within the personality. By internalizing his parents' commands and taboos and learning to punish himself in advance for his desires to disobey, the child avoids the pain of being punished by his parents. The superego's chief form of punishment is guilt. Freud used an interesting simile to describe the superego. The self, he said, is like a city that is beseiged by an army. After the army (society, parents) takes the city, in order to be spared the necessity of maintaining a siege, it establishes a garrison within the city to maintain order. The superego is the "internal garrison." It is partly conscious, but a large part of it (as in the case of Oedipal fears and guilt) is unconscious.

The *ego* is the rational directing force in the personality. It is concerned with mediating among three parties: the imperative libidinal and aggressive drives of the id; the internalized commands, taboos, and guilt feelings of the superego; and the actual demands of the outer world. Whereas Freud saw the id as dominated by the "pleasure principle," he saw the ego as governed by the "reality principle." More than either of the other functions of the personality, the ego is conscious.

To Freud a large part of individual and social behavior must be understood in terms of a number of psychodynamic devices through which the personality tries to resolve the four-way tension of id, ego, superego, and outer world. These have been identified by Freud and his followers. Not all social scientists would accept all the content Freud gave to these devices, but a large number agree that they exist and are important. They are key concepts that deserve study, for we shall encounter them again throughout this book.

Repression

Repression occurs, we have seen, when an impulse is not only inhibited, but pushed out of consciousness. In a sense it is "got out of the way," but seldom very satisfactorily, because it continues to seek fulfillment. In one of his lectures in the United States, Freud compared the "return of the repressed" to the ejection of a disorderly person from a meeting hall. The person is removed but remains in the vestibule, hammering on the door. The problem of repression is not only an individual but a mass problem. For, to Freud, the growth of civilization requires an increasing denial ("suppression, repression, or something else?") of libidinal and aggressive impulses on the part of everybody.

Introjection

Introjection is the turning inward of impulses, mainly aggressive ones, against oneself to escape the danger of attacking the outer world. We can see the germs of this reaction in a frustrated child who gets so angry that he hits himself. The German philosopher Friedrich Nietzsche, before Freud, had described this kind of behavior.

All instincts which do not find a vent without, turn inwards. . . .

These terrible bulwarks, with which the social organization protected itself against the old instincts of wild, free, prowling man became turned backwards against man himself. . . . It was man who, imprisoned as he was in the oppressive narrowness and monotony of custom, in his own impatience lacerated, persecuted, gnawed, frightened and ill-treated himself; it was this animal in the hands of the tamer, which beat itself against the bars of the cage. . . .[15]

Guilt is an important form of introjected hostility, the punishment of oneself instead of someone or something else. Again, Freud saw this device increasing with civilization in that the price of progress in civilization was paid by forfeiting happiness through the heightened sense of guilt.

Fixation and regression

As we have seen, Freud regarded the achievement of adulthood as a very difficult struggle. If the going is too rough, one may find it easier to remain psychologically a child, to fixate in his development. Or he may try to return, or regress, from an achieved adulthood.

In the Freudian view, development may be blocked so that oral and anal interests retain a dominant significance. For example, compulsive eating, drinking, smoking, or talking may represent failure to develop emotionally beyond the point where one's chief source of pleasure was his mouth. A person strongly marked by these traits is called an oral character. Again, chronic constipation, chronic preoccupation with the bowels, persistent use of "dirty" language, and compulsive preoccupation with order and cleanliness may represent failure to leave one's anal pleasures and anxieties behind him. Such qualities may mark the anal character. In less complicated terms, we all know people (including in

15. Friedrich Nietzsche, *The Genealogy of Morals*, Edinburgh and London, Foulis, 1910, pp. 100, 101.

some degree ourselves) who just have not quite grown up.

Stressful situations are likely to produce regressive behavior, which may have the meaning of "going back" to mother or father to be passive and cared for. In serious illness patients are likely to become dependent and infantile. Imprisonment causes regression in sexual behavior in probably the large majority of inmates of penal institutions. Bruno Bettelheim, a psychoanalyst who was imprisoned in the Nazi concentration camp at Buchenwald, relates the strong tendency of prisoners to admire their captors and become dependent upon them. Some inmates even searched out and put on old Gestapo uniforms so that they could be like their guards. Crowd behavior is very likely to be regressive, and in "war hysteria" whole nations may become seemingly infantile in their behavior. Adulthood always involves a tension between progressive and regressive tendencies. There are few if any people who will not regress if enough pressure is put upon them.

Displacement
Displacement is the transfer of aggressive impulses from the frustrating object to an innocent party. A child, angry at her father for putting her to bed, hits her beloved dolly. In Danny Kaye's rendition of "The Inspector General," there is a sequence which beautifully illustrates displacement. A colonel barks an order to a major, who says an obedient "Yes, sir," and barks it at the first lieutenant. He in turn says, "Yes, sir," and barks it at the second lieutenant. Finally the order gets to the buck private, who says "Yes, sir" to his sergeant, turns around, and kicks a little dog. The "scapegoat," who was loaded with the people's sins and banished, is a classic example of displacement. The Nazis used the Jews as scapegoats, many poor whites use Negroes, the Communist nations may use "capitalist imperialists," and some capitalists may blame everything on Communists.

Earlier we saw that there is a close link between peace in the in-group and hostility toward an out-group. Freud held that all religious groups must be hostile toward nonbelievers, for only by displacing their in-group hostilities can they love their fellow believers. Sometimes the device of displacement is manipulated. The Southern novelist Lillian Smith has an imaginary conversation between Mr. Big and Mr. Little in a Southern white community. Mr. Big tells Mr. Little that if he will just let Mr. Big run the town, he can treat Negroes any way he likes.

Sublimation
Sublimation is the turning of a blocked impulse into an attainable form of expression. We know how a person bereaved, or disappointed in love, or separated from a loved one may "lose himself in his work." Freud saw sublimation in many forms of work. A woman incapable of having children may become a teacher or open a nursery school. Homosexual desires to be a woman may be sublimated in a career of designing women's clothes. Sometimes hostile as well as libidinal tendencies may be sublimated. A person with *sadistic* tendencies may act out part of his impulses in a socially useful way as a surgeon. (Not all surgeons are sadists, any more than all dress designers are homosexuals!) Freud considered that a large part of aristic production consists of sublimation of frustrated drives. He wrote a book exploring the case of Leonardo da Vinci. The paintings of Van Gogh, in which he expressed the tortures of his spirit, are certainly an example of Freud's contention. Sublimation may be the final triumph of the human spirit in situations of seemingly hopeless frustration. In a dark cell in Auschwitz concentration camp was found painted on the wall a picture of green mountains, a house with shutters, and in the middle of the shutters, hearts.

Compensation
Whereas in sublimation one expresses the same impulse in another form, in compensation the impulse is gratified

through a different kind of activity. A good example is a university guidance counselor's report on a student: "He is not outgoing enough, but he will learn to compensate by high grades for his lack of social skills." We have seen how the authoritarian personality may turn his lack of love into the drive for status and power. Hitler's compensations for his frustration as a painter and a man are a dramatic example. An early psychoanalyst, Alfred Adler, stressed the way in which inferiority feelings—the famous "inferiority complex"—may lead to compensatory efforts for power. He felt that a sense of physical inferiority was very important. Cases come to mind. Caesar was epileptic, Napoleon was short, Theodore Roosevelt was sickly as a child and Franklin Roosevelt a polio victim, Stalin had a withered arm.

As these cases of political leaders suggest, compensation is a mass as well as an individual phenomenon. Not only Hitler but a large part of the German people compensated through the doctrine of Aryan superiority for national defeat in World War I and for the economic deprivations of the Depression. The white, lower-class "redneck" farmer in the American South is generally one of the strongest supporters of "white supremacy." As one "red-neck" was quoted, he is " . . . on the underside of the plank with nothing between him and the bare black ground. He's got to have something to give him pride. Just to be better than something."[16]

Identification

When a person cannot gain satisfactions on his own, he may seek them through becoming "one" with another person, group, or institution. We have already discussed the role of identification of a child with his parent, teacher, coach, or cultural hero. We saw how, through imitation of his model, the child learns techniques for growing up and enjoying the satisfactions the

16. Robert Penn Warren, *Segregation*, New York, Random House, 1956, pp. 43, 44.

model now has. There is a second and more immediate gain through identification. The accomplishments and gratifications of the object of identification come to be experienced as one's own.

Consider the child's "My Daddy can lick your Daddy." Unconsciously, if not consciously, a young child is likely to believe that his Father is the greatest and most powerful person in the world. This belief gives him a sense of security, and also of power which he shares. The thought that some other Father might be able to beat up his own is thus a threat to his own ego. In identifying with the Gestapo by putting on their old uniforms, the prisoners at Buchenwald were, like the young boy, borrowing power. Identification is an important device in social as well as individual psychology. People tend to identify with city, school athletic team, company, class, race, nation. By so doing they acquire traits of power and significance which as individuals they do not have. Should "their" team lose a game or "their" race be insulted or "their" nation lose a war, it is taken as a personal blow.

Identification may clearly be a form of compensation. It is also a form of introjection in that one "incorporates" a part of the outside world into his own ego.

Transference

Transference is closely related to identification. Attitudes held as an infant or young child toward one's parents are transferred in later life to figures, or other entities, which remind one of his mother or father. The child tends to regard his parent as he later regards God, as omnipotent and omniscient. Fal, age five, one of the children studied by Piaget, believed that his father had invented the game of marbles. He also believed him to be older than his grandfather and older than God! In transference the qualities of omnipotence and omniscience tend to be attributed to other people in authority. This transfer tends to be accompanied by an ambivalent attitude:

one is worshipful of the parent substitute, but he is also resentful and rebellious.

Thus teachers, coaches, physicians, priests, kings, and presidents tend to seem as parents and to become targets for both adoration and hostility, even if they themselves may merit neither. Freud developed the concept of transference out of his own experience that patients turned the analyst into a father (or mother). The idea of transference, if not the word, has become popular enough so that we now commonly speak of a political figure like Franklin Roosevelt, or Eisenhower, or Adenauer, as a "father figure."

Institutions also tend to become objects of transference. It is no mere accident of words that the Catholic believer speaks of Mother Church, while accepting the Pope (literally, "papa") as his spiritual leader. God as conceived by many people is an anthropomorphic (human-like) figure, based upon the father image. Nations tend to be symbolized as either masculine or feminine. France is La Belle France (feminine), Germany has historically been the Fatherland, Russia is still Mother Russia. When we speak of defending the United States we usually use the pronoun "she."

We can see that transference involves either fixation or regression—that is, we react to figures and symbols in adulthood as though we were children.

Projection

We can say that we project upon figures and symbols the images (not necessarily realistic) which as young children we had of our parents. Projection is the opposite of introjection. We attribute to the outer world something that is actually inside us.

Interesting illustrations of what we mean by projection are found in the psychological testing devices known as projective techniques. Essentially these confront a person with an "unstructured" situation and ask him to give it form. One such device is the Rorschach test, in which a person is asked to tell what he sees in a series of ink blots. What he does "see" will be largely a projection of what he is. In the Thematic Apperception Test (TAT), one is presented with a series of pictures so indefinite in detail that they leave much room for imagination. For example, the picture may simply show outlines of two people, one older and one younger. Such different responses as "The father has just punished the child" and "They are going for a nice walk in the woods" will tell much about the persons responding.

Studies of college students have shown that students rated as stingy are more likely to see others as stingy. One mental illness, paranoia, is particularly marked by projection in the form of delusions that one is hated and persecuted. "I hate and distrust everybody" becomes "Everybody hates and is out to get me." Psychiatrists like Erich Fromm and Jerome D. Frank think that there is a large element of paranoid projection in the behavior of the great political powers. Every nation accuses others of "aggression," proclaims its own innocence, and insists that its own military activities are purely for defense. Its image of its "enemies" is based in part upon fact, but partly upon a projection of its own aggressive aims.

Since it is obvious that Freud's views are highly debatable, and debated, some evaluation is due at this point. From the foregoing pages, it should be clear that the author is not among those people—of whom there are some of repute—who consider Freud's ideas to be on the whole worthless or harmful rubbish. It is his opinion that Freud is one of the greatest contributors to our understanding of society. Let us briefly examine, however, several aspects of Freud's ideas.

1. Of all Freud's theories, there is probably greatest acceptance of the general idea of the unconscious (which Freud did not originate) and of the psychodynamic devices that we have just discussed. There is not necessarily

agreement with the content that Freud found in the unconscious or its devices.

2. There are many critics who feel that Freud was not scientific. There is much in Freud that is questionable and bizarre, and some that is clearly false. In general, however, these critics are likely to have a too narrow view of science. Clinical experience of therapist with patient—which furnishes most of the evidence for psychoanalysis—is different from quantitative laboratory experimentation, but both can be sources for valid scientific conclusions.

3. Some critics claim that Freudian therapy—upon which we have only touched here—has been no more successful than other less expensive, less time consuming, and less complicated methods for treating neurotic people. Some claim that people are just as likely to recover with no treatment at all. There have been a number of studies of this problem. Such comparisons are difficult, for it is hard in the first place to determine what a successful treatment means. There is, however, no clear proof that Freudian therapy is unusually successful. Critics claim that it should be if the theory is sound—"by their fruits ye shall know them." Certainly the record of therapy does not suggest that Freudianism has anything like all the answers.

4. There is much disagreement with the stress given to sexuality in general, to the sexuality of children, and to the Oedipus complex. It is this writer's opinion that sexuality is as important as Freud saw it to be, but that he underemphasized the importance of other things. We shall see shortly what these are. The same is true of the sexual interests of children.

Science will in the long run probably accept the importance of the Oedipus complex, but not in as universal a sense as Freud thought. Human life almost universally occurs in families. It is therefore very likely that the first strong emotional ties will be incestuous ones. These are bound to be partially frustrated and to create deep emotional reactions which must later be unlearned. It is likely, however, that Freud generalized too far from the family structure he knew best—the nineteenth-century, Victorian, patriarchal, upper-middle-class, Jewish Viennese family.

This was the contention of the anthropologist Malinowski, who tried to see whether the Oedipus complex could be found in a very different kind of society. The one he knew best was the Trobriand Islanders, of Melanesia. Here the father, instead of being the head of the family, was simply the wife's husband and a kind companion for the children. His biological role in producing children was not even known. The mother's brother wielded the rewards and punishments. Malinowski found that in the dreams and folklore of the Trobrianders, there appeared to be strong repressed hostilities toward the *uncle,* but not toward the biological father. He concluded that Freud had rightly pointed to a "nuclear complex" present in all societies, but that he was wrong in supposing that it took the same form everywhere.

The psychotherapist Wilhelm Reich, a follower of Freud and an admirer of Malinowski, suggested that the Oedipus complex is actually a form of pathology which develops in family systems characteristic of the Western world. Here children are forbidden to express their sexual interests freely in play with other children. They therefore turn them back abnormally into their families. In a society like that of the Trobrianders, where sex play was freely allowed, Reich thought that children would not have to form intense Oedipal attachments.

5. Freud properly emphasized the role of conflicts in childhood in shaping later life. In so doing he underestimated the role in personality of later cultural conflicts of a nonsexual kind. The psychoanalyst Karen Horney (1885–1953) rejected much of Freud's emphasis on sex and the Oedipus complex, holding that the source of

neurotic disorders lies much more in conflicts within the values of society. In our society, for example, we teach children in church and synagogue to be loving and cooperative, and then throw them out into a "jungle" world of cutthroat competition. Neurotic difficulties, Horney thought, grow more out of such problems than out of childhood experience as such. Erich Fromm (1900–   ) has emphasized the increasing separation of man in the Western world from nature, work, and his fellow man. He sees this as the chief source of personality conflict. Harry Stack Sullivan, also a psychoanalyst, held that the source of emotional problems must be found not primarily in childhood sexual conflicts, but in the "interpersonal relations" of adulthood.

These three people have all been "neo-Freudians"—so called because they have still considered themselves members of the Freudian tradition. Unfortunately, they have not been able to accept the fact that *both* they and Freud might be largely right. In pointing out Freud's omissions, they have tended to "throw the Freudian baby out with the bath."

6. The most serious criticism of Freud is that he considered the spiritual dimension of personality to be unreal or compensatory. He tended to see people as rather helpless victims of their biological imperatives. One of Freud's younger contemporaries, Carl Jung (1875–1961) accepted the role of the libido as life energy, and in general accepted the idea of the unconscious and its devices. He held, however, that the basic problem of man is more than the release of sexuality and the reduction of tension. To him man's essential problem is that of giving to his life a significance in the universe. It is failure here, Jung said, which is at the heart of emotional conflict. In his experience, he claimed, no patient who did not solve his religious problems ever really got well. Freud, by contrast, considered religion a neurotic illusion.

A more recent Viennese psychiatrist, Viktor Frankl, who spent a long period in a Nazi concentration camp, likewise insists on the inadequacy of Freud's theories to explain and deal with people's really human problems. Like Jung, he sees each person's psychological task as that of finding the unique meaning of his own life. This may lie—as was his own experience in Auschwitz—not primarily in gratification of biological imperatives, but rather in exercising one's unique human capacity to find meaning in spite of frustration or even death.

Clearly Jung and Frankl also point to a dimension lacking in the Freudian view. It is unfortunate that they too have felt it necessary to play down or reject Freud's sexual discoveries rather than to include his truth within their own.

PSYCHOLOGY AND CULTURE

Our discussion in this chapter has posed many problems about the relationship of the individual to society. In the next chapter we shall examine the cultural basis for human life. Let us note some key questions which we shall want to carry forward into that and later chapters.

Question 1. Can there be a society which satisfies basic human needs? There is plenty of evidence that most people find their experience with society to be somewhat less than completely rewarding. If our social institutions did not frustrate many needs and desires, we would not have so much murder and suicide, crime and delinquency, neurotic difficulty and psychotic breakdown, escape into frantic "fun," alcohol or LSD, slow suicide through addiction to tobacco, violent rebellion by high school and college youth, or an increasing incidence of the degenerative diseases of stress.

Clearly we must have social organization and culture. Is it possible to have them without frustrating the important imperatives of human beings? There are three basic positions on the matter.

One view, that of extreme cultural relativism, says that there need be no necessary conflict because human needs are themselves created by society. Thus, in a properly organized society, people would want only what the society was able to provide. We have seen, however, that this view leaves out the biological and other imperatives whose form of expression is shaped by culture, but which can be neither created nor eliminated by culture.

A second view is pessimistic. Human drives are by nature in conflict with the demands which any society must make. This view is historically associated with the English philosopher Thomas Hobbes, who held that society serves to keep in check man's naturally selfish and antisocial human nature. Freud believed that both man's love impulses and his destructive drives must inevitably be frustrated in any kind of advanced society.

A third view is again optimistic. Culture at present frustrates human needs, but this is the fault of culture. This view is especially associated with the French philosopher Rousseau. "Man," he said, "is born free, but he is everywhere in chains." A better society would, however, make possible the gratification of natural drives.

Question 2. Why is there so much destructiveness in the world? Fifteen years before the atomic bomb, Freud pointed out that "men have brought their power of subduing the forces of nature to such a pitch that by using them they could now very easily exterminate one another to the last man." Why is destructiveness so great that human beings, all of whom desire life and happiness, threaten to extinguish all society and human existence? Again, there are three major answers.

One holds that human aggression, hostility, and violence are the expression of an inborn drive toward destruction. This, as we have seen, was Freud's view. In this case we can only hope, as Freud did, that the more posi-

tive forces in human nature may somehow hold the innate destructiveness in check. This picture is not very hopeful.

A second view maintains that hostility does not exist for its own sake, but is a response to frustration. This distinction is not much different from the first viewpoint, since society must inevitably so frustrate people that their hostility must be just as great as if they had a destructive instinct.

A third position also holds that hostility is a response to frustration, but denies that society must frustrate people severely. Taking issue with more pessimistic views, the psychiatrist Jules Masserman, for example, holds that "hostilities among human beings . . . spring from the frustrations and the anxiety-ridden inhibitions of their persistently barbaric culture."[17] It is clear that Masserman does not think that culture need be so repressive.

Question 3. What is the relationship of the psychologically healthy person to society? Does psychological health mean complete conformity to one's cultural pattern? Or is it possible for the conformist to be psychologically sick? Does psychological health perhaps mean the ability to gratify one's drives, all the way from the biological to the spiritual, even if society would suppress them? Is it necessarily neurotic behavior to be against the institutions of one's society? On the other hand, is rebellion necessarily healthy? What leads a person to be a nonconformist? Is it healthier to seek a life in which all one's tensions are resolved or to try to heighten one's tensions? Does the psychologically healthy person seek to reduce the stress (wear and tear) in his life to a minimum, or does he seek stresses that are meaningful to him?

Question 4. How is the psychology of individuals related to social organization and culture? There are some

17. Jules Masserman, "Experimental Neuroses," *Scientific American*, March 1950, p. 43.

Scene in a public park: suppression of the individual or preservation of culture?

tions of "national character" developed in early childhood. One such view "holds that the infant's early experience in feeding and toilet training determine his adult character, and that this character, in turn, determines the nature of his culture, since most adults in any culture have received similar training during childhood." One study of the Japanese people, for example, attributed a large part of their culture to the fact that Japanese children were trained for the toilet early, and thus developed strong anal traits in their national character. Critics have referred to this as the "Scott tissue theory" of culture.

The truth would seem to be somewhere between these two views. In an earlier chapter, we saw that a society is more than the people who carry it forward at any time. It is an ongoing system of technology, values, and institutions. Each new generation must, however, acquire the social pattern. It does this not through instinct, but through socialization (learning of basic, human, social relationships) and enculturation (learning of the specific culture pattern). This experience of learning is a psychological process. National character clearly does influence culture. If the growing-up experience of a whole population is such as to make people predominantly authoritarian or democratic in personality, we cannot ignore this fact in studying their economic, political, or other institutions. The Freudian psychodynamic devices throw much light on all aspects of social behavior. If large numbers of a population have need for a scapegoat, this fact must be taken into account in studying their class, caste, and religious institutions, and probably their political foreign policy. In short, to know culture we must understand people as well as institutions.

people who will think that this chapter is largely irrelevant in a book on social science. To them, individual psychology is one thing, and social organization is another. The pattern of society is determined by geography, resources, political power relations, and cultural traditions, but not in any important way by the psychodynamics of individual lives.

On the other hand, there are those who believe that social organization and culture are little more than reflec-

Suggestions for further reading

The student who has come this far will feel that all psychology is social psychology, that individual behavior can never be understood apart from the social behavior in which it is involved. In this he would agree with RAYMOND H. WHEELER, who pioneered this view among psy-

chologists in The Science of Psychology (*Crowell, 1929*). *Wheeler's book is a good general supplement to Chapter five.*

On the subject of how we learn, JOHN B. WATSON's Behaviorism (*rev. ed., University of Chicago, Phoenix Books, 1930, paper*) *is a strong, if somewhat overstated, argument for the power of conditioning. A point of view which places more stress on purpose and insight is* EDWARD C. TOLMAN's Purposive Behavior in Animals and Man (*Appleton-Century-Crofts, 1969, paper*). *General works on learning are* ERNEST R. HILGARD *and* GORDON H. BOMER, Theories of Learning (*3rd ed., Appleton-Century-Crofts, 1948*) *and* MORRIS L. BIGGE, Learning Theories for Teachers (*Harper & Row, 1964, paper*).

Two fundamental books on the physiological interaction of the organism with its environment are WALTER B. CANNON's *presentation of homeostasis in* The Wisdom of the Body (*Norton, 1932*) *and* HANS SELYE's The Stress of Life (*McGraw-Hill, 1956, paper*).

GEORGE HERBERT MEAD's *important view of how the self develops in the game—first referred to in Chapter four—is found in* Mind, Self, and Society (*University of Chicago Press, 1934, paper*). The Moral Judgment of the Child (*Free Press, 1932, paper*) *presents* JEAN PIAGET's *experiments on how the self-sense develops from constraint to cooperation. How the sense of one's sexual role is developed by cultural influences is described by* MARGARET MEAD *in* Sex and Temperament in Three Primitive Societies (*Dell, 1967, paper*) *and* Male and Female (*Dell, 1968, paper*). The Psychological Frontiers of Society (*Columbia University Press, 1945, 1963, paper*), *by* ABRAM KARDINER *and* RALPH LINTON, *is a joint description by a psychoanalyst and a cultural anthropologist of the* basic *personality structures of three cultural groups, including the midwestern United States.* THORSTEIN VEBLEN's The Theory of the Leisure Class (*Mentor, 1954*) *was a pioneer work in describing how economic forces shape individual personality and psychology.*

An excellent introduction to psychoanalysis through FREUD's *own work is* The Basic Writings of Sigmund Freud (*Modern Library, 1938*). *Outside of Freud's own work, perhaps the most important book in basic psychoanalytic theory is* WILHELM REICH's Character Analysis (*Noonday, 1949, paper*). *Here Reich, while insisting on the importance of sexuality, emphasizes cultural factors which Freud overlooked. An important criticism of Freud by a cultural anthropologist appears in* BRONISLAW MALINOWSKI's Sex and Repression in Savage Society (*World, 1955, paper*). ALFRED ADLER's *presentation of the inferiority complex in* Understanding Human Nature (*Fawcett, 1968, paper*) *was one of the first important deviations from Freud by one of his students.* C. G. JUNG's *deviation toward emphasis on religion appears in* Modern Man in Search of a Soul (*Harcourt Brace Jovanovich, paper*). *In* Escape from Freedom (*Avon, 1969, paper*), ERICH FROMM *insists on the role of cultural (as against sexual) factors in psychological problems.* KAREN HORNEY's The Neurotic Personality of Our Time (*Norton, 1937, available in paper*) *stresses the conflict between cooperative and competitive impulses as the main source of personality disturbance in our society.* VIKTOR E. FRANKL's *"third Viennese school of psychoanalysis" (the first two were those of Freud and Adler) is presented in* Man's Search for Meaning (*rev. ed., Beacon, 1963; Washington Square Press, paper*).

Chapter six
The cultural basis: I

Culture, we have seen, is a pattern of group habits passed by learning from one generation to another. It includes the ways in which a group of people make a living, bring up their young, settle conflicts, treat illness, make love, play games, paint pictures, worship God, and do many other things. We have referred to culture at a number of points already. Now we shall deal with it systematically.

CULTURE, BIOLOGY, AND SOCIETY

First, let us remember that culture is transmitted to each new generation by learning. It is thus different from those patterns that are biologically transmitted. Skin colors of different racial stocks are, for example, not cultural differences, for they are passed down in the genes. Racial differences in speech, in habits of marriage, or (for the most part, at least) in intelligence are the result of cultural differences. All are primarily the product of social, not biological, heredity.

We need to ask also how culture is related to society, or social organization, to which we have devoted a chapter. Society refers to the pattern of roles, statuses, expectations, and values by which the ongoing life of a group is organized. It is thus very closely related to culture. We might say that a society is an organized group that *has* a culture. Sometimes the two seem so close that the terms are used almost interchangeably. For example, we may speak of "the Hopi culture" or "Hopi society," or "the American culture" or "American society," using either term to refer in a loose way to the whole way of life which characterizes each group.

There are, however, other cases where it is clear that society and culture are not quite the same. Since most of us are not going to be professional social scientists, we shall not spend too much time on fine distinctions, but let us at least pay note.

First of all, there may be aspects of social organization that are so new that there has hardly yet been time for them to pass from one generation to another. This is likely to be true in a modern, rapidly changing, highly technical society. Since 1945, for example, a large number of working social relationships have developed around production of, defense against, and agreement for control of atomic weaponry. No one would say that these relationships are not important, yet they have hardly been with us long enough to be transmitted as culture. This is perhaps true of a good many technicways, as distinguished from folkways and mores.

We can, moreover, find human groupings that possess a culture but do not constitute a society. In the United States we have a number of groups that have many distinct cultural traits: Jewish, Italian, German,

Some immigrant groups maintain distinct "subcultures" within American society.

Swedish, Polish, Greek, and other immigrant peoples, and to a considerable extent Negroes. But none of these is a society, in the sense of being an ongoing and more or less independent social organization. Negroes in Africa and Jews in Israel do constitute societies, but neither the Jewish nor Negro ghetto, nor Little Italy, does so in this country. Some Negro leaders would like to establish an independent Negro society within the United States, but they are far from having done so. Within American society we refer to such groups as "subcultures." They are culturally but not socially distinct.

There can, on the other hand, be well-developed social organization with very little or perhaps no culture. In Chapter four we saw that many subhuman groups have a fairly complex and highly organized social life. The anthill and beehive are examples. We cannot say that they have no culture, for we do not know for certain whether these patterns are transmitted biologically or by learning. We do know, however, that if subhuman animals have some socially transmitted learning, it is very simple compared with human culture. It also lacks the unique quality of human cul-

ture: it does not grow or accumulate in the same way.

CHARACTERISTICS OF CULTURE

Now let us examine some central points about human culture: *growth, diversity, similarity,* and *integration*.

Although we speak of them as comparatively static, even primitive cultures change and grow by comparison with any animal culture. It is in the mainstream of civilization, however, that we can really see the uniquely human characteristic of cultural growth. One anthropologist has suggested that we may measure the growth of culture in terms of the amount of energy available to the average individual. The hunter and gatherer could call only upon the limited energy of his own body. Agriculture enabled man to trap more of the energy of plant growth and to harness animal power. The development of machines, culminating in the Industrial Revolution, enormously increased the available per capita energy. The physicist Millikan estimated in 1939 that the average American expended about

13½ horsepower hours of electrical and internal-combustion-engine energy per day. The splitting of the uranium atom made it possible to release 20 million horsepower hours of energy from a pound of uranium, and atomic fusion has increased the human energy potential still further.

Clearly, energy growth is not the only measure of culture. It tells us nothing (directly at least) about development in social relationships or spiritual self-realization. When we consider the possible uses of atomic power, it is clear that energy growth cannot be separated from such other values. Yet per capita energy does afford one measure of the uniquely human capacity to master the environment.

How does culture grow? One of the two main ways is through discovery or invention. To discover is to become aware of relationships that already exist. To invent is to combine existing relationships so as to produce something new. If one of our cave-dwelling ancestors came upon an animal that had been trapped and roasted in a forest fire, tasted it, and conceived the idea that he also could cook meat, this was a discovery. On the other hand, when an ape trained by the psychologist Wolfgang Kohler learned, in a famous experiment, how to join two short sticks to reach an inaccessible banana, this was for him an invention. United States law recognized the distinction: an ultraviolet lamp (invention) was patentable, but the courts denied a patent to a process for using ultraviolet rays to improve the vitamin content of foods (discovery).

As we saw in Chapter one, human civilization rests upon a fairly limited number of basic inventions and discoveries which have enhanced man's ability to manipulate his environment: fire, tools, the plow, the harnessing of animals, the use of wheeled vehicles, the calendar, the use of numbers, the use of metals, the alphabet, and steam, gasoline, electric, and atomic power. Upon these have been developed social inventions—ways of ordering economic life, government, religion, art, education, family life, sports, healing. These inventions were seldom consciously planned. They much more often happened accidentally. Neither have big jumps often been made suddenly. Each invention or discovery has usually involved only a small change in existing ways.

Indispensable as invention and discovery are, no society has invented more than a small part of its culture. The anthropologist Ralph Linton estimates that there is probably no society that has invented more than 10 percent of its cultural ways. The rest are borrowed, acquired by diffusion from other cultures.

The plow, as we saw earlier, was apparently invented in Egypt and Mesopotamia before 3000 B.C. From there it had spread by A.D. 1500 over Europe, Asia, and northern Africa. Since then it has diffused to most of the rest of the world. The alphabet appears to have been invented around the Sinai Peninsula of Palestine in about 1000 B.C. It was transmitted from there to the Phoenecians of Asia Minor. They took it by sea to Greece and Rome. From there it diffused into northern Europe. It took 2000 years to reach Scandinavia. Eventually it spread to virtually all the civilized world except China. The spread of tobacco is an interesting case of diffusion. Apparently Sir Walter Raleigh did bring it to Europe, whence it diffused to the South Seas and Asia, then to Siberia and into Alaska. After it had thus traveled around the world, the Eskimos, who had been only 1000 miles away from tobacco-using Indians, adopted it for the first time. Maize (Indian corn) apparently was first used in Mexico. It diffused from there to the Southwest of the United States, the Mississippi Valley, and the East, and eventually to Europe, but was hardly adopted at all by the Indians of southern California. It is an interesting historical note that the American Indian, whom we visualize as a natural horseman, in fact invented neither the domestication nor the rid-

 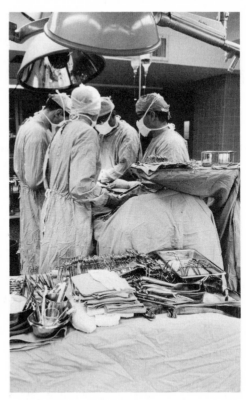

*The witch doctor and modern surgery: approaches to healing that illustrate a
dramatic contrast between two cultures.*

ing of horses, but borrowed both from
the Spaniards.

It is not, probably, for lack of inven-
tive talent that isolated people like the
Bushmen, the Australian aborigines,
the native Tasmanians, and the South
American Fuegians are still culturally
in the Stone Age, before the use of
metals. The reason for their technical
backwardness lies rather in lack of
contact which would have enabled
them to share in the mainstream of
human culture. For those who do share
in that stream, Linton's famous description of the "one hundred percent
American" should be a good antidote
against ethnocentrism and exaggerated pride in the achievements of any
particular culture. If we can learn anything from cultural diffusion, it is that
culturally the human race comes very
close to being "one world." All cultures share by borrowing in a human
cultural tradition to which each culture

adds but a small fraction of what it
takes.

It is as important for us to recognize
the variety of cultures, however, as it is
to see their common roots. "We have
done it all ourselves, with no one's
help," is one mistaken form of ethnocentrism. "Our way is human nature,
the only possible right way," is equally
mistaken. Perhaps the greatest contribution of anthropology has been to
show the immense diversity of ways in
which people can solve human problems. Ruth Benedict has said that we
can imagine a great arc, on which are
ranged all the possible ways in which
human beings might work, eat, love,
raise families, maintain order, play,
teach, heal, learn, worship. No one culture can embody more than a small
part of this arc of possibility. On the
other hand, if we will look into the
records of anthropological research,
we will find that almost every imagi-

nable way of doing these things has been practiced somewhere by some people at some time.

We have already observed a number of beliefs and practices in other cultures which challenge our ethnocentrism because they contradict ways of thinking and acting which we are likely to take for granted. We have noted the inability of the nonindividualistic Australian aborigines to understand how one could be expected to take a test alone, the reluctance of the Hopi to win any contest, the inability of some Eskimos to comprehend war, the absence of status among the Wintu Indians and Trobriand Islanders, the Zuni's giving away of extra property, the reversal of our sex roles by the Tchambuli. We could also add at this point the assumption of the Navaho Indians that accumulation of wealth is evidence of stinginess, lack of responsibility toward one's relatives, or possibly witchcraft, and their reluctance to become leaders or foremen because they feel there is something fundamentally indecent about one person's making decisions for another. Or we could examine the beliefs and practices of those many people who think that we cannot love our children, else we would not punish them, or the widespread belief in American Indian tribes that there must be something wrong with an obedient child.

In classical Greece homosexuality was so respectable that in Plato's writings we find Socrates and other male characters openly making passes at one another. To the Trobriand Islanders, the idea of homosexuality was absurd—why would anyone want a member of his own sex when he could be heterosexual? Throughout much of the Mohammedan world women still veil their faces. According to Sumner's *Folkways,* among the primitive Tuareg the men were veiled and would not uncover their faces even when sleeping, but the women's faces were bare. Suicide may be so common in a culture that a person will kill himself over a slight disappointment or be so foreign to a people that the very idea of it gives rise to "incredulous mirth." Among one Indian tribe a girl at puberty is considered so unclean that she is segregated for three or four years and the very sight of her is considered dangerous. In another tribe the first menses are considered so sacred that the priests will get down on their knees before the pubescent girl to receive the blessing of her touch. In native Samoa, however, puberty and adolescence traditionally passed almost unnoticed.

Among some African tribes fatness was traditionally so associated with beauty that young girls were sent to "fatting houses" to be filled with sweets and fatty foods. Some Javanese have traditionally believed that rice has a soul and sexual feelings. Men and women would engage in ritual intercourse to arouse the passion of the rice and ensure a good crop. (This connection between plant fertility and human sexuality is widespread throughout history.) There have been peoples whose duty it was to kill their first two children, and many others where children have had a duty to put their parents to death when old. Among some Polynesians and Eskimos it has been customary for a host to offer his wife and daughters sexually to a guest, and to reject the offer might be as much an affront as refusing the meal offered by the host. Among the Lovedu of Africa, if one man killed another, he and his descendants might be bound to atone for the offense by offering their sisters as brides to the family of the victim. The Polynesian Tikopia bury their dead under the floors of their houses and hold casual conversations with them. Among them it is an expression of sociability to share with another person one's half-chewed wad of betel nut.

In one culture we find that there are almost no thirteenth floors in hotels because of superstition connected with the number. These people practice mouth-to-mouth kissing, a habit viewed as very unsanitary and disgusting by a number of other cultures. At the same time, for many years they did not use the most effective method of resuscitation (mouth to mouth) because the contact was too intimate. After defecation, these people do not wash their anuses but only wipe them with a piece of paper, a habit considered shockingly unclean by many Hindus. A large number of the members of this culture build houses of worship to a Prince of Peace but maintain the world's largest collection of weapons of war—an institution which some cannibals consider too morally offensive to be understandable. This last culture is, of course, our own.

Behind the wide diversity of cultures there is, however, an underlying similarity. In Chapter four, comparing the Bushman and the New Yorker, we pointed out that both are, after all, human beings with essentially similar hereditary equipment, working out similar problems under essentially similar environmental conditions (see pp. 112–119).

What is true for these two very different peoples is true for all human beings. There are nine essential institutions present in all societies, which grow primarily out of folkways and mores passed down by cultural inheritance. These nine areas of life present in every culture are economic, political, familial, religious, educational, scientific, therapeutic, recreational, and artistic.

After this and the following introductory section, we shall devote the rest of

---

Our solid American citizen awakens in a bed built on a pattern which originated in the Near East but which was modified in Northern Europe before it was transmitted to America. He throws back covers made from cotton, domesticated in India, or linen, domesticated in the Near East, or wool from sheep, also domesticated in the Near East, or silk, the use of which was discovered in China. All of these materials have been spun and woven by processes invented in the Near East. He slips into his moccasins, invented by the Indians of the Eastern woodlands, and goes to the bathroom, whose fixtures are a mixture of European and American inventions, both of recent date. He takes off his pajamas, a garment invented in India, and washes with soap invented by the ancient Gauls. He then shaves, a masochistic rite which seems to have been derived from either Sumer or ancient Egypt.

Returning to the bedroom, he removes his clothes from a chair of southern European type and proceeds to dress. He puts on garments whose form originally derived from the skin clothing of the nomads of the Asiatic steppes, puts on shoes made from skins tanned by a process invented in ancient Egypt and cut to a pattern derived from the classical civilizations of the Mediterranean, and ties around his neck a strip of bright-colored cloth which is a vestigial survival of the shoulder shawls worn by the seventeenth-century Croatians. Before going out for breakfast he glances through the window, made of glass invented in Egypt, and if it is raining puts on overshoes made of rubber discovered by the Central American Indians and takes an umbrella, invented in southeastern Asia. Upon his head he puts a hat made of felt, a material invented in the Asiatic steppes.

*On his way to breakfast he stops to buy a paper, paying for it
with coins, an ancient Lydian invention. At the restaurant a
whole new series of borrowed elements confronts him. His plate is
made of a form of pottery invented in China. His knife is of steel,
an alloy first made in southern India, his fork a medieval
Italian invention, and his spoon a derivative of a Roman original.
He begins breakfast with an orange, from the eastern
Mediterranean, a canteloupe from Persia, or perhaps a piece of
African watermelon. With this he has coffee, an Abyssinian plant,
with cream and sugar. Both the domestication of cows and the
idea of milking them originated in the Near East, while sugar
was first made in India. After his fruit and first coffee he goes
on to waffles, cakes made by a Scandinavian technique from wheat
domesticated in Asia Minor. Over these he pours maple syrup,
invented by the Indians of the Eastern woodlands. As a side dish he
may have the egg of a species of bird domesticated in
Indo-China, or thin strips of the flesh of an animal domesticated in
Eastern Asia which have been salted and smoked by a process
developed in northern Europe.*

*When our friend has finished eating he settles back to smoke, an
American Indian habit, consuming a plant domesticated in
Brazil in either a pipe, derived from the Indians of Virginia, or a
cigarette, derived from Mexico. If he is hardy enough he may even
attempt a cigar, transmitted to us from the Antilles by way of
Spain. While smoking he reads the news of the day, imprinted in
characters invented by the ancient Semites upon a material
invented in China by a process invented in Germany. As
he absorbs the accounts of foreign troubles he will, if he is a good
conservative citizen, thank a Hebrew deity in an Indo-European
language that he is 100 percent American.*

—Ralph Linton, The Study of Man, *New York, Appleton-Century-Crofts, 1964,
pp. 326–327.*

---

this chapter to examining the role played by each of these nine areas of culture in the whole scheme of human culture, looking under each area for both diversities and similarities.

THE INTEGRATION OF CULTURE

We shall also look for evidences of the integration of culture. A culture is not just a collection of odd customs that have no relationship to one another. William Graham Sumner, in his book *Folkways,* spoke of how the mores of a culture are all

> *. . . subject to a strain of consistency with each other, because they*
> *all answer their several purposes with less friction and antagonism when they cooperate and support each other. The forms of industry, the forms of the family, the notions of property, the constructions of rights, and the types of religion show the strain of consistency with each other through the whole history of civilization.*[1]

We can see how this happens by looking at some integrating themes in our own culture. Material goods are for the most part produced in large factories by mass production methods.

1. William Graham Sumner, *Folkways,* Boston, Ginn, 1940, pp. 5–6.

This theme has tended to spread to almost all parts of the culture, so that today food production, education, communications, entertainment and recreation, sport, education, and even religion are mass production industries. None of these aspects of our culture very closely resembles the way it was carried on in 1770, but all resemble one another. Or we may consider the theme of competition. Ideally, at least, our economic system is based on free competition. So, in practice, are to a large extent our political campaigns, our patterns of courtship, our educational system, our organized sports, our scientific efforts, and our world of literature and the arts. In this respect, too, all these activities looked quite different two centuries ago, but they have a consistency with one another today.

The pattern of our culture may be highlighted by taking an illustration from Sumner—the contrast between the cultures of Orient and Occident, East and West. Each, he felt, was so different from the other that "if two planets were joined in one, their inhabitants could not differ more widely as to what things are best worth seeking, or what ways are most expedient for well living. . . ." (The idea—"East is East, and West is West, and never the twain shall meet"—was probably somewhat of an exaggeration.) Each culture, Sumner said, was "consistent throughout," each had "its own philosophy and spirit."[2]

Hsu's profiles of East Indians, Chinese, and Americans, cited in the previous chapter, will suggest what Sumner meant. The life of the Occidental American appeared to be organized around the active, individualistic mastery of the outer world through technology. The life of the Oriental seemed to be organized around the more passive mastery of the inner world and the world of social relationships. In each case, the dominant theme tends to color all activities. Of course, conditions have changed much since Sumner's time (1900). In much of China, Japan, and the rest of the Orient today, one no longer finds the integrated way of life of which he spoke.

Changes in culture furnish good illustrations of how the parts of a culture hang together. Ralph Linton has illustrated this in the case of the Tanala of Madagascar. Up until 200 years ago, the Tanala culture was based on the growing of rice on dry land. Because the soil was frequently exhausted, the Tanala were always on the move and never achieved permanent settlements. Private ownership of land never attained great importance. The land tended to be worked by large families of several generations. There were no marked social inequalities, and there was no slavery. Warfare was primitive, for there were no permanent settlements to fortify and defend. We can see how all the cultural life tended to integrate around the dry-rice farming.

Then the method of food getting changed to wet-rice cultivation in flooded fields. These did not lose their fertility. Thus settlement became permanent. Private property in these valuable, now-permanent plots became important and an object of competition. Social inequalities began to develop, with those who had the best rice fields holding top positions. Slavery emerged as a way of growing the more profitable wet-field crop. Those who could not get good wet land were likely to migrate. The big families began to split up. Permanent settlement gave rise to permanent fortification and the development of systematic warfare. We can see how the new basis of subsistence tended to change the whole culture pattern into one consistent with the new wet-rice cultivation.

Diffusion of a culture trait may also illustrate cultural integration. Generally a trait is borrowed not exactly in the form in which it originated, but in a form which fits the pattern of the borrowing culture. When Christian missionaries preached the concept of the Holy Ghost to the Tsimshian Indians of

2. *Ibid.*, p. 6.

British Columbia, part of whose religion consisted of possession by spirits, the Indians put on frenzied dances four or five days long in which they were "seized" by the Holy Spirit. This was the form which gave the concept meaning in their culture pattern, though hardly that intended by the missionaries. Another missionary to the Tsimshian, knowing that cannibalism was still part of the culture of the Northwest Coast Indians, omitted the Christian ritual of communion (eating of the body of Christ) from his services for fear of what it might mean to the Tsimshian.

One of the most famous studies of cultural integration is found in the book *Patterns of Culture,* by the anthropologist Ruth Benedict. The author describes three primitive cultural patterns, all distinctively different, but each governed by a central theme.

The Pueblo Indians of the Pacific Southwest emphasize moderation in everything, avoidance of exuberance and excitement, and suppression of one's individuality in the group. In this they are strikingly different from almost all other American Indians, who were traditionally given, for example, to wild, ecstatic dancing, and placed great emphasis upon supernatural visions. The theme of the whole life of the Dobu Islanders of the South Pacific seemed to be mutual hostility and suspicion and pleasure in harming others. "The Dobuan lives out without repression man's worst nightmares of the ill-will of the universe." The Kwakiutl Indians of Vancouver Island, British Columbia, centered most of their efforts on asserting status through display of possessions. One of their famous practices was the *potlatch,* a feast at which chiefs tried to outdo one another by displaying and destroying blankets, sheets of copper, oil, and even houses. "All the motivations they recognized centered around the will to superiority. Their social organization, their economic institutions, their religion, birth and death, were all channels for its expression."

We can see the integration of the Pueblo, Dobuan, and Kwakiutl cultures by looking at how some universal human experiences were differently regarded by each, in ways consistent with its dominant culture pattern.

To the moderate Pueblo, economic life was a matter-of-fact cooperative effort. To the hostile Dubuan, it was a way of getting the better of others. To the status conscious Kwakiutl, its purpose was to establish one's superiority. To the Pueblo sex was a natural experience to be enjoyed; to the Dubuan it was marked by fear and hostility; to the Kwakiutl it was a way to improve one's status. Suicide was unknown among the Pueblo; among the Dobu it was a common way of expressing hostility; among the Kwakiutl it frequently followed social failure. The religion of the Pueblo was one of felt oneness with the universe; Dobuan religion consisted mainly of magic for aggression or self-protection; the Kwakiutl expected the gods to be hostile and tried to humiliate them as they did their fellow men. The Pueblo regarded death as a part of the course of nature; the Dobu considered it the result of magic or witchcraft; the Kwakiutl regarded it as defeat and shame. The ideal Pueblo was a cooperative, self-effacing person; the ideal Dobuan, a person who had cheated another of his place; the ideal Kwakiutl, one who had outdone others in possessions.

The question now arises: If all aspects of a culture are related in a pattern, are any one or more aspects of greater importance in shaping the pattern? We can clarify the question by looking at the two problems of (1) explaining the past and (2) influencing the future.

How do we write history? Those of us who studied American or world history a generation or more ago are likely to have been presented with a succession of kings and battles. Underlying this approach was probably the assumption that political and military affairs are the central aspect of culture. More recently new approaches have become more prevalent. A historian may stress primarily the course of economic activities and development. The writer may or may not be a follower of Karl Marx, but this kind of history has been more prevalent since Marx and Engels stressed the materialist interpretation of history, that is, the central importance of material production and distribution. On the other hand, a historian may emphasize intellectual history, or the history of ideas. The assumption is that the way people think is central to cultural life. The influential nineteenth-century German philosopher, G. F. W. Hegel, held that the most important thing about any culture is its central "idea" or "spirit." A historian may feature religious development, perhaps seeing religious beliefs as the central force that shapes culture. Or history may be written as social or cultural history, in which culture is dealt with as a whole but no attempt is made to single out any factor, or factors, as more important than others.

The same problem appears if we wish to influence future events. If we would like to change aspects of a culture, where shall we begin? Suppose we are concerned about crime and juvenile delinquency. Shall we emphasize the raising of living standards, provision of more jobs, or the clearing of slums on the assumption that the economic factor is primary? Shall we try to put better public officials in office? Shall we try to convert criminals and delinquents to new moral and religious standards? Shall we institute recreational programs, or take slum children to concerts, museums, and other cultural opportunities? Shall we try to improve family life so as to avoid the results of broken homes? Or must we begin everywhere at once?

If we would like people of the economically underdeveloped nations to become more democratic, shall we try to democratize them by military force? Shall we send specialists in government to teach them the theory and techniques of democracy? Shall we help them to achieve economic independence and a higher living stand-

ard? Shall we send missionaries? The answer we give depends on our view of what forces in the pattern of culture are primary.

The question of how to weigh the elements of culture has been one of the most perplexing problems of social science. Some people would, for example, give economic factors a weight of perhaps 2, political and religious factors a weight of 1, recreation perhaps a weight of one-half. Others would follow a quite different weighting. Some would weigh all aspects about equally. Probably most social scientists would agree that no one formula can be applied to all cases. Different factors have different importance in different cultures, or in different times and situations in the same culture.

Clearly this problem is of practical importance in any effort to change society, for the better we judge the right point or points at which to take hold, the more effective we shall be in grappling with any practical problem. We shall not answer the question at this time, nor shall we finally resolve it at any point in this book. However, the rest of this chapter and the chapters to follow should give us some new perspectives upon it.

Now that we have discussed at some length the integration of culture, we should make a qualification. There is also much inconsistency in culture. Ruth Benedict, one of the strongest exponents of the theme of cultural integration, warns that not all cultures are as well integrated as the Pueblo, Dobuan, and Kwakiutl. We might wonder whether even her accounts of these peoples, which make each seem almost entirely single-minded, may not be somewhat oversimplified. For example, an important autobiography of Sun Chief, a Pueblo of the Hopi people, makes Pueblo life sound more complex and full of conflict than the usual reports of anthropologists.[3]

3. Leo W. Simmons, ed., *Sun Chief: The Autobiography of a Hopi Indian,* published for The Institute of Human Relations, New Haven, Yale University Press, 1942.

The Tokyo Hilton

Technically advanced cultures are likely to be less closely integrated than primitive ones. We can find plenty of inconsistencies in our own. There is often a sharp contradiction between our democratic ideals and our actual treatment of minorities. The sexual mores we preach are often quite different from those we practice. We espouse religions of brotherhood in church and synagogue but very often cut our brother's throat in the marketplace. We praise the virtues of our free, competitive economic system when economic power is actually concentrated in a relatively few hands. We believe in everyone's right to an excellent education, but pay teachers so poorly that many of the best qualified people do not enter the profession. Each student can expand this list of inconsistencies.

Perhaps the most important way in which a culture may lose integration is through change. Sudden contact with another group may be quite destructive to the integration of a primitive culture. When the Pueblo culture came in contact with white civilization and its money economy, its members were confronted with the choice of holding on to their cooperative values or making money by pushing themselves ahead individualistically. To do the latter meant giving up most of the values of tribal life based on submerging oneself in the group. The same kind of thing has frequently happened to the integration of African tribal life.

In technically advanced cultures, the rapidity of change may make it almost impossible for the parts of the culture to remain in harmony. The sociologist William F. Ogburn, who was chairman of President Hoover's Commission on Social Trends, coined the term "cultural lag" to describe the situation where one part of a culture changes and others do not. One of Ogburn's illustrations was the way in which destruction of American lands and forests went on for many years before a program of conservation was finally launched. Social provisions had lagged behind the physical need. Ogburn felt that it is generally "material culture," that part which deals with the physical environment and technology, that changes first. There is a lag before the nonmaterial culture of social ideas, laws, and institutions catches up. We can find plenty of illustrations: the failure of highway systems to keep up with the increase in cars, the absence of effective programs for control of pollution, the lag of school construction behind the explosion of school population and of recreational facilities behind the increase in leisure, the inability to create political machinery for peace when military technology has made war potentially suicidal for all.

We must question Ogburn's idea that it is always the material culture that leads and the nonmaterial culture that lags behind. Can we not say that our nonmaterial ideals of peace are far ahead of our lagging material technology of destruction? This lag has existed since the Hebrew prophet spoke of, but did not succeed in bringing about, the beating of swords into plowshares. Are not our nonmaterial ideals of a just economic system, free from poverty, far in advance of our lagging material arrangements for producing and distributing goods—whether under capitalism, communism, or something else? Is it not our ideals of racial brotherhood that are out in front and our physical patterns of racial segregation that lag behind? Would it not be best simply to think of cultural lag as any kind of lag between the parts of a changing culture?

We have still another problem. A "lag" sounds bad. Is cultural lag necessarily undesirable? If mechanical transportation increasingly replaces human muscle, what shall we say of those rare individuals who continue to walk? If everything seems to be getting bigger and more concentrated, are we to regard the existence of a small corner grocery, a small family farm, or a small college as necessarily undesirable? If industrial development is the established pattern for success, what of a community which refuses to admit heavy industry? If accommodations for tourists all over the world become so "Hiltonized" that one can travel everywhere and never really leave home, is this "progress"? If personal and sexual responsibility are on the decrease, how shall we judge those who remain responsible? If a culture becomes increasingly irreligious, what of those who continue to believe in God? How we view such matters clearly depends upon how we regard the direction in which things are going. If we question the pattern of change, then we may well consider the disharmony of cultural lag to be positive and healthy.

THE MAIN AREAS OF CULTURE

In the rest of this chapter and Chapter seven, we shall examine in turn each of the nine major areas of life which underlie all cultures. These are, again, the economic, the political, the familial, the religious, the educational, the scientific, the therapeutic, the recreational, and the artistic. In each case we shall try to do three main things.

1. We shall try to indicate why the area is found in all human culture. This will involve describing the functions it performs in serving the needs and interests of human life. For example, why have all cultures had some form of economic life?

2. Having defined the functions which make this area of culture part of the universal culture pattern, we shall then describe the main forms which it has assumed in the history of human culture. For example, what are the most important different ways in which human beings have organized their marriage and family life?

3. We shall try to give a number of specific illustrations of how the area is related to the other areas of culture. These illustrations will give us a stronger sense of the integration of culture. For example, how has art been related to economic life, religion, and so on?

THE ECONOMIC ASPECT OF CULTURE

"The first task of life," said Sumner, "is to live." All people are equipped by nature with needs that must be met if they are to survive. Almost all, at least, live under conditions where the means for satisfaction are more or less scarce and require effort to obtain. The South Sea Islands where all food drops from the trees or is otherwise available for the asking are rare, if not nonexistent. When absolute life needs have been met, other needs and desires tend to arise, and often they become almost as urgent. The economic aspect of culture, in the broadest sense, is concerned with organizing human energies for overcoming the scarcity of nature.

Everywhere people *produce* and *consume* goods and services. Goods are tangible, desired objects. Services are desired activities performed by one person for another. Since very few people are isolated and totally self-sufficient (even Robinson Crusoe had his man Friday), economic life is almost always concerned with the *exchange* of one person's goods and services for those of another. It is necessary to have some system for *distributing* the goods and services that are produced. Economic activity almost always involves some form of *technology:* tools, machines, weapons, processes of metalworking, modes of travel and transportation, sources of power. It involves some system of *organization* of work, in which leadership is provided and tasks are distributed. It includes some kind of arrangements for the ownership of *property.* It is related to certain *values* concerning economic activity. The traditional Pueblo values centered around tribal cooperation, for example, whereas the white American's values center around individual pursuit of gain.

In Chapter eight we shall concern ourselves with those principles governing economic behavior that are the special interest of economists. Here we shall be more generally concerned with the role of economic behavior in culture.

The ways in which people have organized their economic life are as various as their cultures. Nevertheless, all human economic activity can be grouped under a limited number of arrangements. These we may relate to two events of overwhelming importance in the history of mankind. The first is the development for the first time, around 3000 B.C., of an economic surplus, that is, a quantity of production beyond that necessary to meet the minimal needs of life. The second is the technical revolution which brought our vastly productive modern industrial world.

Two kinds of economic arrangements preceded the development of an economic surplus. The *hunting and gathering economy* has occupied by far the largest part of human experience. It was the only form of organization from the beginnings of man until about 7000 B.C. Archaeologists refer to this as the Paleolithic (Old Stone Age) economy, because its technology consisted of only the crudest stone and

wood tools and weapons. Small groups wandered and foraged over large territories. They were governed largely by custom rather than formal organization. There was not much specialization. Social classes had not developed. There was no surplus production beyond that necessary to meet basic needs. What was available tended to be distributed equally or on the basis of need. No one went hungry as long as there was food.

Some hunters and gatherers lived in fairly settled communities. It was the agricultural revolution, however, that made settled *village economy* the dominant form of organization. This has been the prevalent form through all of recorded human history. Increased productivity made it possible to support much larger populations in villages, but there was still no great surplus above survival. This economy rests on the cultivation of plants, domestication of animals, pottery, carpentry, textiles, and mining. The village economy goes back to Neolithic (New Stone Age) times, when stone implements were well developed, but metals were still absent. Good examples of Neolithic villages are found along Swiss lakes, dating back to about 2500 B.C. Village economy still prevails throughout a large part of the world. It is typical today, for example, of countries like Yugoslavia, Albania, Brazil, or Cambodia. Most primitive peoples now live in this way.

By about 3000 B.C., the adoption of the plow had so increased productivity that the land could support not only farmers but city dwellers. On this basis there arose in Egypt, Mesopotamia, and Assyria a *temple town economy* built upon this surplus. Two classes of people controlled the surplus. The masses of people supported the priesthood and the temples where they functioned, because the priests were believed to have supernatural power to protect or harm. Political rulers, who maintained order internally and waged war externally, also claimed part of the surplus for their services. The great cities of Greece and Rome were like-wise built upon economic surplus. Although they were especially marked in the historic cultures, these developments have also occurred elsewhere. The Inca and Aztec nations produced a large surplus with development of temple towns and a ruling class. We noted how changes in rice cultivation brought about the development of a ruling class in Madagascar. Among preliterate peoples and African tribes, in particular, ruling classes based on surplus have developed. The description of Dahomey depicts this development.

With the fall of Rome, the classical city society gave way to the *feudal economy*. As the central government of the empire broke down, life became concentrated on estates, or manors. The lord of the manor held his land in exchange for money or services rendered to the king. The manor was largely self-sufficient, dependent upon growing its own food and providing for other goods through the services of craftsmen. Around the manor house clustered the dwellings of freemen and serfs, who secured the protection of the lord in exchange for obligations to serve him. The serf could not leave the land unless he was able to buy his freedom. In this economy the economic surplus was controlled by the feudal lords, the kings, and the church. Feudalism remained the basis for the economy of Europe for almost a thousand years.

Within the feudal economy, however, there gradually arose the *guild economy*. Instead of being attached to the manor, merchants and craftsmen began to cluster in towns, most of which were survivals of Roman days. There they organized in guilds, which controlled the growing market for goods and the services of shoemakers, silversmiths, glass workers, weavers, and other trades. The guild usually monopolized the sale of its craftsmen's products. Guilds regulated working conditions, established a just price for goods, endeavored to maintain high standards of craftsmanship, and performed fraternal services, such as burial for their members. As trade and production revived and the use of money became more widespread, the town economies based upon guild organization attained an increasing importance, while the feudalism of the isolated rural manors, which could not compete with the attractions of town life, declined.

From the fifteenth to the eighteenth century in Europe, there was increasing trade and demand for goods, which gave rise to a new *commercial economy*. The voyages of discovery by Portuguese, Spanish, Dutch, and British seamen opened up new trade routes for raw materials and manufactured goods. New gold supplies stimulated business activity. The guild economy was too local and inflexible to meet this situation. Guild production gave way to domination by large business enterprisers, who organized large numbers of workers, at this stage usually in their homes. Vast trading companies arose to carry on commerce. The local manorial and town economy gave way before the rising importance of the national state. Colonies which furnished raw materials and markets for goods were developed. Control of the economic surplus by the church and the manor lords had already slipped with the rise of the town guild economy. Now the control passed further into the hands of a powerful class of urban organizers of production, merchants and bankers. This class became known as the *bourgeoisie*—the "burghers," or inhabitants of the city (burg). The stage was set for the second great revolutionary development in economic history—the vast increase in the economic surplus through the rise of industrialism.

We have already described the character of the *industrial economy* in Chapter one. Large organization, urbanization, high specialization, and a large economic surplus are characteristic of all developed industrial economies. Given these similarities, there have been four important forms of industrial economy, in terms of who owns industrial facilities and, to a large extent, who controls the economic surplus. In the *capitalist* economy, industry has been primarily owned by private individuals and groups independent of the state. In the so-called *communist* economies, industry has been primarily owned and operated by the state. Under *democratic socialist* economies, there is usually a mixture of state ownership and regulation with private ownership. In the *fascist* economies, formal ownership has been for the most part in the hands of private individuals or groups, but these have been so organized and controlled by the state that their rights of ownership have been severely limited. Later we shall devote some time to each of these types of industrial organization.

Interrelations

Let us now examine some specific interrelations between economic life and the rest of cultural organization.

A good illustration is the widespread change wrought by the development of an economic surplus in Egypt, Mesopotamia, Assyria, and India around 3000 B.C. (and later in Inca Peru, Aztec Mexico, Madagascar, and Dahomey). This change manifested itself in eight ways. (1) It gave rise for the first time to a society sharply organized in social classes, some controlling a large part of the surplus and others controlling little. (2) As workers became capable of producing substantially more than was needed for their upkeep, it became for the first time advantageous to capture and hold slaves. (3) War became significant as a way of seizing the surplus and the labor power of others. (4) The political state developed, as organized rule by groups controlling a large part of the surplus. (5) It became possible for the first time to subsidize temple building and a professional priesthood on a large scale. (6) Part of the surplus went into supporting nonagricultural people in cities. (7) The surplus made possible the leisure for some people to pursue

science, philosophy, mathematics, and the arts as careers. (8) Relaxation of the urgent necessity of making a living made possible the development of individuality distinct from the mass. Clearly no aspect of culture was unaffected, and the change has continued to the present time.

We have already noted how the second great economic revolution, the introduction of industrialism, spread its effects over all modern culture. The rest of this chapter will illustrate this further. We have already stressed the importance of economic relationships in shaping the self.

Now let us look at the reverse situation—where economic relations are shaped by other aspects of culture. The relationship of government to economic life is an example. Some people speak as though economic affairs would be best if there were no government at all, but every economic system, from the most primitive to the most modern, operates within a framework of political norms. Government may not, it is true, own industries or businesses as it does in a Socialist or Communist economy. It may, indeed, give them a very free hand. Yet even where it governs least, government ensures that the contracts men make will be observed. It restrains those who would blow up their competitors' stores or factories or otherwise use violence to keep them from selling their goods. Government legalizes certain types of economic organization, such as corporations or labor unions, and protects them in the exercise of their established rights. It is not, therefore, a question of whether or not politics enters economic life, but of how much and in what way, for without politics no economy could go on.

Economic life also takes place within a framework of ideas and values. Most social scientists agree that a very important part of industrial society has been the system of values that we call the "Protestant ethic." This is associated especially with the German sociologist Max Weber. Let us examine it.

In order for a commercial and industrial economy to have arisen after the Middle Ages, certain things were necessary. Production of material goods had to have a high value. People had to be motivated to work hard and energetically. They had to learn to specialize on particular jobs. They had to save the economic surplus for reinvestment in new production. Prices of goods had to be free to vary according to supply and demand.

The society of the late Middle Ages furnished a number of obstacles to such development. Many people were more interested in Heaven after death than in this world or felt that individual religious experience was more important than material things. Hard work was often regarded as an unfortunate necessity, but not as a positive good. Accumulation of wealth was likely to be regarded with suspicion; it was thought to be hard for a rich man to enter the kingdom of Heaven. Charging interest for the loan of money was spoken of as "usury" and considered sinful. An additional difficulty was the doctrine of the just price, which held that there is only one right natural price for every good and that it is sinful to charge more or offer less.

The commercial, and eventually industrial, economy that arose out of the Middle Ages would have been impossible without a great change in this framework of ideas and values. This change did take place. It came from many sources, but today we think that probably the most important single source was the Protestant religious philosophy of John Calvin.

In a world where people were gravely concerned about their eternal salvation, Calvin held that only a few, a small "elect," were predestined by God to be saved. How could one know whether or not he was one of the elect? By the kind of life he led. What was the right kind of life? One in which one neither spent his time in the pursuit of worldly pleasure nor retreated into mystical meditation, but engaged himself actively and continually in the everyday affairs of practical life. The member of the elect would not be a jack-of-all-trades, but would rather have a specialized role in life, a definite calling or vocation. If he applied himself seriously in hard work in his vocation, it was very likely that he would make money. This was wrong if one spent his earnings in pleasure for himself; wine, women, song, card playing, and the theater were all forbidden, as they were in the later Calvinist philosophy of Puritanism. But if one saved his earnings and invested them in more production, wealth was not necessarily sinful at all. On the contrary, getting rich was more likely a sign of God's favor. A new view of charging interest was necessary. Calvin held that the Old Testament prohibition on usury applied to a tribal society where loans were person-to-person affairs in time of need, but that the taking of interest was different and necessary in an impersonal business world. Likewise the doctrine of the single just price no longer held after Calvinism became influential.

The Protestant ethic thus laid the groundwork for the commercial and industrial economy of modern times. One Protestant writer, Abraham Kuyper, claims that

> scarcely had Calvinism been firmly established in the Netherlands for a quarter of a century when there was a rustling of life in all directions, and an indomitable energy was fermenting in every department of human activity, and their commerce and trade, their handicrafts and industry, their agriculture and horticulture, their art and science, flourished with a brilliancy previously unknown, and imparted a new impulse for an entirely new development of life, to the whole of Western Europe.[4]

All this is history. Today not so many people take formal religion as seriously as they did in Calvin's day. Yet the underdeveloped nations of the world,

4. Abraham Kuyper, *Calvinism*, Grand Rapids, Mich., Erdmans, 1931, p. 73.

These ruins are at Machu Picchu, site of an ancient city built by the Peruvian Incas, a preliterate people who developed an advanced governmental organization. (Courtesy of the American Museum of Natural History.)

as they become industrialized, seem almost inevitably to develop something very much like the somber, hard-driving, Puritan Protestant ethic. This has been true of Russia, China, Africa, and other parts of the world.

THE POLITICAL ASPECT OF CULTURE

All societies have some form of machinery for maintaining an orderly life in the community. Political organization, as part of the total culture pattern, has three important characteristics. (1) It is related to a particular territory. (2) In this territory other institutions—families, corporations, labor unions, schools, even churches—may also exercise powers of control, but political institutions are the final authority. (3) Their power is not final primarily because they have greater force at their command, but because it is recognized as legitimate. Political organization is believed by its subjects to have a final right to enforce its will, which no other organization has.

How did government originate? We referred earlier to the once upon a time story of the social contract, which holds that men at some historic time abandoned a completely individualistic state of nature to form civil society under government. According to this theory, they formed the political contract because they saw it to be ration-

ally to their advantage. The social contract theory was prominent in the writings of the influential English political writers Thomas Hobbes (1588–1679) and John Locke (1632–1704), and in a different form, in those of the French thinker Jean Jacques Rousseau (1712–1778). We can be quite sure now that the theory of social contract was wrong. There has never been a state of nature in which human beings lived without some kind of common rules.

The political organization of a society is only one aspect of *social control*, the wider pattern by which all societies have guided and coerced their members. Earlier we saw that folkways, mores, and technicways may exercise strong social control without any formal machinery for enforcing the control. We saw that formal institutions and laws grow out of the folkways and mores and always rest upon them. Political organization, or government, begins when individuals or groups become designated as having special rights in enforcing social control over a whole society.

From observing preliterate peoples, we can guess the general way in which government originated. The oldest human grouping is probably the extended family, or clan, made up of related individuals descended from common ancestors. Perhaps the earliest government was the authority of the oldest male, or males, to settle disputed cases or formulate rules for clan members. In time leaders of several clans may have formed a council of elders, which in turn chose a leader, a tribal chief or king. At first the office may have been temporary, only later to become hereditary.

Among hunters and gatherers and simple farmers and herders, who have not acquired an economic surplus, government must be fairly limited and amateur, for there is no extra wealth to support a professional ruling class. Chiefs among the Bushmen receive no tribute in money and have no special dress or mode of life to distinguish them. The central Eskimos respect the man who has special knowledge about game, but do not feel obliged to obey his orders. Among the Selk'nam of Tierra del Fuego, the only authority is in the family; beyond this there is only moral force. Among the Caroti of South America, the chief has no power to appropriate the resources of the community. Among the Siriono of Bolivia, the highest official has to do everything anyone else does, only better. Among the aborigines of Queensland, the elder is highly respected, but there is no individual who directs affairs. The Murngin of Australia do not have organized tribes or the position of chief.

None of the American Plains Indians is known to have had a hereditary chieftainship. The Council of Seven Chiefs of the Omaha organized communal buffalo hunts, confirmed leaders, made peace with other tribes, and generally administrated tribal affairs. They did receive certain gifts in recognition of their position and by virtue of the fact that they were too busy to make their own living by taking part in the hunt, but they did not form a separate privileged class.

Matters are likely to be quite different in societies that have developed an economic surplus. Then a fully organized political state is likely to emerge. Although the greatest development of the state has taken place in the historic cultures, advanced governmental organization may occur among the more affluent preliterate peoples. The best examples are found in the historic Incas of Peru and in modern Africa, Malaya, and Polynesia.

The Inca state was a federation and supported a large bureaucracy. A careful census made everybody subject to

*When thou art come unto the land which the Lord thy God giveth
thee, and shalt possess it, and shalt dwell therein, and shalt
say, I will set a king over me, like as all the nations that are
about me;
Thou shalt in any wise set him king over thee, whom the Lord thy
God shall choose: one from among thy brethren shalt thou
set king over thee: thou mayest not set a stranger over thee, which
is not thy brother.
But he shall not multiply horses to himself, nor cause the people
to return to Egypt, to the end that he should multiply horses:
forasmuch as the Lord hath said unto you. Ye shall henceforth
return no more that way.
Neither shall he multiply wives to himself, that his heart turn not
away: neither shall he greatly multiply to himself silver and
gold. . . .
That his heart be not lifted up above his brethren, and that he
turn not aside from the commandment, to the right hand, or to the
left: to the end that he may prolong his days in the kingdom,
he, and his children, in the midst of Israel.*

—Deuteronomy 17:14–17, 20.

*But the thing displeased Samuel, when they said, Give us a king
to judge us. And Samuel prayed unto the Lord.
And the Lord said unto Samuel. . . .
Now therefore hearken unto their voice: how be it yet protest
solemnly unto them, and show them the manner of the king
that shall reign over them.
And Samuel told all the words of the Lord unto the people that
asked of him a king.
And he said, This will be the manner of the king that shall reign
over you: He will take your sons, and appoint them for himself, for
his chariots, and to be his horsemen: and some shall run
before his chariots.
And he will appoint him captains over thousands, and captains
over fifties; and will set them to ear his corn, and to reap his
harvest, and to make his instruments of war, and instruments of his
chariots.
And he will take your daughters to be confectionaries, and to be
cooks, and to be bakers.
And he will take your fields, and your vineyards, and your
oliveyards, even the best of them, and give them to his servants.
And he will take the tenth of your seed, and of your vineyards, and
give to his officers, and to his servants.
And he will take your menservants, and your maidservants,
and your goodliest young men, and your asses, and put them to
his work.
He will take the tenth of your sheep, and ye shall be his
servants.
And ye shall cry out in that day because of your king which ye
shall have chosen you; and the Lord will not hear you in that day.*

—I Samuel 6–18.

taxation and the draft of his labor. Government income was used to build public works—roads, bridges, aqueducts, storehouses. The ruling group was maintained in luxury, but goods were so distributed that no one was allowed to want.

The traditional society of Dahomey, in West Africa, was stratified into slaves, serfs, free farmers and artisans (who furnished the soldiers and officials), and the upper class of priests and rulers. All subjects were liable to military service and to taxes on field crops, palm groves, livestock, hunting, and the use of toll roads. There was also a sales tax. The income was used to support the king and his followers, the army, and officials.

In Polynesia the bounty of the tropical climate has made an economic surplus easy to obtain. Tahitian rulers were the highest of three social classes. The chiefs were regarded as descended from the highest class of gods. They had extensive lands, separate dwellings, and a large staff of servants from the lower class. The Tahitians themselves expressed relationships within their society by an analogy with cooked breadfruit. The skin was for the people, the meat for the *arii* (rulers), and the core for *manahune* (commoners without property).

The state as we know it in the modern world arose along with social class distinctions, slavery, war, and an economic surplus appropriated by rulers.

The accompanying quotations illustrate the contrast between political organization before and after the economic surplus, as found in the Old Testament. In the selection from Deuteronomy, the Israelites are told to select a leader who will not "be lifted up above his brethren." In the excerpt from Samuel, the prophet tells the people of all the ways in which their king will set himself apart and reign over them.

As rulers came to be above rather than of the people, the function of political organization became more complex. In the simpler societies, government could be described as an agency serving common interests of the society. Once a surplus had arisen, however, it came to serve also the special interests of a minority of rulers, often against the interests of the majority. There have been three important views of the function of the state in society.

One sees the state as representing the general welfare, a consensus of the interests of its subjects. This was the view that underlay the notion of a social contract entered in by all members for their common good.

A second view sees the state as representing the interests of a minority ruling class that uses government to dominate and exploit the mass of people. This view has been held especially by Marxists and anarchists. It was summarized, for present times, in the famous statement by Marx: "The state is nothing but the executive committee of the bourgeoisie"—that is, government serves the political interest of the capitalist class.

A third view sees the state as holding a balance of power among a number of special interests. It is seen as neither the agent of a single group nor the servant of an abstract general will. In the Federalist Papers, James Madison expressed this view concisely:

> Those who hold and those who are without property have ever

formed distinct interests in society. Those who are creditors, and those who are debtors, fall under a like discrimination. A landed interest, a manufacturing interest, a mercantile interest, a moneyed interest, with many lesser interests, grow up of necessity in civilized nations, and divide them into different classes, actuated by different sentiments and views. The regulation of these various and interfering interests forms the principal task of modern legislation.[5]

We shall discuss this problem in more detail in later chapters. Here let us say that there is some truth in each view. The common welfare view probably describes fairly well the simple governments that have generally existed before the rise of an economic surplus and a distinct political state. The view of government as the agent of an exploiting class certainly has a great measure of truth for most historic governments—the ancient states of Egypt, Assyria, Mesopotamia, Rome, Carthage, the national empire states which arose in Europe after the Commercial Revolution, and twentieth-century totalitarian states. Where do democracies, such as that of ancient Athens or the modern United States, fit in? We must remember that Athenian democracy admitted to participation only a small minority, and that at the time of the American Constitution only three to four percent of the population was entitled to vote. As the vote has been extended in modern liberal democracies, perhaps the view of the state as holding the balance of power among many special interests is closest to the truth.

All these questions are, however, debatable. For example, most Americans are likely to see German Nazism and Russian and Chinese communism as domination by minorities. To the

5. Henry Steele Commager, *Living Ideas in America*, New York, Harper & Row, 1951, p. 166.

The family is the basic unit of social organization.

Nazis, however, the Third Reich represented the highest true interests of the German people. To the Russian or Chinese Communist, his government may represent true democracy, as compared with what he sees as disguised class rule in the capitalist countries.

We need to elaborate a little on one point which was made at the beginning of this section, for it complicates this discussion. No government can stay in power long through sheer force and intimidation alone. To remain it must have the active consent, or at least the passive assent, of the governed. It must be regarded as legitimate, as having the right to rule.

This recognition may not be hard to get, even though a particular form of government may seem clearly to be against the interests of most of its subjects. In the preceding chapter, we saw that all societies subject their members to a cultural brainwashing in the process of growing up. Thus even people who would seem clearly to be exploited and oppressed generally accept the rule of their oppressors.

It is an interesting fact that when rulers use part of the economic surplus of society for extravagant display of their affluence and power, while the masses remain poor, this display does not usually turn their subjects against them. Rather—from the kings of Dahomey to the British royalty or the Russian Soviet bureaucracy—display by rulers tends to unite the people more strongly behind them. Their subjects appear to identify psychologically with this display and to be glad to be subject to such wealthy and "legitimate" rulers.

Interrelations

The relationships between government and other parts of culture are easier to see than some other connections. It will be necessary only to mention some of them briefly.

We have seen that government furnishes a framework of protection, property rights, obligations of contract, and the like, which are necessary for organized economic behavior. It is also obvious that other aspects of culture operate within a political framework. In our society, although by no means in all, marriage requires state action for its beginning and its termination by divorce. Law enforces obligations of support upon parents and limits their power to punish their children. Education, in most technically advanced nations, is an important function of the state. In England the church is an official agent of the state. Although the United States Constitution forbids "the establishment of religion," legislative bodies and the military forces have chaplains, and money carries the insignia "In God We Trust." In big, modern states, a large part of science is subsidized by government for state purposes. Health and recreation are likewise subject to state support and control.

The state is also obviously shaped by other aspects of culture. We have seen how the development of government has been related to economic surplus and the groups that control it. As the quotation from Madison indicates, economic interests are always a strong factor in shaping government. Money clearly has power to influence political campaigns and elections and to sway legislation through expensive organized lobbying. The family plays an important part in creating acceptance of government. This can be seen clearly in totalitarian states like Nazi Germany and the Soviet Union, but it is true everywhere. Formal education teaches patriotism through rituals such as the flag salute and through history books that exalt the merits of the prevailing form of government. Religion is also likely to play an important part in legitimizing government. In primitive and modern societies alike, disobedience to law is believed to be not only a crime but a sin.

Let every soul be subject unto the higher powers. For there is no power but of God: the powers that be are ordained of God. Whosoever therefore resisteth the power, resisteth the ordinance of God: and they that resist shall receive to themselves damnation.[6]

6. The Apostle Paul in his Epistle to the Romans 13:1–2.

THE FAMILIAL ASPECT OF CULTURE

The family is the basic unit of social organization. Human beings, compared with other species, have a long period of infancy and helplessness. This is related to the human characteristic of learning rather than inheriting behavior patterns. It is a source of the flexibility which makes for culture. The long dependence of the human animal requires a continuing relationship between child and adult. Because of the intimate organic tie of mother and infant, the elemental family unit is mother and child. But this is not enough. The human female, though more durable than the male, is less physically strong. Under primitive conditions she needed a male for physical protection of herself and her child, especially during pregnancy. Thus arose the core family—a woman, a child, and a man to take care of them.

Mother and child are a natural symbiotic unit. To stay together is physiologically and psychologically necessary for the child and also strongly beneficial for the mother. But why did a man become attached? Not because he felt a responsibility as father of the child. Even if a primitive male knows what responsibility means, preliterate peoples do not all know the relationship between intercourse and pregnancy. But the woman may have made care of herself and her child a condition for continued sexual intercourse with her. Family life would provide regular sexual relations otherwise difficult for an unattached male. Once he had joined the mother and child, the male would tend to develop affectionate feelings for both. We know that among existing preliterate peoples, fathers may have very tender and even "motherly" relationships with their children. Affection for the woman would tend to strengthen the sexual and familial relationship. From the evolutionary standpoint, we can be sure that a society in which the mother-child-father family did not develop could not have survived long, or even in all likelihood have developed at all.

During the late nineteenth century, when social scientists first began studying the family systematically, there was great dispute about its origins. One group held that in the beginning there were no permanent sexual ties between men and women, that everyone shared mates indiscriminately in a kind of sexual communism. Opposed to this theory of "original promiscuity" was the theory of "original monogamy," which held that the normal relationship for human beings has always been that of one man and one woman. These opposing views had strong political overtones. The idea of original sexual communism was promoted especially by Socialists and Communists, who attack the "bourgeois" family and its sexual mores. The idea of natural monogamy tended to be supported by more conservative people who favored the prevailing mores.

Of course, we can only speculate about the beginnings of the human race, for evidence is scanty. Preliterate peoples now existing give us only limited help, for they are all far advanced in terms of man's long past. Nevertheless, no clear cases have been found of communal sex relations without separate families. There is little reason to think that they ever existed in the more distant past.

On the other hand, it is clear that monogamy is far from universal. Polygamy (Greek, "many mates") has been fairly widespread in human experience, and people who have practiced it have considered it as natural as we are likely to consider monogamy. Polygamy has two forms: polygyny (one man and several wives) and polyandry (one woman and several husbands). Of the two, polygyny is far more common. It is found, among many other places, in the Old Testament. There are a very few cases of group marriage of several men and several women. Because the sexes are approximately equal in number, monogamy will probably always be the marriage form for most people, for under normal conditions widespread polygamy would leave large numbers of people mateless. There are probably also, for sensitive people at least, gratifications in a monogamous relationship which are difficult to find where affections are spread among several people.

We can see three functions which make the family the very important institution that it is.

The family *protects* and *orients* the child during his years of physical and social dependence. It is by far the most important agent in transmitting culture. The family, or something like it, is thus indispensable to both individual and society. Since it has such great power over the child, the family can, however, also be very damaging. For this reason some people have advocated abolishing the family and substituting some other way of orienting children. It has been proposed that upbringing by professionals in child guidance would be better than orientation by "amateur" parents. In Israel the cooperative farms (*kibbutzim*) to a large extent take children away from parents and raise them in group dormitories, mess halls, and work and play programs. It is fairly certain, however, that any such plans can succeed only if they are able to furnish both the guidance and the personal sense of love and belonging which families at their best provide.

The family is also the center of *sexuality* and *procreation*. Very few cultures have limited sex to marriage, as our traditional mores have tried to do, but all societies have sexual controls centering around the family. Premarital sex may be recognized and approved, but it is expected that eventually youth will settle down and raise a family. Extramarital sex exists in every society, but so does some kind of feeling that adultery threatens family and society. All societies, also, have incest taboos against sex relations in the immediate family other than those of husband and wife.

The family is, in addition, the center of *nutrition.* Even in our urban world, where people eat a great deal in restaurants, this is still so. It is clearly the case in primitive societies. In her important book, *Hunger and Work in a Savage Tribe,* Audrey Richards has studied the relationship of the family to nutrition among the African Bantu. Food, for a primitive people like the Bantu, is the most urgent concern of life. It is the family that grows gardens and stores and prepares the food. It is the immediate family who eat together. Since there are no grocery stores or snack bars, the child or adolescent can get food only from the family supply. Withholding of food can thus be a powerful weapon in discipline. The child learns his group relationships largely in terms of nutrition. His first sense of his family is that of a group that eats together. Only later does he become aware of the larger clan or tribe, as he becomes responsible for participating in the hunt or other group food-getting activities.

In discussing the functions of the family, we need to understand clearly that its role in our society today is quite unlike the role of the family in most other societies throughout history and prehistory. Our industrial, urban, secular culture creates quite a different family situation from that which exists in a primarily agricultural, rural, and religious culture.

Throughout most of history, the family unit has been not the separate family of mother, father, and children, but what we call the extended family, or clan. This consists of the living descendants of common ancestors and generally includes at least three generations. This is the family as we find it among the Old Testament Hebrews, among most primitive peoples today, and among the European peasant immigrants who came to American cities one, two, and three generations ago.

The extended family has typically been a productive unit. The members have not gone away from home to hold jobs. They have worked together on the land or in simple crafts which are carried on in the home. This has meant that each child is an economic asset. In the American frontier family, for example, each new male child very early furnished a strong back to help his father with the work of the farm. Each new girl very early learned to help her mother with cooking, dishwashing, sewing, housecleaning, and the care of younger children. Houses were large and food largely homegrown, so one more child was likely to add less to the cost of the homestead than he could contribute to it. In a society with no public social security system, one's children are his insurance in old age, and the more children he has, the more secure he is likely to feel economically. Thus the economic nature of the extended rural or village family tended strongly in favor of a large number of children.

In organization the extended family has tended to be patriarchal, with the strongest powers of authority in the oldest male. This we find in the Old Testament and in the European immigrant family in this country. When the family was organized for physical struggle against nature and other men, power tended to rest in those who were strongest and least handicapped by pregnancy. The patriarchal organization tended to continue even when these primitive conditions of physical struggle no longer existed, as, for example, in the non-Negro ghettos of American cities. In the traditional Chinese family, a woman was always subordinate to some male: first her father; if he died, her brother; then her husband. It is easy to oversimplify the power of the male, however. In Roman law, for example, the power of the father (*patria potestas*) theoretically allowed him to punish his wife and children at will, even by death. Actually, there are no cases on record where the *patria potestas* was exercised in this extreme form. In the patriarchal family, responsibility tended to be divided into the area of men's work and that of women's work, and in the work of house and kitchen the woman ruled to a large extent. Also, women have always been able to use their sex and other qualities to exercise power over men even where males theoretically have the authority. Nevertheless, as long as the extended patriarchal family was dominant, women were usually inferior in legal rights over their persons, over property, and in formal group decision making.

Children were also inferior. The patriarchal family was typically authoritarian. The role of the young was expressed by such slogans as "Children are to be seen and not heard," and by the belief that a child's will must be broken through rigid discipline. Although, again, actual relationships were often gentler than the formal rules, not many patriarchal families voiced the modern complaint that it is the children and not the parents who run the household.

All this reflected the fact that life was centered on the family group rather than upon individual development and self-expression. Economic and physical survival was central, and children very early learned to take their part in hard work. The long-range planning of a person's life was determined more by interests of the family than by personal taste. On the frontier, for example, it was likely to be assumed that the oldest son would stay on the land and inherit the farm and responsibility for it.

Choice of mates was no exception to this emphasis on group rather than individual. In old China a young man and woman might never even see each other before the wedding. Girls in India used to be betrothed and married as children. In large numbers of primitive and historic peoples, it has been customary for large gifts of money, cattle, or other goods to be exchanged by the families of bride and bridegroom. A good match was likely to be one that brought generous gifts and enhanced the prestige and property of a family. It may be hard for many of us today to believe that most people have never married—indeed, do not marry today

—primarily on the basis of personal attraction or love, but because the marriage has been an advantageous arrangement for their families. Some of us who are still not far from the extended patriarchal family may find it easier to understand.

The organization of the extended family has generally been rooted in religious values. The roles of men and women, the relationship of parents to children, the subordination of the individual to the clan, the high value on fertility, and the patterns of sexual control have all been supported by religious hopes and fears. They have not been regarded as conventional or merely convenient patterns, but as part of the nature of things and of the will of God.

How has all that we have been discussing changed over the last 200 years, as our society has become more industrial, urban, and secular?

First of all, the extended family has tended to dissolve into separate households which no longer have the kind of close emotional and social relationships that formerly existed. This change has often been dramatic and tragic in the case of immigrant groups. As they have abandoned the language and customs of the mother country, the children and grandchildren of immigrants have broken away to establish their own identity in separate households confined to one set of parents and children. In the third generation, typically, the grandchildren have rejected alike the mother tongue and the clan loyalties of the extended family.

The main reason for this is that the family has ceased to be a productive unit. This is true also of the separated family group. The male breadwinner now goes away from the home to work. His wife may do the same. Child labor laws have made it difficult or impossible for the young child to contribute to the family income, although the girl may still be able to help in the home. Thus children have tended to become economic liabilities rather than assets; they must be supported, perhaps through college, with little paid back in return. Fewer children are likely to be born under such circumstances. On the other hand, those who are born are more likely to be wanted for other than economic reasons.

As careers outside the home have become available to them, women have ceased to be dependent upon males for support. Thus both parties to marriage have become economically able to "take it or leave it." Under such circumstances women have lost most of their inferior status both in and out of the home. In the suburbs, where the man may commute long distances and be almost a stranger at home, the family may seem to be a matriarchy (ruled by the mother) rather than a patriarchy.

As relationships between men and women have become more nearly equal, so have those between parents and children. When the family contains only a few children deliberately chosen rather than many who perhaps were unplanned or even unwanted, more attention is likely to be given to the needs and personality of each child. When family relationships become more democratic, parents are likely to be less authoritarian and more permissive toward children, to rely on reason and persuasion more than upon punishment.

As women and children rose in "value," and the newlywed couple split off from the extended clan, personal needs and interests came to be more important than family loyalties and obligations. Before the last fifty years, a Chinese youth who emigrated to the United States might feel obligated to send a regular contribution from his meager earnings to his family back in China and to write frequently about how his heart was really still with them. Today the college student of immigrant stock may resent being asked to visit his grandparents once a year. Public social security for the aged has greatly increased the ability of the young to put their own interests first rather than those of parents and grandparents.

Courtship and marriage have become primarily matters of individual rather than family choice. Romance has taken the place of clan convenience. Whereas it used to be assumed that love, if it appeared at all, was something that grew after marriage, now it is assumed that love is a precondition for marriage. Romantic love was, of course, not invented in the nineteenth or twentieth century. It has its roots in the Middle Ages, primarily in the extramarital affairs of wandering knights with ladies of the manor. In fact, there is probably no culture where personal romantic attraction has not had some place. Epics of the Trobriand Islanders, for example, celebrate the devotion of a pair of lovers who went to their death. But it is only in our modern society that it has become almost unthinkable for most people that a couple should marry without being in love.

Finally, religion has come to play a much smaller part in shaping family organization and values. Marriage is regarded not so much as a sacred bond as a contract which may be revoked when it ceases to be gratifying for either or both parties. Sexual behavior is governed less by absolute standards whose violation brings a sense of guilt and more by practical consideration of consequences. A girl today may decide to refuse premarital intercourse because she is afraid of pregnancy or because she feels she wants to wait for a psychologically deeper relationship than is offered. Or she may deliberately decide to have a premarital sex life because she believes that chastity is psychologically unhealthy. Her great-grandmother very likely just considered sex before marriage a sin.

Interrelations

Because personality is formed there more than by any other aspect of society, the family has a very widespread influence on all areas of culture. An example is the formation of attitudes toward authority.

In the preceding chapter, we saw how parents tend to be regarded as all-powerful, all-knowing, and all-right. We then saw how, by the operation of transference, this attitude tends to be projected upon other parent figures. There is no aspect of culture uninfluenced by such attitudes toward authority developed in the family.

In political life, public figures such as kings or presidents derive some of their power from being regarded (mostly unconsciously) as parent figures. Presidents Franklin Roosevelt and Dwight Eisenhower are good examples. One's country is likely to be symbolized as either fatherland or motherland. A good deal of the legitimacy of government comes from the fact that to it are transferred ideas of parental authority, which cannot be disobeyed. Parent attitudes are particularly likely to be transferred to military superiors.

The projection of familial authority plays a central role in religious institutions. The minister, rabbi, or priest, the Pope, and God himself are all Father. The Virgin Mary is the protecting Mother, and in some religions God is conceived as both Father and Mother.

In economic life bosses are likely to be regarded as parent figures. Sometimes one is referred to as "the Old Man." Employees are likely to develop toward bosses (as toward all authority figures) ambivalent attitudes of both admiration and hostility.

In the educational area, substitute parental authority has played an extremely important part in the role of the teacher in the classroom. In the German preparatory and university system, Herr Professor has always been a strong father figure—demanding, for example, that students rise when he enters the room. Parent projection is less important in democratic school environments than in the traditional authoritarian ones. In recreation, high school and college, coaches are particularly likely to play the role of admired substitute parents.

In our therapeutic institutions, doctors tend to play the role of strong father figures. People who are sick are likely to feel helpless and infantile and to attribute to physicians the almost magical powers that young children usually believe their parents possess.

In the aesthetic aspect of our culture, artists are likely to give unduly great respect to certain great masters and often have difficulty in developing their own styles if they conflict with the authority of these powerful figures.

Even in science, where objective observation and experiment are always supposed to be the final standard, the authority of dead and great men is often hard to challenge. It may often have power in the face of repeated and indeed overwhelming objective evidence to the contrary.

The family, like other social institutions, reflects economic changes. We have already seen in some detail how family structure has been influenced by the economic events of the Industrial Revolution.

Another good case of cultural interrelationships is the influence of early Christianity upon the family. In general we can say that the Christian tradition has created negative attitudes toward the body, marriage, sex, and women.

Early Christianity was strongly influenced (partly through the Greek philosopher Plato) by the "mystery religions" of the East, which held that the body is inferior to spirit and that salvation lies in overcoming the flesh. This influence is reflected in the advice given by the early church father, Jerome, who said that he could not advise mature young women to take baths, since they should be ashamed to see their own bodies.

Marriage was viewed with doubt by early Christians. Probably this was in part true because many of them expected the early end of the world. The very influential apostle, Paul, held that bachelorhood (which he himself practiced) was the best state and marriage an inferior condition. Clearly this was because marriage involves a bodily sexual relation. Paul's famous statement, "It is better to marry than to burn," did not refer particularly to hell fire, but to his idea that for "weaker" individuals, it was better to marry if necessary than to suffer the unrelieved "heat" of sexual desire. This advice was not, however, for the strong. Very interesting is the view of some early church fathers that marriage itself may be good, but that ideally even married people should live sexually "like brother and sister." Needless to say, even at that time this idea was not very widely practiced.

Under the influence of Paul and others, women were the object of suspicion and attack. Paul had admonished women to obey their husbands and required them to cover their heads in church. Many early churchmen, who held sex to be evil and indeed the source of all human trouble, blamed woman for man's fall. All women were, the influential bishop Tertullian said, "daughters of Eve," who "degrade God's image, Man."

Any brief description of the influence of Christianity on family life must, of course, be oversimple and one-sided. There is, however, little doubt that the attitudes just described have had a powerful effect in shaping family and sex mores in the Western world down to the present, especially when they have been combined with the later Puritan attack on enjoyment and pleasure.

THE RELIGIOUS ASPECT OF CULTURE

Our discussion of the economic, political, and familial aspects of culture has inevitably led us into the religious dimension. The social nature and function of religion are more difficult to define than the aspects that we have analyzed so far. Let us approach them by looking at several views of the function of religious behavior.

One view sees religion as arising in *animism*. This is the belief that objects are animated by souls or spirits. According to this view, religion began in primitive man's mistaken interpretation of certain universal experiences. In dreams, reflections in water, and shadows we seem to have a second self. When dreaming, one may travel widely while an observer will see his body remaining on his bed. The idea thus arose of a "double" or a less material self or spirit. Then, according to the animistic view, man began to attribute to other animals the same kind of spirit which he thought he had found in himself. Eventually he also projected his experience upon trees, rocks, the wind, and other objects and forces of nature. Finally he might project a great universal spirit.

A great French sociologist, Emile Durkheim, thought that he had found the source of religion in *collective representations*. Religion involves a sense of the sacred or supernatural, a feeling of holiness or "moreness" which becomes attached to objects or events. The Polynesians used the term "mana" to describe this supernatural quality. How does the sense of mana originate? In occasions and activities, said Durkheim, where group activity is raised to a peculiar pitch. In preparing for critical events, such as the hunt or battle, for example, a primitive group may engage in dances and other group activities that carry them out of themselves. The group life seems to have acquired a special, extraordinary quality which distinguishes these experiences from ordinary, secular life. (We may be helped in understanding this if we think how group ritual generates school spirit before an athletic event.) Sensing this change, the primitive believed that a supernatural mana had descended upon the group. He then began to connect this same mana with certain "totem" animals which became sacred to the clan or tribe. In time he might also have attributed mana to extraordinary objects or events—the sea, overwhelming mountain ranges, winds, and streams. Or mana might have been personified in immaterial spirits or deities.

One of the most widely held views sees religion as primarily an expression of fear. Faced with a threatening environment which he could neither understand nor control, primitive man decreased his anxiety by attributing the events of his world to beings whom he could in at least some measure comprehend and influence. That is, he invented gods. Many exponents of this view regard religion as a part of the childhood of the human race. They feel that as they become civilized, adult, and rational, people should be able to live without such primitive myths.

Two expressions of the fear theory have been especially influential. In the nineteenth century, the German philosopher Ludwig Feuerbach wrote a book called *The Essence of Christianity.* In this he maintained that religion clearly fits deep human needs. It is thus subjectively real, useful, and perhaps even necessary. But the fact that it fulfills human desires does not make it objectively true. Rather, the fact that religion is such an obvious wish fulfillment should lead us to expect that the gods are only projections of human fantasy.

Early in the twentieth century, Freud wrote a book called *The Future of an Illusion.* In this he held that human beings wish to maintain throughout life the sense of gratification and security that they believed parents provided in their childhood. Religion perpetuates this sense of security by projecting parent figures as gods. But this, said Freud, is only fantasy. Hard as it may be to do so, mature human beings must learn to endure life without illusion.

The main role of religion, according to the *exploitation* theory, is the function it plays in the class structure of society. According to this view, religion serves to keep the masses of people content with their lot to the advantage of their rulers. By focusing attention on bliss after death—"pie in the sky"—religion diverts people from protesting against their lot in this life. An English clergyman, Charles Kingsley, was one of the first to express the exploitation theory. He wrote, toward the middle of the nineteenth century, that religion too often served as a narcotic to dull

industrial workers to the evils of the Industrial Revolution. Karl Marx and Friedrich Engels expressed this idea in their famous slogan, "Religion is the opiate of the people." Since that time the exploitation theory has usually been associated with Marxist thought. The German philosopher Friedrich Nietzsche later attacked Christianity for having taught the masses of people a morality of submission which prevented them from revolting against their rulers.

The anthropologist Malinowski saw the core of religion in *life crises* which it serves to "sacralize" (make sacred). The ordinary events of life may be regarded in a matter-of-fact and secular way, but certain crucial events are so important to society and to the individual that they must be linked to the supernatural.

Pregnancy and birth are essential to group survival, and are thus surrounded with ritual and invocation of divine help. At puberty the passage from childhood to adulthood must be made successfully by each new generation if the group is to continue. It is thus usually marked by sacred rites and ceremonies. Preparation for the hunt and warfare, both events involving danger to the individual and deeply connected with the welfare of the group, are likely to invoke supernatural aid. Successful harvest, among people close to the margin of subsistence, generally gives rise to some kind of ceremonies of gratitude and thanksgiving to Providence. Marriage, the key ceremony in the family structure, is ceremonialized as a concern not only of the individual but of the group and of the gods. Finally, death is a threat not only to the individual but to the group, for each member's passing would demoralize and threaten to disrupt the group were the threat not counteracted by the religious belief in immortality. Religion overcomes the crises.

There are parallels between these primitive and universal life crises, as described by Malinowski, and the sacraments of the Catholic Church. Malinowski was concerned with describing the function of religion in society. He tried to show wherein it is necessary. Unlike Feuerbach and Freud, he did not contend that because religion can be shown to fulfill deep human needs, we must necessarily conclude that it is an illusion. On the other hand, he did not hold that it is necessarily true.

Other interpreters might agree that religion can include all the elements just described, but they hold that it is something more than all of these. It is the vehicle through which men give ultimate *meaning* to their lives. From this standpoint one's religion is that which is of ultimate value to him— whether it be truth, beauty, or God; money, power or fame; or even the deliberate gratification of the physical senses which he worships. In this view communism is the Marxist's religion, just as the Jew or Christian or Buddhist has his religion. Concern for humanity as the highest value may be the atheist's religion. Devotion to country, right or wrong, may be the religion of the nationalist.

Other people would say that men's ultimate meanings are extremely varied, from the most selfish to the most altruistic, from the highly materialistic to the most supernatural. All of them can hardly be religion. There must be some significant difference between religious and nonreligious meanings. This view would find the meaning of religion in love as a way of life. "God is love" is a theme common to many religions. Religion may be primarily the effort to convince oneself that the universe loves him. Then one feels himself saved from fear because he is loved. Or religion may emphasize the effort to give love on the widest possible scale as a way of life. Through this giving— to other people, to social causes, to God—one also overcomes fear. "Perfect love casteth out fear." One "finds himself" by "losing himself."

A North American Indian totem pole.

It is not easy, out of these conflicting views, to arrive at a clear statement of the social functions of religion. Almost certainly each of them contains some truth. Perhaps some of the pieces will begin to fit together if we suggest that religion is *men's ultimate effort to feel at home in their universe.*

There are many reasons why human beings should not feel at home in this world: hunger, pain, illness, the seeming insignificance of man in the face of enormous natural forces, the ever-present threat of death, and the certainty of ultimate death. This not-at-homeness, this sense of alienation and separation, men experience as fear or anxiety. Our present age has been described as the Age of Anxiety (combated by psychiatry, alcohol, tranquilizers, drugs, and many other means). But this is nothing new. Our Puritan ancestors lived in fear of witches and, of course, of cold and starvation. The Middle Ages were marked by waves of mass hysteria. Primitive man lives on the brink of violence by beast or inanimate forces and in fear of his own natural end if he is fortunate to live that long. Ultimate fear, then, would seem to be the lot of man.

Religion, however, offers a solution, at least partially, for anxiety. Man may believe that he is in contact with the forces that govern the unknown and unmanageable. He feels that by coming to terms with these forces he may be able to control his own fate.

Control may be through *magic.* By performing certain acts, man feels that he can, with fair certainty, bring about desired results. Sticking a pin in a wax image, for example, may cause an enemy to sicken and die, or intercourse with his wife on a newly planted field may ensure a good crop. Strictly speaking, magic is hardly religion. In a sense it is more like science, for in magic as in science, one believes that if he only performs the proper act, its consequence must follow.

One may, however, deal with the universe through *petition* and *prayer.* Sacrifice may play an important part here. The desired results—good crops,

protection from enemies, cure of disease—are no sure thing, as they are believed to be with magic, but one feels that if he can stay in the proper relationship with the gods, he will be taken care of.

The relationship to the gods or to God may be essentially that of child to parent in the authoritarian family. The power, or powers, that control the universe may be regarded as arbitrary, jealous, and demanding. Salvation from fear then depends upon pleasing the whims of the gods. The fear of God perhaps best describes this relationship. In many respects the Old Testament Jehovah was a god of this kind:

I the Lord thy God am a jealous God, visiting the iniquities of the fathers unto the third and fourth generations of them that hate me, and showing mercy unto thousands of them that love me and keep my commandments.[7]

There is, however, another kind of relationship of man to God. Here God is conceived of as loving his people, even in spite of their shortcomings. What he asks is that they commit their lives to his service—that they love him, and other people, as God loves them. For some religious people, the God who loves them and is loved by them is still thought of in personal terms. They may believe in a separate supernatural realm and in personal immortality. For others, the relationship is more impersonal and naturalistic. At the farthest extreme, religious faith may be simply a belief that if one does not let the universe down, it will not let him down. Such a faith may reject both the supernatural and personal survival after death. This belief is held by many people who call themselves humanists, or even atheists.

We can name three important methods by which relationship to the divine may be sought or expressed.

Ritual is the repetition of acts that have become traditional—chants,

7. Exodus 20:5–6.

dances, pronouncement of sacred words, actual or symbolic sacrifices. No religious practice, from the most primitive to the most sophisticated and modern, is without ritual. Ritual evokes the religious spirit in those who practice it by connecting the present with significant traditions of the past. The Catholic mass is a clear example. It is felt that ritual is pleasing to God and brings men into a relationship of closeness to the divine. When men believe that repetition of certain words or performance of a ritual act will inevitably bring a desired result, ritual may come close to magic.

Most religions call their followers to express their love of God in some kind of *social action.* The great religious seer, Buddha, found the way to union with God (Nirvana). At first he thought that he should do nothing but enjoy this union, but then he remembered all the people who had not found the way and was impelled to return among men to help them. The Old Testament writers, especially the prophets, repeatedly call for a better society: "Blessed is he that considereth the poor: the Lord will deliver him in time of trouble." The call to social justice is repeated in the New Testament: "Be ye doers of the word, and not hearers only. . . . Pure religion and undefiled before God is this. To visit the fatherless and widows in their affliction. . . ." Einstein saw science itself as serving humanity in the spirit of the Hebrew prophets. Many people in all faiths have overcome fear by losing themselves in service of others.

A third way in which men try to make themselves at home in the universe is through personal *mystical experience.* Whereas the way of social action leads one out into the busy outer world, the search for deeper personal union is likely to involve quiet retreat from the world and concentration upon one's inner experience. Mystical communion may be as simple as the practice of the individual who has a quiet hour of meditation each day or the group that goes to the seashore or woods or mountains for a retreat of reflection

and renewal. It may be a more intensive search which involves special techniques, such as withdrawal into extremely isolated surroundings, fasting, concentration of attention on objects or symbols, control of breath and bodily musculature. Or it may involve frenzied dancing, as among the whirling dervishes and some American Plains Indians. Among the best known examples of mystics have been a number of Catholic saints, the Hindu Yogis, and the exponents of Zen Buddhism. Recent interest in LSD and other psychedelic drugs has been based on the belief that they widen religious experience.

We have seen something of what religion means for the individual. What now is its function in society? We may be helped in understanding its role by a distinction made by the French Protestant religious scholar, Auguste Sabatier. He distinguished between the religion of authority and the religion of the spirit.

The religion of authority is likely to be found in formally organized religion. In the Judaeo-Christian faiths, this is found in the synagogue and church. It embodies a body of tradition which links the present to the past. Emphasis is likely to be upon a rather fixed body of rules which is believed to be eternal and unchangeable. In the language of the Bible, this is "the law." The relationship of the believer to the law and to God is likely to be that of the child in the authoritarian family. This authority gives support to the rules. The most important individuals in the religion of authority are the priests who promote the law. Practice centers around ritual. The religion of authority is closely related to the established folkways and mores. It strengthens them and is thus a powerful conservative force in culture.

By contrast, the religion of the spirit is likely to be a revolutionary force. It is generally found outside organized religion or among those who revolt against established religious and cultural authority. As opposed to the priests of the religion of authority, the central figures in the religion of the spirit are critical and often dramatic prophets. We find such figures as the Hebrew prophets, Jesus, Saint Francis, Martin Luther, the Quaker George Fox, and today figures like Mahatma Gandhi and Martin Luther King. Exponents of the religion of the spirit are likely to charge religious authority with having distorted the true spirit of religion, of having corrupted even the law. They are likely to emphasize the individual's inner light rather than external commands and taboos, to stress personal conscience rather than traditional authority. Thus mystical experience of God is likely to be more important than traditional ritual.

Much the same distinction has been made by the German historian of religion, Ernest Troeltsch, between a church and a sect. A church is an established institution that represents majority sentiments, accepts the prevailing stardard of ethics, emphasizes the importance of an established body of doctrine and an official clergy. A sect is a new, separatist group that represents a minority, criticizes prevailing social ethics in the name of a wider religion, stresses personal emotional experience, and relies on inspiration of laymen or ministers rather than formal training. Examples of churches are the Roman Catholic Church, Orthodox Judaism, and the Lutheran, Episcopal, and Congregational churches. Historically the Quakers, Baptists, and Methodists have been sects, only to form churches. Groups like the Jehovah's Witnesses and the Pentecostal groups are sects today.

Religion thus plays no single role in culture. In one form it is one of the strongest bulwarks of established authority. In another form it may be one of the most radical instruments for social change.

Interrelations

We have already seen a number of ways in which religion shapes culture: the influence of the Protestant ethic in the rise of industrial society, the role of

Christian sex and family attitudes on family structure in the Western world, the part played by religion in legitimizing government through the doctrine that "the powers that be are ordained of God."

The accompanying selection illustrates the relationship among religion, economic surplus, and government in the primitive African state of Dahomey. We may ask ourselves whether there are any parallels in modern states of which we know.

Religion is shaped by culture just as clearly as it shapes culture. One of the most thorough studies of this subject is a book by H. Richard Niebuhr entitled *The Social Origins of Denominationalism.*

Niebuhr looks at the various religious groups, primarily Protestant, in Europe and the United States and asks how we can explain their differences. Are they simply due to disagreements about the nature of God and of religion, or do the denominations represent different economic, political, and social backgrounds and interests? Niebuhr believes that both cases are true.

The clearest example of the social origins of religious differences is found in the separation of Negro and white churches in the United States. In 1929, when Niebuhr wrote, over 90 percent of American Negroes were in segregated churches. The number is somewhat lower today. This separation was not due primarily to differences over religious doctrine. It was the result of the fact that white Christians would not admit Negroes to their churches, or if they did so, would not admit them as equals. The separation of the major American churches into northern and southern denominations, at the time of the Civil War or earlier, was likewise mainly based on social and political rather than religious differences. Only recently have most of the major denominations been united.

Established state churches, such as the Church of England, are, of course, a clear example of how politics affects religion. The church receives state support and the clergy are in effect state employees. State churches can clearly be expected, on the whole, to teach a traditional body of doctrine which does not challenge existing institutions. They will stress ritual rather than personal emotional experience, which is likely to be regarded as dangerous. H. Richard Niebuhr found clear social class differences in the European religious groupings that followed the Protestant Reformation. Christianity began as a religion of the poor. After it became successful and wealthy, the Catholic Church had always had to deal with heresies, such as those of the Albigensians and the Franciscans, which attracted the poor and uneducated. As the idea of the Protestant ethic suggests, the Calvinist churches—Presbyterian and Reformed —which arose out of the Reformation enrolled mainly the rising or successful business classes. In England the Church of England represented established values. Luther, who began as a radical critic of Catholicism, soon denounced peasant revolts and made it clear that he intended no economic or social revolution. The poor and "disinherited" had to go somewhere else, and they did so—into sects such as the Anabaptists, Baptists, Mennonites, and Quakers. The overthrow of the monarchy in England brought to power Cromwell, a representative of the Puritan middle classes, but it also brought into being a number of sects of the poor, such as the Ranters, Levellers, and Seekers. In the eighteenth century, Methodism arose with a strong appeal to the poor.

At times, on a market day, a crier would be dispatched by the chief priest of the feared and powerful spirit of a sacred river, the Halan, to apprise the populace that this spirit had threatened a poor harvest and an epidemic among the livestock. Every man and woman was, therefore, instructed to bring to the palace within three days a cowrie shell for each of his animals to appease the wrath of this being—one shell for each goat, one for each head of cattle, and one for each sheep—and to deposit the shells for each kind of animal separately. Before the cowries were brought, each animal was to be touched with the shell representing it, in order that the threatening danger might be transferred to the shell. A ritual fringe of palm fronds was also to be placed about the neck of each beast to make the spiritual quarantine more effective.

Since the people complied in all haste, these results were achieved: as something having value was given, there was an assurance that no more than the correct amount of cowries would be accumulated; as the value of one shell was extremely slight, no economic burden that might of itself have been resented was imposed. The shells thus collected made an impressive total, and the king, not unmindful of its effect, demonstrated his concern by doubling this number before the entire sum was sent to the chief priest who had issued the warning. All benefited, therefore; the royal bureaucracy, by retaining an equal number of pebbles as the number of shells forwarded to the priest, had an accurate count of the animals kind by kind and village by village, on which to base their fiscal computations; the people received reassurance that a threatened danger would be avoided, and at an extremely low cost; and the priests received their due in remuneration and gratitude from the monarch with whom they cooperated and from the people whom they served.

*The identical device could not, of course, be employed time
after time. Variations were introduced on the principal theme. For
instance, a different category of goods would become incensed
with the people, and for differing reasons. Or different methods of
making the supernatural ill will known, often in themselves
indirect, were employed, as when dead animals were found at
various crossroads, and their owners, seeking out the diviners,
discovered "independently" why these misfortunes had come
upon them. The procedure in averting continuing disaster was
invariably the same; the process of assuring income to the
kingdom was facilitated, the support of the king, in so far as this
type of tax was concerned, was aided, and the priests were
the more richly rewarded for their services in directing affairs
according to supernatural will.*

—Melville J. Herskovits, Economic Anthropology, *New York, Norton, 1965,*

In the United States, according to Niebuhr, churches have continued to represent economic and social interests. Here the Episcopal, Presbyterian, Unitarian, Christian Science, and Congregational churches have traditionally been strongest among the middle and upper classes, especially in the urban East. Methodists, Baptists, Quakers, and the Disciples of Christ have had appeal among lower-income groups, the rural areas, and much of the West and South. As in Europe, the sects and churches of the less established classes have generally been more democratic in organization, more emotional in their experience of religion, and more critical of established social institutions. Since Niebuhr wrote, many of the lines have become more blurred. Some of the most powerful social protest, for example, now comes from within the Episcopal church, and some of the strongest opposition to change comes from groups like lower-class southern Baptists.

Suggestions for further reading

Chapters six and seven constitute a unit dealing with the unity of culture. Therefore a single list of readings appears at the end of Chapter seven.

Chapter seven
The cultural basis: II

THE EDUCATIONAL
ASPECT OF CULTURE

Education is the whole process by which an individual, in interaction with his culture, collects information and develops techniques, attitudes, and values. Since the child can obviously become an adult participant in culture only after a long educational experience, we are likely to think of education as pertaining to children. But the existence of adult education as an institution in our society bears witness to the fact that education is actually a lifelong activity which is never completed.

In technically advanced societies, we have separate educational institutions. We shall see that this is not ordinarily true among primitive peoples. In either case, however, education is an activity of the whole society. One writer, discussing "how the community educates" in the contemporary world, lists sixteen different influences in addition to the school: home, neighborhood, playground, nature, religion, work, civic conditions, the street, travel, beauty and ugliness, group membership, authority or lack of it, sickness and accident, punishment, longing and aspiration, and reading.

In the broadest sense, education is everything that happens to promote the development of an individual. A major part of education is socialization (transmission of the basic techniques of cooperative living) and enculturation (transmission of the folkways and mores of the culture). Education also includes learning one's social role, that is, the behavior considered appropriate to the subgroups to which he belongs—his class and his race, for example. It includes also the specialized techniques necessary for his part in the division of labor.

Education may allow the individual to continue in the station of life of his parents, or it may be the avenue through which he learns how to be upwardly mobile in his society. In relatively static cultures, education mainly transmits the tried and true ways of the past. In changing societies, however, it must perform the double task of transmitting the old ways and at the same doing something to enable the individual to face the new. Finally, since each person is an individual and never a mere rubber stamp of his culture, education may also help him develop his potentialities for uniqueness as a person. Since most cultures have been more concerned with perpetuating themselves than with individual development, this last function of education has not usually been very prominent.

It may be useful to look at educational institutions in terms of three kinds of historic social situations. Education in primitive societies is largely informal and not institutionalized. Education in preindustrial civilizations has generally been formal education for a class minority. Industrial civilization, on the other hand, generally leads toward formal mass education.

We have seen that in primitive societies the tasks of life are relatively

Education in three stages of society: **top left,** *informal learning of hunting skills among the primitive Bushmen (courtesy of the American Museum of Natural History);* **top right,** *a private school for the well-to-do in Colonial America;* **above,** *formal mass education today—a high-school language lab.*

simple and change little from one generation to the next. Since there is no written language, the traditions to be learned are limited to those that can be passed down by word of mouth (or other means of expression, such as the dance). There is, therefore, no need for formal educational institutions. Parents, aunts and uncles, and grandparents are able to do most of the job of educating the young. Perhaps skilled matrons will give girls special instruction in the tasks of women, and experienced hunters or warriors may teach their trade to the boys. At puberty, in many but not all primitive cultures, the young go through *rites de passage* in

which they are initiated from childhood into adulthood. These usually involve learning of tribal traditions, as well as tests of skill and courage. (Christian confirmation rituals and the Jewish Bar Mitzvah are parallels in our society. Some people have also seen a similarity in our examinations for candidates for advanced degrees.) The only specialized training in a primitive society may be that given to the priests or medicine men.

The development of civilization increased the division of labor and generally brought fairly rapid social change. It also introduced written language. The priests needed to master writing in order to transmit and interpret the sacred texts upon which their position in society now depended. Literacy for other people became helpful or necessary in meeting the demands of a more complicated society. Thus formal educational institutions arose.

Between 3000 and 2000 B.C., in the complex urban civilization of the Sumerians in the Tigris-Euphrates Valley, writing was probably invented. The Sumerians had a formal educational system separated into elementary and advanced divisions, with graded steps. By the fourth or fifth century B.C., Athens had a well-developed educational program. Education in Greece was strongly influenced by the Spartan system of military training. The Hebrews stressed character training and the Jewish social ethic more than the science and philosophy that were prominent in Athenian education. The Romans, in their educational system, introduced the study of foreign languages and contemporary literature. Already in the days of Confucius (551–478 B.C.) formal schools played an important part in China, and through many centuries the ruling class in that country was selected on the basis of intellectual performance in competitive examinations.

With the decline of Rome, education and literacy dwindled in most of Europe. Early Christian education was primarily church-centered, with emphasis on traditional values rather than intellectual development. However, the Middle Ages made one highly important contribution to formal education: the universities which arose in the twelfth century to teach theology, the liberal arts, law, and medicine. These were generally dominated, however, by the philosophy and method known as *scholasticism:* logical argument from authority and accepted theological premises rather than objective study of events. Meanwhile, the Eastern Empire at Constantinople carried on the tradition of Greek and Roman education in its universities. Science, philosophy, and mathematics played an important part in formal education in the urban and religious centers of the Muslim world.

From the Renaissance to the Industrial Revolution, the broad trend was toward more secular and widespread education. Already in the late Middle Ages, town schools had developed in the towns and cities which were dominated by the rising bourgeois class of craftsmen and merchants. The Renaissance and the Commercial Revolution brought a general widening of experience and a more critical attitude toward existing institutions. After the fall of Constantinople in 1453, refugees to Italy brought the classical educational traditions of Greece and Rome back to western Europe. The medieval spirit gave way to the philosophy of *humanism,* which stressed the development of human powers in this life rather than preparation for the hereafter. The writings of humanists like Francois Rabelais (died 1553), Michel de Montaigne (1533–1592), Juan Vives (1492–1540) and Desiderius Erasmus (1466–1536) all stressed the importance of educating for practical life through real-life experiences. The invention of the printing press in the fifteenth century made possible the mass production of reading matter and thus stimulated a demand for more widespread education.

The Protestant Reformation, with its stress on individual religious experience rather than church authority, also promoted the widening of education. Luther broke with the Catholic Church in encouraging the reading of the Bible by laymen in their native language. To promote this Lutheranism sponsored general primary education, secondary schools, and universities. Under Calvin in Geneva, the community became responsible for an educational system with primary schools at the base and college education at the top. The Protestant clergyman Jan Amos Komensky, known as Comenius (1592–1670), was almost three centuries ahead of his time in arguing for mass education in practical subjects as the best way to bring all men to glorify God. Spurred by the Reformation, the Catholic Jesuit order developed a systematic program of instruction for the young. The trend toward education for individual development was strengthened by the writings of John Locke, who taught that all men are born with equal potentialities which must be developed by social experience, and Jean Jacques Rousseau, who held that experience with nature is especially important in enabling the individual to develop his individual powers and criticize existing institutions.

With the rise of *nationalism,* which accompanied the coming to power of the largely Protestant middle classes, there was an increased demand for systems of publicly sponsored education. This was an ideal of the French Revolution and was gradually put into effect in France after 1833. In Prussia in 1763, school attendance became compulsory from ages five to thirteen or fourteen, and the Civil Code of 1794 stated clearly that education from primary school to university was a responsibility of the state. In the United States, public education has, of course, been sponsored primarily by the states rather than by the federal government.

As suggested earlier, tendencies toward mass education were greatly strengthened by the spread of industrialism. The Industrial Revolution raised the general standard of living, thereby making available a greater "surplus" for education as well as other cultural pursuits. Literacy and formal education for social roles became necessary in order to fit the individual into a more complex and specialized society. In turn industrialism organized the masses of workers, who then made universal public education one of their strongest political demands.

In the most advanced industrial nation, the United States, we have a spectacular example of this widening of formal education. In 1900 about 1 percent of young people went to college. Today the figure is about 50 percent. Even in most Western industrial nations, the percentage going to college is still closer to the 5 percent figure. Thus in this country we have had a spectacular change from class education to mass education. In 1900, when only about one youth in twenty finished high school, college education still stressed the traditional classics— Greek, Latin, philosophy, literature, mathematics, rhetoric, and a little science. This kind of college experience trained a young man (and a few young women) to take their places in the upper-middle or upper class. Today in the United States a college education is coming to be looked upon as everyone's birthright—in fact, almost a necessity for a job with any prestige. Other industrial countries are likely to follow the lead of the United States. England, for example, now is building "red brick" colleges for the middle classes to supplement upper-class universities like Oxford and Cambridge.

The unprecedented expansion of mass education in the United States has created problems and conflicts which are still far from resolved.

Formal curriculum versus "education for life." The traditional classical education, intended for a leisured upper class, is not the kind of education needed by a majority of the population. In the 1920s, under the influence of John Dewey and others, there arose a demand for "progressive education" which would be more concerned with daily life. It would stress preparation for participation in a rough-and-tumble, dynamic society rather than preoccupation with books, traditions, and formal curricula. The danger in progressive education is the tendency to encourage "meaningful experience" rather than to transmit basic skills and knowledge, such as writing ability or the habit of rigorously examining evidence.

The cultural heritage versus preparation for social change. This is related to the first problem. Those who are satisfied with the status quo are likely to say that the job of the school is to pass down known tradition and not to be an agency for "propaganda." Such conservatives are often dominant in the community and prominent on school boards or boards of trustees. Others say that in a society where change is inescapable, it is disastrous simply to teach from the past. But if education is to prepare the student for change, what kind of change should it prepare him for? Should it simply make him flexible enough to adapt to a variety of possibilities? Concern with what (if any) the goals of education in the United States really are has been stirred by the presence of the Soviet system of education. Whatever one thinks of its goals, the Soviet goals seem to be fairly clear.

Liberal versus specialized education. With every field of knowledge becoming more complex, there is pressure to begin fairly narrow specialization as early as possible. Since the Depression formal education has become the chief method for climbing the economic and social ladder. It is, in fact, almost the only way up for a lower-class or lower-middle-class youth. Students are likely to want to get ahead as fast as possible with preparation for their vocation. They are likely to regard anything that seemingly does not deal with their trade (such as sometimes social science!) as a positive barrier to their ambitions. A few employers and professional schools, on the other hand, will insist that what they want is not the narrow specialist who is ignorant of almost everything except his trade, but the person rounded by a solid general education.

Social adjustment versus individual development. The former president of the University of California, Clark Kerr, suggested that the university is a factory whose product is human material equipped to fit social and economic roles in an industrial society. Indeed education has become big business; it is one of our largest industries. But student protest in our colleges and universities has centered around just this conception of education. It has been directed against the mass production methods (as seen in large, impersonal classes) that often implement it. Education, many of the protesters feel, should concern itself first with enabling the individual to develop his potentialities to the full. Such education, they feel, requires personal contact on a face-to-face basis. Many teachers and administrators agree.

Personal versus impersonal instruction. Production line methods are themselves largely a result of the widening of education. It would probably cost no more than it did 25 or 50 years ago, it is true, to give a student a personalized education, but it is hard to get the money to do it, and there is a strong tendency to spread cheap and impersonal methods of instruction once they have been introduced. This is especially true of general or liberal courses, when pressures are strong to spend money for advanced specialized training. The desire for specialized library and laboratory facilities tends to favor big schools which can afford such facilities. Thus the small, personalized school or college tends to get squeezed out of existence. The pressure toward "factory" education will become stronger as increasing numbers of the young people born in the post-1945 baby boom become of high school and college age.

Such problems have caused many people to take a second look at the whole program of mass education. One of its results has been the prolongation of economic infancy. Youth is able to take a mature place in society at increasingly older ages. This is especially true of those whose vocation requires post-graduate training, and their number is increasing. This postponement is justified on the ground that longer preparation is needed in a complex and specialized society.

Some critics have questioned, however, whether the prolongation of education usually meets the need of such a society. They wonder whether we may not have spread our education out thinner so that the average A.B. degree today may be no better than a high school diploma was fifty years ago, or an M.A. no better than a bachelor's degree was then. To what extent, some ask, are our hours and years of education really used? To what extent have our public schools, colleges, and universities become public baby sitters, keeping young people off the streets and off the labor (or marriage) market until there is a place for them?

Can mass education, they ask, do otherwise than thin education down? With 40 percent of youth going to college, is it possible to maintain the standards that existed when only five percent went? Should everybody have the right to go to college, or may the needs of most people be met by stopping earlier (and perhaps continuing in their spare time in adult education programs)? This would not have to mean a return to upper-class education, for the smaller number going to college could be selected from all social levels. It may be, on the other hand, that the original 5 percent were not selected mainly on the basis of intellectual capacity, but simply on the basis of class membership. The average student in our high schools and colleges today may therefore be as good as, or better than, his predecessors. To this very central question we do not have an answer.

Interrelations

No aspect of culture is uninfluenced by the educational process, for all cultural attitudes are shaped through education, formal or informal. Let us examine the relationship of education to economics, politics, and religion.

As we have seen, formal education in our society plays a major part in preparing people for their part in the economic process and for their social class role. Education is also influenced by occupation and class. The largest percentage of school dropouts, for example, come from low-income and low-status groups. Although education is our chief ladder of upward mobility, the dice are still generally loaded against lower-class youth. Teachers with middle-class values are likely to be biased, consciously or unconsciously, against children who are not so clean, or orderly, or careful of their money, or quiet, or restrained in their violence and sexuality as are middle-class youth. Grades and recommendations are likely to reflect this prejudice.

Schools are dependent upon economic support for their existence. There is always the question of how education will be influenced by those who support it financially. There is a strong tendency for donors to believe that schools should comply with their wishes and, sometimes, prejudices. Where this is the case, withdrawing or threatening to withdraw government funds, church subsidies, foundation grants, or private donations may be a strong factor shaping what is taught. Administrators and school boards almost always have an ear for how school policies and programs will influence sources of income. Freedom of education depends upon an adequate supply of funds that has no strings attached.

Schools are a powerful force in shaping political attitudes. In the totalitarian countries, it is taken for granted that this is as it should be. Many people in the avowed democracies also believe that this is what education should do. Legislators and legislative committees sometimes take this point of view. In the United States, they feel that schools should be propaganda agencies for the American way of life, which usually means private enterprise capitalism, and formal democracy. If rival political systems such as communism are studied, it should be for the purpose of exposing their faults, never their virtues. These people believe that since they are agencies of the government, schools should have no place for critical examination of that government. Opposing views hold, of course, that the aim of education is not to propagandize but to seek truth. They maintain that the purposes of democratic government and society will in the long run be best served by objective examination of all institutions.

The relationship of education to religion is equally close and difficult. Formal education probably began in primitive societies as training for the priesthood. Throughout civilization it has more often than not been associated with religious indoctrination. Now, in the United States, the Constitution forbids the "establishment of religion," that is, the state cannot promote any religious belief. Thus public educational institutions, as agencies of the state, cannot actively engage in religious practices or religious training. Actually, the matter is more complex than it might seem. Religion is a question of one's ultimate view of his universe. Thus everything that is taught in some sense influences religious beliefs, positively or negatively. If religion is forbidden in the schools, what is likely to happen is that education is slanted toward agnosticism or atheism. These are themselves religious ideologies, answering the question of the ultimate nature and meaning of things. Thus it is difficult or impossible to make the schools religiously neutral; they will almost certainly be biased toward one or another kind of religion or irreligion.

A possible answer is to have all religions presented and discussed objectively and impartially. This involves the problem of representing all religious points of view equally and adequately. Moreover, since religion is an emotional experience, it is doubtful whether it can be communicated adequately by an objective, intellectual presentation. Yet to allow all religions (including atheism) to be experienced emotionally by youth in public schools would almost certainly raise again, on the part of unbelievers, the cry that the schools were teaching religion.

THE SCIENTIFIC ASPECT OF CULTURE

"Man by nature desires to know," said Aristotle. Thus science (Latin *scio,* to know) has always been a part of culture. Primitive man inhabited, as do we, a strange and awesome universe. It confronted him with the rising and setting of the sun, the rotation of seasons, flood and drought, thunder, lightning, and storm; the movements of the planets and stars; accident, disease, and natural death. Thus he had an inescapable desire for pure science, knowledge that might not have any immediate practical result, but that would make his universe at least somewhat more predictable. He needed to have a map for the earth and heaven, to be able to trust day to follow night and spring to follow winter, to be able to explain in some way the catastrophes that threatened him, for ignorance has always meant fear, and knowledge of the unknown has meant some relief from anxiety. The known is less terrifying than the unknown.

Primitive man also needed applied science. The Trobriand Islander fishing for his living in a delicately balanced outrigger boat in the waters around his home needed reliable knowledge of the physical principles of balance, of the movements of tides and of sea life, of the behavior of sails in wind, of the prevailing breezes and destructive storms. When he planted the yams which constituted the other largest item in his diet, he used knowledge of the growing seasons, of methods of selecting yams and preparing ground, of watering, cultivating, harvesting, and storing. Both at sea and in his garden, he performed ritual ceremonies (magic) and prayed to his gods (religion) for protection and success. But neither in garden nor at sea did he rely on magic or prayer alone. Like all primitive peoples, he also had practical scientific knowledge.

Science has two main sources. The priest, shaman, medicine man, and later philosopher have developed broad explanations of the universe. From these explanations have grown, especially, astronomy and mathematics. The practical craftsman, interested in techniques that will work in his trade, has learned some of the general principles that govern the behavior of physical materials, plants, animals, and man. One of the most important craftsmen has been the healer (usually in the beginning the priest or medicine man), practicing the craft of medicine out of which grew knowledge of biology and chemistry. At all times scientific prediction that can be tested objectively has been mixed with magic and superstition. Always, however, in any culture, both the pure and the applied interpretations of reality have contained some measure of testable truth, without which no culture could survive.

The agricultural revolution was a turning point in the development of science. The hunter and gatherer lives largely from day to day without much foresight. To plant seed which will be harvested months later requires prediction and an act of faith in the uniformity of nature, a trust that what has happened once will happen again. This is the basic faith upon which science rests. Agriculture in Egypt, which depends upon the annual overflow of the Nile, illustrates the relationship between cultivation and science. The Egyptians discovered very early that the course of the star Sirius, or Sothes, through the sky during the year could be used to predict the flow and overflow of the Nile. After a few years of charting Sirius, it was possible to predict the inundation six months in advance. Such records probably led to what the Egyptian expert, James Henry Breasted, called the first date in history: the creation of the Sothic calendar in 4236 B.C. The calendar was the first major example of scientific prediction.

Science began as man's effort to locate himself in space and time. Einstein called science "the study of space-time under the aspect of eternity." To the primitive each day was a crisis, for at noon the sun began to set. Would it rise tomorrow? Each autumn brought a similar crisis, for the nights began to lengthen. Would spring come again? Spring itself brought crisis, for then came the planting of crops, with all its uncertainty. In autumn came also the harvest and (in northern climates) storage for the long, uncertain winter. Each crisis called forth religious ritual to make certain that time would remain on a course favorable to man. Man's calendars foretold these sacred times and thus enabled him to take ceremonial action to stave off disaster and win divine favor.[1]

Thus in Sumeria around 3000 B.C., the temple was a center not only of religion but of astronomy, which may have begun there. In Egypt at the same time, one of the important functions of the king was that of astronomer. The Egyptian pyramids and the Babylonian ziggurats (pyramidal temple towers) served as markers for observing the stars. The strange collection of vertical stones at Stonehenge in England was probably an astronomical observatory. The stars enabled man to control time. They were also claimed to control human events in ways we doubt today. Astrology was basic to Babylonian, Persian, and late Greek science, and spread to China. Newspapers still print horoscopes. Astrology had a scientific element—the signs of the zodiac may have been the herdsman's first calendar.

The stars also enabled man to control space. As he began to trade and navigate unknown seas, the heavens helped him find his way. The stars guided the sailor as well as the priest and farmer. In the fourteenth century B.C., the first known map was constructed in Egypt.

Mathematics developed as an instrument for controlling space and

1. Noah Edward Fehl, *Science and Culture,* Hong Kong, Chung Chi College, 1965, p. 24.

The ancient Egyptians built these pyramids to serve as markers for observing the movement of the stars.

time. It is an important example of the power of abstraction which is so important to science. "It must have required many ages," said Bertrand Russell, "to discover that a brace of pheasants and a couple of days were both instances of the number two."[2] One of the earliest mathematical documents is from around 2000 B.C., again from Egypt. It is entitled "Directions for Obtaining Knowledge of All Dark Things." The practical use of mathematics is shown in the pyramids. With only the simplest of tools, the Egyptians were able to make the four sides so close to absolutely square, and to locate them so precisely along the directions of the compass, that it would be difficult to duplicate their work even with modern instruments.

The first high point in science came in ancient Greece. (The second was the period after the Renaissance, and the third the twentieth century.) The invention of the alphabet by the Phoenecians about 1200 B.C. made written communication far easier for the Greeks than it had been in the hieroglyphic language of the Egyptians and Babylonians. Much of the work of Greek scientists continues in our heritage today.

Hippocrates (born 460 B.C.) remains one of the great figures in all scientific medicine. Euclid's *Elements of Geometry,* published about 300 B.C., is still a mathematical classic. Aristarchus (310–230 B.C.) placed the sun at the center of the solar system, with earth among its circling planets. It took science almost twenty centuries to catch up to him. A large part of the reason was the opposition of Aristotle (384–322 B.C.). Although he happened to be wrong about the important matter of the solar system, Aristotle was profoundly right about many other things. For example, he foreshadowed by 2000 years the theory of natural selection developed by Darwin.

Why . . . should . . . our teeth . . . come up of necessity—the front teeth sharp, fitted for tearing, the molars broad and useful for grinding down the food—since they do not arise for this end? . . . Wherever . . . all the parts came about just what they would have been if they had come to be for an end, such things survived, being or-

*ganized spontaneously in a fitting
way; whereas those which grew
otherwise perished and continue to
perish.*[3]

Darwin himself, given a copy of Aristotle's writings late in life, said that as biologists, compared with Aristotle, his idols Cuvier and Linnaeus were mere schoolboys. In the fourth century B.C., the brilliant mathematician Eudoxus laid the foundation for scientific astronomy. Theophrastus (born 372 B.C.) began the systematic study of botany. Geography was systematically developed in the late Greek period. Pythagoras (about 584–495 B.C.) founded a school for science and demonstrated that the earth is round. Scientific thought to the present day could not conceivably be the same without the work of the great philosopher Plato (427–347 B.C.).

By the time of Aristotle (the fourth century B.C.), the main outlines of science, especially geography and astronomy, had spread in a belt from the European Atlantic to the Pacific coast of China. With the eclipse of Greece and the rise of Rome, science on the whole declined. For the most part the Romans borrowed rather than developed new scientific ideas. It is often thought that the medieval church was responsible for the decline of science. This is true in part, but science had begun to fail long before the fall of Rome.

In 1200 A.D., toward the end of the Middle Ages, science was more advanced in China and the Mohammedan world than in Europe. The Byzantine Empire and Moslem science preserved Greek mathematical science, as they preserved Greek educational principles. In India the zero and decimals were discovered in the sixth century A.D., thus making mathematical calculation much easier than it had been for the Greeks. The medieval church, on the other hand, opposed mathematical science, which seemed to make abstractions more important than the fate of individual men.

Yet the groundwork was being laid for the great development of science after the Renaissance. By 1300 the invention of convex lenses and the development of spectacles promised to double the reading life of man. Toward the end of that century, Nicholas of Cresme debated the geocentric (earth-centered) theory of the solar system, thus foreshadowing the revolution in astronomy, by which Nikolaus Koppernigk (Copernicus, 1473–1543) and Galileo (1564–1642) were to change men's conception of the universe. Nicholas of Cusa, in the fifteenth century, believed in a moving earth and a boundless universe. As early as the sixth century, John Philoponus of Alexandria had experimentally refuted Aristotle's view that bodies fall with a speed proportional to their weight. The rediscovery of this behavior of falling bodies by Galileo a thousand years later was one of the cornerstones in the development of physics. Philoponus had said:

For if you let fall from the same height two weights of which one is many times as heavy as the other, you will see that the ratio of the times required for the motion does not depend upon the ratio of their weights, but that the difference in time is a very small one.[4]

Jean Buridan, rector of the University of Paris, had by 1330 developed the idea that inertia and gravity keep the earth in its orbit. (Inertia is the tendency of a body at rest to remain at rest, or in motion to continue in motion in the same direction, unless acted upon.) Thus the great keystones of the modern conception of the universe—the heliocentric theory, gravity, and inertia—were all discovered, though not systematically developed, in the Dark Ages.

The seventeenth century brought a

3. *Ibid.*, pp. 183–184.

4. *Ibid.*, p. 347.

tremendous burst of development in science, as in all of culture (it was the century of Luther, Shakespeare, and Milton). Copernicus had mathematically demonstrated that the earth rotates around the sun, but his book on *The Revolutions of the Heavenly Bodies* failed to sell its first printing of 1000 copies. The idea was contrary to common sense, and even Galileo rejected it for a long time. Johannes Kepler (1571–1630) was a brilliant astronomer; among his many achievements were the concept of a scientific hypothesis and the idea that the planets are guided in their orbits by a force which operates at a distance.

Galileo was more of a popularizer of science than an original thinker. The heliocentric theory, for which he stood trial by the church, was (as we have seen) 2000 years old. The law of falling bodies had not only been stated by Philoponus a thousand years earlier, but had been demonstrated by Simon Stevin in the sixteenth century. Galileo, however, belonged to a world where the time was ripe for a new view of nature. The commercial revolution called for a new science to keep pace with production and trade. Already in southern Germany and northern Italy, in the fifteenth century, there had been a surge of technical development. Galileo himself developed a telescope and was able to back up his theories with direct observations. The Renaissance, as we have seen, had brought a new and more secular attitude toward man and nature. As the two accompanying paintings, one medieval and the other Renaissance, suggest, the Renaissance had introduced a new three-dimensional, solid concept of space. The medieval painter worked without perspective in two dimensions.

Thus Galileo's *Discourses Concerning Two New Sciences,* published in 1638, changed the Western world's way of thinking about the physical world. It paved the way for the organization of physics and astronomy by Isaac Newton (1642–1727) around the universal concept of gravity. Newtonian

Galileo demonstrating his telescope.

physics was the basis for modern science until the twentieth century.

Other sciences now began to move forward. Already William Harvey (1578–1657) had established scientific physiology by studies that led to discovery of the circulation of the blood. At the great Italian University of Padua, where Harvey was a student while Galileo taught, the clinical thermometer and an instrument for measuring the pulse were also developed. Chemistry had originated in the late Greek period in the form of alchemy, the effort to transmute base metals into gold. It was not systematically developed, however, until the eighteenth century, with the work of the French chemist, Antoine Lavoisier (1743–1794). The nineteenth century was one of development in geology and biology. Geological investigation established the long history of the earth and overthrew the doctrine of the recent creation of the world. Biological research led to formulation of the theory of organic evolution by Charles Darwin (1819–1882) and Alfred Russel Wallace (1823–1913).

The twentieth century will undoubtedly be remembered as another great revolutionary period in the history of science. The static, well-organized, solid material universe of Newton, governed by inexorable laws, is no more. In twentieth-century physics, everything is in flux, matter is no longer solid, all observations are relative, and even the idea of strict causation is in question. The dominant figure in this revolution has been, of course, Albert Einstein (1879–1955). Actually, most science is still more in the age of Newton than in that of Einstein.

Accompanying the change in the underlying content of science has been an equally revolutionary change in organization. No longer is the scientist an amateur, literally, doing his work out of love or the excitement of the quest. Research is now conducted almost entirely by highly specialized and trained professionals, working in large universities, industry, or government. No longer does the economic and industrial system wait for discoveries and inventions to occur. Inventions are planned as needed and carried out in subsidized laboratories, usually by teams of scientists.

Interrelations

Science has always been the product of a scientific community, and the community has been an intimate part of the whole culture. Every great scientist must say with Newton, "If I have been able to see further it is because I stood on the shoulders of giants." He must also pay tribute to the fact that the time (that is, the cultural situation) was ripe. When it is not ripe, the scientist and his work are usually forgotten. Leonardo da Vinci invented an airplane in the

fifteenth century, but the world was not ready for it any more than it was ready for Aristarchus' heliocentric view of the universe in the third century B.C. When the time is ripe, however, discoveries and inventions are likely to come forth in abundance.

In 1920 in his book, *Social Change,* the American sociologist William F. Ogburn tabulated a large number of discoveries or inventions made at or near the same time by two or more people. Among these simultaneous discoveries were the planet Neptune, sun spots, decimals, logarithms, the calculus, the law of gases, the telescope, the microscope, photography, the thermometer, the law of conservation of energy, the law of inertia, the electric motor, the grain harvester, the telegraph, the microphone, the phonograph, the electric light, the telephone, antisepsis, anaesthesia, the theory of organic evolution, the theory of the emotions, and the theory of color. It will be very instructive to study the whole list in Ogburn's book.

Three of the most important aspects of the climate of science are the economic, the political, and the religious.

The scientific and economic aspects of culture are very closely related. Science furnishes techniques for production. On the other hand, nothing stimulates science like the demand for new technology. We have seen that the livelihood of the ancient farmer, herdsman, and sailor was closely tied up with astronomy and geography. There were very interesting relationships between seventeenth-century British science and the needs of shippers who were now making long voyages to India, the American colonies, Russia, and Africa. Newton's theoretical studies in physics and astronomy were closely connected to his interest in three basic problems of navigation: measurement of longitude at sea, determination of the time of the tides, and principles of hydrodynamics which would make possible faster and more seaworthy ships. There is also considerable evidence that the greatest interest in science in

England was found among the Puritans, who made up a large part of the business class. The Puritans were only a small minority in the English population, but they constituted 62 percent of the original Royal Society of Scientists. It is unlikely that the Industrial Revolution could have taken place in the eighteenth century without the scientific developments of the seventeenth. Both the practical background in mechanics and the new rationalistic approach to problems were necessary. Nor would these developments in science have burst forth so spectacularly had not there been the atmosphere necessary for great technological changes.

Science, like education, can progress only as long as someone is willing to pay the bill. Modern industry has definitely benefited from the advancement of science, but until recently, especially in the United States, industry has not been very generous in supporting basic research. Sometimes business had definitely discouraged science, as when inventions have been held off the market because they might make products last too long. In recent years government contracts, especially for the military, have made up an increasing part of the support of science. There is, however, no automatic guarantee that the interests of business or military necessity will be the best long-run interests of science. Those who pay the bill may take the same point of view toward basic research as that satirized by a British scientist in describing pure mathematics, "This subject has no practical use; that is to say, it cannot be used for promoting directly the destruction of human life or for accentuating the present inequalities in the distribution of wealth."[5]

The relationship of science to politics is clearly close and important. The great chemist Lavoisier lost his head on the guillotine during the French Revolution in part because of the un-

popularity of his scientific views. An outstanding American physicist, Robert Oppenheimer, was hampered in his work because his political connections and opinions were suspect. In the Soviet Union, the biologist Lysenko has won fame for his unorthodox views on genetics because they support the Marxist party line (although they may not be so absurd as generally thought in the West). The German Nazis proclaimed "not objective science . . . but the heroic science of the soldier. . . . "

This last connection, between science and the military, has always been important. Archimedes' discovery of the principle of the lever derived from work on military weapons. The concept of force behind moving bodies probably grew out of the study of military projectiles, such as cannon balls. Leonardo da Vinci, in applying for a job with the Duke of Milan, stressed his ability to build bridges, drain moats, mine fortresses, dig tunnels, and make light cannon. As an afterthought he mentioned that he could also construct public buildings, make statues, and paint. Galileo was able to sell the telescope because of its use in naval warfare. Lavoisier was in charge of explosives for the French government arsenal. The smelting of iron by coal and the use of the steam engine were developed for needs of artillery. Wilkinson bored steam engine cylinders with techniques learned in boring cannon. The Bessemer steel process was developed to meet the need of stronger steel in rifled cannon.

Today the influence of the military upon science is greater than ever before. The twentieth century has introduced the idea of science as a tool of national interest. Before this century science was considered an international, human concern and the scientific community a world community. Actions supported this belief. During the eighteenth and nineteenth centuries, free scientific exchange took place even in wartime. The British scientist, Humphrey Davy, visited

5. J. D. Bernal, *The Social Function of Science*, London, Routledge & Kegan Paul, 1939, p. 9.

France during the Napoleonic Wars and was honored by Napoleon, even though some of his work had been of military utility. Today scientists in all the major nations are limited in what they can study, how they can study it, and how they can communicate their findings by considerations of national security. Some people have refused to do classified research because they feel it is contrary to the vocation of the scientist.

The relationship of science to religion is complex. Through most of human experience, science (the study of nature) and theology (the study of God) have been considered a single subject. The scientist has considered his work to be the interpretation of God as manifested in nature. The primitive medicine man has generally been both priest and scientist. In the early civilizations, the temple was the center for science. Even when science was separated from formal religion, as in Greece, Plato began his study of science with God's creation of the universe. In the medieval world, it was assumed that the scientist studied God's world. Copernicus was a monk and Kepler a devoutly religious man. Newton begrudged the time that natural science took from his main concern, which was theology. Francis Bacon, who summarized scientific knowledge early in the seventeenth century, spoke of the function of science as "the glory of the Creator and the relief of man's estate."

The revolution in science that began in the seventeenth century divided science and religion. Instead of being located at the center of creation, man was now an insignificant inhabitant of a minor planet. The revolution in geology undermined belief in a sudden divine creation. The theory of organic evolution made the whole development of species, including man, the result of a series of accidents rather than of a divine purpose. Neurological research revealed the close relationship between the nervous system and mental activity and brought into question the idea of an immaterial soul.

More important than this, the great scientists who established the scientific revolution had driven a wedge between nature and man. They depicted nature as a mathematical mechanism. Newton's universe was a system of hard spheres held in relation to one another by a mechanical force called "gravity." Galileo saw the world as consisting of quantities, which can be measured by science, and qualities (such as the emotions or the sensory experience of color or sound), which are outside science. The influential philosopher René Descartes (1596–1650) divided the universe into two worlds, that of nature and that of man. The first was to be understood by mathematics, the second by psychology. One observer has said that before Galileo, man, God, and nature were an undivided unity. After Galileo a mechanical, inanimate nature became the important reality, and both God and man were pushed to the sidelines.

Since then science and religion have been in conflict a large part of the time, and many times religion has fought scientific advance. Not all the fault has been on the side of religion. Reasonable religious views can never be the same as they were before Copernicus and Darwin, yet the picture of the universe constructed in the seventeenth century was not the only one possible. Historically men have represented reality by at least three models (many more are, no doubt, possible). One is that of a machine. When this model dominates, life and mind as well as inanimate nature are reduced to machines. It is by no means certain that this model explains the facts best. Plato used the model of an organism, a complex system of mutually interdependent parts. This may be closer to the field theory of modern science (see Chapter five) than is the model of Galileo, Newton, and Descartes. A third model sees the dominating fact in the universe as mind. Before we dismiss this model as fantastic, we may remember that Einstein said the cosmos seemed to him less like a great machine than like a great intelligence. Religion is certainly much more at home with Einstein than with Newton.

THE THERAPEUTIC ASPECT OF CULTURE

According to Francis Bacon, the purpose of medicine was to bring the parts of man's body into harmony. Health is an ecological problem involving the balance of an organism in relation to its environment. Disease is a failure to maintain this balance. The function of the therapeutic aspect of culture is to preserve the integrity and vitality of the body in the face of all the stressors it encounters. In Chapter five we listed some of the stressors with which we live. They are cold, heat, humidity, deprivation of oxygen, thirst, hunger, overeating, overexposure to sunlight, wounds, poisons, bacteria, frustration, repression, fear, anger, excitement, boredom, disappointment, depression, grief, famine, economic insecurity, economic competition, population crowding, war and threat of war, status anxiety, overstimulation, suppression of personality, intoxication of food, air, and water.

This outlook on health and disease is as old as the great Greek physician Hippocrates and as new as the recent work of Selye and others on stress. It is important to have this broad view so as to avoid the danger of oversimplifying the picture by overemphasizing any single factor (such as, for example, bacteria). This conception suggests that the therapeutic aspect of culture has two main tasks. One is to maintain conditions that will keep disease from occurring. The other is to treat it when it occurs. Of the two, the first is far more important, although the unfortunate use of the term "medicine" to describe all prevention and therapy would suggest otherwise. In Greek mythology the preventive aspect was symbolized by the goddess Hygeia, the aspect of treatment by the god Aesculapius.

Among primitive peoples (as among all people) knowledge about health is both scientific and magical. Health to the Melanesian, says Malinowski, is a natural state of affairs unless tampered with. Preliterate men know that the body can be damaged by poisons, wounds, burns, falls, cold, heat, overstrain, overeating, and too much sun. They may use such natural remedies as rest, massage, steaming, or warming at a fire. They have also developed drugs, most of them herbs or vegetables. Many of these do not, so far as we know, have any therapeutic effect of a biological or chemical nature. However, some ancient medicines, from primitive and other cultures, do have known functions. Examples are cod liver oil; boiled toads, whose skins contain a substance which acts on the heart like digitalis; ground up dinosaur bones, a good source of calcium; and burnt sponge, whose iodine content helps goiter.

On the other hand, a large amount of disease cannot be explained scientifically or pseudoscientifically by primitive men. For the Trobriand Islander, says Malinowski, this is true of most causes of illness and death. These the primitive is likely to attribute to black magic, or sorcery. One is ill because someone has put a spell or curse upon him or an evil spirit has visited him. Therapy then consists in finding the offender and removing the curse or driving away the spirit. The medicine man is a specialist at this kind of white magic.

Our earliest record of the healing arts among civilized peoples is from Egypt of 4000–5000 B.C. The Code of Hammurabi tells us that medicine was regulated by the Babylonians by about 2500 B.C. The ancient Hebrews, in their dietary laws and sanitary codes, began the science of preventive medicine. With the Greeks medicine was separated from religion. Temples for healing were dedicated to the god Aesculapius. Hippocrates began the practice of clinical medicine with his detailed observations and reports of cases. These were not equaled in the next 1800 years. In his writings he established the philosophy of prevention and healing which is still followed by the best practitioners today.

After Hippocrates the practice of healing never reached the same high point in Greece or Rome. The Romans, one of whose strong points was engineering, did however introduce important public health measures: clean streets, pure water provided through aqueducts, and sewage disposal. Only after the Industrial Revolution was this advance equaled. Celsus compiled a medical encyclopedia which was still in use in the Renaissance. Dioscorides, a Greek army doctor, originated the *materia medica* (systematic list of drugs). Aretaeus recorded excellent clinical observations of pneumonia, tetanus, empyema, and epilepsy and gave the first accurate accounts of insanity. Galen (A.D. 131–201) performed physiological experiments that were not equaled until Harvey's work on the circulation of the blood in the seventeenth century. Unfortunately, Galen, like Aristotle, became established as an absolute authority whose writings were rarely questioned until the late Middle Ages.

Little progress in healing was made in Europe during the Middle Ages. The Arabian physician Rhazes (852?–932?) gave excellent clinical descriptions of smallpox. In the eleventh and twelfth centuries, under Arab influence, secular medicine was taught in the medical school at Salerno, in Italy. In the fourteenth century, Henri de Mondeville perfected methods of cleaning and treating wounds. He was bitterly opposed, for Galen had taught that pus in wounds was natural and healthy. Equally bitterly Mondeville wrote, "God did not exhaust all his creative power when he made Galen." His discovery was not accepted until it was put forward in the nineteenth century by Semmelweiss and Holmes, over equally strong opposition but with more success.

The refugees from Constantinople who brought new educational and scientific ideas to Italy after 1453 also brought the influence of Hippocrates, which stimulated European medicine. Paracelsus (1493–1541) was an exotic figure who promoted the use of the usually stronger (and also more dangerous) mineral medicines instead of herbs. In this sense he set the trend for modern pharmacy. He was the only prominent person between the fourteenth and nineteenth centuries to advocate keeping wounds clean. Andreas Vesalius of Padua (1514–1564) was the first important anatomist (Leonardo da Vinci was forbidden by the Pope to practice dissection in a hospital, and Michelangelo did dissection secretly as training for his sculpture.) Ambroise Paré (1510–1590) was a great surgeon who introduced artificial eyes, massage, and the truss for hernia.

The seventeenth century was very productive in medicine as in astronomy. Harvey's discovery of the circulation of the blood was outstanding. Anton van Leeuwenhoek (1632–1723), a janitor and dealer in cloth, developed the microscope and saw protozoa. This was obviously a very central advance. An Italian anatomist, Marcello Malpighi (1628–1694) saw capillaries under the microscope and thus showed how blood makes its way back to the heart. Thomas Sydenham (1624–1689), called the "English Hippocrates," gave clinical descriptions of gout, scarletina, dysentery, malaria, and cholera. He prescribed cinchona bark for intermittent fevers, iron for anemia, and cool drinks for fevers.

The Industrial Revolution established the character of modern medicine. The crowding of people into industrial cities, with provisions for housing, water supply, and sewage disposal far inferior to those of the Romans, led to massive health problems. Industrial development gave the scientific push of which nineteenth-century medical development was a part.

Edward Jenner (1749–1823) employed the experimental method to demonstrate that inoculation with cowpox immunizes against small pox. Rudolf Virchow (1821–1902) used the microscope to establish the science of cellular structure. The first practical use of anaesthesia (the word was coined by Oliver Wendell Holmes in 1846) brought a revolution in surgery. After the introduction of antiseptic cleansing of wounds by Holmes and Ignacz Semmelweiss (1818–1865), Joseph Lister (1827–1912) developed the technique of asepsis (sterilization of the operating room and the surgeon's equipment). Asepsis made practical for the first time surgery of the abdomen, joints, chest, and brain. Gregor Mendel (1822–1884) contributed his epoch-making study of the mechanisms of heredity. Florence Nightingale (1820–1910) organized the profession of nursing. Louis Pasteur (1822–1895) and Robert Koch (1843–1910) demonstrated the germ theory of infection. Charles Brown-Séquard (1817–1894) put forward the idea that body chemistry is controlled by glands of internal secretion.

This brings us to the twentieth century. At this point we should look carefully at our therapeutic institutions as they fit into the total social picture. Of the medical developments of this century, perhaps the most revolutionary have been advances in knowledge of the endocrine glands, scientific knowledge about nutrition including vitamins, development of vaccines against a number of specific diseases, development of antibiotics, and the concept of stress as related to disease. Some of the trends have been spectacular. Infant mortality has been drastically reduced. Infection and death in surgery have been largely controlled. Some diseases—smallpox, scarlet fever, diphtheria, polio, measles—seem all but abolished. There is a tendency to attribute all the gains to such advances as the germ theory of disease, vaccines, and miracle drugs. We need, however, to take a longer and somewhat more cautious view of twentieth-century medicine.

In an excellent book, *Mirage of Health,* Rene Dubos has shown that most of our advances in disease pre-

Inoculation of children in the early nineteenth century.

vention began long before vaccines, antibiotics, or even the germ theory. This was true of leprosy, plague, typhus, and sweating sickness. Yellow fever, diphtheria, scarlet fever, and measles had been conquered or were less severe before modern wonder drugs. Some of this progress was due to general improvement in conditions of life. The introduction of inexpensive cotton undergarments easy to launder, and of transparent glass that allowed light into most dwellings, contributed more to the control of infection than did all drugs and medical practice. Nutrition had begun to improve and working-class children to become bigger before 1900.

Positive public health programs had often had dramatic results. In 1804 and 1827, Barcelona and Alciente eliminated yellow fever by antifilth campaigns. In the 1830s a "Health of the Towns" movement began to clean up England's industrial cities. From 1880 to 1898, Max von Pettenkofer conquered typhoid in Munich by bringing in clean water and controlling sewage. Even in the twentieth century, one of the most effective childbirth programs has been that of the Frontier Nursing Service, which has depended on delivery by midwives in the homes of Kentucky mountaineers. Only in recent years has the medical profession so reduced maternal and infant mortality. Dubos compares the idea that all recent progress has been due to twentieth-century advances with the fantasies of the small boy playing by the sea. "When the tide is receding from the beach it is easy to have the illusion that one can empty the ocean by removing water with a pail."[6]

Moreover, the diseases that were not dealt with somewhat successfully in the nineteenth century are, for the most part, not being controlled today. In the case of the so-called degenerative diseases—such as arthritis, diabetes, cardiovascular disease, and cancer—the situation is getting worse in spite of some medical advances. The life expectation of an American at 45 today is not significantly greater than it was several decades ago.

Twentieth-century medicine tends to be dominated by an oversimple and one-sided view of disease. Pasteur, on the contrary, emphasized that when he encounters bacteria, a person's reactions are a result of his heredity, his state of nutrition, climate and other environmental factors, and his mental state. He knew that not every encounter with germs results in disease. In one village in the Punjab of India, nearly every person was once found to have a positive Wasserman test, indicating the presence of syphilis germs, yet there were no visible signs of syphilis. Around 1900 the Russian physiologist Metchnikoff drank, without serious harm, several tumblerfuls of culture isolated from fatal cases of cholera. Large numbers of people carry the herpes virus, which causes fever blisters, but have blisters only when other harmful conditions exist. Dubos says:

> Bacteria such as tubercle bacilli, streptococci, or staphylococci, many types of viruses potentially capable of producing influenza, intestinal disorders, or various forms of paralysis, all kinds of protozoa and worms, are commonly present in the tissues of individuals who consider themselves hale and hearty.[7]

He points out that when a population first encounters a new germ, as South Sea islanders once did with the measles virus, the results may be disastrous, but in time the population generally develops a working balance between predator and host, in which people are able to live with bacteria without disease or with only mild illness. He feels that such a balance is mainly responsible for the lessening severity of diseases like scarlet fever, measles, tuberculosis, and diphtheria.

A far too simple view of the germ theory plus some remarkable successes with vaccines, antibiotics, and surgery have led to overemphasis of "specific causation" and treatment and neglect of total bodily hygiene. It is easy for this to happen in a society that is separated from nature and often worships technology. Many people look upon a doctor as someone who can work a miracle when they have broken all the rules of health. By concentrating on spectacular therapies, many physicians have encouraged this view.

A prominent public health official, Dr. Herbert Ratner, has said that medical practice suffers from activism. A large part of disease, if left alone, will heal itself. He points to Hippocrates' view that the gods [that is, nature] are the real healers. Thus the task of the doctor is (1) to help nature to heal, (2) to use medicines only if necessary, and (3) to use surgery as a last resort. Modern medicine, says Ratner, almost reverses this order. Drugs are poisons

6. Rene Dubos, *Mirage of Health*, Garden City, N.Y., Doubleday, 1959, p. 31.

7. *Ibid.*, p. 71.

and are given only because it is hoped that their beneficial effects will outweigh their damaging side effects. This is true of serums and vaccines as well. Surgery is a dangerous treatment even at best. Yet all these remedies are prescribed almost routinely. Ratner says that the majority of patients who see a physician would do just as well without seeing him, and even better if the physician happens to interfere too much. A prominent student of the aging process, Dr. Martin Gumpert, has said that the average American is so overmedicated that it is almost impossible to know how a healthy body reacts.

If we accept the Hippocratic concept of health and disease put forth at the beginning of this section, we must agree that most doctors are entirely too narrowly trained. Most physicians will now agree that up to 90 percent of the patients they see suffer not primarily from organic disorders, but from psychological or social stresses. Yet the training of the average physician gives him no adequate background in psychological or social science. A considerable part of illness can without a doubt be attributed to modern dietary habits, as described in Chapter three, but the typical doctor has only the spottiest acquaintance with modern nutritional knowledge. A Harvard University clinician, Dr. Maxwell Finland, has stated that every approach toward preventing and managing disease, without the necessity of drugs, is an advance in favor of humanity and scientific medicine. A large body of knowledge of this kind already exists, but most medical students and their teachers are too preoccupied with medication and surgery to be interested in it.

Narrowing of knowledge in this respect is due to a large extent to the high degree of specialization of most doctors. The great nineteenth-century physician William Osler said that it was more important to know what sort of a patient had a disease, than what sort of a disease the patient had. He also said that even tuberculosis was a social disease with medical aspects.

But the general practitioner who did see the whole patient has virtually disappeared, and the typical specialist rarely encounters the whole individual. The result is a dehumanization of the relationship between doctor and patient. To this is added the fact that most doctors will not make house calls and tend to hospitalize their patients routinely. The patient is then likely to become a "case" who fits into a routine convenient to the hospital and the physician. There is, without doubt, need for specialization in medicine, as elsewhere. Ratner maintains, however, that most practice should be conducted by general practitioners, outside hospitals, with specialists called in only for those rare cases which the ordinary doctor seldom sees.

Depersonalization and commercialism usually go hand in hand. When there is no personal relationship, a profession tends to become a business. Most enlightened physicians would agree that at least 50 percent of surgery is probably unnecessary, and that one of the reasons for many operations is the simple desire for a fee. They would also agree that while many doctors are dedicated and idealistic, a considerable number are in the profession mainly because there is an undersupply of doctors, and incomes are therefore very high. Specialization has tended, in many cases, to make fees very large. Fee splitting—rebate by a specialist to the doctor who refers a patient—is still a common abuse. In California not many years ago, it was found that most ophthalmologists were getting rebates from opticians to whom they referred patients. It is common for ophthalmologists to make considerable income themselves from selling spectacles, and in a number of cases physicians own drugstores and make a profit on their own prescriptions.

Even when this last problem is absent, the medical profession is in a strange relationship with the drug industry. This industry originated in the nineteenth century, with Edward Robinson Squibb (1819–1900) a leading figure. The congressional investigation headed by the late Estes Kefauver disclosed that profit margins in the drug industry are among the highest anywhere. As profit-making enterprises, pharmaceutical companies have an interest in encouraging the indiscriminate use of drugs. The same kind of thing is true of the surgical supply industry. So extensive has the drug industry become that a large number of doctors no longer formulate their own prescriptions personally. Instead they take recommendations of drug salesmen as to the efficacy of their products and write prescriptions for their prepared medicines. In most cases today, these drugs are so new that there has not been time for adequate testing.

The operation of modern medicine is related to its organization. The American Medical Association (AMA) is, in effect, a strong monopoly to which most, although not all, physicians belong. Those who do not may experience difficulties, such as reluctance of hospitals to admit their patients. The AMA is dominated by high-income urban specialists. In 1938 it was successfully prosecuted by the federal government for denying access to hospitals to physicians who had served a medical cooperative in Washington, D.C. This action was in line with the AMA's policy of opposing all forms of what they deem socialized medicine. The organized medical profession has continually campaigned against competing forms of treatment, such as osteopathy, chiropractic, and naturopathy. In one case it was successful in closing the clinic of a nationally known nonmedical practitioner, in spite of affidavits by medical doctors and other evidence that he had successfully treated internal and external cancer.

The AMA has campaigned vigorously against nutritionists who have tried to spread advanced knowledge about foods. It was, on the other hand, long silent on such vital matters as the widespread addiction to tobacco and the commercialization of this addiction. The organized medical profession opposed Sister Kenny's use of physiotherapy in the treatment of polio until the evidence was overwhelming in her favor. In this it was no different from doctors in the past, who have opposed most of the significant advances in medicine—for example, the theory of circulation of the blood, the introduction of the stethoscope, the cleansing of wounds, and the use of asepsis in surgery.

We can suggest some factors underlying these current problems in the healing arts. (1) Medicine is overspecialized and depersonalized as part of a general trend in modern society. (2) Those responsible for human helath and life have a natural tendency to be conservative, though this tendency is hardly shown in the indiscriminate use of inadequately tested remedies. (3) The doctor practices in a society which is more at home with physical and chemical technology than with natural processes. (4) There is an acute shortage of physicians. (5) As the influence of religion has declined, the physician who can save life has acquired some of the unquestioned authority that was once given to the priest who could save one's soul.

Interrelations

As in other areas of culture, many problems in the healing arts are intimately related to economics. For one thing, there are far too few doctors to meet the demand. The result is inflated incomes for physicians and crowded and impersonal waiting rooms and hospitals for patients. There is no reason to think that the cause lies in a shortage of talent. It lies, rather, in a shortage of facilities for training doctors. The average medical student cannot pay his way, and there has not been support for an adequate number of medical schools. Here again is a paradox of the affluent society: the public comes close to worshiping the physician and his services, yet it allows a constant shortage of doctors to persist.

There are clear class differences in health and treatment. The disease rate goes up as one goes down the economic ladder. As long as medical care must be paid for "as one goes," a large amount of illness is not going to be treated, and people will wait to seek help until they are seriously ill. Private and public medical insurance plans tend to relieve this problem. It is argued, on the other hand, that they result in considerable unnecessary treatment, and that tendencies toward overactivism and overmedication may be increased.

Medical practice may become a function of government, as in Britain and other countries. Opponents of socialized medicine argue that the quality of medicine is reduced if the doctor becomes an employee, that the personal relationship between physician and patient is destroyed, that medical matters are decided by unqualified officials instead of by doctors, that a large part of the doctor's time is consumed in bureaucratic red tape. Advocates contend that it is a poor doctor who becomes less effective because he is on a fixed salary rather than private fees, that doctors under free enterprise medicine are actually controlled by a powerful medical monopoly and by pharmaceutical interests, that specialization and depersonalization of private medicine have already destroyed the old doctor-patient relationship, and that under socialized medicine many people receive medical care that they never got before.

Relations between medicine and religion have been extremely varied. In primitive societies medicine, magic, and religion are usually inseparable. Priest and physician are likely to be the same person. With the development of secular medicine, there has often been antagonism. When James Simpson used anaesthesia in childbirth in nineteenth-century Scotland, for example, the clergy attacked him on the grounds that God had intended women to bear their children in pain. Simpson quoted scripture back by showing that God had put Adam into "a deep sleep" before removing his rib to create Eve!

Another connection between medicine and religion lies in the effect of hope and faith on healing. No doctor would suppose that telling a patient he is likely to die or be permanently crippled will hasten his recovery. Recent discoveries in psychosomatic medicine have added to what physicians have always known. One surgeon who specializes in the attachment of detached retinas in the eye writes, for example, that the most important single factor in the success of this operation is the emotional confidence of the patient. There is good evidence that even cancer is more likely to develop in a deeply negative and unhappy person. Interesting in this connection is a 1969 television commercial by the AMA showing the contents of a syringe being injected into a patient and announcing that he was being treated with the most potent medicine—Faith!

Whatever one thinks of its objective truth, strong religious belief is probably the most powerful source of hope and confidence available. There is much conflicting evidence about faith cures of disease. However, it is certain that faith helps recovery in any illness and that it is particularly effective in illnesses that are largely psychological in origin. The most radical example of reliance on faith is Christian Science, which originated in the late nineteenth century. It rejects medical treatment entirely and relies for health on faith, prayer, and religious study alone. In recent years there has been in some orthodox churches a rather strong interest in spiritual healing. Special healing services are likely to play a part. Usually they are intended to supplement medical therapy rather than to substitute for it.

THE RECREATIONAL ASPECT OF CULTURE

To observe play is to look deeply into culture. The Halloween mask and the masked ball are survivors of sacred rites common to most societies. The top was originally a magical device. In Korea the kite was once used as the ancient Hebrews used the "scape-

goat," as an object on which to banish the sins of the community. "Mulberry bush" is a May Day dance which goes back as far as the Greeks. The game of London Bridge survives from human sacrifice at the building of a bridge. The child's game of tag is probably a survival of a primitive flight from an evil spirit or of the terrifying choice of a sacrificial victim.

Play is certainly found in all cultures. There have been many attempts to explain it. According to one view, play takes place because people have surplus energy to expend. Another approach regards it as a repetition of age-old experiences of the race. Fascination with tree climbing, for example, may be a survival from our simian ancestors. Other people have seen play as a preparation for adult life. Children's mechanical games prepare for the technology of adulthood, their athletic contests for the competition and struggle of maturity. Still others have seen play as chiefly a release for the tensions of ordinary (that is, nonplay) life, and a re-creation of one's spent powers. Plato related it to the young animal's and child's need to leap!

All these ideas are in part true. Taken together, they probably furnish a rather good explanation of play. In another sense, however, play needs no explanation because it is almost certainly the elemental life activity out of which work branches because of ne-

cessity and to which life normally returns when work is finished. Since work has been so important and time consuming for most human beings, we are likely to think of play or recreation as what one does with his leftover, nonwork time. Play is, however, more than this, for in most of the world's most serious activity, we also find elements of play.

It is not just an accidental matter of words that one's line of work is sometimes referred to as the "game" he is in, or that in a competitive society the contestants ordinarily respect the "rules of the game." Except when international agreements and conventions break down, this is as true of warfare as of business. We have spoken of science as motivated by the pure thirst for knowledge and the practical need for applied technology. There is also a third motivation; one may view scientific experimentation, theory spinning, mathematical manipulation, as a game. Philosophy is in part "playing with ideas," literature a "playing with words," and the other arts play with their respective media. A recent best seller, Eric Berne's *Games People Play,* analyzed the way in which the often unconscious playing of games permeates our interpersonal relations.

One of the most thorough students of play has been the Dutch historian Johan Huizinga (pronounced "hite-zin'-

ga''). Play, he says, is free activity which we consciously think of as outside ordinary life. We regard it as a game, make-believe, not serious. At the same time, we can be entirely absorbed by it. As such, play involves no material interest, brings no monetary profit. It has fixed spatial boundaries (the stadium, the chess board, the stage, the ring for marbles, the hopscotch squares, the shuffleboard court). It is also definitely organized in time; it has a beginning and an end and proceeds in an orderly manner according to fixed rules.

Roger Caillois, a French sociologist, has analyzed play in a very systematic and thought-provoking manner.[8] He thinks that play falls under four headings: contest, chance, mimicry, and vertigo.

Contest is the assertion of the self in the desire to win. Its typical form is sports, including such indoor contests as bridge and chess. In real life the spirit of contest is found in such activities as economic competition, competitive examinations, and advertising.

Chance also represents the desire to win, but by submission of the self to luck or fate. It is found in private poker games, church bingo, casinos, parimutuel betting, and state lotteries. (Contrary to Huizinga's definition, chance definitely does involve the hope of material gain.) In real life chance is found in such activities as "playing the market."

Mimicry is play through imitation of another. It includes animal imitation, childhood role taking, all forms of the drama, and hero worship (identification with an athlete, movie star, or royal figure). In real life it appears in the wearing of uniforms or in ceremonial etiquette.

Vertigo expresses the desire to escape from real life by temporarily destroying one's equilibrium, to escape from ordinary perception, to lay aside one's conscience. It is sought through swinging; ecstatic dancing;

8. See Roger Caillois, *Man, Play, and Games,* New York, Free Press of Glencoe, 1961.

speed on skis, motorcycles, in cars or boats; carnival rides; mountain climbing; alcohol and drugs (ants and caterpillars also deliberately intoxicate themselves). In real life it is expressed in professions such as acrobatic tightrope walking, whose appeal is control of tendencies to vertigo. (Caillois' book was published before the vogue of rock music; in this, especially in acid rock, we might well find elements of vertigo.)

Neither Huizinga nor Caillois has, of course, said the final word on play. All that we have said so far should, however, give us a background for looking at play historically.

People in all societies have certainly played in ways common to all higher animals: running, jumping, wrestling, fighting, eating, drinking, and sexual advance. Adults in many proagricultural societies may have little separate leisure, but work is almost inevitably accompanied by joking and horseplay as in our society. The more tropical peoples have had more free time because food is easier to get. Everywhere children have usually had leisure for play. Ceremonial drama plays an important part among preliterate peoples. This is generally of a religious nature, associated with the critical changes of season and critical points in the individual's life development. These we have already discussed. As people begin to practice agriculture, acting out of seasonal changes may be believed to help along the desired results, such as return of the sun or a good harvest. Vertigo plays an important part among primitive peoples. One form is periodic periods of license in which taboos are relaxed and almost "anything goes." Another form of vertigo is the holy frenzy of religious rites, such as occurred in the dances of the Plains Indians.

Economic surplus brought an increase in leisure, at least for the upper classes. Among the historic peoples, we know that the Egyptians played ball 4000 years ago. Assyria, Persia, Egypt, Greece, and Rome had parks for public recreation. The first planned physical exercises and gymnastic programs were in Persia, where they prepared young men for military service. In Sparta physical education was extended to girls. The Greeks had a strong sense for play. Plato wrote that

> *man is made God's plaything, and that is the best part of him. . . . What, then, is the right way of living? Life must be lived as play, playing certain games, making sacrifices, singing and dancing, and then a man will be able to propitiate the gods, and defend himself against his enemies, and win in the contest.*[9]

The contest, or *agon*—the striving to excel—was very important in Greek culture. Everything became occasion for it. There were contests in beauty, in singing, in solving riddles, in keeping awake, in eating and drinking. Political satire was a highly developed form of *agon.* The theater, which first achieved organized prominence in Greece, centered around a contest among playwrights for honors. In sports contest culminated every four years in the Olympic Games.

The Roman culture was not generally lighthearted. Every city had, however, its arena, where gladiatorial combats and other contests furnished diversion for the masses. There were also public baths, theaters, and games. Medieval life was more relaxed. It was, says Huizinga, "brimful of play, the joyous and unbuttoned play of the people." For the upper classes, there were tournaments, courtly love, and the whole game of chivalry. The Renaissance upper class lived in a world of poetry and art and imitation of Greek culture. The Renaissance man was the well-rounded individual who devoted his leisure to the joyous development of all his human powers. The rollicking satire of Rabelais expressed an age which was also "unbuttoned." The Baroque period, whose height was in the seventeenth century, was marked by a playful extravagance in architecture and style of life. It was, for example, the period of the wig. Romanticism, beginning around 1750, to a considerable extent "played" with fantasies of a Utopian society and a return to nature, at a time when the Industrial Revolution was just beginning to lead the world far away from nature.

The main influences that have shaped play in the modern world seem, however, to be Puritanism and industrialism. As we saw in the section on economic aspects, the two appear to be closely connected.

The ethic of Puritanism, which arose in the seventeenth century, was generally antiplay. The great Protestant leader Luther had been much interested in music and gymnastics. We have suggested, however, that the Puritans tended to look with suspicion upon everything except work and church going. An extreme of this type of attitude was the view of the eighteenth-century German educator Franke, who held that all play should be forbidden and children taught its folly and wastefulness. When Puritanism, as Max Weber said, "turned with all its force against the spontaneous enjoyment of life," among the things banned were the pub, the card game, the dance hall, most sports, and especially the theater. The only recreation allowed was that which clearly promoted physical efficiency. Karl Marx observed that the Protestants had abolished most of the holidays that are so numerous under Catholicism. The English Puritans came into sharp conflict with Kings James I and Charles I over the Book of Sports, which legalized certain games on Sunday. Puritanism was prominent in New England and has strongly influenced our American tradition and our attitudes toward enjoyment of leisure.

Industrialism has affected play as thoroughly as it has influenced other aspects of culture.

Leisure. The shift from farm to factory and office and the mechanization of the

9. Johan Huizinga, *Homo Ludens,* London, Routledge & Kegan Paul, 1950, pp. 211, 212.

home have freed most children from work and given women more leisure. Older people no longer wait until they are incapacitated to retire. Shortening the workday has brought increasing free time to the employed. Regular vacations for the average worker are almost entirely a matter of the last hundred years. We may expect a steady increase in leisure.

Organization. With industrialism leisure has become the concern of formal social institutions. The massing of people into cities often left little room for play and recreation unless they were specifically planned.

The first outdoor gymnasium—the beginning of organized athletics, gym, and sports in the United States—was set up in 1821. The YMCA, now an important urban center for recreation, began in 1844. In 1853 New York City set aside Central Park, and by 1901, 796 cities in the United States had land for parks. The first "little" community theater was established in Paris in 1887. The first American community center for slum areas, Hull House in Chicago, was founded in 1889, four years after Toynbee Hall in London. Community playgrounds began to develop around 1900. The spread of organized community recreation is illustrated by California: in 1905 there was one local recreation department, and in 1940 there were 44 departments. In 1945 North Carolina established the first adequate statewide agency to coordinate community recreation. Philadelphia, in 1961, became the first major city to set forth an overall plan for developing recreational facilities. In 1962 the President and Congress received a comprehensive series of 27 scientific reports summarizing and forecasting the development of outdoor recreational facilities in the United States.

Commercialization. With city life, organization of play, and rising incomes, play has become increasingly something for which one pays. Commercial-

ized professional sports largely began with baseball around the end of the nineteenth century. Already in 1892, however, an English visitor had been impressed by newspaper coverage which gave one column to the death of the poet Whittier and twelve columns to the Corbett-Sullivan prize fight. The motion picture industry arose in about 1914. The automobile put recreation on wheels in about 1920; the first state gasoline tax was passed in Oregon in 1919. Radio broadcasting became a solid part of American culture in the 1930s and television in the 1950s. By 1955 more time was spent by Americans in watching television than in any other single activity except sleeping.

Professionalization. Commercialization of recreation creates a division of labor between the performer and the spectator. Specialists in sports and other commercial recreation actually cease to be players and become workers. Professionalism stresses increasing perfection of performance. This drives even amateurs to become workers. Spectators also cease to be players, except by identification with the performers. For many the "hot stove league"—sedentary exchange of sports lore and statistics—replaces actual participation in play.

Play in today's world. Some writers have taken a dim view of the future of play in the modern world. In the mid-nineteenth century, the philosopher Henry Thoreau wrote from his rural retreat at Walden Pond, "A stereotyped but unconscious despair is concealed even under what are called the games and amusements of mankind. There is no play in them, for this comes after work."[10] Huizinga believed that nineteenth-century industrialism, with its emphasis upon efficiency and profit, began to destroy the spirit of play. Production became all consuming, and play itself ceased to be recreation.

10. Henry David Thoreau, *Walden and "Civil Disobedience,"* New York, New American Library, 1960, p. 10.

Ever since the last quarter of the nineteenth century games, in the guise of sport, have been taken more and more seriously. . . .

In the case of sport we have an activity nominally known as play but raised to such a pitch of technical organization and scientific thoroughness that the real play spirit is threatened with extinction. . . .

More and more the sad conclusion forces itself upon us that the play element in culture has been on the wane ever since the eighteenth century, when it was in full flower.[11]

Others take a more optimistic view. They believe that we have outgrown the Puritan fear of fun and are moving into an Age of Sport. We no longer feel guilty about enjoying ourselves, and we will have more and more time in which to do it. True, recreation has been organized, commercialized, and professionalized. But people are not mere spectators. In many forms of recreation—from hobbies to little theater to family camping—these people argue, we are learning to "do it ourselves" and are thus revitalizing the spirit of play.

Interrelations

Economic relations and play are intimately related. The competitive *potlatch* in which the Kwakiutl earned prestige by giving away or destroying goods is similar to the "game" of displaying possessions competitively in our society. Competitive American sports both express and prepare for the intensity of competition in real life. Branch Rickey, who was a devout Protestant, once defined his ideal ball player as one who would break both legs of anyone standing in his path to second base. Baseball player and manager "Birdie" Tebbetts, a college graduate, once said that if he couldn't hate an opponent the concept by which he lived would be destroyed and

baseball would have no purpose. A top golf pro explained that when he readied his swing, he thought of somebody he disliked and got so mean he almost wanted to hit himself. Football coach Jim Tatum offered the comment that winning was not the most important thing—it was the only thing. On the other hand, the team spirit helps prepare for the cooperative aspects of team behavior in economic and other life.

Play also compensates for the tensions and frustrations of economic life. Caillois observes that people who at work make only one part of a machine may enjoy immensely making scale models of the whole machine in their spare time. Spectators "let off steam" at athletic events. People who know they are not going to make it in the real-life struggle for money and status may compensate by fantasies of striking it rich through gambling or television contests. One observer has commented on the tendency of immigrant groups, who have been discriminated against economically, to find a substitute channel in sport. Thus minority groups have furnished an unusually large number of athletes. Nonathletes then identify with successful stars. By serving as such a safety valve, sports may keep tensions from building up into social protest or revolution.

Play has a very important role in political life. The modern Olympic Games are intended to promote international good feeling, but have become intense contests at which national prestige and power are held to be at stake. Politics is a continual contest, and for some people the "game" itself, with its stratagems and manipulations, is at least as fascinating as the results. Law and justice were originally a game in which cases were decided by the drawing of lots or by a contest. In the Old Testament, Saul settled a case between himself and his son Jonathan by casting lots. Among some Eskimos the drumming match, in which each contestant in a case at law tries to outdo the other in insult and abuse,

11. Huizinga, *op. cit.,* pp. 197, 199, 206.

is the only way of making a decision, even in the case of murder. Courts are now supposed to seek an abstract, objective justice, but the courtroom is still clearly an arena of contest.

It has already been suggested that war is usually a game played within rules. In the Biblical book of Samuel, Abner describes a battle: "Let the young men now arise and play before us." This is suggestive of modern television coverage of warfare, which brings it into the living room much like an athletic contest. The term "pitched battle" originally referred to warfare that took place on a previously marked-off field. Historically war has often been thought of as a test of fate in which victory indicates God's judgment in favor of the winner. There are also close connections between nonmilitary sport and war. It was once said that the wars of England were won on the playing fields of Eton (a "public" school). Former West Point football coach Earl Blaik has said that football was the closest to war of any game invented by man. Gridiron heroes often transfer the game spirit to the battle front.

We have already seen that a good deal of religious expression is ritual (for example, the drama of the Mass) or vertigo (as in the search for ecstasy through dance or drugs). Philosophy probably originated in primitive contests in solving riddles about natural and supernatural phenomena. The search for knowledge is still to a very large extent polemics, that is, an effort to destroy the arguments of an opposition. The accompanying selection suggests an interesting relationship between athletics and the structure of the school. (The language is simple but abstract, and we will do well to think of concrete illustrations. We may also ask to what extent this description, written in 1932, is still true.) Art, particularly dance and poetry, is close to play, although the two are not the same.

By furnishing all the members of the school population with an enemy outside the group, and by giving them an opportunity to observe and participate in the struggle against that enemy, athletics may prevent a conflict group tension from arising between students and teachers. The organization of the student body for the support of athletics, though it is certainly not without its ultimate disadvantages, may bring with it certain benefits for those who are interested in the immediate problems of administration. It is a powerful machine which is organized to whip all students into line for the support of athletic teams, and adroit school administrators learn to use it for the dissemination of other attitudes favorable to the faculty and the faculty policy.

In yet another way an enlightened use of athletics may simplify the problem of police work in the school. The group of athletes may be made to furnish a very useful extension of the faculty-controlled social order. Athletes have obtained favorable status by following out one faculty-determined culture pattern; they may be induced to adopt for themselves and to popularize other patterns of a similar nature. Athletes, too, in nearly any group of youngsters, are the natural leaders, and they are leaders who can be controlled and manipulated through the medium of athletics. Those who are fortunate enough to be on the squad of a major sport occupy a favored social position; they are at or near the center of their little universe; they belong to the small but important group of men who are doing things. They have much to lose by misconduct, and it is usually not difficult to make them

*see it. They have, too, by virtue of their favored position, the
inevitable conservatism of the privileged classes, and they can be
brought to take a stand for the established order. In addition,
the athletes stand in a very close and personal relationship to
at least one faculty member, the coach, who has, if he is an
intelligent man or a disciplinarian, an opportunity to exert a great
influence upon the members of the team. The coach has
prestige, he has favors to give, and he is in intimate rapport with
his players. Ordinarily he uses his opportunities well. As the
system usually works out, the members of the major teams form a
nucleus of natural leaders among the student body, and their
influence is more or less conservative and more or less on the
side of what the faculty would call decent school citizenship.*

—*Willard Waller,* The Sociology of Teaching, *New York,
Russell & Russell, 1932, pp. 103–119.*

We may observe two final relationships between play and social and cultural life in general.

A large part of relations among people consists of role playing. Both Shakespeare and some modern psychologists have suggested that we may learn a great deal about social life by regarding it as a theater in which everyone is acting parts. Traditional Japanese culture seemed built on the idea of social relations as play. In the language used to address people of higher rank, "You arrive in Tokyo" can best be translated "You play arrival in Tokyo," and "I hear that your father is dead" as "I hear that your father has played dying."

The spirit of fair play, says Huizinga, and of playing the game by the rules underlies all civilization and all society. Without this concept the world would be a jungle. When they cease to be controlled by this play spirit, business or international relations do become a jungle. Play is thus a great culture former. This would seem to agree with Mead's and Piaget's studies of the child's experience in learning the game of life.

THE ARTISTIC ASPECT OF CULTURE

The artist is a person who tries to say something by creating beauty of form.

Art is a way of communicating experience, a language. It is older than written language. In fact, writing almost certainly began in art, in stylized pictograms such as make up the original symbols of the Egyptian, Babylonian, and Chinese languages. Art, like mathematics, is a way of saying things which cannot be duplicated by ordinary language. No quantity of words can evoke the experience of the Mona Lisa, or the Parthenon, or even the United Nations building. When we say that the artist tries to express himself through beautiful form, we shall have to get along for the present without a final definition of beauty. However, all of us would certainly have to reject as absurd the opposite proposition that the function of the artist is to create ugliness.

We distinguish various kinds of art. The *fine arts* generally include painting, sculpture, music, literature and drama, and architecture. The *useful* or *practical arts* are ones like basketry, weaving, pottery making, and work in metals. By this distinction we do not mean that the fine arts are useless. Except for architecture, however, they do not serve an immediate practical objective as does a basket, a piece of cloth, a pot, or a fine metal bowl. We also speak of *commercial art,* which is mainly connected with the styling, decorating, or advertising of mass-produced objects. We also often distinguish the fine arts from primitive art and folk art. Primitive art is, of course, the art of preliterate peoples. Folk art is the art of the ordinary people in civilized societies, whereas fine art has traditionally been the art of a leisure class. A Greek or Guatemalan skirt may be folk art. A Bohemian peasant dance is folk art. Woven into a symphony, a folk dance becomes fine art. Finally, we have to distinguish between representational and abstract art. Representational art depicts an object or tells a story. Abstract art tries to present more or less pure form without depicting anything. A realistic portrait or landscape is representational; a painting composed entirely of geometric forms is abstract. An opera is representational music; most nonvocal music is relatively abstract.

What is the function of art in human life and society? Art, like play, seems to be an elemental human activity (monkeys and chimpanzees, indeed, also can draw pictures). If given a chance, all normal human children will spontaneously produce simple artistic forms. Art, as we have said, is a language, in which shape, line, and color are used to communicate experience that is very often on a deep unconscious level. Art is also skill, that is, the ability to do something with grace and simplicity. In this sense every skilled person is an artist.

Art is a social bond. Music, especially the dance, is a powerful unifying force. The building of the great cathedrals, which were communal projects, is another example of the socially unifying power of art. Art may be magic. Making an image of a hunted animal may be thought to cause the species to multiply; making an image of an enemy, to cause him to die. Art may be religion. A large part of art has been part of worship; a central function of art in India has been to evoke the mystical experience called *rasa*. Art is often a class symbol—the ability to own or understand and appreciate objects of art is often an important badge of social status. Art may also be propaganda. It may support the status quo, as did medieval painting when it made figures large or small according to their social rank, or as does Socialist realism in Russia, which is supposed to depict only the virtues of Soviet life. On the other hand, the writings of a Jonathan Swift or the engravings of a Goya may satirize the social order. The paintings of a Delacroix or the music of the Marsellaise or the Internationale may glorify revolution. The poetry of a Yevtushenko may raise doubts about the perfection of Soviet communism.

If we look back to primitive art, we will see why we must always beware of making "primitive" mean "backward." The Western world has recently come to appreciate African sculpture. Almost 20,000 years ago, on the cave walls of south central France and northern Spain, our ancestors painted magnificent pictures of animals and men. Not, perhaps, until the Cretan civilization, 15,000 years later, did artists depict living forms with such immediacy and naturalness. The skill of these artists has led some people to call them the "Paleolithic Greeks."

Most primitive art is less outstanding. There is little or no economic surplus to free time for artistic activities. Nevertheless, a study of the Australian aborigines showed that they painted in bad weather, and primitive peoples generally do get a good deal of art work done. It is limited by the fact that they are on the move: there are no architecture, theaters, concert halls, symphony orchestras, mural paintings on large buildings, large statues, or fragile glass. They can produce small carved figures, drawings, leather work, basketry, pots, simple weaving, personal jewelry, folklore, and songs transmitted verbally.

Primitive art serves a variety of functions. It decorates people and their surroundings, increases technical skill, and frightens the enemy. Poetry, music, and dance inspire warriors. Ancient Chinese lore held that they also force nature into treating man well and keep the world on its course. Most primitive art is not representational, as are the famous cave paintings. It is more likely to be a stylized simplification of real objects, as is the case with Australian aborigines.

In primitive cultures art is not the product of a special artist class which is set aside from nonartists. Among the Australian aborigines, there is no specialization of artists. Some primitive peoples do specialize to some degree. In either case the typical situation is that of the Balinese, among whom everyone produces art of some kind. Indeed, there is no word in Balinese for "art," and this is typical of preliterate peoples. It is so much a part of the total group life that it is not even thought of separately. Nor is art likely to be thought of as an individual performance. One anthropologist relates how, in an African tribe, when he tried to make a chair or stool and set it aside, on returning he would always find that someone had "helped" him. Art is part of a sacred communal tradition, and the artist may be allowed to deviate very little. In nonreligious art, however, there often seems to be more room for originality than we would expect.

The agricultural revolution brought an economic surplus which made more expensive and professional forms of art possible in the ancient civilizations. It has also been suggested that the loss of the manual skills associated with hunting accounts for the fact that the heights of realistic painting attained by the Paleolithic cave painters were not reached again for many centuries. The range of material in all the arts makes it impossible to attempt even a sketchy account of their development in the historic civilizations. We can only describe some of the high points that art has reached in expressing human experience and aspiration.

The art of ancient Greece expressed the richness of Greek culture, which we have already touched upon in other areas. The highest point was perhaps the Age of Pericles, during which the Parthenon was built between 448 and 432 B.C. We do not know a great deal about Greek music and painting. The first is extremely perishable, and the second less durable than sculpture or architecture. It was in these two latter fields, and in poetry and drama, that the Greeks made their great contribution.

At the height of Greek culture, for the first time, statues were made capable of standing freely (*contrapposto*). This development was coupled with the quality called *pathos*—suffering conveyed with nobility and restraint—and the Greek delight in the human body. The result was a presentation of human personality and form never before achieved. The Parthenon was the classic example of the Doric temple; the other two forms, Ionic and Corinthian, were also named for their types of columns. Theaters were another architectural achievement; the amphitheatre at Epidaurus is still used today, and the author can testify that the acoustics are so excellent that the striking of a match in the pit can be heard on the topmost row of seats. In probably the ninth century B.C., Homer's poem, the *Iliad,* which has been called "the poem of force," gave one of the world's great depictions of the tragedy of human violence. In drama the Greeks established the two major forms: tragedy (Aeschylus, Sophocles, and Euripides) and comedy (Aristophanes). In the great fifth century B.C., Sophocles' *Oedipus Rex* dealt with the tragic theme which Freud later enlarged upon.

The Romans contributed the arch and the vault to architecture, and the artists of the Byzantine Empire did unequaled work in mosaics. The next peak in architecture after the Greeks came, however, in the twelfth and thirteenth centuries in the building of the Gothic cathedrals. This was the ultimate expression of the Middle Ages, which have been called the "age of faith." Here was expressed, as never before or since in architecture, man's upreach toward God.

The circumstances are an interesting example of the interconnection of politics, religion, and art. Between the years 1137 and 1144, the abbot Suger rebuilt the Abbey Church of St. Denis, now on the outskirts of Paris. This was the church of the French king, whom Suger wanted to strengthen against the nobility by building a shrine of great religious power. His architect achieved this goal by supporting the roof on thin walls and inserting large window spaces. The result was an intense sense of upward thrust and a luminescent quality inside the new abbey. Within the next century the Gothic style spread, cities collected donations for building or reconstructing cathedrals, and communities rallied to their construction. Among other Gothic cathedrals were Notre Dame de Paris (begun in 1163), Notre Dame de Chartres (1194–1220), Amiens Cathedral (1220), and Reims Cathedral (1225–1299). At Chartres magnificent stained glass windows, which still survive, brought the peculiar Gothic luminescence to its height. The Gothic cathedral spread, with variations, to England, Germany, and Spain.

As in all areas of life, the Renaissance brought a great burst of growth in art. As Athens had been the cultural center of the ancient world, so the Renaissance centered in Florence. Giotto (1276?–1337?), Masaccio (1401–1428), and Leonardo da Vinci replaced the flat, medieval painting with perspective and three-dimensional space. This reflected, and made possible, a more natural approach to human life and painting. These innovators were followed by Raphael, Titian, and other great painters. Donatello (1386–1466) created the first free-standing statue since the ancient world. Michelangelo (1475–1564) combined the technical skill of Donatello and the Greeks with a range of passionate emotional expression that the

ancient sculptors had not achieved. The sixteenth and early seventeenth centuries brought the plays and sonnets of Shakespeare, and the later seventeenth century Milton's *Paradise Lost.* The development of techniques for blending many parts (polyphony) gave an entirely new range to vocal and instrumental music and paved the way for the symphony and other new musical forms.

In discussing art, much more than in dealing with science and technology, it is important to try to avoid ethnocentric biases. We cannot leave out the art of the East as inferior to the art of the West. The historian Will Durant, writing of the beautiful Indian tomb, the Taj Mahal, says that if time were intelligent, it would destroy everything else, but would leave this evidence of man's nobility as consolation for the last man.

Probably the period of the T'ang and Sung dynasties in China (618–1279) should be ranked with the great productive periods in art. While Europe was in the Dark Ages, eighth-century China produced two great poets, Li po (705–762) and Tu fu (711–770), whose verse ranks with the world's most beautiful. This period also produced the great painter Wu Tao-tze (born about 700). The accompanying later landscape, by Fan K'wan, was done about the year 1000. The art historian H. W. Janson suggests that no one in Europe at the time or even much later could have appreciated its pictorial and emotional subtlety. Durant calls Chinese porcelain the summit and symbol of Chinese civilization and one of the noblest things ever done by man. In the Sung dynasty, the Ming dynasty (1368–1644), and the later reign of the Emperor Ch'ien Lung (1736–1796), Chinese craftsmen in porcelain produced work which no European potter has been able to duplicate.

We have seen that nineteenth- and twentieth-century technology has revolutionized Western culture. What has happened in art? Recent years, says the English art critic, Herbert Read,

Primitive sculpture by the Bambara people of Africa (*University of Pennsylvania Museum*)

Goya's series of etchings The Disasters of War expresses the barbarism of all wars. This scene is called simply "What For?" (*Metropolitan Museum of Art, Schiff Fund, 1922*)

Landscape by Fan K'uan (*Museum of Fine Arts, Boston*)

Claude Monet, a master of French impressionism, shows the impressionist fascination with capturing the effects of light on canvas in his painting entitled The Snow at Argenteuil (*Museum of Fine Arts, Boston*)

Minoan fresco at Knossos, Crete, c. 1500 B.C. (*Heraklion Museum*)

Animals painted on a cave wall in Lascaux, France, by prehistoric artists almost 20,000 years ago

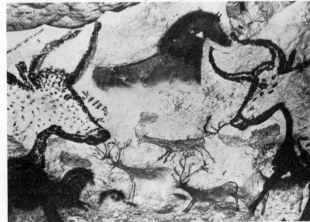

The Cathedral of Notre Dame de Chartres, superb example of Gothic architecture

The Taj Mahal (1648), Indian jewel of architecture

Picasso's Girl Before a Mirror, 1932 (*Museum of Modern Art, New York, Gift of Mrs. Simon Guggenheim*)

Michelangelo's expressive statue David. Renaissance sculpture equalled that of the ancient Greeks (*Brogi–Art Reference Bureau*)

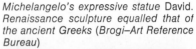

The Parthenon at Athens, built in the fifth century, B.C., during the Age of Pericles

have freed painting from perspective and the need for representation. This, he believes, opens up new possibilities for painting as a language. Freud's illumination of the unconscious has given the artist new materials with which to work. The trend away from representation was seen in late nineteenth-century impressionism, which suggested a scene rather than actually drew it. Twentieth-century surrealism brought painting whose form was more that of dreams than of objective reality. Some twentieth-century painters, like Mondrian, eliminate subject matter entirely in favor of pure geometric forms. James Joyce broke the traditional rules of the novel in *Ulysses,* which follows the stream of consciousness rather than sequence in logic or in time. Musical composers like Schönberg reject the traditional rules of melody and harmony. In architecture design is stripped down in many cases to the barest geometric necessities.

Some observers see twentieth-century trends as part of one of the great creative revolutions in the history of art. Others feel that much of modern art is simply a flight from the task of representing reality, which has perhaps become too complex or painful for the artist.

How, now, are art and the artist related to the development of culture? Many artists, and other people, insist that art is a free, spontaneous, inspired activity and that the artist is not dependent upon the culture pattern as are businessmen, the politician, the scientist, or even the priest or prophet. The very influential eighteenth-century philosopher, Immanuel Kant (1724–1804), held, for example, that artistic skill or talent could not be taught, but was endowed by nature. The twentieth-century writer, Aldous Huxley, said, "Every artist begins at the beginning. The man of science, on the other hand, begins where his predecessor left off."[12] The twentieth-century poet,

T. S. Eliot, argued that literature is really independent of cultural development. "The whole of the literature of Europe from Homer has a simultaneous existence and comprises a simultaneous order."[13]

It is true that no simple cultural interpretation can explain an artistic genius like Homer, Shakespeare, or Michelangelo any more than it can explain genius in any other field, or fully explain *any* person. It also seems that the artistic impulse in general is independent of culture, in the sense that in young children it is very much the same in all societies. A number of tests of drawing and painting have indicated that children begin by scribbling, then produce abstract designs, and finally draw representations of objects, and that this development is very similar everywhere.

However, art seems clearly to be subject, first of all, to an "immanent" development, that is, one within itself. Although perhaps not so much as the scientist or technician, the artist does build on artists who have gone before him. No primitive music, for example, has polyphony, which could have originated only in fairly recent times after a long development in the use of sound. The vaults of Gothic cathedrals could not have been suspended on relatively thin walls without the very much earlier invention of the arch and its gradual development over many centuries.

It appears that all the arts have, through time, become more complex. This is true, for example, of modern poetry or the modern novel, if we compare them with earlier forms of poetry or story telling. This is not a simple matter, for primitive African sculpture, for example, is much more complex than some products of modern culture, and the Gothic cathedral more complex than much modern construction. Also, art may go in cycles. The anthropologist Kroeber showed that this tends to happen with women's fashions—skirt length goes from long to

12. Thomas Munro, *Evolution in the Arts,* Cleveland, Cleveland Museum of Art, n.d., p. 26.

13. *Ibid.,* p. 152.

short, and then repeats itself. Nevertheless, taken as a whole, art seems to have moved from simplicity to complexity.

In addition, art is *not* insulated from the surrounding culture. The artist is limited and shaped by available materials and techniques. Mexican weavers who have carried down their tradition over centuries can no longer repeat some earlier patterns because looms are no longer constructed to produce them. Had the common stone in Greece and Italy been granite instead of the more easily worked marble, sculpture would have been quite different and probably other arts would have become prominent instead. Technological developments in oil paints since the Renaissance have made it possible for painters to use techniques that were previously impossible. More recent development in pigments seem, incidentally, to have shortened the life of paintings, because the colors fade faster. The use of perspective in painting (as contrasted with flat medieval and Oriental painting) is related to developments in science. The luminescent use of light by nineteenth-century impressionist painters like Turner and Monet was influenced by scientific theories of color and light.

Furthermore, art is shaped by cultural themes and values. Homer's *Iliad* and Shakespeare's *Macbeth* are works of genius which have meaning in all times and places. Yet they are also built, respectively, out of Greek and Scottish legends and traditions. Notre Dame cathedral clearly represents the upward aspiration toward God of a highly religious age, just as a modern office building expresses a secular in-

---

What we must recognize is that for one reason or another the centralization of the arts in a city like London or Paris creates an ambiance or an atmosphere that exercises an irresistible attraction on the young artist or poet. Who among us blessed, or it may be, cursed with creative aspirations but born in the provinces, does not remember a sick and desperate yearning to get to "the center of things"? Here in London or Paris, we imagined, was the only arena in which we could gain fame, the only gladiators against whom we could measure our own skill.

This state of mind may well be an illusion. In a metropolis we may, indeed, sharpen our wits and polish our manners, but we may lose more than our innocence. Before I explain what I mean I would like to glance at a few artists who by exception matured their genius away from metropolitan centres of culture, and who yet, by general consent, were great artists. I will keep to the nineteenth century, which is far away enough to insure objectivity, and yet near enough to exhibit all the features of centralization.

In drama there is the outstanding figure of Ibsen. We may differ in our estimate of Ibsen's genius, but in the past I think our differences were due largely to the controversial issues which were raised in his dramas, and not to any purely aesthetic judgments. Now that the controversial issues have died . . . we can recognize Ibsen as essentially a poet and dramatist, and as one of the greatest the world has ever known. Certainly he had no equal in the nineteenth century. We are then confronted with the significant fact that Ibsen's genius was matured in one of the smallest and poorest countries of Europe, and even then not in its capital city, but in the provincial town of Bergen.

*In painting I would ask you to consider the case of
Cezanne. . . . Cezanne is inconceivable without his Provencal
background: he grows out of that regional landscape like
one of its olive trees. His genius would have wilted in a
metropolitan atmosphere. . . .*

*Cezanne, who was the antithesis of a bourgeois, and was a very
great painter, was never drawn into the centralized intellectual life
of Paris. He was born and remained a provincial, with a provincial
accent and a complete inability either to dress or behave like a
gentleman.*

*I might quote many other instances of great geniuses who have
matured on the periphery rather than at the center of our civilization
—a particularly interesting example is Emily Bronte. . . .*

*We are dealing with a sociological issue, namely, whether art
in general is best fostered by a centralized and metropolitan
culture, or whether it grows deeper and stronger roots in a regional
soil. Historically the answer is clear: the greatest artists have arisen
in an overwhelming majority in situations or under social
conditions which we should now consider regional. The two
greatest epochs of art—Greek art and Gothic art—drew their
vitality from confined and relatively isolated localities, and even
the art of the Renaissance . . . was an art inspired by local
rivalries. . . . Sociologically, centralization spells devitalization,
. . . devitalization of spiritual forces. . . .*

—Herbert Read, The Grass Roots of Art, *New York,
Meridian, 1961, pp. 123–126.*

---

dustrial culture. Dickens' novels cannot be separated from the impact of the Industrial Revolution. Jazz, as a musical form, is clearly related to the rapid and uncertain tempo of an urban, industrial society.

Even more specifically, art is shaped by the fact that somebody pays the artist. Michelangelo's career as a sculptor is shot through with his efforts to express himself in spite of his patrons. Shakespeare's plays bear evidence that they were written in part for mass audiences; an example is the drunken porter scene in *Hamlet.* It is hard for us to conceive that as late as the eighteenth century the great German composer Haydn wore livery because his status as a musician was that of a hired servant. Beethoven was distressed at much of the music he had to write in order to make a living. Much of the contemporary painter Picasso's early work was for an appreciative minority, but in recent years he has frankly catered to the taste of those who will buy. Novelists who want to sell their work may have to do the same.

All this suggests that culture both forms and confines the artist. The nineteenth-century German sociologist of art, Ernest Grosse, has said that nearly every great work of art was created against the prevailing taste and nearly every great artist was rejected by the public. This is probably somewhat exaggerated, yet it speaks a truth not only about the great artist but also, as we have seen, about creativity in science, medicine, or religion. Study of the spontaneous art of children suggests, in addition, that all of us originally possessed great capacity for creativity, not only in art but in other fields, that has largely been stifled by cultural brainwashing.

We have indicated that there are elements in urban, modern, industrial culture favorable to art. The large city furnishes an exciting and stimulating environment for the artist. There are, however, important factors that are strongly unfavorable. Art seems to have arisen as part of a natural relationship among people in a community—the primitive tribe, the peasant village, Athens, Florence, Chartres. The modern world has to a large extent eliminated close communities. Art has also grown out of participation in the natural processes of the physical and biological world. The modern world separates man from nature and makes his home one of machines. In the accompanying selection from his book, *The Grass Roots of Art* (note the significance of the title), Herbert Read contends that large city life is unfavorable to the highest artistic development. Historically, also, most art has been associated with a religious view of the universe. The urban industrial world is largely secular. Already art has become largely a specialty: the artistic impulses of the average person simply no longer develop. Can the artist himself continue to be creative in a world largely separated from community, from nature, and from religious values?

Interrelations

With art it has been peculiarly necessary to discuss the whole question of how far it really *is* a part of culture. In doing this we have already dealt with many of its important interrelations.

Art is clearly related to the economic and technological level of a culture. Like the scientist, doctor, teacher, priest, and politician, the artist must also make a living.

In the history of art, secular art has been the exception rather than the rule. Primitive art is largely religious. Among the Tiv of Nigeria, the word *gba* means (1) working in wood, and (2) God's creation of the world. The Acropolis was a religious site, the Gothic cathedrals an avenue to God. Even the great Renaissance painters and sculptors were religious men dealing mainly with religious themes.

On the other hand, secular art (and sometimes sacred art) may come in conflict with organized religion. The Catholic Church has frequently censored art as contrary to morals or decency. The whole atmosphere of Puritanism has been a censorship of art. As we have seen, Puritanism has tended to regard everything except work and worship as, at best, wasteful. It has opposed the theater, and the naturalistic presentation of sexuality. Reacting against Catholicism, it has rejected much of religious art, such as stained glass windows, other church ornamentation, and complex music.

Art is related to play. Both represent deep and universal tendencies. Art, however, requires the construction or appreciation of a definite *form*. This requires discipline and control. Thus the player who becomes an artist ceases to play freely, even though he may enjoy himself intensely. Creation is work.

Suggestions for further reading

The purpose of Chapters six and seven has been to bring home repeatedly the fact that no element in human life can be understood apart from the whole culture in which it appears. The suggestions which follow include books which illustrate the general integration of culture and books which show the relationship of specific institutions to the whole. All these books should help students to think in such a way as to find cultural integration in their own personal experience.

An easily read, comprehensive, and humane account of the development of culture by a

cultural anthropologist is The Tree of Culture *by RALPH M. LINTON (abridged ed., Random House, 1959, paper). Another book which many students find fairly easy and quite fascinating is RUTH BENEDICT's* Patterns of Culture *(Houghton Mifflin, paper). SUMNER's* Folkways *(see Suggested Readings for Chapter four) was written before the term "culture" was generally used, but insists throughout on the integration of social institutions, and is full of rich, interesting, and concrete material.*

Hunger and Work in a Savage Tribe by AUDREY RICHARDS (Free Press, 1948) and

MELVILLE J. HERSKOVITS' Economic Anthropology *(Norton, 1965, paper) deal with the role of economic institutions in preliterate cultures. Two important books are concerned specifically with the relationship between economic life and religion in modern society. They are* The Protestant Ethic and the Spirit of Capitalism *by MAX WEBER (Scribner's, 1931, available in paper) and* Religion and the Rise of Capitalism *by R. H. TAWNEY (Mentor, paper). Another older book,* Lectures on Calvanism, *by ABRAHAM KUYPER (Eerdman's, 1931), also treats the relationship of religion to economic development and general culture since the Protestant Reformation. FRANZ OPPENHEIMER's* The State *(English translation, 1914) is a very important analysis of the relationship between economic interests and political development.* A Social History of the American Family *by ARTHUR W. CALHOUN (Barnes & Noble, 1945, paper) is a fascinating account of the relationship of family institutions to American culture from colonial times to the present.*

BRONISLAW MALINOWSKI'S Magic, Science, and Religion *(Doubleday, 1954, paper) treats the relationship of these three institutions in the preliterate culture of the Trobriand Islands.* EMILE DURKHEIM's *The Elementary Forms of* Religious Life *(Free Press, 1954, paper) explains religious experience as an expression of the individual's sense of membership in his society. LUDWIG FEUERBACH's* The Essence of Christianity *analyzes religious belief as a projection which satisfies the needs of people in society.* The Religions of Authority and the Religion of the Spirit *by AUGUSTE SABATIER (McClure Phillips, 1904) is concerned with the different ways in which emphasis on authority in religion and emphasis on individual religious experience color the quality of life.* The Sociological Study of the Bible *by LOUIS J. WALLIS (University of Chicago Press, 1927) is a scholarly treatment of Old Testament religion as an expression of Hebrew culture and experience. In* The Social Sources of Denominationalism *(Meridian, 1957, paper), H. RICHARD NIEBUHR traces the social class origins of religious groupings in our culture.*

J. D. BERNAL'S Science in History *(3rd ed., Hawthorn, 1965) deals with the development of science as an integral part of the development of culture. The same is true of NOAH E. FEHL's* Science and Culture *(International Pub. Service, 1965).* HOMO LUDENS, A Study of the Play Element in Culture *(Beacon, 1955, paper), by JOHAN HUIZINGA, treats the role of play in the human enterprise. Another very interesting book on the same subject is* Man, Play, and Games *by ROGER CAILLOIS (Free Press, 1961).* The Grass Roots of Art *(Meridian, 1961, paper), by HERBERT READ, asks primarily how artistic production is related to simple folk experience (the "grass roots") and to the complexity of urban industrial culture. ARNOLD HAUSER'S* The Social History of Art *(Random House, paper) relates art to the cultural milieu from Stone Age cave painting down to mid-twentieth-century developments in the making of films. Literature is analyzed in its social context by VERNON L. PARRINGTON in* Main Currents in American Thought *(Harcourt Brace Jovanovich, 1928, paper).*

Part three
Scarcity and power

Without judging that these are the central aspects of social behavior, we can safely say that no solution of our social crisis will be possible unless we can handle successfully the problems of scarcity and power. People always have more desires than the earth and its resources can readily satisfy. This fact gives rise to two kinds of activity. People organize in order to pool their efforts in mastering the environment. They also organize to insure themselves satisfactions by depriving other groups of access to them, that is, they engage in economic and political behavior. It is seldom or never possible to separate one from the other. This part will deal with economic and political institutions in their complex interrelationship.

Chapter eight
The economic process

At the time of World War I, a noted psychologist was discussing with a social scientist the merits of American intervention. As they analyzed the various factors underlying the war, the psychologist was asked what he thought of the economic aspects. "I am a psychologist," he answered, "and I have no competence to discuss the economic aspects of the problem." His answer was, of course, no answer. No one can afford to plead this kind of ignorance about such a central aspect of the world he lives in. To be uninformed about economic matters is to be ignorant of one of the basic roots of all our life.

In this chapter we shall explore some of the fundamental areas and concepts with which one must be familiar in order to have an intelligent layman's comprehension of the economic aspects of society. This will not be a course in technical economics, but it is intended to clear up some of the mystery which seems to surround economic questions. Some people appear to be afraid of the very word "economics." Like any other subject, economics can become extremely technical if pursued far enough, but there is no reason why a beginning understanding of economic relationships should be any more difficult than an understanding of any other social institution.

THE BASIC DECISIONS OF ANY ECONOMY

The first thing we need to see in understanding the economic process is that there are certain basic economic decisions which all peoples must make if they intend to go on living. Their economy may be one of hunting and gathering, like that of the African Bushmen. It may be one predominantly of agriculture, like that of the United States in the days of George Washington, and of most of the world even today. Or it may be that of a highly industralized nation, like the United States, England, West Germany, the Soviet Union, or Japan. The economy may be feudal, capitalist, Socialist, Communist, or Fascist. But whatever the form of organization, the same fundamental problems must be solved.

What are these problems? What are the decisions that have to be made?

The first decision to be made is: *What shall be produced?* The things people can desire are infinite, but the energies and resources of any society are limited. A few things must be done, a few desires satisfied, and many things must be left undone. Now how do we make this decision as to what to produce? In a highly complex society, it is certainly a complicated and difficult decision. Yet, just as in simpler societies, it does get made. Let us look at three possible ways of making this first decision, and all the other decisions.

One is through *tradition*. In this system the answer to the question "What shall be produced?" is "What our great-grandfathers produced." The chief products of the Trobriand Islanders, when the anthropologist Malinowski did his famous study of

Their societies all have the same basic economic problems. (Top photo courtesy of the American Museum of Natural History.)

them during World War I, were yams, fish, and a number of objects that were exchanged as ritual gifts from one island group to another. As long as the islands were not influenced by the white man, there was no real question as to whether to grow many more yams, or catch many fewer fish, or make more or fewer ritual gifts. All this continued to be done as it had always been done. On the medieval manor, certain lands were traditionally allocated for different uses, and a certain number of artisans—shoemakers, tailors, carpenters, goldsmiths—were attached to the manor house. Sons, to a very large extent, carried on their fathers' occupations. In such a society, as we saw earlier, change was very slow and the idea of progress hardly

existed. What was to be produced was determined here, also, by traditional usage.

In this chapter we shall not be concerned primarily with such traditional economies, but rather with two other ways of making the basic economic decisions.

The next way is through the *market*. The term, of course, originally referred to a place where people came together to buy and sell. In its social science usage, it refers to the *relationships* among buyers and sellers. We all know what we mean when we speak of the fluctuations of the stock market (not of the building where stocks and bonds are sold), or say that there are too many high school graduates for the labor market, or say that there is a

MILK		
DEMAND	PRICE	SUPPLY
6500	20	2000
5800	22	2500
5300	24	3000
4200	26	4200
3500	28	5000
2700	30	6000

Figure 8.1. A supply-demand schedule.

bumper crop of apples this year and that the market will be poor for apple growers. In the last case, we mean that the relationship between buyers and sellers, or between supply and demand, will bring a low price to growers.

When we say that what is produced may be determined by market mechanisms, we mean that it may be determined by forces of supply and demand. Let us see how this may happen by looking at the simple economic model called a "supply-demand schedule." Suppose we take the market for milk around a middle-sized Wisconsin city in the dairy belt. How much milk will be produced, at what price? Let us set up in the center column of our schedule a series of possible prices per quart. On the left side are the numbers of quarts of milk which would be offered for sale by milk producers at each price. Obviously, the higher the price, the more milk farmers are likely to produce. In the right hand column, let us list the number of quarts which would be bought by consumers at each price. Clearly, the lower the price is, the more milk consumers will tend to buy.

We will notice that there is a certain price at which the milk offered for sale will equal the milk bought. At this price, the market is in equilibrium. If less milk were offered, the demand would drive the price up and encour-

age more milk production. If more milk were produced, there would be a surplus, the price would drop, and eventually dairy farmers would produce something else instead. Perhaps they would raise beef cattle instead of dairy cattle, or perhaps they would even sell out and get industrial jobs in Milwaukee or Chicago.

Thus the forces of supply and demand determine how much of the resources of this part of Wisconsin will go into milk production. This is a small part of the whole decision of what shall be produced. The most important thing to notice is that nobody has planned this. A decision has been reached simply by letting people buy and sell. As the great economist Adam Smith put it, the decision is made as though guided by an "invisible hand."

Now suppose that instead of thinking of milk in Wisconsin, we imagine all the possible products that could be made in the United States—milk, wheat, automobiles, houses, hair driers, overcoats, TV sets, bombers, rubber tires, children's toys, and on *ad infinitum*. How much of each will be made, at what price? Now we have to think of a vast market—actually worth close to a trillion dollars—in which all possible products are competing for consumers. *How much of each will be produced will depend upon how many people demand it.* One way of putting this is to say that in a market economy, production is determined by the "ballot box of the market place." Just as political candidates are elected or rejected according to the number of votes they get, so potential products are "elected" by the dollars (or pounds, or francs, or marks) of the consuming public.

We will note that market decisions require free competition, what is also called "free enterprise." We do not have decisions by the invisible hand of supply and demand if the visible hand of government intervenes. The spending of one-sixth of the American national income for military purposes is not, for example, a free market decision. Nor do we have a free market decision if private businesses become so big that they can fix prices and quantity of production, as seems, for example, to be the case in the American drug industry.

A free market could exist only in an economy where all businesses were small, so that none could dominate the market, and anyone with a little capital could move in or out of any line of production fairly easily. This is obviously not the case in the United States today in the markets for automobiles, tobacco, meat, rubber, aluminum, steel, and many other commodities. It was more nearly true in the days of Adam Smith (who published his great book, *The Wealth of Nations,* in 1776), although government sponsorship of big corporations limited competition even then. The British and American economies today are far from a free market society, just as are all large industrial economies. Nevertheless, the concept of the free market is a useful one, just as in physics we find useful the concept of a vacuum, which never exists in pure form in reality, either.

We come now to the third way of deciding what is to be produced, which is by *planning.* One case which we have already suggested is the one where businesses cooperate to restrict free competition. Any of us can observe, for example, that the prices of all regular brands of gasoline are about the same and generally rise and fall together. Usually this happens because of an unwritten agreement by gasoline producers not to undercut one another. In later chapters we shall discuss in much more detail such planning by *oligopoly* (control by a few firms) or *monopoly* (control by one firm). In the days of Hitler and Mussolini, German and Italian business, though privately owned, was organized into national trade associations which planned each line of production. Under the National Recovery Act in the United States during the Depression (a program ultimately declared unconstitutional) there were also national organi-

zations for the purpose of coordinating each line of manufacture or trade. All these are examples of planning by essentially private business.

The type of planning which contrasts most sharply with the free market is direct government planning. Under the policies of *mercantilism,* which preceded free capitalism in England and was opposed by Adam Smith, large private enterprises (such as the British East India Company) were chartered as monopolies by the government. We have many examples of direct government planning in the American economy. Municipal power, garbage collection, and bus services, the federal post office system, the Tennessee Valley Authority, the public parks system, and the allocation of the military budget are all examples of production decisions by government. During the Depression the federal government introduced a number of public programs to combat unemployment. Under the 1946 Employment Act, it became the stated responsibility of the federal government to keep careful record of the progress of the economy and to take measures when necessary to prevent unemployment of workers and resources. Public ownership of railroads is one widespread example of government planning in many European economies. The greatest contrast to the free market method of making decisions is found in the so-called Communist countries. In the Soviet Union, all production is planned periodically, and indeed constantly, through a central agency called the *Gosplan* (State Planning Commission). Of this we shall also say more in a later chapter.

We must note that, just as there are both private and government planning in the United States economy, so there are market mechanisms in the Soviet Union. Indeed, these have been accentuated in recent years. Under economic reforms initiated by the economist Yevsey Liberman, for example, factories now must compete with one another for consumers, rather than being assured the sale of their planned quota of product. All this will suggest that there are no purely planned or market economies, that in reality all present economic systems are mixed economies. However, we usually think of a society like that of the United States as stressing the market, those of the USSR and Communist China as stressing planning, and use the term "mixed economy" for systems like those of Britain, the Scandinavian countries, France, India, and Israel.

The second major decision which all economies must make is: *How shall resources be allocated?* Actually, this is a subhead of the first decision, for to decide what is to be done is to decide, to a large extent, that resources are to be used in one way rather than in another. However, this second large decision involves specific kinds of choices. Let us see how they affect three major factors of production which economists have traditionally distinguished. These factors are *land, labor,* and *capital equipment.*

Land includes all those natural resources that have not been produced by man. Any economic system must decide to what uses to put its land. As an example of a market decision, let us take the case of Pinellas County, Florida. Twenty years ago a considerable part of this county was orange groves. Today a large number of these groves have been bulldozed away and replaced by subdivisions. How did this change take place? With the development of the cities of St. Petersburg, Tampa, and Clearwater, land became more valuable as building sites than for agricultural use—thus the bulldozer and residential construction. No person or organization planned this change. On the other hand, land use is restricted by public zoning policy in this county as elsewhere. Even if a filling station or an industrial plant would represent the most profitable use of a certain piece of land in a residential area, the land cannot be so used. If it wishes to build an expressway over it, the state can take the land through its right of eminent domain. Both zon-

ing and the principle of eminent domain represent planned allocation of land. In Stockholm, Sweden, a large degree of public planning of land use is possible because most of the land is owned by the municipality rather than by private individuals.

Labor may similarly be allocated by either market or planning mechanisms. A sailor in the merchant marine, faced by the prospect that ships will be automated, may retrain himself to be an airplane mechanic. Large numbers of farmers and unskilled workers have left the Appalachian area in the hope of finding better jobs in cities. Scientists have moved from the underdeveloped countries to the Western nations, and from Europe to the United States, in such numbers that the phenomenon has been called the "brain drain." Such changes all represent allocation by the pull of the market. On the contrary, slave labor camps, the military draft, and compulsory national service all constitute allocation of labor through planning. Government employment exchanges and job retraining programs, such as exist in both the United States and the USSR, are a less drastic form of government planning of the labor supply.

The same principles hold for managerial talent, which is a specialized form of labor. In the American economy, capable executives and managers tend to be drawn into those activities which will yield the highest income. In the planned Soviet economy, they are more likely to be assigned by government planning agencies. In the industrial capitalist countries, however, government is also able to influence the allocation of managerial talent through its ability to draw it away from private enterprise into government jobs. The President's cabinet, for example, usually includes a number of people drawn from private industry.

Capital equipment includes all those products of human labor with which other products are made. They are also called "instruments of production." Factories and the machinery they contain; highways and the equipment of airlines, railways, trucking, and steamship lines; and farm buildings and machinery are some of the most important forms of capital equipment in an industrial economy. A good example of the market allocation of capital equipment is the historical movement of industry to the southern part of the United States under the pull of lower wages and other lower costs (although this is not so common as it used to be). Federal corporation taxes are an example of planned allocation. By taking away corporate profits, taxes make it possible for the government to invest money in highways, or parks, or military bases instead of allowing industry to use them to build new plants. Thus corporation taxes shift the creation of capital equipment from the private to the public sector of the economy. In the Soviet and Chinese economies, almost all allocation of capital equipment is a part of central planning.

Allocation of capital equipment presupposes that the third major decision of any economy has already been made. This is the *choice between present and future goods* or between *consumption and investment.* Although it also usually involves the spending of money savings, investment in this sense refers primarily to the creation of new capital equipment.

There is no society so simple that it puts all its work time into directly making or getting goods to be consumed. Even the Bushman spends some time making the simple tools with which he digs roots or hunts game. The time taken for making diggers, bows, and spears must be subtracted from the time available for hunting or digging. The tools are made because, in the long run, more food can be obtained by taking a little time in the short run to make the tools. Thus one of the characteristics of production in all societies is a certain amount of *roundaboutness.* The more complex the society, the more roundabout production is likely to

be, that is, the greater the importance of capital equipment as compared with simple labor.

In capitalistic societies capital equipment is largely privately owned. In Socialist or Communist economies, most is collectively owned. But both types of economy must decide, all the time, how much of their energy and resources to apply directly to producing goods for consumption, and how much to apply to making things which will not be consumed themselves, but used to make other goods. Capital investment is usually of two kinds. Since existing equipment wears out, some resources and energy must always be devoted to replacing it. In addition, every growing economy is constantly adding to its stock of equipment. If too little is set aside for investment, the economy eventually suffers from lack of capital equipment. If too much is set aside, there may be an immediate shortage of consumer goods; then in the longer run, much productive equipment may lie idle because of a lack of demand for its products.

Where market mechanisms prevail, the choice of how much to withdraw from consumption for purposes of investment is made primarily through a large number of decisions by private individuals or corporations. In planned economies it is made primarily by the planning agencies. We may note that different types of economies have different kinds of problems of consumption and investment. The poor, underdeveloped countries—including most of South America, Africa, and Asia—have the problem of trying to save for investment in a situation where most of the people may not even have enough to eat. A new industrial economy like the Soviet Union has to choose among investment for future production, the demands of military expenditure, and the demands of citizens for consumer goods, in short, among factories, guns, and butter. The highly industrialized American economy, unlike any of these others, is potentially so productive that no one should need to be poor in order to support invest-ment. However, military expenditure consumes about one-sixth of our national product. We have the peculiar problem that, except in wartime, we are rarely able to employ all our re-sources, either people or capital equipment. In addition, our system of distribution allows many people to be poor even when there is more than enough to go around.

We are led to the fourth major deci-sion of all economies: *How should in-come be distributed? Who should get what?* Let us examine three possible standards which may be used for de-ciding how income is to be distributed: equality, need, and contribution.

Equality has always had a strong appeal, not only to the self-interest of those who are on the short end of inequality, but also to men's sense of justice. Many voluntary communities, including those of the early Christians and the modern Israeli collectives (*kib-butzim*), have tried it. Carl Sandburg, in his poem "The People, Yes" suggests some of the possibilities and also some of the difficulties of equal distri-bution.

> "So, you want to divide all the money there is and give every man his share?"
> "That's it. Put it all in one big pile and split it even for everybody."
> "And the land, the gold, silver, oil, copper, you want that divided up?"
> "Sure—an even whack for all of us."
> "Do you mean that to go for horses and cows?"
> "Sure—why not?"
> "And what about pigs?"
> "Oh to hell with you—you know I got a couple of pigs."[1]

What the poet is saying, of course, is that while the have-nots may think equality would be a pretty good thing, the haves are likely to have doubts.

1. Carl Sandburg, *Complete Poems,* New York, Harcourt Brace Jovanovich, 1950, p. 481.

There are other problems. If everything were divided up equally, how long would things stay that way? Would not people with more intelligence, or more energy, or fewer scruples soon have a larger share again? If there were no possibility of achieving a larger in-come, what incentives would there be to prepare oneself and work hard? Would not the economy slow to a standstill for lack of motivation?

There are also strong arguments in favor of equality. Unequal reward seems to assume that people are un-equally worthy. Who is to judge a hu-man being's worth? If we do not have equality of income, then the children of those with a higher income start life with an advantage. How can there be equality of opportunity if people do not begin the race of life at the same start-ing point? As for lack of motivation, the advocates of equality might answer that man does not live by bread alone. People work for reasons other than the mere hope of gain. There is another strong argument, if not for complete equality, at least against too great in-equality. If too much goes to a few people of wealth and the mass of people have little income, who is going to consume the products of the econ-omy? This question will return to con-cern us later.

A second answer to the problem rejects equality in favor of *need*. A man with a family needs more than a bache-lor. A family with special health prob-lems needs more than a family in perfect health. A scholar may need books, a musician scores or instru-ments in which a manual laborer is not interested. Again, questions arise. Per-haps we can agree that every person needs certain things just to stay alive and keep working, but few of us would settle for that. The wealthier the econ-omy, the more things seem to be nec-essary. Is a car a necessity for us? a separate bedroom for each member of the family? Are color TV and an annual vacation luxuries or necessities? How do we distinguish needs from mere wants? Yet can we be unconcerned if any of our fellow human beings lack the basic necessities of life?

The third possible standard is *contribution*. Let a person be rewarded according to what he has added to the welfare of society. Certainly there is merit in this criterion. Is it not reasonable that society should reward those who have served it well? Immediately the question arises, however: How shall we measure each person's contribution? The market system has an answer. Let each person offer his talents on the market, and the demand for his services will measure his contribution. But is the sale price which one's services can demand necessarily a measure of his social usefulness? Is a baseball or football star worth more to society than a United States senator who may make less? Moreover, the market measures only in a very short run. What about those who contribute not only today but to future generations? Is a popular movie or TV actor or a night club celebrity worth more to society than an Einstein or a Gandhi?

There is another question here. How much of one's ability to earn an income can be attributed to him? We have already seen that we start the race of life with unequal chances. Each of us is also heir to all the advantages of a rich and technologically developed society. Isaac Newton once said that he could contribute to science as he did because he "stood on the shoulders of giants." Who would be what he is if he had been born in another place, or time, with a different skin, or with parents with a different income? Is it just to reward a person for having the right parents or skin color, for being born at the right place and time?

Let us now see how the market and planning try to answer such questions as we have raised about distribution of income. In its pure form, decision by the market mechanism makes one's marketability almost the only standard in rewarding him with income. This has been the traditional American way of free enterprise. To this philosophy attempts at equality are pernicious, for they stifle enterprise. It is one's responsibility to care for his own needs, and if he cannot or will not, it may be a concern for private charity, but not for public policy. Today, of course, this rugged individualism has been modified, and both equality and need form a part of our public policy of distribution. Minimum wage laws set a floor under income. Social security provides that minimum needs of the aged shall be met. Public welfare provides something for most of the unemployed. The proposal that everyone should have a guaranteed minimum income, regardless of work, is based on ideas of need and equality rather than contribution.

The most highly developed planned economy, the Soviet Union, has theoretically based its distribution on the policies of Lenin.

According to these, there would be two stages of development in distribution. The first was described by the phrase, "To each according to his ability, from each according to his work." "Work" might sound much like "contribution" in the capitalist economies, but to Lenin it meant socially useful work in the service of social revolution. It excluded as socially useless, and parasitic, many activities which earn large incomes in capitalist countries. Income was to a large extent set by planning agencies. In the second phase, the motto would be, said Lenin, "From each according to his ability, to each according to his needs." He looked forward to a society so affluent that reward according to contribution would no longer be necessary, since there would be enough for everyone's needs. The average Russian's material needs are undoubtedly much better cared for than before the revolution. Yet our estimates of Russian incomes suggest that distribution in the Soviet economy is far from Lenin's goal.

Sweden illustrates a different combination of standards of distribution. It is a much more affluent country than the Soviet Union, being close to the United States in per capita income. It is also unlike the Soviet Union in that about 90 percent of its enterprise is privately owned. But a considerable part of this 90 percent is made up of consumers' and producers' cooperatives. They are in considerable measure responsible for the philosophy of public responsibility for distribution which is summarized in the phrase "welfare state." Sweden has been so successful in establishing minimum standards of need that we can say, for all practical purposes, that no one lives in poverty. This is possible because of high taxation which also insures that there are very few rich people. From these taxes come public funds which ensure almost cradle-to-grave security, benefits to mothers, nursery school services, sickness and unemployment insurance, and retirement benefits amounting to two-thirds of the income of one's fifteen most productive years. Thus Sweden has combined a market economy with the elimination of great inequality and provision for most basic needs.

Which is a better way to make the basic decisions of an economy— through the market or through planning? Advocates of the market insist that this is the only democratic way to make them. They argue, also, that the market stimulates more energetic efforts and thus produces a more dynamic type of economy. Advocates of planning say that the market is not democratic, inasmuch as one "votes" as a consumer not on the basis of equality, but on the basis of income. Those with high income dominate this "ballot box." To the planner political planning by bodies chosen on the principle of "one man, one vote" is far more democratic and rational. As we have seen, every modern economy to some degree employs both methods. Our later chapters will give us further basis for evaluating them.

NATIONAL INCOME

Everyone who would be socially informed today needs to be able to think in terms of national income. This means simply that we need to be able to think of the economy *as a whole.* We need to be able to ask such questions as: What is the total level of employment? of investment? of production? of money income? How do they compare with what they were a year ago? five years ago? with what we might expect them to be ten years from now? How does our situation compare with that of other countries? What would be a normal level of employment, investment, production, and income? What policies might help us to attain and maintain that level?

The fact that almost all modern social scientists think this way reflects the fact that we live in a world where planning is playing an increasing role in the making of economic decisions. A little history will perhaps make this clearer. Before the Depression of 1929, economic thinking was dominated by the idea of the self-regulating market. It was assumed that the economy worked best when guided by no overall policy other than the invisible hand of individual decisions by buyers and sellers. What was then important was the activities of the individual business or firm. Thus the dominant economics was what we call *microeconomics*—a study of how the typical small unit in the economy, the individual business, is supposed to operate.

The Depression was a shock from which this type of thinking never recovered. It had been assumed that, like everything else, depressions were a natural part of economic life and, most important, that if we simply let the invisible hand alone, the market would work its way back to prosperity. This was the policy of laissez-faire ("leave it alone"). However, four years of leaving it alone, from 1929 to 1933, seemed only to make things worse, to the point where in 1933 the United States and much of the world faced economic disaster and possibly political revolution. The Roosevelt Administration, coming to office in 1933, gradually rejected the idea of laissez-faire in favor of the idea that government must play an active part in bringing about recovery. The whole New Deal program of public works and other government spending grew out of this change in philosophy. The 1946 Employment Act, as we have seen, explicitly rejected pure laissez-faire in favor of a continuing government responsibility for maintaining investment and employment. Some people, it is true, still maintain that we did not wait long enough for the invisible hand to work things out. They feel that the New Deal made things worse and that what we need now is to return to laissez-faire as we had it before 1929. No serious national political candidate could advocate this today, however, either in the United States or elsewhere. It is noteworthy that Republican administrations in the United States and Conservative administrations in England have largely continued the economic policies introduced by Democratic and Labour parties.

Once it came to be assumed that leaving matters to the decisions of many individual firms was not enough and that we need to think in terms of the whole economy, a new type of economic thinking came to the fore. This we call "national income economics," or *macroeconomics,* to indicate that it is primarily concerned with the total economic picture rather than with the detailed parts. This does not mean that social scientists have ceased to be interested in the microeconomics of the individual firm, but that the major emphasis is elsewhere.

The study of national income can be extremely complex, but we shall need to grasp only a few basic ideas. When we speak of national income, we are ordinarily speaking of one of two things (or both): (1) the total production of an economy in a given period (usually a year), (2) the total flow of money during this period. We shall see soon that both figures are approximately the same, and we shall see why this is so. In order to avoid confusing

A bread line during the Great Depression of 1929.

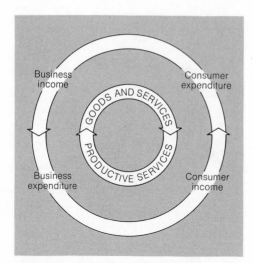

Figure 8.2. The basic wheel of wealth.

these figures with others which are sometimes used in more complex calculations, we usually speak of the total national production as gross national product (GNP).

When we look at GNP more closely, we find it to be composed of a number of elements with which we should familiarize ourselves. We made the distinction between *consumer goods* and capital equipment, or *producer's goods,* in the previous section. *Agricultural goods* and *manufactured goods* distinguish two important sectors of the economy. It is important to be familiar with the distinction between *single-use goods,* which obviously are used up rapidly, and *durable goods,* which survive a number of uses. With the growth of government, the distinction between *private goods* and *public goods* has become increasingly important. Finally, GNP is composed not only of tangible goods, but also of intangible *services.*

The different elements are summarized graphically in the accompanying chart, which should be studied carefully. It is also important to notice that the same good can fall in more than one category. For example, an automobile owned by a government agency is a public, durable, manufactured, consumer good. The orange you eat for breakfast is a private, agricultural,

single-use, consumer good. An oven used in a commercial bakery is a private, manufactured, durable, producer's good. It will be good for you to think of other items and classify them.

To be able to deal with national income easily, one must have not only an intellectual grasp of concepts, but a feeling for what is going on. He must have the sense of (1) a flow of productive human activity (2) which never begins or ends (3) in which goods, services, and money are constantly being interchanged. Two models (in this case, schemes for representing social processes through relationships that we can visualize) may help us to get this feeling.

The first of these is the wheel of wealth. This, we will note, is actually two wheels, one within the other. We have said that national income can mean either a flow of goods and services or a flow of money exchanged for them. The outer wheel in the wheel of wealth represents the flow of money. The inner wheel represents the flow of goods and services.

Note that these two wheels are moving in opposite directions. If we think of our own transactions in earning or spending money, it will be clear why this is so. If one works in a filling station, for example, there is a constant flow of productive services going from him to the station, and a reverse flow of money from the station to him. If one goes to the grocery store, there is a flow of money at the check-out counter from him to the store, and a reverse flow of goods from the store to him. On a large scale, this is most of what we have to know to undertand the wheel of wealth. Money flows in one direction throughout the entire economy, goods and services in the opposite direction.

Let us now look at the four points on the wheel: consumer expenditure, business income, business expenditure, and consumer income. Suppose we make these concrete by considering a specific transaction—your purchase of this textbook.

When you went to the bookstore and

handed it across the counter (consumer expenditure), your money became business income for the bookstore and the publisher. Gradually it moved into business expenditure, as it was used to make payments to individuals or groups involved in the production of the book: bookstore employees, people working in the publisher's office, owners of the buildings involved, printers, suppliers of paper and ink, the author, and the bondholders and stockholders of the businesses. Looked at from the standpoint of those who received it, this money became consumer income. In turn all of these people, from janitors to stockholders, eventually spent (or will spend) the money in one way or another on consumer expenditure for rent, groceries, clothing, entertainment, travel, education, and so on.

Thus the outer wheel has come full circle from CE, through BI, through BE, to CI, and back again to CE, from whence it begins another circle. We can see what we mean by saying that this is an endless process, in which *one act of production furnishes the money which creates the demand for another act of production, and so on without end.*

Let us see what has happened to the inner wheel. As CE passed from you to the publisher (thus becoming BI), consumer goods (the book) passed from the publisher to you in the upper half of the wheel. BI became BE, and then passed from the publisher to people who participated in the process of making books, thus becoming CI. In exchange productive services passed from them to the publisher.

We may think of a year's national income as the total of all the transactions taking place on such a gigantic wheel of wealth over a period of 365 days.

We can add to our understanding by looking at our second model. This time we will, as it were, straighten out the wheel of wealth into a continuous stream of production. Let us see what this looks like.

Consider a simple producer's good, a cotton print dress. Let us try to follow the process which finally resulted in its hanging in a girl's closet. Let us try to find where and when this process began. We are taken back first to the store at which the dress was bought, and then back to the wholesaler. From there we are led to the clothing factory in New York or Chicago or Miami where the dress was made, and from there to the mill in South Carolina where cotton was woven into cloth. From there we go further back to the cotton field in Texas where the cotton was grown.

Now let us break down each stage in the process of production. It will immediately become clear that the production of a dress is far more complex than it would seem at first glance. The retail store and the wholesale warehouse had to be built in order that the dress might be marketed. This required cement, steel, glass, and lumber, each of which must in turn be produced. All the acts involved in producing these in the cement factory, the glass factory, the steel mill, the lumber yard, and the forest are part of the process of bringing the dress to the consumer. So are those which lie behind the construction of the dress factory and the cotton mill. The factory and the mill use machinery, for which power must be generated. The machinery itself must be made out of metal mined in the hills of Minnesota, and other ingredients. The cotton was harvested by a cotton picking machine powered by gasoline, refined from oil originating in Arabia, and running on rubber from the plantations of Malaya. The raw cotton must be transported from field to cotton mill, the cloth from mill to dress factory, the finished dress from factory to retail store. All the vehicles involved must be built and maintained. In the town where the girl bought the dress, and in New York, in South Carolina, Texas, Minnesota, Arabia, Malaya, workers have to be fed, housed, clothed, and provided with other necessities and luxuries. The provision of coffee, orange juice,

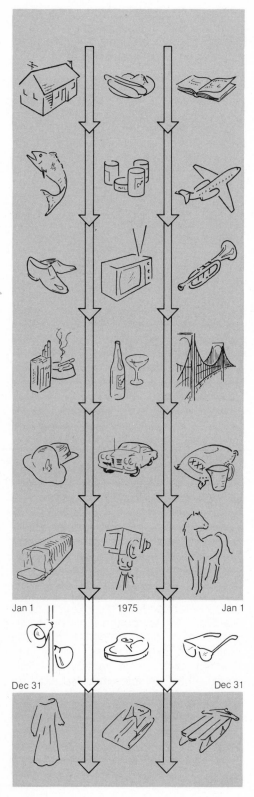

Jan 1   1975   Jan 1

Dec 31   Dec 31

wheat, beefsteak, salad greens, and other food items alone sets in motion another chain of production in far removed places. So now the whole process of producing a dress begins to look like Figure 8.3.

Where did the process begin? In the dress factory? in the cotton mill? in the Kansas wheat field whence came the flour for the breakfast wheat cakes that powered the man who drove the cotton picker? In the jungles of Malaya, or those of Brazil, where grew the dress salesman's morning coffee? Or hundreds of millions of years ago, when nature began to form the oil that powered the cotton picker, or the coal that generated the electricity for the cotton mill and for the blast furnace that purified the ore out of which was fashioned the sewing machine which made the dress? We can see that the production of a dress is interwoven with a multitude of other productive acts whose beginning is before the dawn of history.

When will the process end? If we go back to the principle of the wheel of wealth, we know that the dollars paid for the dress will ultimately be divided in a vast number of ways among the many people at all stages who contributed to its production. They, in turn, will spend this money, generating demand for new acts of production, which will in turn generate others, with no end in sight.

Again, instead of taking a single transaction and tracing it to its beginnings and into the future, we may think of the total stream of transactions which make up all the productive activity going on from day to day and year to year in an economy. These transactions are as intricately interlinked as are the processes involved in making the dress. If we now cut into this stream, so as to isolate that flow which takes place between January 1 and December 31 of a given year, we shall

Figure 8.3. The flow of goods and national income.

COMMODITY FLOW METHOD	EXPENDITURE METHOD
Products of farms	Personal consumption
Products of factories	Personal saving
Value of services	Corporate and public saving

INCOME PAYMENTS METHOD

Total payrolls

Dividends and interests

Cash rents

Profits of farmers and self-employed

Figure 8.4. Three methods of calculating national income.

have isolated one year's national income.

How does one actually measure the annual flow of national income? Let us go back for a moment to the wheel of wealth. Here we saw that whenever there is production of a good or service, there is ideally a corresponding money payment by a consumer. In an exchange economy, that is, one based on money rather than on direct barter, this is only common sense. We should, therefore, be able to reach a national income figure either by getting data on the *value of all production* or data on *all purchases* by individuals and groups. Or, going back to the wheel, we can see what again is common sense: that for every expenditure there is first an income. Thus we might arrive at the national income figure by adding together data on *all incomes* of individuals and groups.

These three methods of calculating national income are the *commodity flow* method, the *expenditure* method, and the *income payments* method. Each measures a different point on the total national wheel of wealth: the commodity flow method measures the upper half of the inner wheel, the expenditure method measures CE on the outer wheel, and the income payments method measures CI. Figure 8.4 shows

the data which are used by each method of computation. In actual life there are complications (such as buying on credit or carrying over inventories from year to year) which will lead the three figures to come out approximately rather than exactly the same.

There is one more device used in analyzing national income with which we should be familiar. This tells us how the output of each line of production is divided among all kinds of uses.

Suppose we want to know what might be the effect of a one billion dollar military cutback upon different sectors of the American economy. We could go to an *input-output* table, as developed by Wassily Leontiev. This, again, is a model expressing social relationships. In structure it is similar to the distance chart on a road map, which as we know lists each city on the left hand margin and again across the top. We then calculate the distance between any two cities by finding the point of intersection. In the input-output table, of which we see a sample section, we find listed instead different lines of economic activity. Any point of intersection then shows how much of the output of a given area at the top of the table contributes to another area on the left of the table.

For example, if we read across the

	Electric power	Coal	Petroleum	Iron and steel	Machinery
Electric power					
Coal					
Petroleum					
Iron and steel					
Machinery					

Figure 8.5. A simplified example of an input-output table.

top until we reach the item steel, and down until we intersect the row marked automobiles, we will find the figure for the amount of steel going into the production of cars. If we read across the top again to the item rubber, we can read down to the rows indicating uses in auto tires, foam rubber mattresses, or surgical supplies. Or to return to our original problem, if we will read across to the headings aircraft, electronics, steel, rubber, food, and so on, and then down to military operations, we will find how much production from each industry goes to the armed forces. We might thus calculate how much each industry would be affected by a military cut.

In a table for the whole economy, the total of all output figures equals the national income, as does the total for all input items, for every item in the national income is produced by someone, and ideally it is bought by someone. Such a table is, of course, a tremendous project. It is undertaken better by computers than by direct visual representation.

This last statement has a direct bearing on the question of market and planning decisions discussed in the previous section. Not very long ago defenders of the market system claimed that overall national economic planning could never work because no group of human beings could keep in mind all the data that would be necessary. Today computers that can manipulate large amounts of national input-output data have apparently made this argument obsolete. Criticism of planning will in the future probably have to be on other grounds. Overall national planning may or may not be desirable, but with our modern techniques for handling national income data, it is almost certainly possible.

THE INTERNATIONAL ECONOMY

So far we have been dealing mainly with economic life within a single country. The same fundamental principles apply to economic relations that involve several nations. However, trade among nations differs from trade within a single country in several important ways. These make it necessary for us to examine international economic relations separately.

International trade is a special example of trade among different geographical areas. This follows in general the principle of division of labor, or specialization. Plato said that "there are diversities of nature among us which are adapted to different occupations." He was speaking of individuals, but he could just as well have been referring to areas of the earth's surface. Different regions tend to specialize in the things they can do best and to rely on other areas to provide other things more cheaply. Florida does not try to grow apples, nor do Michigan or the state of Washington attempt to raise oranges. Some areas specialize in growing one or another type of food-stuff. Others produce various raw materials for industry. Both food and raw materials may be shipped to other areas that specialize in various kinds of manufacturing.The United States imports rubber, tea, coffee, and bananas from the tropics, for example, in exchange for manufactured goods which we can produce easily.

Ideally, economic life tends to spread over the globe so that the particular resources of each part of the world are used to serve the advantage of the whole human population. Reality, however, falls somewhat short of this ideal. The main reason lies in the barriers erected by the organization of the world into sovereign national states.

While trade within a single country is relatively simple because there is a common medium of exchange, international trade is complicated by the fact that each nation has a separate system of money. Anyone who has traveled abroad knows that the first thing he must do before he begins to move about in a new country is to visit the local currency exchange (England), *bureau de change* (France), *Wechsel* (Germany), *cambio* (Italy), or the equivalent and change his dollars into local currency. If we have ordered something by mail from abroad, we have had the experience of having to translate prices and then arrange for some kind of international draft which will convert our currency into the seller's own money.

An illustration may clarify some of the problems involved. Suppose that you are an automobile dealer and sell to an Englishman a car worth $2500, or about 1000 British pounds. How are you going to get paid? Let us suppose that at the same time an American importer buys from England a shipment of woolens worth 1000 pounds. The Englishman to whom you sell the car gives you a draft (check) on his London bank for 1000 pounds. You sell

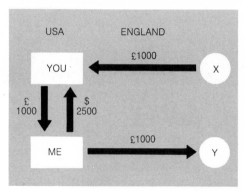

Figure 8.6. A schematic representation of international exchange.

the draft to the American importer for $2500. He then sends it to his British supplier, who deposits it to his account in London, or receives the cash in pounds.

This is a very oversimplified, yet essentially accurate, account of how we handle the problem of separate monies. In actual life you would probably not be so fortunate as to encounter an importer who needed in pounds exactly the amount you were receiving. You would instead probably sell your London draft to your American bank for dollars. The bank would then be able to sell it, in whole or in parts, to importers needing British pounds.

What has happened here is actually a roundabout barter. The exported car has been paid for by imported woolens. We are led to a very important point about international trade. *Goods exchange for goods.* To many people it would seem desirable for a country to sell more goods abroad than it buys. But this is not true, for in the long run, our exports must be paid for by imports.

What would happen if a country should, over a long period of time, have either a so-called favorable balance of trade (more exports than imports) or a so-called unfavorable balance, or what would happen if the United States and England traded only with each other?

The rate of exchange between the

PAYMENTS		RECEIPTS	
Imports	$23.1	Exports	$28.3
Foreign aid	4.1	Repayment of loans	1.3
Private investments	3.9	Foreign investment	
Other	0.9	in U.S.	0.6
Total	$32.0	Total	$30.2

PAYMENTS (Itemized)	$32.0
RECEIPTS (Itemized)	$30.0
DEFICIT FROM ABOVE	$ 2.0

Figure 8.7. The national balance of payments in 1961 (*figures in billions of dollars*).

United States and England is now about $2.50 to the pound. Suppose that the United States continues to export more to England than it receives in return. There will be many more Englishmen going to their banks trying to exchange their pounds for dollars than there will be Americans wanting to exchange dollars for pounds. Just as a short supply of milk drives up the price of milk, so a short supply of dollars will drive up the price of dollars. Instead of getting $2.50 for his pound, the Englishman might get only $2.30. This would mean that American goods had become more expensive (it would take more pounds for an Englishman to buy them). Under these circumstances fewer Englishmen would buy American goods, and the balance of imports and exports would tend to be restored. In the opposite case, that of a surplus of imports from England, Americans would bid against each other for British pounds, driving the price up to perhaps $2.75 to the pound. The greater cost of British imports would again tend to restore the balance of trade.

Our example has so far involved only two countries. Actually, international trade is much more complex. Imports do not have to balance exports for every country with which we trade. It may be enough that our *total* imports from all countries balance our exports. Imbalances with a number of other countries may cancel one another out. Consider the kind of relationship shown in the "triangle of trade." Country A buys $100 million a year more from Country B than it sells to it. Country B stands in the same relationship to Country C, as does also Country C to Country A. A can pay off its debt to B with the surplus of sales it makes to C; B pays off C with its surplus from A; C pays off A with its surplus from B.

The picture is further complicated by the fact that for a short time, a change in the rate of exchange can be prevented by shipping gold. During the early 1960s a persistent unfavorable trade balance caused a great drain on the American gold supply, but any nation's supply of gold is limited, and eventually a balance of exports and imports will have to be restored in one way or another.

Figure 8.7 gives a concrete picture of what is involved in the international economy. This is the balance of payments for the United States in 1961. We have been talking so far about importation and exportation of goods, but international receipts and payments actually include quite a bit more. We can see that Americans' international transactions include not only goods physically transferred to or from American territory, but also

> *goods and services bought to maintain American troops overseas,*
> *purchases of capital equipment abroad by investors,*
> *goods and services bought by tourists abroad,*
> *payments for the service of transporting goods on foreign ships,*
> *payments for goods and services bought abroad by foreign aid,*
> *payments of interest and principal received on loans to other countries,*
> *profits earned from sale of goods and services produced by investments abroad.*

It is interesting to note that although the United States exported $5.2 billion worth more goods than it imported, the other items created an unfavorable balance of trade which amounted to $2 billion. A good deal of this was covered, as has been said, by shipment of American gold reserves overseas, a solution which, again, could not continue indefinitely.

We may note here a point which bears on the next section of this chapter. Since a nation's exports must ultimately be paid for with imports, it is to its advantage to have other nations able to produce goods for exchange. The United States, for example, sells a great deal to Canada, which is a relatively productive country. It can sell little to poverty-stricken areas of Brazil or to the Congo. If these areas become more productive, however, it could. It is true, of course, that they might also become competitors on the world market. But in general, it is shortsighted,

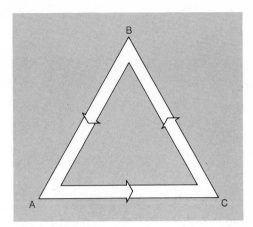

Figure 8.8. The triangle of trade.

even in business terms, for the rich nations to allow parts of the world to remain economically underdeveloped.

International economic relations are complicated not only by the problem of different monies, but by the fact that nations set up barriers against one another's goods. A mother country may use its political power to limit its colonies' trade with other nations, as England did during our colonial days. Economic aid may be given on condition that it is spent in the donor country, as has been the case with some American assistance in Latin America. A government may require permits to export or import, as did Germany during the days of Hitler. The most widespread barrier is the import tax, or tariff.

Within each country we ordinarily have a free trade area where goods are exchanged without tariffs or other import restrictions. Between countries there are generally tariffs. These are of two kinds. A revenue tariff is low enough so as not to be a serious barrier to trade and serves to bring income to the taxing nation. A protective tariff is high enough to make importing difficult or impossible. Its purpose is to keep goods out or to allow them to be imported only at such a high price that they cannot compete with local goods.

If we look at American history, we can see the difference tariffs make. Before the adoption of the federal Constitution, we were, in effect, thirteen different nations, each with trade barriers against the others (we also, incidentally, had thirteen different currencies). One had to pay a tariff, for example, to import firewood from New Jersey to New York. Part of the economic success of the United States today is due to the fact that we now constitute such a large free trade area. Western Europe, a smaller area, has traditionally been divided into many separate and often hostile nations with tariff restrictions and separate currencies. How different would economic life be in the United States today if we were still operating under the Articles of Confederation, as fifty separate countries!

We have tariffs to keep the most efficient producers from commanding the market, and the tariffs often accomplish this task admirably. One of the arguments advanced for protective tariffs is that new industries need protection until they can get on their feet. Through much of our history, the United States generally maintained a wall of high tariffs. This was defended to a large extent on the ground that, without it, older industries abroad would be able to prevent American industrial development by flooding the country with their cheaper goods. Tariffs are also justified on the ground that they protect a country with a high standard of living and high wage costs (such as the United States) against competition from countries with lower standards (such as Japan).

Both justifications have some merit. In some cases a no-tariff policy might keep a young country from ever developing efficient production. Infant industries are, however, usually unwilling to give up their privileged position even when they have grown to maturity. The competition offered by countries with cheap labor can be exaggerated. Generally a country with a high living standard has more capital equipment and more efficient workers and is thus able to produce more cheaply in

spite of the lower wages of its competitors. In the 1960s, for example, a Bell and Howell executive was quoted as saying that he was confident that his company's efficiency would enable it to more than hold its own against foreign camera producers. In a large number of cases, those who argue for protective tariffs simply want to protect their own inefficiency against more efficient competitors.

When we understand that a country must import in order to pay for its exports, we can see that a high tariff wall must cut down on its ability to sell abroad, as well as cut down the flow of international trade in general. Recognition of this fact has led toward a lowering of tariff barriers in the past twenty-five years.

The United States, long a high tariff nation, began negotiating tariff reductions with other countries during the Roosevelt Administration. One of the most important recent developments in tariff reduction has been the formation of common markets. Two of these are in western Europe. The European Free Trade Area (known as The Outer Seven) includes Austria, the Scandinavian countries, the United Kingdom, Switzerland, and Portugal. The European Economic Community (also called The Six, or The Common Market) has as its members Belgium, the Netherlands, France, Luxembourg, West Germany, and Italy. By 1964 both groups had gone 60 percent of the way toward eliminating tariffs. Perhaps in the not distant future they will form an economic United States of Europe. On a smaller scale, the Central American nations of El Salvador, Nicaragua, Honduras, Guatemala, and Costa Rica have formed the Central American Common Market. In 1960 nine other countries (Argentina, Brazil, Chile, Colombia, Ecuador, Mexico, Peru, Paraguay, and Uruguay) organized the Latin American Free Trade Association. These two groups may eventually form a single Latin American free trade area of 200 million people. Meanwhile other international negotiations constantly seek a lowering of tariff barriers.

Another important difference between national and international economies lies in the fact that international trade is linked with military policy. Nations are afraid of being involved in war and having their foreign trade cut off. Thus they are likely to try to be more or less self-sufficient. They are likely to try to produce all the things essential to their people and to their military policies regardless of how much more cheaply they might be bought elsewhere. Germany during the Hitler period made many ersatz (substitute) products at home in place of imports; for example, the Germans synthesized fuel to take the place of natural oil. Underdeveloped nations today are likely to feel that they must develop their own heavy industries—steel, machinery, building materials, transport, and weaponry. They must act like great powers even though they could much more economically import these things and concentrate on smaller industry that required less drain on their resources.

International trade is not only shaped by political rivalries and wars; it is a central part of them. Conflicts among nations are not *just* struggles for economic opportunity, as some Marxists have thought, but no realistic account of political conflict can leave out the international struggle for economic advantage.

We cannot understand the Peloponnesian Wars between Athens and Sparta (and Persia) without taking into account rivalry for trade routes through the Gulf of Corinth to Italy and Sicily. Underlying the Punic Wars between Rome and Carthage was conflict over trade with Sicily and Spain. The story of the Crusades is incomplete without an understanding of how Christian victory over the Moslems gave the Italian cities of Venice, Genoa, and Pisa a virtual monopoly over Mediterranean trade and shut out their rival, Constantinople.

The political history of the modern world is a succession of conflicts among empires involving command of world trade. Portugal and Spain once divided the earth between them. The voyages of discovery which opened up the Western hemisphere grew out of their competition for trade and wealth. Britain succeeded them and dominated the scene for over 300 years. In American history we can read the account of her conflict with the Dutch, the Spanish, and the French. War in the Americas was only part of worldwide trade rivalries. The defeat of the Spanish Armada put an end to the economic ambitions of Spain in 1588. Waterloo marked the victory of Britain over France's bid for domination. In the late nineteenth century, Germany rose as a threatening industrial power, with dreams of economic expansion in the Near East through a Berlin-to-Bagdad railway, but she was twice defeated in World Wars I and II. By that time, however, Britain's economic supremacy was already passing to the United States.

Today the United States dominates the world economy. In a recent year, we produced about 60 percent of the world's locomotives, 40 percent of its civilian aircraft, 20 percent of its metal cutting tools, 20 percent of its farm machinery, 18 percent of its buses and trucks, and 15 percent of all farm products. In 1958 about one-seventh of all the imports in the world came into the United States, and about one-sixth of all the exports left it. We provide 25 percent of all farm exports. The United States consumes close to one-half of all the raw materials produced outside the Soviet Union. Canada, Venezuela, the Philippines, and Brazil all send from one-fourth to one-half of their exports to us. It is easy to see why "when the United States sneezes, the rest of the world gets pneumonia."

Nevertheless, our supremacy does not go unchallenged, and the result is the kind of trade warfare that has gone on all through history. Russia has organized her eastern European satellites into a Council for Mutual Economic Assistance (Comecon), while the United States seeks to expand trade with these countries.

Japan has become a major industrial power. In 1963 she led the world in the production of ships, photographic materials, transistors, sewing machines, motorcycles, cotton cloth, and silk. She is a world leader in the export of textiles, textile machinery, cement, ceramics, and toys. In ten years, ending in 1963, her industrial production quadrupled.

In Latin America the United States is threatened by the aggressive economic policies of Japan, West Germany, and France. From 1957 to 1962, for example, United States exports to Latin America dropped by about 30 percent, while from 1959 to 1962, those of France rose about one-third, West Germany's about 15 percent, and Japan's almost 60 percent. The Alliance for Progress has sought to hold or regain Latin American markets in the face of this severe competition. The west European free trade areas are to a considerable extent an organization against the United States. We know, of course, of Chinese economic rivalry with the United States in Southeast Asia. We are perhaps not so aware of France's interest in tin, coffee, tea, fruit canning, and brewing in this area which it once dominated. Economic rivalry here and in Latin America underlie many of the sharp political differences between France and the United States.

In 1965 Secretary of State Rusk said that "it is the ambassador's job, and the job of everyone with him, to accept the notion that the expansion of American trading interests is a central function of diplomacy."[2] What he said could be involved in a realistic job description of a diplomat of almost any country now and through history.

In 1958 Clarence B. Randall, a steel industrialist who was once special

assistant to President Eisenhower, stated to a Detroit audience which contained a large number of industrial leaders:

The United States is becoming more and more dependent upon the importation of raw materials for our industry. That needs no documentation to a Detroit audience. The vast undisclosed, undiscovered national resources of the world lie in the new countries. It is therefore tremendously important to our future that those resources be available to us and not excluded from us by a new "curtain." The second part of our economic future is that in the great new and uncommitted countries lies the vast markets of the future for American goods. I say to you that our grandsons will not hold us blameless if we permit these great resources and these great markets to be swept into the other camp by our own apathy and ineptitude.

Speaking of the Cold War in 1961 to a congressional committee, the then Secretary of State Christian Herter said, "The immediate objective in this war is the control of the contested countries, more than three score and ten in number. The ultimate objective is the control of the world. The struggle will be relentless, irreconcilable, merciless." This but follows, it would seem, the reasoning of the previously quoted statements. It is our modern-day version of an old story.

Trade relations, however, sometimes cut across the main lines of apparently "irreconcilable" economic and political conflict. In 1967, for example, China was denouncing Western "imperialists" and "fascists," and the United States and Australia were opposing Chinese policy in Vietnam. Yet the Chinese government was apparently importing large quantities of goods from Australia, carrying on an active underground trade with South Africa through French agents, and selling steel through Hong Kong for

2. Department of State Bulletin, vol. III, No. 1343, Publ. 1845, March 22, 1965, "Some Fundamentals of American Policy," by Secretary of State Dean Rusk.

American military installations in Vietnam.

Cartels, international alliances between corporations, have existed for a long time. One of the most famous was the cartelization of the oil market by Standard Oil and the German I. G. Farben Company, a relationship which continued after Hitler came to power. In the last twenty years, there has been a large development of multinational corporations. In 1963 one-third of all the automobiles and almost all of the computers made in Europe were manufactured by partially or wholly American firms. The president of Abbott Laboratories, a drug firm with plants in 22 countries, expressed a new multinational point of view: "We are no longer just a U.S. company with interests abroad. Abbott is a world enterprise, and many major, fundamental decisions must be made on a global basis." A very significant recent development has been cooperation between private American corporations and Communist governments in carrying on different lines of production in eastern Europe. While we may question the philosophy that puts economic interest above all other considerations, it may be a good thing when it limits competitive nationalism.

THE UNDERDEVELOPED NATIONS

In Chapter one we discussed, among the great areas of social change in our world, the "revolution of rising expectations" which is taking place among the economically underdeveloped areas. We saw that our own kind of economic development is something new, and still relatively rare, in human history and that the underdeveloped nations still make up the large majority of the human population. We shall now examine more specifically the economic and social problems that these areas must overcome if they are to attain the kind of economic development we have experienced. After we have dealt with these problems of the underdeveloped majority, we shall consider in the next section the also very real problems of the developed minority.

A useful framework for thinking about this problem has been furnished by Walt W. Rostow, formerly Policy Planning Chief for the United States State Department. Rostow divides the process of development into five stages.

The first stage is the *traditional society.* This is represented today by most of Central America, Africa, and Southeast Asia. On the Bushman–New York continuum which we set up in Chapter four, these peoples fall toward the Bushman end of the scale. We can, therefore, describe them as relatively preliterate, technologically simple, unspecialized, nonhistoric, static, isolated, immobile, primary, homogeneous, and close to nature. A good many of these characteristics must, obviously, be changed before economic development can take place.

The second stage sets the *preconditions for take-off* into economic development. Today Ethiopia, Kenya, Thailand, Afghanistan, and perhaps Indonesia are at this point. Traditional attitudes are beginning to give way to more modern ones. Scientific ways of thinking have been introduced. People are beginning to think of time as something to be carefully planned, to give great importance to money and the things it can buy, to view work as positively valuable, and to consider individual advancement as a proper and important goal. They are beginning to adopt the Puritan ethic.

The third stage is the *take-off* itself. The classic illustration is England at the time of the Industrial Revolution. The United States after the Civil War and Russia in the 1920s and 1930s are other examples. Today Mexico, Puerto Rico, and possibly Brazil and Argentina are at this stage. The economy is able to create a good deal of its own capital equipment—5 to 10 percent of the GNP is being reinvested. Railroads are developing and industry is producing substantially for both domestic and foreign markets.

After the take-off there is a *drive to maturity* which lasts about three generations. In the United States, this was roughly the period between the Civil War and World War I. From 10 to 20 percent of GNP is plowed back into the economy. Development takes place in railways, steel mills, ships, chemicals, textiles, electric power, and machine tool products. The country is becoming urbanized. The more conservative bureaucrat is replacing the adventurous pioneer. Some people are beginning to question whether it has all been worthwhile.

The final state is that of *high mass consumption.* The United States reached this point in the 1920s, western Europe and Japan in the 1950s. The Soviet Union is about to enter it. In the United States the beginning of this period was marked by stress on automobiles, single-family dwellings, durable household goods, mass produced foods, and electrification of the economy. In this stage the emphasis has shifted from producers' to consumers' goods. The sternness of the Puritan ethic is giving way to an emphasis on spending, on consumption, on "the good life." People are beginning to wonder whether the economy can continue to grow, whether it will be possible to find new economic frontiers for investment.

Rostow's stages are an attempt to analyze economic development as it has occurred historically. It remains to be seen how far newly developing countries will follow the same pattern. Countries that develop later have the advantage, for example, of being able to move much faster because they can draw on the experience and technology of the already developed countries. This was true for the United States, which drew on England, and the Soviet Union, which drew on the United States and other countries.

Let us make clear the task of an underdeveloped country. It is to become productive enough so that an increasing number of its resources can be devoted to making capital equipment rather than merely providing the bare necessities for survival. Almost all the people in the underdeveloped countries are likely to be occupied in merely staying alive. To change this, agriculture must first become more efficient so as to release some people from full-time work on the soil. These people can then make machinery, which can then be used to produce manufactured goods. Some of these goods can be used to raise living standards at home. Others can be exported to pay for consumer goods, capital equipment, and raw materials from abroad. Once enough has been saved to make a start on capital equipment, economic development tends to snowball. The first step is the hardest.

What are the obstacles to economic development?

The most basic one is the low productivity of *agriculture.* In the United States, one farm worker feeds 27 other people. In Africa it takes from 2 to 10 workers on the land to feed one non-farmer. In 1955, in spite of the fact that rice is the staple crop of Southeast Asia, the United States produced three times as much rice per acre as did Vietnam. There are many reasons for such differences. The underdeveloped nations have very little farm machinery. Their farmers often lack knowledge of good farming practices. They are not likely to have modern methods of seed selection and are very often short of water and fertilizer. Their plots are often too small for efficient farming. Overcoming these problems requires both knowledge and capital.

How can an underdeveloped country release people from the land to start making capital equipment and manufactured goods? In India, for example, most of the people are so poor that many are already starving. Would not reducing the number of farmers just make things worse? Not necessarily, because most underdeveloped countries actually have too many people on the land. Removing a considerable number of people might actually raise their agricultural productivity. A recent experiment carried out near Cairo suggests that the present crop output could be produced by approximately half Egypt's present rural population.[3] We are not suggesting a totalitarian mass removal of people to cities, where they would only swell the number of unemployed and homeless. We are saying that there are enough people in most underdeveloped countries to begin doing the work of economic development if it is organized intelligently.

No program of economic development can go very far, however, without control of population growth, as we can see in the following example. The Aswan Dam in Egypt will be a monumental project in economic development. As high as a 30-story building and three miles long, it will provide irrigation for 2 million new acres of agricultural land, provide three times as much electricity as was previously consumed in Egypt, and increase agricultural production up to 45 percent. It has been estimated, however, that in the ten years required for construction, the population of Egypt will have increased by just this same figure, 45 percent. In twenty years the population of Latin America is expected to increase by about 80 percent, from 200 to 360 million. India's increased production as a result of industrialization has barely, if at all, kept pace with her population growth. Without birth control economic development is literally a case of having to run constantly faster in order to stand still.

Certainly one of the gravest barriers to economic development is *malnutrition* and *illness.* Josué de Castro, in *The Geography of Hunger,* attributes most of the traditional apathy of the Latin American peon to simple lack of adequate food. It is well known now that pellagra and other deficiency diseases for a long time sapped the

3. See Robert Heilbroner, *The Great Ascent,* New York, Harper & Row, 1963, p. 76.

energy of the American southerner. Probably a good deal of the resignation which we associate with India and other parts of the Orient is due to semistarvation. It is estimated that until recently, about 5 million people a year in the underdeveloped nations developed tuberculosis and that about 50 million contracted yaws, a disfiguring disease resembling syphilis. About 450 million were estimated to suffer from trachoma, a serious disease of the eyes, and about 15 million from leprosy. In Africa it is estimated that 12 percent of the population die from malaria before maturity. They live long enough to eat, but not to produce. There are African villages where no child born in recent years has lived to the age of one.

There are no simple answers to this problem. Parasites and bacteria and their carriers have been controlled by better sanitation, nutrition, and medical techniques. But studies by Price, McCarrison, and others suggest that a good deal of the ill health of the underdeveloped world is itself due to contacts with more developed nations. The colonial system substituted the cheapest and least nourishing civilized foods for more varied native diets and thus undoubtedly tended to lower resistance to disease. The more developed nations have introduced to native peoples the degenerative diseases of civilization, such as heart disease, diabetes, arthritis, and cancer, which they rarely suffered from before. These are almost certainly related to diet, stress, and physical inactivity. Wholesale adoption of Western ways would be an entirely too simple solution for the problem of health in the underdeveloped world.

Our discussion of the Bushman–New York continuum described certain attitudes typical of traditional societies which must change if development is to take place. One of these is the conservatism of the tested. For people on the brink of starvation, to try a new type of seed or a new method of plowing may seem to be gambling with disaster. Yet development requires willingness to give up many of the practices handed down by one's forefathers. Modern technology, upon which development depends, demands a scientific attitude toward relationships of cause and effect, but this may require much relearning. The novelist Richard Wright relates how a Ghanian, driving downhill a truck heavily loaded with lumber, slammed on the brakes. The momentum of the load carried the lumber through the cab and crushed him to death. Another driver, who had seen the accident, took the truck, drove it downhill, slammed on the brakes, and was similarly crushed. He had attributed the first disaster not to natural physical forces, but to witchcraft.

Technological development requires close coordination of the activities of many people. It is impossible to do this without following schedules. This demands an attitude toward time that is different from the traditional one. In Liberia an observer found that a church service scheduled to begin at 11 o'clock might start at any time before one. This slackness of schedule is related to the *mañana* ("tomorrow") attitude found in much of Latin America. One of the frequent complaints lodged by visitors from underdeveloped countries to the United States is against the constant rush to be "on time."

Development requires related habits of self-discipline. A day laborer on his way to work in an underdeveloped country may stop at a stream, remove a fish from a net he set the night before, and never show up for the job. He has met his needs for the day. This example also illustrates the traditionalist attitude toward money. In a modernized society, we assume that it is human nature to want to make money and get ahead. The traditionalist attitude is to work just hard enough to earn an accustomed wage. Thus, says Max Weber, in a modern society, raising the rate per piece of work done is likely to make people work harder because of the chance to earn more.

Traditionalist peoples, on the contrary, are likely to work less hard because it takes less work to earn the amount to which they are accustomed. The desire for personal gain is not, of course, the only alternative to traditionalism. People may also perform disciplined work, as they do, for example, in the Israeli cooperatives, out of a dedication to communal ideals.

In most underdeveloped countries, the *class structure* stands in the way of economic advance. Typically land wealth, and power are held by perhaps 3 to 5 percent of the people. The rest of the population is an illiterate, propertyless, and poverty-stricken peasant mass. There is generally no substantial middle class in between. In Brazil, for example, a thin layer on Rio de Janeiro's gold coast lives in the utmost of modern affluence and sophistication. On the hills overlooking Rio, the inhabitants of the *favellas,* or slums, live in wretched shacks without modern sanitation (see the photograph on page 256). Farther away in Pernambuco Province of Brazil, millions of peasants work for a few wealthy landholders under conditions resembling those of medieval serfs. To the vast majority of people in the underdeveloped world, ideologies like democracy and communism are abstractions with little meaning, but land reform, which would redistribute the soil so as to give them farms of their own and a sense of belonging in their society, is the first interest of the masses almost everywhere. Groups as different as the Communists, the American Alliance for Progress, and the Catholic Inter-American Cooperative Program are agreed that economic and political development for countries like Brazil requires a drastic redistribution of wealth and social power.

Around 1960 it was estimated that in the next ten years in Nigeria 20,000 top-level administrators, executives, technicians, and managers would be needed. Where are such people to come from? Not from the depressed masses. At present 50 percent of the underdeveloped world is illiterate. In Africa the figure is from 80 to 85 percent. When Libya became independent in 1949, there were only 14 university graduates in the country. The situation in the Congo was similar when it attained independence. Not only are the destitute majority unequipped for the task of development, but so are most of the propertied class, who are likely to be preindustrial in their way of thinking, to look upon industry and business as beneath them, and to be interested in land speculation, profiteering through trade, and financial manipulation rather than in production. Even those underdeveloped peoples who become educated may be more interested in personal power or high-level political manipulation than in the hard work of economic advance. Of all the students in the United States from the underdeveloped countries, for example, only about 4 percent were recently reported to be studying agriculture. A substantial number of scientists and professional people join the brain drain to developed areas.

Another obstacle is the heritage of *colonialism.* Many underdeveloped countries owe most of the economic development they have to the nations that colonized them. The colonizers brought capital. In the better colonies they brought opportunities for education. They brought the idea of economic advancement. In many cases they brought the ideology of political freedom. But they came primarily to use the natives as instruments for their own profit and power. They came as masters who regarded, and treated, native peoples as inferior and often as subhuman. In the less advanced colonies, their fear of revolt led them to keep the people depressed and illiterate. Where educational opportunities were offered to natives, those who were educated were very often used to keep their own people down.

Since the colonizers were primarily interested in profit and not in the balanced development of colonial areas, development was very often so one-sided as to lay a poor foundation for future independence. In Venezuela,

---

To begin to understand economic development we must have a picture of the problem with which it contends. We must conjure up in our mind's eye what underdevelopment means for the two billion human beings for whom it is not a statistic but a living experience of daily life. Unless we can see the Great Ascent from the vantage point of those who must make the climb, we cannot hope to understand the difficulties of the march.

It is not easy to make this mental jump. But let us attempt it by imagining how a typical American family, living in a small suburban house on an income of six or seven thousand dollars, could be transformed into an equally typical family of the underdeveloped world.

We begin by invading the house of our imaginary American family to strip it of its furniture. Everything goes: beds, chairs, tables, television set, lamps. We will leave the family with a few old blankets, a kitchen table, a wooden chair. Along with the bureaus go the clothes. Each member of the family may keep in his "wardrobe" his oldest suit or dress, a shirt or blouse. We will permit a pair of shoes to the head of the family, but none for the wife or children.

We move into the kitchen. The appliances have already been taken out, so we turn to the cupboards and larder. The box of matches may stay, a small bag of flour, some sugar and salt. A

*few moldy potatoes, already in the garbage can, must be hastily
rescued, for they will provide much of tonight's meal. We will
leave a handful of onions, and a dish of dried beans. All the rest
we take away: the meat, the fresh vegetables, the canned goods,
the crackers, the candy.*

*Now we have stripped the house: the bathroom has been
dismantled, the running water shut off, the electric wires taken
out. Next we take away the house. The family can move to the
toolshed. It is crowded, but much better than the situation in Hong
Kong, where (a United Nations report tells us) "it is not uncommon
for a family of four or more to live in a bedspace, that is, on a
bunk bed and the space it occupies—sometimes in two or three
tiers—their only privacy provided by curtains."**

*But we have only begun. All the other houses in the neighbor-
hood have also been removed; our suburb has become a shanty-
town. Still, our family is fortunate to have a shelter; 250,000 people
in Calcutta have none at all and simply live in the streets. Our
family is now about on a par with the city of Cali in Colombia,
where, an official of the World Bank writes, "on one hillside alone,
the slum population is estimated at 40,000—without water,
sanitation, or electric light. And not all the poor of Cali are as
fortunate as that. Others have built their shacks near the city on
land which lies beneath the flood mark. To these people the
immediate environment is the open sewer of the city, a sewer
which flows through their huts when the river rises."†*

* Social Aspects of Urban Development, *Committee on Information from Non
Self-Governing Territories, March 10, 1961, p. 129.*

† *"The Cauca Valley," unpublished World Bank memo by George Young.
(With the kind permission of the author.)*

—Robert L. Heilbroner, The Great Ascent, *New York,
Harper & Row, 1963, pp. 33–35.*

---

for example, according to Robert Heilbroner, oil makes up 92 percent of all
exports. In Chile copper makes up 66
percent, in Bolivia tin is responsible for
62 percent, in Honduras bananas are
52 percent of all exports, and in Colombia coffee makes up 77 percent. A
country that is dependent on the sale
of a single product is likely to be at the
mercy of those who buy or market the
crop and of sharp changes in world
demand for it.

With such conditions as a background, the departure of the colonial
powers left grave problems. One-sided
development was one problem. Profound unpreparedness for self-government and independence, as in the
Congo, was another. Since one tends

to view himself as others see him, centuries of being regarded as inferior or
subhuman often left strong feelings of
inferiority and self-doubt. On the other
hand, release from colonial control has
sometimes led to excessive national or
racial self-pride, sometimes to distrust
and hatred of all white people. These
reactions are not likely to encourage
the developed nations to offer the help
which the underdeveloped countries
need so much.

Although actual political ownership
of underdeveloped lands by foreign
powers is disappearing, foreign economic and political control has not
gone. The underdeveloped nations
have frequently been pawns in the rivalries and ambitions of the great pow-

ers. The Communist nations give economic aid and try to stir up social revolution not primarily to help the native peoples, but to strengthen their own power positions. The non-Communist powers often seek to dominate the underdeveloped nations in order to secure markets, raw materials, and military bases. They may, as the United States has done in Latin America and Southeast Asia, give verbal support to land reform and other changes in class structure. In actuality they are likely to support the ruling minorities. Both businessmen and diplomats are likely to feel more in common with the affluent, modernized few than with the poor and backward many. Typically they also resist social change as dangerous to their own economic and political interests.

THE DEVELOPED ECONOMIES

While the underdeveloped countries are struggling to develop enough resources to meet the tremendous needs of their people, the chief problem of the developed nations seems to be maintaining demand for all that they can produce. This is a strange problem, for human desires would seem to be so limitless that there would never be a problem of keeping resources busy. Yet except in wartime, the industrial nations—particularly the market economies—have rarely used all their manpower or other resources. This difficulty appears to become more pressing in the late stages of the drive to maturity and in the age of high mass consumption (in the United States, roughly the period from World War I to the present).

The problem has two aspects. One is that the beginning of economic development in the Western world, the Industrial Revolution, was also the beginning of *business cycles.* The curve of the industrial economies from the late 1700s has been not a steady upward line, but a wavy succession of troughs and crests, prosperity and de-

pression. In the troughs factories close, people are out of work, store shelves may be empty, and land may lie idle, even with great human need for goods. Figure 8.9 shows the history of business cycles in the United States. Preindustrial economies have had their fat and lean years too, since Joseph dealt with the problem in ancient Egypt, and others before him. But these are not the same thing as the business cycles of an industrial economy. Marxists claim that these cycles are inevitable under capitalism, but are not necessary to successful industrialism. They point, for instance, to the fact that the Soviet Union did not experience the Great Depression which involved all the capitalist world and has not had cycles like those of the capitalist industrial nations.

The second aspect of the problem is a tendency toward long-run *stagnation.* When development is new there always seems to be a shortage of resources for the big tasks to be done. Rising population demands constantly more consumer and capital goods. Development starts in one area (textile manufacture in England and the United States), and only gradually spreads to embrace almost all economic life. This gradual extension is what Rostow calls the "drive to maturity." Maturity is reached when industrialization has become general. As growth approaches maturity, there may be an increasing problem in keeping the economy going at full capacity. This is not the same thing as the alternation of good and bad times. It is the failure of the economy to use all its resources even in good times. This is depicted in the accompanying chart. It has been a problem in the United States in the twentieth century, and it seems that as it approaches maturity, the Soviet Union may also have this problem.

Let us look at the developed world in 1965. The United States was enjoying an affluence without parallel in history. There were more people at work than ever before, yet unemployment had been a persistent problem. In 1963 the

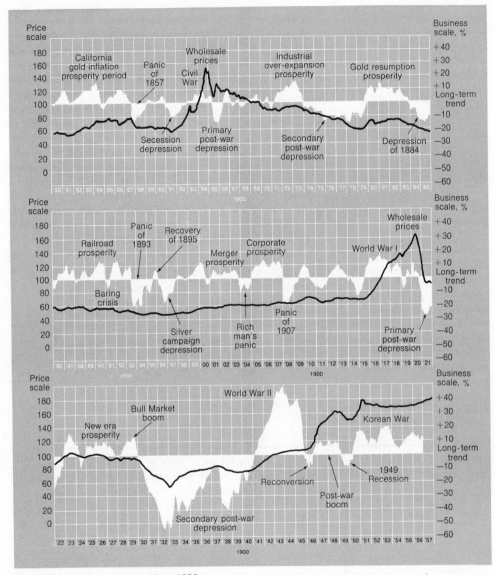

Figure 8.9. Business cycles since 1850.
Source: The Cleveland Trust Company.

United States Bureau of Labor Statistics compared unemployment in the United States and seven other industrial nations.

The 1963 unemployment rate for the U.S.—at 5.7 percent—was still five times greater than in Japan, where the rate was 1.1 percent. It was more than ten times as great as in West Germany, where it was 0.5 percent. And it was more than three times as great as Sweden's rate, more than twice as great as Italy's and well above the rates in France and Great Britain. The only country whose unemployment rate was close to the U.S. rate in 1963 was Canada.[4]

In 1963 the New York Herald-Tribune had reported that there were no more

4. "Unemployment in the U.S. and Other Industrial Nations," AFL-CIO American Federationist, August 1965, p. 13.

jobs in manufacturing than ten years before and no more jobs in transportation than in 1929. Good authority had predicted that it would be necessary to create 2 million jobs a year to replace those eliminated by automation alone.

Western Europe was showing signs of a business slump. After World War II there had been a tremendous demand to replace the damage done by the war. Backed by Marshall Plan aid from the United States, this stimulated a new take-off with high production, perhaps accounting for the low unemployment rates. By 1965 the rise may have been leveling off. The British economy was in a serious slump. There were signs that the postwar boom in West Germany was slowing down. Thousands of workers were unemployed in Italy. France was experiencing a spreading recession. Far around the world, Japan's sensational industrial growth had slumped. Warehouses were overstocked, goods were unsold, there was talk of layoffs, and university graduates were expecting to be unemployed.

In the Soviet Union, an economic periodical reported that the unemployment rate in Leningrad and Moscow was 6 to 7 percent and that it was higher in the rest of the country. The figure given for Siberia was more than 25 percent. This journal advocated public relief for the jobless. The government was establishing labor exchanges and job retraining programs. Automation seemed to be creating some problems similar to those in the United States. There appeared to be an "other Russia" as well as an "other America."

We will be in a better position to evaluate the problem of the developed economies if we return to the wheel of wealth and look at some theories of how it works, or fails to work, under different conditions. Let us examine four different versions of the wheel, as shown in Figure 8.10.

The first shows the economy as it was described by the influential French economist, Jean-Baptiste Say (1767–

1832). We have seen that the central problem of developed economies seems to be that of maintaining enough demand to keep all their resources employed. From where does demand come? Why might it fall short? According to Say's Law, demand comes from previous production: "A product is no sooner created, than it, from that instant, affords a market for other products to the full extent of its own value."[5] This sounds familiar. We might diagram this: BE CI CE. Here we can see Adam Smith's invisible hand working to ensure that nothing that is produced shall go unsold. If demand should fall short, it must be because something has interfered with the free operation of the market.

Say denied that there could be, in the ordinary working of the economy, any such thing as too little consumption. There was, however, the hard fact that the business cycle periodically created troughs or depressions in which not everything produced was bought or all resources used. Marx and the Socialists developed the view that this happened because there was not enough money in the hands of consumers to buy back all the products. How could this be? Say was wrong, these economists said, in assuming that all the income received in the process of production is necessarily spent. One can also withdraw his earnings from the stream of wealth by saving them. There can thus be goods produced for which there is no market.

If such saving happens on a large scale, the result can be a major failure of demand and a business depression. Poor people, these economists said, are not likely to create such a result by too much saving, for they have little to save. With the rich it is different. The cause of depression, they believed, lies chiefly in the maldistribution of income. Too much goes to the rich, who

5. Jean-Baptiste Say, *A Treatise on Political Economy*, 3rd Amer. ed., trans. from the 4th ed. of the French by C. R. Prinsip, Philadelphia, John Grigg, 1827, p. 78.

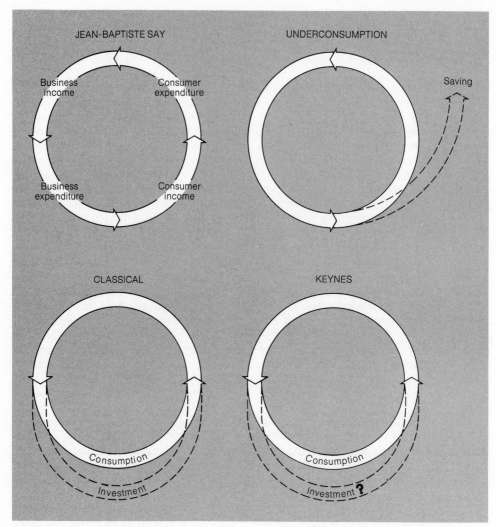

Figure 8.10. Four wheels of wealth.

save too much, thus causing a failure of demand and unemployment of workers and other resources. Moreover, since we can (in the view of these economists) expect wealth to become increasingly concentrated, depressions will become increasingly worse until the market system will be unable to survive.

This underconsumption theory (see, again, Figure 8.10) has been very widespread among Socialists and other social radicals and liberals. A modern example is a television interview with Walter Reuther, late president of the United Automobile Workers, on auto-

mation. When asked if he was worried about who will pay union dues when men are replaced by machines, he answered that he was not especially bothered about the dues, but what really worried him was who was going to buy the cars.

Economists more optimistic about the market system were quick to offer rebuttal to the underconsumption theory. The underconsumption theorists, they said, assume that money saved is withdrawn from the stream of production, but this is not generally true. If one makes more than he wants to spend, he can, it is true, simply hide it

Figure 8.11. Employment rates in Great Britain before and after World War I.
Source: William H. Beveridge, *Full Employment in a Free Society,* Norton, 1945, pp. 42, 48.

away. But most people do not do this. More commonly they do one of two things. They may invest it in new capital equipment, which will in turn create demand for new jobs. Or they may put it in a bank. In this case it will be available for borrowing by other people who want to invest. If too much should be saved, the invisible hand will be at work, for just as the price of milk falls when there is a surplus and thus corrects the oversupply, so the price of borrowing money (the interest rate) will fall if oversupply occurs. Thus saving does not generally reduce demand. It is simply an alternative way to create demand. Figure 8.10 also shows this view of the wheel of wealth.

This was the orthodox view generally accepted up to the time of the Depression of 1929. As we have seen, the shattering impact of mass unemployment caused many people to reexamine their assumptions. Two British economists were particularly important critics of the traditional view.

Sir William Beveridge (1879–1963) had for many years held rather orthodox views on unemployment, but his observations of the British economy led him to question them. For example, he saw that after World War I, high unemployment had seemingly become a normal thing in Britain. He was espe-

cially impressed by the contrast we see in Figure 8.11. From 1860 to 1920, the *lowest* employment rate ranged from 90 percent up close to 100 percent. From 1920 to 1937, the *highest* rate was barely above 90 percent. Beveridge concluded that there was a long-run trend toward permanent unemployment—long-run stagnation—in Britain.

The most influential critic of the orthodox position was John Maynard Keynes (1886–1946). He did not believe it inevitable that demand should equal production. He restated the underconsumption theory in a way which took into account the objections raised by the orthodox view. How much of income becomes demand, said Keynes, is related to the *propensity* (tendency) *to consume.* The higher a person's income, the lower his propensity to consume, the higher his propensity to save, that is, the larger the percentage he is likely to save, the smaller the percentage he is likely to spend. This conclusion seems to be borne out by actual studies of the spending of different income groups. The larger the percentage of the national income that goes to upper-income groups, the greater the possibility that income may not become demand. It is also likely that the wealthier an economy becomes as a whole, the greater the propensity to save—thus the greater the problem of keeping the wheel of wealth going as the economy approaches maturity. This last idea is not so certain, however, as the first one.

All this would make no difference if savings were all certain to become investment, but this is not true, said Keynes. Whether or not people will invest their savings depends largely upon their *expectations,* that is, when they see good times and a large chance of profit ahead, they are likely to invest. When they are pessimistic about the chance for future profit, they are likely to be reluctant to invest. The orthodox answer had said that a fall in the price of money in bad times would keep savings from piling up unspent. Actually, Keynes held, expectations are generally more important than the interest rate in people's decision to invest. When prospects of profit are very good, people will tend to borrow and invest even if the interest rate is high (because they expect profit to be even higher). When prospects are bad, they are reluctant to borrow even if money is very cheap (for why borrow even cheap money to finance a possible future loss?). Yet in time of recession or depression, when spending and investment are most needed, this is exactly how things are.

Thus there is no automatic regulator to ensure demand for all that the economy can produce. It is quite possible that demand could stay so low that an economy would more or less permanently have a substantial proportion of its resources unemployed. This would seem to describe Britain's situation in the 1920s and 1930s.

We come back then to where we were in an earlier section. According to Keynesian economics, the wheel of wealth cannot be counted upon to run itself. Full use of resources will require constant vigilance and active intervention by government. This will be of two kinds.

The first, which we call *monetary policy,* has been used even in orthodox market economies. It involves changes in the availability of money for spending and investment. In the United States these changes are guided by the Federal Reserve banks. When there is too much spending and investment, the government makes money harder to borrow. When spending and investment lag, the government may make borrowing easier. The Federal Reserve banks may raise or lower the interest rate that they charge to local banks for loans to them. This is called the "rediscount rate." Like any retailer whose wholesale prices rise or fall, local banks are likely to change their interest rate to their clients accordingly. There are also more complex monetary policies for making the money supply tighter or looser.

According to Keynes, however, changes in the price of money may be relatively ineffective at certain times when they are most needed. Then monetary measures need to be supplemented by *fiscal policies.* These involve government taxation and spending. In time of recession, government may counteract the slowness of business by cutting taxes (thus leaving more money free for spending and investment). The Johnson Administration did this in 1965. Or government may increase its spending through public works and other measures and thus supplement and stimulate investment by private individuals and businesses. The Works Progress Administration (WPA) program under Roosevelt put money in the hands of the unemployed. The Public Works Administration (PWA) under the same administration created new demand for steel, cement, and other building materials for dams, post offices, and large public construction projects. The interstate highway program, although not necessarily intended primarily for this purpose, has been a similar spur to the economy. On the other hand, if overinvestment threatens, government may raise taxes or cut back on its own public works and other spending.

Today the views of Keynes have become to a large extent the orthodox economics. Many Keynesians believe that application of their policies in the United States during the past thirty years has smoothed out, if not completely prevented, the troughs of the business cycle. They also feel that by management of the economy we have kept employment at a high level and avoided stagnation. This has been done while preserving a basically market economy and the system of private ownership.

In addition to the continuing criticism of conservatives, there are, however, some other important questions which remain to be answered. Have the Keynesian policies which have been pursued by the government since 1935 really solved the problem of recession and stagnation? In March 1933, when Roosevelt took office, there were 14,-762,000 workers unemployed. After seven years of the New Deal, in January 1940 there were still 9,163,000 people, or 16 percent of the labor force, out of work. It took World War II to restore full employment and, indeed, create a shortage of resources. The Cold War began shortly after the end of hostilities. It has continued to call for extremely high military budgets, which in recent years have amounted to at least one-sixth of the whole national income. Yet unemployment has generally continued fairly high, though not near depression levels, and recessions have threatened periodically.

What would happen if military spending were to be discontinued (this is very unlikely) or drastically reduced? In 1945 an economist, Walter Oakes, wrote an article entitled "Toward a Permanent War Economy." In it he reasoned that the American economy had not been able to maintain itself in peacetime and that we could therefore expect large military spending to become a permanent part of our life. This would be necessary to support the economy even if not for military reasons. In 1965 Gerard Piel, the editor of *Scientific American,* expressed the opinion that "we are stuck with an arms industry because it is the only

way to prop up an outmoded economy." President Eisenhower once commented that since we had never known real peace since the Depression, we had no way of knowing whether our economy could function without large military expenditure.

A second question has to do with social needs that have not been met. John Kenneth Galbraith, a leading economist and former ambassador to India, contends that our success in meeting the needs of most individual consumers has not been matched by equal success in dealing with those public needs that cannot be met by single consumers. We have put two cars in a large number of garages, but how are we to cope with the problem of mass transportation, especially in urban areas? With more people needing public recreation, how are we to keep our remaining public wilderness and beach areas from passing into private hands? How can we make any real impact on the pollution of air and water? How can we keep our landscape from becoming increasingly ugly? How can we rebuild the one-fifth of our houses that are inadequate or worse? Passing from public back to private needs, how can we elevate out of poverty the 35 million people who make up "the other America"?

A third question is whether Keynesian methods can handle the problem of automation. Suppose that automation is as revolutionary and as far-reaching as many people think, and that large masses of workers continue to be displaced. To what extent will private industry be able to find new job-creating opportunities for investment of its profits? Will there be markets for the goods produced? To what extent will government be required to develop enough public works to fill the gap? Will it be able to do so, or will automation create a permanent mass of nonworking people, perhaps supported by an annual income guaranteed by government? If so, will theirs be a dignified and rewarding life?

A number of critics feel that the

Keynesian approach is too limited to be able to deal constructively with these three problems. They believe that maintenance of a peacetime economy, provision for major public needs, and constructive use of automation all require a far larger and more positive role than government has yet played. In 1963, for example, Seymour Melman, professor of industrial engineering at Columbia University, proposed that the United States undertake a long-run peace budget of $330 billion, which would plan for a large private and public investment in crucial areas of our society.[6] His proposal was to spend the following amounts in various programs:

Education	*$30 billion*
Highways	*75*
Housing	*100*
Water and conservation	*60*
Health and hospitals	*35*
Other (air pollution, etc.)	*30*
	$330 billion

In 1966 a large group of economists and other citizens presented a "Freedom Budget" for the decade 1966–1975,[7] calling for a balance of private and public investment toward the goals of

abolition of poverty,
guaranteed full employment,
full production and high economic growth,
adequate minimum wages,
farm income parity,
guaranteed incomes for all unable to work,
a decent home for every American family,
full educational opportunity for all,
modern health services for all,

updated social security and welfare programs,
equitable tax and money policies.

There is a difference of opinion among such critics as to whether this kind of comprehensive program could be successfully carried forward without government's undertaking directly activities that have up to now been left to private enterprise. There may be similar differences of opinion as to whether private ownership will in the long run be suited to large-scale automation or whether the best technical and social use would be achieved by government ownership of large automated industries.

In the United States the most recent solution to the Keynesian problem has been an attempt to have the best of all worlds: to maintain a large military economy while at the same time expanding welfare spending and to do both without cutting into the affluence to which middle- and upper-class consumers have become accustomed. The most striking results of trying to do all three things simultaneously has been not a shortage of demand, but an excess, which has created an inflationary rise in prices. Frequently there seem to be both excess of demand and shortage—severe inflation coupled with danger of serious recession.

Another question about economic maturity: What constructive role can the developed nations play in the underdeveloped countries? They can recognize first that development of the underdeveloped world is required by the humanitarian values they profess (whether democratic, capitalist, Communist, or other). Development is also required by their long-run self-interest, both in the advantages of trade and in a stable and peaceful world. They should realize that few if any of the underdeveloped countries will be able to do the job alone, any more than the United States or the Soviet Union was able to mature economically without foreign aid. The assistance required will consist of capital and various kinds

6. Seymour Melman, *The Peace Race*, New York, George Braziller, 1962, p. 87.
7. *A "Freedom Budget" for All Americans*, New York, A. Philip Randolph Institute, October 1966.

of technical help—the services of teachers, engineers, agricultural specialists, population experts, physicians, physical and social scientists, and so on.

It must be realized that the returns will come slowly, especially if the population problem is not successfully dealt with, and that in some cases economic maturity may not come at all in the foreseeable future. It is necessary to be aware that many of the underdeveloped nations, having been long kept in a kind of childhood, are now going through an economic and political adolescence. No more than parents of adolescents should the developed nations expect that the process will always be orderly, or efficient, or peaceful, or that the underdeveloped countries will try to view the problem objectively.

At the same time it must be clear that the developed nations can only help provide the physical equipment and technical skills to get economic development started. Providing India with wheat illustrates how relief cannot be permanent. The main long-run effort must be carried through by the underdeveloped people themselves. This requires that the mass of people be admitted to economic, political, and social participation in their societies. For the developed nations, this means that their aid should be given so as to reach the ordinary people and not only to enrich the already wealthy few. This effort is helped if a large part of the aid can be given directly, in the form of capital or technical help, to local projects in which the people participate and exercise control, such as, soil improvement; housing construction; clinics and hospitals; birth control programs; building of dams, roads, and electrical power stations and lines; clearing of swamps; and establishment of small industries. It is helped, too, if the aid comes personally, as has been the case with the Peace Corps, through the participation of individuals who are willing to identify with the local people by sharing their life and their problems.

The developed nations will have to get used to the fact that the political and social forms that development takes may not be those which they most approve. It is quite clear, although it is hard for Americans to accept, that few if any underdeveloped nations will take the way of free enterprise capitalism. The writer was once talking with a high-level diplomat from a Near Eastern country, one which was a strong supporter of the United States in the Cold War. He asked the diplomat whether he felt that development in his country could be carried forward by private enterprise. "You Americans," said the diplomat, "are obsessed with this idea of free enterprise. We take it for granted that projects like large-scale irrigation, electric power, or railroad construction have to be undertaken by the government." This view is fairly typical of the underdeveloped world, yet this diplomat was strongly opposed to totalitarian communism.

Others are not so decided about their opposition to communism. The underdeveloped world is much impressed by the economic achievements of both the Soviet Union and China. Not having experienced any kind of political democracy, many countries are not seriously troubled by its absence under communism. Leaders may feel that their illiterate masses will not be ready for self-government for a long time in any event. They may feel that democracy, even if possible, would be too slow and inefficient for the great leap forward which they are in a hurry to make. However, many, like the late President Nasser of Egypt, prefer an independent, native nationalism to dependence on the Soviet Union and China. They have experienced manipulation by the Communist powers, and they do not like it. Americans are prone to believe that if one is not a free enterprise capitalist, he must be a Communist. This is not the case.

In rural areas of the underdeveloped countries, there is a strong fear and distrust of the city and of centralized authority, of whatever kind. This is the way, for example, the average South Vietnamese has for a long time felt about Saigon. In Africa tribal leaders often strongly oppose efforts of nationalistic governments to destroy their tribal separateness. This was one of the issues at stake in the bitter Biafra conflict of 1969. No doubt the leaders feel this way partly because they do not want to lose their power, but they also feel that the traditional village and tribal life possesses strong values which they do not want to see replaced by the impersonality, the excessive materialism, or the frantic stress of Westernized urban life. If this opposition to centralization of power is supported by land reforms, opportunities for education, and local industries which will raise mass standards of living, development may well move toward some form of democratic middle way.

WORK AND LEISURE

We need now to look at the economic process in terms of the experience that people have at work and away from work. So far we have been discussing economic activity as a means for earning the necessities and perhaps luxuries of life. But work is not only a means. The time we spend at work is life itself. Indeed, for most human beings work has always been most of life.

What does work mean to people? We must be careful not to jump to the conclusion that work, always and everywhere, means what it does to us in our world. To many of the Greek philosophers, contemplation was the highest form of life, and work was fit only for slaves. To the monk in the medieval monastery, on the other hand, work was a way to worship God. A Brazilian peon may see work as a way to make the income he has always expected. A Hopi Indian may regard work as a cooperative activity for the common good. The peon's brother in São Paolo, and the Hopi's Americanized cousin may both see work as an

avenue to getting ahead. The experience of work is different in an agricultural society and an industrial economy. It may again be changed drastically by automation.

A good way to make the problem personal is for each of us to ask himself, "If I were guaranteed an annual income of $5000 for the rest of my life, what would I do? Would I never work again? Would I spend my time in loafing, or in travel? Would I work at something other than my present job, or than the career I am planning? Or would I stay in the same line of work?" Each person's answer will tell what work means to him.

The first meaning of work always has been, and still is for most people: *survival.* We do not need any complicated reasons to tell us why most human beings have worked. They have had to, if they were not to die. The Greek word for work is best translated "drudgery." In the Judaeo-Christian tradition, Adam's sin doomed his descendants to earn their bread by the sweat of their brows.

Most of the human race, like the African Bushmen and the vast majority of inhabitants of the underdeveloped countries today, have been the victim of scarce resources and primitive technology. Others, in more advanced economies, have been slaves or serfs, legally bound to work for others to avoid physical pain or death.

We should not be misled, however, by the fact that most people in the developed countries have not been legally enslaved. Large numbers of the legally free can best be described as wage slaves. In the mines of England in the early Industrial Revolution, women sometimes worked naked. In the United States, 40 to 60 percent of all factory work before the Civil War was done by children. In his famous defense of slavery before the United States Senate in 1839, John C. Calhoun contended that slaves had better working conditions, better relations with their employers, and more economic security than the free workers in

European and northern factories. His reasoning was not totally wrong.

Migratory workers in the United States today generally live in the poorest of sanitary conditions with few legal protections and substandard wages. The present condition of many factory employees is accurately described by the writer Harvey Swados, who worked on an automobile assembly line to gather material for a novel. Most of the workers he knew, said Swados, hated their jobs and worked only because they had to. He added that if one hears a strange rattle in his new car or smells a strange odor, it may be only a batch of bolts or the remains of the lunch which a worker has thrown into the car as it went by him on the assembly line. He has taken the only available way to him to express how he feels about his job.

As people attain the necessities of life, their desires usually do not cease. If you were offered $5000 a year, you would be relieved of the pressure of sheer survival, but you might well argue that you would not have enough to develop yourself fully as a human being. Your ability to travel, and thus share in the whole gamut of human experience, would be limited. One cannot support a family and buy very many books, records, or original paintings, or attend many plays or concerts, on $5000 a year. He will find it hard to give his children a first-class education. Many people, given a better-than-survival income, would choose to go on working in order to attain a considerably higher *standard of living*.

There are other kinds of desires, too. For many people it is very important to attain a certain *status* in society. This, to a large extent, requires the ability to spend in certain ways. In the last year of the nineteenth century, the sociologist and economist, Thorstein Veblen, in a fascinating book called *The Theory of the Leisure Class,* coined the term "conspicuous consumption." This described the behavior of people who consume, not for survival, not even for immediate personal enjoyment, but for the sake of their appearance in the eyes of others. Since that time many sociologists have studied status seeking.

Middle-class and upper-class status require the ability to live at a certain kind of address, in a certain kind of home, to dress and furnish one's home in a certain way, to drive a certain car(s), to send one's children to certain schools, to entertain in a certain manner, to belong to certain clubs and organizations, to support certain charities and other community activities, to vacation at certain places in certain ways, and to keep abreast of constantly changing fads and fashions in all these things. To do so requires money, which generally demands work. The advertising media encourage one to buy "the most expensive perfume in the world," to drink the beer that will elevate one's status, to live in a "prestige community." Sometimes they frankly announce that a product is a status symbol.

All our meanings of work have so far been related to what one's earnings can buy, but man does not live by bread alone; work also has less material meanings. Rather closely related to status is *identification* with the organization for which one works. We saw in an earlier chapter how in-group membership may enable a person to "borrow" the power of the group. In an organizational society, where organizations are big and powerful and the individual is small and powerless, one may gain a sense of power through the very submission that is required of him. This is not at all the same as satisfaction in working for a company that makes a good product.

The author once used to be visited by a college book salesman who was very proud of being a member of one of the largest firms in publishing. He boasted, indeed, that his company's representatives had the highest rate of ulcers in the business! The United States Marine Corps develops this kind of intense identification on the part of its members with the reputation of the corps for discipline, toughness, and masculinity.

In his novel *Women in Love,* D. H. Lawrence describes brilliantly how this kind of identification operated when a British coal mine was mechanized and the men "reduced to mechanical instruments." "The joy went out of their lives," but they submitted, and "even got a further satisfaction."

> There was a new world, a new order, strict, terrible, inhuman, but satisfying in its very destructiveness. The men were satisfied to belong to the great and wonderful machine, even whilst it destroyed them. It was what they wanted. . . . They were exalted by belonging to this great and superhuman system which was beyond feeling or reason, something really godlike. Their hearts died within them, but their souls were satisfied.[8]

Some people appear to be driven to work, and in work, by an inner *compulsion.* The author once worked in the service room of a large cafeteria, where food was prepared for the cafeteria line. The workers were poorly paid, and the mangement had not hired enough people to do the work. The workers resented both these things. They would seem to have had good reason to do no more than a "good day's work," at most. Yet the crew leader maintained a feverish pace, and the rest of the crew followed. Often no one stopped to eat his own meal, or one grabbed it while he worked, standing up. The author once said to the crew leader, "Why don't you slow down? They could hire more men. You're driving us all crazy." The only reply was, "We've got to get the work done."

Another example comes from the other end of the income and status ladder. In 1963 the American Management Association did a study of 335

top executives, with an average salary of $68,000 a year. One might have supposed that they would have earned the right to take it easy. Yet the survey showed that "almost every one of a president's waking hours are devoted to the job." These executives had virtually no leisure time for family or recreation. Even vacations were work-oriented.

Perhaps both these groups, without really knowing it, were expressing the Puritan ethic of work. Perhaps they were carrying out the older scriptural instruction, "Whatsoever thy hand findeth to do, do it with thy might." Perhaps they were suffering from a neurotic compulsiveness.

Yet the corporation presidents, at least, might have claimed another motive. A different group of executives was asked a question similar to the one we posed at the beginning of this section, "If you were given the choice of retiring now at your present salary, would you keep on working?" Ninety percent said yes. A good number of them, no doubt, would have spoken of their *love for their work,* for this is a part of work experience which is probably as old as the motive of survival. Let us examine some aspects of the love of work.

One is the aesthetic pleasure in craftsmanship. When primitive men painted on the cave walls of Spanish Altamira and the French Dordogne valley (see page 248), what was the function of their art? Almost certainly a large part of it was very immediately concerned with survival. Perhaps their drawing was an anatomy lesson which prepared their eyes and muscles for the hunt. Probably also, by reproducing an image of their game, they expected magically to multiply the quantity of animals or to bring them under their power. But practical ends alone cannot explain the playfulness, the lightness of touch, and the evident delight in their work which went into these paintings. Through 20,000 years since then, innumerable workmen of all kinds have shared their joy of craftsmanship.

8. D. H. Lawrence, *Women in Love,* New York, Modern Library, 1922, p. 263.

Closely related to the aesthetic aspect, but somewhat more somber, is gratification in mastery of one's environment. We can see this tendency very early in the child's mud pies and sand castles, his dams and bridges. Alexander Graham Bell once defined an inventor as, "A man who looks around upon the world and is not contented with things as they are." This is a motive very strong in modern Western culture. We often call it "Faustian," after Goethe's eternally restless figure of Faust. The psychoanalyst Robert Lindner has suggested that man differs from all other animals in that they adapt themselves to their environment, but man adapts his environment to himself. He calls this urge the "instinct of rebellion."

> *Because of the instinct of rebellion man has never been content with the limits of his body: it has led him to extend his senses almost indefinitely, so that his fingers now probe space, his senses magnify the nuclei of atoms, and his ears detect whispers from the bottoms of seas. Because of the instinct of rebellion man has never been content with the limits of his mind: it has led him to inquire into secrets of the universe, to seek the very mysteries of creation. Because of the instinct of rebellion, man has never been content, finally, with the limits of his life: it has caused him to deny death and to war with mortality.*[9]

Work also gives the gratification that comes from cooperation with others. In a northern state one October afternoon before the first frost, the author picked green tomatoes which were to be spread out on tables to ripen. His 6-year-old nephew, entering the room where the sorting was in progress, exclaimed with gleaming eyes, "Oh boy! Work!" He felt, no doubt, some of the urge to manipulate things of which

9. Robert Lindner, *Must You Conform?*, New York, Holt, Rinehart and Winston, 1956, pp. 175–176.

Lindner spoke, but also the pleasant prospect of doing this as part of a happy group. For centuries farmers have transformed the work of planting, harvesting, and building by doing it as communal activity. Craftsmen have developed close personal relationships in their small shops. Industrial engineers have repeatedly found even today that the social relations in which people work may be more important in determining how well they work than are their physical surroundings.

There is another kind of human bond in work—the desire to serve one's fellow man through what he produces. We tend to be cynical about motives, to ask of any person who seems to be altruistic, "What's in it for him?" Yet the simple desire to serve others may explain more than anything else the life work of many physicians and nurses, priests and rabbis, Peace Corps workers and VISTA volunteers, teachers, scientists and engineers, psychiatrists and social workers, artists and craftsmen, executives, public servants, revolutionary leaders. Einstein once said that ideally the scientist carries out the great commandment of the Hebrew prophets, to make the world a better and more just place. At their best all the great religions, at least of the West, have given this compelling meaning to work. One's activity becomes not a job, but a calling, a vocation; his attitude toward it a dedication and a commitment. One need not, of course, be formally religious to find such a meaning for his work and life.

We have said that the meaning of work is different under different situations. How is it affected by the great change from a preindustrial to a modern industrialized economy?

Consider a society like that of Europe in the Middle Ages, or the United States at the time of George Washington, or most of the underdeveloped world today. Most of the people are engaged in farming, and a few are small scale craftsmen. Most struggle on the edge of survival, for their technology is very primitive. The tools used by American farmers at the time of Washington, for example, had not changed very much from those used in Egypt 5000 years earlier. Neither have those used in most underdeveloped countries today. In this kind of society, farmer and craftsman turn out their product with their own hands and these few simple tools. The peasant lives in a small, fairly close community, where most people are accustomed to work together. The craftsman works alone or employs a small number of helpers. The market for the products of both farmer and craftsman is small. The farmer produces for his own use, or for his landlord, or for occasional small markets or fairs. The craftsman works (as in the early Middle Ages) for a nobleman or (as later) for a local market in a small town or city. Thus the relationship of both farmer and craftsman to product, to fellow worker, and to customers is likely to be a personal one. Each of us may think back to the meanings of work described earlier and ask himself which of them are likely to be present here.

The most obvious change brought about by industrialism (England after 1775, the United States after 1870, Japan today) is the substitution of machines for human muscle. The first obvious effect of mechanization is increase in output. Nowhere has this been more glowingly described than by Marx and Engels in *The Communist Manifesto:*

> *The bourgeoisie, during its rule of scarce one hundred years, has created more massive and more colossal productive forces than have all preceding generations together. Subjection of nature's forces to man, machinery, application of chemistry to industry and agriculture, steam navigation, railways, electric telegraphs, clearing of whole continents for cultivation, canalization of rivers, whole populations conjured up out of the ground—what earlier century had even a presentiment that such productive forces slumbered in the lap of social labor?*[10]

This increased production should make the problem of survival less pressing for everybody, but such has not usually been the case. The first effect of the Industrial Revolution in England was unemployment of many workers whose place was taken by machines. Some found new jobs, but some never did. Thomas Malthus and economists who followed him questioned whether industrialism can permanently raise the living standard of the masses of people. They put forward an "iron law of wages," which held that as living standards tend to rise, increase in the number of children of workers will cancel out the gains. Thus overall wages cannot rise in the long run.

The spread of birth control techniques in the later stages of industrialism has clearly raised living standards in the most developed nations. Yet in those underdeveloped countries where population growth exceeds growth in GNP, the iron law of wages is still a grim reality.

Almost a century after the Industrial Revolution, the English philosopher, John Stuart Mill, could say that it was doubtful whether the overall lot of man had been improved by the Industrial Revolution. In the United States, the economist and philosopher Henry George, in his book *Progress and Poverty* (1879), argued that industrial progress had elevated the upper-income groups but worsened the lot of large numbers of poor people.

The use of large and expensive machinery leads to a new form of social organization of work—the massing of people into factories or other large business organizations. Workers are detached from the land and brought together in cities. Both at work and away from work they are likely to lose

10. Karl Marx and Friedrich Engels, *Manifesto of the Communist Party,* Great Books of the Western World, vol. 50, Chicago, Encyclopaedia Britannica, Inc., 1952, p. 421.

the close personal relationships of a rural community or small town and to feel part of an impersonal mass. At the same time, the volume of production increases enormously. The worker who formerly produced personally for his own use or for a small local market now produces for a horde of faraway customers whom he neither knows nor even sees.

The substitution of machines for human labor relieves much of the physical strain and drudgery of labor, but it is likely to change the relationship of the worker to his work in another way. The tool, which men used before industrialism, is an extension of the power of a man. It is his servant, under his control. But the machine tends to make the man, instead, *its* servant. He may feel that the machine controls him rather than vice versa. This seems to have been the feeling of the assembly line workers described by Swados.

This is especially true because the machine greatly increases the division of labor. In *The Wealth of Nations,* Adam Smith tells how the making of a pin, previously the work of skilled craftsmen, is broken down into many operations in a pin factory. No writer since Smith has added much to his brilliant description of how, and why, the division of labor enormously increases output. But Smith also saw another side of this specialization.

> *The man whose whole life is spent in performing a few simple operations . . . has no occasion to exert his understanding, or to exercise his invention. . . . He naturally loses, therefore, the habit of such exertion, and generally becomes as stupid and ignorant as it is possible for a human creature to become. But in every improved and civilized society this is the state into which the laboring poor . . . must . . . fall, unless government takes some pains to prevent it.*[11]

11. Adam Smith, *The Wealth of Nations,* London, Routledge, 1890, p. 613.

America's poverty belt in Appalachia would uphold Mill's view that industrial progress does not improve the overall lot of man.

We see that there have been in industrialism strong tendencies toward the *alienation* of the worker from his work, his fellow workers, and his customers. By alienation we mean a loss of the sense that any of them are his own. The last 75 years have in some ways modified this situation. It had seemed in the nineteenth century that industrialism was going to reduce most of the population to an unskilled mass, but this has not happened. The development of machine tools has restored some control and skill to the operator. The percentage of unskilled workers has decreased, the proportion of people in factories has declined, and there has been a great increase in the number of sales people, government employees, white-collar workers, salaried professional people, technicians, and other people trained in the physical and social sciences.

But there is another factor in the modern economy which alienates the worker. This is the fact that the worker

CLASS DIVISIONS IN THE UNITED STATES: 1870–1940

(in thousands)	1940	1930	1920	1910	1870
Farmers	5,265	6,012	6,387	6,132	3,100
Owners	3,227	3,463	3,594	3,864	2,325
Tenants	2,038	2,549	2,433	2,268	775
Working class	29,518	25,813	22,665	19,730	6,035
Industrial	16,124	16,198	15,118	12,982	3,225
Manufactures	9,250*	9,150	9,450	7,425	1,812
Mining	824	887	982	862	179
Transportation	2,950*	2,961	2,386	2,204	465
Construction	3,100*	3,200	2,300	2,490	768
Farm laborers	2,312	2,606	2,217	2,658	1,500*
Other workers	11,082	7,456	5,329	4,089	1,310
Middle class	16,633	14,884	11,682	8,870	2,289
Old—enterprisers	3,863	3,751	3,350	3,261	1,532*
Business	3,382	3,304	2,943	2,895	1,304
Professional	481	446	406	366	128
New—salaried	12,769	11,580	8,332	5,609	756
Technical-M'g'rial	2,062	1,966	1,527	999	129
Professional	2,660	2,413	1,581	1,179	204
Clerical	3,889	3,345	2,719	1,403	68
Sales people	3,347	3,003	1,877	1,595	282
Public service	439	418	290	208	48
Upper bourgeoisie	240	300	200	—	—
Total	51,656	47,457	40,935	34,733	11,424

* Partly estimated.
Source: Lewis Corey, "Problems of Peace: IV. The Middle Class," The Antioch Review (Spring 1945), p. 69.

typically does not own or participate in controlling either the instruments with which he works or the product he creates. At the time of Thomas Jefferson, 80 percent of all Americans were self-employed. In 1950 only 13 percent were their own bosses. The rest were typically employees of rather large organizations. Their labor had become a *commodity,* bought and sold on the market like any other good or service.

Let us look at how this development of an employee society affects the experience of work. First, a comparison. In a simple, preindustrial capitalist economy, where one owns his own small farm, shop, or business, he can have a sense of immediate control over his life. This is the ideal of the market system. Even if he is one of a few employees in a small shop, he may have a good deal of this sense. On a *kibbutz* in Israel, where almost everything is cooperatively owned, one does not personally own the instruments of production, but may have a strong sense of involvement in a common enterprise. In a cooperative store or factory in Sweden (or England, or even the United States), one again does not personally own the capital equipment with which he works, but as a member of the cooperative, he may feel that collectively he does. In a Yugoslavian factory, the nationally owned plant is theoretically, at least, controlled by a local council of workers. Some of the same feelings are probably present. Many people who work for the Tennessee Valley Authority in the United States seem to feel a sense that this publicly owned corporation and its activities represent their interest. Many individuals in a new, revolutionary, "planned" society like Cuba or China undoubtedly feel that they are working for goals which are their own.

When one has a sense of participation, in any of these forms, it may be possible for him to have a feeling of gratification and creative meaning in his work, even if his job is mechanical and routine. But these situations are not typical in the largest economies.

Undoubtedly many Russians today feel that they are working meaningfully for the revolution, but there are without doubt large numbers who feel that they no longer work for themselves or for any real interest they share, but rather to enhance the power and wealth of privileged bureaucrats over whom they have no control. In the large corporations in the United States, one clearly works for the profit of stockholders and controls neither his tools nor his product. One may become an organization man and keep some sense of belonging by identifying his life with the impersonal enterprise. But large numbers of people almost inevitably feel alienated from their whole work experience.

Under such circumstances the simple motives of craftsmanship, fellowship, and service are likely to disappear. Work is likely to become mainly a job, a way in which one compulsively pursues money and status.

How will automation affect the meaning of work? We must not be carried away by exaggerated science fiction accounts of a completely automated future. As far ahead as we can see, there will certainly be large areas of life—in business, the professions, services, public employment, and industry itself—where neither automation nor highly advanced mechanization will apply. Nevertheless, the possible effects of automation are immense. At present automated machinery has not been introduced as widely as it could be because of fear of what might happen if masses of workers are displaced. If we can find ways to overcome these fears, by spreading the gains of automation, we shall undoubtedly be on the brink of one of the great revolutions in human history.

Automation can go much further than advanced mechanization in turning the burden of hard physical work over to machines. It can never, as has been said, completely eliminate it. Automation can enormously increase our productivity. Thus it can alter all our relationships of work and leisure. Adam's curse may well be removed—we may no longer have to earn our bread by the sweat of our faces (Genesis 3:19). Leisure can be enormously increased. By the beginning of the twenty-first century it is quite conceivable that the American work week could be reduced to fifteen hours or less. We could probably do this while increasing our living standard and providing large amounts of capital and equipment for the underdeveloped world. Up to now the vast majority of people have assumed that work is the major part of life and have hoped to salvage a few crumbs of leisure. After automation the situation may well be reversed. In the mass consumption economies, leisure may occupy most of people's time, and work for money may require only a few odd hours.

The revolution of leisure will require a drastic revision in all our thinking. It would seem that leisure should be no problem, that the only real problem is work! With all the things to be done in the world, how could one ever have too much time? Yet since the Industrial Revolution, conservatives have always argued against shortening the work week on the ground that the poor will not know what to do with their leisure. There has been considerable ground for this fear. People who have known nothing other than incessant work and have never been educated for anything else often devote what little free time they have to the cruder forms of sex, violence, and escape. Learning how to use leisure creatively may be for them a slow process. This is one reason why it will probably be much better gradually to spread leisure by reducing the work week for everyone than suddenly to create a class of workless people, even if they are given a guaranteed annual income. This will enable public schools, adult education programs, and public and private recreational agencies to help everyone prepare for the new experience of free time.

It is not only the poor who will have to revise their attitude toward leisure. Retired people of all classes, of whom we already have an increasing number, very commonly do not know what to do with their time. Sometimes the shock of being thrown into a sudden vacuum of leisure actually leads them to an early death. In modern Western society, large numbers of people have been strongly guided by the Puritan ethic of more or less compulsive work. We have been inclined to regard leisure as waste or even sin. If the curse of Adam is eliminated and machines take over a large part of our work, we shall have to learn to give more value to "just living," to life which is not a means to money, or status, or any other end outside itself. Otherwise, we shall find ourselves feeling bored, restless, guilty, or seeing leisure only as an opportunity to make more money by moonlighting on a second or third job.

As automation is extended, we should expect people to seek in leisure many of the values that men have previously found in work. As we have seen, industrialism has removed many of the most immediate work gratifications. Automation generally demands relatively light and fairly skilled work, but in most cases it is very far from the work of the craftsman. By turning most of our lives into leisure, automation may enable us to recapture these pre-industrial values.

People will be able to expand the role played by their hobbies, by do-it-yourself interests, by arts and crafts, and by teaching and learning of all kinds. Leisure will give more time for the social satisfaction of doing such things together. It should expand the opportunity for deliberately choosing to serve others. With a 15-hour week, groups of people might voluntarily devote unpaid overtime for production earmarked for disadvantaged peoples. More people might follow the lead of the Peace Corps, the medical ship *Hope,* and Quaker and other service organizations in volunteering time for service in underdeveloped countries. Intelligently used, the increase of leisure can mean a great widening of all human horizons.

Suggestions for further reading

Those interested in contrasting the basic points of view of market and planning should make (or renew) at least a passing acquaintance with ADAM SMITH'*s* The Wealth of Nations *(2 vols., Irwin, 1963, paper) and* The Communist Manifesto *by* KARL MARX *and* FRIEDRICH ENGELS *(Penguin Pelican, 1968, paper). Recent factual criticisms of the market economy appear in* MICHAEL HARRINGTON'*s* The Other America *(Penguin Pelican, 1962, paper).* JOHN KENNETH GALBRAITH'*s* The Affluent Society *(New American Library, paper) and the collection entitled* Poverty in America, *edited by* LOUIS A. FERMAN, JOYCE L. KORNBLUH, *and* ALAN HABER *(rev. ed. University of Michigan Press, 1968), are also helpful. A very widely read (and debated) attack on the idea of planning appears in* FREDERICK HAYEK, The Road to Serfdom *(University of Chicago Press, 1944, paper). A more recent discussion favorable to free enterprise is* Capitalism and Freedom *by* MILTON FRIEDMAN, *a University of Chicago economist (University of Chicago Press, 1962, paper).*

Few people talk these days about the problems of economic development without some reference to WALT W. ROSTOW'*s* The Stages of Economic Growth *(rev. ed., Norton, 1962, paper). A readable and very competent book on this subject is* The Great Ascent *by* ROBERT HEILBRONER *(Harper & Row, 1963, paper). The cultural problems of economic development are illustrated in a number of case studies in* Cultural Patterns and Technical Change, *edited by* MARGARET MEAD *(New American Library, paper). It would be hard to find a more insightful and brilliant treatment of this topic than appears in* Black Power, *the late Negro novelist* RICHARD WRIGHT'*s account of his 1953 visit to the African Gold Coast (Harper & Row, 1954). Those interested in the political aspects of development may like the collection by* GABRIEL ALMOND *and* JAMES S. COLEMAN, The Politics of the Developing Areas *(Princeton University Press, 1960).*

A strong presentation of the Keynesian approach to the mature economies is Full Employment in a Free Society *by* SIR WILLIAM BEVERIDGE, *the author of the British social security system (2nd ed., Hillary, 1960). Sharp disagreement is expressed by* HENRY HAZLITT *in* Failure of the New Economics: An Analysis of Keynesian Fallacies *(Van Nostrand Reinhold, 1959). Closer to the new economics is* C. E. AYRES' The Theory of Economic Progress *(Shocken, 1962, paper). Its scope is indicated by the subtitle:* A Study of the Fundamentals of Economic Development and Cultural Change. *Its theme is the constant conflict between technical progress and the resistance of tradition. An extensive research study by* SEBASTIAN DE GRAZIA *on the changing balance between work time and free time is summarized in* Of Time, Work, and Leisure *(Doubleday, paper).*

Chapter nine
The political process

The political aspect of society, we saw in Chapter six, involves decisions that have (1) authority (2) within a given territorial area (3) because it is felt that they are rightfully or legitimately made. It is one aspect of the total process of social control, which also involves folkways, mores, technicways, and social institutions other than the political. In primitive cultures the political aspect is not sharply separated from the rest of society. With the development of an economic surplus, however, political activity tends to become specialized in a separate group, which operates through special machinery of government.

In this chapter we shall study the political system in greater depth than was possible earlier.

LEGISLATIVE, EXECUTIVE, AND JUDICIAL FUNCTIONS

A central part of the political process in all advanced societies is the formal machinery of government, which tends to divide itself into three functions: legislative (the making of laws), executive (the administration of laws), and judicial (the interpretation of laws). In the American political system, there are three governmental branches corresponding to these three functions.

This is not the place for a beginning course in formal American government; we can only review the outlines. Congress is primarily a legislative body, divided into two houses. A large part of its work is done in committees, some

of which have great power to influence legislation. The president's main function is executive. Under him is the cabinet, consisting of the various secretaries who head the chief administrative departments. The main judicial functions of the federal government rest in various levels of courts, with the Supreme Court at the top. In general the formal organization of the three functions on the state level parallels that of the national government. Municipal and other local governments have more varied structures. In the American federal form of government, certain powers are reserved for the states, others for the federal government, and some are exercised by both. The power of the central government has increased in various ways with the passage of time.

The separation of powers in distinct governmental branches is largely peculiar to modern representative governments. Absolute monarchies do not have separate effective legislatures or an independent judiciary. The same is largely true of modern totalitarian governments. We should, moreover, beware of exaggerating the extent to which the three powers are separated in our own government. In studying political matters, we need especially to recognize that what is formally true on paper, may not very well represent what actually happens.

The executive branch of government, for example, performs many legislative functions. The power of the president, or governor, to veto laws may give him as much weight in the law-making process as many legislators combined. Cabinet departments or other administrative bodies established by the legislature may possess wide powers to interpret the law through administrative orders and rules. The Employment Act of 1946, as an example, established only a broad framework, within which the president's Council of Economic Advisors was given wide powers. President Eisenhower was able to desegregate the armed forces by executive order.

The president customarily proposes an extensive program of legislation in his State of the Union messages. Congress is under considerable pressure to adopt this program, although it may resist some of the pressure. There are many ways in which the executive may exercise persuasion on legislators. Uncooperative individuals may not receive the support of the executive or the party machinery when they seek reelection. They may find that bills for expenditures in their districts are not passed because of executive pressure. They may be given inferior committee assignments. The executive may make legal or other expert help available to legislative committees involved in drafting legislation. The president may go on television or make public speeches for or against pending bills.

In military affairs, the president or the Defense Department may take over large areas of policy making on the grounds that in the national security area Congress cannot be as competent as military specialists. An extreme illustration is the waging of major war without the congressional declaration required by the Constitution. To a lesser degree, other executive departments will argue that their superiority in technical knowledge makes them best fitted to shape policy. In an age of specialization, there is considerable logic in their arguments, and thus the executive tends to take over an increasing number of legislative functions.

The judiciary is in a similar situation. In theory courts are supposed only to interpret the law, not to make it. They measure a case up against the law as one would measure a bolt of cloth against a yardstick. For them to do any more is to exceed their proper role. Thus, for example, in the *Brown* v. *Topeka* case invalidating school segregation, the federal Supreme Court justices were charged by some conservatives with having acted as sociologists rather than jurists.

Common sense will tell us that the theoretical view of the function of the judiciary is not and cannot be realistic. There are few cases on which a competent lawyer cannot put up some kind of fairly reasonable argument for his client because the meaning of the law is almost always subject to different interpretations or there is a question as to what law fits the case. As society becomes more complex, legislatures are more likely to pass laws laying down a general framework, with details to be filled in by experience. When they interpret such laws, judges are really making the law, often just as much as the legislature which originally passed it.

We can illustrate the legislative function of the judiciary by considering the history of the interpretation of the Constitution by the federal Supreme Court. In theory the Court simply reads the Constitution and measures a case against it. The actual fact may not quite be as one Supreme Court judge once suggested, that the Constitution is like a Jello mold into which the judges can pour anything they wish. However, the Constitution is a document drawn up nearly 200 years ago in a preindustrial society which was still 90 percent rural. Sometimes judges try, through historical research, to determine what writers of particular Constitutional clauses actually intended at the time. Seldom is this crystal clear. At other times they are more inclined to ask what the founding fathers would mean if they were alive today. This leaves even more room for interpretation. The result is that the judges are constantly "making" the Constitution and in so doing cannot help being influenced by their own personal and partisan biases.

It has been suggested that the Supreme Court has played three roles in American history. (1) Up to the Civil War, its decisions mainly strengthened the federal government against the states. This, on the whole, represented the interest of eastern industrial and financial groups against the farmers of the South and West. (2) From the Civil War to about 1937, the Court strongly favored business. Laws passed by legislatures pertaining to child labor, minimum wage, and workmen's compensation were, for example, declared unconstitutional. In the 1930s there was strong criticism of the Court as a group of prejudiced conservatives. An influential book was *The Nine Old Men,* by Drew Pearson and Robert S. Allen. President Roosevelt tried, unsuccessfully, to change the Court by enlarging it. The criticism did, however, contribute to a change in Court decisions. (3) Since 1937 the Court has handed down a number of decisions involving civil rights and civil liberties. Examples are the school desegregation decision and the decision that Jehovah's Witnesses cannot be required to salute the flag. The segregation decision, in particular, brought strong criticism of the Court, especially of Chief Justice Warren— this time as a group of prejudiced liberals. Again, criticism seemed to have its effect, and decisions became somewhat more conservative.

All this should not be taken to mean that judges simply forget their oath of office and vote their biases. On the contrary, the records of Supreme Court justices indicate that it is rather difficult to predict, from his previous behavior, how a man will vote on the Court. Justice Hugo Black, whose nomination was opposed on the grounds that he had once belonged to the Ku Klux Klan, became a very liberal judge. We can say, however, that judges do create laws by interpretation and that their interpretations tend to reflect their personal experience and the temper of the times.

The executive and legislative branches also exercise judicial functions. Administrative agencies may actually assume a good many functions of courts. The National Labor Relations Board hears charges of violation of established labor procedures, and the Fair Employment Practices Commission does the same in the case of equal rights in employment. Local Selective Service boards and appeal boards bear a resemblance to courts. The Constitution gives the Senate the power to sit as a court in impeaching the president. It also enables Congress to regulate courts. In the post–Civil War case of *ex parte McCardle,* the Supreme Court was forbidden by Congress from hearing the case on appeal at all.

Congress and the state legislatures do perform more legislative than judicial or executive functions, and the same principle holds for the main functions of the other branches. What we have seen, however, is that only in a general way are the three functions segregated. There is another important point at which the political process is much more than appears on paper. To limit the political aspect of society to the formal organization of government would be to miss most of the reality of political life. Let us therefore see now what lies behind the activities of legislatures, administrators, and courts.

How are political decisions and policies related to the whole community? Theoretically the legislative and executive branches are elected by the people, and the judiciary is generally selected by these branches. Therefore, all serve as delegates for the people. Is this true? Does government serve some kind of general interest or does the democratic process disguise the power of minorities who actually run society? This is a question which we raised in Chapter six when we posed the three views of the state: (1) as representative of a general will, (2) as the agent of a ruling class, and (3) as a balance of power among pressure groups.

If we examine the literature of political science in the past forty or fifty years, we find that one of its great accomplishments has been the demonstration of the multifunctionalism of modern political institutions. Thus it has shown that the courts not only adjudicate but also legislate; that the bureaucracy is one of the most important sources of legislation; that legislative bodies affect both administration and adjudication; that pressure groups initiate legislation and participate in administration; and that the media of communication represent interests and sometimes initiate legislation.

—*Gabriel Almond,* The Politics of the Developing Areas, *Princeton, N.J., Princeton University Press, 1960, pp. 17–18.*

INTEREST AND PRESSURE

Let us approach the problem by looking first at groups which are especially able to shape the political process in their own interest. Such pressure or interest groups shape public opinion through access to the mass media. They are able to influence elections through campaign contributions and other support of favored candidates. They help shape legislation through lobbying activity. They try to get their own members or people favorable to them appointed to administrative bodies and to influence their decisions. They also try to influence judicial appointments and are able to shape the law by providing legal talent to argue cases.

In local communities one usually finds business and industrial interests playing a major role in politics. Banks, power and light companies, department stores, real estate corporations, and particular local industries are likely to carry a great deal of weight. Labor unions usually have some power, especially the craft unions which are concerned with such matters as building regulations. Negroes and other minority groups may be visibly represented and push their special interests. The clergy may be somewhat important, at least as window dressing to give respectability. The press usually plays a rather powerful role. News-

papers depend upon advertisers for a large part of their income and are reluctant to offend them in their news or editorial policy. At election time newspaper recommendation of candidates may be a powerful influence on the voter perplexed by long slates of candidates or complicated issues.

While some students of the subject question some of his conclusions, Floyd Hunter's study, *Top Leadership, U.S.A.,* certainly contains much truth:

> *A small group of men in any particular community become known as top leaders, policy makers, opinion leaders, or decision makers. As a top-drawer circuit of influential persons, they most often represent the largest local industries, banks, law firms, commercial houses, and newspapers. A fringe group of ranking politicians, educators, clergymen, and occasionally one or two labor leaders may be called upon to sit in council with the nuclear group when a community-wide project or issue is up for discussion.*[1]

On the state and national level, business interests are organized into trade associations. Among the influential ones are the associations of retail

1. Floyd Hunter, *Top Leadership, U.S.A.,* Chapel Hill, The University of North Carolina Press, 1959, pp. 5–6.

druggists, bankers, retail dry goods dealers, railroads, insurance companies, brewers, coal mine owners, cement and iron manufacturers, and aircraft industrialists. Most of these, in turn, belong to the United States Chamber of Commerce. Organized in 1912, this includes also local chambers of commerce and has as its slogan, "What Helps Business Helps You." The other major business interest group, the National Association of Manufacturers (NAM), was founded in 1896 to oppose organized labor and antitrust legislation. Theoretically it includes only manufacturing firms, and these on the basis of individual rather than group membership. The NAM has been strong through the years in defending its concept of free enterprise. Until the Depression it represented primarily small industry, and it still likes to present this image. Since that time, however, big business has become more prominent. This element tends to be less conservative than the small business element, and the NAM has not always been able to present a unified position.

Organized labor has in recent years become a significant force on the American political scene. It is represented primarily by the AFL-CIO. The Political Action Committee (PAC) of the CIO has for many years publicized the voting records of candidates, supported friendly candidates, and physically helped to get voters to the polls. Unlike business, labor as an interest group has had to work against dominant cultural forces. A 1945 poll showed radio network opinion 5–1 in favor of management against labor. A little later, between 1947 and 1957, only 7 percent of United States senators were children of low-salaried workers, wage earners, servants, or farm laborers. Labor's main strength lies in its alliance with the Democratic Party.

Farm interests have political power out of proportion to their numbers. To a large extent this has been true because rural areas have traditionally been overrepresented in the legislatures and Congress. (Reapportionment of electoral districts, ordered by the Supreme Court, is changing this.) The so-called farm bloc, formed in the 1920s, is a strong, conservative force serving primarily the interests of large farmers; it centers around the National Grange and the Farm Bureau Federation. The latter has close ties with the United States Department of Agriculture. The farm bloc has generally opposed unions, welfare legislation (including medicare), laws to protect poor farmers, control of farm prices, and foreign aid. It has generally favored farm price supports, which have mainly benefited large farmers. In these activities it has often worked closely with the NAM. By contrast, the National Farmers' Union, whose membership consists mainly of smaller farmers, has been liberal and prolabor.

Two professional groups, the American Bar Association and the American Medical Association, have considerable political power. The Bar Association has tried, with some success, to have its opinion consulted on appointments to the United States Supreme Court. It exercises similar powers in state judicial appointments. In theory it wishes to pass only on the professional qualifications of appointees, not on their politics. We have already described some of the organization and activities of the AMA. It was undoubtedly influential in holding back medicare for many years. The AMA and the organized drug industry have a large amount of influence in the national Food and Drug Administration. Another professional organization, the National Education Association, has less political power, but does endeavor to promote educational standards and pay for teachers. In 1968, for example, it became embroiled in a bitter controversy with the governor and legislature of Florida.

The major religious bodies are active in politics. The National Council of Churches (Protestant) has lobbied in behalf of social legislation, civil rights, and disarmament. One experienced observer said in 1961 that only once in a generation had legislation opposed by the Catholic Church been approved in New York City or the state legislature. Catholic pressure supported Franco in the Spanish Civil War. It has been active in movie censorship and in support of federal aid to parochial schools. Jewish organizations have opposed discrimination, anti-Semitism, and the use of released time for religious instruction in public schools. Of the partition of Palestine between Jews and Arabs, which established the basis for the Jewish state of Israel, President Truman said, "I do not think I ever had so much pressure and propaganda aimed at the White House as I had in this instance."[2]

Groups with a military interest have also usually been a conservative force in American politics. The largest veterans' organization, the American Legion, has opposed public housing, prolabor legislation, and compulsory health insurance, and has favored legislation friendly to the military and veterans. In foreign policy it has been consistently hawkish. The Legion is dominated by active and retired army officers. At one time one-third of the members of Congress were Legionnaires. The smaller American Veterans' Committee, which grew out of World War II, is by contrast generally liberal. There is also a liberal minority in the Legion. Other promilitary groups such as the Air Force Association and the Aerospace Industries Association may carry considerable weight in promoting their special interests.

We have already discussed the political power of racial groups. As early as the 1940s, the threat of a march on Washington by Negroes influenced the creation of the Fair Employment Practices Commission. The NAACP has successfully argued civil rights cases in the courts through the years. One of these was the *Brown* v.

2. Harmon Zeigler, *Interest Groups in American Society,* Englewood Cliffs, N.J., Prentice-Hall, Inc., 1964, p. 214.

Topeka desegregation decision. By placing scholarly articles in law journals, the NAACP has built up a body of legal opinion favorable to its point of view and has thus influenced the courts. The direct action programs of the more militant civil rights organizations have not only forced local desegregation, but have been a strong pressure behind federal civil rights legislation.

Let us summarize, with illustrations, some of the specific ways in which such pressure groups operate. Sometimes a group may directly sponsor legislation. The Employment Act of 1946 was an important legislative measure of the Farmers' Union. Other groups may vigorously oppose measures. The NAM placed propaganda against this bill in teachers' mail boxes in Fergus County, Montana. Conservative congressmen received aid from General Motors, the Machinery and Allied Products Industry, and the U.S. Chamber of Commerce in preparing for hearings and redrafting legislation. Of industry opposition to a pollution control bill, one congressman said, "I've never seen such lobbying." Pressure groups may exert strong influence on legislative committees. In Florida in 1963, the House Committee on Public Health waited for the Florida Dairy Products Association to speak on a milk-pricing bill and then followed its recommendations. In Illinois this kind of procedure appears to be standard in some committees. In 1961, when it was proposed to reduce the influence of southern Democrats by enlarging the federal House Rules Committee, Chairman Howard Smith held meetings with the NAM, the Chamber of Commerce, the AMA, and the American Farm Bureau Federation, all of whom opposed the changes.

Interest groups may be very closely tied into administrative agencies. The Veterans Bureau comes close to being run by the American Legion. During the Eisenhower Administration, business was successful in getting business-oriented appointments to the National

Labor Relations Board. Labor and liberal groups had been successful under Democratic administrations. Agencies set up to regulate may find themselves virtually taken over by the interests they are regulating. This is largely true of the Interstate Commerce Commission, which has promoted the interests of the railroads against truck and water freight carriers. The Florida Milk Commission, a state agency, and the Florida Dairy Association, a dairymen's association, are almost identical. One writer says that in the case of government regulating bodies, "Few policies have been pursued unless they have been approved by the well organized groups who are being regulated."[3]

There has been similar influence on the judiciary. In the period after the Civil War, railroad interests were very powerful in shaping court decisions. In 1931 the NAACP and liberal organizations succeeded in defeating Senate confirmation of federal judge John J. Parker to the Supreme Court on the ground that he was anti-Negro. Justices Brennan and Goldberg were appointed to the Court only after consultation with the American Bar Association.

Interest groups are likely to make much of their power to punish or reward at the polls. They may do this through campaign contributions, of which an example is support of three consecutive Florida governors by the DuPont interests. In the Bryan-McKinley campaign of 1896, industrial workers were told that there would be no jobs for them if Bryan was elected. Both the NAM and, as we have seen, the AFL-CIO publicize voting records and back favored candidates. A good deal of the power of pressure groups comes through alliance with political parties. The AFL-CIO is an important part of the Democratic Party machinery, just as NAM support is important to the Republican Party. Through the power of advertising, moneyed

interests can throw the great influence of the press and other mass media behind their candidates. Democratic presidential candidates generally have to run against a hostile national press.

In the long run, the most important influence of pressure groups is probably in shaping the climate of public opinion. Legislators, administrators, and even judges are occasionally intimidated or bribed into voting against their convictions. The most important influence of pressure groups is, however, in enlisting and supporting those who agree with them. If antilabor lobbies are successful in dealing with senators, for example, it is largely because of the senators' antilabor background. One student of pressure groups says:

> Many legislators vote their own consciences and would be affronted by attempts of conservative organizations to exert direct influence on their votes. What they fail to recognize is that their consciences have been previously conditioned by the climate of values assiduously cultivated by these same conservative pressures. It is there, not in campaign contributions, direct lobbying, and letter campaigns, that the real and enormous power of the conservative lobby rests.[4]

The same would hold true of the pressures on administrators and judges and of the influence of liberal interest groups.

What is true of formal governmental machinery is true of the public. Voters can be intimidated or bought, but more important are the pressures that shape the mind of the voter over a lifetime. The antilabor public sentiment reflected in the poll cited earlier is more important than political pressures in a particular election. The greatest effect of interest groups is in shaping the political enculturation of citizens, that

3. *Ibid.,* p. 119.

4. Stephen K. Bailey, *Congress Makes a Law,* New York, Columbia University Press, 1950, pp. 148–149.

Portrait of Thomas Jefferson by Charles Willson Peale.

is, the development of their basic political ideas and ideologies.

In this the mass media play a significant role, beginning in early childhood. All interest groups try to reach the public mind through newspapers, radio, movies, and television. The schools are another central area of political enculturation. Conservative organizations try to see that the schools teach "the American way" of free enterprise. Negro organizations try to inject the role of the Negro into history and civics books. Labor furnishes teachers with material that it hopes will find its way into the minds of pupils. Churches, likewise, are subjected to pressures and propaganda. In reaching these shapers of public opinion, those interest groups with the most money are likely to be the most successful in promoting their particular brand of cultural brainwashing.

Of the relationship between interest groups and formal legislative bodies, one student of politics has written that "the legislature referees the group struggle, ratifies the victories of the successful coalitions, and records the terms of the surrenders, compromises, and conquests in the form of statutes."[5] This statement underestimates somewhat the amount of independence which legislators—as well as administrators and judges—may sometimes have, but it points to an important truth.

POLITICAL PARTIES

Especially at election time, political pressures are likely to focus on, or be focused through, political parties. By contrast with the multiparty systems of some other countries, the United States has generally had a two-party system. We now need to look at the interests that have been expressed by these parties, historically and at the present time, and also to take note of the history and functions of minority parties on the American scene.

The Democratic tradition goes back to Thomas Jefferson, who represented the primarily agricultural interests of the rural South. He did not think highly of industry and favored a decentralized society based upon the principle that "that government is best which governs least." A second wing of the early Democratic tradition (which, confusingly, was at the time called Republican) was made up of the urban workingmen of the North. This interest was represented by Aaron Burr. The party became truly democratic with Andrew Jackson. Although himself a rich planter, Jackson drew a large part of his support from the poor backwoods farmers of the South and West. Part of his view of democracy was the spoils system, through which political rewards were distributed not on the basis of merit but to the victor's supporters. Much of this tradition continued in the urban Democratic machines. Today the Democratic Party still remains primarily a party of the rural South and the urban North, dominated by southern planters and city bosses.

5. Earl Latham, *The Group Basis of Politics*, Ithaca, N.Y., Cornell University Press, 1952, p. 35.

The Republican Party has a somewhat more complex history. It goes back, first of all, to the Federalists, who at the time of the Constitutional Convention desired to form a strong central government to protect and promote business and industrial interests. The most important figure was Alexander Hamilton, who was a political conservative with a strong distrust of the masses and of democracy. Hamilton's *Report on Manufactures* in 1791 was a comprehensive and imaginative plan for the development of the United States as an industrial nation. The Federalists sought to promote this growth through such measures as a protective tariff against competing foreign goods. The Jefferson party, with agricultural products to sell abroad, opposed such a tariff. This clash on the tariff continued into the twentieth century.

The Federalists were succeeded in 1834 by the Whigs, headed by Henry Clay, who developed in opposition to Jacksonian democracy. The Whig Party represented some large southern planters, farmers and businessmen of the North, and some of the richer farmers of the West. They stood for industrial expansion and internal improvements, such as canals and railroads, which would be sponsored by the federal government and would advance industrial and business interests. The Republican Party as such arose before the Civil War, as a mixed party unified by opposition to slavery. Its great symbol has been Lincoln. In the industrial takeoff after the Civil War, however, it became the party of big business and of the rural Midwest and has remained so to the present.

After the Civil War, the character of the two major parties was largely set. The Republicans dominated the national scene from 1850 to 1900, the period from 1900 to 1932 was mixed, and since that time the Democrats have generally been dominant. We should note one very important change which has taken place since the days of Jefferson and Hamilton. At a time when capitalist business and industry

Portrait of Alexander Hamilton by John Trumbull.

were just getting started, the Hamiltonians wanted a strong federal government to protect and promote these interests. The Jeffersonians feared this concentration of urban business power and favored decentralization. In the late nineteenth century, however, the tables began to turn. Now firmly established, the business and industrial interests called for a policy of governmental "hands off," while small farmers and the urban poor began to look to government for help. Since then the Democrats have become the party of strong central government.

If we now relate the two parties to the interest groups discussed in the previous section, we will find a lineup which looks like this:

Democratic

AFL-CIO
Farmers' Union
NAACP and other civil rights groups
American Veterans' Committee

Republican

NAM, Chamber of Commerce
Farm Bureau, Grange

American Legion
AMA, American Bar Association

This alignment, of course, represents dominant tendencies, not the affiliations of all members. We shall discuss religious groups separately in a little while.

We can learn a good deal more about interest and pressure in American politics by seeing how party allegiance is related to population characteristics. Many of the data are taken from *Parties and Politics in America,* by the political scientist Clinton Rossiter.

Section. The South, southern New England, and the far West have been predominantly Democratic areas. The upper Mississippi valley, northern New England, and Oregon have been generally Republican.

Since the late nineteenth-century rise of Tammany Hall and other urban political machines, the city has been a Democratic stronghold. The Democrats became a majority with urbanization. The political analyst Samuel Lubell says that an observer, noting before World War I that three-fifths of all school pupils in the major cities were the children of immigrants, could have predicted a major Democratic wave when they came of voting age. This, in fact, happened in the Al Smith campaign of 1928, when Smith carried the major cities for the Democrats for the first time. Except for the South, rural areas tend to be Republican, as do also the suburbs, although migration from the central cities brings more Democrats.

Social and economic class. Clinton Rossiter says that "class has now become the most important single factor in shaping the political behavior of Americans and . . . consequently, class is the most reliable single index to political allegiance."[6] Lubell remarks that one generally need only

6. Clinton Rossiter, *Parties and Politics in America,* Ithaca, N.Y., Cornell University Press, 1960, p. 89.

drive through any area of a city to know whether it will vote predominantly Democrat or Republican. Labor is the strongest single factor for the Democrats. The old middle class of independent business and professional people is generally Republican. The new middle class of white-collar workers, salaried professionals, technicians, service employees, and government workers—which has mushroomed in the past 75 years—is predominantly Democratic.

Ethnic groups. "Old Americans" (English, Scotch, German) tend to be Republican, and "New Americans" (central, eastern, and southern European) to be Democratic. Jews are Democrats by about 3 to 1; Negroes by about 4 to 1.

Religion. In the past Protestants have been mostly Republican. Catholics have been strong in the Democratic party.

Age. Younger voters are more likely to be Democratic.

Education. People with more formal education are likely to be Republican. However, a 1955 study showed college social-science teachers to be Democrats by 2 to 1.

Sex. Women have a slightly greater tendency to be Republican.

These are long-run trends, and some of the differences may not hold true at a particular time. For example, a 1963 Gallup poll on Kennedy versus Rockefeller showed Kennedy carrying all population groups. In the 1960 presidential election, the manual workers had been the only major occupational group to support him.

It is interesting to note how changes in composition of the population have affected and are likely to affect the balance of Democratic and Republican strength. Among the factors favoring the Democrats are (1) the large increase in the new middle class, (2) the coming to voting age of the "new Americans," (3) the urbanization of the nation, (4) the coming to age of a wave of young people, and (5) the enfranchisement of the Negro. On the other hand, the trend toward suburban living is likely to produce new Republicans, as is also the industrialization of the South, which is creating an urban, upper-middle-class Republican Party.

Some facts of American political life require us to modify the idea that we have a two-party system. The South has not traditionally had two parties, although as just noted, this is changing. On the local scene, this one-party system may not be as completely undemocratic as it seems. In some cases it may mean no more than that candidates who would elsewhere be Republican run as opposition within the Democratic Party. On the national scene, it does make an important difference, however. Assignments to important committee posts are generally made on the basis of seniority. Because they are very often unopposed for reelection, southern senators and congressmen are likely to stay in Congress longer than those from other states. The South thus heads far more important committees than its numbers would justify, and these chairmanships enable it to promote or sidetrack legislation. In the Senate especially, Senator Joseph Clark has shown, a conservative establishment wields great power in this way.

In his book, *The Deadlock of Democracy,* political scientist James McGregor Burns has suggested that there are, in fact, four parties on the national scene rather than two. Each major party is divided into a presidential and a congressional wing. The presidential party controls, in each case, the quadrennial national conventions. It centers around the president or the last presidential candidate as head of the party. The congressional party is dominated by party congressional leaders and has its greatest strength between elections.

Support for the presidential parties generally comes from people of lower incomes, who are less educated, more in favor of welfare legislation, more urban, more internationally minded, and less involved in ordinary politics than supporters of the congressional parties. On a scale of liberalism and conservatism, the four parties would line up as shown above.

The presidential Democratic Party is the party of Roosevelt, Truman, Stevenson, and Kennedy. Its strength is in the urban Northeast and the Middle West. Its political slant is best represented by the *Washington Post.*

The presidential Republican Party is the party of Willkie, Dewey, Eisenhower, and Nixon. It is strong in the metropolitan suburbs. Before its failure, the New York *Herald Tribune* represented its point of view.

The congressional Democratic Party has been the party of John Garner, Howard Smith, and Harry Byrd. Its strength is primarily in the South. Burns believed that its position was best reflected by the *New York Times.* This paper may be too liberal to say this today.

The congressional Republican Party is the party of Taft, Dirksen, and Hickenlooper. It is strong in the rural North and the rural Middle West. Its philosophy is represented by the *Chicago Tribune.*

There is a strong tendency for congressional Democrats and congressional Republicans to line up together against the presidential Democrats, with the presidential Republicans sometimes taking one side and sometimes the other. At this point the four-party idea is valuable, for we can hardly have a realistic picture of Congress if we suppose that the major lines are always between Republicans and Democrats.

Along with the two dominant parties, third parties have had a role in American politics. This has not been because of any great success in getting elected to office, especially on the national level, but because of the power of third-party protest to influence the programs of the major parties.

All the significant third parties have been variations on one theme. In the late nineteenth century, western and southern farmers, with some labor support, revolted against the growing power of eastern banks, railroads, and industrialists. This general movement was called Populism. It supported inflation of the money supply to help debtors, it called for nationalization of the railroads to curb their power, and it advocated the right of the people to initiate laws directly (initiative) and to vote directly upon them (referendum). In the 1892 presidential election, the Populist Party carried several states and got 22 electoral votes. In 1896 the Populists backed the Democratic candidacy of Bryan and lost; Bryan's defeat represented the victory of big business.

However, Populism continued into the twentieth century as a reform program. The Progressive movement, under Theodore Roosevelt—"Populism with its whiskers shaved"—stood for direct election of senators, conservation, establishment of a Department of Labor, an eight-hour day, and the vote for women. In 1912 Roosevelt ran as a third-party candidate for the presidency and got 88 electoral votes. In 1924 Robert M. LaFollette ran on a third-party ticket and polled nearly 5 million votes, as compared with 8 million for the Democrats, who ran second. LaFollette called for government ownership of railroads, relief for

farmers, abolition of the injunction in labor disputes, and a popular referendum on war. He was supported by farmers, railway union officials, intellectuals and liberals, and the Socialist Party.

The Socialist Party had been organized in the 1890s. They differed from the Populists in calling for a general nationalization of the major industries. They tried, rather unsuccessfully, to appeal to industrial workers. Their main strength was in the western Populist areas. In 1912 the Socialists elected more than 300 state and municipal officials. Eugene V. Debs got about 900,000 votes in 1920, and in 1932 Norman Thomas polled about 800,000 votes. His strength undoubtedly influenced the Roosevelt New Deal to some extent. The last significant left-wing third-party movement was the Henry Wallace Progressive Party of 1948, which got 1.2 million votes, mainly in urban areas.

Again, the degree of success of Populism, Progressivism, and Socialism in the American party system can largely be measured by those aspects of their programs which have become part of our political scene through major party programs.

COMMUNITY POWER STRUCTURE

Let us now return to our earlier question: To what extent does government represent (1) decision by the people as a whole, (2) decision by a unified ruling group, or (3) a balance among pressure groups?

In 1915 the political writer Robert Michels put forward his now famous "iron law of oligarchy" (rule by the few). In any large organization, he said, we cannot have decision by the mass of people. Any political change therefore merely substitutes one minority group, or elite, for another. Other students of politics, while perhaps agreeing that the mass of people cannot rule directly, have held that it is possible to have a pluralistic political system in which a number of groups compete for power without any single one becoming dominant. This was the idea of James Madison, quoted in Chapter four. The economist John Kenneth Galbraith has put forward the idea of "countervailing power." The power of business is counterbalanced by that of government agencies, by organized labor, by the farm bloc, and so on, so that we have not one power center, but many.

The most influential elitist view was that of Marx. He held that since the rise of an economic surplus, each state in history has been dominated by a ruling class. In capitalist society the state is the agent of the capitalist class. The sociologist C. Wright Mills applied the basic Marxist idea to contemporary society and developed the idea of a "power elite." This is a threefold ruling group consisting of top businessmen and industrialists, government leaders, and representatives of the military. Mills felt that such a power elite makes most of the central decisions in our society.

A number of social scientists have studied power relations on the community level. Before and during the Depression, Robert and Helen Lynd did two famous community surveys of Muncie, Indiana ("Middletown"). They reached the conclusion that decisions in the Muncie community were largely shaped by the Ball family, which controlled the Ball Mason Jar Company. Not only politics, the Lynds concluded, but also the churches, the schools, leisure, philanthropy, and public opinion were strongly influenced by the Ball interests. They also found some power exercised by other individuals who had been very active in political and community service organizations or had otherwise identified themselves strongly with community affairs. The Lynd survey was not popular in Muncie at the time, but forty years later the Lynds were called back to "Middletown" for a dinner in their honor.

Floyd Hunter published his report, entitled *Community Power Structure,* based upon a study of Atlanta. As in the case of Muncie, the city studied was disguised, this time as "Regional City." Hunter began his study by interviewing people prominent in four groups: business, government, civic associations, and society activities. He asked them to name people whom they considered leaders in the community. From their replies Hunter secured a list of 175 leaders, which further research cut down to 40. On the basis of this research, he reached the conclusion quoted earlier that a small number of representatives of industry, banks, law firms, commercial houses, and newspapers shaped the important decisions in Atlanta.

Hunter then tried to apply his method to the United States as a whole. His results are reported in *Top Leadership, U.S.A.* He began with a list of 1093 national associations. A panel of informed people reduced these to 106, whom they considered most influential. Questionnaires were then sent to these organizations, asking them to name leaders in their own and other groups who were influential in the national power structure. The same questionnaire was also sent to chambers of commerce and community chests. Interviews were held with community leaders named by all these organizations. A questionnaire was sent to 500 selected leaders. This study, which took more than four years, led Hunter to the conclusion that the concentration of community power on the local level is repeated in the country as a whole. He believed that about 200 men in some thirteen cities constituted a "national power structure" of great influence. He further concluded that

> The major coercive organs of power at the national level are two major configurations, formal government and the economic corporation. . . . In combination with other elements of organized community action the members of these two leading organs of power formulate top national policy.

From empirical observation it seems reasonable to say that the corporate enterprises are the most potent single forces on the American scene. They reach into every cranny of American life, and their patterns of operations parallel and intertwine with every American institution. Through selected members they collectively control the political machinery at all levels of government, when control is necessary to their functioning.[7]

Hunter's findings have been criticized by some social scientists. His method of determining leaders was "reputational." He gathered opinions about people who were in a general sense felt to be decision makers, without examining actual community decisions and how they were made. In a study of New Haven, published under the title *Who Governs?,* Robert Dahl concluded that there was no evidence of a single unified group of decision makers. He did not, however, find much direct evidence of real popular participation in decision making. In Bennington, Vermont, Harry Scoble concluded that no single power structure existed in the city. In Syracuse, New York, L. Freeman and others studied how 39 community decisions were made. This method contrasted with Hunter's reputational method. They found no unified core of power leaders. They also found, however, that less than three-tenths of one percent of the adult citizens of Syracuse participated directly in making these 39 decisions.

One of the most important studies of community power structure is *Men at the Top,* by Robert Presthus. This reports a comparison of power structures in two New York state communities called Edgewood and Riverview. In each community Presthus studied how five major decisions were made.

Edgewood is a relatively wealthy community, two-thirds Republican.

Most of the population is native-born, and the foreign-born are mainly of Anglo-Saxon stock. Presthus found that three groups were involved in decision making: people with economic power, politicians, and specialists of other kinds. Thirty-six people were active in the five decisions, "individuals who have over time demonstrated their ability in such tasks as fund-raising, legal matters, command of mass media, political negotiations, control or possession of financial resources, organizing ability, and positions of ethnic or religious leadership."[8] These leaders had a large number of memberships in the chamber of commerce, the country club, and the Greater Edgewood Industries. Forty percent of them participated in two or more of the decisions. Thus Presthus concluded that the power group was rather unified. Of the leadership groups, economic leaders had higher income, higher social status, and belonged to more prestigious organizations. Their influence outweighed that of either the politicians or the specialists.

The Edgewood power structure seemed to fit the Marxian picture of domination by economic interests. Riverview was different. It is a poorer community, with low-paying industries and a large working-class population, many of them from non-Anglo-Saxon origins. Some leaders belong to the chamber of commerce and the Industrial Development Committee, but by contrast with Edgewood, there are more leaders found in the Moose, Elks, Masons, and veterans' organizations, which represent lower-income levels. Most decisions centered in the Democratic mayor and his Republican city attorney. Since the community is poorer than Edgewood, Riverview depends for community improvements— in health, education, housing, and flood control—upon aid from the state and federal governments. This the mayor is in a position to deliver, as

7. Hunter, *op. cit.,* pp. 187, 252.

8. Robert V. Presthus, *Men at the Top,* New York, Oxford University Press, 1964, p. 136.

long as he continues to provide Albany and Washington with a Democratic majority in a Republican country. Economic leaders play a secondary role in decision making in Riverview.

Presthus drew several conclusions from the *Men at the Top* study. Other things being equal, he felt, economic leaders have an advantage over politicians, since economic power is exercised continuously, while politicians ordinarily go in and out of office. Also, economic leaders are likely to be better educated and of higher income and prestige. Where the community is poor, as in Riverview, politicians have the advantage of contact with outside political interests, which control economic resources not available in the community itself.

Whether governed primarily by economic or political elites, both communities seemed to have great centralization of decision making. Some students of politics have felt that participation of citizens through a number of effective social, service, patriotic, labor, professional, business, or political groups may keep power from being concentrated. Almost 150 years ago, the French observer Alexis de Tocqueville, in his book *Democracy in America,* had commented on the great capacity of Americans for such voluntary organizations. A 1953 study by C. R. Wright and H. H. Hyman found, however, that "voluntary association membership is not a major characteristic of Americans. Nearly half of the families (47 percent) and almost two-thirds of the respondents (64 percent) belong to no voluntary associations."[9] In neither Edgewood nor Riverview did Presthus find many people participating effectively through voluntary groups. There may be a tendency for voluntary community organizations to be more effective, and power less concentrated, in larger cities. There is little evidence in the Presthus study or in others, however, that the mass of citizens in any community are able to match the weight

9. *Ibid.,* p. 240.

carried by one or another kind of power elite.

PROPAGANDA

One of the important specific aspects of the political environment is propaganda, which is to a very large extent a product of this century. It is true that the term "propaganda" originated in the organized efforts of the Catholic Church to "propagate" the faith. There has been no more effective pamphleteer than was Tom Paine in the Revolutionary War. Both Union and Confederacy had effective propaganda organizations in the Civil War. Distortion of news about the sinking of the battleship *Maine* played a large part in involving the United States in the Spanish-American War.

It was only in World War I, however, that the major nations, including Great Britain and the United States, mobilized for all-out propaganda efforts upon their public. Much World War I propaganda, especially the atrocity stories, was very crude. In the 1920s Russia, under Lenin, began a systematic thought-control program. The Italian Fascists bought out the Stafani News Agency, and the Japanese government adopted a centralized information policy. The American New Deal, beginning in 1935 with the entry of government into the economy and society on a new scale, was accompanied by organized government efforts to publicize and sell their program. The output of government press releases was increased many times. In 1933 the German Nazis embarked on a massive brainwashing of their people.

World War II led again to centralized control of information by all governments. The United States Office of War Information had bureaus for distributing propaganda through books and magazines, graphics, motion pictures, newspapers, and radio. After the war the United States undertook, with the Voice of America, a systematic overseas propaganda program to counter

Communist propaganda. By this time "information making" by advertising and public relations experts had become a major part of all industrial nations. Government had learned to make use of these facilities. In 1946, for example, a massive propaganda campaign for a permanent draft made the United States Army the third largest advertiser in the nation. Political candidates have increasingly used the mass media. Since 1952 all major presidential campaigns have been managed by professional advertising agencies. The amount and range of government releases in the United States have greatly multiplied, with a large increase of classified information, off-the-record speeches by government officials, and charges that government has managed and censored information. China since 1949 has refined many previous propaganda methods in indoctrinating her population.

This development is far from accidental. The increase of government propaganda is, first of all, only part of an increase of propaganda in society as a whole. The development of mass society has weakened the primary groups within which people once lived and has tended to make them individual atoms in a world of large organizations. They have become dependent upon these large organizations for factual information, for example, about the vast array of consumer goods. They have also become dependent for values and ideologies to replace those that were once absorbed in family, church, and neighborhood. Mass media, including those influenced by government, tend to fill the gap.

Scientific development of media—news gathering, radio, moving pictures, and television—has made such mass information possible on a hitherto unimaginable scale. Control of the media has become increasingly centralized. Modern psychology and sociology have given public relations and propaganda specialists new techniques for manipulating the public. Literacy itself has made people more susceptible to propaganda. Lenin, an astute propagandist, realized that mass literacy would be necessary for the Soviet propaganda machine to be most effective. Illiterate and culturally backward peoples are hard to reach with mass propaganda. The Nazis, for example, found this to be true of the backward areas of Germany. Mass education may make people not less, but more, open to propaganda. A contemporary French writer on propaganda, Jacques Ellul, has said that "the most obvious result of primary education in the nineteenth and twentieth centuries was to make the individual susceptible to superpropaganda."[10]

On top of all this, the size and scope of government have vastly increased in our century, largely because of the greater complexity of industrial society. If citizens are to know about government activities, an increased amount of government information is inevitable. The most important factor of all has probably been the increase in the importance of the military. Massive mobilization for hot or cold war creates a situation where extensive secrecy, censorship, and management of information can easily be argued to be not only justifiable but essential.

What is propaganda? Many definitions have been offered by students of the subject. None of them agrees entirely; nor will the one we shall offer. It may be useful, however, to define propaganda as *the influencing of belief and action by presentation of stimuli which are one-sided, oversimplified, and appeal to irrational motives rather than reason.*

We may note two things especially. Propaganda defined this way is distinguished from true education, which seeks to present (1) all sides (2) in their complexity and (3) in a way that encourages reason. We should also recognize, however, that much—indeed, perhaps most—organized education is propaganda rather than education in this sense. Secondly, the definition is not restricted to propaganda that is conscious and intentional. We shall see that perhaps the most important propaganda is, in fact, not consciously planned or intended.

Most of our organized knowledge of the techniques of propaganda is an outgrowth of the work of the Institute of Propaganda Analysis, which was founded at Yale University in 1937 and lasted through World War II. The institute and its work grew to a large extent out of disillusionment with the exaggerated propaganda put forth in World War I.

We may open the subject of propaganda methods with a list of "earmarks of propaganda" offered by the sociologist Emory S. Bogardus, and then examine some of the methods more intensively. Among other earmarks by which propaganda may be recognized, Bogardus lists:

> unguarded enthusiasm;
> a sentimental and folksy approach;
> an intolerant air or tone;
> use of broad generalities;
> wholesale condemnation of opponents;
> use of pressure;
> testimony by authorities outside their field;
> insinuations against opponents;
> concealment of sources;
> presentation of both sides from one point of view;
> doctoring the facts.[11]

In analyzing methods we must note what propaganda can and cannot do. It cannot stand up long against clear facts to the contrary. One of history's most effective propagandists, the Nazi Joseph Goebbels, was relatively helpless once the German armies really began to lose. Nor can propaganda usually change deep-seated attitudes. Those who are most influenced by propaganda are those who are at least halfway ready to hear it. It is not likely to influence those who are strongly opposed. One student of the subject suggests that the best subsidized and ablest Baptist propaganda agency could never hope to convert the Roman Catholic College of Cardinals. As long as they had strong group morale, the German armies in World War II were relatively immune to Allied propa-

---

10. Jacques Ellul, *Propaganda,* trans. Konrad Kellen and Jean Lerner, New York, Knopf, 1956, p. 109.

11. Emory S. Bogardus, *The Making of Public Opinion,* New York, Association Press, 1951.

ganda. Russian propaganda which urged invading Nazis armies to overthrow Hitler strengthened rather than weakened enemy morale. For this same reason, fear of Communist propaganda in the United States, where the population has a long history of procapitalist feeling, is greatly exaggerated.

The effective propagandist tries to tie onto existing tendencies and to relate them to attitudes and actions which he wishes to evoke. Paul's approach to the Athenians is a masterpiece of this kind: "Ye men of Athens, I perceive that in all things ye are too superstitious. For as I passed by, and beheld your devotions, I found an altar with this inscription, TO THE UNKNOWN GOD. Whom therefore ye ignorantly worship, him declare I unto you."[12] Since, as depth psychology has shown us, people are very complex and usually have contradictory attitudes, the skillful propagandist usually has a great deal to work with even in seemingly hostile people.

Propaganda always involves distortion. Hitler became famous for his doctrine of the "big lie," which he expressed in Mein Kampf: "In the size of the lie there is always contained a certain factor of credibility, since the great masses of people . . . also lie sometimes in little things, but would certainly still be too much ashamed of too great lies."[13] A large part of World War I propaganda was made up of lies. However, Ellul claims that Goebbels, Hitler's propaganda minister, constantly attempted to make propaganda as accurate as possible. Both Lenin and Mao Tse-tung have held that the spreading of outright falsehoods is bad policy. The United States propaganda manual in World War II said, "When there is no compelling reason to suppress a fact, tell it. . . . When the listener catches you in a lie, your power diminishes. . . . For this rea-

son, never tell a lie which can be discovered."[14] Failure to observe this rule played a large part in the "credibility gap" of the 1960s. Repeated incidents like the denial of U-2 flights over Russia and of the Bay of Pigs invasion of Cuba led one correspondent to say that reporters never really believed a story until it had been officially denied.

Avoidance of outright lies does not mean, in any case, that propagandists tell the whole truth. One way of telling less than all the truth is through *oversimplification.* Goebbels said:

The ordinary man hates nothing more than two-sidedness, to be called upon to consider this as well as that. The masses think simply and primitively. They love to generalize complicated situations, and from their generalizations to draw clear and uncompromising conclusions.[15]

One way of oversimplifying is through black-white thinking. The real world usually consists of shades of good and evil, but for the propagandist it is likely to be populated with angels and devils. When Fidel Castro's sister was asked on American television to name some positive accomplishments of her brother's regime, she replied, "None." Such wholesale condemnation makes no sense, for there is no regime in history that has not accomplished some good. Enthusiasts on both sides are likely to see no middle ground between capitalism and communism. Such thinking is likely to lead to oversimplified slogans: "Make the world safe for democracy," "Better dead than red" (or capitalist). Black-white oversimplification leads to *scapegoating,* in which the world's ills are blamed on communists, fascists, bankers, capitalist imperialists, Jews, outside agitators, munitions makers, or even omnipotent propagandists.

Card stacking is another form of

12. Acts 17:22–23.
13. Adolf Hitler, *Mein Kampf,* New York, Reynal & Hitchcock, 1940, p. 313.

14. Ellul, *op. cit.,* p. 53.
15. *New York Times Magazine* (February 14, 1937), p. 27.

oversimplification. Here one lists truths, but omits other truths. When the *Lusitania* was sunk in 1915 by German U-boats, it was true that many neutral American civilians were victims. Indignation over this fact was an important factor leading the United States toward war. What was not generally known was that the *Lusitania* was carrying munitions and was therefore a fair target under international law and that the passengers had been warned in advance by the Germans. Russians and Chinese use card stacking to build up a one-sided picture of the United States. It is true that we have race riots, gangsters, promiscuous movie stars, war-minded arms makers, and corrupt politicians. It is also true that all these are only part of the whole story. Outright censorship is a long-range form of card stacking through which only favorable truths are allowed to reach the public.

Deceptive statistics may be an effective form of distortion. Major governments now rarely publish completely false figures, but many tell less than the whole story. It may be possible to know how many Americans are killed in a day in a jungle war, but it is not possible to know exactly how many of the enemy die. Yet seemingly accurate figures are given for "Communist" dead (here is another distortion, for not all enemies are communists). Statistics for a whole area may show average losses of Americans to be very light and disguise the fact that the average includes a whole combat unit that was wiped out. United States government figures for unemployment in the 1960s, while not false, probably underestimated the number of unemployed because they did not include people who had given up trying to secure work.

Stereotyping, a term we may credit to Walter Lippmann, is a form of card stacking that creates an oversimplified and distorted image of a group. Negroes may be stereotyped as lacking ambition, Jews as being competitively aggressive, capitalists as being concerned only with profit making. These

stereotypes are not total falsehoods. Lack of opportunity during 300 years of second-class citizenship has dulled the ambition of many Negroes. Discrimination and exclusion from many occupations has led many Jews to be aggressive in protecting their financial and other interests. In order to survive in a competitive economy, capitalists may sometimes have to put profit above honesty or social concern. What the stereotypes leave out is (1) the fact that not all Negroes, Jews, or capitalists possess these characteristics, (2) the historical and cultural reasons why many do possess them, (3) the fact that members of other groups may also possess them, and (4) the fact that even those Negroes, Jews, and capitalists who do seem to fit the stereotype may also possess many other more desirable traits.

A group of propaganda techniques uses essentially irrational appeals to give prestige to the propagandist's cause. These may involve *glittering generalities.* The cause may be described as One Hundred Percent American (a scientific impossibility in view of cultural diffusion). Communists may be urged to support the People's Democracies (which are not democratic), and capitalists to support the Free World (much of which is under dictatorship).

Testimonials may borrow the magnetism of prestigious figures—movie and television stars endorse advertised products, and their support is a powerful asset to political candidates. The *transfer* device may attach to the cause the emotions associated with certain symbols. Even subversive political meetings may display a flag. Politicians are likely to campaign "in the name of home, mother, the little red school house, and the spirit of liberty."

The *plain folks* technique borrows the prestige of the group by associating an individual with it. A political candidate may show himself to be "just one of the crowd" by telling jokes about himself. The fact that he had failed in business (like many other people) was at times a positive asset to Harry Truman. The *bandwagon* says, in effect, "Come along—everybody's doing it." Political candidates like to show that things are going their way, and that their opponent is a loser. Finally, *name calling* gives a reverse prestige by discrediting the opponent: "red sympathizer," "nigger lover," "Uncle Tom." A meeting organized by the author was once picketed by Communists and others bearing signs reading "No free speech for Fascists."

Repetition plays an important part in propaganda. Experimental psychology shows that stimuli that are repeated are more likely to change responses. (It is also true that if some stimuli are repeated too much, a person may cease to be influenced.) Goebbels advised:

> In the long run only he will achieve basic results in influencing public opinion who is able to reduce problems to the simplest terms and who has the courage to keep forever repeating them in this simplified form despite the objections of the intellectuals.[16]

Alex Inkeles, in a study of public opinion in the Soviet Union, reports that "one of the most striking facts about Soviet mass communication is its repetitiveness."[17] Students of Communist China tell us how impossible it is to escape the incessant, repetitive blare of radio. In the United States, there is no single government propaganda line, but no one knows the total effect of constantly repeated exposure on all media to reports of war and foreign affairs, all with varying degrees of pro-American bias.

The sources of propaganda can be either revealed or concealed. In "white" propaganda, the source is known; in "black" propaganda, it is disguised. In 1915 the British government was fortunate in having the distinguished historian, Lord James Bryce, to head a German Outrages Inquiry Committee. No disguised propaganda would have been likely to have the impact of the extravagant atrocity stories which came from this highly respected source. On the other hand, if a propagandist wants to insinuate that a Catholic president will put the United States under the power of Rome, or that a Christian Scientist as president will discriminate against the medical profession, he will probably do best to spread unacknowledged rumors.

Editorials suggested or planted in newspapers are likely to be far more effective than paid advertisements. Wendell Willkie's presidential candidacy in 1940 was more convincing because it appeared to arise out of a grassroots movement at the Republican convention ("We Want Willkie"), although it was actually planned by interest groups. A good illustration of "black" propaganda is the activity of the Hamilton Wright Organization, a recognized agent for Chiang Kaishek's Nationalist China from 1957 to 1962. The Wright agency distributed stories, news articles, photographs, and movies about China. Its clients included NBC, CBS, ABC, and Sunday supplements. Seventy-five percent of

---

16. Frederick C. Irion, *Public Opinion and Propaganda,* New York, Thomas Y. Crowell, 1950, pp. 35–36.

17. Alex Inkeles, *Public Opinion in Soviet Russia,* Cambridge, Harvard University Press, 1950, p. 320.

the contracts specified that neither the editor nor the reader would know where the material originated.

Finally, propaganda may be either intentional or unintentional. In defining propaganda we have not included intent in our definition. If we think of propaganda in terms of intent, we are likely to stress the activities of conscious manipulators of public opinion, often big liars. Intentional propaganda is very important, but to emphasize it alone is to overlook the most widespread and significant distortions of public opinion. If parents, teachers, newspaper writers, radio and television broadcasters, and film makers all present a slanted version of reality, it may matter little that they may not intend to distort.

"Propaganda," says Jacques Ellul, "is a good deal less the political weapon of a regime (it is that also) than the effect of a technological society that embraces the entire man."[18] What he is saying is that we must include as propaganda a large part of cultural brainwashing. Ellul feels that China and the United States are two major examples of the direction in which mass shaping of public opinion is moving in the modern world. Chinese propaganda, is, of course, planned, centralized, and intentional. The shaping of American opinion has no conscious center, but from all sides technically developed mass media sell us—and, indeed, much of the world—on the American Way of Life. We cannot clearly say how much more effective the one kind of propaganda is than the other.

LEGITIMACY

"All governments," says the Declaration of Independence, "derive their just powers from the consent of the governed." We might also add, "and their unjust powers," for, as we have seen, even the most tyrannical government cannot rule by force alone. Most of its

subjects must also feel that it has the right to rule them. What is the nature and origin of this sense of legitimacy?

First we must say that, in a certain sense, governments are not the only organizations regarded as legitimate. The Catholic Church is clearly felt by its members to have the right to prescribe rules which they must follow. Political parties, even though not having governmental power, may sometimes be felt to have even a proper power of life and death over their members. People may feel that a factory owner has a right to run his plant as he sees fit. Labor union members may feel morally bound to carry out the strike orders of their union. The sense of legitimacy may exist in any organization toward which its members have strong emotional feelings.

With government, however, there is an important difference. Governments are deemed to have supreme authority over the territories they rule. The right of other organizations to rule over their members within an area is limited. They must give way before the authority of government. Government is supposed to represent the interests of the whole population of its territory, whereas any other organization represents only a partial interest. Therefore, only government in the final sense is considered to have the legitimate right to rule.

We need now to go a little deeper into the mechanisms by which government is legitimized, for after all, people will give up for government their money in taxes and their lives in war. To produce such results, feelings of legitimacy must be quite deep.

A useful starting point is the distinction, by Max Weber, of three forms of legitimacy. (1) Legal, or rational, legitimacy rests on the idea that government is rationally pursuing unquestionable goals. (2) Traditional legitimacy rests on the belief that what has survived for a long time deserves to be followed. (3) Charismatic legitimacy is the "magic" which attaches itself to government because of magnetic leaders.

18. Ellul, *op. cit.,* p. xvii.

Let us begin with the rational form of legitimacy. Here it is believed, first, that the government represents principles that are above debate. Secondly, it is believed that the government's daily acts are expressions of these principles.

What kinds of principles are beyond dispute? The government may represent the *will of God* on earth. The clearest example of this kind of legitimacy is a nonpolitical one: the authority claimed by the Catholic Church as the result of a direct grant of power given by Christ to Peter and thence to succeeding popes. But Paul also said of existing government, "Let every man be subject to the rightful powers, for the powers that be are ordained of God." The British philosopher Thomas Hobbes argued the "divine right of kings." God had established kings to bring order out of the chaotic and violent "state of nature." To disobey the monarch was to disobey God.

A second source of authority may be the *law of nature.* In the Middle Ages, Thomas Aquinas worked out a great statement of Catholic principles based on natural law. Behind this law was still, however, God. This was not the case at the time of the French Revolution. The revolutionary regime claimed to embody the rights of man, which were part of the natural order of things. The American Revolution had found men "endowed by their Creator with certain inalienable rights," but many of the founding fathers were not traditionally religious, and the American republic came closer to being founded on an impersonal order of nature than on a personal God.

A third source may be *scientific law.* At one time the Mexican dictator Diaz is said to have based his rule on the idea that it embodied a scientific system of action. The best example, however, is scientific socialism. Marx believed that his revolutionary system was based on the application of modern scientific method to the economic and social order. The legitimacy of the Soviet regime in the USSR, as of other Communist regimes today, is founded on the claim that the political system is derived from scientific Marxian principles.

Finally, government may base its claim to legitimacy upon the *will of the people.* The lawyers of the Roman emperor Augustus went to great lengths to demonstrate that his regime was actually founded on a grant of power given by the citizenry of Rome. For obvious reasons this basis for legitimacy is most likely to be used by governments that are democratic in form. Since officials and policies are subject to periodic approval or disapproval in popular elections, it is claimed that government represents the popular will. (And it was once said that "The voice of the people is the voice of God"!) Our discussion of pressure groups and community power structure suggests that the real facts may not be quite so simple. Minorities may use the myth of the "will of the people" to legitimize their own undemocratic control, just as minorities under other systems employ the other myths.

It is not enough that the government be believed to rest upon infallible principles; it must also be believed that its daily acts express these principles, otherwise the principles may themselves be used to question the legitimacy of an existing administration. This is, in fact, what almost all revolutionary leaders do. When he denounced the Catholic hierarchy, Luther did not claim to be following new principles, but to be preserving the true Catholic faith against those who had forsaken them. When he denounced Stalin, Trotsky did so in the name of true Marxian socialism, which he claimed Stalin had corrupted. Jesus expressed the point of view of all such critics, "Think not I am come to destroy the law or the prophets: I am not come to destroy, but to fulfil."

To protect themselves against such attacks on their legitimacy, governments must have ways of proving that they really are carrying out fundamental principles. To a large extent this is done by judges and courts, who are supposed to reach their decisions by going back to first principles and applying them to the particular case. In actual fact, as has already been suggested, they may do almost the opposite. "The judges judge backwards" said one law professor; "decisions first, rationalizations to follow." In the school segregation case, a good argument could be (and has been) made that the Supreme Court decided what would be socially desirable or politically expedient policy and then found constitutional principles to justify it. An equally good case could be made for earlier conservative decisions, such as those invalidating child labor laws. Insofar as this is true, the courts serve to legitimize political decisions by surrounding them with the aura of the Constitution.

Thurman Arnold, a high government official in the Roosevelt Administration, once wrote a book developing the idea that theology, economic theory, and legal jurisprudence all perform essentially the same functions in the church, the economic order, and government. In each case the myth is that they provide principles according to which decisions are made. In fact, said Arnold, the decisions are made largely on the basis of expediency and are then justified in terms of the principles. This view is only a half-truth; it is just as true that judges make decisions by measuring cases against principles and precedents as that they find principles to justify expediency. But probably no more true. Courts and judges do play an important part in giving the acts of government legal, or rational, legitimacy.

The second major basis for legitimacy is tradition. "What was good enough for our grandfathers is good enough for us." In the United States, this appeal is likely to be strongest in the South or in some parts of New England. It is strong in the British upper classes. Those who defend existing government on these grounds are likely to have a great deal to say about

the Constitution, founding fathers, Magna Charta, and the like.

Other things being equal, that which has existed for a long time tends to be thought of as right. It has stood the test of time. Says the Declaration of Independence, "Prudence, indeed, will dictate that governments long established should not be changed for light and transient causes. . . ." Especially since the evolutionary view became popular, it is likely to be argued that institutions that have survived over a long period represent a survival of the fittest. They must have satisfied the needs of most people or they would not have survived. Here tradition becomes the voice of the people.

There is usually what we may call a "presumption in favor of the status quo." In court of law, a prisoner is presumed innocent, under Anglo-Saxon law, until proved guilty. The burden of proof is upon the prosecution. Similarly, there is likely to be a presumption in favor of traditional institutions, and the burden of proof is upon those who would change them. For example, it is not usually considered enough merely to criticize existing institutions; one must also be constructive. There are some good reasons for this. In collective life, as in individual life, habit is essential. We cannot think out anew every morning how we shall dress, brush our teeth, or get to school or work. Similarly, we cannot constitute government (or any other institution) afresh every morning. Also, there is the conservatism of the tested. Survival at least proves that the traditional way is a way of getting things done, and this has not yet been proved of any alternative proposal. Thus we hesitate to rock the boat.

We inevitably develop emotional attachments to accustomed ways. The Swedish monarchy, for example, performs no significant political function; the ruling Social Democratic Party is on record as favoring a republic; yet no one seriously considers dethroning the king and queen. Even when a relationship has been mainly unpleasant—an ugly home, a frustrating job, a bad marriage—if it has persisted long enough we may find it hard to give up. The same tends to be true of political institutions. Where public matters are concerned, there is also likely to be a collective "editing" process which strengthens our ties to the past. Just as the individual mind tends to banish unpleasant memories, so in the history of our political institutions we tend to remember only the difficulties mastered, the wars won, the noble causes fought for. The history textbook writers and the Fourth of July orators tend to gloss over the lost wars, the inglorious causes, the political and social disasters. Thus the public has an unduly favorable memory of the traditional ways.

The arguments for the legitimacy of traditional institutions are by no means airtight, but they may not have to be logical to be effective. Survival does not prove that tradition is the only way or the best way to do things—only that it is a possible way. Governments can exist for decades or centuries because people are too hungry, too ignorant, too depressed, or too unorganized to revolt. They may not be serving basic human needs in any real sense. The fact that institutions have survived demonstrates only that they have been more or less workable up to the present. They may not work in the future. The tested traditional habits of national sovereignty and military armament seem very likely, for example, to lead to nuclear disaster. In such cases perhaps the burden of proof should be on those who would continue the traditional ways rather than on those who advocate changing them.

The third form of legitimacy is that due to the charisma of a leader. Charisma is an undefinable, magical quality which some political figures and other people possess. Examples of charismatic leadership in modern times are Roosevelt in the United States, Hitler and later Adenauer in Germany, De Gaulle in France, Churchill in England, Mao Tse-tung in China, and Castro in Cuba.

POLITICAL LEADERSHIP

To examine charismatic legitimacy we must study briefly the characteristics of political leadership. We should note in the beginning that not all the phenomena of leadership we shall describe are solely political. The same mechanisms may be found underlying leadership in any aspect of social life. Leadership tends, however, to come to a focus in politics, because this is the center of legitimate power.

What, first of all, is the relationship of the leader to the social and political climate? Do the times make the leader or does the leader make the times? Extreme answers of both kinds have been given. Some people believe that great men are largely independent of their society and would have been great regardless of their times. Such people are likely to see history as written largely in terms of heroes. Others claim that the great leader is simply a person who happened to come along at the right time. Had he not appeared, someone else would have.

The truth is somewhere between the two extremes. To be an outstanding political leader one must live at a time when there is a great political need or opportunity. Otherwise he may possibly be great, but not in the field of politics. On the other hand, times of great need for leadership may or may not produce individuals equal to the occasion. If they do arise, leaders adequate to the challenge may then play a very considerable personal role in shaping political history.

The civil rights leader Martin Luther King, one of the great political figures of the twentieth century, illustrates the interaction of social situation and personal qualities. In the late 1950s, the time was ready for a revolution of the Negro masses. This, as we have seen, was part of a worldwide revolution of rising expectations. There was the possibility that it could take either a violent or nonviolent form. Pent-up frustrations came to a head in the form of a bus boycott in Montgomery, Alabama. King, a Baptist minister still in his twenties, was drawn into leadership. Although well educated and disposed to nonviolent techniques and philosophy, at first he leaned rather heavily on pacifists who were experienced in the struggle for peace and civil rights. They undoubtedly influenced, also, the eventual broadening of his program to include foreign policy and economic change as well as civil rights.

As the civil rights revolution spread, King came to symbolize the spirit of courageous, nonviolent love as an instrument of social change. His personal magnetism and an eloquence bred in the Southern Baptist ministry made him a truly charismatic figure not only for millions of Negroes but, as his assassination showed, for a large part of the American public. His leadership clearly shows the interplay among (1) the ripeness of the times for a leader like King, (2) the concrete shaping of the leader to the specific needs of the situation, and (3) the personal contribution of the unique qualities of a magnetic individual. Certainly this combination gave an almost irresistible sense of rightness and legitimacy to the Negro movement in the eyes of large numbers of both Negroes and whites.

Let us look at a number of types of political leaders. These types are not intended to exhaust the subject; they should start our thinking rather than close it.

One type is the *machine man.* His main asset is connections. This person owes his prominence almost entirely to his place in a powerful political organization rather than to personal qualities or public services. Over a considerable period of time, he has come to know a large number of people, particularly key organization people. He has been able to put a considerable number of people in his debt through the patronage of political office—jobs, government subsidies, and other favors which he is able to distribute. He keeps his political fences in order. At election time he receives party endorsement and party financial support, and the organization musters itself on his behalf. From the standpoint of the party, he is safe just because he has no outstanding qualities or principles. Such a person may come to prominence and power just because he is a nonleader. Probably the majority of political office holders are of this type. Occasionally this kind of person becomes a presidential candidate or even a president. Warren G. Harding is perhaps the most recent example of such a machine man in the presidency.

The *organizer* owes his prominence not primarily to personal qualities, not to position in political organization, but to his ability to accomplish things. His strength is in know-how. By contrast with the machine man, whose platform is likely to be pleasant but empty generalities, the organizer promises specific accomplishments and attains leadership through his ability to deliver. Whereas the magnetic, charismatic leader is likely to arise in dark times of crisis, the organizer tends to come to the front when the crisis is over and the task of practical rebuilding is at hand. Thus in Russia the Khrushchevs, Kosygins, and Brezhnevs occupy the place once held by Lenin and Stalin. The charismatic war leader Churchill was succeeded in Britain by the colorless Labour Prime Minister Attlee, who did, however, carry through a program of nationalization which no succeeding regime has dared to undo. In the civil rights movement, the magnetic figure of King contrasts with the organizer Roy Wilkins, who has made the NAACP part of the national power structure. Nelson Rockefeller is perhaps an example of a nationally prominent political figure whose strength lies not mainly in personal flair but in a reputation for getting things done.

The *father figure* is a very important kind of leader. His main asset is transference (see Chapter five). When Franklin D. Roosevelt died, some patients in psychoanalysis committed suicide, and others openly said, "I feel as though my father had died." Dwight Eisenhower, whose personality fit his conservative political platform, was a good case of the father figure. Konrad Adenauer, known as Der Alte (the Old Man), who served as West German chancellor to almost the age of 90, is another clear example. Kings are usually viewed as fathers. The pope (the title is from the same root as "papa") is also clearly a father image.

Freud analyzed the role of the father figure in the army and the church, and sometimes wrote as though all significant leaders were father figures. This would be a great oversimplification. Nevertheless, we have seen that early experience with authority tends to shape later experience. Young children tend to feel that their parents know everything, can do everything, and are always right (their acts are "legitimate"). These attitudes tend to be transferred to later authority figures. Political leaders are a very important example.

What are the characteristics of the father figure? In general they are the same traits that distinguish the real father in the eyes of the child. A certain amount of age is necessary; a very young man can hardly play the part. On the other hand, aging alone is likely to turn a "young Turk" into an "elder statesman," a paternal figure. Position itself tends to make one a father figure, regardless of personal qualities. This is true of a king or a president. Power tends to breed in followers the dependent and respectful attitudes of young children toward parents. Masterful traits are likely to build the father image—imposing stature and build, striking or fearsome appearance, verbal ability, poise, ease in handling people. Self-confidence, the assurance of rightness, unquestioned conviction of one's capability and significance, all tend to put other people in the role of children. Access to knowledge not available to followers tends to foster attitudes of dependency.

In general the qualities which build the father image are those which tend to re-create the early situation of child and parent. Sometimes this relationship is played upon deliberately. The executive or bureaucrat will keep people waiting, even when his office is empty, so as to magnify his importance. Guards in Nazi concentration camps put inmates in the position of children by arbitrarily granting or denying them access to toilet facilities. In Norman Mailer's *The Naked and the Dead,* the authoritarian General Cummings describes how he uses arbitrary power to strengthen his father image:

> *There was the old myth of divine intervention. You blasphemed, and a lightning bolt struck you. . . . If punishment is at all proportionate to the crime, then power becomes watered. The only way you generate the proper attitude of awe and obedience is through immense and disproportionate power.*[19]

The leadership of the *ideologist* rests on ideas. It is not enough for people to be discontented; they must be able to express their discontent. Here the man of ideas plays an important role. John Locke was one of the most important ideologists behind the American and French revolutions. Adam Smith furnished intellectual justification for the rising capitalist class. Karl Marx conceptualized the frustrations and aspirations of the industrial workers. Henry Thoreau furnished the revolution of rising expectations with the philosophy of civil disobedience.

On the other side, established regimes cannot ordinarily silence ideas with naked power alone, but must meet them with other ideas. Thus the idea maker always performs an important role in legitimizing the status quo. Generally the most influential idea makers are on the side of the established order. Edmund Burke put forth powerful arguments against the French Revolution. The most prominent Western economists have supported modern capitalism against socialism. Until re-

19. Norman Mailer, *The Naked and the Dead,* New York, Holt, Rinehart and Winston, 1948, p. 283.

cently most intellectuals, like most other people, regarded civil disobedience as an illegitimate disruption of law and order. Students of revolution have found that loss of allegiance of the intellectuals is one of the strongest signs that a regime is losing its grip.

Another important type of leader is the *hero.* His strong point is the show of courage. He is a person, usually relatively young, who stands up against established authority. In terms of the deep emotions involved, the model for this kind of leader is the child who challenges his parents, teachers, policemen, or other authority figures. Sometimes the child performs an "initiatory act" which others fear to perform. He thus enables them to do it also, because he has done it first. The act may be swearing, masturbating, playing hooky, stealing, smoking "pot," or the like. By contrast with the father figure, who is likely to strengthen his charisma by being somewhat distant and aloof, the hero is likely to stress the plain folks device of being "just one of the boys." In his speech he may depreciate himself and direct humor at himself.

Eugene McCarthy in the 1968 presidential campaign, alone daring to challenge Lyndon Johnson in the New Hampshire primary, illustrates very well the hero as initiatory actor. Robert Kennedy, who was then able to follow McCarthy into the race, is an excellent example of a leader who had consciously played the role of the young hero. So did his brother, John Kennedy. When he took up the cudgels against "malefactors of great wealth," Roosevelt became in part the hero as well as the father image. Harry Truman, who in his senatorial days had been aligned with small business against monopoly, continued to play the hero role in his successful 1948 presidential campaign against the "do-nothing Eightieth Congress." His opponent, Thomas Dewey, had been a hero in his younger days as a fearless crusader against crime, but time and youth had now run out on him.

Few leaders are of any single, pure type. Probably the most effective leader is one who is able to combine a number of appeals. Hitler was, to many Germans, a reprehensive and tyrannical father, but to others he was a hero who cast off restraints imposed by the Treaty of Versailles and enabled individuals to release repressed impulses. He was also successful in reorganizing an ineffective German economy. Roosevelt, as we have seen, played the roles both of the father and the initiatory actor. The hero role of John and Robert Kennedy has been supported by a great deal of the pure power of a well-financed political machine. When McCarthy seized the hero's mantle in 1968, Robert Kennedy was forced to a considerable extent to fall back on this source of strength. In the same campaign, Hubert Humphrey, once a liberal hero, became the candidate of the old-line machine politicians.

Not all types of leadership have equal charisma or equal power to confer legitimacy on political regimes. In general the father figure and the hero are likely to tap the deepest emotional springs and furnish the purest type of charismatic legitimacy. The intellectual rarely catches fire with the mass of people. His important contribution is likely to be rational rather than charismatic. The machine politician does not as such possess much charisma. Nor is this the strength of the organizer. It is true that the man like Lenin, Hitler, Churchill, or Roosevelt, who can get things done in a time of great crisis, is likely to receive great popular adulation and an unquestioning following. Such a leader, however, usually has other strong charismatic qualities in addition to organizing ability.

Finally, it should be clear that the appeal of charisma depends at least as much upon the follower as upon the leader. Charisma, like beauty, is largely in the eye of the beholder. The authoritarian personality studies show that the authoritarian individual is more likely to be swept away into uncritical followership than the more democratic

Russian soldiers demonstrate in Moscow during the revolution of October 1917.

person, who is likely to be more objective and critical. The same is true for the other mechanisms of legitimacy. Piaget's studies show that unquestioned reverence for tradition is characteristic of the mentality of the very young child, who is subservient to external constraint and authority. As he loses his uncritical respect for authority, the child becomes more objective about tradition. In an important book, *Law and the Modern Mind,* Judge Jerome K. Frank applied the same principles to rational legitimacy. The immature mind seeks a system that will provide absolute certainty and is peculiarly drawn to political orders, or other social systems, which claim to provide it. The more mature mind recognizes that no human statement of principles is absolute and no administration perfect. Thus in all aspects, the more mature individual will examine more critically all claims to absolute legitimacy.

THE PROCESS OF REVOLUTION

Not all leaders simply perpetuate an old political order, and no legitimacy lasts forever. Change is always taking place, even in the most apparently static societies. We analyzed some of the processes in Chapter seven. Sometimes the change is slow and relatively peaceful. At other times it is rapid, disrupts much of the society, and replaces one old system of legitimacy by a new one.

Political revolution is not something that descends upon a society like a bolt from the blue. In fact, it probably takes several generations to develop. It represents a failure of the established order to meet the felt needs of a sufficient number of its members. Political systems ordinarily escape revolution because (1) the process of enculturation teaches people to accept the legitimacy of the status quo, and (2) the system provides a certain number of real gratifications. When enough people feel that the gratifications are insufficient and begin to question the values they have been taught, then government can stay in power only by the increasing use of force. Ultimately force is likely to prove ineffective, and with it the government.

Periods before revolution show a

March of the women on Versailles, October 1789.

number of common characteristics. There is an *improvement in economic conditions.* Alexis de Tocqueville, writing of the French Revolution, was one of the first to notice this when he wrote, "It was precisely in those parts of France where there had been the most improvements that popular discontent was highest."[20] When utterly degraded, people are too tired and demoralized to revolt. All revolutions are really revolutions of rising expectations, but these expectations are not realized fast enough, at least by a substantial number of people. New classes on their way up find that there is "no room at the top." This was clearly true of the middle classes before the English and French revolutions. The lower classes become newly aware of their exclusion from the good things of the society.

There tends to develop an *ideology of frustration,* a "social myth" which undermines the legitimacy of the existing government. The myth usually holds that the present regime has usurped power illegitimately. It cites history to show that frustrated groups are really superior people who have been robbed of their rights. It usually calls for return to a true natural order of things. "All great revolutions," says Lyford P. Edwards, a prominent student of revolutionary change, "are 'religious' revolutions in the original, etymological sense of the word. They are carried through by men who feel themselves to be, in a special manner, 'tied' or 'bound' to 'God,' the 'Universe,' or the 'Ultimate Power' conceived in some fashion."[21] This is true even if, as in the French and Russian revolutions, the movement attacks organized religion.

The development of the social myth is likely to mark the *desertion of the intellectuals.* We have already noted that this is one of the strongest signs that the status quo is in danger. In the Reformation, Thomas More, Erasmus, Luther, and Calvin became critics of the established church. The English political leaders, Edmund Burke and William Pitt, took the side of the American colonies. Gogol, Pushkin, Kropotkin, and Gorki became critics of the czarist regime.

20. Chalmers Johnson, *Revolutionary Change,* Boston, Little, Brown, 1966, p. 62.

21. Lyford P. Edwards, *The Natural History of Revolution,* New York, Russell & Russell, 1965, p. 91.

Meanwhile, there is a growing *disintegration in the ruling group.* Shortage of money and unpopular taxation to raise money were part of the English, American, French, and Russian revolutions. The government is unable to meet the demands of changing times. Sometimes the personality of rulers plays an important part. George III, Louis XVI, and Nicholas II were all weak or stupid rulers at the time their countries revolted. Sometimes the rulers are simply stubborn in their refusal to change. Most important is their loss of confidence in themselves and in the legitimacy of what they are doing. "Is it not a simple fact," asked Plato, "that in any form of government revolution always starts from the outbreak of internal dissension in the ruling class?" When such demoralization sets in, rulers are likely to be unable to take simple steps of self-protection. In 1784, for example, the French censor wavered for a long time and then permitted de Beaumarchais' bitter antigovernment satire in *The Marriage of Figaro* to be shown.

With these developments, the actual revolution will probably begin with an act that might otherwise be relatively unimportant: Luther's theses against the church, the Boston Tea Party, the storming of the Bastille, bread riots in the streets of Petrograd. This act is likely to dramatize the existing regime's *inability to use force effectively.* It may be shown that a substantial number of the police or army have lost their morale or have actually turned against the government. Defeat in war is a powerful factor in producing such demoralization. Such defeat preceded, for example, the Russian Revolution, the overthrow of Mussolini in 1945, and the Chinese Revolution of 1949. The critical point in the Russian Revolution came in Petrograd when the soldiers of the Volinsk regiment fired into the air instead of at rioters. Behind their action lay defeat in World War I. Sometimes the fault may lie more with the rulers themselves than with the police or army. Louis XVI was just unable to realize that what was happening at the Bastille was revolution. Most of its students agree that revolution cannot succeed as long as force in the hands of the ruling group is intact and effective.

The first stage of a successful revolution is likely to bring rule by a fairly moderate group. The revolutionary Jacobins in France, one historian notes, were really middle-class people very much like modern Rotarians.[22] On the two sides of the moderates are conservatives, to the right, and radicals, to the left. The beginning of moderate rule is generally a period of optimism. Wordsworth wrote of these days in the French Revolution,

*France standing on the top of golden
    hours,
And human nature seeming born
    again.*[23]

The moderates are, however, immediately beset by problems. A new regime cannot create a completely new administrative bureaucracy, police courts, or army. To a large extent it must rely, for carrying out its policies, upon people from the prerevolutionary regime. Either deliberately or from long unconscious habit, these people are likely to oppose or twist the policies. Alexander Groth has stated this well:

For if every new regime inherits at least some survivals of the old, then also to the extent that the new differs from the old it has to contend with a residue of "dual power": the predisposition of "inherited" officials and sundry decision makers to use their powers so as to thwart and oppose the new sovereign.[24]

22. Crane Brinton, *The Anatomy of Revolution,* Englewood Cliffs, N.J., Prentice-Hall, 1952, p. 99.
23. William Wordsworth, *The Prelude,* Book Sixth, II, 340–341.
24. Alexander Groth, *Revolution and Elite Access: Some Hypotheses on Aspects of Political Change,* Davis, Calif., Institute of Governmental Affairs, University of California, 1966, p. 17.

The revolutionary leaders really have three choices. (1) They can try to convert the "old guard"; this is difficult and takes time. (2) They can modify their policies in a conservative direction; this defeats many of the purposes of the revolution and antagonizes the radicals and perhaps the masses. (3) They can use force, and appeal to the masses, to override the old guard; this policy antagonizes the conservatives and strengthens the likelihood of a counterrevolution.

What usually happens is that the conservatives move out of the picture. Partly they emigrate voluntarily and partly they are driven away or underground by the moderates. In the English Revolution, the new regime passed the Root and Branch Bill against conservative Episcopalians. The French revolutionary leaders passed the Civil Constitution of the Clergy to cripple the Catholic Church. The Russian Bolsheviks tried to eliminate conservative influence in the army by Order II, which democratized the armed forces. Elimination of the conservatives removes, however, a barrier against the radicals, who cry for more extreme action. They claim that a stronger government is needed to carry through a real revolution. They undermine the regime by such tactics as spreading propaganda; getting control of printing facilities; infiltrating the government, the militia and the courts; and organizing workers in the factories. The moderates are, moreover, reluctant to suppress them. They still consider the radicals their allies. If they do act to stop them, the radicals cry that their liberties are being invaded.

Eventually the radicals are likely to take power, as they did in the Bolshevik overthrow of the moderate Kerensky government in Russia in October 1917. The extremists are usually a small minority. In the American Revolution, perhaps 10 percent of the people actively supported the Declaration of Independence. In Russia the Bolshevik party was about one percent of the population. The extremists have the advantage, however, of lacking the scruples which held back the moderates. The leaders are likely to combine high ideals with freedom from political inhibitions: for the revolutionary cause, anything goes. Such leaders have been called "philosopher killers," by comparison with Plato's concept of the ideal rulers, who would be philosopher-priests.

The radicals are helped by the fact that a large number of people drop out of the political process. One of the reasons has probably been pressure from extremists against using the voting procedures established by the moderates. Thus the radicals establish a dictatorship, but with the argument that they are really serving the people. Robespierre called his revolutionary government in France the despotism of liberty against tyranny. In Russia Trotsky said, "Those against the insurrection were 'everybody'—except the Bolsheviks. But the Bolsheviks were the people."[25] Having taken power from the moderates, the radicals are likely to liquidate any opponents who have been even more extreme. Thus the government that had beheaded Charles II in England silenced the radical Levelers, Robespierre guillotined anarchists, and Trotsky eliminated the anarchists only to be himself murdered by Stalin. The whole situation is likely to be intensified by foreign invasion; in both the French and Russian revolutions there were foreign plans for dividing up the revolutionary country.

The height of the radical regime is the reign of terror. Even in the relatively mild American Revolution, loyalists were executed at Kingston, New York, and after the battle of Cowpens, South Carolina. The terror is not usually, however, nearly so bloody as is thought at the time and in the near future. Carefully managed fear is more typical than wholesale massacre. A fairly small number of executions are magnified to create the impression that everyone's life is in immediate danger.

25. Brinton, *op. cit.*, p. 167.

Cromwell, for example, carefully staged and publicized two spectacular massacres which took 4200 lives in Ireland. By so doing he probably avoided a war which might have cost 40,000. The French revolutionaries announced that the city of Lyons and its population were to be utterly destroyed. Wrecking crews were sent in and tore down a few buildings, and news of the total demolition spread by rumor over France. The number of actual deaths in the Russian terror was fairly small.

Along with the reign of terror is what historian Crane Brinton has called the "reign of virtue." Enthusiasm for the "religious" ideology of revolution reaches its height. It is at this time that some of the characteristics of revolution named by Eric Hoffer are most intensified: a sense of power, a sense of drama, a sense of absolute rightness, hatred for the old order and for counterrevolutionaries. Renaming marks the new era: a new calendar for France, revolutionary instead of czarist names for Russian cities. The "surrender of the self to the whole," as Hoffer calls it, results in the invasion of private life: everybody lives in a goldfish bowl. "Lenin," said Maxim Gorki, "was a man who prevented people from leading their accustomed lives as no one before him was able to do."[26] In contrast with the moderate period, in which there is a loosening of moral codes and emphasis on enjoyment of life, the reign of virtue is one of downgrading the present. Enjoyment is held in check by a new Puritanism. This was marked in the Puritan Revolution in England. The Reign of Terror in France attacked brothels, gaming houses, and drunkenness. Lenin called for austerity in language that could have come from an English Puritan or a Calvinist: "Carry out an accurate and honest account of money, manage economically, don't loaf, don't steal, maintain the strictest discipline in labor."[27]

This intensity is too great. Also, the government of terror and virtue, which is usually run by a committee, is not very efficient. Sooner or later a new leader comes to power, this time usually a conservative dictator. Cromwell in England, Napoleon Bonaparte in France, Stalin in Russia, and possibly Washington in the United States represent this change. Against the resistance of the revolutionary minority, much of the old governmental machinery is reestablished. This development has been called the "Thermidorean reaction," after the fall of Robespierre on the ninth of the month Termidor in the French revolutionary calendar. A new ruling group takes power. Political amnesty is granted to a number of prisoners and refugees. Formal religion, if it has been in disfavor (as in France and Russia) begins to return. At the same time, the revolutionary myth loses its intensity. So does the virtue; there may be an alternation between restraint and moral freedom.

The preceding sketch is, of course, an abstract pattern, a model which no actual revolution has followed exactly. What it does show is the tendencies in the revolutionary process which are likely to lead from step to step. Some actual revolutions abort or end in a takeover by counterrevolutionaries. This was true of some revolutions in Europe in 1848 and of the Paris Commune of 1871. In some revolutions power remains in moderate hands without passing on to radicals. For the most part, this was true of the American Revolution, which never reached the intensity of the English, French, or Russian revolutions.

Alexander Groth has pointed out that the form of revolution depends considerably on how far the revolutionary group is away, in organization and ideology, from the elites in power. When the revolutionary group is able to adjust fairly easily to the old administrative and power structure, the transition may be fairly smooth and the establishment of the new regime fairly easy. This was what happened with Mussolini in Italy and Hitler in Ger-

26. *Ibid.*, p. 200.
27. *Ibid.*, p. 207.

many. They moved in with much of the old power structure, primarily politicians and industrialists to whom fascism was not totally repugnant. This old guard hoped to use Mussolini and Hitler, and the budding dictators in turn hoped to use the old guard for their purposes.

The Russian Revolution was quite different, for there was little common ground between the Bolsheviks and the administrative and power structure carried over from the czar. Thus the new regime had to try to replace the old machinery as rapidly as possible by training, for example, their own army officers and industrial managers. In general the establishment of the Bolshevik regime was a much slower, more turbulent and bloodier process than the establishment of fascism and Nazism.

It is very important, in concluding this chapter, that we see revolution not as something apart from the ordinary political process, but as one expression of the conflicts of power and the forces of change which are always present within it. Revolutions are never made primarily by outside agitators (although conservatives almost always think so), or even by inside ones. They express the fact that the existing social and political structure has failed to provide for needed change by more peaceful means.

Suggestions for further reading

Many social scientists believe that the objective study of government as a social process can be dated from ARTHUR F. BENTLEY's The Process of Government, *first published in the early years of this century and reprinted by the Harvard University Press in 1967. Some feel that there is still no better introduction to this subject. Recent, concrete, and realistic books on how government operates in the United States are* The Governmental Process *by DAVID B. TRUMAN (Knopf, 1951); V. O. KEY, JR.'s* Politics, Parties, and Pressure Groups *(5th ed., Thomas Y. Crowell); and* Parties and Politics in America *by CLINTON ROSSITER (Cornell University Press, 1964, paper).*

A fascinating analysis of how American voting has been related to class interest is SAMUEL LUBELL, The Future of American Politics *(rev. ed., Harper & Row, 1965, paper). The first sociological studies of community power structure were* Middletown *and* Middletown in Transition, *by ROBERT M. LYND and HELEN LYND (Harcourt Brace Jovanovich, paper).* The Power Elite, *by C. WRIGHT MILLS (Oxford University Press, 1959, paper) contended that the United States is dominated by a minority of top businessmen, politicians, and military brass. FLOYD HUNTER's famous Atlanta study,* Community Power Structure *(University of North Carolina Press, 1969, paper) and its extension to the national level,* Top Leadership, U.S.A. *(University of North Carolina Press, 1959, paper) give a similar picture of minority rule. The Edgewood and Riverview studies of community power relations in New York state, by ROBERT V. PRESTHUS, are reported in* Men at the Top *(Oxford University Press, 1964, paper). ROBERT DAHL's New Haven report,* Who Governs? *(Yale University Press, 1961, paper) presents a more optimistic view of the possibility of democratic community control.*

A long-accepted work on propaganda is LEONARD DOOB's Public Opinion and Propaganda *(2nd ed., Archon Shoe String, 1966, paper). More recent is* Propaganda, *by the controversial French writer JACQUES ELLUL (Knopf, 1965), who sees propaganda as an inevitable part of the technological society. Two provocative books on how political rule is legitimized are* Law and the Modern Mind *by JEROME H. FRANK (Peter Smith), and* The Folklore of Capitalism *by THURMAN W. ARNOLD (Yale University Press, 1937, paper). Both authors were high-ranking judges in the New Deal days of Roosevelt. Two very important studies of how revolution takes place are* The Natural History of Revolution *by LYFORD P. EDWARDS (Russell & Russell, 1927; reprinted, 1965) and CRANE BRINTON's* The Anatomy of Revolution *(Vintage, 1957, paper). ERIC HOFFER's* The True Believer *(Harper & Row, 1951, paper) is a longshoreman-intellectual's view of social movements. The reader will find more pithy, insightful observations than systematic analysis.*

The kind of government we can expect in our impersonal culture is discussed by WILLIAM KORNHAUSER in The Politics of Mass Society *(Free Press, 1959). A detailed statistical survey of the same subject is reported by GABRIEL ALMOND and SIDNEY VERBA in* The Civic Culture *(Princeton University Press, 1963). Almond and Verba studied political participation in five countries—Britain, West Germany, Italy, Mexico, and the United States.*

Chapter ten
The political spectrum

We shall examine in this chapter the forms that government has taken and might conceivably take. There have been in history only a fairly limited number of ways of organizing political life; perhaps only a limited number of political arrangements are possible. Each of the forms has two aspects. (1) Objectively it is a system of social relationships. (2) Subjectively it has an ideology, a system of beliefs and myths by which it is justified, or legitimized.

We have seen that government, as a distinct social institution, begins with the development of economic surplus after the agricultural revolution. Aristotle already saw some of the chief forms of government: monarchy, aristocracy, and timocracy (rule based on property). He felt, also, that each of these systems had a degenerate form. Kingly government, he said, can easily become tyranny. Aristocracy can become oligarchy, a form of collective tyranny. Timocracy can degenerate into democracy. Of the degenerate forms, Aristotle felt that tyranny is the worst, democracy the least dangerous.

AUTHORITARIANISM

Since the development of the political state, the most common form of government has clearly been *authoritarianism*. Externally this has represented Aristotle's first and second types—rule by an individual or a small group. Here we find absolute monarchies; rule by dictators like Caesar, Cromwell, Hitler, Stalin; or rule by a small minority, as in medieval feudalism, modern Ethiopia or South Africa, or the Soviet Union. In actuality we could probably say that all authoritarianism has been the rule of a minority group (aristocracy or oligarchy), for no single king or dictator is so capable or so powerful that he can rule a country absolutely alone. Under authoritarianism the mass of people remain forever political infants, without any direct participation in their government. The government is a law unto itself: the individual citizen has no rights (such as due process of law) that limit the government's right to do with him as it pleases. Internally authoritarianism is based on a relationship between ruler and ruled which repeats that of parent and young child in the traditional authoritarian family. There is no sense that the people have any right to control the government, any more than children in a patriarchal family have a right to participate in family decisions.

The authoritarian regime is held together, as one writer has put it, by guns, grandparents, and God. Since the authoritarian government is not bound by legal procedures, its monopoly of force can be used effectively to terrorize people into submission. In addition, tradition is strong, and people are likely to feel it is wrong to rebel against the political system that served their ancestors (thus, traditional legitimacy). Finally, the traditional society is usually a religious one, so that people are easily convinced that their rulers are the representatives of God. We have seen Thomas Hobbes' classic argument basing absolute rule on the divine right of kings (rational legitimacy).

The typical authoritarian government is part of a society that is postprimitive, but premodern. Thus it dominated the period from about 3000 B.C. to about A.D. 1800. Authoritarian government can mature only when an economic surplus has given rise to specialization, separation into distinct classes, and separate machinery of government. On the other hand, it begins to run into difficulties in a technically advanced society, with its rising standard of living, widespread education, and rising expectations. Because it is typically premodern, the authoritarian society as such is not really totalitarian (although all totalitarian societies are based on centralized authority). Totalitarianism, which is the regimentation of all life into the mold of a single political ideology, requires modern techniques of mass propaganda and brainwashing. It is a twentieth-century product.

LIBERALISM

Liberalism arose in the seventeenth and eighteenth centuries out of the individualism of the Renaissance. More immediately, it was a manifestation of the desire of merchants and manufacturers for freedom from authoritarian constraint by kings, landed aristocrats, and the church. The British, American, and French revolutions represent the political triumph of the liberal philosophy.

The rising middle classes of England, the Continent, and the United States clashed with the whole structure of premodern society. The Protestant Reformation and the Protestant ethic created, as we have seen, a climate and a justification for individual profit seeking. Political liberalism turned in the same way against the authoritarian state. The ambitious capitalists found

themselves, first of all, excluded from participation in governments ruled by kings and landed gentlemen. They found their interests hindered by tariff barriers, by special charters granted to monopolistic companies, by laws artificially maintaining agricultural prices, by restrictions on importation of raw materials, and by government regulation of manufacturing processes, sometimes down to minute details. Harry K. Girvetz says:

> In the preliberal era . . . prices, interest rates, the condition of work, the quality of merchandise, the relationships of vassal to lord or journeyman to master, all these were determined, not by a contract or agreement representing the upshot of a bargain or negotiation among the parties to the transaction or relationship, but by preestablished rule and practice.[1]

Against restrictions of all kinds, liberalism preached the freedom of individual activity. In his book *Liberalism,* the distinguished British social scientist, L. T. Hobhouse, suggested the main planks in the liberal platform.

Liberalism stands for the *rule of law,* which makes both ruler and ruled subject to a political constitution, a written or unwritten higher law which neither can legitimately violate. The British Magna Charta and the Bill of Rights in the United States Constitution furnish such a framework. Also central is the principle that all those who are charged for the costs of government should also have the opportunity to participate in government—no taxation without representation. A third aspect of the liberal program is guarantee of *civil liberties*—individual freedom of religion, assembly, petition, speech, and association. Liberalism also calls for equality of *social opportunity.* Each person should, so far as possible, be able to strive for social and economic

1. Harry K. Girvetz, *The Evolution of Liberalism,* New York, Crowell Collier and Macmillan, 1963, p. 71.

John Locke

government leaves people to pursue their individual interests with the least possible interference. Adam Smith's idea of the invisible hand which guides the laissez-faire market is an example of this concept of natural harmony.

To understand the liberal idea of harmony we need to examine the liberal view of man. The individual is a social atom. Society is an association of separate organisms who are more or less complete in themselves. The idea that the individual is to a large extent a product of society is rejected. The great English liberal philosopher, John Stuart Mill, specifically denied that society has any different properties from its individual members. He rejected the idea that in combination people might create a new compound, as hydrogen and oxygen produce water.

The individual atoms of liberalism are naturally passive, unless stirred into action by some external force. Effort is painful. The English philosopher, John Locke, who was very influential in the development of liberalism, held that the human mind is a blank slate which is given form only by events which happen to it. Thomas Malthus spoke of "the acknowledged indolence of man." To the historic liberal view, man is not stimulated to socially useful activity by any natural joy in being usefully active. He can be motivated only by the spur of powerful individual selfishness. "Everyone but an idiot," said a much read eighteenth-century liberal, "knows that the lower classes must be kept poor or they will never be industrious." By the same standard, the middle and upper classes will rest on their oars unless motivated by the hope of more and more profit.

rewards without discrimination on the basis of birth, race, nationality, religion, or any standard other than ability and merit.

Economic opportunity involves the ability to contract freely with others to buy or sell goods, services, or labor. This means that the liberal economy will be one of free competition. The liberal platform also includes the principle of *self-determination*. Localities shall have a maximum of home rule as against control by central government, and nations shall have the right to decide their form of government without coercion from other nations. Liberalism implies, finally, the deliberate effort to build an *international community* based on liberal principles and a rejection of empire building and of efforts at nationalistic domination through military power.

Every political ideology has a view of man and society. The authoritarian view holds that man in a state of nature is violent and untrustworthy and that a strong hand is needed if social order is to exist. Liberalism, on the other hand, believes in a natural harmony among men, which will work itself out best if

Man, in the liberal view, is then a pure egoist. As a separate social atom, he is moved only by self-interest. He is also highly rational. He is forever calculating the most intelligent way to serve his atomistic selfishness. The idea of economic man, always scheming how to make the most profit, is a central part of this conception. Another great nineteenth-century liberal, Jeremy Bentham, referred to the "felicific calculus." He meant that people are always calculating how to gain for themselves the greatest possible felicity, or well-being.

The natural social harmony must be, then, one of *atomistic individuals rationally pursuing their separate ends under the spur of personal gain.* If the common interest of society is to be served, it is through enabling people to follow their selfish desires, not by persuading or forcing them to renounce them. "Private vices, public virtues," said the liberal Bernard de Mandeville. Said Adam Smith,

It is not from the benevolence of the butcher, the brewer, or the baker, that we expect our dinner, but from their regard to their own interest. We address ourselves, not to their humanity, but to their self-love; and never talk to them of our own necessities, but of their advantages.[2]

A twentieth-century version is by economist Milton Friedman, "There is only one responsibility of a corporation—to make as much money as possible within the rules of the game."

We may note that very little of this liberal view of man and society finds much support in modern social science. Our knowledge of the relationship between culture and personality does not agree with the idea of isolated social atoms. Our discussions of play and work suggest that interested activity, not inertia, is the natural condition of all animals. We now consider social impulses to be at least as basic as egotistical ones. Our modern emphasis on the uncertain and irrational elements in human personality does not fit the model of man as a calculating, rational machine. Nor does our study of society give us reason to believe in a natural harmony of selfish interests. There is little evidence in

2. Adam Smith, *The Wealth of Nations,* London, Routledge, 1890, p. 11.

modern social science that laissez-faire will produce the best of all possible worlds. We doubt, as one social historian put it, that free competition is an automatic substitute for honesty, or for social concern.

One more aspect of the historic liberal view is important. This is *utilitarianism,* whose chief spokesman was Jeremy Bentham, and whose slogan was "the greatest good for the greatest number." If we ask why liberalism expressed so much concern for the individual, we will find two answers. One lies in the idea of natural rights. The Declaration of Independence held that the rights to life, liberty, and the pursuit of happiness are "self-evident." This idea was powerful in the French Revolution. In the nineteenth century, however, the doctrine of natural rights became less popular among liberals, and the utilitarian idea tended to take its place. This held that the freedom of the individual should be respected, not because he has any natural right to it, but because this is the best policy for society. Through individual liberty—economic, political, and social—the natural harmony is best achieved, the greatest good realized for the most people.

In the eighteenth, nineteenth, and twentieth centuries, liberalism has had a tremendous impact upon political and social institutions. It has been the dominant philosophy in three great national revolutions which have changed the world. It broke down mercantilist regulation of production and restrictions on free competition. It lowered tariff barriers and encouraged free trade among nations. It has spread guarantees for civil liberties and the rule of law. It has extended the vote to the middle and lower classes. It has removed a great many class barriers to economic and social mobility. It has weakened political colonialism throughout the world.

In the same period, however, liberalism has itself undergone a great change. The eighteenth- and early nineteenth-century liberal had a very

John Stuart Mill

negative view of the state. In the late nineteenth century, liberals began to support child labor laws, minimum wage and maximum hour laws, accident compensation laws, and other types of social legislation. In the twentieth century, liberalism is associated with the welfare state—in the United States, with the New Deal and now the Great Society. Today's liberals seem to be as positive in their view of government as their ancestors were negative. In some senses the liberal of today seems almost the opposite of the old-time liberal. What has happened?

Some old-style liberals and other critics would say that today's welfare state liberal is no liberal in anything but name, that he has sold out the liberal cause. There is another way of looking at the matter, however.

In this other view, the liberal has always been concerned with the freedom and development of the individual. Two hundred years ago he rebelled against arbitrary authoritarian controls by government. It seemed that if these could only be removed, a healthy society might develop. In the nineteenth century, however, it became apparent that the removal of govern-

ment regulation had opened the door to another form of arbitrary control, that of powerful private economic interests. In the face of large corporations, the individual worker, consumer, or small businessman was powerless. Even Adam Smith had said that the ordinary worker in an industrial society must become ignorant and degraded "unless government takes some pains to prevent it." A hundred years later many liberals felt strongly that only a positive role for government could establish conditions for real freedom and development of the individual. This kind of thinking led John Stuart Mill, one of the most powerful exponents of liberalism, to become virtually a Socialist in his later years. It is behind liberal support for a vastly extended role of government today.

There are many who think that the twentieth-century liberal state poses as great a threat to human individuality as did the authoritarian state of the eighteenth century, or perhaps even a greater one. This raises questions to which we must return later. It is clear, at any rate, that in two centuries the meaning of "liberal" has changed enormously.

SOCIALISM

The nineteenth-century development of capitalist industry, which made welfare liberals out of laissez-faire liberals, also gave rise to the more radical philosophy of socialism. Some thinkers like Mill were led far in this direction. Others found it no longer possible to accept capitalism at all.

The term "socialism" is very loosely used. It is correct to think of socialism as *socialized control of the means of production.* Ownership of capital goods is no longer in the hands of private individuals or corporations. The means of production may be owned by the state (nationalized), they may be in the hands of semi-independent public corporations like the TVA, or they may be in the hands of producers' or consumers' cooperatives. Socialism may also include some private ownership of capital goods, provided the units remain very small. This is the case in Yugoslavia, for example. It is very important to note that under socialism only capital goods are socialized. Consumption goods continue to be the property of individuals.

Socialism is more than a legal change in ownership, it is also a shift in actual control to democratically responsible bodies. The socialized means of production may be governed by administrative agencies, as with the post office or the TVA; by workers' councils, as in Yugoslavian industry; or by cooperative society meetings, as in England, Sweden, the United States, and many other countries. Such democratic control is quite different from the authoritarian nationalization of capital goods under Russian communism or under German and Italian national socialism. Neither modern communism nor fascism is in the true tradition of socialism, although the former nationalizes almost all means of production, and the latter nationalized some.

At this point we need to distinguish between socialism and communism. (1) The distinction may be that communism socializes consumption as well as production. This is the case in the primitive communism of some preliterate societies, in the early Christian communities, and in a number of voluntary Utopian communities which have adopted the principle of holding all goods in common. (2) In this sense communism may also refer to a final state of development, which will be reached after a preliminary stage of socialism. This has been the theory in the Soviet Union. In the end it is held that Russian society will move toward a communality of goods which will be primitive communism on a grand scale. (3) Historically Communists have often been distinguished by their emphasis on the need for sudden and violent revolution, while Socialists have stressed the possibility of a peaceful transition from capitalism. (4) As suggested, the term "communism" is now used to describe nationalized political regimes that are neither communistic nor even socially controlled. Democratic Socialists stress that genuine socialism (or communism) must involve popular control of the means of production and of all political processes.

In the socialist tradition, we must distinguish two forms: utopian and scientific (or Marxist). Utopian socialism grew out of the French Revolution and the social effects of the Industrial Revolution. As the name suggests, it was based on the idea that one could construct an ideal society in the mind and put it into effect by appealing to intelligence. We see here some of the belief in human reason that we encountered in liberalism.

The French nobleman Henri de Saint Simon (1760–1825) constructed a blueprint for society in which property was nationalized; the landed, idle class abolished; and control lodged in a 3-chamber "industrial parliament" of engineers, poets, scholars, musicians, physicists, philosophers, and industrial managers. Saint Simon's plan was highly centralized and not at all democratic.

On the other hand, Charles Fourier (1772–1835) projected a decentralized society which would be a federation of communities of about 1800 people each, called "phalanges." Fourier distrusted and disliked cities, and the phalanges were to return man to the land. Actually his plan was not socialistic, since it did not abolish private ownership of capital goods, but it was very influential in stimulating Utopian communities, especially in the United States. The famous community at Brook Farm, which attracted the philosopher Ralph Waldo Emerson and his associates, was a Fourierist experiment.

Robert Owen (1771–1858) was a Scottish manufacturer who first turned his factory at New Lanark into a model of industrial relations, and then founded a Utopian community at New Harmony, Indiana. Owen's influence in the United States was great enough so that he was invited to speak before Congress.

Mainly as an outcome of the ideas of Saint Simon, Fourier, and Owen, from 1 to 200 experimental communities with socialistic leanings were established in the United States at one time or another during the nineteenth century. It has been estimated that the number of participants may have run into the hundreds of thousands.

To the scientific Socialists, the programs of the Utopians were sentimental and out of touch with historical realities. The major figures in scientific socialism were Marx, Engels, and Lenin. Their central doctrine was historical materialism, the view that material factors are the most important in shaping society.

Critics of Marxism often confuse historical materialism with philosophical materialism (the doctrine that only matter is real) and ethical materialism (the view that only material values are important). Marx may have been a philosophical materialist, but ethical materialism has never been held by Marxists. Erich Fromm has, in fact, made a good case that Marx was really a humanist in the tradition of the Renaissance, who desired above all else to expand the freedom and dignity of the individual. As a young man Marx was much influenced by Christianity. Acceptance of the role of spiritual ideas and values did not mean, however, that noble ideals are enough to bring a good society. "Men make history, but they do not make it out of the whole cloth." Ideas and ideals can be effective only as they mesh into the dominant material conditions of their time.

The most important condition, for the Marxist, was the class struggle. In their view, as we have seen, history is a succession of stages, each dominated by a ruling class which is, in its turn, overthrown and succeeded by another class. Each stage is marked by a dialectical process. This means that each period of class rule creates contradic-

tory forces which will eventually undermine it.

Feudalism, through its need for the products of craftsmen, gave rise to cities and to the bourgeoisie, who eventually abolished it. Bourgeois rule, in turn, masses together a propertyless proletariat who will eventually bring capitalism to an end. This must happen, said Marx, as workers finally become sufficiently aware of their real situation: labor has created all the value of production, but the capitalist pays the worker only a part of this value and keeps the rest (surplus value) for himself. We need not evaluate the much debated labor theory of value (which Marx did not invent) or theory of surplus value to see how they fit into the Marxist scheme.

To the scientific Socialist, then, realistic action is class action. Noblemen like Saint Simon and benevolent industrialists like Owen can never bring about fundamental change through rational plans or isolated Utopian experiments. Only the organized working class has the power, at this stage in history, to create a Socialist society. Members of other classes can be effective, if at all, only as they join the movement of the workers. Ideas and ideals can be effective only as they fit into the actual needs and possibilities of the moment.

In the Marxian view, passage from one historical stage to another requires a revolutionary process. Privileged classes have never given up their privileges without severe resistance. No more can it be expected that the capitalist class will permit socialism to come peacefully. The working class must therefore be organized for powerful and decisive action. This may involve such direct action as a general strike or the seizure of public offices. It is conceivable that socialism might be voted in through regular legislative procedures. Even should it come to power peacefully and legally, it will be resisted with sabotage and violence. In order to check this counterrevolution, there must be a "dictatorship of the proletariat." In actuality this will be a dictatorship *for* the proletariat by an intellectual elite of scientific Socialists who know the real needs of the workers better than they do themselves.

In time, as the old capitalist class dies off (or is killed or emigrates) and the rest of the people are educated in the ways of socialism, the dictatorship will no longer be necessary, and the political state will wither away. The class struggle will have come to a close, for when those who work productively control the means of production, there will be no one to exploit. In time production may become so plentiful that all important goods will become free, and the ideals of communism will be realized. Then, in the words of Lenin,

Karl Marx

> *freed from capitalist slavery, from the untold horrors, savagery, absurdities and infamies of capitalist exploitation, people will gradually become accustomed to the observance of the elementary rules of social life that have been known for centuries and repeated for thousands of years in all school books; they will become accustomed to observing them without force, without compulsion.*[3]

For many years after Marx, scientific socialism seemed to dominate the Socialist camp, and the Utopians to be discredited. Today, however, Socialists (and non-Socialists) are taking a new look at the problem. Tremendously spectacular political achievements have been made, it is true, in the name of scientific socialism, but the most spectacular of them seem to have led to a new class authoritarianism which is neither Socialist nor Communist, and embodies few of the humanistic ideals of liberalism or of Marx or Lenin. If the great "Communist" societies of today are to become either Socialist or Communist, it appears likely that they will

do so only through another social revolution not programmed in the scientific Socialist book.

Scientific socialism, as developed by the so-called Marxist parties, has tried to fit social reality into theories entirely too narrow and rigid to contain it. Probably if he were alive today, Marx would reject a large part of what has been written and done in his name. In his early writings, there were strong Utopian elements. At one time he expressed impatience with some of his followers, saying, "I am not a Marxist." Democratic Socialists and some members of the New Left of today continue to support the economic and humanitarian goals of socialism and to appreciate the great insights of Marx, but they have adopted a flexible and experimental approach which is closer to Utopian socialism than to Marxist orthodoxy.

CONSERVATISM

The rise of liberalism and socialism led to a political reaction in the form of

3. V. I. Lenin, *State and Revolution,* New York, International Publishers, 1932, pp. 73–74.

Edmund Burke

modern conservatism. Beginning in the late eighteenth century, this has actually had two phases. The first, a *precapitalist conservatism,* stood for the old order of kings, landed gentry, and church against the new industrial society and its political expressions. This agrarian conservatism is still with us today—in parts of the American South, for example—but has lost a large part of its power. As the capitalist industrial class established its dominance, conservatism shifted from a rightist attack on capitalist liberalism and became instead a defense of capitalism. *Laissez-faire conservatism* (we might almost call it "liberal conservatism") opposes both socialism and welfare liberalism, but in the name of capitalist values which the old conservatives fought bitterly.

There have thus been two conservatisms, just as there have been two liberalisms, and for essentially the same reason—the success of modern capitalism. Let us look at some of the basic principles that underlay the old-style conservatism and then see to what degree they have changed as the meaning of conservatism has changed.

Continuity. When a conservative speaks, one usually hears references to the past: the Hebrew prophets, the Greek philosophers, Jesus, the Middle Ages, the founding fathers, and the Constitution. The conservative believes strongly in the legitimacy of tradition. To him there is little really new under the sun. Most significant human problems have been encountered long ago, and some kind of workable solution has been achieved through long and painful experience. The institutions of the status quo represent the accumulation of this experience. These neither should, nor indeed can, be easily changed. An example of this view is the statement by a great American conservative, William Graham Sumner, on "The Absurd Effort to Make the World Over." Edmund Burke (1727–1977), who opposed the French Revolution on the grounds just described, made another classic statement of the conservative view. Burke is often considered the father of the conservative tradition.

The last sentence of Burke's statement emphasizes a point very important to conservatives. Society is more than the sum of the individuals living at any given time, and society's interests more than their interests. Therefore it is wrong to emphasize the individual, or even a single generation, at the expense of the longer social concern.

The conservative thinks of himself as profound by contrast with the liberal or radical, whom he judges to be superficial. He considers himself to be a person with deep roots in history. The liberal or radical is detached and rootless. The conservative feels that the liberals and radicals oversimplify social problems, while he understands their complexity. The radical or liberal, he believes, is full of abstract and irrational dreams, while the conservative is in contact with hard reality.

We will notice that in the quotation from Burke he uses the words "society" and "state" interchangeably. This indicates the traditional conservative attitude toward government. Society is a body of institutions that have been proved necessary by time and experience. The state is one of these institutions: it is the arm by which the order won over centuries is preserved. We shall see that the later laissez-faire conservatism took a new view of government.

Property. A second main point in the conservative program is the defense of property. In the French Revolution, conservatives like Burke saw revolutionaries running roughshod over long-established property rights. Today conservatives see welfare liberals threatening the sanctity of property. John Locke, primarily a laissez-faire liberal rather than a conservative, laid down the primacy of property rights: "The great and chief end . . . of men's uniting into commonwealths, and putting themselves under government, is the preservation of their property." Two centuries later Sumner asserted, "At bottom there are two chief things with which government has to deal. They are, the property of men and the honor of women. These it has

to defend against crime." Few conservatives, perhaps, would go as far as one candidate for the governorship of Florida in 1964: "Government's function should be limited to protecting the possessors of property against those who possess nothing."

To the modern liberal, the conservative seems to value property above human rights (as, for example, when a storekeeper's right to run his own business is placed above a Negro's right to be served). To the conservative, however, the right of property is simply the first human right. All other rights will eventually fall if property is not protected.

Religion. In his *Reflections on the Revolution in France,* Burke said of the people of England, "Church and state are ideas inseparable in their minds, and scarcely is the one ever mentioned without mentioning the other." Today, when issues such as prayer in the public schools are contested, conservatives are generally found supporting religious exercises, and liberals supporting the separation of church and

---

If this poor old world is as bad as they say it is, one more reflection may check the zeal of the headlong reformer. It is at any rate a tough old world. If we puny men by our arts can do anything at all to straighten [it], it will be only by modifying the tendencies of some of the forces at work so that, after a sufficient time, their action may be changed a little and slowly their lines of movement may be modified. . . . The great stream of time and earthly things will sweep on just the same in spite of us. . . . It is only in imagination that we can stand by and look at it and criticize it and plan to change it. . . . Every one of us is a child of his age and cannot get out of it. . . . The things which will change it are the great discoveries and inventions, the new reactions inside the social organism, the changes in the earth itself on account of changes in the cosmical forces. . . . The men will be carried along with it and be made by it. The utmost they can do by their cleverness will be to note and record their course as they are carried along. . . . That is why it is the greatest folly of which a man can be capable, to sit down with a slate and pencil and plan out a new social world.

—*William Graham Sumner, "The Absurd Effort to Make the World Over,"* from Sumner Today: Essays of William Graham Sumner, *ed. Maurice R. Davie, New Haven, Conn., Yale University Press, 1940, pp. 109–110.*

*Society is indeed a contract. . . . The state ought not to be
considered as nothing better than a partnership agreement in a
trade of pepper and coffee, calico or tobacco, or some other such
low concern, to be taken up for a little temporary interest, and to
be dissolved by the fancy of the parties. It is to be looked on
with other reverence. . . . It is a partnership in all science; a
partnership in all art; a partnership in every virtue, and in all
perfection. As the ends of such a partnership cannot be obtained
in many generations, it becomes a partnership not only between
those who are living, but between those who are living, those who
are dead, and those who are to be born.*

—Edmund Burke, *Reflections on the Revolution in France (vol. 24 of
The Harvard Classics), ed. Charles W. Eliot, New York, Crowell
Collier and Macmillan, p. 232.*

state. Conservatives like to think of religion as the moral cement which holds
society together. They think of government and society as part of an eternal
moral order. They consider liberals and
radicals irreligious relativists, who
recognize no absolute values, and
materialists, who have no use for
higher spiritual concerns.

Aristocracy. To the conservative the
liberal naively denies one of the most
obvious of facts, that men are unequal
in their capacity to rule. Alexander
Hamilton, perhaps the most outstanding single individual in the first days of
the United States, and not a complete
conservative, said before the Constitutional Convention:

> *All communities divide themselves
> into the few and the many. The first
> are the rich and well-born, the other
> the mass of the people . . . [who]
> seldom judge or determine right.
> . . . Give therefore to the first class
> a distinct, permanent share in the
> government.*[4]

John Adams, the second American
president, whom one student of conservatism has called the outstanding
American conservative, held a similar
view.

*By the law of nature, all men are
men, and not angels—men, and not
lions—men, and not whales—men,
and not eagles—that is, they are all
of the same species, and that is the
most that the equality of nature ad-
mits to. But man differs by nature
from man, almost as much as man
from beast. . . . A physical inequality, an intellectual inequality, of the
most serious kind, is established un-
changeably by the Author of nature,
and society has a right to establish
any other inequalities it may judge
necessary for its good.*[5]

This view is echoed, for contemporary conservatives, by Ortega y Gasset
in *The Revolt of the Masses:*

> *Society is always a dynamic unity
> of two component factors: minorities
> and masses. The minorities are indi-
> viduals or groups of individuals who
> are specially qualified. The mass is
> the assemblage of persons not
> specially qualified.*[6]

Ortega did not hold that qualified individuals are confined to any one social
or economic class, but he did insist
that they are a distinct minority.

4. Papers of Alexander Hamilton, Columbia University Press, 1961, vol. IV, p. 200.

5. John Adams quoted in Clinton Rossiter, *Conservatism in America*, New York, Knopf, 1955, p.
114.
6. José Ortega y Gasset, *The Revolt of the Masses*,
New York, Norton, 1932, p. 13.

The conservative, then, has been traditionally *antiegalitarian* (denying the political equality of men). He has been *antimajoritarian* (like Hamilton and Ortega, he distrusts the masses). He believes in *indirect rule,* which makes effective mass democracy less likely. (Election of the president by an electoral college, rather than by direct vote, is an example of indirect rule.) Believing in inequality, the conservative is likely to stress command and obedience. He is likely to have little patience for those who challenge established authority. He is also likely to put liberty above equality (especially freedom of economic enterprise). The conservative position against sit-ins as violation of the liberty of storekeepers illustrates this view.

Original sin. The conservative takes a dim view of human nature. This is one of the main reasons why he distrusts programs for social improvement. The theological doctrine of original sin holds that all men share in the fall of Adam. Not all conservatives share this particular theology, but they are likely to agree with John Adams, who said that anyone wishing to form a state and make the necessary laws for the government of it must presume that all men are bad by nature. Freud was in many ways a revolutionary figure, but he expressed a deeply conservative point of view about the possibility of social progress. His view has greatly influenced modern thinking.

> The natural instinct of aggressiveness in man, the hostility of each one against all and of all against each one, opposes this program of civilization. . . . And it is this battle of the Titans that our nurses and governesses try to compose with their lullaby song of Heaven.[7]

We see here in Freud the typical contempt of the conservative for the opti-

7. Sigmund Freud, *Civilization and Its Discontents,* trans. Joan Riviere, New York, Jonathan Cape, 1930, pp. 102, 103.

mism of liberals and radicals. Reinhold Niebuhr, one of the most prominent modern theologians, and usually described as a political liberal, nevertheless expresses a profoundly conservative view of original sin. "There is no force in human culture, no technique in government, and no grace in the human spirit which can completely overcome the power of human egoism."

The conservative's pessimism about human nature reinforces his skepticism about the masses. Only a few rare people, if any, can rise above their selfish nature and achieve some degree of altruism and rationality. The conservative is thus extremely skeptical about the possibility of any real social progress. Because "you can't change human nature," history cannot do much more than repeat itself. *Plus ça change, plus c'est la même chose* (the more things change, the more they're the same). Believing that social progress is unlikely, the conservative is likely to see the only real hope in individual self-cultivation and self-improvement.

There are surface similarities between the conservative's view of human nature and the laissez-faire liberal's view. On the face of it, Niebuhr's statement about human egoism could have been made by an eighteenth- or nineteenth-century liberal, and was made by a man who considers himself a twentieth-century liberal. But the liberal, if in the beginning he had little faith in individual love and altruism, did believe in individual and collective reason. He felt that even man's innate selfishness can be so directed by intelligent social policy that all things will eventually work out for good. Thus the liberal view has always been essentially optimistic, whereas the conservative view is pessimistic and tragic.

Some modern conservatives might not entirely recognize themselves in the picture we have painted. Perhaps this is because of the change in the nature of conservatism to which we have referred. The original conservatism was the ideology of "the original gentlemen and landed property," as Burke described it, of late nineteenth-century England. It took a strong foothold in the United States in the Old South, with John C. Calhoun as its most prominent spokesman.

With the breaking of southern power and the success of liberal capitalism, conservatism became the ideology of successful businessmen, industrialists, and bankers. Conservatives appealed, and still do, to the eternal order of nature, against welfare liberals and radicals who would tinker with it. But the eternal order is the capitalist "struggle for existence," not the aristocratic life of kings and nobility. We can see this appeal in John D. Rockefeller, Jr.

> The growth of a large business is merely a survival of the fittest. . . . The American Beauty Rose can be produced in the splendor and fragrance which bring cheer to its beholder only by sacrificing the early buds which grow up around it. This is not an evil tendency in business. It is merely the working out of a law of nature and a law of God.[8]

To this laissez-faire conservatism, the state was not the servant of nature and God, but an obstacle. Rather than quote Burke, it was likely to quote Jefferson: "That government is best which governs least." The clash between this new capitalist conservatism and the old conservatism of land, king, and church was expressed by Henry Adams (great-grandson of John) in his autobiography, in which he said of himself:

> He had stood up for his eighteenth century . . . as long as any one would stand up with him. He had said it was hopeless twenty years before, but he had kept on, in the same old attitude, by habit and taste, until he found himself altogether alone. He had hugged his antiquated distaste of bankers and capitalistic society until he had become little better than a crank.[9]

In today's conservatives we find a blend of laissez-faire conservatism with the principles of Burke. It refers to "constitutional government" and appeals for continuity with the tradition of the founding fathers against liberal and radical change. It opposes "big government" as interference with the natural order of things, although this is a change from the traditional conservative view of the state as preserver of traditional institutions. The right of property (now primarily capitalist property) is still to them the central human right, and its protection the central purpose of government. Conservatives generally oppose the separation of church and state and continue to identify their program with eternal moral and religious values. They are not so openly aristocratic as in the days of "the original gentlemen and landed property," but still distrust the masses. Underlying this is the old distrust and pessimism about the nature of man.

The two strains in present-day conservatism are not completely fused. In the United States today, both keep some of their original form. A good deal of American conservatism is laissez-faire conservatism, an across-the-board defense of the existing capitalistic status quo against government action by liberals and radicals. The world that this philosophy would conserve is not free competition, but control by a relatively few large private enterprises (who sometimes support it financially). In its extreme form, this laissez-faire conservatism shades into an authoritarian and undemocratic far-rightism (which we shall explore in Chapter fourteen). An example of this extreme conservatism would be Senator Joseph McCarthy's campaigns against subversives in the 1950s.

---

8. John D. Rockefeller, Jr., quoted in Rossiter, *op. cit.*, p. 152.

9. From *The Education of Henry Adams,* quoted in *ibid.*, p. 170.

Such defense of the status quo is much the same as another kind of liberal conservatism, which stands for the values of eighteenth- and early nineteenth-century liberalism. Its ideal is a society of small landowners and merchants. A prominent example of this type of conservatism was President Eisenhower's deep-grained belief in the simple virtues of a capitalist past which existed at some time to some degree in rural, small town America.

From this conservatism, the hero of which is Thomas Jefferson, we move to a Burkean conservatism totally discontented with modern industrial society (big industry, big government, and other aspects of the revolutions of technology and organization). This "preindustrial conservatism" is not content with the status quo. Rather, it wishes to turn back the clock to a past which has disappeared. Its strongest expression has been among the southern agrarians. A group of southern agrarian writers issued in 1930 a manifesto entitled *I'll Take My Stand,* a defense of the primarily agricultural way of life against "what may be called the American or prevailing way." The southern agrarians have felt that they stand for "the cause of civilized society" against "the new barbarism of science and technology controlled by the modern power state."

A somewhat less thoroughgoing exponent of eighteenth-century conservatism is William F. Buckley, Jr., founder of the conservative magazine *National Review* and host of the television program, "The Firing Line." Buckley opposes collectivism, centralization, "populism," secularization, "mass culture," internationalism, "progressive education," liberalism, and people who are "soft on communism."

Another old style conservative is Russell Kirk, known for his book, *The Conservative Mind.* Kirk is Barry Goldwater's favorite political thinker. He has been described as "a man who has lost patience with the course of American development in every field from art to politics."

Somewhat peculiarly, as we move from idealistic laissez-faire conservatism to Burkean rejection of modern mass society, the conservative comes close to the anarchist. The anarchist would say that the difference is that he wants to move forward from industrial society, while the Burkean conservative is a reactionary who would like to go backward. Later in the chapter, we shall see where the anarchist does want to move.

FASCISM

As the so-called Communist state is the totalitarian distortion of socialism, so fascism is the totalitarian distortion of conservatism. The extreme left and extreme right have many similarities, especially their rejection of democratic political procedures and their effort through modern communication techniques to shape all life into a single mold. There are also important differences. While the Communist governments at least pay lip service to democracy and preach the "withering away of the state" as an ideal, fascism rejects democracy and accepts totalitarianism, in principle, as an ideal way of life.

The two outstanding examples of fascism are Hitler's Germany and Mussolini's Italy. In both cases fascism arose in a turbulent postwar world as an extreme movement against the left —liberalism, socialism, and communism. In both cases fascism came to power with the cooperation of conservatives—landowners, industrialists, and militarists—who did not completely trust either Hitler or Mussolini, but feared liberalism and radicalism more. They were especially terrified by the Russian Revolution. The Fascists were willing to use methods of violence and terror which conservatives would not themselves employ, but would tolerate or support as the lesser evil. Fascism was thus only an extreme form of programs which conservatives had supported in both countries.

Hitler and Mussolini inspecting an honor guard in Munich.

Fascism also had conservative support abroad. Churchill, for example, once said that should England ever face such a situation as faced postwar Italy, he hoped she would have a leader of the caliber of Mussolini. Many conservatives in the West saw Hitler, in the beginning, as a bulwark against Communism. Had not substantial and powerful interests in the democratic world felt this way, Mussolini and Hitler would probably have been stopped without World War II.

In addition to powerful conservatives, the Fascists also appealed to frustrated members of the lower middle class, who had been hit hard in both countries. Italians fought in the trenches of World War I for a victory in which they shared little and came back to an unstable economy. Ex-soldiers, office workers, teachers, civil servants, small businessmen, and independent professionals attached themselves to the banner of Mussolini. Germany had been saddled by the Treaty of Versailles with guilt for World War I and with reparations payments to the victorious Allies. She had then encountered the Great Depression which hit all the Western capitalist world. The lower middle classes suffered severely.

Both Mussolini and Hitler appealed to these classes, in the beginning, with an attack on large landowners and big business and industry. Here was the socialism in the National Socialist platform. As they moved toward power, however, both played down this part of their program and emphasized that part which appealed to landed aristocrats, big industrialists, and the military. "We cannot confiscate the property of landlords; we are Fascists, not Socialists," said Mussolini.

Economically, Italian and German fascism for the most part maintained private ownership of the means of production, but with extensive state controls. In Germany, for example, the government controlled all exports and imports. In both countries each line of business or industry was organized into a compulsory trade association. Each association was actually a vehicle for handling government regulations. The associations were generally dominated by big firms at the expense of little business and industry. In Italy these industry-wide associations were called "corporations." Thus the Fascist economy has been described as the corporate state, a system different from both Communist nationalization and capitalist private enterprise.

The main targets for fascism were

liberals and radicals. In Germany the Nazis were able to eliminate the political power of the Communists by blaming them for setting fire to the Reichstag (the national assembly building). The Jews in Germany became a symbol of internationalism, liberalism, and socialism—all of which they did tend to stand for—and were therefore a special target for the Nazis. Anti-Semitism never reached the same level in Italy. In both countries, however, non-Jewish liberals and radicals suffered. The aim of the Fascists was to wipe out everything "left of center" in whatever form. Thus arose the genocidal Nazi effort to exterminate the Jews, and their less-known extermination campaign against the Russian nation.

Two central aspects of historic fascism were racism and nationalistic aggression. For Mussolini war against the "inferior" Ethiopians took the place that anti-Semitism held in Germany. In the two cases, Ethiopians and Jews served as scapegoats on whom to project all of people's frustrations. Both Fascist regimes were prime examples of the displacement of aggression through foreign war. Hitler did have some success in relieving the economic ills of Germany, such as unemployment. Mussolini was less successful. Neither could, however, stabilize his hold on society except by putting it on the footing of a permanent war economy. Mussolini and Hitler raised the specter of being threatened by enemies on all sides, and also within, and the hope of great conquests for the nation. They were thus able to quiet dissent at home. Thus, militarism was a necessary part of fascism.

Why did fascism arise in Germany and Italy, and under what conditions might it arise again, there or elsewhere? We should note, first of all, that one of the things most deplorable about fascism, from the standpoint of democracy, is also one of its great strengths. People give up their individuality to the mass in exchange for a profound ethnocentric experience of collective power and aggression. The

Fascist theory, as the accompanying quotation from the Italian Fascist philosopher, Alfredo Rocco, indicates, asserts the supremacy of the state and the insignificance of the individual. A number of students of fascism have felt that this submergence of the individual has a strong appeal for many people.

Erich Fromm, in his book, *Escape from Freedom,* has held that man in the modern world has lost the ties that he had in the precapitalist community and desires to "escape from freedom" by submerging himself in a mass movement. In *The Origins of Totalitarianism,* Hannah Arendt similarly suggests that industrial society has given people a sense of rootlessness and destroyed their identity. Thus it has made them liable to irrational mass movements which will restore a sense of identity and belonging. The authoritarian personality studies relate the Fascist personality to deep anxiety, hostility, and dependency resulting from childhood experiences of lovelessness. Wilhelm Reich, in *The Mass Psychology of Fascism,* claimed that authoritarian controls over man, especially his sexuality, have destroyed his self-confidence and individuality and created a deep reservoir of hate. Under adverse social conditions, Reich believed, man everywhere is open to the programs of hate-mongering dictators.

All these explanations undoubtedly tell us something about why fascism is appealing. They do not tell why it broke out at particular times and places, and not at others. The interpretation of fascism by historian John Weiss, in a book entitled *The Fascist Tradition,* may throw some light on this question.

Three conditions, says Weiss, are favorable for the development of fascism in the modern world: (1) a strong conservative element, (2) a strong liberal and radical element, and (3) disturbed political and economic conditions which conservative measures cannot solve, and which, therefore, drive the country toward liberal, or socialist, or communist solutions. Under these conditions the extreme right is

For Liberalism, society has no life distinct from the life of the individuals. . . . For Fascism, the life of society overlaps the existence of individuals and projects itself into the succeeding generations through centuries and millennia. Individuals come into being, grow, and die, followed by others, unceasingly; social unity remains always identical to itself. For Liberalism, the individual is the end and society the means; nor is it conceivable that the individual, considered in the dignity of an ultimate finality, be lowered to mere instrumentality. For Fascism, society is the end, individuals the means, and its whole life consists in using individuals as instruments for its social ends.

—Alfredo Rocco, "The Political Doctrine of Fascism," International Conciliation, *Carnegie Endowment for International Peace,* October 1926, n.p.

---

able to capitalize upon the discontent of lower-middle-class groups and the desperation of conservatives who are willing to give totalitarian violence a last chance against the left. The fascist regime is really incapable, in the long run, of creating a stable society. Thus, the country is driven into more violent measures against real or imagined enemies at home and abroad. In the world of modern communications and rising expectations, tolerance will enable liberals and radicals to gain a following. Therefore, only thoroughgoing totalitarian repression can keep the extreme right in power.

Weiss points out two different situations in which Fascist elements tried but did not gain a foothold. In England a long-established liberal tradition, tinged with socialism, had influenced even the conservatives, so that they lacked the narrowness and stubbornness of other conservative groups. Although a Fascist movement did develop during the Depression and the Hitler period under Sir Oswald Moseley, it never had a serious chance of gaining power. In Spain after the Spanish Civil War, and in Hungary before Hitler, on the other hand, there was no effective liberal or radical organization. Conservatives under Franco in Spain and Horthy in Hungary were therefore able to maintain control by traditional authoritarian methods, without resorting to the totalitarian extremism of fascism. The Fascist organ-

ization in Spain never became a serious political threat, and in Hungary the Horthy regime actually took severe repressive measures against its own right wing.

What is the possibility that fascism will again come to power? Some of the general underlying elements suggested by various writers are present throughout the Western world today: a sense of alienation, loss of identity, frustration of sexual and other organic needs, authoritarian personality structure. Some of the specific conditions are present in many places.

In the United States, in the South, there is a social system on its way out, marked by a landed aristocracy and a frustrated lower-middle and lower class of whites. These elements have at times tried to hold on to the status quo with an almost Fascist violence and repression. There are in various parts of the country armed spokesmen of the extreme right. There are many people who feel severely threatened by liberals and leftists, whom they consider to be identical. There is racism directed against Negroes and Jews, which is part of a general pattern of authoritarian ethnocentrism directed against all "different" groups. Many people feel that repressive measures are in order against all these enemies within. They also feel encircled by a world which they believe to be almost totally Communist or near-Communist. They advocate an extreme military crusade against enemies abroad. In this they have considerable support in high military circles. These radical rightists receive substantial financial support from a few wealthy industrialists.

All these are potentially Fascist elements. Could fascism come to the United States or other Western nations? Whether it becomes a serious threat will probably depend upon how well liberal or socialist reforms succeed in meeting the deep problems of an age of change.

ANARCHISM

There is a final political heritage without which we cannot really put into perspective some of the most significant events of the past decade—Negro sit-ins, student riots, draft resistance, and other manifestations of civil disobedience. This is the anarchist tradition.

To most people the word "anarchy" means violence and chaos, but anarchism as a political philosophy does not necessarily imply either. The goal of the anarchist is a society which will regulate itself without coercion by formal authority (Greek: *an,* not; *arche,* government). Actually, the ultimate goals of both laissez-faire liberalism and communism are anarchistic: the self-regulating market society and the "withering away of the state."

Let us look at some basic anarchist principles.

Decentralism. Anarchism has arisen within the last few centuries as a protest against the centralized national state and against centralized control over the means of production. Politically decentralism calls for local control, as against control by centralized bureaucracy. Economically it means control of production by the people directly engaged in it—a system closer to the guild organization of the Middle Ages than to modern centralized industry. In terms of residence, it means the breakup of cities and return to a life closer to the soil. More broadly, anar-

chism opposes the Establishment, bigness in any form, the large impersonal power of a mass society. In education, for example, it would favor the small, decentralized cluster college rather than the massive educational factory.

The simple life. With the passing centuries, modern society has become increasingly complex, with increasing strain upon its members. It is often said that this is the price that must be paid for the highly specialized organization which produces the modern standard of living. The anarchist has always questioned this and held that a society based upon simpler and more immediate relations would be efficient enough and much more desirable. The early hippie culture, for example, made much of flowers, held love-ins, and urged people to "make love, not war."

Optimism about man. Contrary to the opinions of both traditional conservatives and liberals, the anarchist believes that man is fundamentally loving and social. If he acts otherwise, it is because a badly arranged society has distorted his real nature. The anarchist is likely to agree with Rousseau that "Man is born free, but he is everywhere in chains." If the chains can be broken, man will become generous and social.

Belief in natural reason and justice. Like the liberal and the conservative, the anarchist believes in a natural order. This is not, however, based on authority and command, as is the conservative's order, or upon a harmony of individual selfishness, as is the liberal's. It is more equalitarian than authoritarian, more cooperative than competitive. Like Lenin (whose ultimate communism is an anarchist vision) the anarchist sees the "breaking of the chains" as liberating man's natural capacity to build a society grounded on justice and reason. It is true that anarchism has developed two different pictures of the good society. One is a society of individual, property-owning small producers (this is the typically American version). The other is a federation of cooperative communities (this is the European model). Both versions anticipate good will and neighborliness rather than authority and selfishness.

Direct action. The anarchist has always been skeptical about official political processes of change. Government, he has held, is largely the tool of the status quo. To try to get freedom through legislation is largely to play with stacked cards. It is usually more effective, he believes, to take direct steps, such as demonstrations, strikes, boycotts, and disobeying unjust laws. Government operates mainly by pressure, not reason. Confronted with direct action, it may make changes that would otherwise be denied. We have seen this philosophy at work in the civil rights, student protest, and draft refusal movements.

Nonviolence. Most people, if asked to imagine an anarchist, will conjure up a wild-haired figure with a bomb. As we shall see, they are not entirely wrong, for there has been a very important violent strain in anarchism. Violence is not typical, however, of the anarchist approach as a whole. Believing in the essential goodness of man and in the possibility of a just and reasonable society, the anarchist has generally been opposed to forceful coercion. He has also distrusted violence because of its connection with organized government. In this century the Gandhian philosophy of nonviolence has strongly influenced many people with anarchist leanings.

We may be helped in getting the flavor of anarchism by some thumbnail sketches of individuals who have influenced this philosophy. The term "anarchist" was not coined until the nineteenth century, and even since that time not all these figures would have called themselves anarchists. But it is the point of view that is important.

Sir Thomas More (1477–1535) was the hero of the play *A Man for All Seasons.* His book *Utopia* ("Nowhere") was an impassioned plea against the excesses of the commercial revolution and the dispossession of peasants from the land. The central figure in the book is Raphael Hythlodaye, who argues that the political state is a conspiracy of the rich. In Utopia there is no money. Goods are held in common. There are no locks on the houses. All dwellings are exchanged every ten years to make certain that no one gets too attached to property. There are few lawyers, and war is inglorious. The disregard for conventional values is indicated by the fact that gold is used to make urine pots.

Gerrard Winstanley (1609–1652), an English tailor, was involved in perhaps the first sit-in (or rather "dig-in"). He was a leader in a radical group in the Cromwellian revolution. This group became known as the Diggers because of their way of protesting the revolution's lack of concern for the poor. In 1649 they took possession of St. George's Hill at Walton-on-Thames and planted carrots, parsnips, and wheat. Troops eventually dislodged them. Winstanley considered authority bad and private property, evil:

> So long as such are rulers as call the land theirs, upholding this particular property of mine and thine, the common people shall never have their liberty, nor the land be freed from troubles, oppressions and complainings; by reason thereof the Creator of all things is continually provoked.[10]

Winstanley believed in the inner God in man, which prompted man to be reasonable, in direct action, and in nonviolence.

In 1793 William Godwin (1756–1836) wrote in *Political Justice,* "With what delight must every well-informed friend of mankind look forward to the dissolution of political government. . . ." England was at war with the French

10. Gerrard Winstanley, quoted in George Woodcock, *Anarchism,* New York, World Publishing, 1962, p. 46.

revolutionary government, the press was censored, Thomas Paine had been banished for his revolutionary sympathies, and Godwin defended the revolution. He believed government and authority evil and even disapproved of legal marriage on this ground. He held that man is shaped by his environment and under the right conditions is "perfectible" and capable of reasonable behavior. He advocated communal ownership of property. *Political Justice* was one of the best selling government books of all time. Godwin strongly influenced his wife, Mary Wollstonecraft, an ardent advocate of women's rights, and his son-in-law, the poet Percy Shelley.

The first person to call himself an anarchist was Pierre-Joseph Proudhon (1809–1865). He coined a famous phrase, "property is theft." He distinguished ownership of the means of production (property) from personal possessions: property is the creation of the community and of many generations of culture, but the owner treats it as his own. "This it is, above all other things, which has been so fitly named the exploitation of man by man." Proudhon was an associate of Marx, but disagreed with Marx's belief in dramatic revolution and his willingness to use the machinery of the state to bring about change. Proudhon preferred to appeal to men's capacity for justice: "the central star which governs societies, the pole around which the political world revolves, the principle and regulator of all transactions." He was obviously speaking of the world as it might be, not as it is.

The idea that anarchism is violent derives from Michael Bakunin (1814–1876). He was a dramatic Russian who once smoked 1600 cigars in a month in jail and lost all his teeth from scurvy in prison. Like Proudhon, Bakunin was associated with Marx, but was opposed to politics and central organization. His anarchism was one of secret societies, conspiracies, and the "revolution of the deed"—individual terrorist acts against heads of state or industry.

Henry David Thoreau

To his influence we can charge the kind of anarchism that led to the assassination of William McKinley, French president Carnot, and Prince Umberto of Italy, and the attempted murders of steel magnate Henry Clay Frick and President Franklin D. Roosevelt. On page 135 we quoted his idealistic belief in the creative power of violence.

A quite different figure was the gentle New England philosopher, Henry David Thoreau (1817–1862). "That government is best," he said, "which governs not at all." His most famous contribution is his essay "Civil Disobedience," in which he proclaimed the right and duty to disobey immoral laws. "Let your life be a counterfriction to stop the machine." "There will never be a really free enlightened state until the state comes to recognize the individual as a higher and independent power." Thoreau's influence on the twentieth century has been great. Gandhi owned much to "Civil Disobedience," and the American civil rights movement was influenced both by Gandhi and directly by Thoreau.

Less known, but also very important, is the contribution of Randolph Bourne (1886–1918), a student of the philosopher John Dewey and a writer for radical magazines. Opposing American participation in World War I, Bourne coined the phrase, "War is the health of the state." War, he said, is always attractive to governments, because during wartime the herd impulse is strongest and dissent is most easily crushed. In his book, *The State,* Bourne said,

> *War is the normal activity of states; diplomacy is the wheedling and the bargaining of the worn-out bullies as they rise from the ground and slowly restore their strength to begin fighting again. . . . We cannot crusade against war without crusading implicitly against the State.*[11]

Bourne's argument that only an anarchist approach can hope to do away with war, is one that cannot be lightly dismissed in the nuclear age.

A final figure, Peter Kropotkin (1842–1921), is clearly identified with the anarchist movement. Born a Russian prince, he turned down a high government post to go as a geographer to Siberia. There he became interested in cooperation among animals and developed material for his classic work on the role of mutual aid in evolution (see Chapter four). This book gave a new factual basis for belief in the possibility of a noncoercive society. An important part was his study of mutual aid in the medieval towns. Kropotkin also pointed out, around the beginning of the twentieth century, that the development of light and mobile electric and gasoline power and of rapid communication made decentralization technically possible. He lived to see the Russian Revolution, and his response to the Bolshevik terror was typical of an anarchist, "This buries the revolution." When he died in 1921, his funeral procession, despite Bolshevik repression,

was five miles long. Banners carried in scarlet letters on a black background, the message, "Where there is authority, there is no freedom."

Of what relevance is anarchism today? Obviously it is Utopian, an ideal that will not be reached in any time we can foresee, and perhaps never. Just as clearly it has something to say about great problems of a mass society which must be solved—the bigness and impersonality of government, of military power, of vast impersonal factories, of huge industrial combinations, of monster universities, of overwhelming mass communications.

The question we must always ask the anarchist is, "How can we coordinate the affairs of a modern industrial society without strong centralized coercion?" The easiest answer is that there is no way, that the Industrial Age has moved forward and molded society in its image, and that "you can't turn the clock back." A harder, but perhaps truer, answer is that the Industrial Age is only in its infancy, that mass society may be a poor and crude first effort at using modern technology, and that in the long future we may discover newer and more decentralized ways. To these the philosophy of anarchism may contribute.

POLITICS AND MASS SOCIETY

At the end of our two chapters on politics, let us look at the direction which political organization may take in the near future.

First, with the spread of the commercial and industrial economy over the globe, simple communal governments of the kind which exist before an economic surplus will continue to disappear. The national state will become the prevalent form of government everywhere, although in underdeveloped areas such as parts of Africa, it may have competition from strong tribal governments. The result might entail some kind of compromise, with tribes holding power of a kind not known in the West.

11. Randolph Bourne, *The State,* New York, Resistance Press, 1946–1947, pp. 14, 20.

Second, mass communications and the revolution of rising expectations are likely to bring an end to the old simple authoritarian governments ruled by more or less absolute kings or oligarchies. In a book on *The Politics of the Underdeveloped Areas,* published in 1960, James Coleman illustrated this kind of transition: traditional oligarchy (Ethiopia, Yemen), colonial or racial oligarchy (Southern Rhodesia), modernizing oligarchy (Pakistan), terminal colonial democracy (Tanganyika, Nigeria), political democracy (Philippines). Tanganyika and Nigeria have since then become completely independent.

Third, whether modernized societies will develop along the lines of liberalism and democratic socialism, on the one hand, or totalitarian communism or fascism, on the other, is a complex and uncertain question.

(1) Industrialization and urbanization tend to produce conditions favorable to democratic government. In *The Politics of Mass Society,* William Kornhauser reports that Communist parties tend to be unsuccessful in highly urbanized societies, in societies where per capita energy is high, and in societies with a high per capita income. Although Communist support tends to be urban and Fascist support rural, in general Fascist movements are strong in those countries where Communist movements are strong, and weak in the more urbanized and industrialized countries where Communism is weak. Gabriel Almond and Sidney Verba's study of five political systems in *The Civil Culture,* cited in the previous chapter, would seem to show citizens participating more freely in the urban and industrial societies of Great Britain and the United States.

(2) Urban industrial society makes it increasingly difficult for the single citizen to influence government as an individual. In the face of this fact, there are two possibilities. One is that democratic control will increasingly lose out to a centralized power elite of one kind or another. This seems to have been shown in some of the studies of community power structure. It is also possible that widespread membership in informal voluntary associations—churches, labor unions, lodges, farm organizations, civic clubs, political organizations, ethnic organizations, professional associations, and the like—will keep power spread and maintain a pluralistic political structure. Some people see great hope for democracy in this direction. Others point to the fact that many people do not belong to organizations and that many voluntary associations (such as labor unions, veterans' organizations, and sometimes even churches) are not very independent of the prevailing power structure.

(3) Crisis tends to weaken liberal and democratic Socialist governments and make one or another form of totalitarianism more likely. Although urbanization and industrialization seem in the long run to be favorable to democracy, their very rapid introduction may not be. If large numbers of people are displaced from their jobs by machines or are torn from primary groups and crowded in urban slums and ghettos, the chance of totalitarianism increases. Depression or the aftermath of war, particularly a losing one, may have the same effect. Continued massive preparation for war is one of the most likely ways for liberal governments to lose their democracy. Again, then, avoidance of totalitarianism depends largely upon the success of liberal and Socialist governments in meeting human needs without militarization.

Suggestions for further reading

A comprehensive discussion of the liberal tradition by a British scholar is Liberalism by L. T. HOBHOUSE (Oxford University Press, 1964, paper). ARTHUR SCHLESINGER, JR., a historian and friend and adviser to President Kennedy, has written of twentieth-century liberalism in

The Vital Center (*Houghton Mifflin, paper*). *An important book on socialism by a distinguished British Marxist is G. D. H. COLE's* The Meaning of Marxism (*University of Michigan, 1964, paper*). *The Socialist ideal as seen by an artist is depicted in "The Soul of Man Under Socialism" by OSCAR WILDE (Crescendo, 1969, paper). For the Socialist view of an active revolutionary, see ERNESTO "CHE" GUEVARA,* Complete Bolivian Diaries and Other Captured Documents (*Stein and Day, 1969, paper*). *The conservative tradition in the United States is very ably presented in CLINTON ROSSITER's* Conservatism in America (*Knopf, 1955, paper*).

The meaning of fascism in the modern world is very thoughtfully analyzed by JOHN WEISS in The Fascist Tradition (*Harper & Row, 1967, paper*). *An inside account is that of HANNAH ARENDT in* Totalitarianism (*Harcourt Brace Jovanovich, 1968, paper*). *A psychoanalyst's interpretation of fascism, based on his concentration camp experience, is found in* The Informed Heart, *by BRUNO BETTELHEIM (Free Press, 1960). Another psychiatrist's account of his concentration camp days is that of VIKTOR FRANKL in* Man's Search for Meaning (*see suggested readings for Chapter five*). *A postwar study by an American of what Germans experienced and thought under Nazism is reported in MILTON MAYER's* They Thought They Were Free (*2nd ed., University of Chicago Press, 1966, paper*). *Two important psychiatric views of fascism are those of ERICH FROMM in* Escape from Freedom (*see suggested readings for Chapter five*) *and* The Mass Psychology of Fascism *by WILHELM REICH (Farrar, Straus & Giroux, paper).*

The authoritative general book on the anarchist tradition is Anarchism *by GEORGE WOODCOCK, a top politician in British Labour governments (World, 1962). Possibly the most influential single document in this tradition is HENRY DAVID THOREAU's* Civil Disobedience (*Harper & Row, 1965, paper*).

Chapter eleven
Power in the American economy

In this and the following chapter, we shall continue our study of power by asking how it is organized in economic systems. This chapter will deal with the role played in the most productive market economy—that of the United States—by four significant economic groups: businessmen, laborers, farmers, and consumers. Our discussion of political pressures in Chapter nine and Woodrow Wilson's statement on the next page indicate that this is a political as well as an economic problem. The next chapter will be concerned with the role of government in the economic power structure of market, mixed, and planned economies.

THE CONCENTRATION OF BUSINESS POWER

Statistics do not ordinarily make the easiest or most fascinating form of reading. Some recent studies of American business are, however, worth a little extra effort. No other form of description can tell us so much about where power actually lies in the economy of the United States. The facts contrast rather shockingly with traditional American ideals of free competition.

In 1932 a famous study by Adolph Berle and Gardner Means called *The Modern Corporation and Private Property* revealed that the 200 largest corporations in the United States—excluding banks and insurance companies—controlled almost half of all corporate wealth. These 200 firms made up 7/100 of one percent of all corporations.

In 1939 and 1940 the National Resources Committee, appointed by President Roosevelt, published a report entitled *The Structure of the American Economy.* In this report they found that 106 of the 250 larger corporations, which contained nearly two-thirds of their combined assets, belonged to eight corporate interest groups. Among them, then, these eight groupings controlled a very substantial part of the entire American economy. The groups designated were Morgan–First National, Kuhn-Loeb, Mellon, Du-Pont, Rockefeller, Chicago (primarily meat packing), Cleveland (primarily steel), and Boston (primarily shoe machinery). Some of the family names are, of course, familiar.

In 1938 and 1939, a special committee was appointed to study the problems of American small business. This committee's report on the concentration of business power was very close to the 1932 findings of Berle and Means. One-tenth of one percent of all American corporations, they found, owned 52 percent of all corporate assets.

In 1949, a committee of the federal House of Representatives under the chairmanship of New York Congressman Emmanuel Celler studied the degree of oligopoly (control by a few firms) in the economy by examining the control

The masters of the government of the United States are the combined capitalists and manufacturers of the United States. It is written over every intimate page of the records of Congress, it is written all through the history of conferences at the White House, that the suggestions of economic policy in this country have come from one source, not many sources. . . . Suppose you go to Washington and try to get at your government. You will always find that while you are politely listened to, the men really consulted are the men who have the biggest stake—the big bankers, the big manufacturers, the big masters of commerce, the heads of railroad corporations and of steamship corporations. . . . Every time it has come to a critical question these gentlemen have been yielded to, and their demands have been treated as the demands that should be followed as a matter of course.

The government of the United States at present is a foster-child of the special interests. It is not allowed to have a will of its own.

—Woodrow Wilson, The New Freedom, *Englewood Cliffs, N. J.,* Prentice-Hall, 1961, pp. 48–49.

---

exercised by the top four firms in different lines of industry. In 46 industries, they found, the "big four" produced more than 75 percent of the total product. In 104 additional industries the top four producers made from 50 to 75 percent. Industries like steel, automobile manufacture, meat packing, and cigarette manufacture are illustrations of such oligopoly.

The same question was asked in 1957 by a Senate committee chaired by Senator Estes Kefauver. This committee found a much wider spread of oligopoly. The "big four," they found, made 75 percent or more of the products in 131 industries, and from 50 to 75 percent in an additional 260 fields.

These statistics make it clear that the United States today is by no stretch of the imagination a free-market society. Orators talk of free enterprise as though we were still in the days of Adam Smith, which were almost two centuries ago. Today there are still some industries—the garment trades are a particularly good example— where the capital investment needed is so small that competition does exist among a large number of independent producers, but this is not typical of the economy as a whole. Oligopoly rather than the free market is the rule. Let us

see how time has changed the world of Adam Smith.

We will remember the characteristics of a free-market economy. There is competition because enterprises are small enough so that it is easy to get into a profitable line or out of an unprofitable one, and no one firm can dominate the market. It has been suggested that poor transportation and communication made the economy of Adam Smith in some respects actually less competitive than today's. With only slow means of getting about and roads rough and sometimes impassable, one might have no other choice than to buy from a local merchant or craftsman. Today one can go to a nearby larger town or buy from a mail order house. Be this as it may, the Industrial Revolution had hardly got under way before a development took place that ended free enterprise as far as it existed in Smith's sense. This was the legalization of what in England was called the joint stock company, and in the United States, the corporation.

Corporations are distinguished from two other types of businesses. Individual enterprises are owned by a single person or family; partnerships are owned by two or more people. Usually, although not necessarily, the corporation involves investment by more people than either other form.

The corporation has three important characteristics. (1) *Immortality*—It can outlive any of its individual members. Harvard University is an example. (2) *Personality*—A corporation is a person under the law. It can sue or be sued. It has some of the legal privileges of real persons. (3) *Limited liability*—This is the most distinctive characteristic. Under ordinary circumstances an individual investing his money in a corporation risks only the amount he invests; his liability is limited to this amount. An individual enterpriser, or a member of a partnership, may be liable for all the debts of the enterprise.

What is the importance of limited liability? It enables the corporation to accumulate large sums of capital from a large number of individual investors. Thus it meets the needs of an industrial system where large-scale outlay for capital equipment is required. Neither of the other forms could ordinarily meet it, although there are important exceptions in the form of family corporations, such as the Ford Motor Company. Clearly, however, large numbers of people would not invest small sums of money in General Motors or American Telephone and Telegraph Company if they might be responsible personally for all the enterprise's obligations.

The corporation had profound effects on the market system. When vast amounts of capital could be accumulated, enterprise became so large that in many cases it was no longer possible for the average individual or group of individuals to compete. This effect spread in several directions.

Smaller competitors tended to be squeezed out. The relationship of management to the worker was changed. In a small, personal shop, the owner might be no more able to get along without a given worker than the worker could do without him. Thus bargaining power was fairly equal. This was not the case with the individual worker and the corporation. Corporate organiza- tion created an inequality of bargaining power which only collective bargaining by unions could equalize. The relationship to suppliers of raw materials changed. Thus farmers, with perishable products to market, might be at the mercy of railroad or grain elevator corporations. Finally, the relationship to the consumer was changed. For a competitive price, set as in our example in Chapter eight, was substituted an oligopoly or monopoly price. Consumers were offered a restricted quantity of goods for which they had to pay more.

In effect, we can say that *free enterprise ceased to exist when the corporation was legalized.*

We can think of a continuum with "perfect competition" at one end and "perfect monopoly" at the other. In between are various forms of "imperfect competition." Toward the monopoly end we encounter oligopoly. This is the direction in which the American economy has been moving. Let us look more specifically at why this is so.

First of all, it must be said that monopoly is not entirely new. We are told that at some time in the seventh or sixth century B.C., the Greek philosopher Thales cornered the crop of olive oil and made a killing. Under the mercantilist policy which preceded liberal capitalism, governments chartered monopolies such as the British and Dutch East India companies. Monopolistic tendencies have particularly flourished, however, under corporate industrialism.

These tendencies are likely to grow out of *efficiencies of plant size.* Some types of production require so much investment that there is really room for only a few big producers. Where both big and small producers survive, bigness has advantages. It makes possible the use of larger and more specialized machinery. It also enables the big plant to make use of other specialized services. Market research, product quality control, advertising, and public relations can be put in the hands of specialists, while a small

Andrew Carnegie

The chain, now holding the whole market, could then raise prices and make up the original loss.

In the United States, the great period of business concentration occurred between the Civil War and the end of the nineteenth century. The war had destroyed the power of the agrarian South and left no serious rival to industrial capitalism. Other circumstances were highly favorable.

The American continent was richly endowed with natural resources—coal, oil, iron, timber, water power, and most metals. It constituted a vast market without internal tariff barriers. The government was very friendly to business enterprise. It owned over half the land of the whole country and made vast amounts of territory and resources available for expansion. Between 1847 and 1872, the federal government gave to railroads grants of land equal to the combined area of Maine, New Hampshire, Vermont, Massachusetts, Rhode Island, Connecticut, New York, and much of Pennsylvania. American conditions seemed to develop a high degree of both technical and organizational skill. The cultural climate was a free and easy one, inclined to excuse morally doubtful practices if they "produced the goods." Business practices, moral and immoral, did. Beard says:

> *In 1860, just a little more than a billion dollars was invested in manufacturing and only 1,500,000 industrial wage earners were employed in the United States. In less than fifty years the capital had risen to more than twelve billions and the number of wage earners to 5,500,000. During the same period, the value of manufactured products had leaped to fourteen billion dollars a year, fifteen times the total at the beginning of the epoch.[1]*

Statistics also show that growth was accompanied by concentration. In 1900 almost half of all the manufac-

plant may not be able to provide its own specialized services. The large plant can buy raw materials in bulk at lower prices. It may get cheaper freight rates for the same reason. There are, it is true, limits; industrial plants, like all groups, have a critical size beyond which efficiency declines. This may be why a large corporation like General Motors has decentralized its production.

Firm size, organizational size of the whole corporation, not technical size of the productive plant, may have advantages for reasons other than efficiency. Their size and resources may enable giant firms to dominate the market, even though other firms are actually more efficient. An example is the process through which chain stores have spread, often at the expense of local, independent grocers. A chain would come into a town and begin selling at a very low margin, or even at a loss. Its resources enabled it to do so. The independent could not meet the competition and had to go out of business.

tured goods in the United States were turned out by less than two percent of all manufacturing firms. In many industries production increased ten or fifteen times between 1865 and 1900, but the number of firms decreased. By 1890 there were monopolies or near monopolies in oil, iron, steel, copper, lead, sugar, and coal.

Steel, the structural basis for the economy, was organized by a Scottish immigrant, Andrew Carnegie. By 1901 he had built United States Steel into a billion-dollar corporation. He had adopted the principle of vertical integration of the industry—from mine to market it was controlled from a single source. He also used the technique of "rebates," by which United States Steel paid established freight rates but received partial refunds which were not available to competitors.

Oil became a near monopoly under the Standard Oil Company, which was organized by John D. Rockefeller. Through high organizational efficiency, and also price wars, intimidation, and sabotage, Standard Oil was able to squeeze out competitors and bring oil wells as well as refineries under its control. At the other end of the process, Rockefeller had a highly efficient and not always scrupulous organization for marketing oil. He got freight rebates and at one time was also on the point of getting refunds on his competitors' shipments.

Electricity, introduced for light and power in the 1870s, became concentrated in two firms: General Electric and Westinghouse. *Meat packing* was largely controlled by Philip Armour, Nelson Morris, and Gustavus V. Swift, who introduced the refrigerated railway car.

In 1860 *railways* were the biggest single economic interest in the country. The three chief figures in centralizing this network were J. P. Morgan, Edward H. Harriman, and James J. Hill. When he combined the Union Pacific and the Southern Pacific, Harriman controlled more than 15,000 miles of track. By 1900 major control of rail-

John D. Rockefeller, Sr.

roads had been taken over by bankers.

This, indeed, was the tendency everywhere: for control to pass from technicians or business organizers to *financiers.* This trend resulted from the increasing size of investment and the dependence of the industrialist upon large financial companies for his capital needs. The two major financial interests at the turn of the century were those of Morgan and Rockefeller. The Morgan interests had brought under their control thirteen railroads, a combination of steamship companies, another combination of harvester companies, and United States Steel. Morgan also had financial interests in such places as Mexico, South Africa, Japan, China, and the Philippines.

We have said that the Protestant ethic has been a strong force in the growth of business and enterprise. Late nineteenth-century America is a

J. P. Morgan

property should do what they like with it. I owe the public nothing." Yet he was a regular member of the Episcopal Church and contributed generously.

The important point is that religion seems to have enabled these captains of industry to pursue wealth, sometimes by highly doubtful means, with a good conscience. When a railroad combination was invalidated by the Supreme Court, Hill complained, "It really seems hard, when we look back upon what we have done . . . that we should be compelled to fight for our lives against political adventurers who have never done anything but pose and draw a salary."[2] When coal magnate George F. Baer refused in 1902 to negotiate with his workers, he was able to say, "The rights and interests of the laboring man will be protected and cared for not by the labor agitators, but by the Christian men to whom God in his infinite wisdom has given the control of the property interests of the country."[3]

By the start of this century, most of the concentration described at the beginning of this chapter had taken place. Competition had given way to oligopoly in large areas of the economy. This concentration was due, first of all, to the technical plant efficiency of the large corporation and to its greater economic power in the market. During the nineteenth century, and since, it has also been brought about by various kinds of alliances among corporations, all of which served to limit competition.

One of the simplest of these was the *gentleman's agreement* by competitors to sell at the same price instead of undercutting one another. By eliminating price competition, all were able to profit at the expense of the consumer. From 1907 to 1911, such gentlemen's agreements controlled 90 percent of the steel industry. In the accompanying

good example, although there were some exceptions, it is true. "Gentleman Jim" Fisk, who milked the Erie Railroad into bankruptcy, loved food, liquor, and women. Of the wrecking of the Erie he said, "Nothing is lost save honor!" However, he was probably an exception.

Jay Cooke, the biggest financial "wheel" aside from Morgan, was a devout church member and summed up his faith: "We must all get down at the feet of Jesus and be taught by no one but Himself." Rockefeller was an ardent Baptist and referred to his earnings as "God's gold." Although Carnegie was a skeptic, his advice followed the Puritan virtues: "Aim for the highest, never enter a barroom; do not touch liquor, or if at all only at meals; never speculate . . . put all your eggs in one basket, and watch that basket." James J. Hill, who built the Great Northern Railroad, was a Protestant, although he richly endowed a Catholic seminary because of the Church's moral training of immigrant workers. J. P. Morgan once said, "Men owning

2. James J. Hill, quoted in *ibid.*, vol. 2, p. 194.
3. George F. Baer, quoted in Foster Rhea Dulles, *Labor in America*, 2nd rev. ed., New York, Thomas Y. Crowell, 1960, p. 191.

excerpt (p. 366), Clarence Randall, former board chairman of Inland Steel, comments on how Judge Elbert H. Gary of United States Steel accomplished this through dinner meetings.

A variation of the gentlemen's agreement was the *pool*. This divided the market, giving a part to each competitor. Each agreed not to try to sell to its competitor's customers. For over a quarter of a century, the meat industry was controlled by such a pool. During this period no firm increased its share of the market. Quality, service, and costs were fixed. Such an arrangement resembled a medieval guild on a vast scale.

Actual spoken or written agreements to restrain competition met with opposition in the courts and tended to give way to more informal arrangements for *price leadership.* One strong firm in an industry becomes established as the leader, and competitors generally follow its price changes. From 1937 to 1939, the Temporary National Economic Committee (TNEC), a congressional body, investigated the methods of monopoly and found price leadership to be one of the most common techniques. Our own experience tells us that gasoline prices may vary widely from time to time, but that prices of different companies generally rise and fall together. The TNEC found that in every area of the country there was a price leader in the oil industry. Price leadership was also the rule in marketing steel, as it was in the crackers, newsprint, anthracite coal, flour, corn syrup, stove, tin plate, cigarette, and milk bottle industries.

Today major producers in most leading industries prefer to compete on other bases than price and standardize prices through some form of leadership.

The most obvious way to reduce competition is through an outright *merger.* Standard Oil developed its power to a large extent by actually buying out competitive oil companies and suppliers of oil. In recent years there have been railway mergers of the New

James J. Hill

York Central with the Pennsylvania Railroad, and Atlantic Coast Line with Seaboard Air Line.

Interlocking directorates have some of the same effect without actual legal combination. In this case a number of the same individuals sit on the boards of directors of two or more corporations. Each of the interlocked companies is then likely to pursue policies favorable to the others. A famous case has been interlocking of Du Pont, General Motors, and U.S. Rubber, a combination which has made it likely, for example, that Du Pont paints and fabrics and U.S. Rubber tires will be given preference for General Motors cars.

The *trust* is an arrangement whereby stockholders in a number of corporations give their voting rights over to a common board of directors, who become trustees for their interests. This device has theoretically been controlled by the Sherman Anti-Trust Act of 1890 and the Clayton Act of 1914. In two famous cases in 1911, the Standard Oil Company and the American Tobacco Company were dissolved by court order. Virtual monopoly in these industries was thus changed to oligopoly. Under both Theodore and Franklin Roosevelt, there were waves of active trust-busting by the government. In general, however, the antitrust laws have been used more frequently against labor, to prevent strikes and boycotts, than against large business.

A *holding company* is an organization that owns portions of the stock of producing companies. It does not itself produce anything. By this device it is possible to control a large industrial empire with a small investment. The importance of the holding company technique is indicated by the fact that some of the biggest American corporations—American Telephone and Telegraph, United States Steel, Eastman Kodak, and General Electric—are nonproducing holding companies.

Consider the accompanying diagram of a holding company operation, in which six producing companies with an investment of one million dollars each are held by holding companies A and B, which in turn are held by holding company C. Just over 50 percent of the investment is the most that is necessary to control a company's policies. Thus an investment of approximately $750,000 can control a capital stock of $6 million. By pyramiding holding companies upon one another, it is possible to reduce the investment much farther, but this kind of practice has been somewhat limited by law. However, our diagram actually overestimates vastly the amount of investment necessary for control.

Most stockholders in large corporations no longer attend annual meetings. Their shares are voted by proxies who are likely to represent important stockholding interests. When proxies are combined with holding company operations, it is possible for a very small investment to have enormous leverage.

We might note that we sometimes hear that business power has been dispersed through stock ownership by many people, who acquire shares through profit sharing and investment plans. This does little, in fact, to change the picture. A study by economist Robert L. Lampman showed that in 1953, 76 percent of all corporate stock was owned by the top one percent of stockholders. Facts like these led a 1963 University of Pennsylvania research project to state that eight or

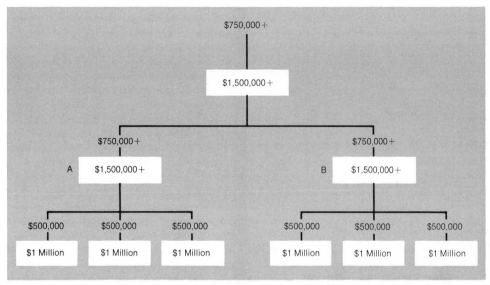

Figure 11.1. Pyramiding of holding companies.

nine men are powerful enough to be able to influence the whole business system of the country.

THE ORGANIZATION OF LABOR

The organization of labor in the United States paralleled, but lagged behind, that of capital. Through the colonial period, America was a preindustrial society, and relationships between employers and workers tended to be personal. The founding of the United States was followed shortly by the beginning of the industrial system. Alexander Hamilton's *Report on Manufactures* in 1791 saw the trend and put forward plans for creating a governmental atmosphere favorable to industry. In New England the corporation became prominent after about 1815. In 1830 Alexis de Tocqueville, the famous French author of *Democracy in America,* predicted that the American aristocracy would consist of manufacturers.

The coming of industry changed the status of the worker to that of one in a number of hired hands, with whom the plant manager might have no personal contact. The relationship of management to workers was especially likely to be depersonalized if the owner ceased to manage his own factory and hired a salaried manager. One factory agent was quoted as saying, "I regard my work people just as I regard my machinery. So long as they can do my work for what I choose to pay them, I keep them, getting out of them what I can."

The physical condition of some of the workers is reflected in a report in 1849 by Dr. Josiah Curtis to the American Medical Association. Curtis stated that "there was not a state's prison or a house of correction in New England where the hours of work were so long, hours for meals so short, and ventilation so much neglected as they were in the cotton mills of that section." Between 1800 and 1860, from 40 to 60 percent of factory hands were children, who worked from 12 to 15 hours a day for wages of $1 to $6 a week (not at present dollar values).

Workers underwent the change in economic status that accompanies industrialization and urbanization. Whereas the small farmer had his land, garden, and livestock to fall back on in time of emergency, the industrial worker had none of these and no source of capital or credit. He thus became dependent upon selling in the market the only asset he had—his labor power. In the United States as a whole, workers did have the advantage that labor was relatively scarce.

At the same time, workers were at a disadvantage legally. In an 1806 case involving the Philadelphia Cordwainers (shoemakers), labor organization was held to be a conspiracy. This was in general its legal position for several decades. It is interesting that there was a political division on this question. The Federalists, with strong urban and industrial elements, favored the conspiracy doctrine, while the mainly agrarian Jeffersonians opposed it.

The Federal Society of Journeymen Cordwainers, founded in Philadelphia in 1794, was perhaps the first permanent trade union. In 1827 Philadelphia also became the site of the first city-wide central union, the Mechanics' Union of Trade Associations. The National Trades Union, founded in 1834, was the first national labor organization of its kind in the world. Its platform included free universal education, public land for settlers, reform of child labor, and a 10-hour day. In 1836 six industrial centers had a total of 300,000 members. Between 1834 and 1837, every organized group struck; the total number of strikes was 173. Part of this activity was due to depression conditions in the Panic of 1837.

As is often the case, these changes in power relations were reflected in legal changes. In *Commonwealth* v. *Hunt,* a case decided in 1842, the Supreme Court of Massachusetts declared that labor unions as such are not conspiratorial. This decision was followed by courts in other states, and it opened the doors for further labor organization.

In 1869 there was organized, under the leadership of Terence Powderly, the Knights of Labor. This national union had extensive membership among unskilled workers. It stood for equal pay for women, abolition of child and prison labor, and formation of a bureau of labor statistics. The Knights looked forward to long-range changes which would bring about a society of independent artisans rather than hired wage laborers. One of the methods through which they worked to do this was the formation of producers' and consumers' cooperatives.

The American Federation of Labor (AFL), which began in 1886, was a quite different type of organization. It featured craft unionism, organization of the skilled "cream" of labor. It excluded not only unskilled workers, but also women and Negroes. Under the long leadership of Samuel Gompers, it established organized labor as a permanent force in American life. Unlike the Knights of Labor, the AFL was primarily concerned with "bread and butter" unionism, promotion of relatively small but immediately attainable goals. It opposed the Socialist movement which was beginning to gain some political strength. In this respect it set the tone for American trade unionism, which, contrary to some charges of communism, has over the years been overwhelmingly procapitalist.

This was not, it is true, the case with the Industrial Workers of the World (IWW). The Wobblies, as the IWW were known, held to the principle of one big union for all skilled and unskilled workers. Their program was revolutionary and "syndicalist," that is, they believed in the operation of industries by the workers themselves. (This type of organization, we may note, has been adopted to a considerable extent in Yugoslavia.) The IWW's membership came mainly from the unskilled masses of labor—lumber, agricultural, and construction workers in the West, and foreign-born industrial workers in the East. In 1912, it won a spectacular strike in the textile mills of Lawrence, Massachusetts, despite the presence of 1400 soldiers brought in to break the strike.

After World War I, labor's membership and power declined. In the boom period of the 1920s, it became harder to organize workers. The Republican

Party was in power, and the climate was antilabor. This changed with the Depression and the Roosevelt Administration. In 1935 Congress passed the Wagner Labor Relations Act, which gave legal protection to the right to organize. Previously management had often been able to cripple unions by firing their leaders. Now a fired leader or organizer could ask for reinstatement under the Wagner Act, probably with lost pay.

This protection was followed by the rise, in 1935, of the Committee on Industrial Organization (later the Congress of Industrial Organizations, or the CIO). The CIO developed first within the AFL, to meet the need for industry-wide organization of low-skilled workers. The AFL did contain industrial unions (organizations of all workers in a given industry, regardless of special skill), as well as craft unions (containing only members of specialized skill). The CIO began, however, much more extensive organization of industry-wide unions. Organizing committees were set up for steel, automobile, rubber, textile, tobacco, and other workers. In 1938 the CIO split away from the AFL. By the following year, its membership was almost as great as that of the parent organization. For the first time, low-skill workers had been effectively organized.

Labor organization in the United States has been faced with many difficulties. One has been the *variety of languages and cultural backgrounds* among workers. As industrialism took over in the last third of the nineteenth century, factories and railways were manned by immigrants. First came the Germans, the Irish, and the Scandinavians. Later came the refugees from eastern and southern Europe, including Jews. Immigrants brought their native languages and also strong nationalistic hostilities.

When immigrant workers spoke little or no English, communication between organizers and workers or within union meetings was difficult. Each new immigrant group tended to become the target for all earlier established majorities and minorities. The Irish, at first the objects of severe discrimination, gradually became assimilated and later turned the same prejudice against the Poles, Czechs, Italians, and Jews. These prejudices and hostilities worked against effective cooperation toward union objectives. Most of these problems have cleared up as European immigrants have become Americanized, but prejudice against Negroes is still a barrier, especially in the South. A number of the old AFL unions continue to discriminate.

A second obstacle to labor organization has been *lack of class consciousness* among workers. In nineteenth-century Europe, the class structure had become so fixed that there was relatively little chance for upward mobility. Most people remained in the class in which they were born. They felt that they belonged to it. When Marx preached "Workers of the world, unite!" he struck a deep chord in the class consciousness of European workers. The situation was quite different in the United States. With much unoccupied land and a shortage of labor, people had strong hopes of being able to rise above the station of their birth. "From rags to riches," "from log cabin to White House," sloganized these hopes. People were more likely to be interested in making it on their own than in organizing to promote the interests of the working class. They identified with the classes above them. They had a bourgeois, not a proletarian, consciousness. This is still the case today with white-collar workers, who have been hard to organize. Semi-professional workers like teachers are likely to feel degraded at the thought of belonging to a union along with "working-class" people.

The *federal structure of government* has also posed difficulties. Traditionally, the courts have severely limited the power of the national government to control labor conditions. Since the Franklin D. Roosevelt Administration, they have been somewhat more liberal.

Combination of capital was regarded as in accordance with natural laws; combination of labor as a conspiracy. Monopoly was good business, and businessmen denounced or evaded the Sherman Act, but the closed shop was un-American. It was the duty of government to aid business and to protect business interests, but government aid to labor was socialistic. That business should go into politics was common sense, but that labor should go into politics was contrary to the American tradition. Property had a natural right to a fair return on its value, but the return which labor might enjoy was to be regulated strictly by the law of supply and demand. Appeals to protect or enhance property interests were reasonable, but appeals to protect or enhance labor interests were demagogic. Brokers who organized business combines were respectable public servants, but labor organizers were agitators. The use of Pinkerton detectives to protect business property was preserving law and order, but the use of force to protect the job was violence. To curtail production in the face of an oversupply of consumers' goods was sound business practice, but to strike for shorter hours in the face of an oversupply of labor was unsound.

—*Samuel E. Morison and Henry Steele Commager,* The Growth of the American Republic, *4th ed., New York, Oxford University Press, 1950, vol. 2, p. 153.*

However, labor has always had to depend to a large extent upon state laws. This has required working for legislation in what are now fifty different state capitals. If favorable legislation was passed by one state, industry could move to states with more lenient laws. A more favorable climate of laws was, for example, one of the main factors leading the cotton textile industry to move from New England to the South.

The federal governmental structure was only one of the *legal difficulties* facing American labor. Until about 1937 the courts were definitely favorable to capital. This was not a peculiarity of the courts; it was simply an expression of a cultural double standard toward capital and labor, which is described in the accompanying quotation from two noted American historians.

The Lochner decision in 1905, which invalidated a New York State maximum hour law, is an example of court action against labor legislation. Invalidation of a 1916 law banning products of child labor from interstate commerce is another. Employers could, until New Deal days, bind workers by a yellow-dog contract, in which a condition of work was that they would not join a union. (The term implied that only a yellow dog would voluntarily sign such an agreement.) On the other hand, in 1890 the Supreme Court found that a boycott of an unorganized firm by the Danbury, Connecticut hatters' union was a violation of the Sherman antitrust law. The union's members were held liable for damages.

An employer could use the lockout, closing of a plant beset by labor disputes, to win his case against a union. If the union struck, he might be able to secure a court injunction to break the strike. This happened in the Pullman Strike of 1894, and again in the railway strike of 1922. Use of the injunction in labor disputes was limited by the Norris-LaGuardia Act of 1932. However, as recently as 1968, the injunction was used against public school teachers in Florida.

Where other obstacles were not enough, labor organization might be prevented by outright *violence.* Labor unions were no better regarded a century ago than were civil rights leaders in some parts of the South in the 1960s, and the repressive measures used were often similar.

Sometimes hired strikebreakers were employed. In 1892, while Andrew Carnegie was on vacation in his native Scotland, a strike broke out at his Homestead, Pennsylvania, steel plant. Pinkerton detectives and state militia were brought in on barges, to which strikers set fire. An open battle followed in which men were killed on both sides. Sometimes troops attempted to break strikes. This happened in Coeur d'Alene, Idaho, in the 1890s, when soldiers confronted armed members of the Western Federation of Miners. It also happened at Lawrence, Massachusetts, in 1912. As we have seen, this strike was finally won. Local police have played their part. In the Chicago "Memorial Day Massacre" of 1937, police shot into a crowd and killed a number of people. In "Bloody" Harlan County, Kentucky, and in adjoining counties of the Kentucky coal mining area, police and sheriff's officers have for decades enforced the interests of mine owners against workers.

Some of the violence has been committed by workers, or attributed to them, with further damage to the cause of labor. In 1875 groups of miners, called "Molly Maguires," in the anthracite coal areas of western Pennsylvania carried on a reign of terror against mine owners. It was marked by savage beatings and some cold-blooded murders. In 1886 a strike took place at the Chicago plant of the McCormick Harvester Company. Several workers were killed in a clash with police. A protest meeting was called, in the course of which a bomb was thrown which killed a policeman. Eight anarchists were brought to trial and four were hanged (one committed suicide), although there was no evidence that any of them had thrown the bomb. The Haymarket Riot nearly finished the Knights of Labor, although they insisted that they had had no connection with it. Similarly, the explosion of a

The Homestead Strike, 1872.

bomb on Wall Street in 1919 resulted in a wave of feeling against the IWW, who were almost arrested out of existence.

In spite of all these obstacles, labor has arrived. Pollster Samuel Lubell points out that in the election of 1928 the Democrats, with Al Smith as presidential candidate, carried the major cities of the country for the first time. What had happened was that the children of the early twentieth-century immigrants to the industrial cities had now reached voting age. In the Roosevelt Administration, this shift in power was reflected in a Congress favorable to labor, and eventually in a change in Supreme Court decisions. Large areas of labor are still unorganized, but advances are being made in organizing white collar employees, and a start is being made toward unions of agricultural workers.

Today labor has become part of the power structure. It would be a mistake to suppose that it is equal in power with organized business or that labor runs the country. Labor leaders do earn salaries comparable to those of business executives, however. They mix on the local and national level with the highest business, political, and military leaders.

The same centralization of power that we have seen in business has taken place in labor organization. In 1900 the average union had 8400 members. In 1944 the figure was 75,000. Obviously the possibility of control by the average member has become less. Of 198 elections for union presidents between 1900 and 1948, only 38 were contested. This means that national labor leaders tend to be reelected repeatedly without opposition and often to be removed only by death.

Union organization generally has four levels: (1) the local union, or "local," (2) the city central labor body, (3) the state organization, and (4) the international union, so called because most national unions have Canadian locals. Most local unions are probably fairly democratic. However, they also generally have little power, for this is usually centralized in the international body.

There are great differences in the degree of centralization or democracy in international unions. Some are historically undemocratic. From 1900 to 1939, the tobacco workers' union never even held a convention. The United Mine Workers, at the peak of their power, were generally ruled with an iron hand by John L. Lewis. The teamsters have been dominated by a series of autocratic presidents, of whom James Hoffa is a recent example. The longshoremen have had a highly centralized structure. The musicians were

for a long time under the authoritarian rule of Caesar Petrillo. The carpenters were governed for many years by "Big Bill" Hutchinson.

Other international unions have had a more democratic history. The typographical workers have a fully developed two-party system. The United Auto Workers have been reasonably democratic, in part no doubt because of the democratic values of their former president, Walter Reuther. The Newspaper Guild, the government employees, and the American Federation of Teachers have had a rather democratic structure. These are, of course, white-collar unions. The International Ladies' Garment Workers Union has been on the democratic side, but its record has been marred by racial discrimination.

The factors behind centralization of union power are the same ones favoring centralization in all areas of life. Size itself has tended to make grass-roots control by locals more difficult. Officials secure power within the union that enables them to reward their friends and punish their enemies. *Grievances* of members against management are likely to be handled by union officials, who can press them or not according to whether the person presenting the grievance is in their favor. Union officials have *patronage*— the ability to make or influence appointments or other rewards to those who have been loyal. Union structure gives officials *disciplinary powers* which may be used, as they were in the United Mine Workers Union during John L. Lewis' administration, against political opponents. Closely related to these powers is control of the union press. Officials may be able to present their views to the membership and censor the views of their opponents.

One of the most important justifications for union centralization is the need to be unified in the struggle against management. Labor-management relations, officials may say, are hostile, and no group engaged in hostilities can afford the luxury of being democratic. Management control is highly centralized, and therefore effective; it is not necessary to consult all the stockholders in order to act. Unions, it is claimed, must be capable of equally rapid and effective decisions.

The manner in which an international union first developed is likely to affect the degree of democracy. Some internationals have arisen from the bottom through consolidation of existing locals. This situation favors democratic control, although it has not always produced it. Other unions, particularly those formed during the CIO Depression drive, were organized from the top down through industry-wide organizing committees. The tendency has been for the power which began at the top to remain there.

Another element in centralization is the tendency of officials to become charismatic father figures; this tendency exists in all organizations. Especially when a leader has been forceful and effective, he is likely to be revered, even though perhaps also hated.

Finally, the composition of membership is important in determining the degree of centralization. Unions composed largely of unskilled and illiterate workers are no more likely to be democratic than are any other groups of this kind. It is significant that, for the most part, the more democratic unions have been those involving high-status and professional workers.

Labor in the United States, then, has progressed from being an outlawed movement against the established order, to being a definite part of the Establishment. As this has happened, it has developed the centralized bureaucratic structure typical of powerful organizations in a mass society. It is not, however, any more authoritarian than business, government, or most other large organizations. Labor has also become conservative. In 1968, at a time when some businessmen were organizing against the Vietnam war and the *Wall Street Journal* was editorializing against it, the National AFL-CIO convention gave the national administration its rousing support.

THE FARMER IN URBAN SOCIETY

Compared with capital and labor in business and industry, the farmer is the forgotten man in our urban society. Management and workers have developed strong organized power to protect their interests in the economy. The average farmer has no comparable organization. The results are shown in his standard of life.

In 1963 the median income per farm family was $4107, compared with $7644 for nonfarm families. The nonfarm income was thus 86 percent higher. In the same year, 43.4 percent —almost half—of all farm families were below the poverty level of $3000, and 28.1 percent were below $2000. The comparable figures for nonfarm families were 17 percent under $3000 and 9.5 percent under $2000. The condition of hired workers is much worse than that of farm owners or renters. In 1961 the average nonmigratory farm laborer made $1083 in money wages, the average nonmigrant woman worker, only $326. The average migrant made $902, the average migrant woman, $340. Flush toilets were missing in 6 percent of urban homes and in 38 percent of farm homes. Bathtubs and showers were both absent in 7 percent of urban residences, and in 37 percent of farm dwellings.

To understand why the farmer lives as he does, we must examine the place of agriculture in the urban industrial economy.

The Civil War marked the turning point for American agriculture, as for American industry. It meant the end of the power of the old agrarian South and was followed by the adoption of mechanical techniques which changed the nature of agriculture. In 1850 farm methods were really very little advanced over what they had been in Egypt 2000 years before Christ. The next hundred years saw more significant changes in agricultural techniques than had taken place in the previous 4000 years.

Before the war Cyrus McCormick had begun to market a reaper for wheat which merely cut the grain and left it in piles. In the 1870s and 1880s, an automatic grain binder came into use, and in the far West a combine which cut, threshed, and bagged the grain in a single operation was sold. By 1870 an improved steel plow was in use. Mechanical corn planters and wheat drills speeded the process of planting. Corn huskers and riding plows also came. The development of the gasoline engine brought the tractor around the turn of the century. These developments, said historians Charles and Mary Beard, "made a change in the cultivation of the soil scarcely less profound than that wrought by the spinning jenny, the loom, and the blast furnace in the methods of manufacture."

Mechanization, beginning with wheat and corn, has spread to other crops. The mechanical cotton picker has revolutionized cotton production. Potatoes, tobacco, nuts, tomatoes—and in Cuba, sugar—can be harvested by machine. Since 1930 the process of mechanization has been greatly accelerated in the United States. From 1930 to 1955, the number of wheat combines increased 16 times, the number of trucks 3 times, the number of milking machines 7 times, and the number of corn pickers 13 times. In the same period the percentage of farm homes with electricity rose from 10 percent to 90 percent.

This mechanization brought a great increase in the efficiency of production. A good general estimate would be that the productivity of the average farmer doubled between 1850 and 1900, and tripled again between 1900 and 1960. In 1850 the typical farm worker supported four nonfarmers; in 1900, seven; in 1950, the number was 23. The recent increases are particularly impressive. From 1947 to 1964, output per man-hour on the farm increased 176 percent. In nonfarm occupations the increase over the same period was only 56 percent.

This great increase in productivity has been accompanied by a depopulation of rural areas and impoverishment of most farmers who have remained. Of the nearly 900 counties in the United States, nearly one-third have lost population for forty years or more, and now have fewer than 10,000 people. This is just the period of greatest gain in agricultural productivity. In 1790 the United States was 90 percent rural; in 1960, it was 9.3 percent rural; in 1965, 7 percent. From 1910 to 1950, the share of the GNP earned by farmers fell from 16.1 percent to 7.4 percent. This change reflected in part the fact that industry and business have simply expanded faster than agriculture, but our earlier figures show that those engaged in agriculture have also failed to share the gains of twentieth-century growth. Certainly the farmer's income has not kept pace with his tremendous recent gains in productivity.

A related result of mechanization has been the same tendency toward concentration that we found in business and industry, although it has not yet gone to that extent. In 1950, however, around 70,000 big farms covered one-third of all the land in the East and two-thirds in the West. From 1949 to 1964, farms with $25,000 or more annual income rose from 1.9 percent to 4.1 percent of all farms. These figures might not be particularly impressive if we did not note that in 1964 these large to giant-size farms did 39 percent of all farm business. The accompanying table gives a concise picture of types of American farms and how they divide farm income. We will note that the figures are for total sales, not net income. Three facts shown by this table are worth pointing out. (1) The majority of farms (noncommercial plus substandard) produce less than 10

FARM TYPES AND INCOME, 1964

FARM TYPE	PERCENT OF FARMS	PERCENT OF SALES
Noncommercial farms	37.0	3.7
(Part-time and residential)		
Substandard farms	18.7	5.6
(Sales below $5000 a year)		
Family-type farms	40.2	51.7
(Sales $5000 to $24,999 a year)		
Large to giant-size farms	4.1	39.0
(Sales $25,000 a year or above)		

Source: Conference on Economic Progress, Agriculture and the Public Interest, Washington, D.C., 1965, p. 19.

percent of all sales. Of course, the noncommercial farmers are not primarily interested in sales. (2) The few large to giant-size farms produce sales quite out of proportion to their number. (3) The family-type farm still produces more than half the sales value of American farms. It is, therefore, far from obsolete.

What are the reasons for the depopulation, impoverishment, and concentration in American agriculture? The first is mechanization itself. Machines were a great help to those who could afford them. To those who could not, they were a curse. The nonmechanized farmer had to compete with the mechanized farm, and this he usually could not do. One illustration will show what has happened. In 1944 on the flat plains of Texas, where power-driven mechanical cotton pickers could be used, cotton could be grown for $.04 a pound. In the hilly country, where machine pickers were not practical, it cost $.19 a pound to produce. It is not hard to see why a large part of cotton production has moved from small farms on the hilly, southern piedmont to large farms in the flatlands of Mississippi, Louisiana, Arkansas, and Texas. The introduction of the wheat combine created the same kind of problem for the small wheat farmer. Mechanization has meant that the farmer has usually been forced either to go into debt to buy machines, to live on a reduced income, or to lose his farm to a larger operator or to a bank or mortgage company.

A second factor, historically, was the closing of the frontier. Up to the end of the nineteenth century, there was plenty of unoccupied territory, and good land could usually be had fairly cheaply. With the 1890 census, it was announced, however, that the frontier was closed. From then on farmers had to compete for land already in cultivation, at higher prices, at the same time that they were borrowing to buy the new farm machinery.

A third, and the most important, reason for the position of the farmer is the market in which he sells his product. Industrial and business management, as we have seen, have developed an oligopolistic system which enables them to command a high price for their products. Unionization of labor has created an oligopoly in the labor market, which keeps wages relatively high. The ordinary farmer has developed no similar combinations to boost the price of farm products. He sells his crops in what is still essentially a competitive market and must buy consumer goods and agricultural capital goods in an oligopolistic market, that is, he must sell cheap and buy dear. This has been his essential problem at least since the turn of the century.

Another peculiarity in the market for farm goods lies in the fact that the farmer's tie to the land makes him less mobile than other businessmen or industrial workers. Low prices for farm products are thus likely to have a peculiar effect. Ordinarily, low prices for any commodity tend to lead sellers to seek other lines of activity. The supply is thus reduced, and the price adjusts itself again upward. But for farmers, farming has traditionally been not only a business but a way of life. Thus when prices fall, instead of reducing production or leaving the farm, they are likely to increase production, to try to compensate in quantity for their poor returns. Surplus production is likely to drive prices still further down.

During World War I, when the United States was shipping large amounts of food to the European nations at war, food prices soared, and farmers mortgaged themselves to buy new land and equipment. When the war was over and foreign nations could again supply themselves, prices fell. Farmers with heavy debts tried desperately to meet their obligations through more production, which reduced prices even further. Incomes declined, mortgages were foreclosed, and an agricultural depression was under way which lasted through the 1920s, at the same time that the rest of the economy was booming.

Before we go further in analyzing the economic and political position of the farmer, let us look at some of the social effects of what has been happening. It is an extremely serious thing for most of a population to lose productive contact with the land. There is, indeed, a serious question whether a civilization can long survive on this basis. When William Jennings Bryan was seeking the presidency in the 1890s on a platform calling for the free coinage of silver, which would inflate prices and reduce the farmer's burden of debt, he put the matter dramatically: "Burn down your cities and leave our farms, and your cities will spring up again as if by magic; but destroy our farms and the grass will grow in the streets of every city in the country."[4]

At almost the same time a Wisconsin historian, Frederick Jackson Turner, put forward the famous thesis that American democracy had rested upon the individualism of the small frontier farmer, which was now being destroyed by the rise of large corporations and the closing of the frontier. In the 1940s a social anthropologist, Walter Goldschmidt, did an extremely important study of the social effects involved in the transition from small owner-operated farms to large absentee-owned farms.

In Dinuba and Arvin, California, Goldschmidt felt that he had found two farm communities that were very similar in all but one respect: size and ownership of farms. In Dinuba, where farms were small and owner-operated, community spirit was high, physical improvements in the community were plentiful, voluntary associations were numerous, there was independent local government, and people had a strong sense of roots in the community. In Arvin, where farms were large and owners typically lived outside the community, there was no independent local government, community spirit was low, voluntary associations were few in number, the physical appearance of the community had deteriorated, and few people felt that they "belonged" in the community.

Goldschmidt felt that this disorganization of community is probably the price that must be paid if the family-type farm is forced out of existence. This he felt would be a loss of values fundamental to American democracy as it has historically been known.

Farmers, like other groups, have continually tried to strengthen their position in the economy through organization. This has taken a number of forms.

1. Through organizing cooperatives farmers have tried to keep for themselves money that formerly went to industrialists, wholesale and retail merchants, and processors. A co-op is owned by those immediately concerned as consumers or producers. Control is usually on the principle of

4. William Jennings Bryan, quoted in Samuel E. Morison and Henry Steele Commager, *The Growth of the American Republic,* 4th ed., New York, Oxford University Press, 1950, vol. 2, p. 261.

A Granger meeting in Illinois, 1873.

"one man, one vote," as contrasted with the "one share, one vote" principle in corporations. Earnings are usually divided according to the amount of business contributed by each member.

The National Grange, organized in 1867, developed the first effective cooperative movement in the United States. The Farmers' Union, founded in 1902, has had development of co-ops as a major objective. Consumers' co-ops, such as the retail stores organized by the Grange, enable members to buy directly from producers or wholesalers. Marketing co-ops, such as cooperative grain elevators or co-op creameries, save for the farmer the profits of processing middlemen. Producers' co-ops, such as the farm machinery and stove factories founded by the Grange, or the oil refineries operated by the Farmers' Union, eliminate profits of producers as well as middlemen on goods important to farmers.

2. Agricultural producers have formed marketing or trade associations. The sugar growers and the fruit and vegetable growers have developed strong national lobbies. The California Fruit Growers Association and Florida Citrus Mutual are examples of marketing associations. Around 1920 an attempt was made to reduce acreage and control prices through organiza-

tion of tobacco producers in Virginia and the Carolinas. Cotton, walnut, livestock, soybean, and milk producers also have national associations.

3. Farmers have at times undertaken direct political action. The Farmers' Alliance, organized in the 1880s in the South and West, furnished the main support for the Populist Party in the presidential election of 1892. The Populist platform called for nationalization of railways and telegraphs, a postal savings bank, a graduated income tax, government warehouses, reclamation of excess land granted to railways and other corporations, shorter hours for industrial workers, the secret ballot, initiative and referendum, and direct election of senators. Although the Populists did not gain many national offices, many of these demands became law within the next thirty years. In the early years of this century, the Farmers' Non-Partisan League won over the government of North Dakota and initiated such measures as state grain elevators. The Democratic Party of Minnesota still carries the full name of Democratic-Farmer-Labor Party.

4. Aside from winning control in elections, farm interests have been somewhat successful in using political influence to balance the power of industrial capital and labor. In the 1870s

the Grange secured regulation of railway rates and establishment of a federal Department of Agriculture. Since 1921 the so-called farm bloc has had a powerful influence in Congress and in farm-state legislatures. The heart of the farm bloc has been the Farm Bureau. In 1919 state legislatures began to establish farm bureaus to cooperate with county agents of the federal Department of Agriculture in work with farmers. These became organized into the American Farm Bureau Federation. The other major organization in the bloc is the Grange.

The farm bloc has successfully promoted farm price supports, government credit for farmers, farmer representation on the Interstate Commerce Commission, exemption of co-ops from taxes, reduction of interest on farm mortgages, and lower railway freight rates. It resisted control of farm prices during World War II. The bloc has been antilabor, opposing regulation of hours and wages, and the union shop. It has opposed the efforts of labor unions to organize farmers. It has generally supported the interests of big commercial farmers. It strongly opposed the Farm Security Administration, established in the Depression to protect poor and substandard farmers. It has objected to controls to protect immigrant migrant workers. It has opposed medicare and other welfare legislation, opposed extensive foreign aid, and generally has cooperated politically with the National Association of Manufacturers.

The Farmers' Union, on the contrary, has publicly declared itself spokesman for the small farmer and the family-type farm. It has stood for cooperation with organized labor and for a society founded on producers' and consumers' cooperatives rather than private profit. The Farmers' Union gave much support to farmers' milk strikes in the 1930s, supported the Farm Security Administration's program for poor farmers, favored protective measures for immigrant farm workers, and was the major sponsor of the 1946 Employment Act.

5. There have been efforts to organize farmers on the model of labor unions or within existing labor organizations. The Southern Tenant Farmers' Union, organized during the Depression, was an unsuccessful attempt. During the same period, both the United Mine Workers and the teamsters tried to organize farmers. In 1959 the Agricultural Workers' Organizing Committee was formed by the AFL-CIO to organize agricultural labor around Stockton, California. Two years later an independent union, the National Farm Workers' Association, was organized by Cesar Chavez. The two unions merged in the summer of 1966 into the AFL-CIO United Farm Workers Organizing Committee (UFWOC), after a major strike among grape workers in the Delano, California, area (incidentally very close to the Arvin and Dinuba communities studied by Goldschmidt). Chavez, a charismatic leader, has been very successful in joining economic demands with "la causa" (the cause) of the oppressed Mexican-American ethnic group. UFWOC's first success was in securing contracts with wine grape growers. These contracts were followed by a campaign to win over table grape producers. A nationwide grape boycott aroused considerable support, which culminated in 1970 in contracts with most table grape growers. The Chavez union has received considerable support from other unions, especially the United Auto Workers. It has had little success in organizing migrant streams in the Midwest and the East, although success in California will probably stimulate organizing effort in these areas. Organized labor intends to make farm labor a major objective in its future organizing campaigns.

About the efforts of farmers to protect themselves through organization, we can draw two general conclusions. The first is that they have not yet been able to produce, on any large scale, a bargaining power equal to that of industry or organized labor. The second is that organized farm power, with the exceptions of the Farmers' Union and recent unionization efforts, has become increasingly conservative and dominated by big owners. In neither respect has farm organization protected adequately the interests of the family farmers who still constitute a majority of farmers, or of the stationary and migrant laborers in the giant "factories in the field."

What, then, is the future of the farm in the American economy? Some observers are very pessimistic. They see substandard and family farms disappearing, leaving almost all farming to absentee-owned "farm factories" manned by agricultural labor which will have no real ties to the soil. To overcome the farm surpluses which we have had in the past, they believe, we actually need further reduction of farm acreage and population.

Not all students of the farm agree. Leon Keyserling, former chairman on the President's Council of Economic Advisors, maintains that we have greatly exaggerated our farm overproduction in the past, and that we really need more production, not less. Many nonfarm Americans still have a substandard diet. If they are to have enough money in their pockets to buy adequate food, and also adequate clothing, more farm acreage will be needed. If the whole economy can maintain full employment and adequate incomes for all, says Keyserling, this will happen. Although the United States cannot feed the world, American agriculture and the whole American economy can benefit by expanded sale of food to needy countries abroad. This might require an increase in foreign aid appropriations to pay for the food in the short run, but it would be a sound humanitarian and economic investment in the long run.

Keyserling estimated in 1965 that, to feed a domestic population with adequate incomes and to help provide reasonable improvement for hungry people abroad, American agricultural production in 1975 would have to be *above* 1964 output by these amounts:

Beef cattle, 43 percent
Hogs, about 10 percent
Poultry, 55 percent
Eggs, slightly less than 15 percent
Dairy cattle, about 15 percent
Wheat, 15 percent
Corn, 12 percent
Rice, 26 percent
Barley, 20 percent
Dried beans and peas, 21 percent
Soybeans, slightly less than 29 percent
Cotton, production would remain about the same.[5]

Such expansion would give opportunity for family-type farms. Since they have been selling cheap in a competitive market and buying dear in an oligopolistic one, farmers have actually been subsidizing urban dwellers. It is therefore only reasonable that a part of this "subsidy" be returned so as to make their income equivalent to nonfarm income. Attempts have been made in the past to ensure farm price parity through price subsidies, that is, to make the ratio of farm to nonfarm prices equal to what it was early in this century. Price parity does not, however, ensure equal income. Moreover, price supports have helped giant farms much more than small ones. (A 1968 study showed that only 4.5 percent of government farm payments went to farmers with $2500 annual income or less, while 54.5 percent went to the 10 percent of farmers grossing $20,000 or more.) Keyserling therefore proposes income supports to needy farmers, rather than continued price subsidies. These would be only part of a general antipoverty program to raise all substandard incomes. Keyserling believes

5. Leon H. Keyserling, *Agriculture and the Public Interest,* Washington, D.C., Conference on Economic Progress, 1965, pp. 83–84.

that if the imbalance in farm and non-farm bargaining power can thus be overcome, and government discrimination against smaller farmers corrected, the middle-sized family farm can hold its own with the large corporation farm in terms of efficiency.

A program to equalize the economic and social power of farmers with that of the rest of the nation might include:

1. Increase in domestic consumption of farm products through elimination of substandard nonfarm incomes

2. Increase in foreign consumption, financed where necessary by increased foreign aid

3. Income supplements to farmers to compensate for their inequality in bargaining power

4. An Agricultural Employment Act to provide, for agriculture, the same overall governmental responsibility that the Employment Act of 1946 provides in business and industry and provision for agricultural advisers on government farm policy

5. Subsidized resettlement of farmers from areas (such as parts of Appalachia) where commercial agriculture does not seem possible to other agricultural or industrial areas

6. Exploration of the possibility of combining agriculture with industry in some areas where farm productivity is low

7. Unionization of stationary and migratory farm laborers.

THE SOVEREIGN CONSUMER

The role of the consumer in the economy requires careful exploration, because fact is so colored by theory. Although, as we have seen, we really live in quite a different world, many people still imagine that we live in the world of Adam Smith. In that world the consumer is supposedly king.

When we were discussing the operation of the market, we saw that in a freely competitive society, the basic economic decisions are supposed to be made by consumer demand. What to produce, how to allocate resources, how to divide between consumption and investment, how rewards shall be distributed—all are decided by the spending of consumer dollars. The whole market for buyers is like a great polling place, where each dollar spent is a vote for this or that commodity, this or that way of organizing the economy. Each consumer, being interested in getting the most for his money, rationally calculates how best to spend his dollars. Thus the best products are continually being chosen, the inferior, rejected. There is always a stimulus to improvement—"if one makes a better mouse trap, the world will beat a path to his door." The decisions of consumers taken together form the most rational and democratic way to make the economic decisions of a society.

Let us examine this theory of consumer sovereignty, or if we wish, the "better mouse trap" theory. To what extent does the consumer today govern the economy in a rational way?

In the first place, we must ask, "Which consumer?" The theory of consumer sovereignty compares the "ballot box of the market place" with the political polling place, but there is a very important difference. In political elections each person has a single vote, regardless of his social and economic status. At the ballot box of the market place, however, everyone votes according to his income. Our discussion of community power structure should have made it clear that citizens actually have very unequal political power. At the voting place, at least, all are equal. This is not true of the economic voting of consumers.

In 1955 the average person in the upper one-tenth of the population received 27 times as much income (after taxes) as the average person in the bottom one-tenth. Thus he had 27 economic votes to one for the poor person. Let us see what this unequal ability to vote means in a specific case.

Consider a fairly wealthy person with $100,000 of free capital. With this money he can "vote" that the resources of the country shall be so used as to buy him a winter apartment in Manhattan, a summer home in the Berkshires, and a vacation house in Nassau. Each will remain idle a considerable part of the time. If this amount of purchasing power had been allocated by voters holding one ballot each in a political election, the result might have been quite different. The $100,000 might have been used instead to build twenty $5000 homes for year-round occupancy by slum families. Whether or not one thinks it is just for people to influence the economy in proportion to their wealth will depend, in part, on how just he considers our distribution of income to be. One thing is clear, however—economic voting in the market is not based on the democratic principle of one man, one vote.

Another aspect of consumer sovereignty is the tendency of the individual consumer to choose private over public goods and services. This point has been especially stressed by the economist John Kenneth Galbraith in his book, *The Affluent Society*. Private goods or services are all those which are bought and used by separate private individuals. Public goods and services are socially owned and used. An automobile is a private good; a highway, a public good. A hairdresser furnishes a private service; a policeman a public one. Galbraith has pointed out that in an economy where decisions are made by private consumer choice, public needs tend to be left out.

Cars will be bought freely, but highways will lag behind. Children will get expensive toys, but the pay of school teachers will be too low. Television sets will be more widespread than bathtubs and showers, but public parks will be inadequate. Consumer goods will be bought at an unprecedented rate, but trash disposal will not be adequate to get rid of the debris. An advanced technological society, says Galbraith, produces an ever-increasing need for public goods and services that will not ordinarily be chosen spontaneously by most independent spenders. Consumer sovereignty in the free market is not designed to make rational decisions about public needs.

So far we have been raising questions about the justice and adequacy of consumer sovereignty through market choices. We need now to ask to what extent consumers in our economy actually behave as the theory of consumer sovereignty says they should.

One important problem lies in *mass production*. Before 1790 relationships between producer and consumer were likely to be direct and personal. The typical producer was a craftsman with a small shop in a small village. The typical consumer was a self-sufficient farmer, or another townsman. If townsman or farmer bought a pair of shoes and was dissatisfied, he could demand personally that the defect be corrected. If he could not get satisfaction, he could spread the word that this shoemaker should not be patronized. Thus the consumer had a very direct control over the producer. Today the consumer buys a pair of shoes mass-produced many miles away by people whom he can never know. He has no way to influence the shoe manufacturer in the same direct manner in which the pre-1790 craftsman could be reached. Of course, he can urge others not to buy from this manufacturer, but the number of customers he can ordinarily reach is limited.

Each individual can, it is true, still exercise his consumer sovereignty by refusing to buy a given product. In this sense he still has control through his economic vote, but here another factor enters in. With mass production has come a great *multiplication of products*. It has become increasingly hard for any of us to form an intelligent judgment about most of the products we consume. If one is to patronize the manufacturer with the better mouse trap, he must first know which mouse trap is better. How can consumers get the information to know? The choice of gasoline is a good example of the problem. Which of us is really capable of judging among the conflicting and skillfully presented claims of rival oil companies? The problem is complicated by the fact that retail gas tanks are not always filled by the company they represent. An independent station may at times be supplied by a truck from a major company. A station bearing the name of a major company may occasionally have its tank filled with an independent gasoline.

How many of us are really able to make an informed choice among such products as watches, power mowers, coffees, sewing machines, electric washers, diet foods, teaching machines, electric shavers, cheeses, milk, or lingerie? Perhaps on one or two of these items each of us may have some real competence. In most cases, however, we probably follow hearsay, of what our neighbors are doing, or the claims of the most persuasive advertiser.

Oligopoly makes the consumer less than sovereign. When prices are fixed through price leadership, the consumer no longer has the opporutnity to choose the most efficient producer. "Fair trade" laws, through which the manufacturer sets a minimum price for retailers, have the same effect by denying consumers the right to buy "fair traded" items more cheaply at discount houses, or elsewhere. Advertising may create oligopolistic restriction of consumer choice. The Temporary National Economic Committee reported an interesting case in 1939. A manufacturer produced a new toothpaste which received a government contract, had the approval of the American Dental Association, would sell at one-half the retail price of leading brands, and would give the retailer twice as large a markup. One would suppose that this manufacturer would have had an instant success. Actually, he failed completely, and had to go into another line of business. He found that to enter the market he would have to spend $100,000, not for an advertising campaign, but for a preliminary market survey to see whether a campaign would be justified.

In such ways oligopoly, which we have seen is more typical today than free competition, sharply restricts free consumer choice. It diverts resources away from the channels that consumers would freely select and into the hands of oligopolistic concerns.

Internal restrictions of rational consumer choice are no less important than the external ones. One of the most important of these is the need for "conspicuous consumption." The term was coined by Thorstein Veblen in *The Theory of the Leisure Class,* a social science classic which has never really been outdated. The conspicuous consumer buys not for the direct use-value of products, but for the status which he will gain in the eyes of his neighbors.

Mrs. Manyrocks spends $100,000 for her daughter's wedding at the Plaza, and Mrs. Allgold must therefore spend $125,000 for her daughter at the Ritz. Some years ago Buick cars were distinguished by the number of holes in the side of the hood—a 4-hole car carried higher prestige than a 2-hole or 3-hole model. "Knowledgeable people drink Imperial"—and of course one wishes to be "in the know." "The uncommon pen for the uncommon man" —and who wants to be common? "Will this be just another summer of Pontiac watching, or are you set to get a Catalina of your own?" There is no happiness for the conspicuous consumer in watching the more fashionable consumption of others.

Unlike the rational "economic man," who always buys cheap, the conspicuous consumer may have to buy dear. "He paid $165 for his suit—his tie, of course, is Wembly." One is urged to live in one of a builder's "expansive and expensive houses." A perfume is advertised, not for its quality of sexual stimulation (which is its biological function), but because it is "the most expensive perfume in the world."

Sometimes the appeal to status is un-disguised; a billboard announces a "prestige community."

Fashion is closely related to con-spicuous consumption. One example is annual models of automobiles. Seldom do these involve significant engineering improvements. Their purpose is mainly to sell new cars by making last year's model psychologically obsolete. It has been estimated that when large Ameri-can cars follow the example of Volks-wagen and eliminate annual models, a consumer will save several hundred dollars on a $3000 automobile. This is the cost of annually retooling a plant.

A dramatic case of the influence of fashion was reported by Color Re-search Institute of Chicago. A large department store stocked a new dress in three colors: turquoise (a blue), fuchsia (a purple), and chartreuse (yel-low-green). The responses of shoppers were observed. Most women "just loved" the turquoise gown. They ad-mired what the fuchsia dress "did for their complexion." The chartreuse gown evoked no such spontaneous re-sponse. It had, however, been adver-tised in *Vogue* as the "color of the moment." The result? Half the women bought the chartreuse gown over the dresses they spontaneously liked. One shopper said, "The color makes me want to vomit," but bought it anyway.

In about 1960 there appeared a rather startling case of the power of fashion. A Texas chiropodist, a medical doctor in good standing, had ampu-tated the last joint on the little toe of a considerable number of women in order to make their feet fit more easily into the very pointed shoes then in style. For those who felt deformed by the loss, there was the consolation that a little red nail polish would help dis-guise the disfigurement when the feet were not covered!

Such social compulsions suggest that the model of the rationally calcu-lating consumer very often does not fit real behavior very well. In recent years a number of social scientists, partly under the influence of Freud, have entered the advertising profession and have attempted to use the findings of depth psychology to make more effec-tive appeals to consumers. These motivational researchers have tried to discover the unconscious factors that lead people to buy. While some of their claims seem exaggerated, many of their findings are very revealing. A number of these are summarized in Vance Packard's book, *The Hidden Persuaders.*

One researcher investigated the emotional responses of women in supermarkets by means of a device which registered the rate at which their eyes blinked. He had supposed that the excitement of being confronted with so many buying possibilities would lead to rapid blinking. He was surprised to find that the blinking rate of the shoppers became, instead, very slow; it was almost that of a person in a trance. Apparently the loaded shelves with their varied colors and designs had an almost hypnotic effect. The women roamed around the shelves in a "hypnoidal" condition, filling up their carts. Only when the bill was finally rung up at the check-out counter did they suddenly begin to blink rapidly!

An equally fascinating piece of in-vestigation dealt with people's choice of cigarettes. The hypothesis of the researcher was that an individual's choice reflects the kind of person he is. If one could get personality profiles of smokers, the investigator reasoned, he should be able to predict their smoking choices from these profiles. He secured a number of responses to the Rorschach inkblot test, a standard technique for diagnosing personality. After inspecting the Rorschach find-ings, he then wrote down for each in-dividual his guess as to the cigarette that person smoked. He was right in almost all cases.

It is possible to name some of the more important appeals made by moti-vational researchers, and by advertis-ers long before them.

One is *power.* A good example is the

case of the "Ford man." In a study of the psychology of car owners, researchers found that the typical Ford owner is a young man, of upper-lower social class, with a good income. He likes to feel that he has a lot of power and speed under the hood at his command. Probably this need expresses some insecurity about his social position and about himself, even though he seems to be on the way up. By contrast, the owner of the De Soto car produced by Chrysler was typically a conservative, responsible, upper-middle-class matron. Many of the appeals to buy status goods are appeals to enhance one's sense of power. In general those who buy for the experience of power are people who experience some sense of powerlessness.

Much advertising appeals to the consumer's need for *regression.* The appeal is not usually made directly; the open pitch is more likely to be to relax. It has been found that milk symbolizes for many soldiers overseas the safety of home and mother. Cigarette smoking (and also drinking) are regressive forms of behavior.

Sexual insecurity is one of the most powerful of all appeals. Many men need to be reassured of their virility; many women of their attractiveness. Marlboro cigarettes, once a red-tipped smoke for women, have capitalized on the male need very successfully with their image of the he-man in "Marlboro Country." An ad for trousers announces that, "He attracts girls like an oil man since he started wearing Mr. Leggs slacks." For those women whose love life is stale or nonexistent, a soap invites them to "plunge into a flirtation with the forbidden." "Men turn, women burn" when one puts on a particular brand of hosiery. A girdle promises, "Instant figure—add you." The makers of Maidenform brassieres have been unusually successful in appealing to usually repressed wishes, "I dreamed I stopped traffic in my Maidenform bra." Some motivational researchers have suggested that the de-

sire to appear in public with few or no clothes is present in most of us, and the ad "represents a beautiful example of wish fulfillment."

The *transfer* device, named by the Institute of Propaganda Analysis, plays a large role in advertising. Favorable emotions associated with one object or situation are transferred to another object which is presented simultaneously. (This is in a way a classic case of the "conditioned response.") Thus Salem cigarettes feature a young man and woman strolling in the spring, amid hills, woods, and streams and pausing to light up a Salem, because it is "springtime fresh." Desires for sexuality and contact with nature are thus harnessed to sell tobacco.

At this point it should be clear that the image of the sovereign, rational consumer, guiding the economy through his free choices, has only a limited usefulness in the real economic world of today. The principle of "one dollar, one vote" means that consumer power is heavily weighted to begin with in favor of those with money. Individual consumer choice is unequipped to serve the increasing need for public goods and services. Mass production and long distance transportation have removed consumers from the direct personal control over producers which they could once exercise. Multiplication of products has reduced the ability of consumers to make informed judgments. An oligopolistic market limits the choice consumers would have in a fully competitive economy.

Cultural and psychological compulsions make the consumer much less than a free agent. Advertising creates a situation where the producer shapes consumer choice at least as much as the consumer shapes production. Advertising cannot, any more than can any form of propaganda, sell a customer something which he does not in some way want. But many consumer wants are unconscious, and many of them are irrational and in conflict with the individual's more reasoned judgment. Whether or not it is more skillful in manipulating these wants than it used to be, advertising is extremely adept.

In the face of this situation, consumers have received some protection from several sources.

Two federal agencies have special consumer interests. The Federal Trade Commission (FTC) is concerned with truth in advertising. It is interested primarily in preventing unfair competition, but in the process it has helped consumers. The FTC has issued cease and desist orders, for example, to a cigarette company which advertised that its brand is "easy on your throat," and to cosmetic manufacturers who claimed that facial creams would build up worn-out cells and that a powder would protect against infection.

The *Food and Drug Administration* (FDA) of the Department of Agriculture is more directly concerned with consumer protection. It was responsible for the famous removal of contaminated cranberries from the market. It forbade the distribution of the drug thalidomide after it had been found to produce birth deformities. The FDA maintains inspection services which have, for instance, seized shipments of butter containing rodent excrement and shipments of rubber contraceptives with holes. The FDA is forced, however, to operate with an inadequate budget. Moreover, like most government regulatory agencies, it is likely to be unduly influenced by the interest it is supposed to control—the food, drug, and chemical industries. The FDA is likely to allow potentially harmful drugs to be marketed until after they have been clearly proved dangerous. It has been very slow in curbing widespread contamination by pesticides.

Two private nonprofit organizations are dedicated to consumer interests. Consumers' Research conducts laboratory investigations of a wide range of products and reports its findings in monthly *Consumers' Research Bul-*

letins, with annual summaries. It has, for example, reported that one well-advertised washing machine may at times tear up clothes, and that another is so constructed that clothes may slip down between the tub and housing, with no way of retrieving them except by dismantling the machine. Consumers' Union puts out similar laboratory reports in its monthly and annual *Consumer Reports.* Consumers' Union has given consumers such information as that the best toothpaste, at one time, was not any advertised brand, but a brand available in dime stores for ten cents. Any consumer contemplating any major purchase will do well, from the standpoint of both quality and cost, to check the reports of both these consumer agencies before buying.

The consumers' cooperative movement has, since the Granger days of the 1870s, been interested in bringing goods to consumers more cheaply by eliminating middlemen. Groups of co-ops have maintained warehouses and factories as well as retail stores. While not nearly so widespread in the United States as in England and Sweden, co-ops are of some significance. They have practiced grade labeling, through which different qualities of a given product are clearly designated. They have not given great attention to such consumer problems as additives and insecticide residues.

It is fairly easy to draw a final conclusion as to the place of the consumer in the structure of economic power. Consumers are the most poorly organized of all important economic interest groups. Today organized capital is clearly the dominant power group, organized labor is in second place, and the farmer is still lagging badly behind. And the consumer has only the weakest kind of protection. The modern American economy has moved from competition among individuals to bargaining among powerfully organized groups. Each of these strives to maintain an oligopolistic market in its own field. It is much easier to conceive and organize the interests of producers than those of consumers. Thus the consumer, being everybody, is in a sense economically and politically nobody. John Kenneth Galbraith has described the situation well:

We have an economic system which, whatever its formal ideological billing, is in substantial part a planned economy. The initiative in deciding what is to be produced comes not from the sovereign consumer who, through the market, issues the instructions that bend the productive mechanism to his ultimate will. Rather it comes from the great producing organization which reaches forward to control the markets that it is presumed to serve and, beyond, to bend the customer to its needs.[6]

6. *The New Industrial State,* New York, New American Library, 1967, p. 18.

Suggestions for further reading

The most influential research report on the concentration of business power in the United States was The Modern Corporation and Private Property *by ADOLPH BERLE and GARDINER MEANS (Commerce Clearing House, 1932). An important recent study is GABRIEL KOLKO,* Wealth and Power in America *(Praeger, 1962, paper). The idea that American business oligopoly constitutes a ruling class is developed by G. WILLIAM DOMHOFF in* Who Rules America? *(Prentice-Hall, 1967). In* Beyond the Ruling Class *(Random House, 1963), SUZANNE KELLER criticizes this approach and also throws light on some of the problems of community power structure raised in Chapter nine.*

The concentration of power in labor leadership was documented by C. WRIGHT MILLS in The New Men of Power *(Kelley, 1969). The history of American labor is written by a university historian in* Labor in America: A History *by FOSTER RHEA DULLES (3rd ed., Cornell University Press, paper) and by a radical activist in SIDNEY LENS's* Radicalism in America *(Thomas Y. Crowell, 1966). Lens's interesting dedication is "to the impractical dreamers who make history while the practical ones revive the jungle."*

Agriculture and the Public Interest by LEON H. KEYSERLING (Conference on Economic Progress, 1965, paper) is a thorough statistical analysis of the situation of the farmer by a former chairman of the President's Council of Economic Advisors. The first writer to bring the migratory farm worker to public attention was CAREY McWILLIAMS in Factories in the Field *(Shoe String, 1969). A very sympathetic account of the work of the United Farm Workers' Organizing Committee is* Sal Si Puedes: Cesar Chavez and the New American Revolution *by PETER MATTHIESSEN (Random House, 1969).* Economics for Consumers *by LELAND J. GORDON and STEWART M. LEE (5th ed., Van Nostrand Reinhold, 1967) is an excellent study of the position of the consumer in the economy.* The Hidden Persuaders *by VANCE PACKARD (Pocket Books, 1970, paper) is a somewhat sensationalized but important and very useful account of the way in which social science knowledge and social scientists have been used by the advertising profession in selling goods to the American public.*

Chapter twelve
The economic spectrum

In Chapter eight and elsewhere, we have discussed the market and planning as alternative ways of making economic decisions. Now we shall examine in more detail the variety of economic systems which range themselves along the continuum from free enterprise to planned society. In order to get the sharpest contrast, we shall begin with capitalist economy, at one end, and then explore totalitarian planned economy at the other. We shall then look at some of the varied forms of mixed economy which fall between.

In Chapter eleven we saw how the development of industrial society has led to the substitution of bargaining among various combinations for competition among isolated individuals. This same development has led to a corresponding increase in the economic functions of government. In the 1930s Franklin Roosevelt once said that an extension of government powers was necessary if big business interests were not to take over the country. Government has increased its economic role as a "countervailing force" to organization of big capital, big labor, and big farming interests, if not big consumer organizations. This means that we do not have in the major nations anything like pure laissez-faire, which is the role which government is supposed to play in a pure market economy. The United States remains the most important nation still basically committed to capitalist free enterprise. We shall begin here and then move next to Japan.

KEYNESIAN CAPITALISM: THE UNITED STATES

So much of our discussion thus far has dealt with the American economy that this section will be a brief review rather than a presentation of new material. This will not be true of the rest of the chapter.

Prerevolutionary America was probably as close to the pure market economy as we are likely to get. It was based on the small farm, small shop, and small store in a primarily rural and village economy. With the growth of industry and urbanization, the world of Adam Smith ceased to be. During most of the nineteenth century, however, government's role was largely that of giving a free hand to rising industrial capitalism. It gave legal recognition and protection to the corporation, did little to curb the combination of corporations into oligopolies, gave lavish grants of public resources to private interests, and favored business and industrial capital over labor and the farmer.

About the turn of the twentieth century, labor and Populist pressures led to some measures against industrial oligopoly, such as the antitrust laws of 1890 and 1911, regulation of railroads under the Interstate Commerce Commission, some regulation of hours and wages in industry, and some compensation to workers for injury on the job. It was not, however, until 1935, after the shock of the Great Depression, that government clearly entered the economic arena as a positive force.

The Wagner Labor Relations Act gave real protection to labor organization for the first time. New Deal legislation embodied a new concept of government: its positive responsibility for the welfare of the economy. No longer was it to stand by and wait for the "invisible hand" to work things out. Crop control and price subsidy under the Agricultural Adjustment Administration, public works under the Works Progress Administration and Public Works Administration, industry-wide planning under the National Recovery Act, direct government operation of business under the Tennessee Valley Authority, establishment of public responsibility for the aged under social security, all expressed a new economic role for government. The Employment Act of 1946 established clearly the view of the economic role of government made famous in the writings of Keynes: it is the responsibility of government to take such measures as private enterprises cannot or will not take to ensure steady full employment of resources. Monetary policy (government manipulation of the money supply through the Federal Reserve banks) was to be supplemented by active fiscal policy (positive use of taxation and public spending as antidepression or antiinflation measures).

The most revolutionary administration since that of Franklin Roosevelt, so far as the philosophy of government and the economy is concerned, was that of Lyndon B. Johnson. Although the Great Society is far from being put into operation, its economic concepts went far beyond any previously advanced. It was affirmed to be the function of government not only to maintain full employment, but also to promote economic welfare in all sectors of the economy where it is lacking. The passage of medicare invaded an area long held sacred to private enterprise. The war on poverty, if in practice perhaps only a skirmish, affirmed government responsibility to end the contradiction of impoverishment in the midst of affluence. The guaranteed annual income, hinted at by radicals at the beginning of the Johnson administration, by the end had come to be almost taken for granted, although there was disagreement as to its exact form.

It should be clear, however, that this is not socialism. It has been said, probably with truth, that a liberal Democrat in the United States is less socialist than a typical British Conservative. All major political factions in the United States favor private ownership of the means of production. Steel and coal, nationalized in Britain, are private property in the United States. So are railroads and communications, which are publicly owned in many other countries. There is no large cooperative sector of the economy to challenge private business, as in Sweden. No political party today could, it is true, call back the revolution that has taken place since Franklin Roosevelt in the role of American government in the economy. This is, however, a Keynesian revolution, not a Socialist one, for the chief significance of Keynes was that he thought he had found a new economic policy which would make capitalism work. This is what government in the United States is trying to do.

SPONSORED CAPITALISM: JAPAN

From 1951 to 1963, the economy of Japan grew at a rate of over 9 percent per year, the highest rate in any non-Socialist industrial nation. As a basis for comparison, the present growth rate of the United States is about 3.5 percent. From 1953 to 1963, Japan's industrial production quadrupled. Earnings were being plowed back so fast into further production that in one year, 1961, over two-fifths of the whole national product was reinvested. Despite the fact that the Japanese per capita income is calculated to be only one-fifth that of the United

Tokyo at night.

States, forests of television antennas meet the eye even in rural areas. Instant food preparations are in wide use, and commonly consumed items include electric blankets, rice cookers, toasters, washing machines, heating units, and refrigerators. Today Japan leads the world in the production of ships, photographic materials, transistors, sewing machines, motorcycles, cotton cloth, and silk. She ranks among the world leaders in the export of textiles, textile machinery, cement, cosmetics, and toys. She is now ahead of Britain; she is the fourth industrial power in the world.

This success since World War II is often pointed to as a dramatic example of what free enterprise can accomplish. In fact, Japan's economic system is somewhat less laissez-faire than that of the United States. The government owns the telephone and telegraph lines, part of the radio and television network, and two-thirds of the railways. It has taken a very active role in promoting investment: a dozen governmental institutions are engaged mainly in financing private investment. In 1960 the government put forward a comprehensive 10-year plan, intended to double GNP during that period.

Nevertheless, by contrast with al-most any major industrial power except the United States, Japan's economy does depend upon private enterprise. The railways and radio and TV network do have a large private sector. Major industries formerly operated by the government—steel, shipping, shipbuilding, oil refining, electric power distribution—were returned to private ownership under the American occupation after World War II. Government's activity in financing private enterprise has declined in recent years. Recent growth is due mainly to the very high amount of private investment. Japan's economic plan is advisory, not compulsory. So strong is the belief in capitalism that even the Socialist Party does not seriously advocate nationalization of industry.

Japanese free enterprise is, however, far from the world of Adam Smith. The concentration of economic power resembles the situation in the United States. For many decades the *zaibatsu,* a powerful group of families, have controlled a large part of Japanese business and industry. In 1958, the top 2.5 percent of all nonfinancial companies had 73 percent of company assets, 58 percent of sales, and 42 percent of all workers. A survey in the same year showed 11 industries in which three

*Within the growing middle class . . . the "Westernization" of
taste proceeds apace. Food preferences, long resistant to change,
are now shifting toward more meat, dairy products, processing
foods, and dining out. Clothing fashions turn toward higher-grade
fabrics, mostly synthetics, and more diversified wardrobes. New
leisure pursuits absorb rising increments of family income. Spending
on movies, baseball, and other such entertainment tripled in the
fifties. Weekend trains and holiday spots swarm with holiday
crowds. The gay life of the Ginza [Tokyo night-life area] prospers
as never before, nourished by ample expense accounts. More
significantly, the average family reads one newspaper a day
and ten weekly journals a month, as people increasingly gain the
benefits of a high-school education. At the same time the Japanese
home is being invaded with mechanical applicances; housemaids
are beginning to disappear except in well-to-do families. TV sets,
washing machines, refrigerators, electric fans, and rice cookers
have become accepted conveniences and status symbols.*

—*William W. Lockwood,* The State and Economic Enterprise in Japan,
Princeton, N.J., Princeton University Press, 1965, pp. 453–454.

firms produced over 90 percent of all output, and another 34 where five firms produced over 80 percent. There is an antimonopoly law and a Fair Trade Commission to enforce it, but both are weak. By 1959 there were 70 major "cartel" agreements to limit and control production and prices in mining, metallurgy, machinery, chemicals, textiles, and other industries. They had met with approval by the antimonopoly commission. Moreover, the general atmosphere is favorable to such oligopolistic agreements and afraid of "excessive competition." To see why, we must look briefly at Japan's economic position in the world.

The great spurt since World War II is only the most recent stage in Japan's Industrial Revolution, which began about a century ago. Until 1868 the country was ruled by a series of hereditary officials known as "shoguns." The mikado, though thought to be a god, was only a figurehead. Since 1603 the shogunate had been held by the Tokugawa family. The society was feudal, dominated by a military caste, and foreigners were forbidden to trade or settle. When he sailed into Uraga Bay in 1853 and demanded that Japan open herself to trade with the West, the American commodore Matthew Perry merely symbolized what was bound to come in one way or another. To many Japanese it seemed that Japan must become a strong industrial power if she was to avoid becoming a Western colony. The Tokugawa regime appeared to stand in the way (although the noted Irish observer of Japan, Lafcadio Hearn, had called it "the happiest in the long life of the nation"). Fifteen years after Perry's visit, the shogunate was overthrown and the mikado Meiji became emperor. The Meiji period, which lasted until his death in 1912, was one of substantial industrial growth.

In the late Tokugawa period there had been, indeed, some of the preconditions for an industrial society. The level of education was high, and bookkeeping and accounting practices were fairly advanced. It is thought that a good deal of agriculture had become commercial. There were some industries—shipbuilding, cotton spinning, and cannon casting. The government played a rather active part in the economy. The Japanese version of Confucianism stressed rational thinking and calculation, a good basis for capitalist industrialism. It also stressed nationalism, thus supporting the desire to industrialize to avoid colonial status.

Japan's take-off might be placed in the 1880s. Although there are disagreements as to the exact figures, one expert estimate is that agricultural production doubled between 1880 and 1915, thus giving a base for industrial growth, which began in the cotton and brewing industries. By the early twentieth century, "the foundations of the shipbuilding, heavy engineering, iron and steel, electrical power, electrical equipment and modern textile industries had been firmly laid." A railway system had been built. Demands for military supplies in the Sino-Russian War gave a boost to the economy after 1905. When European nations were unable to supply themselves with what they needed during World War I, Japan stepped into these markets and experienced another industrial boom. War preparations and export of cheap goods based on low wages led to still another spurt in the 1930s, just before World War II. We can see from the growth rates that the present boom is only one in a series of Japan's Industrial Revolution:

1905–1912	*6.7 percent*
1912–1919	*7.0*
1931–1938	*7.5*
1953–1960	*9.3*

The strong nationalistic drive has led to government sponsorship of economic growth. In the 1880s the government imported British machinery for use in mines. The Bank of Japan was founded in 1885 to provide capital funds. The government promoted the shipbuilding industry in the late nineteenth century and established "pilot plants" for producing cement, plate glass, fireproof bricks, woolen cloth, and cotton yarn. From 1887 to 1936, the government was the largest investor in the economy, providing from 30 to 40 percent of all capital investment. Between 1955 and 1965, the state controlled one-third of all investment spending for purposes such as roads,

land improvement, schools, railways, telecommunications, local undertakings, and loans to private industry.

Another factor has led to both government intervention and concentration of private economic power. Japan has very few of the natural resources for an industrial economy. Only 18 percent of her land can be cultivated. She must import 90 percent of her iron ore, one-third of her coking coal, one-fourth of her steel scrap, and almost all her bauxite, phosphate, cotton, wool, and rubber. As we have seen, in order to import a nation must export. Japan's exports are three times the world average. To export she must compete with nations much better favored with industrial resources and much longer established as industrial powers. Most of the products she exports are highly competitive: cars, heavy electrical goods, machine tools, cosmetics, sugar, paper pulp, toothpaste, soft drinks, hosiery, leather shoes. In addition, there is some discrimination against Japanese goods.

The Japanese economy is thus strongly subject to balance of payments crises—lack of exports to pay for imports. There have been several such crises since World War II. Rapid growth and prosperity have led periodically to an increase in imports and also to home consumption of Japanese goods which would otherwise have been exported. The government has tried to prevent such imbalance by requiring licenses for many imports, the only such import licensing system in the non-Communist world. In addition, there is a strong feeling that only through large industrial combinations can Japan compete effectively, as she literally must do to survive economically.

Such historic and geographic factors have created the situation described by the private American economic research organization, the Committee for Economic Development:

Government economic regulation is clearly more pervasive in Japan than in the United States. Moreover, a much larger sector of industry is controlled by business associations than in the United States.[1]

Three features of the Japanese economy deserve note. One is the dual economy, a contrast between a modernized, mechanized, highly productive sector and a sector of small, traditional businesses with low productivity, low wages, and low technology. This distinction is present in all developing economies, but probably nowhere more so than in Japan. An unusual feature is the amount of subcontracting between the modern and traditional sectors, as between mammoth auto firms and tiny parts manufacturers. Often the big firms exploit the traditional companies. The dual economy is probably intensified by the efforts to force development of heavy industry.

Another important feature is the tendency toward products that use a high percentage of labor to capital (labor-intensive products). This is natural where capital goods may have to be imported, but labor is plentiful and cheap. Thus the strength of the modern sector of the economy has been light industry. The trading pattern has been to import raw materials and capital-intensive products and export labor-intensive goods. Examples of labor-intensive exports are light machinery, electrical and optical equipment, and small vehicles.

We cannot understand recent Japanese growth without relating it to her demilitarization. The policy of trying to prevent a repetition of Japanese aggression has been a great boon to the Japanese economy. Whereas the United States, Britain, and France spend from 8 to 10 percent of their national income for military purposes, and West Germany 4.7 percent, Japan spends less than 1.5 percent. Her ability to put the difference into development of the civilian economy has

been an important factor in her rapid expansion.

Where will Japan go in the future? The main present trends will almost certainly lead her, like all modern industrial nations, farther away from the world of Adam Smith.

Cheap wages will disappear. Japan has now stabilized her once rapidly expanding population. The reduced labor supply will tend to raise wages in the future. Labor organization will have the same effect. In 1964, 36 percent of all Japanese workers were unionized, half of them in the Sōhoyō, the General Council of Trade Unions. Unionization of workers in large industry had been virtually completed by 1949. Before 1960 productivity was rising faster than wages; since then, this has been reversed. Loss of the advantage of cheap wages will probably force more government activity, or more business combination, in an effort to compete in exports. The Sōhoyō labor organization, whose philosophy is mildly Marxist, will exert pressure away from traditional capitalism.

Heavy industry will gain at the expense of small business. Some of the immense industrial concentrations of pre-World War II days have been broken up, but from 1938 to 1961, iron and steel, nonferrous metals, and machinery rose from 20 to 50 percent of investment. The machinery industry expanded fivefold between 1955 and 1961. Productivity in big industry has risen faster than in small industry. The 10-year plan for doubling GNP featured heavy industry. From 1963 to 1965, there was a wave of bankruptcies in small industries. There have been some efforts to get small businessmen to merge workers and technology. A second Industrial Revolution is taking place in Japan. The first revolution, up to World War II, established a dual economy with a modern light industry sector. The second, based on heavy industry, will gradually squeeze out the traditional sector.

1. *Japan in the Free World Economy,* New York, CED, 1963, p. 34.

A Russian machine-testing equipment factory.

Trade liberalization will create strains. Japan has sought to lower barriers against her exports to the United States, western Europe, and elsewhere. In order to do this, she has had to reduce her own restrictions against imports. Removal of these restrictions will put new pressures on Japanese industries, such as those producing coal, automobiles, electrical computers, and large-scale electric generators. Again, there will be the tendency to favor oligopoly or monopoly as the only way of competing.

Growth may level off. In almost all developing countries, rapid population increase has tended to provide a market for expansion and keep wages low enough to allow for large capital investment. Now that Japan's population has been stabilized, there will be fewer new consumers, and wages will rise. Also, a good deal of Japan's rapid growth has been due to the fact that she has been building up her heavy industrial establishment. When this is essentially completed, the question will be the same as in other industrial na-

tions. Can Japan, in shifting from basic technological growth to high mass consumption, keep her economy from leveling off?

STATE SOCIALISM: RUSSIA

At the farthest pole from the free enterprise capitalist economy are the planned economies of Russia and China.

Since 1917 Russia has developed under planning from a backward country to the second largest industrial power in the world. Careful American studies estimate that between 1928 and 1937, the Soviet economy grew at a rate of about 5.5 percent per year. From 1937 to 1958, including the war years when economic resources were actually being destroyed faster than they were built, the rate was about 4 percent. Since the war the growth rate has been about 6 percent a year, as compared with about 3.5 percent for the United States.

This does not prove that Russian planning is necessarily more efficient than American capitalism. It may show only that a young and relatively under-developed economy is likely to grow faster than a more mature one. It does show that a nonmarket economy can produce effectively, something which supporters of capitalism have some-times denied. Khrushchev once pre-dicted that the Soviet Union would catch up with the United States eco-nomically by 1970. The dean of Soviet economists, Stanislaus G. Strumilin, pointed out about the same time, how-ever, that Russian growth had slowed down in the early 1960s and that Soviet production could not be expected to equal American production until after the year 2000. From 1958 to 1963, the growth rate declined annually. We can try to see as we go along what this may mean.

Russian efforts to achieve economic development have been like those of the frog trying to get out of the well, slipping back one step for every two upward. When they took power in 1917, the Bolsheviks were confronted with an economy in which industrializa-tion and modernization had begun, but which was still essentially underdevel-oped. Their first move was to try to in-stall nationalization and central planning overnight. Factories, banks, and transport were nationalized. The peasants took over the agricultural estates. Factory products were allo-cated and rationed by the central gov-ernment. The government requisitioned and distributed farm products. The re-sult was near disaster. Management was inefficient, farmers and workers resisted, and industrial production fell to less than 20 percent of the prewar level. Everything was complicated by civil war and invasion by Allied troops.

The first "war communism" lasted until 1921. Faced with possible failure of the whole revolution, Lenin intro-duced the New Economic Policy, which was essentially a retreat toward capitalism, with a large part of produc-tion carried on by private enterprise and sold in free markets. There was little central planning. Large industry, banking, and foreign trade and transport

continued to be nationalized, but agri-culture and small business and indus-try were largely in private hands. The aim was to return to nationalization gradually as recovery took place. Pro-duction did rise, by 1926, to the prewar level, and by the end of the New Eco-nomic Plan in 1927, most industry had been renationalized.

By this time a great debate had arisen as to how development of the economy could best proceed. It was recognized that, as in all underdevel-oped countries, industrialization must rest upon a surplus in agriculture. The question was how to get it. The rightist group believed that a moderate policy toward the peasants would result in an increase in production, and that peas-ant savings would gradually become available for industrialization. The less moderate leftists felt that industrializa-tion required a drastic national policy that would collectivize agriculture and seize the gains to finance industry. The leftists won, and the forced collectivi-zation of agriculture began. In eight months, between July 1, 1929 and March 1, 1930, the number of peasant households on collective farms rose from about one million to more than 14 million. In the drive to collectivize, 5 million people were deported or shot. The backbone of peasant resistance was broken, as was also the power of independent labor unions. The choice to industrialize by force had been car-ried through.

Russian planners have since then tried to increase agricultural efficiency and develop heavy industry and trans-portation, expecting eventually to be able to provide more consumer goods and services. The first Five Year Plan—an overall national project for develop-ing heavy industry and electrifying the country—was begun in 1928. A second Five Year Plan, before World War II, stressed transportation and agricul-tural planning. The war and the Nazi invasion set back economic develop-ment, and not until 1950 did produc-tion return to prewar figures. Since that time there has been growing pressure on economic planners to provide more consumer goods and services, and they have tried to do so, but progress has been slow.

How does Soviet planning actually take place? We may start with an outline of the formal system of authority. At the top is the State Planning Commission, or *Gosplan,* which prepares yearly (and at shorter and longer intervals) master plans for allocating production. Immediately under the Gosplan are the *ministries* for different lines of production—transport and ferrous metals, for example. Since the operations of a ministry are so enormous, these are usually broken down into administrative units called *glavks,* which may be concerned with specialized branches of production or with functions such as research, procurement of materials, marketing, and the like. Underneath the glavks are combines or *trusts,* consisting of a number of plants or mines. Finally, there is the individual *firm,* a single automobile factory, for example.

In this hierarchy planning is not a one-way street. The Gosplan formulates overall plans and passes them down the ladder. At each level there is a good deal of feedback; plans may be questioned and suggestions for revision offered. A plant manager may say, for instance, that he cannot keep his machinery going without rest for enough hours to meet a projected quota, or that he does not have enough skilled workers, or that he will not be able to get the necessary raw materials. Records show, for example, that an auto plant's quota was changed sixteen times in a 6-month period, and the quota of a major machine-making firm five times in nine months. In general, there is likely to be less leeway for revision in the essential major industries, with central planning looser in less essential production. A large part is played in Soviet planning by technical work called "project making." The Gosplan can decide to generate more electric power or develop certain oil fields, but only engineers and other technicians can develop a working plan with realistic cost estimates.

We remember, of course, that in the market economy the basic economic decisions are made through prices established by free buying and selling. In the Soviet economy, this is not generally the case. We shall see exceptions later. Prices are set by planning authorities, not by supply and demand. What shall be produced, how resources shall be allocated, how much shall be set aside for investment, and how income shall be distributed are decisions made primarily by planning agencies.

The firm manager, given his production quota, must secure his raw materials, his labor, and his capital equipment. For these he will be provided with funds by the central Gosbank. He cannot generally offer a higher price in order to lure materials, workers, or equipment away from some "competing" firm. He will market his product, when it is completed, through state stores at prices set according to plan. How is he motivated to fulfill the plans, if not by prices and profits? Negatively, failure can in extreme cases be tried as a crime against the state. Positively, managers receive bonuses if they fulfill or exceed their quotas. The bonuses, or premiums, may run as high as 10 to 15 percent of a manager's income. What is the machinery through which performance is checked? Each firm has a bookkeeper who represents the state and reports to his superiors. Members of the Communist Party in his plant will prod him to fulfill quotas and will report failures. In the heavy industries, as many as 10 percent of his workers may be Communist Party members. Labor unions may also urge him to meet his norms.

Despite the differences, there are marked similarities between the position of the industrial manager in the Soviet Union and in the United States. In many ways the Soviet manager negotiates and bargains with his superiors, suppliers, workers, and customers as does an American man-

Alexei Stakhanov

ing out of troops. Such strikes occurred in Moscow in 1956, at the Karaganda Iron and Steel Plant in 1960, in the Kermovo industrial area in 1962, and at the Odessa docks in 1963. Ordinarily unions bargain on wages and production norms and provide welfare services similar to those of some progressive American unions—housing, nurseries, dining rooms, stores, sanitariums, clubs, lectures, libraries, and study groups.

The minority of Communist Party members are likely to keep their fellow workers, as well as managers, "on the ball." Socialist competition plays a considerable part in the motivation of Russian workers. There are wage differentials of as high as 4.5 times between different levels of skilled work. Workers as well as managers share in bonuses for exceeding targets. Individual workers with outstanding production records may be rewarded with vacations in the Caucasus or at the Black Sea. A famous program of Socialist competition has been the Stakhanovite movement, which has enlisted workers dedicated to increasing production. The movement takes its name from the coal miner, Alexei Stakhanov, whose crew in 1935 dug 102 tons of coal instead of its norm of 7 tons.

Capital investment, future as against present production, is decided upon by the Gosplan as part of state policy. As in any economy, some of the income of consumers must be diverted from consumption to production goods. How is this accomplished? It would be possible to collect it by selling stocks and bonds to private savers, but this would be too much like capitalism. The main instrument for saving is a "turnover tax" which takes from the producing firm somewhat more than a third of the average retail price charged to consumers.

Agricultural planning has always posed a special problem for the Soviet regime. Farms are now of three kinds. The *state* farms are operated like any state factory. They produce in a few specialized areas, such as wheat, farm-

ager. An administrator in a Soviet automobile trust would probably not find General Motors very unfamiliar. A graduate in business administration from an American university would very likely find most of his training useful in a Russian firm.

Workers also must be motivated to fit into the plans. Russian workers were once virtually tied to their jobs, and during the Stalin period there was considerable forced labor. Now workers are relatively free to change jobs, and positive rather than negative incentives are encouraged. "Each worker has his own dignity," said Khrushchev. "Persuasion is better than shouting and threats."

About 75 percent of Soviet work is paid by the piece rather than by the hour, a system disliked by American workers as a way of forcing production. About 80 percent of workers belong to unions. These do not, as do American unions, have the right to enforce their bargaining position by striking. Since 1956 there have been, however, a number of strikes in Russian plants, some of which have resulted in the calling, and ranching, primarily for sale to state agencies. Their workers are hired like factory hands. *Collective* farms are theoretically managed by and for their members, each being paid according to the "labor days" he has put in. These labor days are based upon hours of time and degree of skill. In addition, each farmer is allowed a *private* plot. Produce from the private farms is generally sold to city dwellers in a market mainly determined by supply and demand. This is, of course, an exception to decision by central planning.

Despite their small size, a surprising amount of Russian agricultural production takes place on the private plots; about 25 percent of all production is from state farms, about 42 percent from collective farms, and about 32 percent from private lands. In 1963 the World Health Organization of the United Nations estimated that these percentages of farm products consumed in Russia were produced by "private enterprise": potatoes, 64 percent; vegetables, 46 percent; fruit, 67 percent; meal, 47 percent; eggs, 82 percent; milk, nearly 50 percent.

We can now look briefly at some of the strengths of Soviet planning, some of its weaknesses, and some of the measures that have been tried in an effort to overcome the weaknesses.

Russian planning has clearly succeeded in producing a high overall rate of growth.

The alternation of prosperity and depression, the business cycle, historically characteristic of capitalist economies, has not been present in the Soviet Union. Russia was not involved in the Great Depression of 1929. We may note here that in recent years Keynesian policies have been fairly successful in smoothing out the business cycle in capitalist countries also.

There are some clear advantages in being able to decide on the amount and direction of investment through central policy, rather than depending upon the decisions of individual investors in the market.

Though cruel to human beings, forced nationalization and forced saving enabled the Soviet Union to solve the problem of accumulating the capital for industrial development. The same result was accomplished in the capitalist Industrial Revolution by depressing the wages of workers to or below the point of subsistence, with perhaps no less suffering.

Central planning is able to eliminate some of the waste of competition, such as the parallel lines of tracks run by competing railway lines in the privately owned American railway system.

On the other hand, Soviet economic performance has in several respects fallen short of what planners might wish. Overall growth figures do not tell the whole story. Soviet agriculture has lagged far behind industrial growth during most of the Communist regime. From 1928 to 1950, there was virtually no increase in agricultural output. In 1963 the gross farm output had risen to about 2½ times that of 1928. This reflected the fact that in 1955 mechanization was seriously introduced on the farms for the first time. Industry and transport previously had priority. Per acre productivity is still low: less than one-half that of the United States in grain, and one-third in potatoes and sugar beets. Per cow yield of milk is about one-half that of the United States. We must bear in mind, too, that with much available land, the United States does not have great pressure for high per acre efficiency and does not have as good a record as some other countries. Agriculture continues to be the most serious Soviet problem. Productivity of workers in mining and industry also lags behind that of the United States. It is about half as high in coal mining, half as high in steel production, and one-third as high in oil refining. This is partly because the Soviet worker has less machinery, or poorer machinery, to work with, but this is not the whole story.

The Soviet Union has only begun to move into the age of high mass consumption, and the rising expectations of her people are far from fulfilled. A 1955 estimate of the percentage of consumer goods available to the average Russian, as compared with the average American, went as follows: meat, 28 percent; milk, 35 percent; hosiery, 35 percent; automobiles, 6/10 of 1 percent; washing machines, 2 percent; television sets, 4 percent. The average amount of space per urban dweller has actually fallen during recent years; in the 1960s it was about one-third of the American average, in spite of the inadequacy of a large amount of American housing. There has been some improvement. A Russian study of 100 families from 1950 to 1956, reported in the *New York Times,* showed the largest increases in expenditure in entertainment, furniture, household appliances, clothing, and shoes. Of these 100 families, in 1950 none had television, washing machines, or refrigerators. In 1956, 42 had a TV, 10 a refrigerator, and 5 a washing machine.

One might remind himself that most countries in the world do not, after all, compare very favorably with the United States, and that in a growing economy things may be expected to get better. However, the economic growth rate has fallen in the past decade or so. As we saw in an earlier chapter, the same problem of unemployment which plagues many capitalist countries has arisen. Unless this situation changes, the urgent demands of consumers are not likely to be met.

At least some of the Russian problems may lie in the nature of their economic system. Along with advantages, decision making through central planning poses some problems that seem more easily solved in a market economy.

Where prices roughly reflect the costs of production, the more costly methods tend to be eliminated. In a planned economy, where prices are set by a planning agency, there is no easy way of comparing the efficiency of different techniques. Thus there seems clearly to have been a lag in Russia in substituting gas and oil for coal as fuel, in substituting oil pipe lines for railroad tank cars, and in replacing steam locomotives with diesels. The way production quotas are established may pose problems. For example, boiler plants which were credited for the square footage of steam boilers they produced were reluctant to substitute a more efficient but smaller boiler. When they were rated by weight of total product, glass factories tended to make sheet glass too thick; when they were rated by square footage, the glass tended to break because it was too thin. Airplane and steel companies have resisted new wing and blast furnace designs because in the short run they would cost more and would make their production reports look bad. In general, there is a reluctance to incur the costs of introducing new models of any kind, and equipment thus tends to be outdated.

Planning raises the whole question of whether a human group is capable of foreseeing and handling the complex interrelationships of a vast industrial economy. These are getting more complex all the time. In the 1930s there were perhaps 20,000 major firms in the Soviet Union. Today there are probably more than 200,000. All these must be taken into account to some extent in planning. The planner deals with firms, not in isolation, but in all their possible relationships with other firms. Thus a tenfold increase in number of firms probably means a hundredfold increase in the complexity of planning. Some observers believe that relatively simple planning methods may have been adequate to keep planning fairly efficient during the early days of the Soviet economy, but that in recent years the job has become too big. They feel that this fact may be behind the decline in the growth rate.

Russian economists and other planners have attempted to meet some of these problems. In 1957 a good deal of decision making was formally decentralized. Regional organizations took the place of most of the national ministries. It was no doubt felt that some of the top-heaviness of planning could be corrected in this way. This change was, however, reversed in 1965.

Another change has been the introduction of some market mechanisms—"consumer sovereignty"—in place of planned controls. We have seen that about one-third of all farm products are privately produced and sold in a free market. There has been some experimentation with allowing collective farms themselves to sell on such a market. In 1964, 400 enterprises manufacturing apparel, textiles, and leather goods were authorized to plan quantity, quality, and style to meet consumer demand rather than to follow directives from above. Some labor is allocated on a competitive basis. To many Russians such moves are a retreat to capitalism. Others believe that no system has all the answers and that some of the more workable features of capitalism can be used to strengthen rather than weaken a planned economy. The most prominent advocate of the new market mechanisms has been the economist E. G. Liberman.

There is considerable interest in the Soviet Union in using input-output tables in planning (see page 272). These tables can be translated into mathematical equations which can then be fed into computers. Another technique of computerizing data, called "linear programming," was first developed in Russia and may eventually be even more useful in planning. As yet Soviet planners have been doing preliminary research with these methods and are not yet ready to trust planning itself to computers. However, they are planning to establish a network of computer centers with one master computer in Moscow, of which Robert W. Campbell says, "The aggregate computing capacity of the system would be something like the joint capacity of all the computers in existence in the United States in the mid-sixties."[2]

2. Robert W. Campbell, *Soviet Economic Power,* Boston, Houghton Mifflin, 1966, p. 52.

Increased use of market mechanisms and computerization appear to be two ways of dealing with the increasing complexity of planning. Consumer sovereignty decreases the number of decisions that must be centrally made. Computers should help handle increasingly complex planning problems when they must be made. Which path will be chosen—or more likely, which combination of the two—remains to be seen.

STATE SOCIALISM: CHINA

Communist China is surrounded by a "bamboo curtain," a policy of limited communication with the rest of the world. The United States has no diplomatic representatives in Peking, and virtually no Americans have visited mainland China. What we know must come from official Chinese publications, which are often of doubtful reliability; from reports reaching Hong Kong through refugees, mainland Chinese visiting relatives, and others; and from records of travel in China by people from other countries.

We do know that in 1949 the Chinese Communists took over a country devastated by invasion and civil war. In the two decades since that time they have developed a growth rate which Western experts think may have soared as high as 18 percent—three times that of the Soviet Union, more than five times that of the United States, at least as high as that of any other underdeveloped nation, and greater than that of Russia in her early days. (Japan reached about the same high figure in 1958–1959.) They have also seen growth slow almost to a standstill. They have tried, with apparent failure, revolutionary experiments like backyard blast furnaces. They have attempted, and failed, to achieve instant communism by gathering farmers into vast centralized communes. They have not solved the problem of agriculture, nor abolished malnutrition, but they have virtually eliminated the actual starvation which has visited China periodically for centuries. Among the underdeveloped nations, they are at present the only one going it alone without any foreign aid.

For a while it seemed as though the Chinese leaders might succeed in creating something like a true communist society more quickly than the Russians, although they began three decades later. Now we cannot be sure where China is headed. Let us look first at the main stages through which the Communist regime has passed, and then at how industry and agriculture have been affected by the revolution.

Roughly the first three years, from 1949 to 1952, were spent in simply establishing the new regime and recovering from the damage of war. China was then one of the most economically backward of the major powers. In 1952 a State Planning Commission was established to undertake railway development and development of northwestern China.

From 1953 to 1957 was the period of the first Five Year Plan, which was modeled on Russian planning under Stalin, with emphasis on the development of heavy industry. During this period most industry and trade were either nationalized or organized into coops under state control.

The second Five Year Plan was scheduled to run from 1958 to 1962. This was the period of the "great leap forward." The aim was to develop industry and agriculture simultaneously. This was to be done, on the one hand, by substituting communes for private ownership of land. On the other hand, handicraft and backyard industries were to be encouraged, and local factory managers were given more freedom. The aim was to integrate industry and agriculture and realize the Marxian objective of eliminating the distinction between town and country. An attempt was made to substitute ideological enthusiasm for material incentives; the atmosphere has been described as like a "perpetual athletic league competition." There was a sensational brief spurt, in which annual growth in GNP rose to 17 or 18 percent. Then industrial production began to decline. Apparently the great leap had just gotten out of the hands of the planners. Agricultural output fell disastrously, in part because of severe drought, and partly because the communes did not work. The situation has been compared to depression in the capitalist nations— underconsumption, overproduction, and unemployment. In 1960 growth in GNP had fallen to 4 percent, and in 1961 it was very low.

The period of recovery after 1961 reminds some observers of the "retreat toward capitalism" under Lenin's New Economic Policy in Russia. In the third Five Year Plan, 1963–1967, agriculture was given first place. It was assumed that it was not possible to force both industry and agriculture forward at once, and that an agricultural surplus must have priority. The Communist Party had now decided that a successfully mechanized agriculture would take perhaps 20 to 25 years. Attention was given to advancing agricultural mechanization. The communes were broken into smaller units. There was more use of markets governed by supply and demand. There was even some advertising. A "great debate," similar to that in Russia in the 1920s, took place between those favoring strong central control and those supporting decentralization.

Let us now look separately at industry and agriculture under Chinese Communism.

Industry was successfully nationalized much more quickly in China than in Russia. By the end of 1953, four years after the end of the revolution, all heavy industry and half of light industry were in state hands. The government had taken over all railways. In 1950 state companies were set up to handle marketing of food, edible oils, cloth, fuel, cotton, industrial supplies, imports, and exports. The government continued to gain control of private industry through rigid government contracts to buy industrial production. The same technique was used to control commercial houses. Another method was joint state-private ownership, under which the state controlled the profits, a large part was set aside for investment, former managers got salaries, and former stockholders got a fixed share of profits. By March 1956, virtually all industry was state-owned or under joint state-private operation. By June virtually all large retail shops were under the same arrangement. By the end of 1956, 65 percent of the craftsmen in small handicraft industries had been organized into 100,000 coops which had a total of 5 million members.

During the first Five Year Plan (1953–1957), industrial growth was rapid, from 14 to 19 percent a year. This rate was exceeded only by Pakistan and Japan. The fastest growth was in electric power, oil extraction, metallurgy, engineering, and chemicals. Steel mills, originally concentrated in the eastern part of China, were built in other sections of the country. During this period China received Russian aid in the form of development loans, complete sets of factory equipment, and especially technical assistance. This aid ended in 1960. In 1956 China produced her first truck, in 1957 her first electric generator, and in 1958 her first tractor. This should make it clear that she was not as yet a major industrial power, although at that time she had hopes of soon surpassing Britain in heavy industrial equipment. The failure of agriculture and of the great leap forward slowed industrial growth after 1958.

Today, in addition to advances in electric power, coal, steel, and oil, China carries on her own production of machine tools, electronic equipment, diesel-electric locomotives, and jet fighters, and maintains technical colleges. She does not, however, as yet have the industrial development either to provide a high level of consumer goods or to support a major military establishment.

Agriculture in Communist China may be looked upon under three aspects: (1) land reform, (2) collectivization, and (3) mechanization.

Welders in a Communist Chinese steel factory.

Redistribution of land from the rich to the poor is a universal demand in underdeveloped countries. It was one of the first changes brought about by the 1949 revolution. The Australian historian, C. P. Fitzgerald, describes the process.

Land reform has passed through three stages under the People's Republic. The first stage was a simple redistribution of landlord properties among the peasants of the village, including the former landlord himself, if he was willing to become an active landworker. . . . The Communists proclaimed "Land to the tiller" as their objective. The redistributed land was granted to the new owners as freehold, a move which won the Communists immediate peasant support.[3]

Estimates of the number of people killed in this first period of the revolution run from "a few tens of thousands" to "close to 50 million." Two or three million would perhaps be a reasonable estimate. Land reform was not in itself a Communist objective, for it simply changes the ownership of private property in land. They did promote it, however, as a first step toward eventual collective ownership. In this way they secured the strongest supporters of the revolution, the poor peasantry.

We can see how collectivization grew by a series of steps out of cooperation in farm functions. The first form of cooperation was "mutual aid," common to farmers almost everywhere. Short-run mutual aid was simply the pooling of work on such tasks as dike or dam building. Long-term mutual aid teams might pool their draft animals or farm equipment, but retain private possession of their land.

Cooperatives as such began in about 1954. In "lower" or "semi-Socialist" co-ops, land was pooled and worked as a unit, but each member was rewarded according to the amount of his land. "Higher-stage," or "advanced-type," co-ops consisted of about 200 families. All land, tools, and animals were pooled. Pay was distributed according to days of labor. Private plots and sale of produce were usually allowed, as were ownership of chickens, pigs, and other farm animals. The "higher-stage" co-ops sometimes joined forces on projects like irrigation operations or small industries.

In 1956 and 1957, farm output declined, and the left wing of the Communist Party conceived the idea of the larger communes. These would contain 4000 to 5000 families instead of 200. Some peasant experiments with larger units gave reason to believe they would succeed. Large-scale organizations were also necessary to operate the decentralized industries which were projected by the central government.

In 1958 the great drive into communes took place. Private farm plots and the free market for agricultural goods were abolished. Collectivization was now complete, for the peasant was no longer a landowner in any sense. Pay was in the form of either straight wages or wages and bonuses plus food; he was now simply a laborer. The communes were supposed to provide to their members the "five guarantees": food, clothing, shelter, medical care, and funerals. They provided mess halls and nurseries to relieve working mothers and homes for the aged. All these were voluntary, and families generally continued to eat and live together. In addition to agricultural functions, the communes also became the government for the county units which usually formed their boundaries. They managed roads, power, medicine, welfare, housing, schools, and banking.

We may note the difference between Chinese and Russian collectivization of agriculture. In Russia the dominant farmers were the middle-class peasants, the "kulaks," who resisted violently. In China the large landowners had been removed, and the land was held by the poor peasants, who largely accepted collectivization.

However, the communes did not solve the agricultural problem. Production of grain in 1960 was probably no greater than in 1957, and China's population was perhaps 30 to 49 million greater. In 1961 close to 6 million tons of grain were imported from Canada, Australia, and elsewhere. At this time a million or more 2-pound packages, presumably food, were being mailed into China monthly through the Hong Kong post office. There was no mass starvation, but there was malnutrition. Meanwhile, the population continued to grow at two to three times the prewar rate, with no control in sight.

3. C. P. Fitzgerald, *The Birth of Communist China,* rev. ed., Baltimore, Penguin, 1966, p. 167.

In the face of these developments, the government reversed the collectivization policy. Agriculture was decentralized to about the lower-stage, or semi-Socialist co-op, with pooling of land for operations but reward according to acreage. The production unit was reduced from the 4000–5000 family communes to the production team of 40–50 households. Larger private plots than before were allowed. Free markets in the form of rural "trade fairs" were established.

Mechanization and other programs for agricultural improvement were pushed forward. The revolution had begun with an "eight character" program for agriculture: water conservation, fertilization, soil conservation, seed selection, dense planting, plant protection, tool improvement, and field management. During the 1949–1952 recovery period, more of the old tools were provided, but few new ones. The first Five Year Plan of 1953–1957 brought semimechanization, with introduction of plows and establishment of tractor stations. During the great leap, efforts were made to provide more of both the old tools and the new machines. By the end of 1960, however, machines were used on only 5 percent of the cultivated land; 80 percent had small but improved implements. In 1962, less than 10 percent of the land was tractorized.

What has Communist China accomplished economically? Where will it go in the future?

The heart of the Chinese revolution is the peasantry. In this respect it is not a Marxist revolution, for Marx saw the industrial proletariat as the force that would overthrow capitalism. In Russia, Lenin and the Bolsheviks claimed to speak for the industrial workers. The Russian Communists have never gotten along well with the peasants. The Chinese have fared much better. They have not succeeded in turning the peasant into a propertyless hired employee of the commune, as they had hoped. Their efforts to integrate industry and agriculture in the country have

so far failed. They have not made agriculture efficient enough to feed all the people adequately all the time, much less to furnish an adequate surplus to support industrialization. They have, however, improved production and distribution of food so as to virtually eliminate actual famine. They have succeeded in getting peasant cooperation on a semi-Socialist basis.

The Communist regime has taken a chaotic and economically backward country, torn by war and revolution, and estalished a solid industrial base which is not likely to be overturned. Over the entire span since the revolution, Chinese industry has grown at a rate that compares very favorably with that of any underdeveloped country.

China has not yet developed an industrial establishment big enough to create the complex mathematical problems of planning which disturb the Russians. Chinese planning has not, however, been very successful. China appears to have a centralized political state, but a rather decentralized economy, with a considerable free market. Despite the claims of the leaders to be the true followers of Marx, the present Chinese economy seems very much like the Russian New Economic Plan, or perhaps like the decentralized economy of Yugoslavia, which the Chinese continually criticize. It is possible that the present loose economic control may lead to a violent centralization of the kind that occurred in Russia in 1928. On the other hand, a way may be found to move forward without this kind of reaction.

STATE SOCIALISM: CUBA

A third example of centralized economic planning is Cuba under Fidel Castro. In 1959 the government of Fulgencio Batista fell before a revolution that represented peasants, workers, students, intellectuals, and a considerable number of middle-class people who were also dissatisfied with the Batista regime. Within a short time, the

A Cuban papaya grower. Under the Castro regime agricultural produce became diversified. Previously most of the land was used for growing sugar cane.

Castro government entered upon an extensive program of nationalization. There are those who believe that Castro was a dedicated Communist who "bided his time" before introducing the program to which he was really committed. Others think that before the revolution he was a nationalistic bourgeois radical with left-wing leanings, who carried the original revolution through with more opposition than support from official Communists, and eventually became convinced that only a system modeled on the Soviet Union could meet Cuba's needs.

The background for the revolution lay in the prerevolutionary Cuban economy. Agriculture was largely cartelized—an oligopoly of large established producers controlled most of land and production. This cartelization prevented adoption of the best agricultural methods—the big owners had a good thing without them, and smaller producers who introduced im-

provements tended to be squeezed out of the market. Industry was likewise controlled by oligopoly. A considerable part of Cuban industry and agriculture was directly owned and operated by United States capital. The rest was dependent upon the United States economy, whose interests tended to come above Cuban interests.

The Cuban economy before the revolution was largely at dead center. Because of strong labor organization, wages in terms of real purchasing power were higher than in any other Western Hemisphere country outside the United States and Canada. But this did not reflect the productivity of labor, which was abysmal. Production and incomes were nearly at a standstill. From 1900 to 1958, the total level of production increased by 1.8 percent per year. Population increased 2.1 percent per year. Thus average income over this nearly 60-year period declined about 0.3 percent annually. Income data were reflected in living conditions. The 1953 population census, under Batista, showed that 65.4 percent of rural houses had palm leaf roofs and dirt floors; 90.5 percent had no bath or shower either inside or outside. According to a Catholic University survey in 1956, 13 percent of the population showed a history of typhoid, 14 percent of tuberculosis, and one-third had intestinal parasites. This background led one writer to say that "socialism was both suitable and possible for closely related reasons." Expropriation of private owners began with the Agrarian Reform Law of 1959. Under this law, by 1963, 46 percent of all agricultural land was distributed to individual farmers, to cooperatives, or to state farms more or less on the Russian model; all agriculture and livestock were under state planning. By 1961, two years after the revolution, about 85 percent of industry had been nationalized. A year later the figure was about 90 percent.

In a 1968 book, Carmelo Mesa-Iago, former director of social security under the revolutionary government, estimated that these percentages of economic activity were in the public sector: industry, 95 percent; construction, 98 percent; transport, 95 percent; wholesale and foreign trade, 100 percent; retail trade, 75 percent; banking, 100 percent; agriculture, 70 percent.

Economic life in revolutionary Cuba is under the control of the *Juceplan,* based on the Soviet Gosplan. This planning body has prepared plans for periods of a maximum of four or five years, broken down into yearly and quarterly plans. So impressed have the Cubans been with Russian planning that at some times their plans have been timed so as to begin on the same date as the Russian plan.

National planning by the Juceplan establishes production quotas down from the national level to each plant or farm, and each individual worker. There are also quality standards as well as quotas regulating quantity. The total income from production is divided into a consumption fund and an accumulation fund. The chief items in the consumption fund are wages and social security. The chief items in the accumulation fund are maintenance and expansion of capital equipment, a reserve against risks, and national defense.

In 1963 a national wage scale was established. Under this pay is different in different areas of the economy: highest in heavy industry, next highest in light industry and food production, lowest in agriculture. Different workers are paid so as to take into account their socially acquired skills and experience and their native aptitudes. Wages are paid according to three different systems: piece rates, based on the number of items finished; hourly rates, based on the time worked; and a flat weekly wage. Every worker must fulfill 100 percent of his assigned quota in order to earn his wage.

What is the relationship of national planning to the ordinary Cuban? Earlier we saw that before the revolution powerful unions had apparently inflated wages beyond actual productiv-

ity. One of the purposes of the Castro government's wage scale was undoubtedly to bring them back in line. Workers and the planners did not obviously see eye to eye on this. Che Guevara reminded workers that the trade union must "learn its new role: that of ally of production together with the managers." Raoul Castro said of opposition to the wage plan, "We will defeat and crush any divisionist who wants to break the monolithic bloc of unity of our people." Lazaro Peña, secretary general of the Confederation of Workers of Revolutionary Cuba, affirmed that "the wage scale is a new conquest of the working class."

Ordinary Cubans do more of the planning in theory, it seems, than in fact. Plans are initiated at the top Juceplan level, then transmitted downward to the local area and plant. Theoretically, there is feedback from the bottom, but a very pro-Castro Latin American observer has said, "Today, the Cuban population does not yet take part in the solution of fundamental problems of economic planning, except by diffuse social pressures."[4] The head of Cuban labor, Lazaro Peña, was more specific about what happens on the local level: "There is generally little time between the notice of meeting and the date it is held, which consequently limits the possibility of preparing matters for discussion. The speaker generally talks at great length. He ends with verbal propositions that are approved without discussion, or at most discussed slightly."

Cuban revolutionary planning has been very consciously and seriously concerned with a question central to all efforts toward communism: Is it possible to achieve production without sacrificing the long-run goals of a Communist society? Communist countries seek, as Khrushchev dramatically announced, to equal or outproduce the capitalist world. At the same time, they also seek to create a new

4. Adolfo Gilly, "Inside the Cuban Revolution," *Monthly Review* (October 1964), p. 37.

kind of man, one who will replace the self-interested "economic man" of capitalism (see the discussion of liberalism in Chapter ten). An example of this man is Fidel Castro's rather idealized description of the new Russian to a group of Russian writers. "We admire the Soviet man, the new man, the creator of a new society, a magnanimous, fraternal man free from the selfish characteristics of a capitalist society." Is it possible to do both things? Or must one appeal to the "selfish, unmagnanimous, nonfraternal" motives which have been central under capitalism?

One of the few things that Marx said about postrevolutionary society was in criticism of the 1875 Gotha Program of the German Workers' Party. In the final stage of communism, said Marx, everyone could be rewarded according to his need, but meanwhile, to make the system go, income must be graded according to productivity. In Russia Lenin gave his answer to the question early. Trotsky proposed to organize local plants on the basis of a simple communism of workers in which all would receive and share alike. Lenin rejected this plan as idealistic, saying that in the transition to communism, reliance on revolutionary enthusiasm and loyalty alone was insufficient. In the years that followed, Lenin's position in favor of material as against moral incentives was affirmed by Stalin and later by Khrushchev. The competitive capitalist incentives introduced by Liberman are an example of this choice. So is the great income inequality of Soviet workers.

When the Chinese Communists came to power in 1949, their new success, like Trotsky's, seems to have led them to hope for instant communism. Since that time they have tended to stress moral revolutionary incentives like pennants, medals, buttons, diplomas, and publicity for outstanding producers rather than the Socialist competition for bonuses and higher paying jobs which has typically been the Russian method. This emphasis

was greatest during the Great Leap Forward of 1958 (the very name suggests moral emphasis).

The Cuban revolutionists did not try immediately to abolish capitalist wage differentials or other appeals to financial self-interest. We have seen that they did establish an unequal national wage scale. However, the issue of material versus moral incentives has been a big one among Cuban Communists. Among the moral programs have been volunteer work (as in the sugar cane harvest), voluntary overfulfillment of quotas, taking of special courses to raise one's productivity, and voluntary programs to reduce lateness and absenteeism.

One of the strongest advocates of moral incentives was Ernesto ("Che") Guevara. His view was expessed in 1963: "We affirm that in a relatively short time the development of conscience will be more favorable to the development of production than material incentives." He added that this could not be regarded as dogma, but must be worked out carefully. On this issue Guevara left (or was exiled from) the government, although his death as a guerrilla in Bolivia was at the hands of CIA-organized and financed troops. Contrary to Guevara's hope, actual efforts to rely on revolutionary spirit in Cuba have led to poor quality work, absenteeism, worker resistance, a return to the Russian method of material incentives, use of penalties from job suspension to imprisonment, and an increase in the number of bureaucrats necessary to keep the system operating.

Carmelo Mesa-Lago, whom we have already identified as a former high official in the Castro government, has diagrammed the problem of Communist incentives in an interesting way. According to Mesa-Lago's interpretation, the effort simultaneously to build production and develop an unselfish Communist man has worked out in different ways in Russia, China, and Cuba. Russia's typical answer has been to fall back on the traditional incentives and to produce sufficiently. China and Cuba have characteristically tried to develop with new Communist motives, and their failure to produce has led to more repression.

How has the Cuban revolutionary economy worked out in terms of production? Clearly there has not been a steady upward trend. Communist sources themselves reveal this. In 1961 Guevara reported these declines in production as compared with 1960: batteries, 50 percent; lumber, 50 percent; tires, 29.6 percent; paint, 13 percent; metallurgy, 25 percent; dentifrices, 61 percent; mineral waters, 32 percent. He also reported declines in petroleum, electricity, paper, charcoal, and ceramics. In 1963 Raoul Castro listed declines in a number of specific agricultural crops, and Guevara reported a 23 percent decline in the industrial sector. The same year Fidel Castro complained that there had been more new construction under capitalism. Rene Dumont, a sympathetic French visitor, reported an "immediate and catastrophic" decline in the quality of Cuban cigars. In 1964 there was a meat shortage, with rationing. Sugar cane production in 1966 was 50 percent below the goal. The Food and Agricultural Organization of the United Nations has said that food and total agricultural production in 1963–1964 were 32 percent below the 1957–1958 level. On the other side, it appears that the Castro government has established itself so strongly that there is no serious likelihood of overthrow in the near future. This it could not have done had it been an economic failure. Furthermore, communism ("to each according to his need") has been achieved to the extent that many services are provided free, including many health services, lower and higher education, many cultural and recreational events, housing, public telephones, and some transportation.

To the extent that the Cuban economy has fallen short of its goals, there are two major answers. One is that the failure demonstrates the inadequacy of socialism or communism. The other is that revolutionary Cuba has not yet been able to overcome the handicaps imposed by its capitalist past.

DEMOCRATIC SOCIALISM: BRITAIN

Britain was the first nation to experience the Industrial Revolution and the first to have that revolution come to maturity in the late nineteenth century. It was also the first country in the capitalist world to embark upon a program of nationalization, planning, and social welfare extensive enough to approach socialism.

In 1945 the Labour Party, dedicated to democratic Socialist ideals, came to power. It inherited a network of rationing, price and wage ceilings, and other controls carried over from World War II. It found broadcasting and overseas airways already nationalized. It was also presented with recommendations, from Conservative dominated committees, calling for nationalization of coal, gas, electricity, and the Bank of England. Nationalization of the Bank had raised no objection from Winston Churchill.

The Labour government was, therefore, not pressing very hard when it set about to nationalize coal mines, railways, electric power, gas, inland canals, London passenger transportation, highway freight, and the Bank of England, all of which were taken with compensation to their owners. The government could reasonably have nationalized fuel, oil, and milk, but did not try to. When it came to nationalizing steel, however, there was a different story. Unlike most of the other industries to be nationalized, the steel industry had been operating fairly efficiently. Its nationalization had not been recommended.

The difference between democratic Socialist and Communist nationalization is indicated by the fact that the Labour government left essentially the same managers in charge of steel plants and asked industry representatives to serve on the Public Iron and Steel Corporation. In 1950 the minister of supply reported the result, "I was informed that every effort would be made to dissuade any important man I might approach from serving on the Corporation. . . . This is concerted action by a number of people for sabotaging an Act of Parliament." In March 1951, the industry publication, *Iron and Steel,* said that the private interests would continue to run the industry "while members of the newly constituted Steel Corporation are learning the difference between steel and slag." The government was thus fairly helpless to control the steel industry, and in 1951, when the Conservatives returned to power, steel was denationalized. Otherwise, nationalization has continued since then under both Conservative and Labour governments.

A second part of British socialism is the most comprehensive program of public social welfare in the world. Like nationalization, this was not a sudden invention of the Labour Party, but was developed under Conservative governments. It was broadened and strengthened after 1945 by the Labour administration.

The program insures against sickness and unemployment from the end of compulsory education to retirement, and provides pension benefits after retirement. It furnishes compensation for injury or illness incurred by workers on the job, and pensions for those permanently disabled. Employed pregnant women receive an allowance during absence from work. Families with more than one child are eligible for cash benefits and supplies, such as food and vitamins. Lunches are provided for elementary and secondary school pupils. There are allowances for widows and orphans, and services and meals for the infirm. The system also provides funeral allowances and death benefits. These programs are paid for through a payroll tax, about one-fifth of which is paid by the employee and four-fifths by the employer.

One of the most significant social services is the program of public medical care, which provides for services of physicians and dentists, drugs, and hospitalization. Four-fifths of the cost is met by a general tax, the rest by a payroll tax. Doctors can participate in the program, engage in private practice, or do both. Although there is a widespread belief in the United States that the program is unpopular with British doctors, a 1956 Gallup poll showed 69 percent in favor of it.

A third aspect of the British system is government planning. Labour governments (1945–1951, 1963–1970) have been generally favorable to planning, the Conservative government (1951–1963) less favorable. Yet it is fair to say that Labour has given up the ideal of complete nationalization in any near future, and the Conservatives have surrendered much of their belief in pure laissez-faire.

Under the influence of Keynes and Sir William Beveridge (1879–1963), an economist who has been called the "father of British social security," the 1945 Labour government was strongly committed to the belief that unemployment and depression can and should be prevented by positive government policy. Nationalization of the Bank of England has given the government somewhat more direct control over the money supply. Control over the nationalized sector has helped government expand or contract spending to smooth the business cycle. Government spending in housing, 70 percent of which has since the war been government built, has likewise been tailored to economic conditions.

In addition, there have been efforts at direct overall planning. In 1947 the Labour government established a Planning Board and a Central Economic Planning Staff. They conducted economic surveys and set up targets for production. In 1947 the Industrial Organization Act gave government the power to establish Development Councils to help modernize industries. In cotton, for example, the government made grants of up to 25 percent for the purchase of new machinery. Under the

Government Responsibility for the British Economy, 1951

Board of Trade: All industries not assigned to another department, of which the most important were textiles, chemicals, rubber, and paper.

Ministry of Supply: Iron and steel, nonferrous metals, vehicles, engineering, explosives.

Ministry of Food: Procurement, distribution, and price control of essential foods and feed stuffs.

Ministry of Agriculture and Fisheries: Farming, horticulture, agricultural machinery, fisheries.

Ministry of Fuel and Power: Coal, gas, electricity, oil.

Ministry of Transport: Transport services other than civil aviation, road building, certain sections of the quarrying industry.

Ministry of Works: Building, civil engineering, building materials.

Admiralty: Shipbuilding and repairing.

Ministry of Health: Medical supplies and pharmaceuticals.

Source: A. A. Rogow, The Labour Government and British Industry, 1945–1951, Oxford, Basil Blackwell, 1955, pp. 54–55.

Labour administration, government was thought to have a general responsibility for economic life, and different ministries were assigned to sectors of the economy. The accompanying chart shows how this looked in 1951. Under the Conservatives interest in planning waned. When Labour came back into office in 1963, however, a comprehensive survey and plan were established to provide for a 25 percent increase in GNP by 1970. This plan was intended to advise industries and give them a framework into which to fit their individual plans, not to coerce them.

How has Britain fared under the Socialist program? Not exceptionally well. One study showed, it is true, that 31 percent of the British people were in poverty in 1936, and only 3 percent in 1950. The year 1936 was, however, deep in the Depression, and hardly a good basis for comparison. The noted British economic historian, R. H. Tawney, was probably right when he said in 1950 that "a more equalitarian society than existed in prewar England, and than exists today in the Soviet Union or in the United States, is in process of creation." The British economy has had, however, one of the lowest rates of growth of any major country, an average of about 2.7 per-cent per year since World War II. France, by contrast, has had a rate of about 4.5 percent. British investment has been a little more than 7 percent of GNP a year. West Germany, in the same period, had 15 percent; Italy, 12 percent; Norway, 20 to 22 percent.

Has Britain's record been poor because of socialism or in spite of it, or for some other reason? One friendly critic of the Labour regime, Sir Arthur Salter, pointed to what he felt to be unsolved problems in nationalization. Under government monopoly, he said, it is difficult to maintain efficiency when there is no competition to stimulate it. Moreover, when public monopoly can raise prices or fall back on public funds for wage increases, it is harder to say no to excessive union demands than when increases must come out of profits. Finally, it is difficult under nationalization to avoid the rigidity and red tape of centralized bureaucracy. Most objective people would agree that Salter has pointed to three central problems which any program of nationalization must face.

However, it is questionable how many of the troubles of the British economy can be attributed to socialism. For one thing, it is not really socialistic. Only about one-fourth of GNP and one-fifth of the labor force are involved in public enterprise. Only about one-half of investment is controlled by the government. A fairly conservative definition of socialism would describe as socialistic an economy where the public sector is "large enough to set the tone for the rest, leaving private industry to operate within a framework of public enterprise, rather than the other way around." This is not the case in Britain; the dominant system is still private enterprise. Of course, the relatively small sector of socialism could be the rotten apple that poisons the barrel!

It seems more likely that Britain's problems grow out of conditions which lie deeper than the question of government ownership and control. Britain is a nation of 55 million people living on a small group of islands. She has historically been forced to import food and to pay for imports largely with manufactured exports. As the first nation to industrialize, she got a jump in the world's markets for industrial goods. She had a favored market in her empire. She served as banker for much of the world. Her ships carried much of the world's trade. All these factors gave her a favorable trade picture. Now the empire has dissolved, and other nations have passed her industrially. Twice she has had to devalue the pound, that is, make British exports cheaper, in an effort to overcome an unfavorable balance of payments.

There is a serious question how large a population and industrial establishment Britain can support with limited resources under twentieth- and twenty-first-century conditions. This seems to be the central problem which Britain, socialist or otherwise, must answer in the future.

DEMOCRATIC SOCIALISM: ISRAEL

Israel is economically one of the world's foremost experiments in democratic socialism. With a private sector limited to a little more than one-fourth of the economy, Israel meets the definition of socialism much better than Britain.

To understand Israel we must be aware of the economic and political ideology of its founders. Although the nation embraces a wide range of beliefs, the single strongest economic element might be described as an anti-market philosophy. Probably the majority of immigrants since the founding of the state of Israel, in 1948, could be called Socialist-Zionist.

The strongest single party is the Workers' Party of the Land of Israel (Mapai). The strongest economic group is the Histadrut, the national labor organization. Organized in 1920 to protect the interests of workers, the Histadrut early sponsored co-ops in agriculture, transport, and other fields. It pressed Jews to employ Jews, subsidized the wages of Jewish workers, and set up industries and other enterprises to employ immigrants. It established the sickness insurance fund, the Kupath Holim, which in 1959 included 70 percent of all workers. The power of the Histadrut reflects the syndicalist color of economic ideas, the concept of socialism as ruled by workers rather than by the central state.

It is also necessary to appreciate the role of the Jewish Agency, the chief Zionist organization. Its main functions have been to promote interest in Israel, to encourage immigration, and to raise funds abroad. Its success is reflected by the fact that Israel receives more aid from overseas than any other nation in the world.

The private sector includes about 27 percent of the economy. Few of the heavy industries are privately owned. Manufacture of potash, glass, cement, phosphates, steel, and metal and concrete pipes is in the hands of either the government or the Histadrut. Even the private enterprise that exists is far from the world of Adam Smith. Almost all private manufacturing industries are dominated by one leader or by a group (cartel) of enterprises who work in collaboration rather than competitively. The Manufacturers' Association, in which membership is almost required, is delegated by the government to control supply, rationing, import, investment, and credit. Most private importers and wholesalers belong to the Chamber of Commerce, whose functions are similar to those of the Manufacturers' Association.

National or municipal industry makes up about 20 percent of the economy. The most important publicly owned industry is electric power, about two-thirds of which goes to industry or irrigation. Workers participate in management.

The largest single sector, 33 percent, is that of Histadrut enterprises. These include industrial and retail trade co-ops, and agricultural co-ops (kibbutzim). Consumers' cooperative societies handle about one-third of retail trade, and a higher percentage of food marketing. Histadrut is represented in publication of daily papers, as a landlord, in manufacture of metal pipes, in import of drugs, in kindergartens, insurance, fishing, oil, auditing, and private law courts. There are three main forms of Histadrut participation in the economy. Ownership by co-ops related to Histadrut is one. Direct ownership by the executive of Histadrut is another. In addition, Histadrut cooperates with government and/or the Jewish Agency in management of a number of enterprises. In general it works closely in an interlocking directorate with the Mapai Party and the government.

The final 10 percent of the economy falls under nonprofit "institutions." These seek material aid outside Israel for academic, political, charitable, cultural, and religious bodies in Israel. The most important of these is the Jewish Agency. The nonprofit institutions participate in such areas as agriculture, banking, building, and shipping.

The Jewish Agency and the state control about 90 percent of all land in Israel. A large part of agriculture is

Young Israeli settlers.

conducted by either *kibbutzim* (singular, *kibbutz*) or *moshavim* (singular, *moshav*). The kibbutz is a cooperative colony in which the land is communally owned. In principle kibbutzim employ no hired hands. Supplies are bought only from co-ops, and marketing is done only through co-ops. The idea of the kibbutz has been strongest in the Socialist-Zionist movement, but kibbutzim have been formed by eight major political groups. In the moshav families own land separately, typically being provided with 2½ to 4 acres of irrigated land, 1 cow, and 50 laying hens. Marketing and other functions are carried on cooperatively. The Jewish Agency has 35 years of experience in organizing moshavim.

Originally the main purpose of kibbutzim and moshavim was colonization of immigrants to Israel. Efficient production was secondary, and mixed farming rather than specialization on large cash crops was favored. The first emphasis was therefore on milk, eggs, poultry, meat, and vegetables for local consumption and the urban market. After these needs were filled, it shifted to wheat, oil-bearing plants, sugar, sisal, cotton, and citrus. This development required mechanization.

For a country committed to Socialist ideals, there is surprisingly little overall planning in Israel. Solicitation of aid from abroad is a major activity, but even this is not very well coordinated. After 1953 a Seven Year Plan for agriculture was scrapped. In 1962 an Economic Planning Authority projected a first Four–Five Year Plan, but it was not very successful. Teaching in economics at the Hebrew University in Jerusalem is dominated by American-trained economists with a bias toward laissez-faire, who are also prominent in government. This fact may be related to the lack of interest and success in planning.

In its output the economy of Israel would seem to be a success. The average annual growth rate from 1950 to 1964 was a solid 6 percent. From 1948 to 1963, Israel was the highest of 19 developing nations in agricultural output per farm worker. She is near the top of the Mediterranean countries in consumption of selected food items and has a general standard of living that compares favorably even with that of highly developed European countries. At the same time, she has achieved the Socialist objective of lessening the income spread. The difference between highest and lowest incomes is among the narrowest in the world.

Appearances may be somewhat deceiving, however, for Israel does not as yet pay her own way. She imports large gifts of goods and capital. In 1957 to 1958, seven-eighths of her imports were subsidized. Saving within the country is low; this is the other side of the high level of consumption. In this respect Israel contrasts sharply with Japan. Imported foreign capital is necessary to make up the gap. The situation is made more difficult by inflation, which is thought by some experts to be Israel's greatest economic problem. Wages rise with prices and pull them still higher, and higher prices then make it harder for Israel to export. To support her efforts to make her own way in the world through exporting, Israel has few natural resources. She does, however, have a high level of education and technical skill and a strong nationalistic pride and determination. At present, diamonds and citrus are the major exports. Other promising possibilities are precision tools, electrical appliances, and the fashion trade. Only when strengthening of her exports enables Israel to stand without continual foreign subsidy will it be possible to judge the success of her experiment in socialism.

MARKET SOCIALISM: YUGOSLAVIA

Yugoslavia today is a Socialist country where no industry is owned by the state and none by private individuals. It has a one-party government, yet operates on the slogan that "the state is the enemy of socialism." It combines long-run planning and socialization of much production with a market which is in some respects more free than those of some capitalist countries. It has achieved substantial agricultural development with a system aimed toward agricultural socialism, but today based firmly on private property in land.

The present regime in Yugoslavia dates back to 1944, when Marshall Tito, with Russian help, drove out the Nazis and established his Partisans as the government in Belgrade. From 1944 to 1949, Yugoslavia was modeled on the USSR, with a terrorist police state and centralization of the economy. Industry was nationalized and centrally planned, and a concerted drive was made to collectivize farmers. In 1948, however, Tito broke politically with the Kremlin, and from that time began the economic changes which have made Yugoslavia an important experiment in decentralized socialism.

The federal government of Yugoslavia is unique in that one of the two chambers of the national legislature is

Freight trains—one of them carrying new automobiles—in Belgrade, Yugoslavia.

a Council of Producers, composed of representatives of industries, commerce, crafts, and agricultural co-ops. Under the federal government are republics, which represent a number of nationalities. The basic governmental unit is, however, the opstina, or commune, of which there are somewhat over 1000. The commune is described by one Yugoslav writer as "that basic cell of the socialist organization which Marx, Engels and all the great socialist thinkers called the free association of free producers." All authority not specifically granted to the republics or the federal government belongs to the commune.

Economically, the communes have most of the responsibility for formulating economic plans and starting new enterprises. They are governed by an elected people's committee, which is itself responsible to periodic general meetings of commune voters. Industries and other enterprises are operated by workers' councils, consisting of from 15 to 200 members, elected by the workers. The workers' councils are responsible to the people's committee of the commune. Actual day-by-day operation is in the hands of a management board of from 3 to 17, elected by the workers' council. A director is chosen by the workers' council, the

commune people's committee, and an industry-wide chamber representing all workers' councils in that field.

In stores and service enterprises, prices and quality may be subject to review by consumer councils attached to the people's committee of the commune. In addition, workers' councils receive recommendations on broad policy from the industry-wide "chambers," which have government representation. There are also industrial groups, called "associations," which are supposed to keep the workers' councils aware of national as well as local interests. Subject to these controls, industrial and business enterprises sell their products on a free market much like that of capitalist economics. One Swedish scholar believes that Yugoslavia's decentralized economic system has "succeeded in blending the principles of free enterprise and collective ownership."

The Federal Planning Institute is in charge of drafting annual and 5-year plans, but they are formulated mainly from the bottom up and are advisory rather than binding. Republics, districts, communes, individual enterprises, and national economic chambers all formulate their plans, which are then incorporated into the national plan. This sets goals for production of capital and consumer goods, for building, for investment, and so on. Making the national plan involves a constant interchange among levels. The national plan has been described as in part "a plan for other plans," and in part a summary of them. Once the plan has been constructed, the federal government does have ways of influencing firms to follow it. It controls large investment funds. It can change taxes and interest rates. It has controls over wages, prices, and foreign trade.

Investment illustrates, however, the decentralization of the economy and the limits of federal control. There is a Federal Central Investment Fund, which can make loans to individual firms. In 1959, however, two-thirds of all investment came either out of republic funds, local funds, or the earnings of individual firms.

In the first years, the government hoped to bring the peasants into collective farms on the Russian model. Even after the break with Russia in 1948, there was an intensive drive for collectivization. It was unsuccessful, however, for 75 percent of the land remained in the private sector. Production was low, and in 1951 large quantities of agricultural products were imported from the United States.

In 1953 agricultural policy was liberalized. Yugoslavian officials decided that for the present, peasant resistance to collectivization was too great and that it would be necessary to leave most land in private hands. At the same time, the government hoped to move the peasants gradually toward socialism and also increase production by making available extensive voluntary cooperative facilities.

Today, in addition to private farms, there are three forms of collective or cooperative agricultural arrangements. The Peasant Work Co-ops are based on the Russian collective farms, but are worker managed and sell in a free market. There are also state-owned farms, operated directly by the government. Most important are the General Co-ops, which serve the landowning peasants.

They began by establishing co-op stores. Most grain is marketed through them. They are the chief distributors of loans and investment funds to peasants. They acquire land and farm it in cooperation with private peasant holdings. Some operate mills, dairies, and wineries. General Co-ops provide to peasants such services as plowing, threshing and harvesting, pedigree stock, hybrid United States corn and high-grade Italian wheat, soil reclamation, flood control, fertilizers, and tractors. To receive co-op services, peasants may have to follow certain practices, such as deep plowing. These co-op programs have been quite successful in raising agricultural yields.

Foreign trade is generally carried on directly by individual firms, who sell their goods on the world market. There has been some licensing of imports, but the direction has been toward free trade. Some of Yugoslavia's chief exports are diesel engines, farm machinery, ocean and river vessels, office machines, electric cables, turbines, and metal goods. At first Yugoslavia traded primarily with the Soviet bloc. Then, after 1948, she shifted to the West. The United States has not only imported large quantities of Yugoslavian exports, but from 1950 to 1959 sent over a billion dollars of economic aid and three-quarters of a billion of military aid. Economic aid has furnished large amounts of food and raw materials. It has aided the development of food production for domestic use and export. It has helped in the development of key industrial projects. All in all, United States aid has not only fed Yugoslavia in time of need, but it has helped provide the agricultural surplus for industrial development, and thus helped wean Yugoslavia away from Moscow. All this has meant that Yugoslavia has tended to run a deficit in her balance of payments; she has been, like Israel, a subsidized nation. However, her policy has been not to try to trim imports, but to hope that an expanding economy will eventually be able to export more.

Yugoslavia's growth record gives promise for the future. From 1953 to 1959, her GNP grew at an annual average rate of 10.4 percent. In 1963 the growth rate was 12 percent, as compared with 2.4 from 1948 to 1952. Agriculture does not yet feed her population, but the agricultural program is bringing results. American corn and Italian wheat, for example, have been very successful in raising output. Although Yugoslavia's standard of living does not compare with that of a neighbor like Austria, the average person is better off economically than before World War II. Electric stoves, refrigerators, and television sets made their appearance in store windows in the late 1950s. In 1960, 35 percent of all wages and salaries went to finance social insurance. Nearly half the population was covered by the maximum insurance—health, disability, retirement, and allowances for children. Yugoslavia has made spectacular gains in raising the level of literacy and in extending educational opportunity.

The Yugoslavian economy has been a pilot project in decentralized socialism, syndicalist in its sector of industry and trade. It has gone very far toward combining social ownership with a free market. The question is asked as to whether the workers' councils and other local organizations actually exercise the power they are given on paper. While home rule may not be quite that complete and there are many ways in which the federal government can exert economic pressure, it seems that the decentralization is real. To a considerable extent it really appears to be true that "both the Yugoslavs and the Americans see in government controls a threat to both economic efficiency and democracy."

Yugoslavia is, of course, still a totalitarian state, in the sense that there is only one recognized party and political line and that political opposition is not among the freedoms guaranteed citizens. Opposition is generally handled somewhat less severely, however, than it used to be. If it is successful, economic decentralization will probably lead to further gains in political liberty.

COOPERATIVE DEMOCRACY: SWEDEN

Sweden is second in the world behind the United States in per capita income. She is second in per capita number of cars, third in life expectancy, and third in production of electric power. She has the highest percentage of unionized workers in the world, has no slums, and virtually no poverty. An extensive social security program similar to Britain's takes one-sixth of all her national income and covers most of her citizens "from womb to tomb." Her system is sometimes called Socialist, yet over three-fourths of the nation's business is in private hands.

There are several keys to Sweden's success. Some are not directly related to her form of economic organization. She is a small country with rich natural resources. These include timber, water power, and the largest deposits of high-grade iron ore in Europe. Lack of coal has in some ways been a drawback, but in others has been an asset. Sweden has been forced to develop her water resources for power. Since electricity came relatively late, lack of coal meant that her Industrial Revolution was also late. Industry was not clustered around coal mines, but dispersed throughout the country. This relieved her of the blight of industrial cities and prevented the development of a sharp division between city and country. By remaining neutral in all the wars of this century, Sweden has preserved her resources from the devastation that has visited other countries.

Government has long exercised ownership and control in the Swedish economy, alongside private enterprise. The Social Democratic Party, which came to power in 1932, is Socialist in philosophy, but has not greatly extended nationalization. Government activity has played several roles. The unplanned exploitation of natural re-

Stockholm, Sweden

sources such as iron ore, water, and timber, which has occurred in other countries, has from the beginning been prevented by the government control or ownership. The government regulates, for example, the cutting of timber. It also operates "natural monopolies": post office and telephone and telegraph systems. It shares ownership of the transportation system with private enterprise, owning most of the railways, about half the bus lines, and part of the airlines system. Monopolies on the import and manufacture of tobacco and on the import and distribution of liquor pay about half the cost of the national social welfare program.

Extensive consumers' and producers' cooperatives are perhaps the most distinctive part of the Swedish economy. Approximately half the Swedish population belong to co-ops. It is easy to become a member. One starts buying, gets "patronage dividends" on his purchases, and applies part of these to the purchase of stock. Consumer cooperatives handle approximately 20 percent of all foodstuffs in Sweden. Most of them are organized under the Ko-operativa Vörbundet (Cooperative Union and Wholesale Society), which was founded in 1899.

At least as important as the con-

sumers' *konsums* are the cooperative factories. In 1956 KV owned 72 of these and had at least half interest in 14 and part ownership in another 28. One of the chief purposes of these factories is to prevent private monopolies, or cartels, from raising prices. KV's first factory, one producing margarine, cut prices by 60 percent. The Luma light bulb factory forced the price of bulbs down 40 percent. KV has conducted other anticartel campaigns by establishing factories to produce flour, galoshes, tires, superphosphate and other fertilizers, pottery, and building materials. KV controls only about 2 percent of Sweden's industrial output. However, careful selection of areas of production where they can control from 15 to 25 percent has enabled them to exert a great influence on the economy.

Farmers' cooperatives are even more extensive than those for consumers, although less well known. Producers' cooperatives handle marketing, transportation, distribution, and credit for farmers. In 1956 the Swedish Dairies Association handled over 95 percent of all milk, butter, and cheese. The Meat Marketing Association receives the farmer's cattle at the slaughterhouse and takes care of slaughtering and marketing. Other producers' co-ops deal with vegetables, eggs, forestry products, furs, starch products, flax, hemp, and oil plant products. Virtually all farmers with any cash products belong to the Federation of Swedish Farmers' Associations.

Although Sweden has come a long way toward providing a secure and comfortable life for her people, some questions are still to be answered.

There are no slums, and Sweden has built magnificent suburban housing developments. Over 80 percent of Swedish homes have been constructed with government assistance. Nevertheless, there has been for years a severe housing shortage. A city dweller may have to wait up to ten years for an apartment. In 1967 a Stockholm newspaper reported the case of a one-room apartment which had been auctioned for $4000. Young people are forced to postpone marriage or live apart. A large population shift to the cities is one reason for the shortage. Rent controls carried over from World War II discourage investment in housing. It is difficult to undertake a necessary housing program when the economy's resources are almost fully employed. When asked in 1967 to advise a young Stockholm couple how to get an apartment, Prime Minister Tage Erlander could only suggest that they either move out of the city or have patience.

A second problem is inflation. In 1966 the price level was rising 8 percent a year. The inflation is apparently related to the full employment of resources. Other countries have had the same problem. When unemployment practically disappears and labor is scarce the price of labor rises. In Sweden in 1966, wages were rising 10 percent a year. When productivity of labor is not rising that fast, wage costs are likely to be paid for through an increase in the prices of goods and services. The only answer appears to be wage and price controls.

A third question is harder to evaluate. Some critics, inside and outside Sweden, feel that the security provided by the welfare state destroys initiative

and interest. They suggest that the high suicide rate and the dissatisfaction and delinquency of many young people indicate an absence of challenge. Some Swedish young people certainly feel that there is wider opportunity abroad. The Swedish economy and society still give the impression, however, that Swedes are aggressive and on the move. The skyline and streets of Stockholm are not those of a city which has stagnated. In any event, as the famous Swedish economist Gunnar Myrdal has said, in terms of social welfare planning, Sweden is probably about where the United States will be in another generation.

LESSONS FOR THE FUTURE

If we can draw any conclusion from our survey of the economic spectrum, it is that the successful economies of the future will not be pure types, but will learn from the experience of past economies and try to incorporate their best features.

Our two capitalist economies, the United States and Japan, clearly show that under certain conditions the market can produce spectacular and sustained growth. They also show the same tendency toward oligopolistic concentration, and thus toward the end of capitalism in Adam Smith's sense. Both seem to indicate that business cycles and long-run stagnation are the great threats to the market system. The United States, in particular, illustrates the effort to solve these problems through Keynesian full-employment policies. These involve the deliberate introduction of planning. Japan, incidentally, demonstrates the economic advantage of not having to carry a heavy load of armament.

Russia and China show that centralized planned economies can also grow rapidly and relatively successfully. Russia, especially, shows that there are some aspects of planning which can probably be done better through market mechanisms, with less effort and an increase in overall motivation and efficiency. Russia also raises the exciting question of the possible role of computerization in planning. The two major Communist economies point up the great problem of fitting the farmer into a nonmarket economy. Russia has clearly failed. China has failed in her extreme attempt at communal organization, but has been relatively successful with a semi-Socialist agricultural cooperation.

Each of our contemporary mixed economies provides some features that may be relevant for economies of the future. Britain was the first working example of a semi-Socialist regime in a major nation. Her comprehensive social welfare program is no doubt a model that will be followed by most affluent economies. Britain's lack of great economic growth may be due to too much socialism, or too little socialism, but more likely to peculiarly

British problems. Israel's two great contributions are the kibbutz, as a model for socialized agriculture, and the wide sector of Histadrut, or union-operated industry. She furnishes a very interesting mixture of economic patterns.

Yugoslavia is a pioneer venture in Socialist (or syndicalist) decentralization of control and planning. She combines planning with market mechanisms and offers a conservative and fairly successful approach to the long-run socialization of individualistic peasants. Sweden again illustrates the economic advantages of peace. Her great contribution is probably the role of the cooperative movement. It has been not only a yardstick to control private industry, but also the source of a philosophy of public concern which runs through the whole economy.

Suggestions for further reading

A recent and important discussion of where Keynesian capitalism is bringing the United States appears in JOHN KENNETH GALBRAITH's The New Industrial State (New American Library, 1968, paper). The State and Economic Enterprise in Japan by WILLIAM W. LOCKWOOD (rev. ed., Princeton University Press, 1969) is a good source on that example of capitalist economy.

An up-to-date and really exciting treatment of the Russian economy is ROBERT W. CAMPBELL's Soviet Economic Power (2nd ed., Houghton Mifflin, 1966, paper). Another long-respected book on the subject is HARRY SCHWARTZ, Introduction to the Soviet Economy (Merrill, 1968, paper).

One of the most informed students of communism in China is the Australian historian C. P. FITZGERALD. See his The Birth of Communist China (rev. ed., Penguin Pelican, 1966, paper). A. Doak Barnett is a rather critical China expert, Felix Greene is a former British journalist favorable to the Mao regime. Works more specifically on the economy of Red China are CHOH-MING LI, ed., Industrial Development in Communist China (Praeger, 1966), and KUO PING-CHIA, China: New Age and New Outlook (Penguin, 1960). Students interested in unusual research may want to look up HUAN-CHANG CHEN, The Economic Principles of Confucius and His School (Columbia University Press, 1911), a doctoral dissertation in which the author demonstrates that Marx's basic economic concepts are found in Confucius. This is a significant study, in light of the fact that Mao

is now said to quote more often from Confucius than from Marx. (Chen is no longer in print, but can possibly be secured on interlibrary loan from Columbia University).

Two critical books on the Cuban revolution are THEODORE DRAPER, Castro's Revolution: Myth and Reality (Praeger, 1962, paper), and CARMELO MESA-LAGO, The Labor Sector and Socialist Distribution in Cuba (Praeger, 1968). A treatment more favorable to the Castro regime is JAMES O'CONNOR, The Origins of Socialism in Cuba (Cornell, 1970).

A. A. ROGOW, The Labour Government and British Industry, 1945–1951 (Basil Blackwell, 1955) is a thorough treatment of the early stages of British socialism. A good source on the Israeli economy is The Economy of Israel by the highly respected Israeli economist DAVID HOROWITZ (Pergamon, 1967, paper). The Yugoslav economy is thoroughly treated in Yugoslavia and the New Communism by GEORGE W. HOFFMAN and FRED WARNER NEAL (20th-Century Fund, 1962). The best known book on the Swedish economy is Sweden, The Middle Way by MARQUIS CHILDS (rev. ed., Yale University Press, 1947, paper). A more recent book is FREDERIC FLEISHER, New Sweden (McKay, 1967).

In Freedom and Necessity: An Introduction to the Study of Society (Random House, 1970) JOAN ROBINSON, a distinguished professor of economics at Cambridge University, presents a thought-provoking survey of the economic spectrum, against a background of economic history.

Part four
Power and freedom

Power relationships are of two important kinds: between group and group, and between group and individual. In Part four we deal with three aspects of group-group and person-group conflict. Chapter 13 treats the organization of group power struggles around national states that have massive destructive capacity. In Chapter 14 we are concerned with the tendency of groups to suppress their individual members when involved in struggles that they deem critical. Chapter 15 asks what kind of social and personal life might make it possible to do two things simultaneously: (1) promote development of persons while (2) maintaining the kind of effective social organization without which individual fulfillment is impossible.

Chapter thirteen
War and its alternatives

One of the most important facts about the world is that it is organized into political units which use violence or the threat of violence to promote their ends. Let us begin our analysis of the international power struggle with a brief look at where it stands today.

At the end of World War II, England's dominance of the capitalist-democratic world passed to the United States. World War II was followed by the Cold War. Soviet troops moved in to establish satellite regimes in eastern Europe. The two great rivals became, and have been most of the time since then, Russia and the United States. In 1949 mainland China entered the scene. Is she united with Russia in a common campaign to spread communism over the world or is she much more interested in promoting her own variety of economy and power in competition with Russia as well as the capitalist United States?

It would be a mistake to regard the struggle among the established great powers in the Cold War as the most important international struggle in the world today. There is, indeed, a significant conflict between West and East, if Russia can be regarded as in part Asian. The more critical struggle is, however, between North and South, not among great powers, but between the developed and underdeveloped nations, between Europe and North America on the one hand, and Africa, South America, and southern Asia on the other.

Over the past four or five centuries this struggle resulted first in the political domination of the underdeveloped world through the colonial system. When it became too crude and unworkable, political domination led to political revolt in the colonies, as in the American colonies in 1776, and in Algeria in 1959. This revolt has become one of the most important facts of the twentieth century. Political imperialism has often been succeeded by economic dominance. Today, for example, France, Japan, and the United States seek economic favors in South America more than they seek political colonies or promotion of political ideology. Belgium, expelled politically from the Congo, tried to hang on to power through continued involvement in mining investments, which led to intervention in Congolese internal politics. In several former British colonies in Africa (Kenya, for example), local nationalists have charged that the British have not really been expelled, but that an economic neocolonialism has continued under new native governments.

The North-South conflict is complicated by the fact that the underdeveloped nations of the South have been drawn into the East-West Cold War as allies and pawns of the great powers. Cuba was used by Russia for her own power purposes at the time of the 1962 missile crisis. Bolivia, Nicaragua, and Guatemala have at times been pawns of United States policy, which has often rearranged their internal economic and political affairs. During the 1960s North Vietnam was used for Russian and Chinese purposes, while South Vietnam was virtually a puppet created by the United States. Much of the international significance of South Africa has come from the fact that she has been strongly anti-Communist in the Cold War and has thereby gained much support in the Free World.

In the world of power politics just described, decisions are finally made and backed up by violence or the threat of violence. This fact has always made power politics a very dangerous part of social life for both those directly interested and those who may be indirectly involved. In Chapter one in our discussion of the weapons revolution, it was suggested that since 1945 we have moved into a new era in the use of violence. The means which have been typically used or threatened in order to settle power struggles have become incapable of really settling anything. In the Nuclear Age the conflicts over power that have been a taken-for-granted part of all human history have become so deadly that the likely or possible outcome of any serious conflict of major powers is destruction of all the powers concerned and also of much of human civilization and life. Thus today all people seriously concerned about social welfare must examine the reasons why these power conflicts occur and thereby try to discover ways in which massive destruction may be avoided.

We shall devote this chapter to analyzing three important aspects of the international power situation. First, we shall look at the idea of nationalism and the political institution of national sovereignty. Second, we shall examine the economic costs and gains of war. Third, we shall look at the relationship of the war system to the people who fight the wars. In each case we shall explore the possibility of alternatives to war as a way of solving problems.

SOVEREIGNTY AND NATIONALISM

According to Walt W. Rostow,

> *National sovereignty means that nations retain the ultimate right—a right sanctioned by law, custom, and what decent men judge to be legitimate—the right to kill people of other nations in defense or pursuit of what they judge to be their national interest.*[1]

Nations fight in wartime or prepare to fight in peacetime on behalf of various interests. One of these is ideology (systems of ideas and values). We would be naive if we took at face value the claims of nations that they are primarily interested in Christianity, Judaism, Islam, freedom, democracy, communism, or any other system of values and ideals. For example, the three main parties to the Cold War—Russia, China, and the United States—all claim to be chiefly interested in promoting their particular ideologies of communism or capitalist democracy. However, their political alliances, such as Russia's with Hitler, and those of the United States with dictatorships in the so-called Free World, suggest that the nations in the Cold War are interested in things other than ideology—economic expansion and political power, for example.

The United States and Russia maintain large nuclear arsenals and worldwide systems of espionage and subversion to back up their political claims, but it is doubtful that the United States is primarily interested in promoting abstract democracy or the Soviet Union in promoting abstract communism. Erich Fromm, for one, has held that the Russian government is, and has been for a long time, not a body of crusaders for Marxism but a conservative dictatorship much more interested in promoting and expanding its power against rivals at home and abroad. Those who follow American foreign policy are likely to hear more about national interest than about making the world safe for democracy. National interest in this connection means primarily economic power and political prestige. China, with its anticapitalistic

---

1. Walt W. Rostow, *The Stages of Economic Growth*, New York, Cambridge University Press, 1960, p. 107.

and anti-American propaganda, would seem to be on some kind of ideological crusade. Facts must question this assumption. We saw earlier that only a few years ago mainland China was carrying on extensive trade through France with apartheid-ridden South Africa and was indeed supplying the United States with concrete and steel for military bases in Vietnam.

We would also be shortsighted to regard ideological claims as nothing but window dressing. People's beliefs are important in determining their actions, if only in the sense that we usually want to give ourselves and others good reasons to legitimize what we do. Ideologies do play a part in the international power struggle, whether as real reasons or as comfortable rationalizations.

Rationalizations for what? In Chapter eight we reviewed the role played by economic interests, primarily markets and raw materials. We must recognize next that nations fight or prepare to fight to preserve or extend their nationalistic self-images.

National sovereignty, in effect, the power of every national entity to do internationally as it pleases, has been closely related to the mass psychology of nationalism, which arose during the period when medieval feudalism was breaking down. Kings (who had wider territorial interests than the nobles on their local manors) were allied with the rising craftsmen and merchants of the towns who welcomed the development of a wider national market with more opportunities than had existed under the feudal system. At the time nationalism was a wider view than the narrow localism of the isolated feudal manor. It was narrow only when contrasted with the wider view well expressed much later by Thomas Paine: "The world is my country."

It is no exaggeration to say that nationalism has become the chief religion of modern man. This is to say that the national state has become the highest object of the average person's devotion and allegiance. In the major powers, as well as the small older nations and the underdeveloped countries, the most important standard by which actions are judged is whether or not they are in the national interest. Neither broad human concerns nor personal morality can stand ahead of national interest. This point of view was expressed in the famous slogan coined in the early nineteenth century by Stephen Decatur: "My country—may she always be right, but right or wrong, my country!" Helpless civilians will be bombed, and nerve gas, botulism toxins, or bubonic plague germs will be used by people in any modern nation, if they are deemed to be nationally necessary. Nationalism breaks through religious boundaries. In any modern war, the institutionalized religions usually support the national policies in all the contending nations. "God," said Napoleon, "is on the side of the largest batallions." In a world of nationalism, God is customarily found on all sides blessing and supporting all national interests simultaneously.

The individual citizen, whatever his personal, moral, political, or religious beliefs, will have to give his political and moral support to these activities, pay taxes to foot the bills, or, as a member of the military, carry them on personally.

What is the nation to whose interest the citizen must subordinate all other interests? It is not his physical country or the people who live in it, or the everyday human activities that go on within it. One writer on thermonuclear war, Herman Kahn, speaks of an atomic war in which a large part of the land of the United States, a large proportion of the people, and many of the farms and towns might be physically wiped out, and yet the national interest, national honor, and our very way of life might survive. As one writer puts it, the nation or state thought of in this kind of way is a mystical entity which has little connection with real everyday activities. In a sense devotion to national interest, national prestige, and national honor may have little to do

*The personified and deified nation becomes, in the minds of the
individuals comprising it, a kind of enlargement of themselves . . .
Dulce et decorum est pro patria mori. [It is sweet and fitting to die
for one's country.] But there would be no need to die, no need of
war, if it had not been even sweeter to boast and swagger for
one's country, to hate, despise, swindle and bully for it. Loyalty
to the personified nation, or to the personified class or party,
justifies the loyal in indulging all those passions which good
manners and the moral code do not allow them to display in their
relations with their neighbors. The personified entity is a being,
not only great and noble, but also insanely proud, vain and touchy;
fiercely rapacious; a braggart; bound by no consideration of right
and wrong. (Hegel condemned as hopelessly shallow all those
who dared apply ethical sanctions to the activity of nations. To
condone and applaud every iniquity committed in the name of the
State was to him a sign of philosophical profundity.) . . .
Identifying themselves with this god, individuals find relief from the
constraints of ordinary social decency, feel themselves justified in
giving rein, within duly prescribed limits, to their criminal
proclivities. As a loyal nationalist or partyman, one can enjoy the
luxury of behaving badly with a good conscience.*

—Aldous Huxley, "Words and Behavior," *The Olive Tree, New York,
Harper & Row, 1937, pp. 99–100.*

---

with affection for one's native land,
people, culture, or community.

An important fact about this mystical
entity is that the ordinary citizen identi-
fies with it. When the nation is glorified,
is enlarged, he is glorified and enlarged, regardless of whatever else
may have been added to, or subtracted
from, his personal merits. The accompanying excerpt from Aldous Huxley
describes graphically some of the
effects of such identification.

Nationalism robs an individual of his
ability to make intelligent and rational
judgments about national and international affairs. The nationalist is intellectually crippled by the fact that his judgments are determined by an accident
of birth rather than by evidence and
reason. William Graham Sumner, the
great student of the folkways and
mores, said, "The patriotic bias is hostile to critical thinking." The nationalist
inevitably is ethnocentric; he views his
national ways as superior because they
are the ways of *his* nation. The real
merits of his country are not so impor-

tant as the fact that it is *his.* Consider
an ardent American nationalist whose
grandfather emigrated from Russia.
Had his grandfather missed the boat,
this person might today accept and repeat all the slogans and justifications
of Russian nationalism.

The nationalist is likely to have a distorted view of the world as divided into
angels and devils, forces of light and
forces of darkness. This is the way
some Floridians view the conflict between Castro's Cuba and American interests. It is the way a very large number of Chinese regard the conflict between Red Chinese political interests
and American imperialism. It is the way
many South Africans look upon foreign
and native critics of apartheid.

American right wingers are likely to
have an angel-devil view. If the real
world includes, as it does today, some
Socialist countries and some left-wing
democracies, far rightists are likely to
be unable to see the difference between light pink and red; they see freedom as totally encircled by universal

The authoritarian personality.

communism. Communists are likely to see all points of view to the right of center as Fascist.

Erich Fromm, among other psychiatrists, has pointed out the role that *projection* plays in this dismal view of the world. The nationalist is likely to attribute to enemy nations all his own evil tendencies and intentions. Some Americans live in fear of an invasion by Cuba, when the only important actual or planned invasion involving the two countries was an invasion of Cuba by the United States (at the Bay of Pigs). The customary science fiction view of imagined visitors from Mars is always that the Martians are hostile. This view attributes to Martians the qualities that earth dwellers would demonstrate if they landed on Mars and behaved as they customarily do on earth.

The studies of authoritarianism show it to be typically linked with excessive nationalistic feelings. The authoritarian personality is an individual who is most at home in a world where "superiors" give orders to "inferiors." He typically worships power. He regards the world as a jungle where only the roughest and toughest, or craftiest, or most dishonest, survive. He generally fears any-

one who is different—in the case of the average American authoritarian, Negroes, Jews, and foreigners. Most important for this discussion is the fact that he is typically a superpatriot. His typical childhood experience in growing up was marked by anxiety, hatred, and the absence of love. The supernationalist is typically a loveless individual.

So dangerous have the psychology of nationalism and the political institution of national sovereignty become that the hope of abolishing them through world organization has arisen repeatedly in the modern world. In 1462 Georg von Podrebrad, King of Bohemia, proposed a federal union of Christian nations with a common parliament. In his Grand Design, King Henry VI of France outlined a political union of all Christian states which he hoped would settle disputes between Catholics and Protestants. Near the end of the seventeenth century, William Penn put forward the idea of a central parliament which would keep the peace in Europe. The French philosopher, Jean Jacques Rosseau, proposed a union for perpetual peace, as did the German philosopher, Imanuel Kant. Ideas were translated into action in 1907 with the formation of the Court of International Justice at the Hague.

At the end of World War I, the League of Nations was founded by the first twenty-six articles of the Versailles Treaty, which ended the war. The league possessed a General Assembly in which each member, regardless of size, had one vote—"a sort of world forum which might deliberate but could not legislate." The League also had a Council of five permanent and other nonpermanent members. (The permanent seats went to the major powers.) Unanimity was required for most decisions by the assembly and the Council. A permanent Court of International Justice became part of the league machinery. There was no league military force, but there was a guarantee of mutual defense if a member were attacked, and provision for economic boycott of aggressors. The league supervised enforcement of many treaties, aided many refugees, and helped insolvent nations. It checked the international opium traffic and collected worldwide statistics on business and labor conditions (one of its most successful features was the International Labor Office), but it was never able to take action against any major power. It could not act when Italy invaded Ethiopia or Japan attacked China or Nazi Germany began its expansion.

At the end of World War II in 1945, the United Nations was established with a General Assembly organized on the principle of one vote for each member. The Security Council, with five permanent and six nonpermanent members, required unanimity. The Soviet Union vetoed action more than 100 times in the first twenty years. The Security Council was empowered to investigate any international dispute, to use diplomatic or economic methods against any aggressor, and, if these were ineffective, to take military action. The UN also included an Atomic Energy Control Commission and a Social and Economic Council. To the latter were attached the International Labor Office, the United Nations Education, Scientific and Cultural Organization (UNESCO), and the World Bank and the International Monetary Fund. The assembly of the UN, which includes all members, has little power, although since 1950 it has been enabled to recommend even military action by a two-thirds vote. The Security Council, like the League of Nations, has been hampered by the veto power —the ability of any permanent member to hold up action.

In a world of nationalistic power struggles, no world organization has yet been set up which has the ability to override the nationalistic interests of any great power.

The League of Nations was established by the victors in World War I without participation by the defeated powers. It served then to balance the interests of the major victorious na-

tions. In 1919 the French Marshal Foch said, "This is not peace. It is an armistice for twenty years."

Of the United Nations, the UN political scientist, R. M. MacIver, has said:

The whole scheme, setting up a slightly disguised hegemony of a few great powers, was a retreat from the conception of an international order regulated by international law. The accent was on established power. . . . The maintenance of peace was made to depend solely on the agreement among themselves of the superpower states. There were no provisions to check the imperialistic designs any one of them might cherish against the others or against the smaller states.[2]

A really independent world government would have the same powers with respect to the individual nations which the United States government has with respect to the separate states. It might have an independent parliament, elected directly by the peoples of the world instead of representing the separate nation-states. It might also have an independent executive branch, capable of exercising police power directly against any individual who violated the international law established by the legislative assembly. An independent judiciary might interpret the law directly in individual cases against persons.

It is not impossible to make gains toward resolving the world power struggle without expanding formal world government. Much has been done, and can no doubt be done, through treaties and other agreements among independent sovereignties. The nuclear test ban treaty is an example. Here it is important to quote Alexander Hamilton: "To expect a continuation of harmony among unconnected, independent sovereignties in the same neighborhood is to disregard the uni-

2. Robert M. MacIver, *The Web of Government*, rev. ed., New York, Free Press, 1965, p. 294.

form course of human events and to set at defiance the accumulated experience of ages."

THE ECONOMICS OF WAR

Relief from the international power struggle clearly requires a vast change in the way in which nations use their resources. When he was secretary-general of the United Nations, Dag Hammarskjold pointed out that the world was spending for military purposes a total of $120 billion a year, or $320 million a day. This amount, if applied to other purposes, would have doubled the income of the poorest 1.2 billion people in the world. At about the same time, the United States Disarmament Commission estimated that world military expenditure exceeded the total gross national product of all the underdeveloped nations.

The United States at the present time spends under ordinary peacetime conditions about $60 billion a year for military purposes. We may compare this drain upon the economy with the $20 to $30 billion of GNP lost per year due to the Depression.

The United States Disarmament Agency has claimed that cities have sacrificed urban transportation to avoid higher taxes upon a population already heavily taxed for military preparation. In 1962 the American Association for the Advancement of Science pointed out that civilian research has suffered because half of all research and development funds went to the military.

A few years ago, the following estimate was given of what could be bought with one-tenth of the annual military expediture of the United States: one school costing one million dollars in each of 3000 countries, a tax cut of one billion dollars, 500 hospitals at $100 million each, $5000 scholarships to 100,000 students.

Sometimes, rather than choosing between military and civilian spending, we try to maintain a high level of both. In Chapter eight we pointed out how the war economy developed by United States involvement in Indo-China has created a major problem of inflation. It has long been suspected that one cannot have "both guns and butter," both an extensive military economy and an affluent civilian economy. What we have learned since the Indo-China war is that if we try to use our limited resources for both purposes, we tend to create an excessive demand. The simplest law of supply and demand tells us that we are likely to have a general rise in prices (inflation).

We also suggested earlier that in another sense we may have no real choice of whether or not to continue a large military economy.

A case can be made that the American economy has never operated successfully on a peacetime basis since 1929. The 1930s was a period of continuing depression, which was sometimes relieved by public programs such as the WPA, but was never solved. The great crash of 1929 was finally brought to an end by Bombers for Britain, the development of an arms industry to supply the British in the war against Germany. World War II was soon followed by the Korean War, and by the more extended Cold War, which became hot in the 1960s in Southeast Asia. The effect of this war was suggested by a May 6, 1963, article by Edwin H. Lahey of the Detroit *Free Press*'s Washington bureau. Lahey said, "The American economy will not provide full employment in this generation, unless there is a war emergency." Gerard Piel, editor of *Scientific American,* once wrote: "The American economy is a sick patient living on injections of deficit financing. The injections have concealed the symptoms, but the patient is still just as sick. We are stuck with an arms industry because it is the only way to prop up an outmoded economy." More briefly, a San Francisco *Call-Bulletin* writer in 1964 described defense industries as "just a glorified WPA."

The effect of guns in providing butter is specifically illustrated by the fact that a few years ago military production made up 82 percent of all manufacturing employment in San Diego, 72 percent in Wichita, and 53 percent in Seattle. It accounts for 10,000 jobs in Orlando, Florida, $.33 of every dollar spent in Jacksonville, and in general for 14.1 percent of all employment in Florida manufacturing.

The impact of the problem was strongly stated by Charles E. Wilson, a former General Motors executive, when he was secretary of defense under President Eisenhower.

> *One of the most serious things about this defense business is that so many Americans are getting a vested interest in it; properties, business, jobs, employment, votes, opportunities for promotion and advancement, bigger salaries for scientists and all that. It is a troublesome business . . . if you try to change suddenly you can get into trouble . . . if you shut the whole business off now, you will have the state of California in trouble because such a big percentage of the aircraft industry is in California.*[3]

That the involvement of the military in the economy creates a serious vested interest in war was pointed out by Wilson's political chief, Dwight D. Eisenhower, in his final address to the nation as president. He made a special point of warning his listeners of the danger of giving too much power to a military-industrial complex.

He was pointing to the tendency of

3. Charles E. Wilson, quoted in Fred J. Cook, *The Warfare State*, New York, Macmillan, 1962, p. 165.

the United States, like other major powers and some minor powers, to become a warfare state dominated economically, socially, and politically by preparation for conflict. This trend has been a departure from a long-standing American tradition.

Before World War I Americans were generally antimilitaristic. From the days when the Pilgrims left Holland in the face of general military service, the United States had been a haven for refugees from military conscription abroad. Although a draft was used in the Civil War and World Wars I and II, until the 1940s permanent peacetime military service never became a part of American life. Traditionally many Americans were isolationists and believed that the United States should remain within its own boundaries and not become involved in what George Washington had referred to as "entangling alliances" abroad. Warfare had for Americans been an unusual interruption of normal peacetime activities. Congress had exercised control over military affairs through its constitutional power to declare war.

In the last twenty years, the situation has changed greatly. Universal peacetime military service for young men has become taken for granted. It is also assumed by many that the United States is properly engaged in military activities and diplomatic activities which may lead to war in any part of the world. War, hot or cold, has become the normal state of affairs, and periods of peace are only exceptions to this condition.

When he spoke of the military-indus-

Until the latest of our world conflicts, the United States had no armaments industry. American makers of plowshares could, with time and as required, make swords as well. But now we can no longer risk emergency improvisation of national defense; we have been compelled to create a permanent armaments industry of vast proportions. Added to this, three and a half million men and women are directly engaged in the Defense Establishment. We annually spend on military security more than the net income of all U.S. corporations.

This conjunction of an immense military establishment and a large arms industry is new in the American experience. The total influence—economic, political, even spiritual—is felt in every city, every state house, every office of the federal government. We recognize the imperative need for this development. Yet we must not fail to comprehend its grave implications. Our toil, resources, and livelihood are all involved; so is the structure of our society.

In the councils of government, we must guard against the acquisition of unwarranted influence, whether sought or unsought, by the military-industrial complex. The potential for the disastrous rise of misplaced power exists and will persist.

We must never let the weight of this combination endanger our liberties or democratic processes. We should take nothing for granted. Only an alert and knowledgeable citizenry can compel the proper meshing of the huge industrial and military machinery of defense with our peaceful methods and goals, so that security and liberty may prosper together.

—*Dwight D. Eisenhower, final address to the nation, January 17, 1961.*

---

trial complex, President Eisenhower was referring to the connection between the official military organization and the economic interests which supply the material for the military forces. The military-industrial complex involves:

1. *The Armed Forces*
2. *The Department of Defense, the executive branch responsible for administering military affairs*
3. *Congress*
4. *Major firms involved in supplying the military.*

The military point of view is likely to be stressed in Congress by congressmen who are themselves military men. Quite recently about 75 congressmen held commissions in the Armed Forces. Among the more prominent recent members with high military commissions have been Senator Barry Goldwater and Senator Strom Thurmond, both holding the rank of general.

Similarly there is a close relationship between the armed forces and the industries that supply them. These industries, which are continually interested in securing military contracts, make a practice of employing retired military men who may have helpful connec-

tions. In about 1960 General Dynamics, one of the major firms supplying the military, had on its payroll 27 retired generals and admirals. This firm totaled 186 military retirees, including a 4-star general, five brigadier generals, one vice-admiral, and nineteen rear admirals. General Dynamics paid its retirees an average of $770 monthly in addition to their military pensions. Companies which held 80 percent of all military contracts employed a total of 261 generals and admirals and altogether 485 retirees above the rank of army colonel.

Not all relations between the military and its suppliers are informal. Senator William Proxmire, formally chairman of the Congressional Joint Economic Committee, reveals that the highest echelons of the Department of Defense meet four times a year with the twenty-one members of the Industry Advisory Council "to discuss mutual problems and draft the nation's defense future."

There are other dramatic illustrations of the close relationship among the different components of the military-industrial complex. A few years ago, a major airplane firm, which had $800 million in military contracts, flew 27 of the highest military brass to the Bahamian Island of Eleuthera. Within thirty days these officers were sched-

Five nose cones for Jupiter missiles at the Army fabrication shop in Huntsville, Alabama.

uled to appear before a congressional committee to testify in support of contracts which contained large amounts for the airplane company which was their host. The group of vacationers included the chairman of the Joint Chiefs of Staff.

According to a congressional investigating committee, over a period of years, the Army, Navy, and Air Force erected millions of dollars' worth of installations on land which were owned, not by them, but by some of their favored contractors. The operation came out in the open when the question arose of selling the installations. The only possible buyers were the owners of the land, who were in a position to dictate the price.

In 1959 Senator Paul Douglas charged that in April and May of that year, the Air Force had flown 1917 influential businessmen, local officials, and community leaders to an air show at Nellis Air Force Base near Las Vegas "to help build up a body of permanent lobbyists for the Air Force and its appropriations." The total flying time was 2338 flying hours, involving 177 military planes at a total cost of $626,000.

Two results of collusion between the military and its suppliers are cost overruns (actual charged costs beyond cost estimates) and supply surpluses (delivery of more items than originally authorized). Says Proxmire,

The disgraceful fact is that neither the contractors nor the Pentagon tell the truth about the cost of the weapons. They deliberately lie about the cost. They deceive Congress. They deceive the public. They purposely underestimate the costs of these weapons systems in order to get them established and to get Congress and the country committed to them.

What is most appalling is the uncritical way in which cost overruns and supply surpluses are accepted by the Pentagon. They treat a $2 billion overrun as if it were small change.[4]

The direction in which the military-industrial complex may be moving was indicated near the end of World War II by Charles E. Wilson of General Elec-

4. William Proxmire, *Report from Wasteland,* New York, Praeger, 1970, p. 7.

tric Company, a high official in the Roosevelt Administration, when he called for "a permanent war economy once and for all, a continuing program and not the creature of an emergency." "It must," said Wilson, "be initiated and administered by the executive branch—by the President as Commander-in-Chief and by the War and Navy Departments. The role of Congress is limited to voting the needed funds. Industry's role in the program is to respond and cooperate in the execution of the part allotted to it." Each large corporation would be expected to have a liaison man with the Armed Forces.

About this time Congressman Carl Vinson stated a typical military view of where power in a permanent war economy should rest. Presidential decisions on armaments and the military budget should be disregarded, said Vinson, because they are "not the military view; . . . our top source for military judgment is the Joint Chiefs of Staff. And as between the Bureau of the Budget and the Joint Chiefs of Staff, I will place my confidence in the latter, in regard to what the national defense needs are." Later the military gained increasing influence over political policy, and the executive gained over the legislative branch.

Wilson's call for a permanent war economy was only a symptom of what was to be a running clash between civilian and military authorities. The 1945 atomic bomb was dropped on Hiroshima and Nagasaki after the military had succeeded in persuading President Truman to override the recommendation of scientists, made in the Frank Report, that a demonstration bomb in an uninhabited area be substituted for demolition of real cities and people. At the end of the war, Donald Nelson, himself a big businessman and head of the War Production Board, was engaged in a bitter fight with the big industries and the military when he tried to cut back to peacetime productions, which would have been disadvantageous to big producers. In the mid-1940s, the Army became the largest single advertiser in the country in an effort to "sell" a permanent draft and was charged by a congressional committee with misappropriation of public funds for a propaganda campaign. Another point of conflict was ratification of the nuclear test ban, which succeeded only after intense military opposition and falsification of scientific test data by the Atomic Energy Commission. In 1960 the Eisenhower Administration was charged by the Air Force with having allowed a missile gap to arise to the advantage of Russia. After this story had been used by the Democrats in the 1960 presidential election of John F. Kennedy against Republican Vice-President Nixon, it turned out that the only missile gap was in favor of the United States. During the Kennedy Administration there was a widespread campaign for extensive fallout shelters against nuclear attack. One eastern governor, Robert Meyner, described the shelter proposal as "a tragic hoax." Many responsible people agreed with him. President Kennedy himself, however, suggested as good reading matter a *Life* magazine article which claimed that an adequate shelter program might save 97 percent of the population. During the administration of Lyndon B. Johnson, there was almost a running battle between the armed forces and Secretary of Defense Robert McNamara, some of whose cutbacks of military projects brought violent opposition not only from the military forces, but from local areas where jobs were lost in plants producing military supplies. In the famous Bay of Tonkin Resolution of 1964, Congress virtually gave President Johnson power to declare war in Vietnam. Johnson's assumption of power was continued by President Nixon, who in 1970 extended the Indo-China war by executive order, over strong congressional opposition.

Another important dimension of the military-industrial complex is education. A considerable part of the work of the military is done in colleges and universities, and in return a substantial portion of the budget of higher formal education is paid by the Defense Department and other war-related government agencies. In 1968 Massachusetts Institute of Technology and Johns Hopkins University had centers for the design of missiles. One-half of the MIT budget and three-fourths of the budget of Johns Hopkins were derived from defense laboratories. Cornell University was developing bombs; the University of Michigan was doing work in photographic reconnaissance and counterinsurgency; the University of Pennsylvania and fifty other universities were engaged in research on chemical, biological, and germ warfare; the University of California at Davis was researching the kinds of methods of defoliating trees which were used in Vietnam; the University of Pittsburgh's Washington center was studying how to sow river and beach mines in 1967. The author's own small university, the University of Miami, without a major graduate school, received about $3 million worth of military contracts. In 1966 the first fifteen universities benefiting from Defense Department money ran from MIT, with $35 million, to Chicago, Syracuse, and Brown Universities, with about $5 million each. In 1967, after student protests, many universities renounced classified research for the military. The president of Princeton at this time announced his position against secret research, while armed guards were patrolling a government financed center for breaking codes.

How the educational system is drawn into the military is described concretely, if caustically, by Senator Proxmire:

The state of Massachusetts, with MIT and a bevy of nonprofit "think tanks," got a third of all contracts going to educational institutions and 15 percent of the Pentagon awards to nonprofit institutions. There, the neoacademics who write for the research organizations located along the Boston bypass have the best of all possible worlds. By settling in Concord or Lexington, they can pretend to be proper Bostonians, avoid the problems of the inner city, and enjoy the luxury of living on Pentagon subsidies. (Occasionally, they bite the hand that feeds them by protesting the establishment of a local ABM site when the reality of the work they do impinges too closely on their personal lives.)[5]

It may be added that Proxmire is a former Harvard professor. Education is supposed to depend upon the impartiality and objectivity of teachers. Institutions that receive large military subsidies are likely to deny that the educational processes are influenced. Of this claim James Ridgeway has said in a book on the business and military relationship of universities, "There is no such thing as dispassionate knowledge that can be requisitioned on demand to serve the interests of entrenched groups like the military. It is too late for the myth. The universities were bought by the Pentagon long ago."

This discussion has, in fact, underestimated the scope of the military-industrial complex. The term, says Proxmire, is itself inadequate.

The complex has more tentacles than an octopus. Its dimensions are almost infinite. It is a military-industrial-bureaucratic-trade association-labor-union-technical-academic-service-club-political complex whose pervasiveness touches nearly every citizen.[6]

About one-sixth or one-seventh of American families, he says, depend directly upon the complex for a livelihood.

This vast complex, says one economist, has "eliminated a large part of the distinction between public activity and private enterprise." Seymour Mel-

5. *Ibid.,* p. 9.
6. *Ibid.,* p. 27.

man, in a book called *Pentagon Capitalism,* maintains that the whole military-industrial establishment is like a vast firm in which the Department of Defense serves as central management and its "free enterprise" suppliers as branches under Pentagon control. Melman believes that this centralized military "state capitalism" originated in 1960 when Secretary McNamara applied the managerial techniques he had developed at Ford Motor Company to organize the whole system of military procurement. Although part of McNamara's interest was in expanding civilian power in his department against that of the military, the main result, says Melman, was to place under more effective central coordination a significant part of the whole economy. This state management, says Melman, has consistently pursued policies which would increase its own power, even when they were in some cases unprofitable for major suppliers, of little or no military value, or damaging to the whole economy. We have here the same kind of problem of locating centers of power which we studied in Chapter nine. Melman feels that the Department of Defense runs the show. Others would believe that Pentagon officials are themselves the pawns of major suppliers or of other powerful segments of the complex.

The political power of the military lies directly to a large extent in the number of people (including educators) who make their living from supplying material for the military forces. In a broader sense it lies indirectly in the importance of military spending in furnishing the purchasing power necessary to keep a mature economy going. The abolition of war will therefore require that we eliminate or greatly reduce this dependence upon war production.

Two historic examples will illustrate the way in which war has historically been related to the economy and also offer some suggestions as to the possibility of reconversion. At the end of the Korean War, between 1953 and 1960, for example, military expenditures in the United States dropped 30 percent, mostly in the one year of 1954. At the time of the first cutback, the average rate of industrial growth dropped two-thirds. Unemployment rose 40 percent over the years 1948 to 1953.

Another historic cutback was in 1945 to 1946, at the end of World War II. At that time the military budget was reduced by $120 billion, and a large number of soldiers were demobilized and thus added to those seeking jobs. This military cutback was handled without any severe recession or increase in unemployment. In 1960 economist Kenneth Boulding (who does not accept the idea that prosperity requires war spending) wrote that "in one year (1945–1946) we transferred an absolute amount of manpower and resources from war to civilian employments, more than twice as much as would be involved in total and complete disarmament at present."

Why the difference in the two situations? During World War II, military goods had been substituted to a large extent for consumer goods—cars, refrigerators, washing machines, and so on. The government had borrowed from citizens to finance the war. With demobilization consumers began to desire the goods they had sacrificed for so long and to cash in their war bonds to buy them. This "deferred demand" enabled the economy to shift back from a military to civilian basis. At the end of the Korean War, the government handicapped reconversion by cutting its own nonmilitary spending and maintaining high taxes which took purchasing power out of the pockets of civilians.

The conclusion that we can begin to draw from these two examples of reconversion is that the militarized nations of the world can prepare domestically for peace only if they can find nonmilitary channels into which to divert the resources, money, and human energy which have heretofore been devoted to preparation for war.

This can be done in part, as in 1946 to 1947, by substituting consumer goods for military goods in the output of firms which have been supplying the military. An example is the conversion of aircraft fabrication plants into plants producing prefabricated panel homes. It can be done in part by national efforts to accomplish large common objectives which have not been adequately met in peace or war. For such purposes California contracted Aerojet in the 1960s "to control all forms of waste including air and water pollution." At the same time the state tried to secure bids for a state-wide system of transportation and for the treatment of criminals and the mentally ill. The United States, for example, has a long way to go to provide adequate income and housing for all its citizens, adequate schooling for all children and young people, adequate recreational facilities for a population with increasing leisure time, highways capable of handling the flood of modern automobile traffic, rapid urban transportation which might make much travel by car unnecessary, and adequate control of air and water pollution. A national program to accomplish these objectives might offset a large cutback in military expenditures. In the middle 1960s, a distinguished group of economists and other citizens advanced a "freedom budget" with detailed annual estimates which would have eliminated gross poverty and major deficiencies in schooling, housing, and medical care by 1975 (see p. 292). It would have done so through a mixture of public investment and of private investment subsidized by public funds.

As part of a long-range reconversion program, the federal government might set up a priority list of public needs to which funds now spent for military purposes could be switched. Any adequate reconversion program would need not only substitute civilian for military spending in the economy as a whole, but also plan to meet the needs of specific local areas now dependent on military contracts. In places like Los Angeles, Seattle, San Diego, Wichita, and Huntsville, Alabama (the rocket capital of the world), specific new industries would have to be brought in as military production was phased out. Workers now in war industries would have to be retrained for new productive skills in their present communities and provided with transportation to new jobs, if necessary.

All this would mean that planning would have to go on from economy-wide reconversion plans proposed, perhaps, by the President's Council of Economic Advisors down to specific community projects initiated by volunteer or public reconversion bodies.

The human aspect of conversion to a peace economy was concisely stated by Dwight D. Eisenhower during his presidency: "Every gun that is made, every rocket fired, signifies in the final sense a theft from those who are hungry and are not fed, those who are cold and not clothed." To the direct destruction wrought by war, we must add the human goods and services that are unavailable because the resources which might have produced them have gone for military purposes. Reconversion of military economies would not only lessen the threat of international violence, but also make it possible to begin satisfying basic human needs which are still demanding to be met on a mass scale.

THE ROLE OF THE INDIVIDUAL

Another alternative to war lies in the possibility that people may personally refuse to fight. In addition to political and economic action by governments there is the question: Suppose they gave a war and nobody came? When service is voluntary, people may simply refuse to volunteer or discourage others from enlisting. In modern national states, whose armies are typically raised by conscription, resistance typically takes the form of draft refusal. Let us look at the background for this in the United States.

Paul Goodman once startled a middle-class temple audience by announcing, "Of course you know that this country was settled by draft dodgers." He was referring to the fact that the Pilgrims, who originally fled religious persecution in England, finally crossed the Atlantic to keep their young men from military service in Holland. A large number of nineteenth-century immigrants also came to escape military conscription in Europe.

At the beginning of the American republic, a number of states used conscription to raise armies to fight Indians and, indeed, the British. But a national conscription program favored by George Washington was rejected. At the time of the War of 1812, perhaps inspired by Napoleon's conscript armies, Congress debated a conscription proposal, which met with fiery opposition by Daniel Webster and other congressmen.

In the Civil War in 1862, Congress required the states to draft men into service, and the next year, adopted a nationwide conscription program. The success of Prussian conscript armies in the Franco-Prussian War of 1870 led to the adoption of conscription by a number of countries. One of these was the United States, which in 1917 rejected volunteering as a method of raising troops for World War I and

adopted a Prussian-type draft. This was repeated for the first time in peacetime in 1940, shortly before World War II. Since that time military conscription has been an integral part of the American scene.

There have always been some Americans who have refused military service. Until the Civil War, these were primarily religious objectors. In colonial days Quakers and Mennonites would sometimes stand aside and repair the breastworks of the forts while their neighbors fought off the Indians. As we shall see, there have been conscientious objectors in the Civil War and both world wars. In the Civil War, Quakers and members of other traditionally pacifist religious groups were placed in noncombatant service. But war refusal had a wider scope than this. When conscription by the states was ordered in 1862, there was violent resistance in Illinois, Indiana, and Ohio. In Milwaukee the draft could be enforced only at gunpoint, and troops were needed elsewhere in Wisconsin. As a result of this resistance, Lincoln suspended habeas corpus for draft resisters. Thirteen thousand people were imprisoned for refusing service or encouraging others to refuse.

When the national government began to draft in 1863, resistance became more severe. In one Ohio town,

429 infantrymen fired on draftees. Enrollers were killed and draft records destroyed in Illinois and Indiana. In Olney, Illinois, 500 draftees laid seige to the town and threatened to burn it if draft records were not released. Congressman Clement L. Vallandingham of Ohio was arrested for making speeches urging draft refusal, denied habeas corpus, and imprisoned. The Supreme Court refused to review the case. In New York City, six regiments of soldiers tried to rescue the city from mob rule for three days. It is estimated that about 1200 people were killed and $5 million worth of property destroyed. The draft riots spread to nearly every major city in the North. Only with the use of troops could the draft proceed. The final result was that, of over 2 million men in the Union army, only 51,516 were draftees.

World War I conscription was more successful. Altogether 2.7 million men were drafted. Again, conscientious objectors were assigned to noncombatant service if they belonged to traditional "peace" churches. The War Department was more lenient than Congress, granting exemption to some objectors with political or personal reasons.

Under the 1940 draft, the basis for objection was broadened to include all objectors "by reason of religious training and belief," regardless of church membership. Conscientious objectors could also reject noncombatant service and be assigned to alternative "work of national importance" in old conservation camps and elsewhere.

Since World War II, the range of protest against war has widened.

(1) Court decisions have broadened the basis for conscientious objection. In 1965 in *U.S.* v. *Seeger,* the United States Supreme Court held that traditional religious belief is not necessary. "A sincere and meaningful belief which occupies in the life of its possessor a place parallel to that filled by the God of those admittedly qualifying for the exemption comes within the statutory definition." The Court's 1970 Walsh decision further legalized objection on grounds of purely personal beliefs, apart from formal religious tradition.

(2) After about 1960 war resistance was joined with the civil rights and other protest movements. A significant event was Martin Luther King's break with his government's war policy and his call to young men to become conscientious objectors. Black power leader Stokeley Carmichael also urged blacks to resist the draft.

(3) In the 1960s draft counseling, originally established by agencies like the American Friends (Quaker) Service Committee to acquaint conscientious objectors with their legal rights, was extended to showing all men of draft age how to find all legal ways out of the draft.

(4) Protest by young men also shifted from individual objection legit-

imized by government to direct draft resistance by either legal or illegal means: draft card destruction, emigration to Canada and Sweden, choice of jail rather than induction. In Union Square in New York City in November 1965, 2000 demonstrators watched four men burn their draft cards. In December 1966 there was a "We Won't Go" conference in Chicago. In October a year later, 320 writers, artists, and educators joined in "A Call to Resist Illegitimate Authority." Dr. Benjamin Spock, the Rev. William Sloane Coffin, and others were brought to trial. In the same year nine draftees in Catonsville, Maryland, and fourteen in Milwaukee burned draft records. In 1970 the war resistance movement became a clear part of the battle of generations in the nationwide wave of campus protests following President Nixon's extension of the Indo-China war to Cambodia, and the killing of students by the National Guard at Kent State University. Another facet of the widened protest was resistance within the armed forces. Examples were the Fort Hood Three, who in June 1966 were transferred to noncombatant service after refusing to go to Vietnam, and Corporal Howard Levy, who in March 1967 was sentenced by court martial for refusing to teach medicine to Green Beret troops.

(5) Another development was the shift from the opposition to any war required by the conscientious objector clause of the draft act, in the direction of objection to a particular war. Such selective objection is illustrated by the 1967 case of David Henry Mitchell, who asked conscientious objector status on the ground that the 1945 Treaty of London, signed by the United States and other World War II allies, made aggressive war a crime and bound all individuals to refuse to participate. (His request was denied by the Supreme Court on the ground that a conscientious objector must object to war "in any form, 'aggressive' or not.") The dilemma of the selective objector is illustrated in the accompanying excerpt from the conscientious objector appeal of a young sculptor who found himself opposed to the Vietnam War and yet unable to be a complete pacifist.

The Sherman case illustrates another recent trend, which in a way reverses the others: from angry individualistic resistance to concern with nonviolence as a way of life and a positive method of social change.

The pacifism which Sherman would have liked to accept not only rejects a particular war that is held to be worse than others, but rejects all wars. This is part of a general rejection of killing and violence as a way of achieving one's goals. The pacifist rejects violence in part because he believes, like Sherman, that to kill or damage people is wrong. He also rejects violence because he considers it an ineffective way to defend worthwhile values or bring about needed change. Nonviolence is more than a negation, more than a rejection. It is an affirmation of a positive method which the nonviolentist believes to be more in keeping with the society based on love and trust

which he wants to build. Thus Mahatma Gandhi, the great Indian practitioner of nonviolence, not only did *not* shoot, bomb, or napalm his enemies, but he tried to confront them everywhere with *satyagraha* (truth force), to meet violence with positive respect and love.

There have been many pacifists without religious affiliation, but nonviolence arises out of values which have been most strongly expressed in religious traditions. Gandhi's programs against the British in South Africa and India had their background in the Hindu doctrine of *ahimsa* (nonviolence). In Chinese Taoist doctrines of Lao-tze: "He who would assist a lord of men in harmony with the Tao, will not assert his mastery in the Kingdom by force of arms. . . . In the sequence of great armies there are bound to be bad years." Isaiah warned the Jews, "Woe to them that . . . stay on horses and trust in chariots, because they are many, and in horsemen, because they are very strong." The medieval rabbi, Isaac Iuria, prayed especially every night for those who had most harmed him. "Love your enemies," said Jesus. "Do good to them that hate you, and despitefully use you and persecute you." The early Christians refused military service as contrary to their religion. Since that

time there have been in the Western world a number of communal movements with a nonviolent philosophy. We saw earlier that one important part of the anarchist movement has been nonviolent. Of this tradition the most influential recent document has been Thoreau's essay, "Civil Disobedience."

Nonviolence is both external action and inner preparation. Among the most important external methods are civil disobedience—the deliberate violation of laws judged to be injust or immoral; the withdrawal of labor power through strike, including the general strike; the withdrawal of buying power through the boycott; and the dramatization of struggle through such symbolic acts as fasting.

No less important is inner preparation. If they are to rely on the power of truth and love, nonviolentists wish first to be sure that truth and love will be in them. Thus they may fast, meditate, and pray for self-purification. They may attempt deliberately to rid themselves of anger, hatred, and bitterness. They will discipline themselves as a group so that unintended violence may not break forth.

These statements are generalizations from the experience of those people who have most dramatically and effectively employed nonviolence

I am not a pacifist. I wish I was. I am a product of a society not geared to this type of thinking. I am not exceptional in this case. I would like to think that it is easier and not particularly courageous to do the right thing. Our society covertly teaches us differently. Intimidation and distrust, whether I like it or not, have colored my reactions to situations. The pacifists, I believe, through their achievement of casting off our society's conditionings, are the hope of ever achieving some sort of peace and love between men.

I am trying to be human. My strength is not, as such, to be completely and lovingly nonviolent. But I am trying to fight an unfortunate human trait of character which I know is wrong. Violence and killing, for any reason, cannot be right. I am trying to clean myself bit by bit.

—Benjamin Sherman, quoted in Lillian Schlissel, ed., Conscience in America, New York, Dutton, 1968, pp. 440–441.

---

and whose experience and example have been particularly appealing to young people in their protest activity: Gandhi, whose defeat of British power contradicts Fanon's thesis that violence is necessary for the liberation of colonial peoples; King, whose civil rights movement achieved substantial results for America's black "internal colony"; Chavez, who has been devoted to nonviolence in promoting the cause of Mexican-Americans; Danilo Dolce, who has rejected violence in the struggle of oppressed Sicilian peasants.

The appeal of nonviolence lies, we have seen, in the hope that it can do two things which it is often believed can be done only by violent methods: defend national territories and liberate dispossessed people. In this light it is interesting to tabulate some of the things nonviolence has accomplished.

In A.D. 259 workers in Rome (plebs), denied political representation and forced into military service, brought about reform by seceding en masse and establishing a separate plebian city.

In the reign of the Roman emperor Caligula (37–41), a lie-down for forty days before the temple at Jerusalem by Jews who left their farms forced removal of a statue of the emperor from the sanctuary.

A consistent policy of nonviolence by the Quaker colonial government of Pennsylvania kept peace with the Indians for about seventy years.

In 1849 to 1867, a broad program of refusing to pay taxes and to accept public offices, and other forces of non-cooperation without the use of arms, liberated Hungary from rule by Austria and restored a constitution and self-government.

In 1920 the Kapp putsch, a dictatorial counterrevolution against the social democratic Weimar government in Germany, was defeated by a general walkout of workers, "perhaps the most complete political general strike in a modern industrial country. German economy was brought to a standstill."

During the Nazi occupation of Norway in World War II, mass refusal by teachers to propagandize for nazism in the schools resulted in revocation of the order and reinstatement of teachers who were sent to a concentration camp for disobedience.

Hunger strikes by conscientious objectors in American prisons during World War II resulted in significant changes in administration of the federal prison system.

In 1953 a nonviolent strike in the Vorkuta forced-labor camp in the Soviet Union resulted in concessions which improved camp conditions.

Extended reports of some of these cases, and others, appear in Milford Q.

Sibley's *The Quiet Battle.* Those who wish to evaluate nonviolence seriously as an alternative to war and violent social change will find Sibley's book well worth studying. How does nonviolence work in cases like those we have related? Let us analyze the forces it may have set in motion.

Economic pressure. Any oppressive system, whether imposed from within or by an outside invader, must supply the economic needs of oppressor and oppressed alike. Refusal of labor power through a strike or refusal of buying power through a boycott weakens the entire system by making it difficult or impossible to carry on its economic functions.

Undermining of legitimacy. We have seen that every political system, no matter how violent and oppressive, exists in a sense only "by the consent of the governed." This is true both of native tyranny and foreign conquest. The point is well put in the excerpted essay by the nineteenth-century French writer La Boétie. The dynamics of the situation were dramatically described by Shelley in his poem "The Mask of Anarchy." If the large majority of people become firmly convinced that the ruling group lacks legitimacy, they can no longer be ruled by it. If tyranny is to survive, it is crucially important that the ruling group itself and its army or police continue to believe in the legitimacy of the regime. The oppressed majority, the oppressing minority, and the armed users of violence who support them may all lack total faith in the rightness of the unjust regime to begin with. Determined nonviolent resistance may serve to catalyze their doubts and perhaps bring down the system.

Strategy of surprise. In the world we know, important contests are usually settled by one or another form of violence. Oppressors and their armies and police are therefore usually well prepared to meet organized violence. Protest which uses a method for which they have not prepared and to which they are unaccustomed may act, as one writer has expressed it, as a kind of moral jiujitsu which throws the oppressive forces off their guard and uses the momentum of their own violence against them. An example is the British soldier who after repeatedly beating Indian Sikhs who had refused either to resist or to submit, threw up his hands and complained, "How can you go on hitting a blighter when he doesn't hit back?"

The moral force of love. When nonviolence is used, not as a very tricky and perhaps useful gimmick, but from moral conviction, the message conveyed is that the nonviolentist values his enemy even more than he desires justice for himself, and thus will not hurt or kill him. He is saying that he believes in his cause so strongly that he will not submit and still will bear violence himself rather than administer

---

Who could believe reports of what goes on every day among the inhabitants of some countries, who could really believe that one man alone may mistreat a hundred thousand and deprive them of their liberty? Who would credit such a report if he merely heard it, without being present to witness the event? Obviously there is no need of fighting to overcome this single tyrant, for he is automatically defeated if the country refuses consent to its own enslavement: it is not necessary to deprive him of anything, but simply to give him nothing; there is no need that the country make an effort to do anything for itself provided it does nothing against itself. It is therefore the inhabitants themselves who permit, or, rather, bring about, their own subjection, since by ceasing to submit they would put an end to their servitude. A people enslaves itself, cuts its own throat, when, having a choice between being vassals and being free men, it deserts its liberties and takes on the yoke, gives consent to its own misery, or, rather, apparently welcomes it. If it cost the people anything to recover its freedom, I should not urge action to this end, although there is nothing a human should hold more dear than the restoration of his own natural right, to change himself from a beast of burden back to a man, so to speak. I do not demand of him so much boldness; let him prefer the doubtful security of living wretchedly to the uncertain hope of living as he pleases.

—*Etienne de la Boétie, quoted in Mulford Q. Sibley, ed.,* The Quiet Battle, *Boston, Beacon, 1963, p. 19.*

*Rise like Lions after slumber
In unvanquishable number—
Shake your chains to earth like dew
Which in sleep had fallen on you—
Ye are many—they are few.*

—*Percy Shelley, "The Mask of Anarchy," quoted in Mulford Q. Sibley, ed.,* The Quiet Battle, *Boston, Beacon, 1963, p. 24.*

---

it. The result may be to weigh the whole system he is opposing upon a moral balance scale against the kind of spirit he is showing. Its presence in all religious systems shows that the ethic of love has deep roots in human nature in various cultures (see Chapter five). Nonviolence may thus win the contest by converting the oppressive violentist into acting according to his own best nature.

The whole matter of war resistance and nonviolence raises an important final question: Why do masses of people who have doubts about the systems under which they live not follow the suggestion of La Boétie and Shelley? Why do they instead commit violence for these systems when they are called upon? Why can almost any national state, no matter what its cause, count upon its people to go to war, right or wrong, at their nation's call? One obvious reason is that cultural brainwashing (see Chapter five) makes them incapable of offering effec-

tive resistance to the important decisions of the power structure when there is a crisis. (Such books as Erich Fromm's *Escape from Freedom* and Wilhelm Reich's *The Mass Psychology of Fascism* will suggest how and why this is so.) Can the reason also lie in the fact that, psychologically, people need to commit violence? Does war serve a deep cultural (or perhaps human) need which our study of social science can help us to understand?

War is an expression of hostilities on the international level. We cannot expect to eliminate war, therefore, without creating the kind of world which will reduce mass impulses toward violence. It is not true, says one noted sociologist, Talcott Parsons of Harvard University, that by knowing the amount of personal frustration and hostility among the people of a nation, one can predict the likelihood that this nation will go to war. War is the outcome of conflicts between complex political institutions, not just a spontaneous

*Aggression in the Western world tends to focus on antagonisms
between solidary groups. . . . There are patent reasons why
nationalism should be the most important and serious focus of
these tendencies. Each [nation-state] tends to have a deep-seated
presumption of its own superiority and a corresponding resentment
against any other's corresponding presumption. Each at the same
time tends to feel that it has been unfairly treated in the past and
is ready on the slightest provocation to assume that the others
are ready to plot new outrages in the immediate future. . . . In
short, the "jungle philosophy"—which corresponds to a larger
element in the real sentiments of all of us than can readily be
admitted, even to ourselves—tends to be projected onto the
relations of nation-states at precisely the point where, under the
technological and organizational situation of the modern world,
it can do the most harm.*

—Talcott Parsons, "Certain Primary Sources and Patterns of Aggression
in the Western World," Psychiatry, 10 (1947).

---

outburst of violence. Yet war making in a society does have some relationship to the amount of frustration, hostility, and violence generated within that society. There can be little doubt that World War II channeled for many Germans an accumulation of frustrations which had piled up after World War I and during the Great Depression. There is evidence, the same sociologist suggests, that there exists in modern nations a reservoir of violence which may, on occasion, be tapped for almost any destructive purpose. Such a reservoir in the United States is suggested by the following titles of articles found in one week's supply of magazines at a small-town bus station.

> *Lust Torture of the Captive Girl*
> *Men, I Hate Their Guts*
> *The Most Sadistic Woman in the World*
> *Evil in My House: My Father Assaulted Me*
> *My Wife Bore a Madman's Baby*
> *Massacre in Your Home: You May Have a Murderer Under Your Roof*
> *I Want a Woman to Kill*
> *You'll Never See Your Wife Alive Again*
> *So Cute, So Nude, So Dead*

> *Nude Cargo: Shipped, Two Female Bodies*
> *A Bay State Chiller: Burn Him, Burn Him*
> *A Kiss Before Murder*

Violence of this kind is free floating in the sense that it can potentially be directed against almost any target. Talcott Parsons has said that the hostilities generated by modern societies in their members tend to be taken out in intergroup antagonisms, such as anti-Semitism, antilabor sentiments, anti-Negro feelings, anti-Catholic hostility, and hatred of foreigners, but especially in nationalistic hostility toward other countries. The studies of the authoritarian personality have shown just this same combination of inner frustration with hostility toward disapproved groups (see page 426 of this chapter). The accompanying excerpt from Parsons resembles the conclusions of these studies.

These relationships suggest that elimination of nationalistic warfare requires elimination or reduction of the inner hostilities which people displace into international violence. This requires that we understand the forces which generate hostility and violence

*The . . . truth is . . . that men are not gentle, friendly creatures
wishing for love, who simply defend themselves if they are
attacked, but that a powerful measure of desire for aggression
has to be reckoned as part of their instinctual endowment.*

—Sigmund Freud, Civilization and Its Discontents, *trans. Joan Riviere,
New York, Jonathan Cape, 1930, p. 85.*

*On the level of history all men are enemies. It is even probably true
that they are . . . beasts of prey. They are in fact worse than
beasts of prey, because they make spiritual and therefore demonic
pretensions for the enterprises by which they satisfy their lusts.*

—Reinhold Niebuhr, "Is Social Conflict Inevitable?" *Scribner's Magazine
(September 1935), p. 168.*

in society. This exploration could well take us back over all the materials of this book.

"From whence come wars and fightings among you?" once asked James, the brother of Jesus. "Come they not hence, even of your lusts that war in your members? Ye lust, and have not, ye kill, and desire to have and cannot obtain, ye fight and war, yet ye have not. . . . " Why do "lusts" war in our members? To James's question, there are two main answers, one biological and the other sociological. The first attributes hostility and violence to the inborn nature of man; the second explains them in terms of the frustrations imposed by society.

The classic example of the first explanation is the answer offered by Thomas Hobbes, who imagined that in a state of nature, man would be a self-centered, greedy creature living in "continual fear and danger of violent death," and that under such conditions we would find "the life of man solitary, poor, nasty, brutish, and short." Two related statements are those of Freud and the modern theologian Reinhold Niebuhr, both of whom find people by nature at war with one another.

Violence among people would be attributed to inborn nature by two contemporary students of the subject, Konrad Lorenz, author of *On Aggression,* who regards aggressive fighting behavior as an expression of a drive natural in animals, and Robery Ardrey, who uses archaeological evidence to argue in *African Genesis* that the really distinctive feature about man is that he makes and uses weapons.

A review of our discussion of war and aggression in Chapter five would be helpful at this point.

Exploration of the sociological view of mass violence could lead us back to any of the revolutions of our time discussed in Chapter one. A number of the more prominent sources of frustration are suggested by the excerpts on pages 445 and 446.

Adam Smith and Karl Marx both describe destructive aspects of the industrial division of labor.

The famous theologian, Paul Tillich, describes the effects upon many people of living in a society where their destiny is not in their own hands.

Erich Fromm speaks of the frustration of being forced to market oneself as a commodity.

The Negro novelist, Richard Wright, tells first of the frustration of being a Negro in a white-dominated society, and secondly of the social frustrations which lead the white majority to violence against minorities.

Wilhelm Reich relates the "sadistic destructiveness" of human beings as we know them to the sexual repression which has long characterized our society.

By contrast with the biological view of aggressive violence (represented, for example, by Freud's theory of the death instinct), the sociological interpretation would agree more with psydualist and physiological psychologist Jules Masserman that "hostilities among human beings . . . spring from the frustrations and the anxiety-ridden institutions of their persistently barbaric culture—not as Sigmund Freud believed, from an inborn suicidal 'death instinct.' "

If we believe with Hobbes and Freud that social (including international) violence originates chiefly in inborn human nature, if we would eliminate the roots of war we must change biology. If we agree with Masserman, we must change social institutions.

The man whose whole life is spent performing a few simple operations . . . generally becomes as stupid and ignorant as it is possible for a human creature to become. . . . But in every improved and civilized society this is the state into which the laboring poor . . . must necessarily fall, unless government takes some pains to prevent it.

—*Adam Smith,* An Inquiry Into the Nature and Causes of the Wealth of Nations, *ed. Robert Hutchins, Chicago, Encyclopaedia Britannica, 1952, pp. 340, 341.*

To subdivide a man is to execute him, if he deserves the sentence, to assassinate him if he does not. . . . The subdivision of labor is the assassination of a people.

—*Karl Marx,* Das Kapital, *Chicago, Charles H. Kerr & Co., 1921, vol. 1, p. 399.*

If human beings feel that their destiny is taken out of their hands, that an objective process on which they have no influence throws them on the street today, draws them into a big machine as parts and tools tomorrow, and will drive them into a war of extinction the day after tomorrow, then no other result than utter hopelessness can be expected.

—*Paul Tillich,* The Protestant Era, *trans. J. L. Adams, Chicago, University of Chicago Press, 1948, p. 263.*

Only in exceptional cases is success predominantly the result of skill and of certain other human qualities like honesty, decency and integrity. . . . Success depends largely on how well a person sells himself on the market, how well he gets his personality across, how nice a "package" he is. . . . A person is not concerned with his life and happiness, but with becoming salable. . . . His feeling of identity . . . is constituted by the sum total of roles one can play: "I am as you desire me."

—*Erich Fromm,* Man for Himself, *New York, Holt, Rinehart and Winston, 1947, pp. 69–70.*

The American Negro has come as near being the victim of a complete rejection as our society has been able to work out, for the dehumanized image of the Negro which white Americans carry in their minds, the anti-Negro epithets continuously on their lips, exclude the contemporary Negro as truly as though he were kept in a steel prison, and doom even those Negroes who are as yet unborn.

It is distinctly possible to know, before it happens, that certain forms of violence will occur. It can be known that a native-born white man, the end product of all our strivings, educated, healthy, apparently mentally normal, having the stability of a wife and family, possessing the security of a good job with high wages, enjoying more freedom than any other country on earth accords its citizens, but devoid of the most elementary satisfactions, will seize upon an adolescent, zoot-suited Mexican and derive deep feelings of pleasure from stomping his hopeless guts out upon the pavements of Los Angeles. But to know that a seemingly normal, ordinary American is capable of such brutality implies making a judgment about the nature and quality of our everyday American experiences which most Americans simply cannot do. For, to admit that our individual experiences are of so low a quality and nature as to preclude the deep, organic satisfactions necessary for civilized, peaceful living, is to condemn the system that provides these experiences.

—*Richard Wright, in Horace Cayton and St. Clair Drake,* Black Metropolis, *New York, Harcourt Brace Jovanovich, 1945, pp. xxvii, xxxiii.*

Sex repression serves the function of keeping humans more easily in a state of submissiveness, just as the castration of stallions and bulls serves that of securing willing beasts of burden. Only the liberation of the natural capacity for love in human beings can master their sadistic destructiveness.

—*Wilhelm Reich,* The Function of the Orgasm, *vol. 1 of* The Discovery of the Orgone, *trans. Theodore P. Wolfe, New York, Orgone Institute Press, 1942, pp. 195, 197.*

Suggestions for further reading

The best known comprehensive history of war as a social institution is A Study of War *by political scientist QUINCY WRIGHT (abridged ed., University of Chicago Press, 1964, paper). An analysis of nationalism by an eminent student of politics is* Nationalism: Its Meaning and History *by HANS KOHN (rev. ed., Van Nostrand Reinhold, 1965, paper). A social psychologist's view is found in LEONARD W. DOOB's* Patriotism and Nationalism: Their Psychological Foundations *(Yale University Press, 1964). For an insider's "no-nonsense" account of how international relations are conducted, see* The Game of Nations *by MILES COPELAND, a former State Department officer and a founder of the CIA (Simon & Schuster, 1969).*

The Warfare State by FRED J. COOK (Crowell Collier and Macmillian, 1962, paper), is the book which opened public controversy over the military-industrial complex. It was followed by The Armed Society: Militarism in Modern America *by TRISTRAM COFFIN (Penguin Pelican, 1964, paper). In 1970 came Report from Wasteland: America's Military Industrial Complex by SENATOR WILLIAM PROXMIRE (Praeger, 1970), and Pentagon Capitalism: The Political Economy of War, by Columbia University industrial engineer SEYMOUR MELMAN (McGraw-Hill, 1970). In 1969 JAMES RIDGEWAY had described the academic segment of the complex in* The Closed Corporation: American Universities in Crisis *(Ballantine, 1969, paper). The concrete human needs to which military spending might be converted are suggested by the 10-year program of private and public investment projected in A "Freedom Budget" for All Americans (rev. ed., A Philip Randolph Inst., 1966).*

A good introductory history of compulsory military service—and resistance to it—in the United States appears in Why the Draft: the Case for a Volunteer Army *(Penguin, Pelican, 1968, paper), by JAMES C. MILLER and others. According to the editors, the first inspiration for this book came from conservative economist Milton Friedman.* Conscience in America: A Documentary History of Conscientious Objection in America, 1757–1967, *edited by LILLIAN SCHLISSEL (Dutton, 1968, paper), is an excellent collection on that subject. In 1952* Conscription of Conscience: The American State and the Conscientious Objector, 1940–47, *by MULFORD Q. SIBLEY and PHILIP JACOB (Johnson Reprint), was designated the outstanding political science book of the year. Later material on war resistance is edited by A. LYND in* We Won't Go: Personal Accounts of War Objectors *(Beacon, 1968, paper). The history of nonviolence is collected by MULFORD Q. SIBLEY in* The Quiet Battle *(Beacon, 1969, paper). The best general work on the theory and practice of nonviolence is* The Power of Non-Violence *by RICHARD B. GREGG (rev. ed., Shocken, 1966, paper). Dramatic accounts of personal nonviolent leadership appear in* My Life with Martin Luther King, Jr. *by CORETTA KING (Harper & Row, 1969) and* Gandhi's Truth *by psychoanalyst and social psychologist ERIK H. ERIKSON (Norton, 1969).*

Chapter fourteen
Totalitarianism and freedom

The economic, political, and social trends of the twentieth century have led many people to wonder about the future of personal freedom. One expression of this concern has been the appearance of "anti-Utopian" novels. By contrast with the earlier Utopias of Thomas More and other writers, which presented an ideal world, these anti-Utopias foresee a nightmare society in which the individual has been swallowed up in the mass.

The first of these gloomy forecasts was *The Iron Heel,* by Jack London, author of the much read nature book, *The Call of the Wild,* and a Marxian Socialist. *The Iron Heel* described a working-class revolution in which socialism was voted into power in the United States. This democratic revolution was crushed by a ruthless counter-revolutionary alliance called the Iron Heel, which kept the American people subject to a brutal dictatorship for 200 years. London's anti-Utopia was in many ways a prediction of later events in Fascist Italy and Nazi Germany.

The next significant anti-Utopian book was *We,* published in 1924 by a Russian poet, novelist, and ship architect, Eugene Zamiatin. The whole world has been organized under a single United State. Everyone has been reduced to a number. All the numbers work on schedule, in unison, without individuality. By ticket, one may have sexual access to a number of the opposite sex, but there are no personal feelings. The United State has sought to make everyone happy by removing

the cause of unhappiness—there is no freedom of any kind. Those who do not adjust disappear quietly into the disintegrating machine. Or they may meet the fate of D-503, who fell in love and even began to develop a soul. He was cured of his fancies by an operation on a "miserable little nervous knot in the lower region of the frontal lobe of the brain."

Brave New World, by Aldous Huxley, takes place in the year 532 A.F. (after Ford). The society is organized on the automobile magnate's principle of mass production. Babies are produced in bottles in decanting laboratories. They are prepared for their high or low statuses in society by control of the amount of oxygen which reaches the foetal brain. After birth they are taken to the social predestination room, where they are perfectly conditioned for their adult life. Art, science, and God have all been abolished, for all these lead people to ask questions and make them unhappy. Minor emotional disturbances are relieved by taking soma, a perfect tranquilizer without hangover. Women's emotional needs are gratified with a pregnancy substitute and a violent passion surrogate. Those who still cannot be happy are exiled to an island populated by other malcontents.

In the mid-1930s, the American novelist Sinclair Lewis published *It Can't Happen Here.* This anti-Utopia was staged in the United States and depicted a Fascist regime brought into being by a demagogue named Berzelius Windrip. The book, written after the rise of Mussolini and Hitler to dictatorial power, was intended to refute the idea that such dictatorship would be impossible in the United States (the message was that it could happen here).

George Orwell's novel, *1984,* depicts the state of the world in that year. It has been completely taken over by three great powers—Russia, the United States, and East Asia. There are three social groups—the Inner Party, the Outer Party, and the Proles (proletarians). The ruling Inner Party is composed of bureaucrats, scientists, professional politicians, publicity experts, sociologists, teachers, trade union organizers, and journalists. The whole society is organized to keep this group in power. A great central figure, Big Brother, is never seen, but his influence is everywhere. The language of Newspeak turns everything into its opposite: "Freedom is Slavery," "Ignorance is Strength," "War is Peace." Everyone is subject at all times to having both his acts and his thoughts watched without his knowledge. "Big Brother is watching you." If one does not continually practice Crimestop, suppression of all dissenting acts or thoughts, he may at any time be liquidated.

These anti-Utopias are clearly not the product of pure imagination. They are an exaggeration of things which are happening in the twentieth century. Do they predict the actual direction in which we are headed? One answer is that it is impossible that all human freedom could be so suppressed. Other people might answer that the anti-Utopias could very easily become reality. A third possible answer might be that we are already living in anti-Utopia and do not know it, that 1984 is not in the future, but already behind us. In this chapter we shall look at some of the important trends which make *Brave New World* and *1984* more than the products of wild imagination.

The problem of individual freedom is posed most sharply in the political dictatorships, where an individual or group rules without machinery for formal check by the people at large.

Edward Everhard, a brawny and brilliant young working-class intellectual, has been invited to the Philomath Club of Berkeley, California, an upper-class cultural club. Here he has damned the upper class as exploiters and predicted their overthrow by workers. Several club members try unsuccessfully to answer him and then a prominent Berkeley industrialist named Wickson takes the floor:

"I have followed the whole discussion with amazement and disgust. I am disgusted with you gentlemen, members of my class. You have believed like foolish little schoolboys. You have been out-generalled and outclassed.

"Believe me the situation is serious. That bear reached out his paws tonight to crush us. He said that there are a million and a half of revolutionists in the United States. That is a fact. He has said that it is their intention to take from us our governments, our palaces, and all our purpled ease. That, also, is a fact. A change, a great change, is coming in society, but hopefully it may not be the change the bear anticipates. The bear has said that he will crush us. What if we crush the Bear?

"We will hunt the bear. We will not reply to the bear in words. Our reply shall be couched in terms of lead. We are in power. Nobody will deny it. By virtue of that power we shall remain in power.

"This, then, is our answer. We have no words to waste on you. When you reach out your vaunted strong hands for our palaces and purpled ease, we will show you what strength is. In war of shell and shrapnel and in whine of machine guns will our answer be couched. We will grind you revolutionists down under our heel, and we shall walk upon your faces. The world is ours, we are its lords, and ours it shall remain. As for the host of labor, it has been in the dirt since history began. And in the dirt it shall remain so long as I and mine and those that come after us have the power. There is the word. It is the king of words—Power. Not God, not Mammon, but Power. Pour it over your tongue till it tingles with it. Power."

—Jack London, The Iron Heel, *New York, Sagamore, 1957, pp. 82–83.*

The problem is particularly sharp where the dictatorships are totalitarian, based on the idea that every institution in the nation must be subordinated to a single dominating idea or purpose. We shall look first at Communist totalitarianism in Russia, and then at the totalitarian regimes in Fascist Italy and Nazi Germany. Not all dictatorships in the modern world have been Communist or Fascist—there are a number in the so-called Free World, the present anti-Communist bloc. We shall examine some of these, especially South Africa.

Not all tendencies toward suppression of individual freedom are found in the political dictatorships. Outside open dictatorships there are strong political tendencies toward suppression of beliefs which do not fit a particular line. There is a great danger to individual freedom in what we may call nihilism (from Latin *nihil,* nothing), the attitude that "if I can't have my kind of world, I won't have any." We shall see that this kind of nihilistic danger comes from both right and left. In the non-Communist countries, as well as in the Communist nations, Communist parties support such a policy. An equally serious threat to individual freedom may be posed by far rightist movements, which are usually outspokenly anti-Communist. We shall look at the activity of such movements in the United States.

The possibility of a brave new world is posed not only by formal political movements, but by tendencies which are a more broad and general part of modern culture. We shall review the way in which the individual is threatened by the rise of nationalism, by the growth of military power uncontrolled by civilian agencies, by control of public information, by the invasion of individual privacy by government and other organizations, and by many of the other tendencies of modern mass society.

POLITICAL DICTATORSHIP

Let us first examine the suppression of freedom in open dictatorships. The first totalitarian society to arise in the twentieth century was the Soviet Union. It was here that Zamiatin's *We* originated. Through a series of political changes in the spring of 1917, the czarist regime was eventually replaced by the moderate democratic Socialist Mensheviks. In the fall power passed to the more radical Bolsheviks, led by Lenin and Trotsky. The Bolsheviks rejected the ordinary machinery of parliamentary government. Their doctrine of dictatorship of the proletariat held that only a strong centralized dictatorship could keep power from shifting back to the old supporters of capitalism. To keep this from happening, they abolished the parliamentary body, the Constituent Assembly, and (in 1918) established a secret police, the Cheka. The Cheka acted principally against people who it was thought might become political enemies of the regime: monarchists, intellectuals, moderate Socialists, and Anarchists. At this time the novelist Maxim Gorky (generally friendly to the revolution) wrote, "Executions continued. Not a day, not a night passes without several persons being executed."

The Bolshevik regime was not only dictatorial but totalitarian. Marxist doctrine held that all the institutions of society generally support the ruling class. In order to bring about a new society free from class domination, it is necessary to keep watch over all forms of social activity. Religion under capitalism was to the Marxists an opiate drugging the people into accepting exploitation. (The Bolshevik view was borne out by the fact that the church had given the support of organized religion to the czarist regime.) Art likewise could not be separated from politics. In a Socialist society, art would promote revolutionary zeal. Thus arose the doctrine of Socialist realism. Only those forms of art can be permitted or encouraged which present revolutionary themes and support the new political regime and glorify its goals and activities.

When Stalin came to power, the secret police turned for the first time against the common people rather than against special groups of actual or possible political enemies. Large numbers of small independent farmers (kulaks) were sent to forced labor camps during the nationalization of agriculture. These camps soon became a central feature of the Soviet system. Under Stalin police power turned also against members of the inner ruling group itself. Between 1934 and 1938, in the Great Purge, a large number of this inner ruling group were brought to trial and convicted. Many were executed. Between 1934 and 1936, approximately one-fourth of the members and candidates for membership in the

Joseph Stalin

Communist Party disappeared from the rolls. Stalin's death in 1953 ended the most severe form of dictatorship. After the Great Purge came a Great Thaw. When he became premier, Khrushchev denounced Stalin and many of his policies. The thaw did not keep Russia from intervening in Hungary in 1956 to put down a popular revolution against the existing Russian-supported dictatorship. Under Kosygin, relaxation of the old dictatorial policies did not keep Soviet troops from doing the same thing in Czechoslovakia in 1968.

As we noted in our discussion of propaganda in Chapter nine, Red China's major contribution to totalitarianism (and thus to the threat of anti-Utopia) has been her thoroughgoing system of political brainwashing. This involves intense saturation with the official "line" in home, school, and public place, through radio, television, posters,

Young Czechs demonstrate, facing the leveled weapons of Soviet troops in Prague, 1968.

propaganda meetings, group "confessional sessions," and the silencing of dissenting voices.

According to Marxist theory, dictatorship was only a temporary practical necessity in order to eliminate the remaining features of the old social system. It was not good in itself. Ideally, it would give way to a society based upon greater self-expression and realization for the individual. Under the Fascist view of society, which came to power in Italy from 1922 to 1945 and in Germany from 1933 to 1945, totalitarian dictatorship is itself a positive good. The state is the most important reality, and the interests and development of the individual are secondary. Individual differences must be subordinated to the interests of the collective state. The most complete development of fascism was in Nazi Germany. Individuals were kept in line by the Gestapo, a highly organized secret police. Dissenters were eventually removed from society to concentration camps. Those who suffered most were likely to be intellectuals, liberals, radicals, and Socialists. Jews, who made up a high proportion of these groups, were most likely to receive the most severe penalties. An

estimated 6 million Jews from Germany and other European countries eventually died in Nazi concentration camps. This treatment was justified by Nazi racist doctrine: a person is to be judged not as an individual according to his character and achievement, but according to membership or nonmembership in a (fictitious) Aryan master race. Fascism glorified the political leader, who was seen as embodying and expressing the glories of the state. In Germany this leader worship reached its highest point in the glorification of *der Führer,* Hitler. The reality of Nazi Germany far exceeded the imaginings of any of the anti-Utopian writers. We saw in Chapter ten some of the other features which made Nazism a real-world model for anti-Utopia: strong nationalistic militarism, based on a permanent war economy; the terror and violence which came from inability to furnish an answer to real social problems; the nihilistic urge to destroy everything which represented the forces by which the Nazis felt themselves encircled.

Many people would find a current version of anti-Utopia in present-day South Africa. One author has said that "South Africa is not the only authoritarian society in the world but it is the only social autocracy." Social autocracy means apartheid (pronounced apart-hate)—the legal separation and segregation of races. The present population of Africa is made up of 1.2 million English-speaking whites, 13 million nonwhites, mainly Negroes (referred to as Africans), and 1.8 million Afrikaners (whites of Dutch ancestry who dominate the government and the society). Blacks are legally required to live in segregated areas and cannot enter white areas, even to work, without an official work pass. They have no representation in the government. Skilled jobs are reserved for whites. Blacks are forbidden to strike. If they do so, they are subject to a maximum penalty of death for sabotage. Blacks cannot hold meetings unless they are officially approved by the government. They are denied equal access to lower and higher education. Many of the Dutch-descended Afrikaners favor territorial apartheid, which would divide South Africa geographically into a white area and black areas. The most important organization promoting apartheid has been the Bruderband, described by one writer on South Africa as the "most powerful single organization within Afrikanerdom." Recently the Bruderband included among its members the prime minister and most of his cabinet. During the Hitler regime, the Bruderband studied, with interest, Nazi methods of organization. At one time it had a Nazi student as a youth organizer. The Bruderband controls most education in South Africa. The Dutch Reformed church in South Africa has generally supported apartheid strongly. Some churchmen and other Afrikaners, as well as English-speaking whites, have however opposed the official policy.

A more recent dictatorship in the "Free World" is that of the military junta which in the spring of 1967 ousted the liberal-democratic government of George Papandreou in Greece. The junta has aroused a wide range of opposition in Greece itself by its attacks on both "leftists" and conservatives. It could probably never have survived without economic and military support from the United States. One of its most outspoken Greek opponents has been actress Melina Mercouri. The most prominent political exile is Andreas Papandreou, son of the former prime minister and himself formerly economic minister. He has related the dictatorship to the trends of our times in *Man's Freedom* (Columbia, 1970). A well-known document on the Greek dictatorship was the movie "Z" (1970) produced by a French film company and based on an incident in Greek resistance to the junta.

RADICAL RIGHTISM

In the United States, as in South Africa, racial fear has been a rallying point for denial of individual liberty. The legal and social system of the South was for many decades very close to South African Apartheid. The weakening of this system, through the Negro civil rights movement and federal government action, has been viewed with alarm by many people who believe that there has been too much tolerance in the country of people who are "different." Thus racism has become a gathering point for movements of the far right.

What is the far right or radical right? In 1955 a national survey showed that 68 percent of the American people believed that a Communist should not be allowed to speak in public. Eighty-nine percent believed that he should not be permitted to teach in a college or university. Sixty-three percent thought that he should not be a radio singer. Over half (51 percent) felt that he should be in jail. Of the same Americans, 60 percent believed that a book critical of the churches and religion should be removed from a public library if a protest was lodged. Eighty-four percent believed that the author should not be permitted to teach in a college or university. Thirty-one percent felt that a person should not be allowed to make a speech favoring government ownership of all railways and big industries (a basic Socialist program). Thirty-four percent believed that a book by a Socialist should be removed from a public library if protested; 84 percent that a Socialist should not be allowed to teach in a college or university. These answers give the flavor, which when exaggerated, makes up the extreme right way of thinking.

The far rightist believes in the traditional "American way of life." This includes the traditional free enterprise business practices. It includes also traditional formal religious practices and institutions. Since the civil rights movement, it is likely to include the traditional patterns of racial separation and discrimination. The far rightist is likely to regard all those who hold different economic, political, religious, and racial views as Communists or else as conscious or unconscious agents of international communism. To the far rightist, people who disagree with him deserve no protection. The answers to the poll we have cited suggest the totalitarian nature of the far rightist way of thinking. The far rightist believes that the educational, religious, and other institutions of society, and also the channels of information and discussion, should be limited to promoting a correct set of beliefs and practices (his own).

Among the more important positions taken by the far right have been opposition to social security, opposition to the income tax (which was proposed in the *Communist Manifesto*, among other places), opposition to labor unions, opposition to school desegregation, opposition to medicare, opposition to the federal Supreme Court, opposition to the United Nations (which is regarded as a "Trojan horse" bringing communism into New York City and into the United States), opposition to foreign economic aid, and opposition to federal aid to education.

What the far right is for, as well as against, is suggested by the Liberty Amendment, a proposed constitutional change which would require the federal government to get out of social security, atomic energy, banking, army construction, veterans' insurance, national forests, and the Tennessee Valley Authority, and to turn such activities over to private enterprise. Rightist political policy was outlined in Chicago in April 1965 at a Congress of Conservatives: United States withdrawal from the United Nations, establishment of new quotas on immigration, repeal of the income tax, and an end to civil rights legislation.

Typical of radical right organization is the Patrick Henry Press of Richmond, Virginia, which mailed half a million copies of a book claiming that school desegregation cannot work because Negroes are biologically inferior. Shades of Nazi racism appear in the appeal of a University of Illinois classics professor circulated from Washington, D.C. by the National Youth Alliance, calling for "the race, called Indo-European or Aryan" to stand up against "alien slime" in the United States—or against "Oriental degenerates" and "the bands of unkempt young derelicts that slouch about in academic silence."[1] Not all rightists are anti-Semitic, but many share the views of the conservative Rat Fink faction (later officially censured by the Young Republicans) which in 1965 circulated the following lines for singing at the New Jersey and National Young Republican Conventions (to the tune of Jingle Bells):

Riding through the Reich
In my Mercedes-Benz,
Shooting every Kike
Saving all my friends
Rat-tat-tat Rat-tat-tat
Mow the bastards down
Oh, what fun it is to have
The Nazis back in town.

The same kind of thinking produced the story, circulated in 1967, that LSD was being smuggled into the United

1. Revilo P. Oliver, quoted in *Covenanter Witness,* July 22, 1970, p. 4.

States from Israel as part of a Communist conspiracy to immobilize American cities. The story claimed that the LSD was being made by the Chaim Weizmann Institute, one of the world's most important scientific institutions. This kind of thinking was behind the statement with which Admiral John C. Crommelin filed his unsuccessful candidacy for the governorship of Alabama in 1958, asserting his opposition to a worldwide "Communist-Jewish Conspiracy" with headquarters in Israel and the United Nations in New York, which was going to turn the whole world into "copper-colored human mongrels" with no race distinctions "except the so-called Jewish race."

Among the chief targets of far rightists have been mental health programs, which are seen as intended to brainwash people into believing liberal and Communist views. In the 1950s a mental health bill in Alaska was attacked on the ground that, under the guise of mental hospitals, it would establish a concentration camp for anti-Communist patriots.

Rightists might justify their position by quoting statements such as this, by liberal psychologist Harry Overstreet:

> *A man, for example, may be angrily against race equality, public housing, the TVA, financial and technical aid to backward countries, organized labor. . . . Such people may appear normal in the sense that they're able to hold a job and otherwise maintain their status as members of society; but they are; we now realize, well along the road toward mental illness.*[2]

Among the methods of the radical right have included radio broadcasting, dissemination of literature, and telephone programs such as "Let Freedom Ring," devised by a Sarasota, Florida physician so as to allow anyone ringing a certain number to receive a rightist message. Rightists have tried to organ-

ize a third party, as in the 1965 Chicago meeting referred to, and also to take over existing political organizations, especially the Republican Party. There was strong far-rightist backing for George Wallace in his 1968 presidential campaign, and for Barry Goldwater in 1964.

The core of the far rightist movement has been, in recent years, the John Birch Society, headed by Robert Welch. Birchers are likely to believe that the United States is in the hands of a conspiracy to sell the country to international communism. All individuals and movements who do not subscribe to a rightist view of economics and politics, and other matters, are likely to be regarded as knowing or unknowing Communists. The Birch Society was founded during the administration of President Dwight D. Eisenhower. At that time such staunch conservative anti-Communists as General George Marshall and Secretary of State John Foster Dulles were labeled as Communist agents, and President Eisenhower himself was described as a conscious member of the international Communist conspiracy. Known liberals and radicals fared much worse. The Birch Society has been widely repudiated by conservatives as well as liberals, and even Welch has somewhat modified his position.

Of rightist efforts to take over his party, former Republican National Chairman Thruston Morton commented, "I am concerned by the fact that the John Birch Society has picked my party as a vehicle to promulgate its monolithic philosophy." This view was similar to that of the noted conservative William F. Buckley, Jr., who described some far rightist propaganda as "paranoid and unpatriotic drivel."

In government far rightist ideas have at times been embodied in the work of the Federal Bureau of Investigation, which collects and uses extended dossiers on large numbers of people without critically evaluating the truth of the evidence or the reliability of its witnesses. Typical of its activities have

2. H. A. Overstreet, *The Great Enterprise,* New York, Norton, 1952, p. 115.

been tapping of the telephone of Martin Luther King and falsification of an interview with Dr. Benjamin Spock to provide material for his indictment on a charge of conspiracy. The House Un-American Activities Committee and the Senate Internal Security Subcommittee, both of which have refused to grant to persons under investigation the ordinary procedures guaranteeing due process of law, sometimes practice far right tactics also. Thus individuals have been refused the assistance of an attorney or been forced to testify to their own legal or political and economic damage, or to answer extended questions from memory without being allowed use of relevant documents.

Rightist ideas have also been embodied in the work of the CIA. In the mid-1960s, much publicity was given to the connections of the CIA with educational institutions, foundations, student groups, and even liberal organizations, many of which, it was revealed, had at times been subsidized to create a propaganda network for a supernationalist view of American foreign affairs. This activity at home supported the work of the CIA abroad in overthrowing or trying to overthrow liberal or radical governments in countries such as Iran, Guatemala, Laos, Indonesia, the Dominican Republic, and Cuba, and supporting dictatorships such as those of Haile Sellassie in Ethiopia and Chiang Kai-shek in Taiwan.

Far rightism achieved great success in the 1950s with the prominence of Senator Joseph McCarthy, who conducted extensive investigations directed at subversives in government. The McCarthy probes damaged the reputations and careers of many people whose only crime was guilt by association. For example, one might have belonged to a cooperative bookstore in Washington, some of whose other members were suspected of being subversive. The total national effect of McCarthy's work was to create an atmosphere of terror in which people were afraid to express radical or liberal opinions, to join organizations to promote them, or to associate with people who advocated them. McCarthy had wide support and wide coverage by the media. It is noteworthy that he never uncovered a person whom he proved to be a Communist.

Sometimes extreme rightist belief has led to violent direct action. The extreme rightist conviction that a conspiracy is seeking to undermine the values they cherish has led groups like the Minutemen to prepare physically to resist the expected take-over by guerrilla warfare. In 1966 a member of the Minutemen testified that his group had discussed plans to assassinate Senator William Fulbright and to put cyanide gas in the air-conditioning system at the UN building in New York. At about the same time, twenty alleged Minutemen were rounded up in New York City on charges of planning to bomb three camps in upstate New York which were held to be centers for leftists and pacifists.

The cause of rightist groups is often aided by support from police and other agencies of law and order. Familiar examples are the 1970 shooting of students at Kent State and Jackson State Universities; the tear-gassing of students by helicopter at the University of California at Berkeley; the activities of a police agent in furnishing weapons to provoke student violence at Hobart College in New York state; the "police rioting" against demonstrators at the 1968 Democratic Convention in Chicago; the actions of off-duty police officers in three cities in attacking or shooting Black Panthers at offices, social events, and in one case in a courthouse during a trial.

Richard E. Rubenstein in his study of mass political violence in the United States (Rebels in Eden, Boston, Little, Brown, 1970) says that illegal police activities may be of four kinds. (1) Police may actually perform illegal acts, as of brutality. (2) Police may discriminate against unpopular groups in enforcing the law. (3) Police may enforce a total political and legal system which is discriminatory. (4). Police may fail to protect one group against the illegal activity of another.

The 1961 report on *Justice* of the United States Civil Rights Commission stated that "Police brutality is a serious problem in the United States," and the Commission on Violence appointed by President Johnson and chaired by Dr. Milton Eisenhower added in 1969 that "this conclusion finds support throughout the literature on police." A sociological study for the Department of Justice in 1966 arranged for observers to accompany policemen on their beats in Boston, Chicago, and Washington. It was found that 38 percent of the officers had expressed "extreme prejudice" against Negroes, while an additional 34 percent had expressed "considerable prejudice" in front of observers. Students and hippies are also targets for police prejudice. An example is part of the radio log of the Chicago Police Department at 1:29 A.M. on Tuesday during the 1968 Democratic Convention:

> *"1814 get a wagon at 1436. We've got an injured hippie."*
> *"1436 North Wells?"*
> *"North Wells"*

From five other cars:

> *"There's no emergency."*
> *"Let him take a bus."*
> *"Kick the fucker."*
> *"Knock his teeth out."*
> *"Throw him in a wastepaper basket."*[3]

In addition policemen are likely to share the conspiratorial view of social protest: it is not a spontaneous response to social injustice, but something stirred up by "outside (or inside)

agitators." Thus, says the Eisenhower Commission, "The police are more likely to believe that 'anarchist' leaders are going to contaminate a city's water supply with LSD than they are to believe that student antiwar or black protest is an expression of genuine, widespread dissatisfaction." This kind of belief fits into the main social role which, as the Eisenhower Commission stated, the forces of law and order have traditionally played as protectors of the status quo against groups who would change it. The commission illustrates the point historically by describing the widespread police repression with which the labor movement had to contend until it became part of the Establishment (see Chapter eleven). The actual role of police in the past, and today with respect to students, blacks, and "peaceniks," contradicts the widely held view that the forces of law and order are a neutral agency representing the public interest against any group interest. The fact is, as the commission suggests, that police have generally served the interest of the ruling power structure, and now serve it. The role of police in the South in enforcing Jim Crow before recent civil rights legislation is an example.

Again, the personality and beliefs of the policeman are likely to fit his role. A description of the British policeman might also be true for the American "cop":

> *The true copper's most dominant characteristic, if the truth be known, is neither those daring nor vicious qualities that are sometimes attributed to him by friend or enemy, but an ingrained conservatism, and [sic] almost desperate love of the conventional. It is untidiness, disorder, the unusual, that a copper disapproves of most of all: far more even than of crime which is merely a professional matter. Hence his profound dislike of people loitering in streets, dressing extravagantly, speaking with exotic accents, being strange, weak, eccentric, or simply any rare minority*

3. *The Politics of Protest: A Report Submitted by Jerome H. Skolnick, Director, Task Force, Violent Aspects of Protest and Confrontation* (1969). The Skolnick task-force report was a supplementary document published somewhat later than the full Eisenhower Commission study.

Demonstrators clash with the Chicago police during the 1968 Democratic National Convention.

—of their doing, in fact, anything that cannot be safely predicted.''[4]

The prominence of Senator Joseph McCarthy is only one case where the far rightist philosophy has been drastically embodied in government action.

4. Colin MacInness in Jerome H. Skolnick, *Justice Without Trial*, New York, Wiley, 1966, p. 48.

A second example is the establishment in 1952 of procedures and camps for detaining persons with unpopular political attitudes.

Title II of the Internal Security Act was known as the "Emergency Detention Act" and provided for government action to be taken in case of (1) invasion, (2) declaration of war by Congress, or (3) insurrection within the

United States in aid of a foreign enemy. The president was empowered to declare an emergency in these circumstances, and the Attorney General was authorized to seize and detain "each person as to whom there is reasonable ground to believe that such person probably will engage in or probably will conspire with others to engage in acts of espionage or sabotage" (not evidence that he has *done* these things).

Specifically to be detained were all people who had been members of the Communist Party, USA, since January 1, 1949, or members of any other organization or political party which seeks to overthrow or destroy by force and violence "the Government of the United States or any of its political subdivisions." In 1952, FBI director J. Edgar Hoover told Congress that "There is a potential fifth column of 550,000 people dedicated to the Communist philosophy."

Under the Emergency Detention Act, the attorney general was under no obligation to present any concrete evidence which might be "dangerous to national security and safety to divulge." The detainee might be held in "such places of detention as may be prescribed by the Attorney General." Specifically, detention camps were established at Tule Lake, California; Avon Park, Florida; El Reno, Oklahoma; and Florence and Wickenburg, Arizona.

Procedures under the Emergency Detention Act were described accurately by Congressman Joe Pool of Texas, himself favorable to the act: "Under a declared state of war we could get the Attorney General to prosecute certain people for sedition and treason. Then if they [Peaceniks] persisted in their actions, the Justice Department could move to put them into concentration camps and leave them there for the duration of the war."

President Harry S Truman, in vetoing the act, said, "It would put the government of the United States in the thought control business. . . . No considerations of expediency can jus-

tify the enactment of such a bill as this, a bill which would so greatly weaken our liberties and give aid and comfort to those who would destroy us."

Senator William Langer of North Dakota commented, "So it is now proposed to have concentration camps in America! We can be absolutely certain that the concentration camps are for only one purpose: namely, to put in them the kind of people those in authority do not like!"

Senator Karl Mundt of South Dakota, always strong in opposition to subversives, said that the act set up "concentration camps into which people might be put without benefit of trial, but merely by executive fiat . . . simply by an assumption, mind you, that an individual might be thinking about engaging in espionage or sabotage."

Senator Pat McCarren, who introduced the original Internal Security Act of 1952, called the detention provisions "a concentration-camp measure, pure and simple."

That the Emergency Detention Act could be used against the antiwar or black liberation movements is indicated by the groups labeled in 1968 by the House Un-American Activities Committee as planning armed insurrection against the federal government: the Communist Party, the Student Non-Violent Coordinating Committee, the Progressive Labor Party, Students for a Democratic Society, and the W. E. B. DuBois Clubs. In 1968 a former FBI agent, Jack Levine, told a New York radio audience of Operation Dragnet, "a very carefully laid out and detailed plan of action set up by the FBI under the Emergency Detention Act for rounding up political dissenters."

Since 1957 no further funds have been made available for maintaining the detention camps. Their use as detention centers has been discontinued. However, in 1967 the capacity of the camps was 26,500, and seven other sites were available.

In November 1968 a suit was filed in U.S. District Court in Washington, D.C., by a number of political dissenters who

The constitutionality of Title II is, to be charitable, highly question-
able. Potentially the Act violates: (1) the First Amendment by being
overly broad and vague, thereby inhibiting the exercise of speech
and assembly rights; (2) the Fourth Amendment by authorizing
deprivation of liberty upon suspicion rather than "probable cause"
and by authorizing detention without judicial safeguards; (3) the
Fifth Amendment by authorizing incarceration solely because of
membership in a political party; (4) the Fifth and Sixth Amendments
by authorizing punishment without trial, by denying the detainee
the right to confront his accusers and to cross-examine the
witnesses against him, and by too severely restricting the scope
of judicial review; (5) the Eighth Amendment by imposing cruel
and unusual punishment where no crime has been committed
and by providing for indefinite detention without the right to bail.

—American Civil Liberties Union, "Of the Emergency Detention Act," Civil
Liberties, 260 (February 1969), p. 9.

might eventually become detainees under Title II.

A more recent illustration of tendencies toward anti-Utopia was House Resolution 14864, the Defense Facilities and Internal Security Act of 1970, which passed the House of Representatives by a vote of 274–65.

HR 14864 would give the secretary of defense the power to screen, with the help of an executive agency, the personnel of all facilities defined as defense related. "Facilities" included any plant, factory, industry, public utility, mine, laboratory, educational institution, research organization, railroad, airport, pier, waterfront installation, canal, dam, bridge, highway, vessel, aircraft, vehicle, pipeline. Under the bill were included all such facilities that would contribute "a substantial portion of the national capacity" or would be in "critical demand in time of emergency." The screening agency would have power to investigate an individual's affiliations, associations, behavior, facts, and conditions, past and present. Causes for denial of a job might include membership on the rolls, or the mailing lists, of organizations advocating peaceful nonviolent change of governmental policies through the ballot. Such advocacy, as well as peaceful strikes or demonstrations, could be defined as "acts of insurrection." A person might appeal refusal of

clearance, but the courts would have no power to stop (enjoin) a refusal of security clearance. Right to appeal could be lost by refusal to answer any question, refusal to authorize others to release information about oneself, or refusal to take a psychiatric examination. People subpoenaed to testify under the act would have to waive their Fifth Amendment protection against self-incrimination. A job applicant would have no right to cross-examine his accusers if the cross-examination might "harm national security," nor in place of this could he have a summary of the evidence against him if, in the judgment of the accusing agency, security would be threatened. If an official of cabinet rank issued a job denial, there would be no right of appeal.

It is not hard to see why the American Civil Liberties Union said of HR 14864 that "1984 will come, blessed by Congressional authorization."

TOTALITARIANISM AND CULTURE

Political and social far rightism is only an organized group expression of broad trends, central to our culture, which threaten the integrity of the individual. In the previous chapter, we saw how the nationalistic spirit tends to sweep the individual into an uncritical and irrational herd. We also observed

The perpetual menacings of danger oblige the government to be always prepared to repel it; its armies must be numerous enough for instant defense. The continual necessity for their services enhances the importance of the soldier, and proportionably degrades the condition of the citizen. The military state becomes elevated above the civil. The inhabitants of territories, often the theater of war, are unavoidably subjected to frequent infringement of their rights, which serve to weaken their sense of these rights; and by degrees the people are brought to consider the soldiery not only as their protectors but as their superiors. The transition from this disposition to that of considering them masters, is neither remote nor difficult; but it is very difficult to prevail upon a people under such impressions to make a bold or effective resistance to usurpations supported by the military power.

—*Alexander Hamilton,* Federalist Papers, *no. 8.*

---

the growth of military influence. Alexander Hamilton in the appended quotation stated very pointedly the effect upon the individual of permitting the military to erode civilian power.

Three further erosions of individual freedom which we have not heretofore specifically mentioned illustrate general cultural forces working toward anti-Utopia. These are the invasion of privacy, the management of news, and the psychology of obedience.

The loss of the right to privacy is, in general, one of the most important experiences of many people today. All societies include privacy, the freedom of the individual from group knowledge and group control of his acts and thoughts. The three major ways in which privacy is invaded are physical surveillance, psychological surveillance, and data surveillance.

Bugging a person through planting on him or his premises a miniature radio transmitter is an example of the listening and watching devices involved in physical surveillance. The author at a party once took a ride with his host, who had left a small radio transmitter hidden in his own living room. The two then listened on the car radio to the conversations of the party guests.

Another example of physical surveillance is closed-circuit television, such as that used to detect shoplifters. This can also be installed in hotel rooms and in private homes. Other listening and watching devices are tape recorders and microphones, hidden cameras, and telephone wiretapping.

Alan Westin, in his important book *Privacy and Freedom*, says,

> *Private use of hidden surveillance devices can be divided into eight major areas of American life in which surveillance has been sufficiently widespread to warrant serious concern: business affairs, labor relations, professional life, personal and family affairs, customer surveillance, civic and political affairs, government agencies, and surreptitious research observation.*[5]

Examples of psychological surveillance are polygraph (lie detector) and personality tests. These have been widely used by government agencies and private corporations in screening applicants and employees. Advanced techniques of psychological surveillance are under development; computer reading of brain waves can tell, for example, whether a person is looking at red or green at a given time. The National Security Agency and the Central Intelligence Agency generally give

5. Alan Westin, *Privacy and Freedom*, New York, Atheneum, 1967, p. 104.

*The most sublime passions of our people were summoned in action
and sacrifice. . . . That total war gave birth to governmentally
organized propaganda. The hates of the people, their courage
and their aspirations could not be allowed to lag in the face of
reverses and suffering. The atrocities and total wickedness of the
enemy had to be constantly illustrated. All governments, including
our own, engaged in it. The heads of bureaus in most
governments have written their confessions with pride in the
lies they invented.*

—Herbert Hoover, in a speech at New Haven, Conn., March 28, 1941.

---

lie detector tests to every applicant.
Speaking of these and other types of
psychological surveillance used for
clearance by government agencies,
Westin says,

> *From the standpoint of privacy, the
> "clearing" procedure demands that
> an individual do for the government
> —and with an impersonal, generally
> insensitive operator—what few indi-
> viduals will ever do in their lifetimes
> for wife, minister, or best friend. The
> individual must bare himself, know-
> ing . . . that the confessional is
> usually observed, recorded, and
> even photographed from outside.[6]*

Examples of data surveillance are
the comprehensive records on consumers maintained by credit-rating
agencies (one agency has dossiers on
42 million people) and the proposal
for a national record bank which would
store on computer tapes records on
essential aspects of the lives of the
whole population. (Already the Department of Defense has 4 million life histories.) A medical data bank clears the
records of 20 federal agencies which
now have 100 million punch cards and
30,000 computer tapes on individuals
and businesses. A 4000-foot reel of
plastic tape could store about twenty
pages of data on every person in the
United States. "The more computers
offer opportunities," says Westin, "to
stimulate behavior, forecast trends,

6. *Ibid.*, p. 154.

and predict outcomes, the more pressure is generated for personal and
organizational information to be collected and processed. In a way we
sometimes only dimly grasp, this is one
of the great changes in modern society."

MANAGEMENT OF NEWS

News management is also worthy of
mention as bearing upon the problem
of individual freedom within modern
society. Within Lyndon Johnson's
presidency, this gave rise to what was
then called the "credibility gap." Freedom of individual action and thought
requires accuracy in the information on
which one acts and thinks. Two factors
in recent times have increased the
problem of the individual at this point.
The first is centralization of the media
of mass information. Newspaper centralization is an example. In 1913, 689
cities in the United States had rival
newspapers. In 1963, there were competing papers in only 52. At the latter
date, 24 states had no competing
newspapers. In 1920, 153 daily papers
were owned by chains. In 1963, the
number was 560. The same tendencies
have been at work in radio and television.

A second factor threatening the accuracy of the individual's information is
the development of government news
management. In 1941 former president
Herbert Hoover reminisced on how
public opinion had been shaped by

propaganda in World War I. His thoughts are found in the excerpt on the opposite page.

Under Franklin D. Roosevelt, public opinion was influenced to a considerable extent by radio saturation through "fireside chats" and other speeches by which the Roosevelt magnetism was broadcast to all radio receivers. Since that time total coverage of many presidential appearances by all radio and TV facilities has become customary. The credibility gap first appeared in the 1960s when the American U-2 plane, piloted by Francis Gary Powers, was shot down over Russia; its mission was denied by the United States government. Of this denial the *Wall Street Journal* said, "like the clergyman caught in nocturnal activities, we will no longer be able to be self-righteous."

A rather spectacular example of the suppression of facts came in the Kennedy-Nixon debates in the 1960 presidential campaign. In these debates, according to his autobiographical book, *Six Crises,* Richard Nixon dealt with a proposal by Kennedy for the overthrow of Castro, and described it as "the most dangerously irresponsible recommendation that he's made during the campaign." What Nixon was dis-

---

From my own experience and observation, I have come to believe that the establishment of military discipline (i.e., the following of orders, adherence to a choice of command, training in weaponry, etc.) should be the first consideration of any organization in the black liberation movement. It provides a means of enforcement or at least a threat of enforcement (which is usually sufficient). It also keeps power and control in the hands of the leadership.

—Earl Anthony, Picking Up the Gun: A Report on the Black Panthers, New York, Dial, 1970, p. 90.

They think they've heard from black power, wait till they hear from white power—the little slob, GI Joe, the guy who breaks his ass and makes this country go. Boy, he's getting sick and tired of all this mess. One day he'll get fed up and when he does, look out!

Asked to define "law and order," an investment adviser in King of Prussia, Pa., said, "Get the niggers. Nothing else."

"Behave yourself and there's no problem," declared a construction worker in Wichita, Kans. "I think of law and order as what I do."

People are fed up that 1 percent of the population is allowed to have legal theft with cops looking the other way. Looters should be shot—if they're 6 foot 9, 2 foot 6, green or yellow.

The U.S. has opened its doors to so many low-classed people. I tell you what: I could get 40 or 50 of my old South Pacific buddies with grease guns and stop all these damn riots.

—Newsweek, October 6, 1969, pp. 29–59.

*We might be the first people to go Fascist by the democratic vote,
and that would be something not even the Germans or the
Italians did. Hitler never got more than 30 percent of the vote in a
free election, but I think the American people now would vote
for almost anything which would put down the so-called peaceniks
and the college kids and the blacks. If our affluent society
turned into one of hardship, I think you'd get by consent of the
people a very right-wing society and a government in which
freedom would be greatly restricted. It would be a sort of
dictatorship by approval.*

—William L. Shirer, quoted in an interview in Awake!, May 8, 1970, p. 30.

guising was the fact that the Eisenhower government had planned the possible overthrow of Castro. In *Six Crises* Mr. Nixon describes the idea that he was "softer" than Kennedy on Castro as "exactly the opposite of the truth, if only the whole record could be disclosed."

The Kennedy Administration itself became responsible for news distortion. The invasion of Cuba at the Bay of Pigs was denied at the United Nations by U.N. Ambassador Adlai Stevenson and denied also at other places.

The policy of new management under the Kennedy Administration led to sharp criticism by the distinguished *New York Times* columnist, Arthur Krock, in *Fortune* in March 1963.

A news management policy not only exists but, in the form of direct and deliberate action, has been enforced more cynically and boldly than by any previous Administration in a period when the U.S. was not in a war or without visible means of regression from the verge of war. . . . Active management of the news by Government can be done by suppression, concealment, distortion and false weighting of the facts to which the public is entitled. It can be done through threats or implication of threats, of shutting off legitimate sources of information to report [ers] who have dug out facts whose publication embarrasses the government for personal policy or political reasons.

About this time Assistant Secretary of Defense for Public Affairs Arthur Sylvester defended news management on the ground that, "It's inherent in government's right, if necessary, to lie in order to save itself when it's going up into a nuclear war. This to me seems basic." During the Johnson Administration, the same Secretary Sylvester once said to a group of newsmen, "If you think any American official is going to tell you the truth, then you're stupid. Do you hear that, stupid?" It was also during the Johnson Administration that the president justified American intervention in the affairs of the Dominican Republic by announcing in a press conference that "some 1500 innocent people were murdered and shot and their heads cut off" by Communists, a statement with no basis in fact. It was during this administration that the American Society of Newspaper Editors charged that "a one-voice philosophy has been extended from the halls of the Pentagon to the military installations in Vietnam."

During the Nixon Administration, the news media themselves (especially television) struck back at the effort to enforce "a one-voice philosophy" upon them. The public statements of Vice-President Spiro Agnew made it clear that in his mind there is no right to dissent against government foreign policy, and Agnew's view received considerable support from the president. What was so totalitarian in this administration's effort to manage news was not so much any particular act as the underlying assumption that on matters of state there can properly be only one voice.

Under the Nixon Administration in November 1969, management of news took on a new dimension—effort at direct censorship. Alarmed by mounting opposition to its foreign policy in the Vietnam War, the administration was particularly disturbed by television coverage of the controversy. The direct suggestion that television censorship might be desirable was made in a speech by Vice-President Agnew, who apparently spoke not only for himself, but with the knowledge and approval of the White House. The Agnew speech was part of a continued tendency of the administration to make dissent equivalent to treason. Underlying this was the totalitarian assumption that no activities can rightly exist which are not in harmony with the policies of government.

THE PSYCHOLOGY OF OBEDIENCE

Much light was thrown upon the degree of independence of the typical American by the famous obedience studies conducted at Yale University in the early 1960s. Yale students and "normal citizens" of New Haven were invited to participate in an experiment which was supposed to check the effect of electric shocks in producing learning. The apparatus provided consisted of a panel of thirty switches of which some were marked "Danger— severe shock" and others beyond them were marked just "'XX." The Yale and New Haven subjects being tested for obedience were told that at different times it would be necessary for them, on order, to correct the errors of an individual visible in another room by administering various degrees of shock. There was no real electric connection, although the subjects thought there was. At times the "learners" (who were actually actors) responded by showing signs of shock, groaning,

screaming, and crying for the experiments to stop, through shouts such as "You're killing me." At such a point those conducting the experiment would tell the people at the "switchboard": "Please continue. You have no choice. You must go on." The students and New Havenites at the switchboard sweated at times, trembled, and swore, sometimes claiming that they would not go on inflicting the "shocks," but 65 percent of the "normal citizens" of New Haven pulled all 30 switches, all the while believing that they might really be inflicting death upon the "learners." Such is the power of obedience to authority.

All these possible foreshadowings of anti-Utopia are expressions of what Theodore Roszak has called the growth of "technocracy." The technocratic society is one that is governed, in somewhat older language, by those who possess "know-how." The techinques used in science and machine technology become the model for all the operations of society, says Roszak in *The Making of a Counter Culture*. All problems are thought capable of being solved by technologists of one kind or another (engineers, social or psychological scientists, and other experts). The growth of military power is argued on the ground that political and diplomatic questions are really only questions of technique which can best be understood and solved by military men. The invasion of privacy is based upon the belief that for people to have private lives is to interfere with the smooth meshing of the organizational machinery in solving our problems. The management of news is based upon the related belief that only that information favorable to the activities of political experts should be permitted to circulate. The pliability of subjects before the suggestions of expert experimenters illustrates the same acceptance of those who possess technical know-how.

Roszak's analysis of technocracy is one treatment of the spread of the organizational revolution. The confronta-

tion of forces for and against an authoritative Establishment has created an explosive situation in our society. It has given rise to two nihilistic extremes, a left which sometimes seems to want no world if it cannot have its kind, and a right which would seemingly rather be "dead than left." Between is a middle majority or "silent majority" which tends to veer somewhat rightward. All forces in the confrontation are reluctant to permit individual development where it involves the right to disagree (with them!).

This kind of individual freedom is threatened by radical students or non-students who run roughshod over other students, teachers, and administrators who (rightly or wrongly) find a value in continuing the ordinary operations of education. It is threatened by the extreme black militant line which insists that whites are no good and reverses the old order of color prejudice. It is threatened by the powerhouse tactics of revolutionary groups—Marxist, pacifist, female, or homosexual—who take over and suppress orderly lectures and discussion in order to enforce their point of view. It is threatened by violent draft resisters who physically restrain others from making a choice to join the Armed Forces. It is threatened by groups like the Black Panthers and SDS Weathermen when they stockpile weapons for revolutionary action.

Individual freedom is threatened by all leftists who consider revolution so imperative that no misguided dissenter should be allowed to stand in the way; it is also threatened by all rightists who consider the suppression of fundamental change so necessary that no consideration should be allowed to interfere. It is also threatened by members of the middle who talk like the people sampled by *Newsweek* in the fall of 1969, during a time of widespread antiwar demonstrations, black militancy, and campus protest.

It was of this right and middle backlash that William L. Shirer, who saw Nazism rise in Berlin, predicted that the United States might be the first country to vote itself into fascism.

In the middle of the spectrum, as on the ends, individual freedom is threatened by the left as well as the right. An example occurred on July 2, 1970, when radio station WXUR, AM and FM, of West Chester, Pennsylvania, was barred from the air by the Federal Communications Commission after a 9-month hearing which followed protests by the Democratic-controlled Pennsylvania legislature, the NAACP, the New Jersey and Greater Philadelphia Councils of Churches, and the AFL-CIO. WXUR was primarily an outlet for right-wing evangelist Carl McIntire. In addition, according to the FCC hearing examiner, it "performed what would normally be considered a wholesome service in providing an outlet for con-

*Many observers who have tried to understand the student
movement and who express sympathy for many of its objectives
find the turn toward confrontation, disruption, and incivility
highly irrational and self-destructive. Increasingly, SDS and the
"new left" are criticized for the style of their actions and
rhetoric. Although many such critics can understand the frustration
which contributes to extreme militancy, they argue that the
strategy of confrontation serves only to defeat the aims of the
movement, and that student radicals ought to exercise self-restraint
if they sincerely wish to achieve their political and social ends.
For example, it is frequently argued that confrontation tactics
accomplish little more than the arousal of popular hostility, thus
fueling the fires of right-wing demagoguery and increasing
the likelihood of government repression. Confrontation tactics in
the university, the critics argue, do not promote reform: they
mainly achieve the weakening of the university's ability to withstand
political pressure from outside, and consequently they threaten
to undermine the one institution in society that offers dissenters
full freedom of expression. Some critics conclude their arguments
by assuming that since in their view the main effect of new
left activity is to create disorder, intensify polarization, increase the
strength of the far right, and weaken civil liberties, then these
must be the results actually desired by the student radicals.*

—Jerome H. Skolnick, The Politics of Protest, *National Commission on the
Causes and Prevention of Violence, Washington, D.C., U.S. Government
Printing Office, 1969, pp. 80–81.*

---

trasting views on a wide variety of subjects" (statement by H. Gifford Irion, quoted in a letter circulated by Carl McIntire). The examiner also said "it is almost inconceivable that any station could have broadcast more variegated opinions upon so many issues than WXUR." He said further, "To impose the fell judgment of removing WXUR from the air . . . could only have the consequence of admonishing broadcasters everywhere that they will act at their peril in allowing robust discussion." He said that the action "could very conceivably result in silencing all controversial discussion on American radio and television." Apparently the liberal Establishment also fears variety of opinion, and offers a threat to personal freedom.

Suggestions for further reading

Totalitarianism: Its Changing Theory and Practice, by CARL FRIEDRICH and others (Praeger, 1969, paper), will give a broad general background to the problem of neo-Utopia in the modern world. The Authoritarian Personality (see suggested readings for Chapter four) is a basic introduction to some psychological aspects of the question.

In The New Class (Praeger, 1965, paper) MILOVAN DJILAS, a top figure in the Yugoslavian regime, criticizes the tendency of Communist bureaucracies to become new minorities exploiting their people. As a result of his views, Djilas, though a respected colleague and friend of Tito, has spent considerable time in jail in recent years. In Darkness at Noon (Modern Library; Bantam, 1968, paper), ARTHUR KOESTLER, a Socialist, uses his own prison experiences as the basis for a brilliant fictional account of life under Stalinist dictatorship. Another important fictional record of prison life under Communism is One Day in the Life of Ivan Denisovich by ALEXANDER SOLZHENITSYN (Praeger, 1963, paper). New China's unique contribution to neo-Utopia is described by EDWARD HUNTER in Brain-Washing in Red China (Vanguard, 1951).

For the contributions of historic fascism, see suggested readings for Chapter ten, especially BETTELHEIM, FRANKL, FROMM, and REICH.

Two South African writers of fiction have portrayed apartheid objectively and movingly. They are ALAN PATON, whose best-known work is Cry, the Beloved Country (Scribner's, 1961, paper), and NADINE GORDIMER, author of The Lying Days (not now in print).

On the Greek junta, see Man's Freedom (Columbia, 1970) by ANDREAS G. PAPAN-DREOU, formerly head of the economics department at the University of California, Berkeley, and himself an immediate personal victim of the takeover.

The United States' experience with concentration camps for Japanese-Americans during World War II appears in Brother Under the Skin by CAREY McWILLIAMS (rev. ed., Little, Brown, 1951, paper). Group invasion of individual life in this country is the subject of ALAN WESTIN's Privacy and American Community Life (Free Press, 1967). A special aspect of this problem is treated by FRED J. COOK (also author of The Warfare State) in The FBI Nobody Knows (Macmillan, 1964). A collection of scholarly selections on rightism in America is found in The Radical Right, edited by sociologist DANIEL BELL (Doubleday, 1963, paper). BENJAMIN R. EPSTEIN and ARNOLD FORSTER have written another book under the same title, The Radical Right (Random House, 1967, paper). Picking Up the Gun: The Story of the Black Panthers by EARL ANTHONY, an expelled Panther, depicts totalitarian trends in this segment of the New Left, as well as arguing feelingly for their necessity. In Push Comes to Shove: The Escalation of Student Protest, STEVE KELMAN, whose formal political affiliation is Socialist, analyzes the role of the New Left in student riots during his Harvard days.

Chapter fifteen
Health in the individual and society

At the end of our study of what *is,* what can we say about what we *ought* to do? In Chapter two we discussed the question of what social science can tell us about values. There we outlined a number of answers which have been given.

1. One view is that values come from sources that transcend scientific investigation. These may, for example, be sacred books which reveal moral or divine law, or they may be the inner voice of conscience, which may also give moral direction. From such a point of view, science is too limited to say anything important about values.

2. A second answer is that science is limited to "if-then" statements, such as "If you want peace you must disarm, or prepare for war." Assuming that we know what we want, science may then be able to tell us how to get it.

3. A third view is that science can dramatize situations and thereby strengthen values which people already hold (as Michael Harrington's *The Other America* probably fortified attitudes against poverty). In this view, while it can bring existing ethical attitudes to a focus, science cannot create them where they do not already exist.

4. A fourth answer is that science can describe the prevailing mores of a culture so accurately that people will be guided in conforming. This view assumes that "Whatever is, is right," in the sense that those who belong to a culture should accept the dominant pattern. By such a standard, if sociological study shows that most people

formally belong to religious organizations or have sex relations before marriage, knowledge of these facts can guide one to premarital intercourse or church membership.

5. A final solution is that science, by describing human situations and human needs objectively, can lay bare basic similarities in the situation and needs of people in all cultures, thereby enabling them to pass judgment on their own and other mores, and making it possible for them to change mores so as to make them more humanly satisfying. In this way science could judge that certain social patterns are healthy and others unhealthy in terms of their success or failure in meeting basic human needs. Thus it may appear that such extremes as excessive Puritanism and excessive promiscuity both reflect failure of a society to gratify sexual needs, or it may appear that religious values, such as compassion and forgiveness, represent common inner tendencies found in all people who have had adequate social experience. The accompanying criticism of the idea that science can stand apart from values comes from an unusual source, a science fiction story written by a Soviet mathematical physicist.

In Chapter two the author expressed the feeling that all these views contain some important truth, but that the last answer was closest to his own. Here he said that in the final chapter he would try to suggest how the materials of the whole book add up in terms of the problem of human and social values.

"You are a scientist, not a politician. . . ."

"I am a man first. It has long been time to tear off the mask of supposed neutrality behind which our scientists try to hide. They look at you naively when it suddenly turns out that the results of their studies are being used for the destruction of millions of human beings. They pretend to be fools who cannot foresee a simple thing—the consequences of their studies and discoveries. They shift all the blame to politicians. If I give a weapon to a madman, then I am answerable for the consequences, not the madman."

—Anatoly Dneprov, "Formula of Immortality," in Ultimate Threshold: A Collection of the Finest Soviet Science Fiction, *ed. and trans.* Mirra Ginsberg, New York, Holt, Rinehart and Winston, 1970, p. 24.

What would a healthy society look like? What would a healthy individual look like? We may be able to throw some light on social and individual health, and at the same time tie this book together, by looking at the problem in terms of the major revolutions of our time with which we began in Chapter one. There we discussed seven revolutions—in technology, population, urbanization, rising expectations, organization, sexuality, and weaponry. Here we may ask of each revolution such questions as: Out of what social and personal needs has it arisen? To what extent is it satisfying these needs? Granted that it has relieved some frustration of needs, to what new frustrations has it given rise? What might be done to preserve the gains which have been accomplished while at the same time avoiding the new frustrations? We can, in answering these questions, use any of the materials covered in this book. Thus we may relate (1) the changing trends of our times to (2) the problem of social goals by (3) utilizing the social science data and principles which have made up most of this book.

To begin with, let us establish a point of departure from which to evaluate our society and where it is going. Our study of society, personality, culture, and the ecological environment should enable us to establish some constant core needs of man as man. How shall we begin to locate these needs?

1. If we examine in all times and places those individuals who have been genuinely socialized, not merely enculturated (for the distinction see Chapter five), we will find them expressing, and in some measure living by, these needs.

2. As we look at the revolutions of our time (and some of the significant counterrevolutions), we will find people specifically giving voice to these needs. As modern society has come to maturity, conflicts between human need and social organization which have always existed have come to a head. In a sense in our generation we are realizing, perhaps more sharply than in any other, the gap, the cultural lag between the kind of world human beings need and the kind they have.

What is the gap? What kind of world have genuinely socialized people always envisaged? Toward what kind of world are the revolutions of our time pressing? *Toward a nonexploitative society.* Sir Albert Howard, a distinguished English student of natural methods of agriculture, has given this diagnosis of the problem: Man began by exploiting, rather than cooperating with, nature. Once this was done, he began to exploit his fellow man. A nonexploitative society would be based, first of all, on a view of man as a symbiotic part of his ecological environment. Secondly, it would regard people as ends in themselves, not merely as means to be manipulated. What does

*There are an almost infinite number of ways to differentiate
between the old and new cultures. The old culture, when forced to
choose, tends to give preference to property rights over
personal rights, technological requirements over human needs,
competition over cooperation, violence over sexuality,
concentration over distribution, the producer over the consumer,
means over ends, secrecy over openness, social reforms over
personal expression, striving over gratification, Oedipal love over
communal love, and so on. The new counterculture tends to
reverse all of these priorities.*

    *It is important to recognize that these differences can not be
resolved simply by some sort of "compromise" or "golden mean"
position. A cultural system is a dynamic whole, resting on
processes that must be accelerative to be self-sustaining. Change
must therefore affect the motivational roots of a society or
it is not change at all.*

—*Philip E. Slater,* The Pursuit of Loneliness, *Boston, Beacon Press, 1970, p. 100.*

this signify in terms of the revolutions in which we are living? Philip Slater has stated concisely the difference between the old culture out of which he sees us as passing, and a new culture which he believes is being born.

Let us look, one by one, at the specific revolutions. As we do this, we must continually remember that, as Slater emphasizes, there are not many revolutions, but one, and that to try to graft new social institutions piecemeal upon an old culture might be disastrous.

TECHNOLOGY

The technological revolution is an extension of man's ability to let tools and machines do his work for him. It is part of his long effort to master his environment in such a way as to satisfy his own needs and desires. The notion that it is good to make the environment satisfy one's needs is not unarguable. There is a point of view which says that human happiness lies in giving up desires, not in gratifying them. This contradicts the view upon which technology rests: that happiness requires satisfaction of basic material needs, those which can be gratified only by master-

ing material nature. The ascetic point of view, that happiness lies in denial, is not likely to be supported by many of the perhaps 2 billion people who go to bed hungry every night. There are people in the world who would argue that it would be more noble for such people to starve than to steal in order to eat, but a Gallup poll of mankind would probably find the vast majority of human beings saying that even man's higher nature requires material satisfactions. This would be a vote for the use of technology in the broad sense.

It is interesting and important to record here one such vote. It occurred in a remarkable interview given in the spring of 1970 to television host David Frost by Abbie Hoffman, one of the "Chicago Seven" tried in connection with disturbances at the 1968 Democratic Convention. After he had described himself as a "heavenist," a believer in the possibility of a "heaven on earth" founded on good will and love, Hoffman was asked what present country he would regard as the best model for his ideal society. "The United States," he replied. When asked why, Hoffman explained, "We have the technology, and that's the necessary foundation for any good society."

Granted that a nonexploitative society will need and use technology, toward what objectives will it be organized?

A healthy society will feel a public obligation to *use technology to abolish material need.* The first ecological fact is that a human being must eat in order to live (must maintain body heat, energy, and structure in order to survive in balance with his environment). It will be an empty ecology to preserve unpolluted air for high-rise dwellers and unpolluted water for the fishing streams and beaches of the affluent if children in the ghetto, or Appalachia, or Guatemala, or Pakistan are unable to stay alive. A healthy society will use its technology to meet people's basic material needs because they are human beings, regardless of what they are able to contribute in return. This will require some rethinking of what John Kenneth Galbraith has called "the conventional wisdom." Until recently, man lived under the "curse of Adam": he had to survive "in the sweat of his face." This is changing. The technological revolution since the eighteenth century has enabled us to transfer a large part of our physical and some of our mental work to machines. With the intelligent use of technology, we may be able before very long to solve the basic needs of the underdeveloped two-thirds of mankind. Automation may speed the process while materially raising the condition of the other one-third. As Galbraith and others have said, we have passed the point where work need be considered a condition for earning income. If human beings are to be regarded as ends, none can be allowed to perish or suffer physically because he or those upon whom he is dependent cannot, or will not, work.

In a sane society, *technology will help supply and distribute leisure.* Perhaps only in a society dominated by the Protestant ethic do we have to apologize for leisure. It may be, as Plato said (see Chapter seven), that man's best life as man is play, and that free time needs no further justification. In any case, individually and socially the "higher" life begins with economic surplus. When all or almost all a person's life must be given to grinding toil, the chances for developing his capacities as a human being are slim. It is only when a society is able to free some of its time from the business of grubbing for a living that it can begin to develop literature, pure science, philosophy, and the fine arts (as well as class exploitation and war).

We can predict that in the future almost all people will have more leisure than at present. Technology has simply made it possible for more of the time of modern populations to be spent in other ways than at work. Free time will create new social problems and tasks. If everyone who were guaranteed annual income were idle, would lives not become meaningless? A healthy society would have to find ways to provide basic economic security and at the same time enable people to find new ways of achieving the creative satisfactions which many have previously found in work. It will be necessary to have available more recreational facilities than at present. We may predict that a good many of these will be furnished at public expense. Another problem to be faced lies in the fact that so many people have learned in the past to expect nothing but work. It will be necessary for people brought up this way to learn to use the new leisure time available to them. This may be accomplished through regular schools or adult education programs, through private welfare agencies, or through government programs. We cannot expect that, without special efforts on the part of society, people who have previously had no significant amount of leisure can learn to use it creatively.

A healthy society will remain constantly aware that work, with or without technology, is more than the means by which man tries to master the environment for his own uses. It is itself a part of the experience of life. Thus any judgment about technology must not only answer the question: How well does it satisfy material needs? It must also answer the question: What does it do to the life experience of the person who uses the technology? Does it make the time spent in work more or less gratifying? How does it affect the worker's relationship to the materials and forces he manipulates? How does it affect his relationship to the people with whom he works? A technology in line with basic human needs must not only produce more, it must also take into account what people experience when they produce. A healthy society will be constantly concerned with finding workable everyday answers to Adam Smith's question.

An intelligent and human organization of technology must also take into account the total impact of technology upon the environment. Technology is part of our ecological relationship to the physical and biological nature in which we live. If it produces more goods by destroying that environment or by making it less habitable, it may subtract from the total amount of human satisfaction rather than adding to it. Some clear examples are pollution of air and water, destruction of natural beauty, extermination of wildlife, exhaustion of the soil, timber, and other natural resources. There are other examples of how technology may disrupt or destroy man's natural ecological relationships. Among these are the physiological stress of crowding in industrial and residential cities and the reduction and destruction of the quality of food through the agricultural, industrial, and commercial processes that increase its quantity. A nonexploitative society will further put technology in perspective by heeding some of the objections of its sharp critics. First, it will seek to be sure that technology is used to satisfy real human needs and not for other reasons.

It will avoid two situations present in the use of technology today. In our discussion of the consumer, we saw that, while the industrial market system theoretically produces to satisfy consumers, in fact it also tends to produce goods and then to persuade consumers to want them. Under a planned economy, use of technology may be similarly guided primarily by the desires of certain industrial managers for income and prestige. Where the profit or power of an interested group becomes the primary reason for using technology and the basic human needs of consumers are manipulated in this interest, technology becomes questionable. Present techniques of market research, if used for broadly social objectives, should be adequate to check such misuses of technology by finding out what people really want.

Another problem is the tendency for technology to become an end in itself rather than a means to human satisfaction. An example is the underdeveloped country that feels it has to imitate the industrialism of the big powers, regardless of how few of its people benefit by vast steel mills, railroads, dams, and arms factories. A British economist, E. F. Schumacher, has drawn upon his experience as a director of the nationalized coal industry to recommend for the developing countries an "intermediate economy" which would avoid both the poverty of the traditional village and also the overwhelming mechanization of heavy industry. He suggests, for example, that the capital used by a worker should not exceed in value the product he can turn out in a year. Another example is the developed country where, as Paul Goodman has put it, technology becomes the object of almost religious worship, and the production of new technical gadgets comes to be valued in itself regardless of what human ends they serve. Under these circumstances consumers will be proud of possessing (or being surrounded by) all the latest gimmicks simply because they are the latest and the most technically advanced.

In this case technology may continue to grind out new products whether or not anyone enjoys them in any direct sense, even if no one profits very highly from their production. "Every advanced country," says Goodman, "is over-technologized; past a certain point, the quality of life diminishes with new 'improvements'!" He mentions the multitude of freeways, high-rise apartments, packaged goods, household appliances, cars which cannot be repaired except by an expert, and even moon shots (which, incidentally, he thinks an exciting and important human adventure).

Another area of safeguard is Roszak's warning against letting technology give rise to a technocracy, the domination of all areas of life by technical specialists. We shall discuss this problem a little later in connection with the organizational revolution.

Work poses the final problem of what forms of ownership and control will provide the most gratifying and most productive organization of work. The possibilities range themselves on a continuum from a pure market economy at the one end, to a purely planned economy at the other end. In between there falls a number of mixed economies. Market economies have generally been subject to severe swings of "boom and bust," and in the best of times have been generally ineffective in maintaining full use of resources without war expenditures. They have also generally been open to the charge that they distribute income, and with it social power, very unequally among their members. The major market economies have therefore been strongly influenced by the theories of John Maynard Keynes, which have enabled them to maintain private ownership of the means of production and at the same time make income distribution more nearly even and avoid drastic swings of the business cycle and long-range underemployment. Planned economies have faced severe problems in organizing large numbers of interdependent productive units and in maintaining the most efficient use of resources without the incentives of competitive profit which operate in the

market economies. They have in some cases experimented with adoption of various competitive market mechanisms. In the Soviet Union, particularly, there has been much interest in the possibility of computerizing the planning process. Mixed economies have included such major powers as Britain and have been more developed in Israel, Sweden, and Yugoslavia. If a mixed economy seems to be the best organization of work, the question remains as to what kind of mix is best: outright government ownership, syndicalist operation by workers' councils, ownership by cooperatives or labor unions or other nonprofit organizations, or continued small- or large-scale private enterprise.

In evaluating different forms of socioeconomic organization, one point should be made clear: Technology is a social product. In our discussion of the anarchist tradition in Chapter ten, we reviewed Proudhon's argument that since the means of production are a product of the common cultural heritage, it is theft for them to be owned and used by private interests for their advantage and profit. The same general point is made by Benjamin Franklin in the accompanying boxed excerpt. Franklin first distinguishes between property for personal use and property in productive capital. Personal property for use is the human right of every individual, he says, but the capital wealth of society is the product of society as a whole and should be controlled in the common interest. No one who has completed a course in social science can argue the central point advanced by Proudhon and Franklin— that capital wealth is a product of the cultural heritage and not of any single individual or group. It is hard to reconcile this basic fact of social science with use and control of the means of production by a social minority (such as, for example, a capitalist minority of private individuals and corporations or a Communist minority of bureaucrats and technocrats). Each student can draw his own conclusion as to what

All property, indeed, except the savage's temporary cabin, his cow, his matchcoat, and other little acquisitions, absolutely necessary for his subsistence, seem to me to be the creation of public convention. Hence the public has the right of regulating descents, and all other conveyances of property, and even of limiting the quantity and uses of it. All the property that is necessary to man, for the conservation of the individual and the propagation of the species, is his natural right, which none can justly deprive him of, but all property superfluous to such purposes is the property of the public, who, by their laws, have created it, and who may therefore by other laws dispose of it, whenever the welfare of the public shall demand such disposition. He that does not like civil society on these terms, let him retire and live among savages.

—Benjamin Franklin to Robert Morris, December 25, 1783, quoted in Jared Sparks, ed., The Works of Benjamin Franklin, *Boston, Whittemore, Niles & Hall, 1856, vol. 10, pp. 45–46.*

particular solution will best fit his version of a nonexploitative society.

POPULATION

However humanely it is organized, the success of technology in reducing human need will depend upon the outcome of the population explosion. All efforts at mastering the environment must ultimately run up against the question: How many people does the earth have room for? To be dramatic, we may recall the predictions quoted earlier that if population increase is not checked, massive famine may result in the underdeveloped areas of the world before the end of this century. This would be the working out of the basic principles laid down by Malthus in his "Essay on Population": human fertility, if unchecked, will exceed man's capacity to support himself. If it is not curbed by active prevention of birth, population will be curbed by famine, disease, or war.

The first aspect of the population question is the one posed in the famous "Essay": How many people can the globe, or any given portion of it, feed? This is not, however, the whole problem. How much space per person is necessary for the quality of life that allows development of human potentialities? The anxiety, hostility, and physical deterioration that result from severe overcrowding obviously reduce the quality of experience. We can safely say that somewhere short of the density which will produce mass starvation is a point where life will be so crowded as to make truly human experience difficult or impossible. A healthy society will not only keep population pressure from producing physical famine, but will also stop it short of emotional famine.

Not only are people in general hurt by uncontrolled population increase, but a particular group suffers especially. Whatever the population situation, it is obviously the women who bear the babies. In early New England churchyards one could still find, only a few years ago, plots where a man was buried with several successive wives who were worn out in childbearing. (New England's population at that time doubled about every generation.) In a society where the race multiplies up to the maximum of its fertility, it is the woman's ability to bear that is pushed to the limit. In effect she becomes a childbearing and childrearing machine. Sexually, she becomes a means to an end rather than a person in her own right. She is first primarily a channel for male sexual pleasure, and as a result a vessel for bringing babies into the world. In the process she tends to lose control over her own body and lose her dignity as a person. As the women's liberation movement has recently urged rigorously, self-realization for the female sex is impossible without control by women over their own fertility.

On the world scene, the values of population control are being weighed against contrary values which are widespread and important. In Chapter one we discussed profertility values: need of children's work, need for future support by children, desire to have heirs to carry on one's name, desire for children as a proof of male virility. Some countervalues are "revolutionary": in the revolution of rising expectations, the claims of some Latin Americans and American Negroes, for example, that population control is a device for reducing the political power of the dispossessed. Some are religious values; one sample is the Biblical command to the Jews to multiply and populate the earth. Another is the view that sex is justifiable only as a way of producing children and not for enjoyment in itself. Another example would be the view that tends to equate birth limitation with murder; if abortion (and contraception) are supposedly used to safeguard the life and personality of the woman, what about the life that is terminated before birth (or before conception)?

Against these countervalues, we must weigh two questions:

1. *Without population control, how can we secure a sound ecological balance of people and resources?*
2. *If people are to be regarded as ends in themselves, how otherwise can the personality of women and the maximum development of both sexes be safeguarded?*

There is good reason to believe that increasing numbers of people are impressed by these questions. Even in a group historically as hostile to contraception as the Catholic Church, many leaders have rejected the traditional position, and there is not clear evidence that ordinary Catholics use "illicit" methods of birth control less than do other groups. In Latin America a good many parish priests openly espouse contraception. It may be that church opposition there is not so great as claimed, but that politicians use the bogey of church opposition to avoid taking a stand on this controversial issue. Experience throughout the world indicates that the poor, who suffer most directly from population pressure, are more likely to ask for contraceptive techniques than to reject them when offered.

How, then, can population pressure be limited? After he had listed famine, disease, and war as the positive checks against overpopulation, Malthus spoke of the prevention of birth through "moral restraint." The Irish Catholic population, which has been kept in control for quite a while, suggests that late marriage plus limitation of marital intercourse might solve the problem under certain limited conditions. The Japanese experience after World War II, in cutting population growth through widespread abortion, raises difficult questions. From the standpoint of the woman, what is the psychological impact of terminating a childbearing process already under way? If abortion is a special way of ending a particular undesired pregnancy, this trauma to the woman may well be balanced by the probable trauma of carrying the pregnancy on to birth. Many people who would favor legalization of abortion by consent of woman and doctor in hazardous or difficult cases might, however, consider the use of abortion undesirable as a general method of population control.

If the alternatives to contraception are questionable, what shall we ask of a desirable method? It should be effective under the conditions in which it will be used. By this standard the rhythm method of avoiding fertile periods in the menstrual cycle (the only method generally approved by the Catholic Church) would have to be rejected; the bulk of evidence is that usually it just does not work. In terms of effectiveness, the pill is probably the most reliable method for a technologically advanced literate population, but may be unreliable in underdeveloped countries among people who cannot count. The intrauterine device (IUD) may work better there. The method should also be safe. The pill has troublesome and dangerous side effects in some cases, and there is no guarantee of complete safety for the IUD. Preferably a method will allow a couple, if they wish, to continue to have children but to space them. Sterilization has the disadvantage that (while sometimes reversible in the male) it may make any future childbearing impossible. The method should also be voluntary. Compulsory sterilization as a general contraceptive technique invades individual freedom in a very important way. Preferably the method should be under the woman's control, as an aspect of control over her own body. The condom, although relatively effective when properly used, would be undesirable from this standpoint.

URBANIZATION

Let us now evaluate the urban revolution in terms of human goals. The city, says the distinguished cultural historian, Lewis Mumford, is a social invention as important as the discovery of language. We are now in the second great historic burst of urbanization— the first urban revolution was 5000 to 6000 years ago. The same reasons that made the city such a great cultural invention still draw people into it and must be weighed against its obvious shortcomings.

The first reasons are technological and economic. The city, we have seen, masses people to perform tasks which smaller groups cannot accomplish.

This is a reason why growth of cities was so important a part of the Industrial Revolution. The city provides a market for a variety of specialized services which more limited markets cannot support. It is thus a magnet for people who wish to develop and market their specialized talents, and for those who wish to buy those talents. There are further sociological and psychological reasons why cities are attractive. The city relaxes the tight control by which the small community keeps the individuality of its members in check. Thus it is an instrument for individual freedom. At the same time, it affords a variety of experience and contacts which are intensely attractive to people living in smaller and tighter groups. Linguistically the word "civilization" is derived from the word for "city" (Latin: *civis*). Civilization and urbanization developed together. The city has typically been the center for man's most uniquely human achievements: science, art, literature, philosophy. If they have not always originated there, they have generally gravitated to the city as the "museum of culture." These functions of the city must be weighed carefully in any scheme of values which stresses individual development as a goal.

The most obvious faults of the city as a setting for human life are ecological: supply of food, water, and other material necessities becomes increasingly complicated. Disposal of waste becomes an even more acute crisis. There is a serious question whether any organism can be crowded as densely as human city dwellers and still continue to function normally. Transport is an added problem: the interdependence of city life requires people to travel long distances for work or play while at the same time making this travel nearly impossible. The city's deepest ecological shortcoming is more general; city life separates man from nature and natural ways of functioning; from fresh air, food and water, plants and animals, and natural bodily activity. It is doubtful

"If technology produces more goods by destroying the environment or by making it less habitable, it may subtract from the total amount of human satisfaction, rather than adding to it."

whether a living species can remain psychologically and socially healthy under such an artificial way of life.

City life also falls short psychologically and sociologically. This is indicated by the maladjustment found in the study of midtown Manhattan, perhaps the urban core of the world. Freedom from small community pressure is bought at the price of weakening the close, intimate relationships which are necessary for a healthy personality. Even the variety and multitude of experiences in the city have another side; a very famous sociologist, Georg Simmel, has said that city life must make people superficial because no one could react intensely to the great number and variety of things that happen to him in the metropolis. We have seen that from the social standpoint, weakening of primary relationships tends to increase crime, delinquency, and other forms of antisocial deviant behavior.

We cannot at this point speak simply of "the city," as though it were a unity. Because of the spatial distribution of population (itself an ecological problem) the city consists of at least two worlds—a core (the central city) in which poor people (mainly of minority groups) are crowded into ghettos with-

out enough income to support either themselves or healthy community functions, and on the fringe the middle- and upper-class suburbs (mainly white). A healthy pattern of life will remedy both the deteriorating slum culture of the ghetto and the often described shortcomings of suburban living.

Any intelligent thinking about the relationship of the city to social and personal health must begin with some technological and economic facts. Large-scale production no longer requires, as it once perhaps did, the physical massing of vast numbers of people. Electricity in a sense made megalopolis obsolete. As Kropotkin pointed out, around the turn of this century, steam power, which required heavy, immobile factory installations, became out of date as a basis for industrial organization. With the revolution wrought by electricity, it became possible to transmit power over long distances and therefore to decentralize industry into smaller and more scattered units. Rapid transportation weakened another reason for city growth. It made the market for specialized services nationwide and even worldwide. In the twentieth century, a Mayo or Menninger clinic, or a Newport jazz festival, does not require a metropolis to support its specialized talents. Granted jet-age or even pre-jet-age transportation, the market for such specialized services extends as far as the remotest physical or emotional invalid or jazz *afficionado*. They can thus be located in relatively small communities. If the market does not come to the service, the service can then go to the market under modern conditions. One need not live in New York to see New York stage productions as long as modern transportation can take them on tour. It can indeed be argued that participation in a local little theater production is a more creative aesthetic experience than going to the city and seeing it done by "pros." Although movie and television are a more remote and second-hand experience than actually being on the scene, modern mass media bring to those in the range of national network coverage many of the intellectual and artistic experiences which originate in large cities. They also spread over the whole population, it is true, some of the shallowest and most questionable experiences and attitudes of urban life.

We need serious rethinking of the whole ecological problem posed by the city. It begins with the food supply. As urban civilization has developed, the qualities which food had when man was a hunter and gatherer have been lost—freshness, wholeness, variety, closeness to their natural state. These are clearly qualities desirable for man's health as a living organism. Would it be desirable, or possible, to reverse the developments brought by agriculture and the commercialization of food so as to make our food more like primitive man's? The federal Food and Drug Administration's ban on the use of the insecticide DDT and cyclamates as sugar substitutes, announced shortly before this was written, are steps toward ecological balance at this point. So is the development of a minor natural foods industry, with markets in health food stores, mostly urban.

The food problem is related to that of waste disposal. Are such procedures as the production of fertilizer out of city sewage a constructive solution to the utilization of wastes? Might such organic fertilizer also restore the natural cycle of decay and growth and thus produce more nutritious food? Would it also be possible to decontaminate industrial wastes on a mass scale in such a way as to avoid pollution of water, air, and the rest of the environment? It seems very clear, for example, that human health cannot long afford massive concentrations of internal combustion vehicles, especially ones requiring lead for their performance. It may therefore be necessary to substitute electric motors, for example, or require decontamination of exhaust. Protectors of health must face the fact that control of pollution will be expensive for those interests which now contaminate the environment, and is therefore likely to continue to be opposed by them.

A genuine campaign to end pollution will probably be impossible as long as not only vested interests, but the public at large, take exploitation of human and other resources for granted as a way of life. Unless this changes, "pollution control" may be a temporary fad. This is an illustration of what Philip Slater meant in saying, "Change must affect the motivational roots of a society or it is not change at all." Because exploitation is so central to the old cultural system, it may well be that Morris Neiberger, quoted in Chapter one, was right in predicting that we will suffocate in our own wastes before we become seriously enough concerned to do anything about them.

Here we come back to a central question about the urban way of life. How can primary communal relationships be preserved or developed in a culture like ours? Some hippies and others will continue to flee to the country and establish communes on the land. The commune may continue to be a model not only for those who leave the city, but for some who stay behind. There have been efforts to incorporate the cooperative communal principles of the kibbutz in some urban housing projects. More people will abandon the central city in hope of a better life in the suburbs. Urbanites, suburbanites, and others will find in sensitivity and encounter groups a meaningful way to establish touch with other people.

RISING EXPECTATIONS

The metropolis today is the most dramatic scene for the revolution of rising expectations, which we shall now evaluate. A little more than a hundred years ago, Henry George found in New York the inspiration for the book *Progress and Poverty,* which described the increase in misery in the midst of affluence. It is not accidental that the city is at the same time the home of the affluent minority who control the instruments by which affluence is produced and the home of the impoverished majority who produce the affluence. At the time of the Depression, a sociologist found in Chicago the contrast between the veneer of the Gold Coast on the lake front and the slum which made up a large part of the city behind the veneer. Today the urban ghetto surrounds the bright light district in which the affluent urbanite plays, and mass media bring pictures of affluence to the ghetto. In Rio de Janeiro the squalid *favellas* of the propertyless poor overlook the wealth and lavish consumption of Copacabana (p. 256), and in Saigon the poor see the contrast between their life and that of the native and foreign minority who control the country.

What can our study tell us about the revolution of rising expectations? When groups are suppressed and denied access to the advantages of a society, the discrimination is usually justified on the ground that the groups are inferior. To take an important recent example, some French psychiatrists held that Algerian blacks were morally and psychologically more primitive than Frenchmen, in fact, that "an African is a lobotomized European" (the reference is to the brain

surgery by which an individual's emotional responses are "flattened" to reduce extreme anxiety).

Social science and the related sciences can tell us that no social groups have been proved superior by heredity in their capacity to contribute to the interests of society or in their capacity to experience and enjoy life. Theories such as the Nazi idea of a superior Aryan race must be discarded by any objective scientific view, as must theories of the biological inferiority of Negroes, Indians, Orientals, Caucasians, or any other racial group. A healthy society will, therefore, allow all groups to participate without discrimination and enjoy access to the advantages of society.

Furthermore, it is no doubt true, as the French Negro psychiatrist Frantz Fanon held in his book, *The Wretched of the Earth,* that success of the revolution of rising expectations is necessary for the psychological health of both the oppressed and their oppressors. Oppression reduces the oppressed individual from a person to a thing. In this sense there was truth in the view that an oppressed African comes to resemble a lobotomized white man; not for biological but for cultural reasons he loses those qualities which make one distinctively human. Lindner is also probably right in his view that "adjustment" to an inferior and oppressed status clashes with an innate "instinct of rebellion." Whether or not we accept the word "instinct," we must recognize that there are tendencies in human beings (also present in all animals) which resist being "cribbed, cabined, and confined" in any way. The poor of the world live, in addition, in a world influenced in the eighteenth, nineteenth, and twentieth centuries by liberal views of the rights of men, and in the nineteenth century by Socialist ideals of economic and political equality. They also live in a world of mass communication where newspaper, pamphlet, transistor radio, movie, and television tell them that a world other than theirs exists for the more privileged, and that this world could be theirs also.

I hear more and more Mexicans talking about la raza—*to build up their pride, you know. . . . Some people don't look at it as racism, but when you say "la raza," you are saying an antigringo thing, and it won't stop there. Today it's antigringo, tomorrow it will be anti-Negro, and the day after it will be anti-Filipino, anti-Puerto Rican. And then it will be anti-poor-Mexican and anti-darker-skinned Mexican. . . .*

—Cesar Chavez, *in* The New Yorker, *June 28, 1969, vol. 65, pp. 43–71.*

We need to establish a system based on the goal of absolute equality of all people, and this must be established on the principle of from each and every person, both male and female, according to their ability, and to each and every person, both male and female, according to their needs. . . . We, the Black Panther Party . . . see it as a necessity for us to progress as human beings and live on the face of this earth along with other people. We do not fight racism with racism. We fight racism with solidarity.

—Bobby Seale, *in* Seize the Time, *New York, Random House, 1970, p. 71.*

On the other hand, those who exercise economic and political power throughout the world have grown up in the same environment of ideas as have the dispossessed. As Gunnar Myrdal suggested of American whites in *An American Dilemma,* they may no longer be able to oppress others so easily with a good conscience. To turn another person into a thing one must in part become a thing oneself, that is, to deprive others of their human qualities, one must deny his own human qualities. This is why Fanon held that the "wretched of the earth," while they struggle for their own souls, also struggle for the souls of their masters and those of all people, living and to be born.

By definition, a nonexploitative society requires success of the revolution of rising expectations. This revolution is a clamor by a large part of the earth's population to be valued as people. It includes the colonial peoples, the "internal colonies" like American blacks and Indians and Mexican Americans, and the poor, the young, the female, the homosexual.

In terms of our valuation of all people as ends, not means, one warning about the revolution of rising expectations should be issued. Fanon suggests it by his argument that the revolution is needed by oppressors as well as oppressed. Seen this way, the goal of the revolution is human dignity for all people. All people means colonial subjects and colonial oppressors, blacks and Indians and whites, hyphenated Americans and unhyphenated Americans, poor and rich, young and old, female and male, gay and straight. An understandable but grave danger in the revolution of rising expectations is that groups which have been dehumanized will react by treating their former oppressors as less than human. Tendencies of this kind appear in some militant blacks, militant youth, and militant women. Leaders in the revolution of rising expectations are likely to lack the wisdom shown by Chavez in criticizing Mexican-American racism, or by Bobby Seale in describing Black Panther objectives.

ORGANIZATION AND COUNTERORGANIZATION

Let us now try to put the organizational revolution in perspective. The last century has been marked by the development of the organizational society, a world where almost all activities of any magnitude are carried on by big organizations. Beginning with the organization of industrial technology, this revolution has spread from the factory to almost all other social institutions.

What does organization do? By answering this question, we may be able to see both why the organizational revolution has spread and why it has been opposed. *Organization patterns the spontaneous and unpredictable flow of life.* For a long time, people (earlier anarchists and today's hippies) have dreamed of a world where organization would be unnecessary and everything would be done through spontaneity and love. It is hard to see how a society of any kind of complexity, with any kind of advanced technology, could operate this way.

In Chapter one we saw how bureaucracy, the "ideal type" of formal organization, patterns the free flow of life. It replaces spontaneous judgments with formal rules. The whole person is replaced by the specialist, who performs a role meshed with other roles. The specialist does not deal with other individuals on the basis of spontaneous attractions and repulsions, but impersonally. He deals with them in terms of a hierarchy of superiors and inferiors. The reason given for freezing the flow of life is that, *within limits,* it promotes rational efficiency, that is, it gets things done.

What are the limits? We see here another side of the patterning of free activity. In Chapter one we saw that bureaucracy is better suited to carrying forward an established order than to promoting change, that is, it is better equipped to freeze an existing status quo than to flow forward into new solutions. In an age of change this is a critical defect. We also saw in Chapter one that bureaucracy is poorly fitted to promote art, science, religion, philosophical contemplation, and deep human relationships, for these depend upon the free play of thought, fantasy, imagination, and movement, and bu-

reaucracy by its nature patterns and freezes all these.

Obviously the bureaucratic patterning of life has two sides. The positive side is stressed by those who see efficient organization as the key to the good life. The negative side is stressed by those who see the organizational revolution as the end of hopes for a good life. At best, the spokesmen of the antiorganizational revolution see organization as a necessary evil, but deplore its tendency to turn whole human beings into means to impersonal ends. They would like us to bear in mind that there are two kinds of organized activity. In one the organization works by reducing individuals to "organization men" who lose their individual personality in the process of fitting into organizational roles. In the other people retain their individuality and voluntarily fit into patterned group activity toward goals which they spontaneously share. Social scientists who have studied organization have found that more spontaneous informal organization may have more to do with getting the work done than does the rigid formal organization. Critics of the organized Establishment would like to see informal, spontaneous cooperation play a larger role in organized activity. Here is where bureaucracy can learn from the antiorganizational revolution.

Positively, the critics of organization believe that life would be better with more of the spontaneity and unpredictability which organization eliminates. What the severe opponents of the organizational Establishment most dislike and fear is the tendency toward technocracy, the tendency for bureaucracy and bureaucrats to forget what bureaucracy is not equipped to do and to freeze all life into bureaucratic molds. They would like to tell bureaucrats to keep hands off those aspects of life where free flow is essential.

The whole problem of bureaucratic organization is part of the general question of the relationship of the individual to his society (social organization). Rebellion against the Establishment is not only rebellion against specific bureaucracies which are deemed oppressive, but rebellion against a whole system of cultural restraints. How is a healthy individual related to his society? On this subject we hear a wide variety of answers. At one end we are told that psychological health for the individual consists in adjustment to his group, that there is something wrong with the person who cannot adjust to society. At the other end, we hear that psychological health consists in nonconformity to the standards of society, which are set up so as to constrict the free development of the individual personality. From this standpoint the worst error is conformity; the adjusted person is looked upon as one who has given up his freedom to gain social acceptance and respectability.

What shall we say? In order to approach a balanced answer to the question, we must do some more exploring of the relationship between the individual person and society. It is clearly true that in no society has anyone ever been able, or will anyone ever be able, to satisfy his every immediate wish without being limited by his group. It is also true that "no man is an island," that human beings are human only as long as they are members of social groups. The idea of the isolated individual is a myth. From birth on it is simply impossible.

It is also true that society as we know it *does* in many ways thwart the development of the individual person. The technological revolution has often turned people into uncreative attachments to machines. The urban revolution has denied many times that kind of natural relationship to one's surroundings which is essential for development as a healthy animal. The conditions which called for the civil rights revolution have deprived a large segment of the population of the status of full human beings. The suppression and repression of sexuality which have given rise to the sexual revolution of our times have in truth deprived people of

development in one of the most critical areas of their lives. The weapons revolution has made the individual person a pawn in the hands of violence-ridden nationalistic states. There are many good reasons for rejecting much of the structure of present human society in the name of individual rights.

No simple formula can resolve this twofold relationship between society and individual: of society as releaser of individual qualities and society as frustrator and inhibitor of the individual. What we as social scientists can suggest is that neither wholesale conformity nor wholesale rebellion is healthy. Each may be sick. A constructive and realistic solution requires that each person first recognize the extent to which personal development is impossible without social membership and participation. Each of us must then distinguish critically between those demands of society which promote healthy personality development in himself and others, and those which make it difficult or impossible.

Such distinctions are seldom made by uncritical conservatives (who are likely to regard the status quo as completely necessary and justified) or by uncritical rebels (who are likely to regard it as totally unnecessary and unjustified). Here we will do well to bear in mind Erich Fromm's description of the revolutionary. The true revolutionary, we might say, is a radical dissenter where irrational cultural patterns are concerned and a conservative with regard to rational patterns. One might, incidentally, say the same thing about the true conservative.

These distinctions are important, but abstract. At this point students should think more concretely—review, for example, our discussion of human needs and drives in Chapter five and ask specifically which cultural restrictions (upon hunger, sex, violence, laziness, the status drive, the quest for meaning, and so on) are reasonable and which arbitrary.

This review will help the student do something that should be done by every person who would be psychologically healthy—"get out his aggression" against his culture. Psychological insight (see Chapter five again) tells us that it is unhealthy to bottle up frustrations within ourselves. Many psychosomatic problems—some gastrointestinal troubles, headaches, colds, and other assorted bodily disturbances —often represent unexpressed frustration and hostility. So do some less somatic emotional disturbances which may make one hard to live with (either for others or for oneself).

Thus psychologists and psychiatrists are likely to advise their patients to express their unexpressed hostilities. The results are often constructive. If they are going to live together as fellow workers, man and wife, lovers, parents and children, brothers and sisters, people will do better if they understand where relationships frustrate them and others. Also, even an irrational emotional explosion may psychologically clear some tension, and with it dispel the psychosomatic and other results.

This method is likely to be incomplete, however, if the therapist or patient lacks a knowledge of basic social science principles, for just as modern physical science cannot be attributed to Isaac Newton alone, but to the whole scientific and cultural tradition on which he built, so one's major woes are usually not ultimately due to his parents, boss, professor, sergeant, wife, husband, or lover, but to the shortcomings of the economic, political, sexual, military, and other cultural institutions in which he and they all live. The therapist who directs his patients' aggression against individuals is likely to be displacing it from these cultural institutions. What happens is suggested by a study of how policemen can become scapegoats. Chevigny says, "For legislators and judges the police are a godsend, because all the acts of oppression that must be performed in this society to keep it running are pushed upon the police. . . . The police thus become

the repository of all the illiberal impulses in this illiberal society."[1]

How will a healthy person deal with his aggression against his culture? First he will become aware of his frustration. This requires becoming aware of himself, of his society, and of his place in it. (It also includes awareness of the ways in which he has displaced his cultural hostilities upon individuals.) Secondly he will distinguish, as suggested earlier, between rational and irrational hostilities. This again requires an understanding of cultural restrictions and of the reasons for them (or given for them). Third he will decide what action to take. The possibilities available run the gamut from explosive nihilistic attack on cultural institutions, to objective and compassionate effort to change these institutions in a more humane direction. People today are taking both courses and all the courses in between. Here again, a good social science understanding, though not indispensable, will be helpful.

One important aspect of the antiorganizational revolution is the effort to reject the Establishment through escape and addiction. This is an important problem of individual and social health. Throughout history, and indeed in nonhistoric and prehistoric societies, some people have found the possibilities offered them by society so objectionable or so narrow that they have sought devices for getting away from it all. In his famous anti-Utopia, *Brave New World,* Aldous Huxley provided a non-habit-forming substance called "soma" which would give a release from the burdens of his totalitarian society. In real life the same function has been performed by substances like opium, alcohol, caffein, and tobacco, and more recently marijuana, LSD, speed, and other semilegitimate mood boosters, and heroin and other hard drugs. In very recent times those who cannot stand to stay put

1. Paul Chevigny, *Police Power: Police Abuses in New York City,* New York, Vintage, 1969, p. 280.

where they are in modern society have sometimes tripped with LSD or other psychedelic drugs. The drug culture is an important part of the antiorganizational revolution. The meaning of a "trip" is double: one gets away to somewhere else, and in so doing he feels that he undergoes a widening of his inner experience beyond that permitted by his society. When any escape of this kind becomes a habit and a necessity, we speak of one's relationship to his avenue of escape as an "addiction." Probably the most important addictions are not the most advertised or the object of the greatest public concern. Many of the adults who are concerned about the younger generation's interest in pot often find themselves unable to bear life without cocktail parties, social drinking in their homes, or an occasional roaring drinking bout. The distinguished anthropologist Margaret Mead recently spoke graphically of the unconscious hypocrisy of adults who stand with a cigarette in one hand and a cocktail in the other criticizing young people for using marijuana. Alcohol, as television commentator Hugh Downs once said, is "our national drug." Addiction to tobacco is probably as important and dangerous as addiction to alcohol, and many people who use none of the more spectacular escapes cannot live through a day without consuming a considerable amount of coffee or Coke.

The culture of escape and addiction raises serious questions (whether it be the grass-acid-speed culture of youth or the nicotine-alcohol-coffee-Coke culture of their parents). First of all, must society be so narrow or intolerable that escape is necessary? Next, is not escape purchased at a high price, if it physiologically or psychologically damages self or others? (This has not been proved of grass, but it has been of acid, heroin, tobacco, alcohol, and Coke.)

In a period when 43,000 Americans died in war in Vietnam, 140,000 others

died at home from drugs. Over the 1970 weekend when four students were killed at Kent State University, seventeen young people died from drugs in New York City alone. In the light of such facts, is the social impact of addiction more a "turn on" or a "cop out"?

SEXUALITY

In our culture sexuality has been one of the sharpest points of conflict between the individual and society. Thus revolt against established sexual mores has been a central part of the antiorganizational revolution.

An evaluation of sexuality in relation to individual and social health must recognize that sexual love is the normal center of a healthy human life. Sexual love here has two aspects: (1) a deep relationship of mutual affection and identification which (2) periodically culminates in orgastic release of tension. Here both asceticism and hedonism are wrong. Asceticism would regard love without sexuality as the highest form of love. As we have seen in early Christianity, this was considered desirable even for married people. Hedonism would disregard the total love relationship between persons and seek only immediate mechanical discharge of tension. Unfortunately, this second one-sided view of sexuality (which can receive no support from social science) has received some apparent support from two recent influential works of sexual research. Kinsey's study of sexual outlets did not necessarily make sexuality mechanical, but had little to say about the interpersonal relations in which outlet took place. Masters and Johnson do not specifically deny the psychological and social nature of sexuality, but one may guess that the sexual response of subjects in the laboratory is something less than the sexual response of lovers in private (even though the subjects may be lovers outside the laboratory).

In answer to both the ascetic and the hedonic views, it must be said that only in a love relationship can sexual experience achieve full gratification, and that if satisfying sexuality is not part of it, a whole love relationship must be disturbed and incomplete. When he attributed neurosis to disturbed sexuality, Freud was saying that emotional health depends upon a gratifying love life. This is the core of what we need to say about sexuality and individual health.

When it comes to social health, we must disagree with Freud. In a famous essay entitled "Civilization and Its Discontents," Freud held that the energy that builds civilization is borrowed or "sublimated" from ungratified sexual impulses. Civilization, he said, requires that people renounce more and more of their sexual desires; sexual frustration is therefore the real price of social progress.

If Freud was right, a person cannot gratify his sexuality without losing some social creativity. Do our own experiences and observations bear this out? Are the socially productive people we know generally people who are sexually frustrated, or is the sexually happy person likely to be the socially most productive person?

Our own experience and the most careful and sensitive scientific study of the problem should tell us that Freud's view is a superficial one. A happy love life is not only the center of individual happiness but also the center of social productivity. A sound evaluation of the sexual revolution should thus show us how we may make sexuality more gratifying so as to accomplish both objectives.

We must begin by recognizing the element of truth in conventional bourgeois sexual morality: the most fulfilling sexual life is found in a deep, enduring relationship between two whole lives. Beginning here, however, we must recognize that a variety of sexual relationships each have their own positive value.

1. *Marriage formally sanctioned by church and/or state.*
2. *Voluntary living together for a long period in a common-law relationship.*
3. *A more or less exclusive prolonged sexual affair without physical living together.*
4. *Sexual intercourse based on casual affection.*
5. *Sexual intercourse based on casual attraction without a strong personal relationship.*

All these kinds of sexual experience have something to contribute to individual emotional stability and social productivity. The same cannot be said of two kinds of sexual experience.

Prostitution is the sale of sexual favors for money or other reward. In this sense the marriage bed may be as much the scene of prostitution (for social position or a wardrobe) as the "house of ill fame." Prostitution is a contractual sale of sexuality between a buyer and a seller rather than a mutual expression of feeling. *Promiscuity* is indiscriminate sexuality, sleeping with anybody or almost anybody. Traditional moralists are likely to call promiscuous any sexuality that violates conventional premarital morality. This is incorrect. The trouble with promiscuity is that, again, sexuality occurs without meaningful interpersonal feeling. In promiscuous relationships the other individual tends to be not a person but a sexual *thing.* The same judgment must be made about all exploitative relationships in which the other individual is depersonalized. An example is the exploitation of immature minors for heterosexual or homosexual purposes.

The exploitation of sexuality is not limited to direct personal sexual contacts. The giving or selling of one's sexuality as a means to other people's ends is as broad as the exploitative culture. The constant presence of sex in advertising is the most obvious example. The breadth of the problem is suggested by theologian Harvey Cox, in his important book, *The Secular City,* when he calls for "searching questions about limiting the deliberate use of sexual stimulation in selling or, even more radically, about the merit of an economic system which seems to require a constant perversion of sexuality in order to survive. Commercial exploitation of sex drives—not the call girl—is our most serious form of prostitution today."

Now let us analyze some specific problems involved in the revolution of sexuality.

The first is adolescent sexuality. This needs to be evaluated in two aspects: as an experience in itself and as a preparation for later sex life. As background for our thinking, we may review a solution to the problem somewhat different from ours. Among the Trobriand Islanders described by Malinowski, sexuality was assumed to be a part of life from the beginning. There was no taboo on nudity for either children or adults. There was no prohibition of masturbation. Children played sexual games, including intercourse, more likely to the amusement than to the horror of adults. At puberty boys and girls began having actual intercourse. This usually involved an invitation for the young woman to visit the young man in the "bachelor hut" which the adolescent boys maintained for sexual purposes. After a short period of "sleeping around," couples usually formed more serious attachments and paired off in monogamous marriage, usually for life.

Among the Trobrianders we may assume that from infancy on, sexuality was enjoyed as an experience in itself in the form appropriate to each age. The results for personal and social adjustment seem to have been good. Malinowski found the Trobrianders a warm, friendly, generous, trusting, cooperative people. As preparation for adult sexual life the pattern seems to have worked: sexual development seems typically to have been a slow maturing to a stable marriage. What can this mean for us? The official mores of our society deny people sexual enjoyment until they are formally married. Adolescence is typically a period of sexual and emotional stress. How does our sexual pattern prepare for marriage? Our traditional mores have held that the marital experience is richer if both parties (especially the woman) save their sexuality for the ultimate partner. What we know does not demonstrate that this works better than the Trobriand pattern of learning sexuality as part of a general learning to love with a number of partners. We have seen that in Kinsey's study the best sexual adjustments in marriage were made by women who had enjoyed orgasm before marriage. Both as experience in itself and as preparation for the future our traditional pattern seems unsuccessful.

Adolescent sexuality involves the possibility of pregnancy. How would a healthy society face this? A society which respects the integrity of the individual will try to establish conditions that will enable him to make his own choices. These would involve, first of all, adequate sex education beginning in childhood. This would relate physiological facts of sexuality to its whole social and moral context. Freedom to choose one's own sexual pattern involves, for the woman, the freedom not to become pregnant. This involves adequate information and adequate contraceptive facilities. By this standard those colleges would seem to be serving their students best which make contraceptive services available to all female students in their health services by consent of the woman, not her parents. It might be further argued that, in a person-oriented society, respect for the individual should carry these services down to the high school level. A counterargument would hold that pregnancy is not the only kind of exploitation which a young girl can suffer, and that if she had contraceptives she could be exposed to use of her body for mechanical sexual outlet before either she or her boyfriends were prepared for more mature sexual experience. Today's students may have to face this problem of contraceptive facilities in the school by the time their own children are teen-agers.

A second important problem which has been brought to a head by the sexual revolution involves homosexual relationships between consenting adults. There are two significant views of this problem. One is that biologically human beings are naturally bisexual, and that the choice of one sex or another is the result of personal experience or cultural conditioning. From this standpoint the fact that most people in our society seem to be heterosexual is due to a form of cultural brainwashing. In this light we should regard homo-

sexuality as a deviant but equally healthy form of expression.

A second view is that healthy people naturally seek heterosexual objects. This view was, incidentally, held by the Trobriand Islanders, who asked naively why a man should want another man when he could have a woman. (According to Malinowski, the neighboring Amphlett Islanders, who had been segregated by Christian missionaries in separate school dormitories, had a different answer. With no privilege of sexual intervisitation, many of the dormitory inhabitants became homosexual.)

The standpoint that views heterosexuality as natural holds that homosexual relationships between consenting adults may have limited value as expressing a form of love, but are incomplete forms of sexual expression. The play and film *The Boys in the Band* depicts movingly both the positive values and the limitations of the "gay life."

An enduring and deep homosexual relationship can have many of the qualities and values of a similar heterosexual relationship, but homosexuality is not "just as good" in either individual or social terms (although it is a possible solution to the population problem). The homosexual chooses his own rather than the opposite sex because he fears the other sex. From this standpoint a healthy sexual revolution will recognize a limited value in homosexual experience without denying that it *is* limited. It will agree with the gay liberation movement that homosexuals have been a cruelly oppressed and dehumanized minority. It will seek to eliminate legal discriminations against homosexuals, and otherwise to establish the moral and legal right to be homosexual. The author shares this view.

We have already suggested some answers to our last question in this discussion of the sexual revolution: What will be the roles of the sexes in a healthy society?

A meaningful answer requires an exploration of the biological and cultural background of sex roles. We start with basic biological facts. Men and women are obviously physically different. (The French say *Vive la différence!*) No man has yet borne a baby. It is theoretically possible, but only a biologically exceptional male could suckle an infant. Men are physically stronger, especially in lifting. For these reasons, long before our civilization, women no doubt typically bore and nursed and cared for children, and men defended them and the children from danger. Work was certainly divided differently in different situations, but everywhere heavy lifting almost certainly fell to men. The difference in physical strength no doubt tended to make males more aggressive. So may the fact that sexually the male enters the female, and she is entered.

Since the urban revolution, the role of women has remained essentially the same, centered in the home, where they have typically been sexual objects, childbearers, and unpaid housekeepers. The world outside the home has been essentially a man's world of competition for survival and prestige in business, industry, politics, religion, and other public activities. From this world women have typically been excluded, or when admitted have been subject to severe discrimination. Thus women are generally paid less for the same work. In some school systems, they may forfeit their tenure rights if they take time off to have a baby. In some churches they have been denied participation in church government. No woman has yet been elected to or received a major party nomination for the presidency or vice-presidency. Female candidates for advanced degrees or teaching positions in universities may be sidetracked if an equally (or less) qualified male comes along. Sexual discrimination goes as far afield as professional athletic and revolutionary movements. A sports writer comments:

When a woman shows intense dedication to a professional sport the rumors begin that either she is subliminating for an inadequate "nor-

mal" sex life or cruising through the locker rooms after other women. Such gossip is usually exchanged at cocktail parties by male officials, newsmen and sporting goods field men and can cause direct harm to a woman angling for some kind of outside endorsement contract. The discussion of male homosexuality is generally taboo.[2]

Even devotion to a radical cause does not ensure a woman against exploitation. An illustration is one Black Panther's conception of a woman's appropriate role: "If you were completely involved in political work, she would work a job and take care of the practical necessities."[3] In both the home and the outer world, a woman is held to be inferior and expected to be passive. Even in bed a woman has been supposed to have less need and capacity for sexual pleasure.

A nonexploitative society must clearly seek to recognize both sexes as valuable human beings, who are neither superior nor inferior, nor identical, but *different*. Thus it will be concerned with women's liberation, but also men's liberation. A case might be made that females have historically exploited males by staying home with kids while their men wore themselves out at the rockpile or office and in fighting tigers and other enemies. As evidence that men have had the short end of the bargain, the fact might be cited that at all ages the male death rate is higher than the female. Elimination of the military draft might be part of a men's liberation program.

Men will not bear children, but women should not necessarily consider themselves less than human because they *do*. They should be protected from excessive childbearing by contraception and abortion with the consent of doctor and mother (and, perhaps, father). Neither will women necessarily

2. Richard Lipsyte, *St. Petersburg Times,* September 5, 1970, p. 3G.
3. Earl Anthony, *Picking Up the Gun: A Report on the Black Panthers,* New York, Dial, 1970, p. 29.

consider it less human to breast feed their babies than to feed them formula out of a bottle. But, as Margaret Mead has suggested, they can be provided with time off and special rooms for suckling their babies during the work day. Women will not consider it degrading to perform other care for their families, but day nurseries with professional help will make it possible for them simultaneously to be mothers and to work. Neither will males consider themselves degraded if at times they do "women's work" of caring for house and children. In truth, they have been less likely to feel degraded since the GI's came back in the late 1940s to wash diapers and keep house while their women went to the office.

In a nonexploitative society, women's personalities will certainly become more aggressive than they now are. Men will probably become softer and more maternal, more like the gentle fathers among the Trobriand Islanders. We can see tendencies toward this softening (not weakening) in today's youth.

What final sex differences in personality will remain when male exploitation and cultural brainwashing have been overcome we can only guess.

WEAPONS

Values oriented toward a nonexploitative world must regard the weapons revolution as the ultimate expression of an exploitative society, and war as the most important obstacle to be eliminated—more important than any of the evils from which weapons are supposed to protect.

Historically, we have seen, exploitation arose with the development of an economic surplus after the end of the hunting-gathering stage of social development. We will remember Toynbee's reminder that war developed along with slavery, as an expression of the struggle for the surplus. Our account of the historic economic roots of war in Chapter eight would indicate that its purpose has not essentially changed. With the rise of modern technology, the nuclear arms race has become the most typical expression of the age of technocracy. Roszak holds that for this reason alone (that the technocrats have created and take for granted as normal a balance of power on the brink of human genocide), youth would be justified in trying to destroy the technocratic way of life.

None of the other revolutions of our

time can ultimately lead to positive social and individual values unless the weapons revolution is intelligently and humanely resolved. A scientific view of the weapons revolution must lead to the conclusion that all-out war with presently available weapons might very likely lead to the destruction of a large part of the human race, and therefore of a large measure of human values. It must also lead to the conclusion that any effort to achieve peace through overwhelming deterrent power in the hands of one nation or a group of nations may quite likely end in such a conflict. This is the more likely if a large number of nations or a significant number of major powers are engaged in an arms race with such deterrence in mind. The scientific judgment must be that under present conditions, any effort at maintaining an armed balance of power in the world will very likely lead to a balance of terror.

Under these conditions a healthy world requires at least two things. (1) Different ideologies or social systems must be willing to live and let live without trying to impose their own way through force and without feeling so threatened that they will adopt potentially disastrous weaponry to protect themselves. (2) Steps must be taken toward limiting the spread of weapons which threaten human genocide and toward mutual arms reduction by those nations which now have them.

Any kind of major arms reduction will have to take into account the degree to which the economic welfare of peoples as well as the political interests of governments are involved in military spending. It will have to provide alternative civilian uses for the manpower and resources now devoted to military purposes. Such a shift will make possible the satisfaction of basic human economic needs which must be neglected as long as military emphasis leads to the replacement of consumer goods and services by military materiel.

Steps toward a healthy world society will require us to abandon the concept of national sovereignty as it has existed up to the present time. Efforts at world organization have, up to the present, been confederations of independent sovereign powers which have insisted upon their right to order their own affairs without intervention from higher authority and to use military methods independently in pursuit of their interests. Experience and study by social science indicate that a world order adequate to cope with the international problems of our age will require that nations surrender their sovereignty to an organized international government with its own legislative, executive, judicial, and police powers.

Social health requires political organization which will keep pace with the fact that the globe has become economically and militarily "one world." Individual health requires that people learn the difference between love of country and nationalism. The first is a feeling for the land, people, institutions, and cultural tradition in which one lives. The second is pride in the power of the political state to which one is subject, in its competition with other states. As was suggested in Chapter thirteen, the state, although equipped with material means ranging from bullets to thermonuclear bombs, is a mystical entity of a semireligious nature. Love of country is natural and healthy; uncritical nationalism is a form of sickness. The extreme case is the supernationalism of the loveless authoritarian personality.

"My country, may she always be right" bespeaks a natural feeling for homeland, but "right or wrong, my country" or "love it or leave it" expresses a psychopathology which the interests of the human race can no longer afford. A healthy German will rejoice in being part of the tradition that produced the music of Bach, Beethoven, and Mozart, the poetry of Heine, and the scientific genius of Einstein. He may be repelled by the strains of *"Deutschland, Deutschland über Alles."* A healthy American may be deeply moved by "America the Beautiful." He may feel no urge to applaud the exploits of the Marines "from the halls of Montezuma to the shores of Tripoli."

The realities of the international power situation make it naive to suppose that we can rely on present sovereign states, individually or collectively, to make the economic, political, and moral changes necessary to deal with the weapons crisis (review at this point the facts of the weapons revolution related in Chapter one). To take a specific case, what national state or states are likely to try seriously to do something about the stockpiling of bacteria for use against other people? In this light individual and mass war resistance take on a new aspect. We are confronted with a situation where the war system is the greatest human error. The Establishment cannot realistically be counted upon to correct it. Possibly the only realistic solution is that suggested by President Eisenhower: perhaps some day the peoples of the world will become so disgusted with the war activities of their governments that they will take matters into their own hands.

There never has been and never will be a society free from conflict between groups. The methods of solving conflicts run along a continuum between two kinds of extremes—at the one end, the possibility of a world thermonuclear war, and at the other, the kind of positive nonviolent philosophy practiced by Mahatma Gandhi and Martin Luther King. In between are a number of possibilities.

In looking at alternatives to the weapons race, we must finally evaluate the future of violence as a way of solving conflicts. What do we mean by violence? It can mean, on the one hand, physical bodily damage or the threat of it. Not all violence is, however, physical. We may do violence to a person also by damaging him psychologically. Poverty is violence. Having to do degrading or ungratifying work to live is violence. Sexual repression is violence. Most present-day enculturation in fact

is violence. As one person has said, violence is that which treats an individual as a thing rather than as a person. The student protester who asserts that "all cops are pigs" is hardly a consistent believer in nonviolent love. Slavery or other forms of involuntary servitude do violence, as may requirements that a person violate his best independent judgment or his conscience. Some people would feel that in these last two senses, military conscription wreaks violence upon a person. Discrimination against a person for reasons other than his personal merits or faults also does psychological violence to his integrity as a person.

There are a number of views as to the necessary and proper role of violence in solving human problems. One view is that violence is justified only in defense of oneself, those whom he loves, or in defense of other helpless persons. This use of violence has been questioned by religious beliefs advocating that even those who are attacked should "resist not evil," but give love in return for harm.

Another view is that violence is justified when used to defend the existing structure of society. According to this view, people do not spontaneously fit into an organized social order and must therefore be coerced into adjusting. For such purposes police and armies exist.

Still another position holds that violence can be justifiably used only to change an evil social system. From this viewpoint the only justifiable violence is revolutionary violence. Black militants and their white sympathizers are prone to believe this today. Fanon in his influential book *The Wretched of the Earth* has held that colonial domination cannot be ended without violence, which is necessary not only for political change, but to change the psychology of both oppressors and oppressed.

Other people would hold that the end justifies the means, that a good cause justifies the use of violence to defend or promote it. Thus violence may be thought right when used in the service of Christianity, Islam, Judaism, democracy, socialism, or other ideologies.

A final view is that violence is never a justifiable way of solving conflicts, that healthy people in a healthy society will seek other means.

From this standpoint violence damages not only those against whom it is used, but those who use it, and the cause for which they use it. In a brilliant essay on the Greek epic, the *Iliad,* Simone Weil has drawn from this great poem the message that the users as well as the objects of violence become turned into *things.* The person who uses material force and weapons to serve good purposes becomes the instrument, and slave, of the methods he employs. They dehumanize and brutalize him. In the New Testament the equivalent is "They that take the sword shall perish by the sword"—not necessarily that they themselves will be physically killed, but that the use of violence will diminish them as independent *persons.* From such a standpoint, the followers of a Gandhi or a Martin Luther King will hold that nonviolent techniques best preserve the integrity not only of the persons they are intended to influence, but also of those who employ them.

The person who uses violence for good ends is caught in the bind that in order to keep people from being "used," he will turn himself and others into things.

But is not the nonviolentist caught in an opposite bind: to avoid turning people into things he will allow the kind of world which dehumanizes people? Can nonviolent methods deliver the results?

When change is needed or a good social order is threatened, can anything but violence produce the needed change or preserve the desirable status quo? Some people these days would point to change in race relations as an example of needed change where violence is necessary. Others would use the example of Israel as a desirable social order which needs to be defended by violent methods. The believer in nonviolence would maintain that violence is so damaging to all involved that Negro rights or the cause of Israel or other humane goals cannot really survive the violence used to defend them. Some young people regard the Establishment as too entrenched to be moved by nonviolent methods. Some people would go back a generation into history and argue that nothing but mass violence could have stopped Hitler. The nonviolentist would retort that totalitarianism is still as great a threat today twenty-five years after the military defeat of fascism.

The greatest possibility of violence in the modern world centers around the revolution of rising expectations. Here we confront one of the most pressing value problems in our world. The underdog may use violence in an effort to shake the Establishment, and the Establishment may use violence in order to keep down the dispossessed. Violence by the underdog is dangerous, both because people may get hurt and because it may make a rational solution more difficult. Looting and rioting by black militants are dangerous. From these standpoints the pouring of blood or excrement into draft files by draft resisters also poses problems. Placement of bombs in university administration offices is dangerous. The collection of arsenals by black militants for revolutionary action against the white majority is threatening. But more threatening to peace and welfare is retaliation or preventive action by the Establishment. The 1969 report of the commission on violence headed by Dr. Milton Eisenhower suggests that police brutality is a greater danger to public peace and safety than the violence of militant groups. Sociologist John Seeley has argued that a large number of adults today regard the conflict of youth and age as all-out war and are so afraid that they will stop at little to curb the threat they see from the young. The treatment of young people by Chicago police at the 1968 Demo-

cratic Convention is an example. As this is written, it has been charged (though not entirely proved) that the American federal and local governments have launched upon a calculated program of exterminating Black Panthers, which bears some resemblance to the genocide (destruction of a group on the basis of ethnic membership) outlawed since the Nuremberg trials.

The greatest social problem we face today is still whether those who possess privilege can surrender it without violence to those who do not.

The question of how to solve the conflicts of our time brings us to the problem of confrontation. This term, which is much used these days by spokesmen for the dispossessed, means essentially three things. (1) Confrontation is making people aware of basic conflicts of interest which have existed but have been denied or ignored. (2) Confrontation is often a dramatic, face-to-face physical meeting or collision between groups with opposing interests. (3) Sometimes this collision takes the form of physical or psychological violence.

Thus it was confrontation when the governments of the United States and the Soviet Union faced each other "eyeball to eyeball" in the 1962 missile crisis. It was confrontation when Montgomery Negroes led by Martin Luther King challenged discrimination in public transportation by refusing to ride the buses. It was confrontation of another kind when George Wallace placed his body in a doorway to challenge integration of the University of Alabama. It was confrontation when Indians under Gandhi challenged British rule by making salt in violation of British law. It is confrontation when peace demonstrators assemble in Washington or New York at a time of international crisis, or when "hard hats" physically challenge the demonstrators' lack of conventional patriotism. It was confrontation when representatives of the women's liberation movement violated established procedures to present their views at Senate hearings on birth control pills. It was confrontation when members of Gay Lib in effect took over a meeting of the American Psychological Association to protest what they felt to be the anti-homosexual prejudices of psychiatrists.

What shall we conclude about the place of confrontation in an age of change? Some people believe that confrontation in any sense should be avoided. Defenders of the status quo are likely to insist that no conflicts of interest really exist and to accuse those who point them out (including even social scientists!) of being troublemakers. Thus for generations conservative southerners insisted that Negroes were happy in a segregated society, or even under slavery. Thus the military prefers not to be reminded by pacifists or others that in the last analysis existing weapons systems are powerless to defend real human interests, and in fact represent the greatest threat to them.

Some people, on the contrary, believe that confrontation of the status quo is essential, and believe, in fact, that it must be physically violent. This is the message of Frantz Fanon, which today powerfully influences many leaders of the dispossessed throughout the world. Others do not insist on physical violence, but do maintain the necessity of psychological violence, such as the denial of self-expression and dignity to opponents. An example was the *putsch* by which the Black Panthers physically took a black cultural center in San Francisco away from other black (not white) groups whom they regarded as counterrevolutionary.

Why do many people believe that physically or psychologically violent confrontation is necessary? It may serve, they hold, to catalyze more moderate people into action. Militant draft resistance may have emboldened members of Congress to oppose the Indo-China policies of Presidents Johnson and Nixon. Black militancy

may have led the middle-of-the-road Kerner Commission to deliver a more radical report on race relations than it would otherwise have produced. Violent confrontation may educate the general public to see how repressive the status quo really is. This was the case in the 1970 confrontations at Kent State and Jackson State Universities. Dramatic physical or psychological attacks may be necessary, it is argued, to mobilize dispossessed people themselves. Thus "all cops are pigs" may reach black ghetto youth who will be left totally unmoved by the idea of "love your enemies."

It is further held that violent confrontation is a valuable liberating experience for those who use it. Middle-class students, for example, have usually been conditioned to fear violent or aggressive behavior. In the process of violent confrontation, they may learn to shed their inhibitions. This, it is argued, is essential if they are to be serious revolutionaries. Finally, violent confrontationists may believe the status quo to be so entrenched and unyielding that no other method will touch it. For example, it is claimed that less shocking methods than those employed by women's and gay liberation would have made no impression in a male- and heterosexual-dominated society.

A third position on confrontation is that of radical nonviolence. From this standpoint we are in the revolutionary transition between two cultures described by Roszak and Slater. The deep opposition between the old culture and the new cannot be glossed over; it must be recognized. This opposition cannot, perhaps, be expressed most effectively in purely objective and unemotional terms. It must probably be dramatized through eyeball-to-eyeball opposition of concrete people in concrete situations. However, if it involves physical or psychological violence, this opposition will be self-defeating and counterrevolutionary. Violent confrontation preserves, in fact uses, one of the most damaging features of the old culture which it seeks to replace. Why it is counterrevolutionary from this standpoint is suggested by the statement of Che Guevara (not a nonviolentist) that the strongest motivation of the true revolutionist is "feelings of great love." How, the critic of violent confrontation would ask, can one build a society of great love by physically or psychologically damaging others? Moreover, the nonviolentist would suggest, violent confrontation may fail because it produces the opposite of the results it expected. The most likely outcome of the gun-carrying stance of the Black Panthers, for example, may be not a nonracist society, but genocidal extermination of the Panthers. So the position of the militant nonviolentist might be summarized: confrontation, yes; dramatization, yes; physical and psychological violence, no.

Here we are led back again to Chapter five and the psychological basis of society. The view of confrontation which the student finally holds will depend upon what he thinks people in our cultural situation are like and what he thinks is likely to move them to intelligent and humane action.

THE POLITICAL SPECTRUM REVISITED

As we finish analyzing social and individual health, it may be helpful to point out that the needs of our age of change require us to rethink the old political concepts of left and right. Let us look briefly at where we have been in our society, in terms of where we may wish to go. It will be good for students to review here the political spectrum in Chapter ten.

Historically, the terms "left" and "right" arose in the French Parlement at the time of the revolution, when the supporters of king and nobility sat on the right side of the house and the representatives of revolutionary capitalist liberalism on the left. The cleavage was between centralized political control and economic and political individualism. As capitalism succeeded

to power in the nineteenth century and was in turn challenged by socialism and communism, the meanings of terms changed. As we have seen, some of the people who had earlier supported capitalist liberalism against Burkean conservatism in the name of human freedom came to see capitalism itself as a barrier to human development. The anarchists, Socialists, and Communists became the left. In 1917 another important development took place: the rise to power of Russian communism, which was in the form of a centralized dictatorship antagonistic to individual freedom. After more than fifty years of Communist denial of the individual in Russia and elsewhere, the question arises again: Who is right and who is left? Today many people feel that all centralized control by political and economic oligopoly should be described as "right" and that the term "left" is properly applied to those who continue to support the ideal of individual freedom and development against both.

Politically, in the 1970s and 1980s, the antiauthoritarian left is likely to be in the tradition of democratic socialism or anarchism or "heavenism"—belief in the possibility of an earthly society based on love and justice. These movements see Burkean conservatism, oligopolistic liberal capitalism, and totalitarian communism as common enemies of the individual. The whole question might be pointed up by suggesting that had Adam Smith (a leftist in 1776) been alive a century later, he would probably have been a Socialist, and were he alive today, he might be a hippie.

Where, in these terms, does the so-called New Left of today belong? Some new leftists are democratic Socialists, anarchists, or "heavenists," but we have suggested that we also have on the left self-styled revolutionary groups which are essentially nihilistic—"our world or none." This approach lacks the respect for opponents and nonfollowers which is essential in a society where people are to be regarded as

LEFT: NONEXPLOITATIVE SOCIETY (PEOPLE AS ENDS)		RIGHT: EXPLOITATIVE SOCIETY (PEOPLE AS MEANS)
1984	Democratic socialism	Nihilistic New Left
	Anarchism	Authoritarian communism
	"Heavenism"	Liberal-capitalist oligopoly
		Landed conservatism
1784	Socialism	Liberal-capitalist oligopoly
1884	Communism, anarchism	Landed conservatism
	Liberal capitalism	Landed conservatism

ends. In terms of the historic meaning of left, these nihilistic new leftists also belong on the right.

The accompanying chart diagrams the trends just discussed. We will see that at each stage left has described opposition to past or present or future forms of coercive economic and political power; right has described defense of these forms. This chart is presented not as the correct answer, but as a basis for thought and discussion on an important question. The choice of the "84" years, including 1984, is with respect to Orwell's famous anti-Utopia, with no suggestion that this year will necessarily turn out as he predicted.

Suggestions for further reading

"New light on the promises—and threats—of our technological age" is thrown by Science Looks at Itself *(Scribner's, 1970), a collection compiled by the NATIONAL SCIENCE TEACHERS' ASSOCIATION with an introduction by the distinguished Rockefeller Institute scientist, RENE DUBOS.*

Two contrasting views by economists on the technological revolution are C. E. AYRES's The Theory of Economic Progress *(cited in suggested readings for Chapter eight) and* Technology and Growth: The Price We Pay *by the English scholar E. J. MISHAN (Praeger, 1970). An important and influential view is also that of BARRY COMMONER, a botanist who seeks a way to "enjoy the fruits of science without destroying the tree of life"; see* Science and Survival *(Viking, 1966). A widely read optimist about the human possibilities of technology is MARSHALL McLUHAN,* Understanding Media *(see suggested readings for Chapter one). Another very important optimistic view is that of the Catholic geologist PIERRE TEILHARD DE CHARDIN in* The Future of Man *(Harper & Row, 1964). So great is Chardin's faith in science that he even sees the development of the atom bomb as a high point in the realization of human values. In* Technological Man: The Myth and the Reality *(Braziller, 1969), political scientist VICTOR C. FERKISS evaluates many views of technology and concludes that in order to master technology for valid human purposes we will have to develop a new kind of human being with a new kind of understanding which has not yet appeared. In* Between Two Ages *(Viking, 1970), ZBIGNIEW BRZEZINSKI, a former high State Department officer and 1968 foreign policy adviser to presidential candidate Hubert Humphrey, takes an optimistic view of "America's Role in the Technetronic Era."*

A provocative book on the future of the population revolution is The Silent Explosion *by PHILIP APPLEMAN (Beacon, 1965). Appleman's approach is striking in that he sees Roman Catholicism and Marxist communism as twin obstacles to solution of the Malthusian problem. For pessimistic views of the urban revolution, see LEWIS MUMFORD,* The City in History, *and MITCHELL GORDON,* Sick Cities *(both in suggested readings for Chapter one). A happier outlook is that of HARVEY COX in* The Secular City *(see also Chapter one). A prominent student of city planning is EDWARD C. BANFIELD, who believes that materially "the present generation of urban Americans is . . . better off than any other large group of people has ever been anywhere" (see* The Unheavenly City: The Nature and Future of Our Urban Crisis, *Little, Brown, 1970).*

Two important documents on the revolution of rising expectations are The Next Generation: The Prospects for the Youth of Today and Tomorrow *by social psychologist DONALD N. MICHAEL (Random House, 1965) and MARJORIE HOPE's "contemporary portraits of the new revolutionaries" in* Youth Against the World *(Little, Brown, 1970). Another is E. FRANKLIN FRAZIER's* Black Bourgeoisie: The Rise of a New Middle Class in the United States *(Crowell Collier and Macmillan, paper, 1962).*

Frazier, a prominent and outspoken Negro sociologist, was dismayed at the behavior of upward-bound blacks who he felt were adopting the worst characteristics of dominant white society.

Thought provoking books on the individual in an organizational society are Growing Up Absurd by PAUL GOODMAN (Random House, 1960, paper) and Must You Conform? by the brilliant late psychoanalyst ROBERT LINDNER (Grove, 1961, paper). Very challenging is the criticism by JACQUES ELLUL in The Political Illusion (Knopf, 1967) of the whole idea that political organization can solve basic human problems. Ellul, the author of Propaganda and The Technological Society, gravely questions the possibility of democratic planning. A fascinating and humane comparison of the attitudes toward the individual held in different societies appears in Harvard anthropologist DOROTHY LEE's essays, Freedom and Culture (Prentice-Hall, 1959, paper). In Culture Against Man (Random House, 1963), another anthropologist, JULES HENRY, asserts that Western society is split between a "culture of life" and a "culture of death." "Death struts about the house while Life cowers in the corner." He investigates how the life-forces might be strengthened against the dominant death-forces. An indispensable document on the escape-through-addiction answer to the organizational world is ALBERT G. MAISEL's article "Alcohol and Your Brain" (Reader's Digest, June 1970). Maisel reports the research of Dr. Melvin Knisely and others, which indicated visible reduction of blood supply to the brain, with presumable tissue damage, after doses of alcohol corresponding to moderate "social drinking." An important affirmation of immediate sensory experience in an impersonal world is that of ALEXANDER LOWEN, in Pleasure (Coward-McCann, 1970). Lowen, also the author of Love and Orgasm (Macmillan, 1965), is a psychoanalyst who has contributed to encounter group programs at the Esalen Center for Gestalt therapy in California.

Lowen's distinction, in both books, between genuine, spontaneous pleasure and the artificial cult of fun is also an important contribution to the sexual revolution. In this last area, several significant books have contributed to the movement for change in the roles of women and men. The three most important intellectual expressions of the movement for women's liberation are The Second Sex by SIMONE DE BEAUVOIR (Bantam, 1961), The Feminine Mystique by BETTY FRIEDAN (Dell, 1970, paper), and Sexual Politics by KATE MILLETT (Doubleday, 1970). The last is a study of the theme of male domination as it has appeared in a number of well-known literary works. An important work in the field of sex roles is American Women, edited by MARGARET MEAD and FRANCES B. KAPLAN (Scribner's, paper), and based on the report of the commission on the subject appointed by President Kennedy and originally chaired by Eleanor Roosevelt.

Directions beyond the weapons revolution are suggested by WALTER MILLIS, a long-time student of war, in World Without War (Washington Square Press, paper). A powerful and learned writer on the subject is political scientist HANS MORGENTHAU. See his Politics Among Nations: The Struggle for Power and Peace (4th ed., Knopf, 1967). Psychoanalyst ERICH FROMM presents his hopes for resolving the international power struggle in May Man Prevail? (Doubleday, 1961, paper). Also important is psychiatrist JEROME D. FRANK's Sanity and Survival (see suggested readings for Chapter one). A systematic outline for genuine world government is put forward in World Peace Through World Law by GRANVILLE CLARK and LEWIS B. SOHN (Harvard, 1968). Clark and Sohn include specific proposals for moving forward from the present United Nations organization.

An extremely significant document is Report from Iron Mountain on the Possibility and Desirability of Peace (Dial, 1967). This claims to be the "leaked" findings of a special study group established by the federal government to examine how the United States might prepare for the onset of peace. The gist of the report is that peace is "probably unattainable" and that it would almost certainly not be in the best interests of a stable society to achieve it. The reason: the study exhaustively examines the economic, political, sociological, ecological, scientific, and artistic functions performed by war, and concludes: "War . . . is itself the primary basis of organization on which all modern societies are constructed." Report from Iron Mountain is presumably fictitious, although it could be a real "leak." In either case, it might furnish a provocative basis for summarizing the whole study of social science.

Index